National Intelligencer Newspaper Abstracts 1849

Joan M. Dixon

HERITAGE BOOKS
2007

HERITAGE BOOKS
AN IMPRINT OF HERITAGE BOOKS, INC.

Books, CDs, and more—Worldwide

For our listing of thousands of titles see our website
at
www.HeritageBooks.com

Published 2007 by
HERITAGE BOOKS, INC.
Publishing Division
65 East Main Street
Westminster, Maryland 21157-5026

Copyright © 2007 Joan M. Dixon

All rights reserved. No part of this book may be reproduced or transmitted in any form or by any means, electronic or mechanical, including photocopying, recording or by any information storage and retrieval system without written permission from the author, except for the inclusion of brief quotations in a review.

International Standard Book Number: 978-0-7884-4182-0

DAILY NATIONAL INTELLIGENCER
WASHINGTON, D C
1849

TABLE OF CONTENTS

Daily National Intelligencer Washington, D C, 1849: pg 1

Army orders: 122-130; 264-267; 483-485
Augustus Porter-Niagara Falls: 232; 239
Bowdoin family: 369
Cadet appointments for 1849: 101-102
Col Fremont-Mexico: 158
Colonization Society: 29-30

Commencements:
    Columbian College: 276
    Gtwn College, D C: 285-287
    St Mary's Female Institution, Chas Co, Md: 315
    Visitation Academy, Gtwn, D C: 291
    Washington Seminary, D C: 281-282

Custis recollections: 163
Deaths of Americans in Matamoros: 385
Descendents of Franklin: 205
Election at San Francisco: 366; 393-394; 468
Fate of R C Gwatkin: 36
Funeral of Mrs Madison: 275
Henry King's letter-Calif: 254
Inauguration of Gen Zachary Taylor: 09
Jennings family: 422
Koscuisko heirs: 494
Licenses issued in Washington: 45-53; 183-191; 350-356
Loss of the brig Floridian: 135
Naval Academy passed Midshipmen: 326
New Territory of Minnesota elections: 323

Officers of the C Devens: 399; Congress: 42; Dale: 327;
Independence: 215; 294; John Adams: 269; Mississippi: 180;
Ohio: 371; Raritan: 103; Supply: 84; 340; Taney: 327; Vandalia: 341

Packet ship Oxford death list: 325
Past Events: 263
Rock Creek: 375
Six wives of Nath'l Thurston: 421
St Louis-ships burned: 217
Signers of the Declaration of Independence: 446
Steamboat casualties in 1848: 153-157
Steamer Empire disaster: 208; 212
Steamer Louisiana disaster: 440; 451
Steamer Memphis disaster: 241
Tavern and Ordinary licenses issued in Washington: 407-409
Tax sale-Gtwn, D C: 43
Vessels cleared for Calif: 387-388
Wash City property to be sold for taxes: 358-364
West Point examination of gentlemen named: 169
Wreck of barque St John-casualties and those saved: 397-398; 399-400

Index: pg 496

Dedicated to our grand-daughter, Stephanie Lynne Mitchell, born June 14, 1987, Silver Spring, Md. Maryland. Our first college grandchild.

PREFACE

National Intelligencer Newspaper Abstracts
1849
Joan M Dixon

The National Intelligencer & Washington Advertiser is hereafter the Daily National Intelligencer. It was the first newspaper printed in Washington, D C; Samuel H Smith, the originator. The same was transferred to Jos Gales, jr on Aug 31, 1810; on Nov 1, 1812, the paper was under the firm of Jos Gales, sr, & Wm W Seaton. The Library of Congress has microfilm of the paper from the first issue of Oct 31, 1800 thru Jan 8, 1870, the final paper. The Evening Star Newspaper of Jan 10, 1870 reports: The Intelligencer is discontinued: the proprietor, Mr Delmar, says that having lost several thousand dollars, & being in poor health, he has resolved to discontinue its publication.

Included in the extractions are advertisements; appointments by the President; Hse o/Rep petitions; passed Acts; legal notices; insolvent debtors; marriages; deaths; mscl notices; tax lists; military promotions; court cases; deaths by accident; prisoners; & maritime information-crews. Also, items or events which might be a clue as to the location, age or relationship of an individual are copied.

No attempt has been made to correct the spelling. Due to the length of some articles, it was necessary to present only the highlights of same. Copy of the complete news item, letter, Chancery record, etc, is recommended.

The index contains all surnames and *tracts of lands/places*. Maritime vessels are found under barque, boat, brig, frig, schn'r, ship, sloop, steamboat, or vessel.

ABBREVIATIONS:

AA CO	ANNE ARUNDEL COUNTY
CO	COMPANY/COUNTY
CMDER	COMMANDER
CMDOR	COMMANDOR
DEC'D	DECEASED
D C	DISTRICT OF COLUMBIA
DWLG	DWELLING
ELIZ	ELIZABETH
ELIZA	ELIZA
MONTG CO	MONTGOMERY COUNTY
PG CO	PRINCE GEORGES CO
WASH	WASHINGTON
WASH, D C	WASHINGTON, DISTRICT OF COLUMBIA

BOOKS IN THE NATIONAL INTELLIGENCER NEWSPAPER SERIES-:
1800-1805/1806-1810/1811-1813/1814-1817/1818-1820/1821-1823/1824-1826/1827-1829/1830-1831/1832-1833/1834-1835/1836-1837/1838-1839/1840/1841/1842/1843/1844/1845/1846/1847/1848/1849/SPECIAL: CIVIL WAR 2 VOLS, 1861-1865

DAILY NATIONAL INTELLIGENCER NEWSPAPER
WASHINGTON, D C
1849

MON JAN 1, 1849
Wash City: First Ward-Mr Easby's ship-yard, at which have been built many fine vessels. Mr Winder's bldg completed & occupied by public ofcs. Second Ward-It is hoped that provision will be made for extending improvement of K westward, & opening 10th from K to N st north. The Hotel erected by the late Mr Fuller, closed for a time, is now re-opened by Mr Thomas, under the name of the Irving House. Third Ward-the Gas Works are in course of erection. Fourth Ward-Large additions to the Bank of Wash. Fifth Ward-It is contemplated to construct a culvert across Indiana ave in a line with the Tiber. The ground around the old Botanic garden has been enclosed & improved, by leveling & embanking the Tiber south of Pa ave. Sixth Ward: Little has been done on the streets. Seventh Ward-The foundry is doing good business, turning out beautiful castings. –John Sessford [The foundation of the Washington Monument has been carried up to within 3 feet of the bottom of the shaft, 80 sq feet at base, & 17 above the ground.]

Ladies with letters in the Post Ofc, Wash, Jan 1, 1849/

Anderson, Mrs E A	Churchill, Mrs Gen S	Herrick, Miss E
Austin, Miss Eliz	Davis, Mrs Ann	Holin, Eliz
Adams, Miss Louisa	Diel, Miss Eliza	Holland, Mrs E L
Ashton, Miss Mary D	Ducket, Lucy	Hanbury, Mrs J G
Blanche, Miss Curly	Delany, Miss Susan F	Hanning, Mrs Mary
Brady, Mrs	Demar, Miss Matilda	Harshorn, Mrs S G-2
Brannan, Mrs E	Davis, Miss Martha	Hood, Mrs Eliz
Bryan, Miss Julia	Dunlap, Miss Sallie S	Hardin, Mrs Sarah
Brown, Miss Mary	Foster, Miss Clara	Johns, Miss Bettie
Butler, Miss Maria	Fletcher, Miss H	Jones, Miss Catherine
Barns, Mrs Mary	Forest, Miss Louisa	Knott, Mrs Cathrine
Bates, Miss Mary	Ford, Miss Lucinda	Kellogg, Miss F L
Banes, Miss Mary	Forbes, Mrs M E	Lucas, Mrs A M
Bulger, Miss M T R	Fairfield, Mrs M A	Lucas, Mrs A E
Brown, Mrs Sarah A	Fisher, Miss Mary E	Lee, Miss Jane
Baxter, Miss Sallie E	Grey, Miss Eliz	Lunt, Miss Julia
Coakley, Miss Ann	Gibbs, Miss Marg't	Lukins, Miss Maria
Corse, Eliza	Gordon, Mrs Susan	Lamkin, Miss S M
Conaway, Mrs E R	Graham, Mrs Danl	Lewis, Miss M
Clark, Miss Marg F	Greer, Miss Isabl's P	Martin, Miss C
Conover, Mrs P A	Howard, Mrs A L	Milligan, Miss E
Cheshire, Mrs R	Hume, Mrs Rebecca	Martin, Miss M-3

Martin, Mrs Sarah
Martin, Miss
McLeod, Miss M
McKenny, Mrs M
Macgowen, Miss E
Nash, Mrs E T
Nicking, Miss S E
O'Reilly, Mary
Proctor, Miss H G
Pickin, Miss M E
Richards, Miss A R
Rose, Caroline
Rodgers, Miss C
Reed, Mrs Kate
Rose, Miss Patsy
Rogers, Sarah Ann
Randals, Miss Emily

Rollins, Miss Louisa
Stevenson, Miss E J
Stewart, Mrs Jane
Stewart, Sarah
Steward, Mrs Susan
Stewart, Mrs D T
Stewart, Mrs Emily
Smith, Miss Eliz
Smith, Miss Harriet
Savoy, Miss Kitty
Smith, Miss M N
Smith, Mrs Marg S
Stakes, Mrs Sarah
Sasser, Mrs M E
True, Miss Ann E
Thornton, Miss Ann
Trezavani, Mrs G

Thompson, Mrs M H
Ungerer, Mrs M-2
Williams, Miss A
Webster, Miss C
Wilson, Miss C E
Withers, Mrs E
West, Mrs Eliz
Woodyard, Miss J
Williams, Miss K J
Williamson, Mrs F H
Wilerson, Miss M
Wood, Miss Phoebe
Wood, Phoebe &
Sylvia Ann
Young, Mrs Ann
-C K Gardner, P M

Iowa State Judges. On Dec 7, Jos Williams was elected chief justice of the Supreme Court, & Geo Green & J F Kinney assoc justices. The election was made by the Legislature.

Criminal Court-Wash: 1-On Wed Jas Oliver, alias McKane, & Randolph Bean were found guilty of assaulting & robbing Geo Caton, in Gtwn, of $10.50. The prisoners were sentenced each to 2 years in the penitentiary. 2-John Coddington, a young man of respectable appearance & connexion, was charged with stealing a cow, the property of Wm Flenner. Jury returned a verdict of not guilty.

Mrd: on Dec 26, in the McKendree Methodist Episcopal Church, Wash, by Rev W Hamilton, Rev Otis H Tiffany, adjunct Prof of Mathematics in Dickinson College, Pa, to Miss Eliza Bruce, daughter of Rev W Hamilton.

Mrd: on Dec 24, by Rev P B O'Flanegan, Mr John B Newton to Miss Henrietta Van Riswick, all of Gtwn.

Mrd: on Dec 26, at the residence of John H Hardesty, by Rev Mr Dalton, Dr Philip R Edelin to Miss Rebecca Clagett, all of PG Co, Md.

Mrd: on Dec 24, by Rev Benj Price, of Queen Ann Co, Md, at **Belle View**, the residence of Col L C Pascoult, Dr J M Gibson, of Wash City, to Carolina, daughter of Chas Dupont, deceased, late Quartermaster Gen of the British Army.

Important from France. 1-Louis Napoleon Bonaparte has been elected Pres of the French Republic, by a large majority. Bonaparte-66; Cavaignac-20; Rollin-6; Raspail-4; Lamartine-3. 2-The Pope has fled from Italy. Ireland was quiet.

Lewis C Suggett, of Ky, is now in Wash, at Mrs Turpin's, on Pa ave, for the winter, where he will attend to pension claims, or any other business entrusted to him.

By writ of fieri facias, I will expose to sale at public auction on Feb 5, the north part of lot 9 in square 246, with improvements thereon, as the property of Thos Joyce, seized & taken in execution at the suit of Nancy Sheehey. –M R Maryman, constable

TUE JAN 2, 1849
Revolution in Rome: M Rossi, the Minister of State, was murdered. He was stabbed in the throat & died immediately. Letter with the following detail: the son of Rossi, standing over the dead body of his father, vowed awful vengeance on the murderer, whom he says he will devote his life to discover & kill.

Mr Freeman, of Schenectady, N Y, was killed on Dec 21 by a collision on the Auburn & Rochester railroad, near Settleville. He was the only passenger in the car attached to the freight train going East. He was conveyed to the residence of Norman Little, where he died in about 20 minutes.

A ploughman lately working in a field at Wendover, in England, turned up an ancient gold bracelet of the intrinsic value of $100. Antiquaries give their opinion that it was deposited at the time of the conflict between the Romans & the sons of the British King Cunobelin.

Mrs Cadet, a widow lady, & a Mr Spegle, a German, were burnt to death in Williamsburg, N Y, on Sat last. The house was on fire, when Spegle rushed in to bear out Mrs Cadet, who was lame; but neither ever appeared alive. Their bodies were found burnt to a crisp. The house was set on fire.

Court of Oyer & Terminer of Schuylkill Co, Pa, last week: John Michl Miller was convicted of arson in burning the barn of John Fisher, near the Scotchman's Locks, on Nov 17 last, & sentenced to 10 years in the Eastern Penitentiary.

Died: on Dec 29, in Wash City, at the residence of his son-in-law, John T Caho, Andrew Barneclo, aged 74 years. Easton & Rockville, Md, papers please copy.

Died: on Dec 31, near the Navy Yard, of croup, Julia, daughter of Anthony & Mary J Addison, aged 14 months & 10 days.

Died: on Dec 23, at New Orleans, Capt David Perkins, formerly of the U S Army, & long & favorably known to the ofcrs of the army & citizens of the U S as sutler of the 3rd Artl.

Died: on Dec 30, at his residence in Balt Co, Md, Dr Saml McCulloh, aged 80 years, brother of Jas W McCulloh, 1st Comptroller of the U S Treasury.

Died: on Dec 22, at Hamilton, Butler Co, Ohio, after a lingering illness of several months, Susan P McD, consort of Col John B Welles, & daughter of the late Wm Taylor, of Va.

Died: on Dec 22, in Fredericksburg, in her 27th year, leaving an infant a few weeks old, Mrs Mary Ellen Gordon, wife of Douglas Gordon, of that place, & daughter of Colin Clarke, of Gloucester Co.

WED JAN 3, 1849
Senate: 1-Ptn of Chas Colburn, asking compensation for his services as a yeoman in the naval service of the U S: referred to the Cmte on Naval Affairs. 2-Ptn of W W Loring, M E Van Buren, & R M Morris, ofcrs of the army, asking compensation for horses lost in the military service of the U S: referred to the Cmte on Military Affairs. 3-Ptn of Hugh Wallace Wormley, asking to be allowed a pension, in consideration of disability incurred while in the military service of the U S: referred to the Cmte on Military Affairs. 4-Additional documents submitted in the case of the heirs of Rusy Ragsdale, deceased: referred to the Cmte on Revolutionary Claims. 5-Ptn of Amaziah Goodwin, on the files of the Senate: referred to the Cmte on Naval Affairs.

Orphans Court of Wash Co, D C. Letters of administration on the personal estate of Peter Feraille, late of said county, deceased. –M A Feraille, admx

THU JAN 4, 1849
Senate: 1-Memorial of Lewis Morris, late capt of volunteers, asking compensation for military services in Mexico: referred to the Cmte on Military Affairs. 2-Memorial of B O Payne, employed in the Ordnance dept as an acting ordnance ofcr of agent, asking a pension in consequence of disabilities received while in the service of the U S: referred to the Cmte on Pensions. 3-Ptn of Roger Jones, Adj Gen of the U S Army, asking the correction of the date of his commission, & the arrears of pay incident to such correction: referred to the Cmte on Military Affairs. 4-Ptn of Mrs Maria L Nourse, asking an allowance for interest on the claims of her late husband, Jos Nourse, deceased, the principal of which was paid under an act of Congress: referred to the Cmte of Claims. 5-Memorial of Vladislaus Wankoweiz, grand-nephew of Gen Thaddeus Kosciusko, asking fot the passage of an act providing for the removal of cases concerning the estate of Gen Kosciusko from the U S Circuit Court for the Dist of Columbia to the U S Circuit Court for the district of Md: referred to the Cmte on the Judiciary. 6-Ptn of Lewis Marchand, asking indemnity for French spoliations prior to 1800: referred to the Cmte on Foreign Relations. 7-Ptn of Wm Jenks, asking the adoption in the military service of an improved firearm, of which he is the inventor: referred to the Cmte on the Militia. 8-Ptn of Jas H Duffer, a U S pensioner, asking an increase of his pension: referred to the Cmte on Pensions. 9-Ordered, that David Butler have leave to withdraw his ptn & papers. 10-Memorial of Saml L Gouverneur, the son-in-law & sole exc of the late Jas Monroe, 5th Pres of the U S, praying that Congress may adopt such measures it may think proper to aid in the publication of the manuscript papers which Mr Monroe left behind him. 11-Cmte on Pensions: bill for the relief of Benj F Bosworth: to be printed. Same cmte: asking to be discharged from the further consideration of the ptn of Wm D & Julia Aikin, reps of Wm Yool, & that it be referred to the Cmte on Naval Affairs. 12-Cmte on Public Lands: ptn of Peter Whitmore Knaggs, asking leave to locate a section of land in lieu of 2 sections which were reserved to him by Indian treaty on the Flint & Shiawassa rivers, made an

adverse report thereon. Samt cmte: ptn of Peter Godfroy for leave to locate a section of land in lieu of section six in the Indian reservation on Flint river, Mich, made an adverse report on the same. 13-Bill for the relief of John P Baldwin failed to be engrossed: lies over.

The dowager Lady Ashburton died at Gosport, England, on Dec 5. She was the daughter of the Hon W Bingman, of Phil, who was, about the time of her marriage, a Senator of the U S for 6 years from the State of Pa.

Jonathan Cole, wife, 3 children, brother-in-law, & servant were ascending Yonge Creek from Maitland, Canada, in a boat, when the boat upset, & all were drowned.

Wash Corp: 1-Ptn of Jas Fitzgerald for the remission of a fine: referred to the Cmte of Claims. 2-Leave given to Wm Rupp to withdraw his ptn from the files. 3-Ptn of A Rothwell, praying remission of a fine: referred to the Cmte on Improvements. 4-Ptn of Richd Tompkins, praying remission of a fine: referred to the Cmte of Claims. 5-Bill for the relief of Robt B Clokey: to lie on the table. 6-Bill for the relief of E G Handy: referred to the Cmte on Police.

House of Reps: 1-Cmte of Claims: ptn of Saml Perry, with a bill for his relief: committed. Same cmte: bill to provide for the payment of the passage of Gen Lafayette from France to the U S in 1824: committed. Same cmte: ptn of John Coates, adverse report thereon: laid on the table. 2-Cmte on the Judiciary: bill for the settlement of the accounts of Capt N M Clarke: committed. Same cmte: ptn of Fred'k Dawson, Jas Schott, & Elisha Dana Whitney, for payment for certain vessels furnished the republic of Texas, & by Texas given up to the U S on her annexation thereto: committed. 3-Cmte on the Judiciary: to be discharged from the further consideration of the ptn of Wyatt Eppes, asking the payment of a bill of costs allowed by the District Judge of the U S for the State of Mississippi: laid upon the table. 4-Cmte on Revolutionary Claims: bill for the relief of the heirs of Wadleigh Noyes, deceased: committed. Same cmte: asking to be discharged from the further consideration of the ptn of Wm H Russell: laid on the table. 5-Cmte on Private Land Claims: bill granting the right of pre-emption to Joshua Holden: committed. Same cmte: bill to satisfy the claim of the legal reps of Jos Reynes: committed. Same cmte: bill for the relief of Jas G Carson, reported without amendment: passed. 6-The heirs of Jethro Wood have leave to withdraw their ptn & papers. 7-Cmte on Invalid Pensions: to be discharged from the further consideration of the ptn of John Barrett: laid on the table. Same cmte: bill for the relief of John Frame: committed. Same cmte: adverse report upon the ptns of Matthew Macklern & John W Howell: laid on the table. Same cmte: to be discharged from the further consideration of the ptn of Geo Gorey: laid on the table. Same cmte: adverse report upon the ptn of Peter Riffle: laid on the table. 8-Ordered that leave be granted to withdraw from the files of the House the papers relating to the claims of Wm C Houneus, John P Boyce, Michl Dowling, Patrick Menan, & Wm Lorillard.

The property in Wash City known as the St Charles Hotel, Pa ave & 3rd st, was sold yesterday at auction to John W Maury, for $11,350.

Obit-died: on Dec 21, in Claiborne, Ala, Hon Jas Dellet, aged 60 years. He was a native of S C, & was among the earlier graduates of the Univ of that State. He removed to Claiborne in 1818, where he continued to reside up to the time of his death. He frequently represented his country in the Genr'l Assembly of the State, & in 1839 was elected to represent the first district in the U S Congress.

The Pres of France. Chas Louis Napoleon is son of Louis, ex-King of Holland. He was born in Paris on Apr 20, 1808. He was a favorite of his uncle Napoleon. Upon the banishment of his family he removed with his mother to Augsburg. He became a citizen of Switzerland. He was again banished from France after the July revolution, 1830. In 1831 he took part in an Italian insurrection against the Pope. The same year he visited England. Again he resided in Switzerland for 2 or 3 years. He was concerned in another insurrection at Strasburg in 1836; was imprisoned in Paris, & sent to this country. In 1837 or 1838 he took up residence in England, where he remained till 1840. For his unsuccessful affair at Boulogne that year he was sentenced to imprisonment for life. In 1846 he made his escape, & again resided in England until Sep last, when he was returned as Deputy to the Nat'l Assembly from the dept of the Seine. His fortunes & conduct since that are as well known to our readers as newspaper reports could make them. Phil Bltn

Died: on Jan 3, at his residence, near Wash City, after a lingering illness, Danl Gold, late & for many years a Clerk in the Clerk's Ofc of the House of Reps, leaving a wife & 2 small children to mourn their irreparable loss. His funeral is today at 2 o'clock, from his late residence.

Died: a few days ago, in the city of Richmond, Va, Chas J Macmurdo, in his 78th year. He was a native of Scotland, & came to this country when a boy of 14; that is to say, about 64 years ago. During the whole of the intermediate time he has been a resident of Richmond, where he was much loved & respected.

FRI JAN 5, 1849
House of Reps: 1-Bills returned from the Senate, each with an amendment: relief of Anthony Bessee; of Jas B Davenport; of John B Smith & Simeon Darden. Also, an act to confirm Eliz Burriss, her heirs or assigns, in their title to a tract of land. The bills passed. 2-Bills taken up & referred: relief of Henry D Garrison; of Thos W Chinn & others. Also, of Maj R L Baker-of the ordnance corps. Also, a bill to authorize the issuing of a register or enrollment to the ship **Annie Tift**.

Missionaries: the barque **Ionia** sailed from Boston on Wed, for Smyrna via Malta. She takes out the Rev Simeon H Calhoun & lady, & Rev Wm F Williams & lady, destined for the mission to Syria; Rev Oliver Crane & lady, destined for the mission to Turkey; Rev Eliphal Maynard & lady, & Rev Edw M Dodd & lady, destined for the mission to Salonica.

In the list of persons of whom the Cabinet has been composed, since the formation of our Gov't, the name of Jas Stoddert, of Md, is put, instead of Benj Stoddert, of Md, who was the 1st Sec of the Navy.

Wanted, a situation as a teacher in a private family, or as assistant in a school, by a young man who is a member of a College in good standing. Address B F Peterson, Washington

The papers state that Peter C Brooke, of Boston, whose death was announced a day or two ago, was the richest man in Boston, if not in the U S. He was the father-in-law of Edw Everett, who, it is said, will now probably succeed to the enjoyment of one of the largest fortunes which ever in this country came into the possession of a man of letters.

Lost or mislaid, a certificate of the value of $900 in the Navy Yard Bridge Co. The transfer is made on the books of the company of the undersigned from the late Em Prout. –Geo B McKnight

Phonographic Reporting Academy. Benj P Worcester, experienced teacher, will open in a few days in the Washington High School Rm, at the corner of F & 14th sts.

Private tutor wanted, in the family, consisting of 5 boys & girls, between the ages of 7 & 15, of a gentleman of Md, residing within 50 miles of Wash. Apply in person to Edw Wm Johnston, at the Intelligencer Ofc.

Mrd: on Jan 1, by Rev Mr Pitcher, Mr Jos Grinder to Miss Mgt Jane Kerby, of Balt.

Senate: 1-Ptn of Catharine Elwes, widow of a naval surgeon, asking to be allowed a pension: referred to the Cmte on Pensions. 2-Cmte on Military Affairs: memorial of Adj Gen Roger Jones, with a bill for his relief: ordered to be printed. This bill allows to Gen Jones the pay & emoluments of his commission as Adj Gen from the time of the reduction of the army in 1821 to Mar 7, 1827, when he was restored to his rank in the staff of the army; provided that the pay & emoluments of captain of artl during the same period be deducted therefrom. 3-Cmte on Pensions: bill for the relief of Jas W Scantland. This is a very extraordinary case: Scantland was severely & dangerously wounded, a musket ball entering his right eye & coming out below the left ear. His wounds, & the care & anxiety which he has since undergone on account of his utter inability to support himself & his family, have induced a pulmonary disease, & that he cannot possibly live but a very short time. He cannot labor. He is entirely dependant for the support upon the appropriation proposed to be made by the bill, & cannot sustain himself without it. Scantland served throughout the whole of the Mexican war, & uniformly displayed great gallantry. His other eye is much impaired. At the last session of Congress he was allowed $30 per month; but was compelled to resort to manual labor. He obtained a clerkship in one of the depts. The surgeon general declared, & certified, that if he continued in any employment, he will lose the use of his other eye. He was shot down, & for some time supposed to be dead. His sufferings have been severe. Some years ago a ptn from Capt Harrison, who served in the Northern war of 1812-13, & who lost a leg, was allowed a pension, it being small, he applied for additional pay. He was allowed $50 per month. Bill was ordered to be engrossed for a 3rd reading, read & passed.

Primary School, #10, for 4th Dist, [Island,] will be opened Jan 8, on 13th st south, directed by Mrs Southworth. Apply for admission to Jas E Morgan, I Mudd, or Wm Ashdown, Sub-Board for 4th Dist.

SAT JAN 6, 1849
Senate: 1-Memorial of Henry C Miller & Philip W Thompson, asking indemnity for Indian depredations committed by the Osage Indians on the Santa Fe road: transferred to the Cmte on Indian Affairs. 2-Ptn of Mrs Priscilla Decatur Twiggs, niece of Stephen Decatur, asking that she may be allowed a portion of the prize money due her uncle on account of the recapture of the U S frig **Philadelphia**: referred to the Cmte on Naval Affairs. 3-Ptn of Jos Kerwin, late a sgt in the 6th Infty, U S army, praying an increase of pension: referred to the Cmte on Pensions. 4-Ptn of Thos & Eliz Armstrong, praying indemnity for depredations committed by the Creek Indians: referred to the Cmte on Indian Affairs. 5-Memorial of Saml Jones. surviving partner & legal rep of the firm of E P Calkins & Co, asking the return of duties exacted of him in the name of the republic of Texas, after her annexation to the U S: referred to the Cmte of Claims. Cmte of Claims made an unfavorable report upon the same, which was ordered to be printed. 6-Documents relating to the claims of the heirs of Joshua Eddy, an ofcr in the Revolutionary army, for commutation pay: referred to the Cmte on Revolutionary Claims. 7-Memorial of the legatees of Thos D Anderson: same to be taken from the files of the Senate & referred to the Cmte on Foreign Relations. 8-Ordered, that Peter Randon have leave to withdraw his memorial & papers. 9-Mr Westcott submitted additional documents relative to the claim of Manual X Harmony: ordered to be printed, to accompany the bill. 10-Cmte on Pensions: ptn of Wm Barton, reported a bill for the relief of Wm Barton & other surviving children of Gen Wm Barton, accompanied by a report, which was ordered to be printed. 11-Cmte of Claims: bill for the relief of the widow of Lt Richd E Cochran, deceased, ordered to be printed. Same cmte: bill for the relief of A C Bryan & others: to be printed. Same cmte: bill for the relief of the legal reps of Robt Fulton, deceased: to be printed. 12-Cmte of Claims: bill for the relief of Theodore Offutt: to be printed. 13-Cmte on Pensions: instructed to inquire into increasing the pension of Isaac W Griffith, of Iowa, on account of the loss of his right arm whilst in the service of his country at Churubusco, Mexico.

Bounty land warrants wanted. The highest price given by J W Simonton, Pa ave, opposite Brown's Hotel.

Boarding School for Boys: Wilmington, Del. Saml Alsop, Principal. References:
Danl B Smith, Phil
Marmaduke C Cope, Phil
Wm Hodgson, jr, Phil
Thos Kimber, Phil
Dr Jno D Griscom, Phil
E C & J Biddle, Phil
Uria Hunt, Phil
Enos Lewis, New Garden
Eli Hilles, Wilmington
Saml Hilles, Wilmington
Dubre Knight

P W Browning, Merchant Tailor, under the U S Hotel, Pa ave, between 4½ & 3rd sts. Measures taken for the sale of Mrs E C Beman's Shirts. Large assortment of ready-made clothing is always on hand.

A Yankee veteran of the turf, John Sherman, of Cambridge, Mass, rode his celebrated mare, Lady Romp, 20 miles within an hour, on Tue, at the Washington trotting course. Including the old man, his saddle, etc, the mare had to carry over 200 pounds, a feat, never before equaled. –Bos Patriot

The Hon Peter C Brooks died in Boston on Mon last. He was 82 years of age, & a native of Medford, which town has been his summer residence for many years past, but from his early manhood he has been a citizen of Boston.

Troops for California: Transport ship **Mary & Adeline** sailed from Old Point Comfort on Dec 27, for Calif, with companies A & F, 2nd Regt U S Infty. Ofcrs of the detachment: Capt H Day, 2nd Infty, commanding
Assist Surgeon C P Deyorle, U S Army
Capt C S Lovel, 2nd Infty, & lady
Capt Delozier Davidson, 2nd Infty, & family
1st Lt Jas W Schureman, 2nd Infty, Co A
2nd Lt H B Hendershott, 2nd Infty, Co F
Passenger, G P Hyslop

Wash Assembly to take place at Jackson Hall, on Jan 9, 1849. Tickets at the Bookstore of Messrs Taylor & Maury, Fischer, & F Taylor, Pa ave. Managers:

Hon Geo M Dallas	Hon T Butler King
Hon R M McLane	Hon I E Holmes
Hon Wm K Sebastian	Hon R K Meade
W W Seaton	Com L Warrington
Gen J G Totten	Capt J E Johnston, U S A
Maj J D Graham	Capt French Forrest, U S N
J Knox Walker	T B Huger, U S N
P Barton Key	Thos Ritchie
John E Addison	Capt J McDowell, U S A
R K Stone	Geo Thom, U S A
J M Foltz, U S N	Aug S Nicholson, U S M C
Hon D M Barringer	W S Walker
Hon E C Cabell	W P Rodgers
Gen Geo Gibson	

Appointments by the Pres: 1-Lorenzo B Shepherd, to be U S Atty for the southern district of N Y, in place of Chas McVean, deceased. 2-Rufus McIntire to be U S Marshal for the district of Maine, from Jan 15, 1849, when the commission of the present incumbent will expire.

Mrd: on Jan 4, by Rev Mr Flannegan, Mr John Mehagan to Miss Janett Rebecca Speiden, both of this District.

Mrd: on Jan 4, at Alexandria, Va, by Rev Mr Jones, Mr Saml T G Morsell, of Wash City, to Miss Susan A Bradley, of the former place.

Mrd: on Jan 4, by Rev Mr Samson, W T Tinsley, of Richmond, Va, to Mrs Bettie T Green, of Hanover.

Died: Jan 1, after a short illness, William A, twin son of Wm A & Francis E Griffith, aged 8 months & 20 days.

Died: on Jan 4, after a short & severe illness, Annie E, daughter of Jacob & Mary A Brodbeck, aged 2 years & 7 months. Her funeral is tomorrow at 12:30 p m, at her father's residence on Pa ave, between 17th & 18th sts.

Neat small farm near Wash City for sale: across the Eastern Branch Bridge, [now free of toll,] on a public road leading to Alexandria. Contains 62 acres; improvement is a 2 story frame house; also, a new 1 story log house. For terms apply to W E Kennaugh & Co, E & 13th sts, Wash.

MON JAN 8, 1849
House of Reps: 1-Resolution for the relief of Saml T Anderson be returned to the House. 2-Leave was granted to Chester Stebbins to withdraw his petition & papers, which at the last session were referred to the Cmte on Public Lands. 3-Motion by Mr Giddings to reconsider the vote by which was ordered to be engrossed the bill for the relief of the legal reps of Antiono Pacheco.

Mr Simon Draper, of Brookfield, died on Dec 28, in his 84th year. He was a soldier of the Revolution, having entered the continental army when quite a youth. He was a member of the Convention of 1820, to amend the constitution of the State, & he served as a member of the Mass Legislature for something like 30 years. The townsmen came up in a body to his funeral, a spontaneous offering of their respect. Mr Draper has left behind him a good name & numerous descendants. One of his sons was appointed consul at Paris by Gen Harrison. Another of his sons, Mr Simeon Draper, jr, is one of the first merchants in N Y C. –Boston Atlas

Mrs Mary Dickson, Postmistress of Lancaster, received an anonymous letter, enclosing $15 in gold. The writer says it was unlawfully taken from her about 10 years ago, for which he ask forgiveness.

The Boston papers announce the death of John T S Sullivan, a son of the late Hon Wm S Sullivan. He was a most accomplished gentleman & scholar, an excellent lawyer, & an author of great ability. His latter years were spent in Phil.

Appointments by the Pres. 1-Lewis Cass, jr, to be Charge d'Affaires to the Papal States, in place of Jacob L Martin, deceased. 2-Consuls: Edw Porter, of Va, for Tabasco, Mexico. Henry A Holmes, of N Y, for Laguna de Terminos, Mexico, in place of Eneas McFaul, jr, deceased. M P Game, of Pa, for Guayaquil, Ecuador, in place of Seth Sweetzer, deceased. Wm H J Anson, of Va, for Chihuahua, Mexico. Thos C McDowell, of Pa, for Bahia or San Salvador, Brazil, in place of A H Tyler, recalled. Jos Graham, of Ohio, for Buenos Ayres, in place of Geo J Fairfield, deceased.

Horace Binney, the eminent lawyer of Phil, has given $1,000 to the city of Burlington, N J, in trust-the interest to be given in aid to the poor of the city by the purchase of fuel.

At New Orleans, on Dec 22, Wm Baily was found guilty of murdering his wife in July, by cruelly beating her just after her confinement, because the child she had given birth was a girl, whereas he desired a boy. The verdict excempts him from the punishment of death, the jury having that power in Louisiana. Did the jury mean to say this was a case of justifiable homicide? If <u>any</u> murder ought to be punished with death, it seems to us that this is just the kind. –Cour & Enq

Died: on Jan 5, in Gtwn, in her 37th year, Mrs Jane E, son of Francis Dodge, jr, & daughter of the late Henry H Chapman, of Md. Her funeral is tomorrow, Tues, at 3½ o'clock.

Died: yesterday, Asbury, youngest son of John & Lucinda Golding, aged 2 years, 10 months & 27 days. His funeral is this afternoon, precisely at 3 o'clock.

The Western Continent, a weekly journal published at Balt, announces that J Smith Homans has become associated with Messrs Garland & J Donaldson in that paper.

Geo W Reeder, well known in the community of New Orleans as a writer of sketches & reporter for the newspapers of that city, died on Dec 26, of cholera. A younger brother was also seized with cholera & died in a few hours. Mr Reeder was a native of St Mary's Co, Md. He has left a wife & a large circle of friends to lament his untimely death. –Delta

I certify that Jas Wilson brought before me as an estray, a Bay Gelding, about 10 years old. Owner is to prove property & take him away. –Jas Wilson, 7th st east, near the Navy Yard.

TUE JAN 9, 1849
Senate: 1-Ptn of Jas Hotchkiss, Simeon Hotchkiss, & Nelson Hotchkiss, asking to be allowed the right of pre-emption of the lands on which they settled in Ill: referred to the Cmte on Public Lands. 2-Ptn of Calvin Blythe, exc of Jesse D Elliot, deceased, praying remuneration for expenses incurred by the testator in receiving & entertaining, while in command of a nat'l vessel, the King of Greece & suite: referred to the Cmte on Naval Affairs. 3-Ptn of David D Porter, lt in the U S Navy, asking compensation for services as political agent of the Gov't in the island of San Domingo: referred to the Cmte on Foreign Relations. 4-Memorial of Wm Bayard & Co, praying a charter for a railroad from the Mississippi river to Calif: referred to the Cmte on Public Lands. 5-Communication from Winthrop W Cheney & S E Guild, excs of Abel Phelphs, addressed to the Cmte on the Library, in relation to the portraits of the early U S Presidents now in the Library of Congress: referred to the Cmte on the Library. 6-Ptn of Patrick Walker, praying for the continuance of his pension: referred to the Cmte on Pensions. 7-Ptn of Rebecca Robeson, on the file of the Senate, be referred to the Cmte on Pensions. 8-Bill for the relief of the legal reps of John Rice Jones, deceased: referred to the Cmte on Private Land Claims.

Circuit Court for Wash Co, D C, yesterday appointed John A Smith permanently to the ofc of Clerk, which had recently become vacant by the death of Wm Brent.

Teacher want to take charge of Frost Royal Academy, Warren Co, Va. –Giles Cook, Pres Board of Trustees.

Mrd: on Dec 6, 1848, in the Parish of Terrebonne, La, by Rev Mr McNair, Col John McGavock, of Williamson Co, Tenn, to Miss Caroline, eldest daughter of Col Van P Winder.

Mrd: on Dec 23, 1848, in Livingston Co, N Y, by Rev W J Bakewell, Mr Wm D Fitzhugh to Annie E Carroll, daughter of the Hon Chas H Carroll.

Died: on Dec 8, at Lancaster, Ohio, Hugh Boyle, in his 77th year. A native of Ireland, he emigrated to America in his early manhood, & in 1798 removed to the Northwestern Territory, where he continued to reside to the close of his useful & blameless life.

WED JAN 10, 1849
Wash Corp: 1-Cmte on Finance: asking to be discharged from the further consideration of the ptns of J A Williams & J A Williams & others: ordered to lie on the table. 2-Ptn from Wm Rupp: referred to the Cmte of Claims. 3-Ptn from Geo Collard, from the trustees of the First Methodist Protestant Church, near the Navy Yard, proposing to sell to the Corp the basement story of the church edifice now occupied by one of the primary schools of Wash City: referred to the Cmte on Public Schools. 4-Cmte on Police: bill for the relief of E G Handy: passed. Same cmte: relief of Wm A Mulloy: passed. 5-Bill for the relief of Robt B Clokey: rejected. 6-Bill for the relief of J Thomas: referred to the Cmte of Claims. 7-Bill for the relief of Saml Cromwell: passed. 8-Ptn of Wm Flinn, praying remission of a fine: referred to the Cmte of Claims. 9-Act to provide for the payment of the balance due Chas Stewart, jr, for laying flag footways: was read. 10-Relief of Preston Simpson: passed.

Galveston News of Dec 28: cholera has been prevailing with great fatality among the troops of the 8th Infty of the U S Army, recently stationed at Port Lavacca. Maj Morrison, commander, removed them into Port Lavacca, & had them quartered in Capt Brower's large bldg, which was used as a hospital for the sick. They were attended by Drs Dallan & Johnson, of Lavacca, but whether they had an army physician we do not learn. Twenty or thirty died each day. Maj Morrison gave them permission to proceed to San Antonio in small parties. Up to yesterday morning there had been 135 deaths. A letter to Maj Tompkins, of New Orleans, Port Lavacca, Dec 25, 1848. On the 23rd 22 men were buried in a pit, & yesterday 28 men were interred near the same spot. Maj Gates command had lost about 20, & no new cases. Dr Mills is with that command. Lt Deaney died last evening, & will be buried today. Lt Fink was sick, but had recovered. -Wm S Colquhoun

Brevet Maj Jas W Penrose, of the 2nd U S Infty, died on the 1st instant, at Plattsburg, N Y, of a disease contracted in the war with Mexico.

The Newburyport Herald of Jan 6 announces the death of Capt John N Cushing, father of Hon Caleb Cushing, in his 70th year. Capt C has been amongst the most enterprosing merchants in Newburyport, & was one of the largest ship-owners in New England.

The ship **Christoval Colon**, formerly one of the packet line between N Y & Havana, sailed from N Y on Sat for San Francisco, carrying these passengers, many of whom belong to the oldest & wealthiest families:

P B Schemerhorn	J R St Felix, jr	L B Lent
Dr J W Ray	M B Thomas	T B Dowling
C H Buckmaster	T G French	Saml L Haven
J H Beckman	J Stanton	W P Bailey
E W Spofford	Henry Livingston	W K Keeney
W J Emmett	W Crockson	G E St Felix
Herman LeRoy Jones	Chas Van Alen	T F Thomas
C S Hatch	Edwin Herrick	J R Garcia
Wm Ledoni	Henry B Livingston	J L Boggs
C J Torbett	Herman R LeRoy	D B D Smith
J Ackerman	Chas H Giles	
J Frothingham	C T Emmett	

Others who intend leaving soon for the enchanted region, are S S Osgood, the artist, C W Holden, of Holden's Magazine, & a son of Chester Harding, the Boston painter. -Tribute.

Mrd: on Monday, by Rev John C Smith, Mr Jas Johnson to Miss Mary D Strange, all of Wash City.

Died: on Jan 6, in Gtwn, Ellen, daughter of Emily & the late Thos Corcoran, in her 6th year.

Died: on Jan 9, Nicholas Travers, at a very advanced age. His funeral is on Thu, at 2 o'clock, from his late residence.

Ofcrs elected at the 34th Anniversary of the Columbia Typographical Society, held on Jan 6.

C F Lowrey, Pres	Jas English, Corr Sec
R W Claxton, V P	Michl Caton, Treas
Thos Rice, Rec Sec	

Anacostia Fire Co election on Jan 5:

Jonas B Ellis, Pres	John D Brandt, Sec
John Ober, V P	Wm Morgan, Sec

House of Reps:: 1-Memorial of Isaac S Keith Reeves, 1st Lt, 1st Regt, U S Artl, adjutant of the Military Academy, praying to be placed on the same footing as dragoon adjutants. 2-Ptn of Danl Palmer for an increase of his pension.

Household & kitchen furniture, & statues, at auction: on Jan 12, at the residence of A A Von Schmidt, on D st, between 6th & 7th sts: includes the celebrated Dancing Canova Statues, with pedestals. —A Green, auct

Senate: 1-Memorial of Fred'k Dant, asking the confirmation of his land claims: referred to the Cmte on Private Land Claims. 2-Ptn of John W Mount, a volunteer in the war with Mexico, asking an increase of pension: referred to the Cmte on Pensions. 3-Ptn of John J Simpson, asking indemnity for damage done to his property by the U S troops: referred to the Cmte of Claims. 4-Ptn of Jos Nock, asking compensation for losses in consequence of the violation by the Post Ofc Dept of his contract for supplying mail locks: referred to the Cmte on the Post Ofc & Post Roads. 5-Additional documents in relation to the ptn of Jas Harley: referred to the Cmte on Patents & the Patent Ofc. 6-Ptn of Saml H Thompson, on the files of the Senate, be referred to the Cmte on Naval Affairs. 7-Cmte of Claims: bill for the relief of Jos Gerard, without amendment.

From Columbus, Ohio. Pittsburg, Jan 9. We have a rumor here that Col Dix, of the U S army, died while a passenger in the stage near Wheeling, of cholera. [Jan 15th newspaper. Death of Lt Col Roger S Dix, U S Army. He was a native of N H, a brother of the Senator in Congress from N Y, & the son of Col Timothy Dix, of the Army, who lost his life in the ill-fated expedition of Gen Wilkinson against Montreal in 1813. He was educated at West Point & completed his studies in 1832. He volunteered his service, & accompanied Gen Scott on the Black Hawk expedition. He was either in Mexico paying troops, or in the U S expediting volunteers to the field. He perished almost without warning with cholera. He has left a little family to deplore his loss. –Union]

THU JAN 11, 1849
Senate: 1-Ptn of Henry W Barnes & Randolph M Cooley, asking compensation for clothing furnished to regts of N Y volunteers, mustered into the service of the U S during the war with Mexico: referred to the Cmte on Military Affairs. 2-Ptn of G W & P E Norton, praying the payment of certain bonds issued by the late republic of Texas, on the ground that, by her annexation to the U S, she has been deprived of her sources of revenue: referred to the Cmte on the Judiciary. 3-Ptn of Francis Barnes, asking compensation for services as an inspector in the custom-house at New Orleans: referred to the Cmte on Commerce. 4-Memorial of Lucretia O Everett, widow & admx of Alex'r H Everett, deceased, late Minister of Spain, asking certain allowances in the settlement of her late husband's accounts: referred to the Cmte on Foreign Relations. 5-Ptn of David Baker, asking an extension of his patent for an improvement in the saw-mill: referred to the Cmte on the Post Ofc & Post Roads. 6-Ptn of Peter A Carnes, a wagoner & forage master in the army of the U S, asking to be allowed a pension in consideration of disabilities contracted in the service: referred to the Cmte on Pensions. 7-Ordered: that the ptn of the legal reps of John

Rice Jones, on the files of the Senate, be referred to the Cmte on Private Land Claims. 8-Ordered: that the heirs of Jethro Wood have leave to withdraw their ptn & papers. 9-Ordered: that Eliz Atkins have leave to withdraw her ptn & papers. 10-Cmte on the Judiciary: bill for the relief of John P Skinner & the legal reps of Isaac Greene: reported the same without amendment. 11-Cmte on Pensions: bill for the relief of Eliz Clapper, of Muskingum Co, Ohio: reported the same without amendment. 12-Memorial of Farley D Thompson, praying to be released from liability as security for a defaulting postmaster: referred to the Cmte on the Post Ofc & Post Roads.

Mount Vernon Sheetings for sale, from the Md Institute for the best manufactured cotton cloth exhibited at the late fair held in Balt. –John Allen, seasonable Dry Goods, Pa ave, between 9th & 10th sts.

Wanted, by a single Frenchman, 30 years of age, who speaks English as well as French, also the languages of the continent of Europe, a situation as valet or head-servant in a family, either to stay or travel about. Address: N Gasne, Depot House, Pa ave, near the Railroad Depot, Wash.

Billiard Saloon & Bowling Alley: on 14th st, opposite Willard's Hotel. –F Burch

Ice-house for sale or rent, on very moderate terms. Apply to Thos Lundy, near the West Market.

The Hon Ambrose H Sevier, Ex-Senator from Arkansas, & recently returned from a mission of Peace to Mexico, died on Jan 1st. His first appearance in the Capitol was in 1827, as the Delegate to Congress from the then Territory of Arkansas; & on the admission of Arkansas into the Union as a State, he became in 1836 one of her first Senators. [Jan 26th newspaper: his death took place at the residence of the Hon B Johnson, his father-in-law, on the 31st ult, & appears to have been wholly unexpectd by the people of Little Rock, to which place his remains were carried for interment.]

Died: on Jan 9, in her 24th year, Mary Althea Sewart. Her funeral will be this evening, at 3 o'clock, from the residence of Mrs Wilson, on Pa ave, entrance on D st.

Died: on Jan 10, Jos Elgar, infant son of Chas E & Mgt A Sherman, aged nearly 2 years. His funeral will take place at 12 o'clock this day.

Died: on Jan 7, after a very brief illness, of congestion of the lungs, Catharine E S Kennedy Lesley, wife of Jas Lesley, jr, of Phil, & grand-daughter of John McKnight, of Reading, Pa.

In the N Y Supreme Court on Fri, Mrs Sarah Dibbin recovered a verdict of $1,500 against Mr Murphy, proprietor of the Bowery line of omnibuses, as compensation for injuries sustained by being run over in Oct, 1847, by one of the defendant's omnibuses. Her arm was fractured in 3 places, which was caused by the carelessness of the driver.

FRI JAN 12, 1849
$3 reward for a cow that strayed from the stable of the subscriber, at the Navy Yard. –Chas H Tavenner.

Housekeeping & fancy goods, & cigars: at auction: on Jan 16, at the store of Wm J Stoops, on Bridge, near High st, Gtwn. –A Green, auctioneer

Senate: 1-Ptn of Wm Green, jr, asking that a patent may be issued for an improvement in the process of manufacturing sheet iron. 2-Ptn of Mary Hall, asking to be allowed a pension: referred to the Cmte on Pensions. 3-Ptn of Rhoda Abney, asking a pension: referred to the Cmte on Pensions. 4-Memorial of Wm Lacon & Lewis H Bates, asking to be indemnified for losses & expenses incurred in consequence of the illegal seizure of a quantity of iron imported by them: referred to the Cmte on Commerce. 5-Memorial of D A Watterston, asking the balance due him for services as clerk to the Surveyor Genr'l of Louisiana: referred to the Cmte on Claims. 6-Cmte on Public Lands: bill for the relief of John Milliken & others, to secure certain rights to pre-emption in Louisiana, & for other purposes: reported the same without amendment. 7-Cmte on Pensions: bill for the relief of Patrick Walker: reported the same without amendment. 8-Bill for the relief of John P Baldwin, owner of the Spanish brig **Gil Blas**: considered. 9-Cmte of the Whole: bill for the relief of the captors of the frig **Philadelphia**. 10-Cmte of the Whole: bill for the relief of Calvin Emmons: referred to the Cmte on Patents & the Patent Ofc: reported back with certain amendments. 11-Bill for the relief of Jas P Seston: passed. 12-Bill for the relief of Wm M Blackford, late Charge d'Affaires to the Republic of New Grenada: considered. 13-Bill for the relief of Ann Chase was considered in the Cmte of the Whole: ordered to lie on the table. 14-Bill for the relief of Sarah D Bingham, wife of Jas H Bingham: passed. 15-Bill for the relief of the owners of the schnr **Ticonie**: considered.

A Faithless Swain. Miss M McClelland, of Bedford, Pa, lately recovered damages to the amount of $3,000 for a breach of promise of marriage from John Vandervert.

Henry Bramall was lately convicted before the Lord Mayor of London of having married 9 wives, all of whom are living. The heaviest punishment which the law awards for this crime is 7 years transportation. The court thought this too light. His Lordship regretted that he could not sentence him to live 7 years with the whole 9 wives, as that would be something like a punishment.

For Calif. 1-The barque **Maria**, Capt Baker, cleared at Boston on Mon for San Francisco, with a large assorted cargo & 22 passengers, among whom is Mr Geo H Davis, of Worcester, Mass, son of Hon John Davis. The **Maria** has on board, a house, painted, & in complete order for immediate erection on her arrival out. 2-The fine ship **Edward Everett**, owned by the Boston & Calif Mining & Trading Co, cleared for the same port on Tues, with 150 passengers. 3-The brig **Forest** cleared on Tues for the same port, with 45 passengers, mostly mechanics, of the old Bay State. The **Forest** has a library on board, partly furnished by her owner, & the remainder by the American Home Missionary Society.

In Chancery. Thos Blagden et al, vs Wm B Jackson, adm of John Little, et al. The creditors of the late John Little are hereby informed that they can receive a 2nd dividend by applying to S S Williams, Trustee.

Orphans Court of Wash Co, D C. Case of Gregory Ennis, exc of Patrick Moran, deceased. The Court & executor of the estate have appointed Jan 30th for settlement of said estate. —Ed N Roach, Reg/o wills

By virtue of a writ of fieri facias, at the suit of Wm McL Cripps, against the goods & chattels of Wm Johnson, to me directed, I have seized one frame house, on Mass ave, between 9th & 10th sts, in square 370, & shall offer for sale the same on Feb 15. —O E P Hazard, Constable

SAT JAN 13, 1849
Senate: 1-Ptn of R M Edwards, asking that soldiers who served in the war with Mexico may not be required to surrender their certificates of honorable discharge in drawing their bounty land: referred to the Cmte on Military Affairs. 2-Ptn of Jas Hook, heir of Jas Hook, deceased, a Revolutionary ofcr, asking to be allowed commutation pay: referred to the Cmte on Revolutionary Claims. 3-Memorial of Jas A Bayard, late Receiver of Public Moneys at Fairfield, Iowa, asking to be released from the payment of certain money of which he was robbed while on his way to deposite the same to the credit of the U S: referred to the Cmte on the Public Lands. 4-Ordered, that the ptn of Caleb Green, on the files of the Senate, be referred to the Cmte on the Judiciary. 5-Ordered, that the ptns of Rowland Carleton & Wm Miller, on the files of the Senate, be referred to the Cmte on Pensions. 6-Ordered, that the ptn of Dorothea Payne, on the files of the Senate, be referred to the Cmte on Pensions. 7-Ordered, that Chas Brenan & others have leave to withdraw their ptn & papers. 8-Cmte of Claims: bill for the relief of Geo Poindexter, reported back the same, with an amendment. 9-Cmte on Public Lands: ptn of Jas Hotchkiss, bill for his relief: ordered to a second reading. 10-Introduced: bill for the relief of Saml J Bayard, late Receiver at Fairfield, Iowa: referred to the Cmte on the Public Lands.

We learn that Roger B Thomas has been appointed Postmaster at Brookville, Montg Co, Md, in the place of R F Speake, resigned.

House of Reps: 1-Memorial of Maj Baker, of the ordnance corps, presenting a plan for the preservation of the interest of the U S in the gold mines of Calif: referred to the Cmte on Military Affairs. 2-Ordered that the heirs of Lt Micah Whitmarsh have leave to withdraw their memorial & accompanying papers from the files of the House. 3-Ordered that Eunice Crossman have leave to withdraw from the files of the House her ptn praying for a pension, & also the papers accompanying the same. 4-Bill for the relief of the legal reps of Antonio Pacheco: postponed.

Died: yesterday, in Wash City, Mr Jacob Acker, after a short but severe illness. He was a native of Bavaria, & was 36 years of age. He was an esteemed citizen, an affectionate husband, & a tender father, having left a wife & 5 children to mourn their severe loss. His funeral is Jan 14, at 2:30 p m, from his residence, in 2nd st, near the depot.

Eastern Judicial Circuit of Florida. Circuit Court, St John's Co. Jan 13, 1848. In Chancery. Prall & others, vs Brush & others-Suit for Partition. Cause to be heard upon the report of Geo Watson, jr, A M Randolph, & Thos C Ellis, Com'rs appointed: report dated Mar, 1848. Com'rs report: the said land so situated that a partition thereof cannot be made without prejudice to some of the owners & a heavy expense to all. It is ordered, adjudged, & decreed, that Geo M Payne, of Micanopy, Alachus Co, Jas Child, of said Micanopy, & Wm A Forward, of St Augustine, St Johns Co, Fla, three suitable competent persons, be & they are hereby appointed Com'rs for the purpose of carrying out the decree of this Court in said cause. Further ordered that the lands be sold at public auction, by & under their direction. The said Com'rs shall in the sale of said lands be guided by the map of said grant made by Messrs Burr, Washington, & Merry, late Com'rs, & shall sell the fractional sections in quantity & forms as laid down on said map. The money from the sale of these lands is to be deposited in the Bank of Charleston, S C. The lands referred to are known as the *Arredondo Grant*, containing 290,000 acres: lies between the 29th & 30th parallels of latitude, nearly midway between the Atlantic & the Gulf. -Geo M Payne, J Child, Wm A Forward, Com'rs

The Washington [Pa] Reporter of Wed brings a confirmation of the telegraphic report of the death of Maj Dix, of the U S Army, who died in Hillsborough, in that county, on last Sabbath morning.

Mr Henry E Waring, of Stamford, Conn, was killed last Fri by his sleigh coming in contact with the railroad train for N Y. His lady, who was also in the sleigh, received slight injuries.

Mrd: on Jan 11, by Rev Smith Pyne, John T B Dorsey, of Elkridge, Md, to Mary Campbell, daughter of Dr Thos Harris, U S N.

Died: after an illness of 18 hours, with croup. Thos Harrison, eldest son of Thos P & Viana Vial. [The Richmond, Va, papers & N Y commercial Adv will please copy.] [No death date given-current item.]

Died: on Jan 5, suddenly, of croup, Eliz, infant daughter of Jas & Eliz Wimer, aged 5 months & 13 days. Also, on Jan 9, of scarlet fever, Kate, eldest daughter of the same, aged 2 years, 2 months & 21 days.

Died: on Jan 12, Wm Hewitt, youngest son of Chas S & Lavinia Wallach, aged 1 year & 9 days. Her funeral is this afternoon at 3 o'clock.

MON JAN 15, 1849
From our foreign correspondent. London, Dec 19, 1848. The election of Louis Napoleon Bonaparte to the Presidency of the Republic of France is the most surprising event which has hitherto occurred in this most wonderful year.

House of Reps: 1-Leave granted for the withdrawal of the ptn & papers of Eliza Tharp. Same for Wm Fuller. 2-Ptn of Bvt Maj Kendrick, relating to ordnance funds lost at Jalapa.

Gen Ruland, of St Louis, who served for a long time as one of Gen Harrison's staff, & was more recently an Indian Agent, died at Jefferson City, Mo, on Jan 5.

Appointments by the Pres. 1-Robt C Ewing, to be U S Marshal for the district of Missouri, from Jan 15, when his present commission will expire. 2-Wm H Marriott, reappointed Collector of the customs for the district of Balt, Md. 3-Andrew B Gray, of Texas, to be Surveyor for running the boundary line between the U S & Mexico. 4-John D Field, jr, to be Coiner of the branch mint of the U S at Dahlonega, Ga, in place of D H Mason, deceased. 5-Thos D Moseley, to be U S Atty for the district of Middle Tennessee, reappointed. 6-Isaac O Barnes, to be U S Marshal for the district of Massachusetts, reappointed. 7-Thos D Condy, to be U S Marshal for the district of S Carolina, reappointed. 8-Justices of the Peace in Wash Co, D C: John Cox, John J Stull, Jas Marshall, Lewis Carbery, Thos Carbery, all reappointed: & Wm J McCormick, & Saml Grubb.

Died: on Jan 13, in Wash City, Mr J Lawson Naylor, in his 34th year. His funeral is this morning at 10 o'clock from the residence of his brother, F Y Naylor, on 2nd st west, in the rear of the Railroad Depot.

Died: on Dec 28, at Welborne Hall, Loudoun Co, Va, at the residence of his brother, John P Dulany, Danl F Dulany, of Fairfax Co. Of the many virtues which adorned his character, let the deep affliction of so an affectionate devoted family speak, & the sorrowing of a widely extended circle of acquaintances testify. -Alex Gaz

Naval Genr'l Court Martial convened at the Gosport Navy Yard, on Wed last, consisting of the following ofcrs: Pres, Cmdor Sloat; Cmders H N Page, J L Saunders, W H Gardner, Saml Barron; Lts A Sinclair & John R Tucker, members, & Simeon Wheeler Judge Advocate. This Court is for the trail of Midshipman DeKoven & such others as may be brought before it.

TUE JAN 16, 1849
M Andraud, the engineer, well known by his works & experiments on compressed air, discovered, at the shop of a dealer in second-hand articles, the electrifying machine of Benj Franklin, which is supposed to have been made at Phil. After 80 years, it is in an excellent state of preservation.

Capt Wm G Marcy, a son of the U S Sec of War, was disposing of every thing in the shape of supplies at his camp, in exchange for gold dust. He had collected 15 barrels of gold ore, & having no means of protecting the treasure, he had buried it, until a vessel of war should arrive on the coast, which is daily expected.

Died: on Nov 13, 1848, at Germanna Mills, Orange Co, Va, after a painful illness, Fred'k F Bowen, aged 28 years. The deceased leaves a wife with 4 small children & numerous relatives & friends to mourn his loss.

Mr Chas Hutchins, a clerk in the Freight Ofc of the Western Railroad, at Springfield, Mass, was instantly killed on Wed. He boarded near the railroad, & as he jumped off the car, a train coming from Boston struck him a fatal blow. It was too dark for him to notice the train.

Senate: 1-Memorial from the Genr'l Assembly of Iowa, asking that Isaac W Griffith, a soldier in the war with Mexico, may be allowed an increase of Pension: referred to the Cmte on Pensions. 2-Memorial of Peter Parker, asking payment of a balance due him for services as interpreter & translator to the U S Agents in China: referred to the Cmte on Foreign Relations. 3-Ptn of the widow & children of John Robertson, deceased, a soldier in the last war with Great Britain, asking that a bounty land warrant may be issued to them in lieu of one which was lost or destroyed: referred to the Cmte on Private Land Claims. 4-Ptn of Hiram Smith, register of the land ofc at Champagnole, Ark, asking to be allowed, in the settlement of his accounts, certain charges for clerk hire & commissions on disbursements: referred to the Cmte of Claims. 5-Ptn of Henry M Rector, asking the confirmation of his title to certain lands in Arkansas: referred to the Cmte on Public Lands.

Died: yesterday, Jas Marshall, after an illness of 10 days, in his 52nd year. He was a native of Pa, & for many years an esteemed citizen of Wash. He was an affectionate husband & tender father, leaving a wife & 3 children to mourn his loss. His funeral is Jan 17, at 2 p m, from his late residence near the Navy Yard. [Jan 26 newspaper: Anacostia Fire Co: resolved that this Company deeply depore his irreparable loss; the Hall is to be hung in mourning for the space of 6 months; the bell of this Company to be tolled whilst the funeral is passing to the place of interment.]

Wash City Ordinances. 1-An Act for the relief of Presley Simpson: the fine imposed upon Simpson for neglecting to take out a license for keeping or harboring of dogs is remitted: provided he pay the cost of prosecution. 2-Act for the relief of Saml Cromwell: to be paid $10, the same having been erroneously paid by Cromwell to the Corp relative to a fine. 3-Act for the relief of E G Handy, police ofcr of the 3rd Ward, to be paid $154.45, said amount being the balance found due to him on the settlement of his police accounts up to Jul 1, 1848, as certified to by the accounting ofcrs of this Corp.

Six & a quarter cents reward, for runaway black boy, Wm Smith. –John Golden

Gen Taylor was 64 years old last Nov. He is hale & hearty, & in the full enjoyment of his natural strong intellectual faculties.

WED JAN 17, 1849
Rev Arsenio Nico de Silva, pastor of the Portuguese refugees recently arrived in this country has died. He was formerly a rich merchant in Madeira, but having embraced the protestant faith, was driven from that island by persecution, & recently arrived here to seek a home in this country for himself & 600 of his expatriated countrymen. –N Y Com Adv

Mr John Lawler, of Whitestone, L I, engaged in procuring ice from a mill-pond, stepped upon some thin ice, & immediately sunk. His body was recovered in about 2 hours. Mr L was overseer of the large estate of the late Mr Leggett, of Whitestone, & leaves a family.

Senate: 1-Ptn of Wm Emmons, adm of Uri Emmons, asking the extension of his patent for a planning machine: referred to the Cmte on Patents & the Patent Ofc. 2-Ptn of Simon Snodgrass, asking the reimbursement of expenses incurred in aiding the removal of the Cherokee Indians west of Mississippi in 1838: referred to the Cmte on Indian Affairs. 3-Additional documents were submitted in the case of E P Guyon: referred to the Cmte on Claims. 4-Additional documents submitted in the claim of Manuel X Harmony: referred to the Cmte of Claims. 5-Cmte on Private Land Claims: bill for the legal reps of John Rice Jones, deceased, reported the same with an amendment: ordered to be printed. 6-Cmte on Pensions: bill for the relief of B O Payne: to be printed. 7-Cmte on Patents: made an adverse report on the ptn of Jas Harley: to be printed.

House of Reps: 1-Resolved, that John J Newton, of Vt, have leave to withdraw his ptn & papers from the files of the Clerk of this House. 2-Resolved, that Henry H Sibley be admitted to a seat on the floor of the House of Reps: as a Delegate from the Territory of Wisconsin. 3-Cmte on Military Affairs: adverse report on the ptn of John Dies: laid on the table. 4-Cmte on Private Land Claims: bill for the relief of the heirs of Semoice, a friendly Creek Indian: read twice & committed. 5-Bills for the relief of Jas P Sexton, & for the relief of Sarah D Caldwell, wife of Jas H Brigham: referred to the Cmte on Private Land Claims. 6-Act for the settling of the claim of Chas G Ridgeley: returned to the Senate. 7-Bill for the relief of Nehemiah Brush: referred. 8-Bill continuing the pension of Patrick Walker: referred. 8-Ptn of Danl Palmer, praying for a law giving him certain back pay & rations, claimed as due him as a recruiting sergeant during a portion of the late war with Mexico. 9-Ptn of Thos Young, of Muskingum Co, Ohio, for a premium for an alleged discovery in hydraulics. 10-The papers of Fred Shaffer were referred to the Cmte of Claims.

Balt American of yesterday contains the following obituary notice. Died, on Jan 10, Mrs Anne Bias, in her 90th year; &, on Jan 12, Mrs Deborah Holland, mother of Mrs Bias, at the advanced age of 110 years.

On Fri week Mr Wellington Stem, of Carroll Co, Md, whilst attempting to cross the Monocacy, at Begg's Fording, in a 2 horse sleigh, was frozen to death during his efforts to extricate his horses from the ice, through which they had broken. When found, he was standing erect, with only his head & shoulders above water, having evidently missed the fording.

Peter C Brooks, the Boston millionaire. The Traveller says the estate will not exceed $1,800,000, & that he has made no bequests of a public character.

G Broadbent, Pa ave, between 8th & 9th sts, intends closing out his stock of Cloaks, Visites, & Mantillas at greatly reduced priced.

Inauguration of Louis Napoleon. The proclamation of the President took place in the Assembly on Jan 20. Gen Cavaignac was in his old seat, seeming anything but down-hearted. One would have said that he was a man relieved of a heavy burden, rather than a defeated & disappointed candidate.

Appointments by the Pres. 1-Chas Eames, of N Y, to be Com'r to the Sandwich Island, in place of Anthony Ten Eyck, resigned. 2-Caleb H Booth, of Iowa, to be Surveyor Genr'l for the district of Wisconsin & Iowa, in place of Geo W Jones, resigned.

Died: on Jan 15, of palsy, Mr Matthias Jeffers, aged 70 years. His funeral is today at 10 o'clock, from his late residence on Missouri ave, between 3rd & 4½ sts.

Died: on Jan 5, at *Atamasco*, the residence of John Patterson, Balt, Co, in her 84th year, Margaret Nicholas, relict of Gov Wilson Cary Nicholas, of Va, & sister of the late Gen Saml Smith, of Md.

Obit-died: suddenly, at sea, on board the steamer **Crescent City**, on her way from New Orleans to Havana, of pulmonary consumption, on Dec 3, 1848, Isaac Shelby, only surviving son of the late Alfred Shelby, & of the present Mrs Dr R J Breckenridge, of Ky. His remains were brought home & interred on Jan 2, at *Traveller's Rest*, the former residence of his grandfather, Govn'r Shelby, of Ky, which this young gentleman inherited. This young man had not quite completed his 21st year; liberally educated; he inherited an ample fortune, & a name honored from the days of the Revolution. –R J B

Last night's Southern mail confirms the death of Col Geo Croghan, the Inspec Genr'l of the Army. He died at New Orleans on Jan 8, of a disease resembling cholera, in his 59th year.

Cincinnati Enquirer: Judge Wiseman, who arrived from below yesterday, states that when the boat **Phoenix**, on which he came, touched at Napoleon, mouth of the Arkansas river, the remains of the Hon Ambrose H Sevier, late Senator from Arkansas, were there awaiting conveyance to his former residence. He had died at Judge Johnson's, about 20 miles below Napoleon, of what I did not learn, but it was not cholera.

Pensacola, Jan 6. Hon Mr Clifford, our Minister to Mexico, & family, arrived here on Thu last in the revenue cutter **Walcott**, from Mobile, & has taken lodgings at Collin's Hotel. A salute of 21 guns was fired by the Yard & returned by the **Walcott**. -Gazette

The brig **Pope** arrived at Honolulu, in 14 days, with a cargo of gold dust. The arrivals from California had produced the greatest excitement among the inhabitants. 200 passengers had left the Sandwich Islands for the gold regions, & many others were soon to follow.

Geo Catlin, the artist, is now in London, stating that the Russian Gov't has made proposals to him for the purchase of his Indian Collection, & the price specified by the artist is $75,000.

Recent arrival in Wash: John Vanderlyn, the Painter of that fine picture in the Capitol entitled "The Landing of Columbus." He occupies one of the Cmte rooms at the Capitol, where, we understand, it is his intention to execute a few portraits.

According to the N Y Express there are no less than 47 vessels loading at the port of N Y for the voyage round Cape Horn. The steamer **Panama** is to sail on Feb 15.

Brevet Maj Hughes, U S Topographical Engineers, late cmder of the Md & D C regt in Mexico, is about to survey a proposed route for a railroad across the Isthmus, from Chagres to Panama, for Messrs Aspinwall & Co, N Y. Capt Lloyd Tilghman, of Balt, has been selected as assistant, & Capt Geo W Brown, of Balt, goes out in some important capacity connected with the camp duties.

THU JAN 18, 1849
House of Reps: 1-Cmte on Naval Affairs: discharged from further consideration of the ptn of Chas Colburn for allowance of wages to the end of the time of his enlistment as yeoman on board the U S ship **Ohio**: laid on the table. 2-Cmte on Foreign Affairs: discharged from further consideration of the ptn of Edw L Young & of various citizens of Norfolk & Portsmouth, Va, praying Congress to pass an act for the relief of said Young for losses sustained in the public service: referred to the Cmte on Naval Affairs. 3-Cmte on Revolutionary Pensions: adverse reports on the ptns of Henry Ballman & John Booystrom, & of citizens of Essex Co, Mass, praying for the benefits of the pension laws: laid on the table. 4-Cmte on Revolutionary Pensions: bill for the relief of Sally Darby: went to the Senate for concurrence. 5-Cmte on Invalid Pensions: to be discharged from the further consideration of the ptns of Saml Cooper, Jos Williams, jr, Jos Farrar, Lorenzo Poelzel, & John English: laid on the table. Same cmte: ptn of Chas Wilson, with a bill for his relief: sent to the Senate for concurrence. Same cmte: ptn of B O Payne, with a bill for his relief: committed to the Cmte of the Whole House. Reconsidered and then laid on the table. 6-Cmte on Invalid Pensions: discharged from the further consideration of the ptns of Geo Casady & John Forest for pensions: laid on the table. Same cmte: ptns of Sally R Johnson & Tabitha Wilder, made adverse reports thereon: laid on the table. The heirs of Dr Louis Wolfley were granted permission to withdraw papers from the files referring to a ptn for a pension. 7-Cmte on Invalid Pensions: discharged from the further consideration of the ptn of Mrs C H Johnson, widow of Capt Hezekiah Johnson, late of the U S army, praying for a pension: laid on the table. Same cmte: adverse report on the ptn of Chas C Cargill: laid on the table. 8-Cmte of Ways & Means discharged from the further consideration of the memorial of Wm Field, clerk of the U S District Court for the district of Arkansas, praying remuneration for services in making an abstract of all bankrupt cases which had been or were pending before said court, in compliance with an order from the Sec of State of the U S: said ptn was laid on the table. 8-Cmte of Claims: discharged from the further consideration of the memorial of David G Bates, Thos Jenkins, & Moses Meeker, praying for the refunding to them the amount of rents paid the U S for lead

mined & smelted on certain Indian lands: laid on the table. Same cmte: bill for the relief of Robt Roberts, which had been recommitted with instructions "to indicate the fund out of which" the claim of said Roberts "shall be paid," with an amendment. 9-Ptn of Geo Fox & Geo Jamison, chiefs, survivors of the N Y emigrant Senecas, in behalf of themselves & of the returned emigrants & the legal reps of those who died in the Indian country & on their way back, setting forth that they are entitled to their share of N Y & U S annuities, where by treaty stipulated to be paid said emigrants at the West, which for certain causes have not been paid, & praying that provision be made for the payment of the same.

Senate: 1-Cmte on the Judiciary: ptn of Caleb Green, late Clerk for the U S District Court for the Western district of Louisiana, asking reimbursement of ofc rent paid by him, reported "that the prayer of the petitioner ought not to be granted." 2-Cmte of the Whole: bill for the relief of David Myerle: question pending being upon an amendment upon the same. 3-Bill for the relief of John P Baldwin: postponed.

Appointment by the Pres: John B Weller, of Ohio, to be Com'r for running the Boundary line between the U S & the Republic of Mexico, in place of A H Sevier, who was nominated to the Senate, & has since died.

From the Western Texan of the 23rd ult. We hear of the death of Judge J E Davis, of Ky, who died at the residence of Col H Grooms, near Austin, on the 11th instant. It will be gratifying to Judge Davis' family to hear that assiduous & unremitting attentions on the part of the family of Col Grooms, alleviated, as far as it was within power of human means, the last suffering of their departed friend.

Extract of a letter, received a day or 2 since, from Lt Ham P Bee, dated Laredo, Dec 7, 1848. The Indians have been in town several times lately, but have killed no one.

Mr Alfred Van Kleek, a member of the firm of R Desha & Co, of Mobile, put an end to his existence on the 9th instant by shooting himself. He has been for some time under aberration of mind, resulting from severe sickness in 1847.

Mrd: on Wed, by Rev Mr Johnston, of Alexandria, Va, Mr Jas Entwisle, jr, of Alexandria, Va, to Miss Catharine A, eldest daughter of Jos Radcliff, of Wash City.

Died: on Jan 17, Mrs Isabella Kelly, in her 63rd year, after a long & painful illness. She was a native of county Tyrone, Ireland, but for the last 30 years a resident of Wash City & Balt. Her funeral is this afternoon at 3 o'clock, from her late residence on 8th near G st.

Died: on Jan 17, of croup, in her 6th year, Caroline, daughter of Benj Beall. Her funeral will take place this day at 3 o'clock from the residence of B F Middleton, on Louisiana ave.

FRI JAN 19, 1849
Liberal reward for return of lost dog, a mouse-colored Greyhound Pup. –Fitzhugh Coyle, 7th st, next door to Latham's Banking-house.

Orphans Court of Wash Co, D C. Letters of adminstration on the personal estate of Jacob Acker, late of said county, deceased. –Caroline C Acker, admx

Senate: 1-Resolution passed by the Legislature of the State of Florida, in favor of a law making compensation to John Tucker, for services as chaplain to a bltn of Florida militia in the Seminole war: referred to the Cmte on Military Affairs. 2-Memorial of Martha Cox, widow of a Revolutionary soldier, asking to be allowed a pension: referred to the Cmte on Pensions. 3-Ptn of Enoch Baldwin, asking the return of the discriminating duties paid by him on a cargo of rum: referred to the Cmte on Commerce. 4-Ptn of Francis G Beatty & Saml Walker, asking compensation for injuries received by the falling of a scaffold while at work on the Treasury bldgs in 1842: referred to the Cmte of Claims. 5-Ordered that Wm Morrow have leave to withdraw his papers. 6-Cmte on the Judiciary: asking to be discharged from the further consideration of the ptn of G W & P E Norton, asking payment of their claims against the late republic of Texas: which was agreed to. 7-Bill for the relief of Chas Wilson, & the bill for the relief of Sally Darly, of Randolph Co, Ga, were referred to the Cmte on Pensions. 8-Cmte on Public Lands: adverse reports in the case of Peter Whitmore Knaggs, & in the case of Peter Godfrey.

Dissolution of the partnership existing under the firm of Worthington & Curtin, by mutual consent. –Thos H Worthington, Thos G Curtin. [New partnership formed under the name of Curtin & Stevens. –Thos G Curtin, R C Stevens]

Files of the Oregon Spectator to Jul 13, inclusive, 3 months later than the Oregon papers last received. 1-Messrs Eels & Walker, missionaries at **Fort Colville**, with their families, had been brought to Oregon city, there to remain until safer times. Their Indians, the Spokans, parted with them with strong tokens of regret & affection. 2-The Rev G Atkinson & lady had arrived from Boston. Rev Thos McBridge was drowned, in June, while attempting to cross the Willamette river. On Sunday last the steamer **Richland**, while on her way from Cheraw to Gtwn, S C, burst her boilers & burnt to the water's edge. Among the 8 or 10 lives lost, was Mr John McFarlan, of Cheraw, & a Mr Davis & his wife. The steamer had on board at the time the body of Mr John Taylor, which was being conveyed to Gtwn for burial. It was consumed. [Jan 23rd newspaper: victims were: Mr John McFarlane, Mrs Henry Davis, her niece Martha Davis, Mr Whitehead, first engineer, Mr Maxy, second engineer, Mr Richd Downing, mate, & 9 blacks. Capt Brock was severely injured in the explosion, as were 3 other white passengers, viz: Mr H Davis, Mr David & Miss Mgt Davis. Capt Brock was rescued from his position by the exertions of Mrs Davis & the stewardess, the former having afterwards perished.]

Mrd: yesterday, at Leamington, by Rev Mr Gilliss, Hudson Taylor, of Wash City, to Christine, daughter of E Lindsley.

Mrd: on Thu, by Rev John C Smith, Mr Wm Murphy to Miss Jane Thomson, of Wash City.

Died: on Fri last, of catarrh fever, aged 9 months, George Anna Derby, daughter of J Goldsborough & Eliza Ann Bruff.

Saml Oakley, trustee of the Illinois & Michigan Canal, on behalf of the State, died at his residence in Tremont, Ill, on Jan 1.

Ezra Keller, D D, Pres of Wittenberg College, Springfield, Ohio, died on Jan 3. He was a ripe scholar & an exemplary Christian.

House of Reps: 1-Ptn of Arthur Hale, postmaster at South Quay, Nansemond Co, Va, for additional compensation. 2-Ptn of Johanna Cockbill & 42 other citizens of Schuylkill Co, Pa, praying for an immediate modification of the revenue laws.

Wash City Item. The funeral of the late Jas Marshall, one of our oldest & most respectable magistrates, took place on Wed. His remains were followed to their final resting place, in the Episcopal Methodist grave yard, [opposite <u>Congress burial ground,</u>] by the members of the Anacostia & Perserverance Fire Companies, & a great number of citizens, who highly respect the memory of the deceased.

SAT JAN 20, 1849
Corp of Wash. 1-Cmte of Claims: bill for the relief of J Thomas was passed. 2-Cmte of Claims: asking to be discharged from the further consideration of the ptn of Geo Seitz: agreed. Same cmte: asking to be discharged from the further consideration of the ptn of Wm Rupp: passed. 3-Cmte of Claims: bill for the relief of M Butler: reported without amendment. Same cmte: ptn of Wm Flinn: ask to be discharged from the further consideration of the ptn. 4-Ptn of Susan J Weeden, praying remission of a fine: referred to the Cmte of Claims. 5-Cmte of Claims: bill for the relief of Wm A Mulloy, police ofcr of the 5th Ward, reported the same without amendment. 6- Nominations by the Mayor for members of the Board of Health:

Dr W B Magruder	J Y Bryant	Dr N Young
H C Williams	Dr J F May	Jas Crandell
Dr T Miller	G C Grammer	Dr J E Morgan
Jas Larned	Dr J B Gardner	J W Jones
Dr J C Hall	J P Ingle	

[Correction of Jan 25 newspaper: Dr R Johnson instead of Dr W B Magruder; Dr W H Sanders instead of Dr Dr J F May; W B Randolph instead of J W Jones]

The fine frig **St Lawrence**, commanded by Capt Paulding, has been displaying the American flag in the North Sea, the Baltic, & in the British Channel. Every where it has been greeted with distinguished attention.

Valuable property for rent: well know property called ***Holme's Island*** or ***Jackson City***, on the south end of the Potomac Long Bridge. Address the subscriber, at Clearspring, Wash Co, Md. –Wm Dodge, Agent

For sale or rent: on the Heights of Gtwn, a beautiful & highly-finished Villa, in the Italian style, at present occupied by Senator Foote. Inquire of M Duffey. Possession on Mar 1.

Senate: 1-Bill for the relief of Saml T Anderson: referred to the Cmte on Naval Affairs. 2-Bill for the relief of Antonio Pacheco: referred to the Cmte on Military Affairs. 3-Bill passed yesterday when the Senate was quite thin, for the relief of Capt Percival. The facts relate to the authority under which duties were said to have been performed, & go to show that the whole business is without any foundation whatever. Instead of this gentleman performing the duties of clerk & chaplain, I [Mr Allen] am prepared to prove that he was appointed as naturalist & astronomer, & also that the purser refused to make the allowance until he was commanded a second time to do so by Capt Percival. Subject may be opened again. 4-Cmte of the Whole: bill for the relief of Fred'k Dawson, Jas Schott, & Elisha D Whitney: considered & postponed.

House of Reps: 1-Act for the relief of Bryan Callaghan: referred to the Cmte of Claims. 2-Ptn of Edw Evans, of Michigan, a soldier of the Revolution, for a pension. 3-Ptn of John Cummins, ordnance sgt of the U S army at *Fort Crawford*, for the usual extra allowance which is made to commissioned ofcrs for doing the duties of acting assist commissary of subsistence. 4-Ptn of Atkins Dyer, for return of foreign tonnage money paid by him. 5-Cmte on the Library to inquire into the expediency of purchasing the diaries & other private papers of Gen Washington.

Valuable property for sale: 3 story brick house on Pa ave, east of Coleman's Hotel, at present occupied by the subscriber as a clothing store & dwlg. Possession can be had on Mar 1 next. Inquire at the store on the premises. –J M Johnson

From Mexico. 1-Miguel Bruno, late chief of the insurrection at Tabasco, has been tried by a court martial & shot, by order of Don Tomas Maria, the present Govn'r of that port. 2-A party of rebels was lately surprised in the Sierra, by Don J Mejia, who killed their leader, Jimenez, & 26 of his men, & made 12 prisoners, who were immediately shot.

The Lancaster Examiner announces the death of Col Christian Jacob Hutter, at Easton, Pa, aged 80. He founded several papers in Lancaster, Allentown, & Easton, continuing as an editor & contributor from 1799 down to 1835. He was for several years also a rep in the Legislature.

Mrd: on Jan 16, by Rev O B Brown, Mr J Thos Clark to Miss Cornelia L, daughter of Mr Wm Cockrell, of Wash.

Galveston Civilian of Jan 6. Affray in Wash Co, Texas, wherein Wayne Barton was killed & Edw Burleson, jr, was badly wounded. The affair grew out of an election at Bastrop the year before last, when a brother of Burleson's was shot by Barton. The parties were brothers-in-law. Gen Burleson, the father & father-in-law of the parties, is well know, having held the ofc of V Pres of the late republic, & other important positions.

Died: on Jan 13, at her late residence, near Orange Court house, Va, Jane Taylor, the beloved wife of Chas P Howard, in her 83rd year.

Thos J Lacy, a prominent member of the Bar at New Orleans, died from an attack of cholera on Jan 11. He was a native of N C, when he emigrated to Ky, & thence to Arkansas, where he served for some time as Justice of the Supreme Court. He was in his 47th year.

MON JAN 22, 1849
New style of boy's clothing at the Fancy & Stationery Store of C A Comly, Pa ave, 3rd door east of 4½ st. Also, at the store of Henry J Rigby, 15½ Balt st, Balt, under the Museum.

Extract of a letter from Thos O Larkin, late Consul, & now Navy Agent of the U S, to the Sec of State, dated at Monterey, Nov 16, 1848, & received in this city on Fri last. The digging & washing for gold continues to increase on the Sacramento placer. I have had in my hands pieces of gold about 23 carats fine, weighing from 1 to 2 pounds. There are many men at the placer, who in Jun last had not $100, now in possession of from five to twenty thousand dollars, which they made by digging gold & trading with the Indians.

Hagerstown [Md] News. On Thu last the house of Mr Christian Hawbecker, in the Clearspring district, was entirely consumed by fire. The wife of of Mr H, for some time past, been a maniac, from which circumstance it became necessary to keep her chained, to prevent injury to herself & those around her. Mr H rushed into the flames to rescue her, took an axe & severed the chain, but she fell backward into the burning bldg. He again attempted by jumping through a window, bearing the object of his devotion & peril. Mrs H was but slightly injured, but Mr H, suffered severely.

Shadrach Barnes, convicted in Madison Co, Ky, of the murder of M Agee, & sentenced to be hanged, committed suicide by hanging himself on Jan 2.

Albany, Jan 10. Yesterday, at the works of the Albany Gas Co in Arch st, Michl Flood & Peter Halpin, long in the service of the company, descended a dry well, & neither came up. Patrick Coyle was lowered into the well, to recover the others, but all 3 died from the gases. The body of Halpin could not be reached. -Argus

House of Reps: 1-Motion for leave to introduce a bill for the relief of Robt B White.
2-Ptn of J P Martin & 76 others, praying for a reduction of postage on letters.
3-Ptn of A G Blanchard, Copeland S Hunt, Theodore Lewis, & others, in relation to the 3 months' extra pay.

Wash City: inquest on Sat on the body of Mgt Evans, who was found dead on Sat near Hertmiller's stables. It is supposed she had frozen to death while in a state of intoxication, she being of intemperate habits.

Mrd: on Jan 17, in Wash City, by Rev Mr Sampson, L A Edmonston, formerly of Wash City, to Eliz Wells, of Balt.

Mrd: on Nov 28 last, at Gibraltar, by Rt Rev the Bishop of Heliopolis, Vicar Apostolic in Gibraltar, & by the Venerable Archdeacon of Gibraltar, Thos Caute Reynolds, of Richmond, Va, to Heloise Marie, daughter of the late Horatio Sprague, of Gibraltar.

Died: on Jan 20, after a brief illness, in his 22nd year, Chas W H Weightman, son of Roger C Weightman, of Wash City. His remains will be removed from the corner of Missouri & 4½ sts, this day at 12 o'clock.

Died: on Jan 21, in Wash City, Theodore Middleton, after long & painful sufferings, which he bore with meek submission, leaving an affectionate wife & 3 children.

Died: on Jan 5, in Wheeling, Va, of a few days' illness, Mr Saml Holtzman, formerly a resident of Wash City, in his 70th year.

Died: on Tue, at his residence in N Y C, Mr John Blake, age 58 years, for nearly 30 years identified with the good & evil fortunes of the Park Theatre in that city.

TUE JAN 23, 1849
Meeting of the Colonization Society, held in Wash City, on Jan 17. The following gentlemen were elected to manage its affairs during 1849: Hon Henry Clay elected Pres of the Society. Elected Vice Presidents:

Gen John H Cocke, of Va
Danl Webster, of Mass
Chas F Mercer, of Fla
Louis McLane, of Balt
Moses Allen, of N Y
Gen W Jones, of Wash
Jos Gales, of Wash
Wm Maxwell, of Va
Elisha Whittlesey, of Ohio
Walter Lowrie, of N Y
Jacob Burnet, of Ohio
Dr Stephen Duncan, of Miss
Wm C Rives, of Va
Rev J Laurie, D D, of Wash
Rev Wm Winans, of Miss
Jas Boorman, of N Y
Henry A Foster, of N Y
Dr John Ker, of Miss
Robt Campbell, of Ga
Peter D Vroom, of N J
Jas Garland, of Va
Rt Hon Lord Bexle, of London
Wm Short, of Phil
Willard Hall, of Dela
Rt Rev Bishop Otey, of Tenn
Gerard Ralston, of London

Dr Hodgkin, of London
Thos R Hazard, of Providence, R I
Maj Gen Winfield Scott, of Wash
Rev A Alexander, D D, of N J
Jas Railey, of Miss
Rev C C Coyler, D D, of Phil
Elliott Cresson, of Phil
Anson G Phelps, of N Y
Jonathan Hale, of Maine
Rev Dr W B Johnson, of S C
Moses Sheppard, of Balt
Bishop McIlvain, of Ohio
Rev P Lindsley, D D, of Tenn
Hon J R Underwood, of Ky
Hon C Marsh, of Woodstock, Vt
Rev J J Janeway, D D, of N J
H L Lumpkin, of Athens, Ga
Jas Lenox, of N Y
Bishop Soule, D D, of Tenn
Hon Thos Corwin, of Ohio
Hon Thos W Williams, of Conn
Hon Simon Greenleaf, of Mass
Rev John Early, of Va
Rev M Pierce, of Ga
Hon R J Walker, of Miss
John McDonogh, of La

Rev Jeremiah Day, D D, of Conn
Theodore Frelinghuysen, of N Y
Rev Dr Edgar, of Nashville, Tenn
Rev Geo W Bethune, D D, of Phil
Rev Leonard Woods, D D, of Andover, Mass
Rev Jas O Andrews, Bishop of the Methodist Episcopal Chr
Rev Beverly Waugh, Bishop of the Methodist Episcopal Chr, Balt

Rev E Burgess, D D, Dedham, Mass
Rt Rev Wm Meade, D D, Bshp of Va
Dr Thos Massie, Tye River Mills, Va
Rev Courtland Van Rensaelaer, N J

Obit-died: on Jan 21, in Wash City, Gen Alex'r Hunter, late Marshal of D C, at age 59 years. His funeral is at his late residence, on 3rd & C sts, on Wed next at 12 o'clock. He was born in Dumfries, Pr Wm Co, Va. Though childless himself, he raised up orphans to adore his name. His robust health & manly frame gave way wholly to paralytic attacks. His father, Nathl Hunter, suddenly ruined in his pecuniary affairs, gave up his fortune to sundry creditors. Not long after that event, he died, leaving the subject of this feeble sketch, just upon the verge of manhood. The manly youth promptly adopted his father's family, & looked upon it as his own. After Gen Jackson became Pres, he treated Gen Hunter as a bosom friend, & made him Marshal of D C.

Civil law of France forbids the marriage of a Romish priest even after he had abandoned the priesthood. M Trivier, formerly a priest in the diocese of Dijon, but now an Evangelical minister, desiring to be married, was refused, on account of his being in holy orders. M Lavelle, a rep of the people, & a member of the municipal council of that town, published the banns, & celebrated the marriage on Nov 16.

The Onondaga Standard states that a few nights since the daughter of R S Costing, of that place, was severly burnt, in her bed, by the clothes taking fire from a light she had been using while reading in bed. She fell asleep & was awakened by the pain occasioned by the fire.

House of Reps: 1-Cmte of the Whole House: asking to be discharged from the further consideration of the bill for the relief of Capt Dan Drake Henrie. Bill was amended & sent to the Senate for concurrence. 2-Payment by the Sec of State, to Wm C Riddall & Wm C Zantzinger, of the sum of $771.41, to be divided equally between them. 3-Payment of $500 to Ezra Williams, a clerk in the bounty land division of the Gen Land Ofc, for extra services rendered out of ofc hours. 4-Ptn of Silas H Hill & other members of the City Councils of Wash, D C, praying Congress to interdict the exterior slave trade in said District, or to empower the authorities of Wash & Gtwn to make laws to that effect. Ptn was withdrawn. To be introduced at the proper time, under the rule. 5-Ptn of Charity Chatfield, of Mich, widow of Joel Chatfield, a soldier of the Revolution, for a pension. 6-Memorial of Jas K McCreary, of Texas, for payment of a slave employed by a quartermaster of the U S army in Mexico. 7-Ptn of John Pierce, jr, late professor of mathematics in the U S navy: referred. 8-Ptn of Fred'k Dent, of St Louis, Mo, praying the protection of his interests against the claim of Carondelet Common. 9-Ptn of Jacob Ream, of Cambria Co, Pa, a soldier in the late war with England, praying for an invalid pension.

Mrd: on Jan 18, by Rev Mr Tillinghast, Edw T Hardy, of Norfolk, Va, to S Lorretto, daughter of John Pickrell, of Gtwn, D C.

Died: on Jan 5, at Middleburg, Loudon Co, Va, Miss Sallie Broun, in her 17th year. A victim of consumption, she suffered protracted & severe pain, yet she bore it with meek submission, & died a peaceful & happy death.

Chas Marsh, aged 84 years, a lawyer of eminence, & formerly a member of Congress, died at Woodstock, Vt, on Jan 11.

The Boston papers advertised for Chas Hall, age 16 years, residing at North Chelsea, who mysteriously disappeared. He was found to have shipped on board a vessel bound to Calif, paying $93, for liberty to work his passage. Those in charge of the vessel communicated with his father, & his jig was brought to a close before it was begun. –Com Adv

WED JAN 24, 1849
A plea for the Red Man of Calif. Is there not something due to the aboriginal race of Calif, at this time? They are the original & rightful owners of the soil in which the discoveries of gold have been made. –A friend to the Red Race.

Senate: 1-Cmte of Claims: memorial of U B Hill, administrator of Gilbert Stalkes, asking payment for the use of the steamboat **James Adams** by the Gov't, during the Florida war: for the relief of the legal reps of Gilbert Stalker: ordered to be printed. 2-Cmte of Claims: House bill for the relief of Jeremiah Moors: recommended its passage. Same cmte: ptn of Thos Linard, asking compensation for corn & fodder furnished a Tenn regt of mounted men, made an adverse report on the same: which was agreed to. 3-Cmte on Private Land Claims: memorial of Moses E Levy, in relation to a tract of land under a Spanish grant, reported for his relief: ordered to a second reading. 4-Ptn of Timothy Cavan, asking for a pension in consideration of an injury received while in the military service of the U S: referred to the Cmte on Pensions. 5-Sec of War to furnish to the Senate any documents or information relative to the claim of Capt Geo E McClelland's company of Florida volunteers, for military services in 1840. 6-Ptn of Geo Whitman, a sutler in the army during the war with Mexico, asking compensation for goods forcibly taken & used by troops of the U S: referred to the Cmte on Military Affairs. 7-Memorial of Wm Henry Bush, a citizen of the U S, asking redress for illegal arrest & imprisonment by the Spanish authorities at Havana, Cuba, while serving on board of an American vessel then lying in that port: referred to the Cmte on Foreign Relations.

Notice: I forewarn all persons not to trade for or otherwise receive a note drawn by Jas Kalahan, payable to Thos Dumphrey, for $100, due on or about Oct 1, 1848, the same having been lost or mislaid. –Thos Dumphry

Obit-died: on Jan 11, 1849, at Woodstock, Vt, Hon Chas Marsh, L L D, aged 83 years. His widow & 4 of his 7 children survive him, among whom is Hon Geo P Marsh, Rep in Congress from Vt. He was born at Lebanon, Conn, on Jul 10, 1765, but removed with his father's family to Vt before the Revolutionary war. His father, Hon Jos Marsh, was one of the leading Whig gentlemen of Vt during that struggle, & was for several years Lt Govn'r of Vt. Chas Marsh graduated at Dartmouth College in 1786, & studied law under Judge Reeve, of Conn.

History of Md, from the first settlement in 1634 to the year 1848, by Jas McSherry, of the Fred'k Bar. 1849, Balt, John Murphy, royal octavo pp 400. The author has added many important facts & incidents to the collections of Bosman & McMahon.

The death of Lt Francis Huger has not been generally announced to the Navy. Lt Huger was a rep of that distinguished Huguenot family so well known in the councils & in the battles of the Republic. He was the son of the gallant gentleman whose chivalric attempt to rescue Lafayette from the dungeons of Olmutz has forever associated his name with that of the illustrious friend & brother-in-arms of Washington. Five years ago an insidious disease withdrew Lt Huger from the discharge of his duties; he died on Jan 6.

Mrd: on Jan 18, in Gtwn, D C, by Rev R T Berry, John M Brewer, of Cumberland, Md, to Miss Mary A Van Lear, of Wash Co, Md.

Died: on Dec 26, 1848, at his residence in St Mary's, Georgia, Maj Archibald Clark, for 34 years collector of that port. He was one of the fathers & founders of St Mary's, & is identified with its entire history, as well as with that of Camden Co. He was appointed collector of the port of St Mary's in 1814 by Pres Madison, & held it to the day of his death.

For sale: 2 story brick house on Pa ave. Inquire of Jos Schwarts, 18th st, 1st Ward.

John Payne, of Wash Co, brought before me a stray dark bay mare colt, that trespassed on his enclosure on Sun last. –J W Beck, J P [Seal] [Owner to come forward, prove property, pay charges, & take her away. –John Payne]

Hon Sidney Breese has resigned his appointment as Regent of the Smithsonian Institution.

THU JAN 25, 1849
Wash Corp: 1-Nominated by the Mayor: Geo H Fulmer as a Com'r of the Asylum in the place of Jas Marshall, deceased. Francis Y Naylor as Com'r of the Eastern Burial Ground in place of Jas Marshall, deceased. 2-Ptn of Z M P King & others for a flag footway across H st, at square 321: referred to the Cmte on Improvements. 3-Ptn of Wm Becket, praying remission of a fine: referred to the Cmte of Claims. 4-Ptn of John W Elliott, praying remission of a fine: referred to the Cmte of Claims. 5-Act for the relief of Wm B Wilson: passed. 6-Ptn of Geo H Oyster: referred to the Cmte of Claims.

Mr David Hale, long known as senior editor & proprietor of the Journal of Commerce, died on Sat last at Fredericksburg, Va, whither he had gone for his health. His age was about 59. He had been sick and inflammation of the lungs ensued, of which he died.

Pierce Butler vs Fanny Kemble Butler: opinion of the Court was delivered at Phil by Judge King. This divorce case will take place in the March term. –Phil Eve Bul

House of Reps: 1-Cmte of Claims: bill for the relief of Solomon T Nicoll & Jas Clinch, of N Y C: committed. 2-Cmte of Claims was discharged from the further consideration of the memorial of citizens of Crawford Co, Ill, in behalf of Delilah Pearson: laid on the table. 3-Cmte of Claims: bill for the relief of Polly Carver, excx of Nathan Carver: committed. 4-Cmte of Claims: adverse report on the ptn of Peter A Carnes: to be printed. Same cmte: bills for the relief of Sayles J Bowen & the legal reps of Washington S Bebee: committed. Same cmte: bill for the relief of Maj E H Fitzgerald, U S army: committed. Same cmte: discharged from the further consideration of the ptn of Saml Reed: referred the same to the Cmte on Private Land Claims. 5-Cmte of Claims: adverse reports on the ptns of Lt Col R E De Russey & J R Callahan & others: ordered to be printed.

Senate: 1-Cmte on the Judiciary: House bill for the relief of Wm Fuller, reported the same without an amendment. 2-Cmte on Military Affairs: memorial of Nathan Weston, jr, late paymaster in the army, asking the extra pay granted by Congress for services in the Mexican war, made an adverse report on the same: ordered to be printed. 3-Cmte on Pensions: ptn of Benj Miller, a soldier in Wayne's army, asking a pension, made an adverse report on the same: ordered to be printed. 4-Cmte on Commerce: ptn of Arnold Naudain, for compensation for superintending the construction of a floating lights while collector of the customs for the district of Delaware, made an adverse report on the same: ordered to be printed. Same cmte: ptn of David L White, of Fla, asking for arrears of compensation & for expenditures for the public service while collector at Apalachicola, made an adverse report on the same: ordered to be printed. 5-Noah Hanson to be placed on the roll of messengers, & pay him the same as received by other messengers. 6-Bill for the relief of Cincinatus Trousdale & John G Connelly, of Ark: referred to the Cmte on Military Affairs.

Emigration to Calif. 1-The <u>Green Mountain Boys</u> are on the move. A company of 10 set out from Vergennes, a little more than a week ago. They are to proceed by ship to Vera Cruz, & thence overland to the Pacific by the way of Mexico. 2-Mr Audubon, jr, the son of the naturalist of that name, is to head an overland expedition, getting ready in N Y, to start for the mines. 3-A ship **Architect** sailed from New Orleans on Jan 17 with a large number of passengers, amongst whom were Dr King, lady & daughter; Jas Taylor, lady, & 2 children; Chas B Caldwell & lady; Mrs Emily Roland & 2 children; Mrs Lack, Henry Josephs, & lady. 4-Pistol trade in New England suddenly stimulated by the Calif fever. Messrs Allen & Thurber, of Worcester, had on hand some $70,000 or $80,000 worth of their self-cocking revolvers, upon the breaking out of the gold mania.

Washington-Chippewa Indians. A delegation from this northern nation of aborigines, consisting of 6 chiefs, 3 warriors, & 2 squaws, with their agent & interpreter, Maj J B Martell, arrived in our city last evening. They have come to visit their "<u>Great Father</u>," the President, to lay before him some grievances in relation to their treaty with the Gov't.

Died: on Jan 24, of catarrh fever, Eliza Virginia, youngest daughter of Jos Sessford, aged 4 years & 2 months. Her funeral will take place from the residence of her father, on C st, on Fri next, at 10 o'clock.

New Orleans: Henry Clay, while walking yesterday, accidentally slipped & fell; his head striking the pavement, producing quite a painful concussion. The venerable patriot was soon surrounded by friends, who picked him up & conveyed him to his residence. He suffered considerably for some time but is not considered by any means dangerously injured. His health otherwise is very fine.

Mrd: on Dec 25, 1848, in Tuscaloosa, Ala, by Rev Basil Manly, D D, Rev John W Pratt to Miss Mary Grace Crabb, only daughter of the late Hon Geo W Crabb, of Alabama.

FRI JAN 26, 1849
The funeral honors of Gen Hunter, formerly Marshal of this District, on Wed, convened at his late residence a large number of citizens of Wash & surrounding country. Religious services were conducted by the Rev Messrs Slicer & L F Morgan, of the Methodist Episcopal Church.

Senate: 1-Additional documents in relation to the claim of Wm Custer for a horse lost in the military service: referred to the Cmte of Claims. 2-Ptn of Danl Doland, a discharged soldier of Col Stevenson's regt, asking extra pay & bounty land: referred to the Cmte on Military Affairs. 3-Ptn of Wm Caton, of Anne Arundel Co, Md, for remuneration for services rendered during the late war with Great Britain: referred to the Cmte of Claims. 4-Memorial of A G Blanchard & others, ofcrs & soldiers, who served in the war with Mexico, asking to be allowed extra pay. 5-Ptn of John Madlam, a soldier in the late war with Great Britain, asking a grant of land: referred to the Cmte on Public Lands. 6-Cmte on Military Affairs: ptn of Marvin W Fisher, for his relief: ordered to a second reading. 7-Cmte on Pensions: House bill for the relief of Chas Wilson, reported the same without amendment. 8-Resolved, to pay John Skirving for his services in ventilating the Senate Chamber during its sessions, together with $1.00 a day for an assistant. 9-Cmte on Pensions: bill for the relief of Salsy Darby. [This pension is allowed to widows of Revolutionary ofcrs & soldiers who were married prior to 1800. This old lady was married in 1794, & entitled to a pension. The party has not been able to furnish proof. The witness, who was present when she was married, is well known by the gentlemen from Georgia, & said to be a person that can be depended upon implicitly. This old lady is now 101 or 102 years of age, & in great need. Bill was passed. 10-Cmte on pensions: ptn of Geo Martin-bill for his relief: to be printed. 11-Cmte of Claims: memorial of Chas Colburn, made an adverse report on the same: to be printed. 12-Cmte on Military Affairs: ptn of Hugh W Dobbin-asking to be discharged from the futher consideration of the same. 13-Bill for the relief of David Myerle: postponed. The Gov't was to pay Merle for water-rotted hemp, at $300 per ton. When the hemp arrived at Boston, it was rejected by the Gov't. 14-Bill for the relief of C Bryan & others, to make compensation for horses that were taken by the Mexicans from Maj Gaines, Maj Borland, & others. The bill has passed the House.

The most authentic map of the U S territory lying between the Cordilleras & the Pacific, is the one drawn from Fremont's surveys, by Chas Preuss, the accomplished naturalist, who accompanied him in his arduous & venturesome undertaking. It is invaluable to all who take the overland route to Calif, & desirable to others. The map was lithographed by E Weber & Co, of Balt. –Balt Patriot

The Rockville Journal says that gold has been discovered on Mr Ellicott's farm, in Montg Co, Md, & sent to the Phil mint, & pronounced genuine.

Thibodaux [La] Minerva, of Jan 6: Mr Dermosthenes Thibodaux, son of the late Col L B Thibodaux, was killed in the woods on Bayous Black, by the falling of a tree.

State of Florida: In Middle Judicial Circuit of Florida-Gadsden Co. Fall Term, 1848. In Chancery. Between Wm H Armistead & John R Armistead, cmplnts, & Alden B Spooner & Matilda W his wife, John E Johnson & Wm R A Johnson, dfndnts, [the last named dfndnt being a minor.] The above dfndnts are non-residents of the State of Florida, they being residents of the State of Virginia, it is ordered, on motion of P W White, solicitor for the cmplnts, said dfndnts are directed to appear & answer the cmplnts' bill of cmplnt by the first Mon of Apr next, [1849,] or that in default thereof the cmplnts' bill be taken as confessed against them the said dfndnts. Copy of this order to be published in the newpapers in Fla, Wash City, & N Y C. The object of this suit is to procure partition of the lands of John C Armistead, deceased, lying in Florida, in which the above cmplnts & dfndnts are interested, & known & described [same were listed in the newspaper.] said land being in the counties of Gadsden & Jefferson, amounting to 1,840 & 32 30-100 acres. Dated Jan 10, 1849. –Thos Baltzell, Judge -P W White, Solicitor for cmplnts. Attest: I R Harris, clerk

Sumter [S C] Banner: Miss Magdalen McCauley, while on a visit at the residence of Dr C W Lesene, & in his absence, swallowed a portion of strychnine in mistake for morphine, which occasioned her death in a few minutes.

Hse o/Reps 1-Cmte on Public Lands: discharged from the further consideration of the memorial of A L Frazer, proposing to construct a railroad from St Louis to San Francisco: laid on the table. 2-Cmte on the Post Ofc & Post Road: discharged from the further consideration on the letter of Burer Simmons, relative to the transportation of the mail from San Francisco to the Sandwich Islands: letter laid on the table. Same cmte: discharged from the further consideration of the memorial of John L Hall & others: memorial laid on the table. Same cmte: adverse report on the ptn of Gwin & McLaughlin: laid on the table. Same cmte: Senate bill-an act for the relief of Thos Rhodes, reported the same back to the House without amendment: bill was laid on the table. Same cmte: be discharged from the further consideration of the ptn of C K Leland & others, & that the petitioners have leave to withdraw their ptns. 3-Bill introduced for the relief of Wm Emmons: referred to the Cmte on Patents. 4-Bill introduced to authorize the coinage of one dollar gold pieces at the U S Mint & its branches. 5-Cmte on Commerce: bill to provide for the settlement of the claims of Henry Leef & John McKee: committed. 6-Cmte on Commerce: discharged from the futher consideration of the ptn of Atkins Dyer, of Truro, Mass, for return of tonnage duty: ptn laid on the table.

A despatch received yesterday from Charleston says that the brig **Fidelia**, of Gtwn, D C, with a cargo of sugar & molasses, lately went ashore & bilged off Tortugas Shoals, & had been taken to Key West by the wreckers.

Obit honors to the memory of Chas W H Weightman, a fellow student. Meeting of the students of the Nat'l Medical College, held on Jan 22, Mr G W Kimberly called to the Chair, & Mr Eusebius Lee Jones appointed Sec. Messrs Young, Lovejoy, & Butt appointed cmte. Announcement by Prof W P Johnston: on Sat evening, Chas W H Weightman, after a few days' indisposition, suddenly expired. He had been attacked with mumps; on Fri he had a convulsion, & was found to be laboring under symptoms of disease of the base of the brain. He rapidly sunk & died.

The fate of R C Gwatkin: Wash, Jan 23, 1849. On Apr 5, 1847, I enlisted Richd C Gwatkin, late of Va, into Co A, Missouri Btln Infty Volunteers, & marched him with the company to El Paso, in the State of Chihuahua, where he was discharged on Feb 30, 1848. He received his pay about Jun 20th, & started for the U S with only one person, Antoine Falcon, in company. At Carisal, Chihuahua, they employed a Mexican to groom their horses; & when they arrived at a watering place about 30 miles of El Paso, the Mexican took Gwatkin's musket while he slept, &, placing the muzzle near his head, blew out his brains; he then took a lance, which he kept for his own defence, & murdered Falcon also. He took their horses & property & went to El Paso, where he boasted of his deeds, & was apprehended, & in jail there on Jul 24, when the U S army passed through. Gwatkin had a large & repectable connexion in Va, but in what town I am unable to recollect. He had become remarkable in Va by killing a very respectable man in a public house at the Mineral Springs in Va some years since, & had been long confined in prison awaiting his trial. Your obedient servant, Elihu H Shepard, late Capt Com A, Mo Bat Inf Vols.

The death of Mr John Loffland, known as the "Milford Bard," is announced. He died in Wilmington, Del, on Mon. At the time of his death he was engaged in the editorial dept of the "Blue Hen's Chicken," a paper published in Wilmington.

Mrd: on Jan 22, by Rev Mr Vanhorsigh, Mr Chas Fraeler to Miss Eleanor E Middleton, all of Wash City.

Died: on Jan 24, in Wash City, Mrs Felicia Rebecca Masi, consort of Mr F Masi, in her 70th year. Her funeral is Sat morning, at 9:30 a m. Her remains will be taken to St Patrick's Church, where high mass will be celebrated.

Died: Jan 15, Cornelius Colison, in his 59th year, late of St Mary's Co, Md.

Geo Pratt, Newspaper Agent, N Y, will soon publish a "Newspaper Press Directory."

Accident on Nov last, by which Mr Owen Conolly, one of the ofcrs, received a very serious injury, by the falling upon him of the ponderous iron gate of the enclosure, while he was unlocking it. He owes his life to the carrier of the Nat'l Intell, Mr McCarty, who was thus early on his accustomed round. It is hoped that time will effect a complete recovery.

Gen Waddy Thompson, of S C, formerly Minister to Mexico, has recently established himself in Wash City, where he will take charge of & prosecute claims against Mexico. –N Y Cour & Enq

The Woodstock party for Calif consists of Capt Bezer Simmons & wife, Capt B F Simmons & wife, Dr Hiram White & wife, Messrs Titus Hutchinson, jr, Fred'k Billings, Franklin N Billings, & Jason B Pierce. Capt & Mrs Simmons, Mr Hutchinson, & F Billings, will sail in the steamer **Falcon** on Feb 1, from N Y to Chagres, then cross the Isthmus to Panama. On Feb 1 the ship **Magnolia** will sail from New Bedford, under command of Capt B F Simmons, & with him his wife, Dr & Mrs White, Mr F N Billings, & Mr Pierce. Mr Chas Spalding, of Montepelier, & others from the vicinity, are expected to sail in the ship **Magnolia**, which will go round Cape Horn. She takes out a full cargo of merchandise, consigned to Messrs Simmons, Hutchinson Co, a house to be established at San Francisco for extensive brokerage & commission business, by Capt B Simmons & Mr Hutchinson, with whom is associated Mr John F Pope, of New Bedford. The party is not a party of gold hunters, probably none of them will go into the diggings. Capt Simmons is the owner of a large real estate in & near the city of San Francisco, purchased on a former visit to that country. Mr White has gone out to practice his profession of medicine, & Mr Billings to establish himself in the practice of law, to which he has been bred. The barque **Hersiles**, which sailed from N Y on Tue, took out an expedition formed by Henry Whitmen & Co, of Providence, for trading & mining, embracing 20 to 30 intelligent men, selected from the different mechanical & trading professions. The ship **Grey Eagle**, which sailed from Phil last week, carried a large number of passengers; amongst whom was Mr Theodore Dubosq, a jeweller, who took with him machinery for melting & coining gold, & stamping it with a private mark.

Wash Nat'l Monument Ofc: On Jan 23, the Board of Managers again met, when the Hon Judge T H Crawford was appointed a member of the Board to fill the vacancy occasioned by the removal of Col Jas Kearny from this city. Benj Olge Taylor was elected to fill the vacancy created by the death of Col Wm Brent.

I wish to engage the services of a Teacher in my family. Direct to Pomonky post ofc, Chas Co, Md. –Pearson Chapman

For sale, the place called *Vaucluse*, in Fairfax Co, containing about 110 acres. The house is in good repair. –O Fairfax, exc of Thos Fairfax

Beautiful residence for sale or rent, in Winchester, Va: recently occupied by the Rev Dr Atkinson. The mansion is a large 2 story brick house; with all convenient outbldgs. Apply to Rev Dr Atkinson, in Winchester, or to the subscriber, near Millwood, Clarke Co, Va. –Jos Tuley

Administrator's sale of household furniture: on Jan 31, at the dwlg formerly occupied by his excellency Mons Pageot, on Pa ave, between 22nd & 23rd sts, all the effects remaining unsold belonging to the estate of the late R W Dyer, deceased. –Stanislaus Murray, adm -E C & G F Dyer, aucts

SAT JAN 27, 1849
The Norfolk Herald announces the arrival in Hampton Roads of the frig **Congress**, Capt Lavalette, from the Pacific. Capt Taylor, who is in bad health, is a passenger on board of her.

Postmaster Genr'l made the following appointments of Postmaster: 1-Lemuel R Bratton, P M, Baven Creek Springs, Somerset Co, Md, vice Saml Bratton, resigned. 2-Elijah Swope, P M, Cavetown, Wash Co, Md, vice Wm C Webb, deceased. 3-Benj Mason, P M, Jarrettsville, Harford Co, Md, vice John W Street, resigned. 4-Jas R Thompson, P M, Warren, Balt Co, Md, vice Jas Miller, resigned. 5-F Finley Horner, P M, Finksburgh, Carroll Co, Md, vice W Horner, resigned.

While Mrs Stallings, son of Mr John Stalling, of Friendship, Md, was employed near the stove on Jan 18, her clothes took fire, & she was so badly burnt that she survived but about 6 hours. She has left a disconsolate husband & 2 small children to mourn their loss. On Monday Mr Wm H Ward, of the same village, left in company with Dr Jacobs & Mr Thos Parks, on a ducking tour at Tracey's creek. While Mr Ward was getting out of the boat into the blind, the hammer of his gun struck the seat of the boat, & the gun went off putting the whole load into the upper part of his thigh. He lived about an hour. Mr Ward was a promising young man, the collector of taxes for the lower district of Anne Arundel Co. He left a wife & 2 small children.

Mr W Chase Barney has established a weekly paper in this city by the title of The Court Journal, which is devoted exclusively to chronicling the events of Life in the Metropolis.

Hse o/Reps 1-Resolved. That the Cmte on the Judiciary, to whom was referred the memorial & accompanying papers of Anson Little, complaining of the official conduct of Alfred Conkling, District Judge for the Northern District of N Y, be authorized to send for persons & papers. Postponed. 2-Cmte of the Whole on the: bill for the relief of Joshua Dodge; of Peter Parker, Sec of Legation & Chinese interpreter at Canton, & Jacob L Martin, late Sec of Legation in France. Also, bill for the relief of: Eunice Crossman. 3-Cmte reported the following bills, with an amendment to each. Bill for the relief of the legal owners of the ship **James Mitchell**; & of John Wilson; of Robt Whittett. Bills without an amendment: bills for the relief of A Baudonin & A D Roberts; of the legal reps of Oliver Lee, deceased; of Israel Johnson; of Edw Myers; of Wm Gove; of Eliz Williamson; of Sarah White; of Polly Aldrich; of Amos Armstrong; of Edw Taylor; of Warren Raymond; of Philip Miller; of Wm P Yonge; of the heirs of Lt Bartlett Hinds; of the heirs of Capt Nehemiah Stokely, deceased; of E B Cogswell; of Jesse Sutton; of Henry Miller; of Lowry Williams; of the legal reps of Darius Garison; of Staunton W Gaar; of Wm Snavely, of Indiana; of Ira T Horton; of Augustus Ford; of Jas Y Smith; of the heirs & legal reps of Presley Thornton, deceased. Bill to provide for the payment of 7 years' half pay due to Sarah Ann Dye, who was the widow of Lt Jonathan Dye, an ofcr in the U S army, & who was killed at the battle of Brandywine. Bills for the relief of Abigail Stafford; of Robt B Mitchell; of Josiah P Pilcher; of Polly Damron, widow of Chas Damron, deceased; of Eliz Kinney; of Mary G Leverett; of Mary Buck; of Wm Whicher; of Francis Tribon; & of Edw Cole. Bill to increase the pension of Henry Clic, of Cocke Co, Tenn. Bills for the relief of: Geo S Claflin; of David Towle; of Henry Childs; of Isaac Downs; of Jos D Ward; of Giles London; of Gardner Herring; of David Murphy; of Saml Graves; of John F Ohl; of Thos I Judge; of Satterlee Clark; of Lewis H Bates & Wm Lacon; of Wm Milford; of Thos H Noble; of John Howe; of the legal rep of Abraham Hogeboom, deceased. 4-Cmte of the Whole reported, without amendment, Senate bills of the following titles: Compensate John M Moore; relief of Creed Taylor; relief of Jos F Caldwell; relief of Thos Douglass, late U S atty for East Florida; relief of the forward ofcrs of the late Exploring Expedition. 5-Act to provide for the settlement of the claim of Henry Washington, late deputy surveyor of the public lands in Florida, was agreed to, & passed. Bill for the relief of the legal reps of Nimrod Farrow & Richd Harris, reported from the Cmte of the Whole, on the 15th ult, with the recommendation that it do not pass; when, on motion of Mr Flournoy, it was laid upon the table. 7-The House took up the bill for the relief of Wm Blake, with an amendment, viz: "Strike out the words 14th day of Jul, 1817, the date of his discharge from the service, up to the 14th day of May, 1845, the day on which his pension was allowed to commence," & insert the words "time of the completion of his evidence of disability." 'Amendment was not agreed to. Mr Fulton moved to amend the bill by striking out all after the enacting clause & inserting: "that the Sec of War be & he is hereby directed to pay to Wm Blake, an invalid pensioner, the sum of $12 per month from the 1st day of Jan, 1846, to the 4th day of Sep, 1848, & at the rate of $20 per month from the latter period during his natural life. Bill passed. 8-It was ordered that leave be granted to withdraw from the files of the House the ptn & papers of Mrs Lydia Lockwood. 9-Ptn of Chas M Reed & others, for an appropriation to construct a light-house at the entrance of Niagara river. 10-Ptn of Cornelius Bates for an increase of pension. 11-Ptn of Esther Scolley, for a pension on account of the Revolutionary services of her husband. 12-Ptn of March Farrington, for remuneration for loss sustained by the receipt of continental money.

Died: on Jan 26, in Wash City, Mr Jeremiah Leary, a native of county Cork, Ireland, in his 62nd year. His funeral is this afternoon, at 2 o'clock, from his late residence on Pa ave, near 4 ½ st.

Household & kitchen furniture at auction: on Jan 30, a the dwlg of J Frazier, on Pa ave, between 17th & 18th sts. –A Green, auct [The house & store is for rent. Inquire of the subscriber. -A Green]

Orphans Court of Wash Co, D C. In the matter of the administration of the personal estate of Henry S Fox, deceased, the court & administrator have appointed Feb 23 next for final settlement & distribution of the assets & the closing of the administration. –Hugh C Smith, adm [Persons interested may apply to J M Carlysle, atty for the adm.]

Senate: 1-Ptn of Abraham L Knickerbocker, praying compensation for an injury received while employed at the U S arsenal at Watervliet: referred to the Cmte on Pensions. 2-Ptn of Robt Rhea, a Revolutionary soldier, praying to be allowed a pension: referred to the Cmte on Pensions. 3-Ptn of the rep of Jos Vidal, on the files of the Senate, be referred to the Cmte on Private Land Claims. 4-Ordered that John Stealy have leave to withdraw his ptn & papers. 5-Cmte on Military Affairs: bill for the relief of Cincinnatus Trousdale & John G Connelly: recommended its passage.

6-Cmte of Claims: bill for the relief of David Shephard: reported the same without amendment. 7-Cmte of Claims: ptn of Asa Andrews, made an unfavorable report on the same: ordered to be printed. 8-Cmte on Pensions: bill for the relief of Timothy Cavan, reported the same without an amendment. He has come from Ohio to attend to his claim, in person, & is in destitute circumsances. It seems that he made application for his pension as early as 1835, but, in consequence of some informality in the testimony that was produced, the pension could not be granted by the Dept. He is now about 45 years of age, & has been an invalid every since the time of his discharge, from an injury he received while in the service on the Canadian frontier. The bill was passed. 8-Cmte on Military Affairs: ptn of Wm R Campbell, Geo Myers, & John Kincart, asking bounty land, reported a bill for their relief. These 3 claimants are 3 very old men; not one is less than 60 years of age; one enlisted as a fifer, the other 2 as privates; they are all poor & deserving men. Bill was postponed.

MON JAN 29, 1849
$500 reward for information, either to myself or to S S Williams, atty, as will enable me to recover the watches, jewelry, & silver stolen from my store on Jan 19.
–Saml Eckel

Appointments by the Pres: 1-Leonard Jones, of Maine, to be U S Consul for the Port of Chagres, in the Republic of New Grenada. 2-M F Bonzano, of La, to be Melter & Refiner of the branch mint of the U S at New Orleans, in place of Pierre A Bertrand, declined. 3-Capt Jas Duncan, of the 2nd regt of Artl, Colonel by Brevet, to be Inspector Genr'l of the Army, in the place of Col Geo Groghan, deceased. Following to be Collector of the Customs: Ephraim F Miller, Salem & Beverly, Mass, vice Jas Miller, resigned. Gersham Mott, Burlington, N J, vice Gershom Mott, deceased. Chas Byrne, St John's, Florida, vice Jas Dell, deceased. Henry E W Clark, St Mary's, Georgia, vice Archibald Clark, deceased.

The last of Braddock's men. The Lancaster [Ohio] Gaz announces the death, at that place, on Jan 4, of Saml Jenkins, a colored man, aged 115 years. He was born a slave, the property of Capt Broadwater, in Fairfax Co, Va, 1734. He drove his master's provision wagon over the Alleghany mountains in the memorable campaign of Gen Braddock, & remained in service at the Big Meadows until its close. He was held a slave until about 40 years ago, when, upon the death of his master, he was purchased by a gentleman who took him to Ohio. Soon after his liberation he settled in Lancaster, when he continued to reside until his death. Although his bodily frame had given way, he retained his mental faculties to the last. It is thought that he was the last man living, either white or colored, who served in Braddock's expedition.

Edwin Bell, editor & proprietor of the Hagerstown Torch-light, takes leave in the last number of that paper. He goes to Calif, to be absent one year. Wm Mettier will have the editorial charge of the paper in the mean time.

A new post ofc is established at Oxford, Talbot Co, Md, & Thos Watts appointed postmaster.

Cumberland Mountaineer: Mrs Timms, wife of John Timms, of Old Town, Md, drowned in Town Creek on Thu last. It appears that she fell from a horse, while atempting to cross the stream, & drowned before assistance could be rendered, although in company with a young brother.

Henry Nash, while a clerk of the steamboat **Ohio Mail**, last summer, killed a hand on board at Bloomington, Iowa, has had his trial at that place. The verdict of the jury was manslaughter, & the prisoner was sentenced to the State Prison of Iowa, at hard labor, for 7 years, & to pay a fine of $10,000.

Wm L Hodge, the worthy proprietor of the New Orleans Commercial Bulletin, has associated with himself in the editorial dept, Isaac G Seymour, formerly editor of the Gerogia Messenger, a gentleman of fine talents.

On Wed week Mr Homer V Morel, of Ellingham Co, Ga, while out hunting, accidentally fell while ascending a hill, & caused the discharge of his gun, which killed him instantly.

Maj Jas Cooper, a much esteemed citizen of Baton Rouge, who had been twice elected Mayor of that city, was accidentally drowned this day 2 weeks. He was on the wharf-boat, awaiting the arrival of a friend, whom he expected from New Orleans. He complained of the saloon being too warm, & said he would walk out on the lower deck. This was the last time he was seen alive. The next day his body was found in the river. He leaves a wife & family to mourn his loss.

Vocal Music Class commences on Wed in the session room of the Baptist Church on E st. –Jos Grigg, jr Mr J H Daniel, whose musical talents are so well known, will also assist in the exercises of the class.

The case of Many vs Sizer et al, for an alleged infringement of a patent for a railroad car-wheel, which has been on trial in the U S Circuit Court at Boston since Dec 28 last, was given to the jury yesterday. They returned with a verdict for the plntf, assessing the damages at $1,733.75. –Boston Journal, 23rd

The Milwaukee Wisconsin notices the death of Thos Williams, aged 90, a distinguished chief of the Iroquois nation, & descended from the Rev John Williams, of Deerfield, Mass, who, with his family & parishoners, was taken captive at the sacking of his native town, by the Indians & French, in the year 1704. The deceased was an active participant in the Revolution, espousing the cause of the British at Bennington & Saratoga. During the war of 1812, by special invitation of the U S Gov't, he placed himself under the protection of its flag, & was present at the battle of Plattsburgh. He had, for many years, mantained the tenets of the Christian faith, & died as he had lived, respected & beloved by his people.

Mrs Fanny Kemble Butler commenced her readings from Shakespeare at the Masonic Temple, Boston, on Fri evening. She selected the "Tempest."

Wash, D C I certify that Wm Gates brought befoe me, as an estray, a brindle cow, found trespassing on his premises, in Wash Co, near Navy Yard Bridge. –Thos C Donn, J P [Owner is to prove property, pay charges, & take her away. –Wm Gates]

Hse o/Reps 1-Ptn of Dorotha L French & 46 others, of Hardwick, Vt, against the extension of slavery. 2-Ptn of O H Platt & other citizens of Windham Co, Vt, in favor of reduction of postage.

Market & Provision Store: adjoining J Hitz's Dry Goods store, on Capitol Hill. -H Gildemeister

The Savannah Republican of Jan 24 announces the decease of Maj Chas Stephens, a gallant ofcr of the war of 1812, Cmder of the Savannah Volunteers in the Florida War, & who had filled with credit several civil ofcs. The same paper announces also the decease of Maj Jas M Kelly, Reporter of the Supreme Court of Georgia.

Mr Wm H Edes, an enterprising merchant of Gtwn, was robbed, some weeks since, during business hours, of a sum of money. Early on Fri, he found a newspaper on the sill, containing the identical money, & about $10 more than lost.

The frig **Congress** arrived in Hampton Roads, from the Pacific. Her Ofcrs:
Capt E A F Levallette, commanding
Lts J W Livingston, R L Tilghman, T P Green, & E G Parrott
Acting Lt John Guest
Acting Master, J F Stenson
Surgeon, D L Green
Purser, Wm Speiden
Assist Surgeons, C Eversfield & W A Harris
Marine Ofcrs, Maj J Zeilin & Capt Robt Tansill
Passed Midshipmen: C M Morris, J M Duncan, C H Baldwin, & N P Harrison
Capt's clerk, Albert Lavallette
Assist to Purser, Geo Tattnall
Purser's Steward, Geo Ott
Boatswain, Geo Smith
Gunner, John Owens
Carpenter, John Southwick
Sailmaker, John Peed
Passengers: Capt Wm V Taylor, Lt Robt D Thorburn, Purser Thos R Ware, Pd Mid S S Bassett, Capt's clerk Geo P Erie, Cmder's clerk J L Rodgers, Carpenter Patrick Dee, Boatswain J H Polley, Carpenter J H Conley, Gunner Edwin Ross.
Geo Christie, bearer of despatches to Gov't from our Com'r at the Sandwich Islands.
Mr Wm H Parks, bearer of despatches from Mr Tod, our Minister to Brazil.

The celebrated Kit Carson, & Moses, the Texan Ranger, will conduct a company to Calif from Independence, Mo, in April next. This offers a fine chance for those desiring to go over the Rocky Mountains safely.

Tax sale on Apr 23, 1849, at the ofc of the Clerk of the Corp of Gtwn:
Lots 32 & 33, on Green st: assessed to John Lee.
West part of lot 101, on Green st: assessed to John Lee.
West part of lot 43, on Green st: assessed to John Lee.
Lot 89: assessed to U S Bank.
S E part of lot 89, Old Gtwn, on Duck lane & Water st, bounded on the north by the porperty formerly belonging to Fr Lownds, now to Messrs Carter & Beall, on the west by the property belonging to the heirs of John W Baker & others: assessed to the heirs of Thos C Wright.
Water lot #34, on Water st: assessed to Thos C Wright's heirs.
Part of lot 75, Old Gtwn, beginning at the intersection with Water st of the east line of that part of said lot 75, formerly owned by Wm Dawson, now belonging to F Dodge: assessed to Stephen West's heirs.
Lot 20: on Green st: assessed to Wm C Conine
Lot 35: assessed to the heirs of Clement Smith.
Part of lot 37, Old Gtwn: assessed to Thos B Williams' heirs.
Part of lot 210: assessed to John B Hilleary.
North part of lot 35, Old Gtwn: assessed to Thos Astley's heirs.
West part of lots 36 & 37, Old Gtwn: assessed to Thos Astley's heirs.
Part of lot 36, Old Gtwn, on Bridge st, between those parts of said lot 36, belonging to respectively to the heirs of Henry Faxall & to the heirs of Geo Goszler: assessed to Thos Astley's heirs.
Part of lot 201, bounded on the west by the eastern line of that part of lot 201 belonging to the heirs of Louis J Lehaul: on the east by the west line of that part of lot 201 belonging to John Mason: assessed to Enoch King's heirs.
Part of lot 251, being bounded on the north by a portion of the south line of Michl Weaver's property; on the south by grounds formerly owned by the late Thos Hyde, now by E A Eliason; & on the west by the grounds now belonging to Henry Kengla, formerly to Chas King & others: assessed to the heirs of Wm Kuhns, otherwise Kontz.

TUE JAN 30, 1849
Panama, Jan 7, 1849. It has taken our passengers 8 days to get from Chagres to this city. At Cruces, several cases of virulent cholera morbus, some think it cholera, appeared among us. Mr Luckett, from N Y, was the first victim; then Capt Elliott, of the quartermaster's dept; & afterwards Mr Birch, of New Orleans, & Mr Geo W Taylor, of Providence. Poor Elliott, who was beloved & admired, lies in consecrated ground, at Cruces.

The Cherokee Advocate announces the death of Mich-an-no-pee the principal chief of the Seminoles, suddenly, a few days since, at **Fort Gibson**. He came down upon business, apparently in the possession of unusual health, but ere the morning he was a corpse.

Died: yesterday, of a lingering disease, Mr John H Smoot, for many years master joiner in the Wash Navy Yard, in his 53rd year. He was an affectionate husband, a kind & tender father, & his loss will be deepy felt by a companion & 5 children whom he leaves behind. His funeral is this afternoon from his late residence on 7th st east, at 3 o'clock.

Senate: 1-Memorial of Horatio Hubbell & John Henry Sherurne, asking the aid of the Gov't in establishing a telegraphic communication across the Atlantic ocean: referred to the Cmte on Commerce. 2-Cmte on Indian Affairs: referred the ptn of Marqueretta Reneau, half breed Osage, made an unfavorable report on the same: ordered to be printed. 3-Cmte on Revolutionary Claims: ptns of John B White, Saml D Davis, & Mary Connelly, asked to be discharged from the further consideration of the same, & that they be referred to the Cmte on Pensions: agreed to. 4-Cmte on Military Affairs, to which was referred the letter of the Sec of War in relation to the maps of the valley of Mexico, from the surveys of Lts Smith & Hardcastle, of the topogaphical engineers: ordered to be printed. 5-Cmte of Claims: ptn of the heirs of Jos Watson, for their relief, with a report: ordered to be printed. 6-Cmte on Military Affairs: ptn of John A Webber, reported a joint resolution allowing an additional compensation to military storekeeper John A Webber: ordered to be printed. 7-Cmte on Naval Affairs: memorial of Priscilla Decatur Twiggs, niece of Stephen Decatur, asked to be discharged from the further consideration of the same: which was agreed to. 8-Cmte on Revolutionary Claims: House bill for the relief of the heirs & legal reps of Joshua Eddy, reported the same with an amendment, of which he asked for the immediate consideration: bill & amendment were read. Mr Eddy was a captain in the Revolutionary war. After having served some time he became insane, & was sent home on furlough. By a resolution of Congress, which passed in 1778, ofcrs in the condition which Mr Eddy was placed were entitled to bounty land & 12 months' extra pay. Mr Eddy remained insane. He disposed, however, by direction of his family, of his bounty land, & never became aware that he was entitled to extra pay. He made application for commutation pay, but that was refused. Two of his sons, who are men of high respectability, made affidavit of the facts. A man by the name of Emory purchased his bounty land. Ir is now something like 70 years since this man left service, & we all know that within that period the Treas Dept has been burned twice & the War Dept once, & the vouchers respecting the settlement of soldiers' claims are necessarily very imperfect. There is evidence that $780 of pay is still due to this man. Bill was postponed until Thu next.

Closed up & squaring up. We have closed our business on 7th st. The books will be in the hands of Thos M Milburn. B Milburn may be seen at Mrs Parish's, Pa ave, next door to A Coyle's shoe store. –T M & B Milburn

Hse o/Reps 1-Bill introduced to authorize the issue of the Treas scrip for $100 to Eliza Johnson, widow of Francis Johnson, late a soldier in the U S Army in Mexico.

Died: on Sun last, in Wash City, Jas Arthur, only son of Jas A & Mgt H O'Connor, aged 4 months & 13 days.

Died: without any apparent reason, at the residence of his son-in-law, Henry Young, near Philemont, Loudoun Co, Va, on Jan 16, 1849, John Combs, a soldier of the Revolution, in his 105th year. -Alex Gaz

Boarding, 2 handsome front chambers, on 4½ st, between C & the avenue.
–M Kerby

Wash City Ordinances: 1-An Act for the relief of Wm A Mulloy: the sum of $78.98 is to be paid to Mulloy as police ofcr of the 5th Ward, to Jul 1, 1848, in full settlement. 2-Act for the relief of J Thomas; fine imposed on J Thomas for alleged violation of law relative to taverns, is hereby remitted: provided he pay the cost of prosecution. 3-Act for the relief of Robt B Clokey: fine imposed for an alleged violation relative to keeping or harboring of dogs, is hereby remitted: provided he pay the cost of prosecution.

Trustee's sale of improved property: by deed of trust from Jas H Chezum, to the subscriber, dated Apr 12, 1846, recorded in liber W B 127, of the land records of Wash Co: sale of part of lot 2 in square 296 on C st; with a well built frame house.
–W Lenox, trustee -C W Boteler, auctioneer

By virtue of 3 writs of fieri facias, I shall expose at public sale for cash, on Feb 7, 1 bay horse, 1 cart, & 1 set of cart gear. Seized as the property of Jas A Wise, to satisfy one judgment in favor of G C Grammer & 2 judgments in favor of John Purdy. –R R Burr, constable

Orphans Court of Wash Co, D C. Letters testamentary on the personal estate of John Landrick, late of said county, deceased. –John J Joyce, exc

WED JAN 31, 1849
Persons who have taken out licenses during Oct, Nov, & Dec-Wash.
Billards: 1-Morse, John E; 2-Provest & Walling'd; 3-Roby, H A
Cart:

Burns, Jas
Brereton, John-2
Briscoe, Henry
Berkley, H T
Barnes, Wm
Barringer, F
Barringer, W
Burgess, John
Burghatter, B
Brown, Robt
Connor, Sarah
Colman, Chas
Caho, J T
Deevers, L
Downey, Mary
Duff, J
Dowell, W
Deneale, W-2
Downing, Jos
Duvall, Thos
Harshman, J
Johnson, Moses
Jarboe, Benedict

Kaufman, C
Kedglie, Thos
Knight, F
Lindsey, Maria A
Langley, W H
McCandless, Julia
Markey, Michl
Mills, John
Mockbee, W
Menze, Herman
McNerhany, E-2
Nelson, Thos H-2
Peters, John
Rose, A L
Railey, Thos
Spurling, J
Stone, Michl
Scott, John-2
St Clair, Geo
Tompkins, Richd
Wise, John
Weser, E

Dog License:
Barrow, H L
Bestor, Chauncey
Bock, M
Burrill, John
Douglass, Wm
Lummons, Susan
Markoe, F
McGarvey, P
Hack:
Adams, Nathl
Braxton, Nancy-2
Burrill, John
Bell, Albert
Boteler, P
Bearley, Jas-3
Beckley, Saml
Bowen, Jas A
Boteler, Philip\
Butler, Jas
Begnam, W
Clarke, Cornelius
Chew, Wm
Costin, W C P
Carey, John
Dulany, Caleb
Dalton, Wm-2
Davis, J R
Deneale, K
Deltro, Thos
Diggs, Judson
Dalton, J
Earle, Robt-4
Fleming, John-2
Fisher, David
Foote, Andrew
Flemming, Pat
Golding, S
Geffers, W J
Gannon, J P
Golding, fred'k
Gothard, Saml
Grimes, C W
Haggerty, D
Harrington, R H
Harrison, Warren
Horner, W

McKean, E
McDermott, M
Munch, C H
Naylor, W
Naylor, Thompson
Rosenstock, M
Smith, J L
Vandrecourt, De A

Henley, Jno
Jamieson, Elias-2
Jasper, Wm
Jones, Robt
Kinsley, Henry
Kelcher, J-3
Kendrick, G H-2
King, Isaiah
Lewis, John
Looby, Terrence-2
Lee, Wm
Mason, Henry
Mullen, Basil
Mullins, J H
Moran, Pat
Mercer, Jas
McNamar, John
Mason, Henry
Mage, R F
Powell, Abm-2
Page, L S
Purcell, Thos
Page, Q L
Painter, Abm
Pynell, R R
Ross, Danl
Riggs, Warren
Raney, R
Smallwood, Dennis-3
Smith, Richd
Sheets, John S-2
Stewart, G
Sutton, Robt-2
Smith, Thos-5
Smithson, John H
Shannon, John
Turner, Henry-2

Turner, Thos
Turner, Galin
Von Essen, P
Valentine, W
Hats, Caps, etc:
Brown T B
Brashears, T M
Bayne, Thos
Barry, sr, F
Burns, Geo
Coyle & Son, A
Crandle, J
Clark, R B
Cammack, C
Cull, Jas
Campbell, D A
Cumly, A C
Davis, Jas B
Eagan & Son, Wm
Edmonston, E
Flenner, W
Griffin, Thos B
Galligan & Son, J
Hercus, Geo
Hoover, S P
Hoover & Son, A
Hall, R B
Harvey & Co, J S
Jennings & Co
Huckster:
Anderson, Thos
Atchison, I
Banks, J
Bowman
Cissell, G W
Ennis, Richd
Edelin, Chas
Gross, John-transfer
Hill, John S
Hatch & Gorham
James, John S
Liquor license:
Aigler, J
Ailer & Thyson
Allen, W
Adams, J G
Adams, Washington
Brady, Michl

Welsh, Thos-2
Wormley, Jas
Wright, Jas
Yates, W H

Jack, jr, Jas
King, Z M P
Mitchell, W
Magruder, T J
Magruder & Co
Mattingly, F
Mann, Chas
Mills, John
Noyes, Wm
O'Donoghue, J P
Rosenstock, S
Randall, G A W
Ruff, J A
Rosenstock, M
Sencheimer, L
Shanks & Wall-2
Staffon, G
Stevens, M H
Todd, Wm B
Wilson, Wm
Williams, Zadoc
Wheatley, Wm J
Young, A H

Kehl, J W
Kibball, A
Lippard, J H
Latham, Moses
Lee, Lucinda
McDonald, J W
Mudd & Edelin
Ragan, Danl
Sheid, E T
Tavenner, Chas H
Webb, A J

Brereton & Br W H
Brunning, H
Bower, John
Bevan, Thos
Bacon & Co, S
Brashears, W B

Buthman, J H
Berry, J W
Brosnahan, C
Barr, J R
Bean, Geo
Boyd, Robt
Brown, John
Cooke, W W
Castel, John
Connor, John
Carlin, J E F
Callan, Lawrence
Cannon, Danl
Clarke, R B
Costigan, J
Donovan, W
Dismond, Dennis
Daly, Jas
Dale & Mountz
Donohoo, JohnA
Duvall, Saml
Dillon, W
Douglas, John
Foller, Thos
Fugitt, F J
Fearson, J C
Ferrall, D W
Frealer, Chas
Frank, Jacob
Fitzgerald, D
Fitnam, Thos
Geffers, W J
Grupe, W
Green, Jas
Greenfield, H C
Goddard, Isaac
Green, Owen
Hercus, Geo
Haggerty, Dan
Hitz, F
Hayne, L
Henning, J
Humes, John
Howell, jr, W P
Harper, W C
Hassler, John
Harvey & Co, J S
Hodge, Mary

Horstkamp, H
Haggerty, Wm
Hines, David
Hall, E
Holmead, A
Hilyard, C
Hughes, W
Handy, S W
Joyce, Michl
Joyce, Susan
Jackson & Bro, B L
Jones, Raphael
Johnson, John C
Iardella, L A
Kane, Patrick
King, Z MP
Killmon, J T
King, Martin
Lord, Wm
Lord, jr, F B
Leddy, O
Lepreux, L & A
Laub, Eliz A
Nesmith, Ann
Nailor, Dickerson
Ober & Ryon
O'Hare, C S
Orme, F
O'Donoghue, Ellen
O'Leary, John
Roemele, J C
Roberts, John
Rice, E V
Reed, B W
Randall, G A W
Rigdon, E
Rochart, Henry
Ryon, J T
Roby, Jane
Semmes & Co, R
Sothoron
Smith, Steward
Stewart, W E
Simms, Elexius
Simms, Ann
Scott, Sarah
Simms, J M
Stoops, Richard

Simms & Son
Semmes & Co, J H
Semmes, T F
Seybolt & Co
Scott, Thos B
Taylor, J H
Thornley, Thos
Trimble, Mathew
Tench, S
Tench, Thos
Travers, E
Merchandise:
Adam, Wm
Anderson, Garret
Allen, G F
Allen, John
Addison & Cockrell
Avery, G W
Allen, L
Beach, S B
Butt, Saml
Brower, Geo
Bartlett, Isaac C
Bates, John E
Brown, T B
Brenner, P
Bayly, W F
Brown, Thos P
Bastianelli, T
Brooke, Gideon
Bergman, L M
Bright, R
Baden & Bro, J W
Bockley, Timothy
Briscoe & Clarke
Brereton, John
Barnes & Mitchell
Berger, J T
Barber, J & C
Browning, P W
Briel, C
Baltzer, M A
Beackley, J W
Clavadetacher, L
Caton, John
Cassel, J T
Clarke, Saml
Campbell & Coyle

Upperman, W H
Willson & Co, O S
Wroe, Saml
Welsh, Catherine
Wall, W L & J T
Wimsatt, R
Webb, A J
Wheatley, Geo
Wright & Son, H
Wilson, Patrick
Young, Alexander

Coyle, Fitzhugh
Callan, J F
Chapin, E M
Carter, Henry
Carter & Co, R W
Clitch, Henreitta
Combs, R M
Comly, C A
Conroy, Mary
Clark, D B
Cochran, Geo W
Columbus, C
Clarke, L F
Caho, J T
Chapman, J
Callan, J
Campbell, Danl
Clagett & Co, D
Cook, W W
Davis, Richd
Davis, Jas B
Dew, G W
Davy, Eliza
Drury, S F
Davis, E C
Deveny, Chas
Delany, M
Duckworth, Marg
Dods, Jos
Davy, Charlotte
Donn & Bro, J M
Doniphan, W T
Delance, M M
Duvall & Bro
Dunn, F A
Ellis, Hannah

Egan & Son, Wm
Edmonston, E
Farrar, J M
Fischer, Wm
Franklin, S P
Fowler, C S
Fitnam, Thos
Farnham, Robt
Fowler, Saml
Funk, N
Galt & Bro, M W
Gautier, J H
Gilman, Z D & W H
Gray, Austin
Gaither, John
Green, A
Hayard, Robt
Higgins, F B
Handley, J
Hyatt & Frasier
Hitz, Ann
Howard, Jos
Hall, R B
Huguenin, A C
Huggins, Jos
Harper & Co, W
Hills, J B
Harbaugh, V
Hall, John
Hepburn, D
Hooe & Co, P H
Hall & Bro
Hall & Co
Honing, John
Heydon, C Q
Holmead, J B
Harrover, W W
Ingle, Jos
James, John S
Johnson, J M
Jones, J H
Jarboe, Benedict
Johnson & Co, T W
Jilliard & Son, J
Knott, Geo A
Kilian, John
Keyworth, Robt
Kibby, W B

Krafft, G
Lawrence, Jas
Luncy, E K
Lindsley, E
Lewis, Saml
Lusby & Duvall
Lane & Tucker
McCarthy, F S
Massoletti, L E
Moran, David
McClery, E J H
Maxwell & Sears
Mickum, J T
Morrison, W M
Masi & Co, F
Morell & Miller
Martin & Wright
Martin, Albert W
Miller, John
Martin, A W
Mortimer, J T
Moore, D
Masi, S
Munch, C H
Miller, Jas
Norbeck, Geo
Nairn, J W
Nailor, F Y
Noell, W
O'Donnell, John
Orme, Wm
O'Dell, T F
Perry & Bro
Parke, W H
Perkins & Dyes
Pursell, Thos
Patterson, R S
Parker, S
Riley, Wm R
Russell & Co, T G
Reid, Andrew
Ridgley & Co
Robinson, J
Rawlings, Wash
Riley, Wm R
Schwartz, A J
Slade, Wm
Shaeffer, J

Skirving, Jas
Stewart, G W
Shuster & Co, W M
Stuck, F F
Simpson, Presley
Shillington, Jos
Savage & Co, J L
Savage, Geo
Shanks & Wall
Shaw, John
Steer, P J
Stott & Co, Saml
Sellhausen, F W
Simms, S
Sweeny, E
Stevens, M H
Tate, J B & A
Taylor & Maury
Templeman, Geo
Thornton, John M
Teeney, Wm
Taylor, Franck
Tucker, W W
Tyson, S E

Tucker & Daniel
Venable, Wm S
Visser, J
Voss, H H C W
Vanzant, Richd
Warriner, C
Walsh, F S
Waterfield, Jas
Wilkins, J L
White & Bro
Wall & Donn
White, N W
Westcott, Jas
Williams, Zadoc
Wheeler, Ephraim
Whittlesey, O
Worthin'n & Curtin
Winter, W H
Wannall, C P
Woodward, C
Wittner, Geo
Williams, F H
Waver, J G

Retail: 1-Dale & Mountz; 2-Hayne, L; 3-Myers, Benj S; 4-Rink, Jos

Shop:
Bully, Alex'r
Brodback, jr, J
Bache, E C
Buete, H
Crane, Michl
Conlan, P
Creutzfeldt, W
Copp, Moses
Connor, John
Davis, Jas
Deckman, Henry
Ehrmantrout, Jos
Fisher, G A
Grayson, Wm
Hoffman, H-2
Jost, B
Kuhl, Henry
Kehrer & Kersey
McGarum, Jas

McIntire, Walter
Nalley, Jas T
Parker, Nathl
Provest & Walling'd
Quigley, Wm
Rollins, Joshua
Ritter, Horace G
Ready, John
Ruppell, G
Rupp, W
Riley, John
Rupert & Lehman
Sweeny, Mary
Samuels, Wm
Todtschinder, J A T
Thomas, Jos
Williams, Zadoc
Ward, Michl

Slave:
Crawford, S C
Fowler, E J
Hill, Mrs
Harding, H
Jones, E A

Jones, C, for Isaac Moore
Swann, heirs of T
Thompson, C F
Young, G W-3
Yeatman, T J

Spirituous Liquors:
Peters, Julius A
Pumphry, Saml
Parsons, Mary L
Phillips, J B

Parker, G & T
Pilling, Jas
Pierce, J M

Stage:
Bohrer, B
Cromwell, Saml
Donaldson, W
Donovan, Danl
Fowler, W R

Golding, W L
Naylor, Thompson-4
Sabastian, C
Turner & Bell

Tavern:
Brown, T P & M
Blackwell, C A
Benter, W
Baker, Thos
Butler, Abram
Branch & Co, D H
Casparis, Jas
Clarvoe, J H
Combs, M R
Corson, Job
Campbell, W H
Cook, H
Dawson, G & J
Dorsey, P W
Donovan, John
Eberbach, J H
Finkman, Conrad
Favier, A
Fitzgerald, Jas
Foy, John
Goldin, John A

Hancock, Andrew
Hendley, J R
Jones, Peter
King, P H
Klomann-transfer
Kleindienst, J P
McGarvey, P
Maher, Jas
Sweeting, Ellen
Shadd, B
Stutz, F
Shackelford
Sheckels, B O
Talty, Michl
Topham, Geo
Thomas, John
Talty, M
Willard, E D & H A
West, John
Williams, John
Walker & Rowlet

Ten-pin alley:
Casparis, Jas-4
Copp, Moses-2
Farrah, John M

Jost, B-2
Topham, Geo

Wagon:
Bell, John
Crocker, Silas
Dyson, Chas
Glick, J H
Gilbert, John

Hatch, Lorenzo
Martin, F W
Mahon, J
McDevitt, j
Roach, Jas

Coal: Fuggitt, J   one night

Commission: Murray, Stanislaus   **Insurance Agency**: Lewis, J C

Concert: Wash's Euterpeans   **Lumber & wood**: Addison &
Concert: Collins, John   Cockrell

Dry Goods: Drury, S T   **Wood**: Cochran, G W

Equestrian: Sands, Lent & Co   **Ventriloquism**: Wyman, John
Ethiopian Concert: Harvey, G W-

Dry Goods-non resident: Broadbent, G
Dry Goods-non resident: Pooder, W P

Persons fined during the months of Oct, Nov, & Dec, 1848, for failing to procure their licenses:

Boteler, C W: retailing
Clagett & Co, D: retailingg
Connor, John: liquor
Coxen, Wm: liquor
Dooley, Patrick: liquor
Davis, Mary: retailing
Eckel, S: retailing
Flenner, Wm: retailing
Hoover, J D: retailing
Howlan, Patrick: liquor
Lee, John: dog-3
-Wm J McCormick, Register

McPherson, W S: retailing
McPherson, R H: retailing
Moore, D: retailing
McCauly, Patrick: liquor
Magee, Owen: liquor
Noell, Wm: retailing
O'Dell, T T: retailing
Scott, Thos: retailing
Tyson, S E: retailing
Welner, Geo: retailing

Died: on Mon last, in Wash City, Geo Lambright, in his 41st year. He has left to mourn his loss a wife, 4 small children, a sister, & a large circle of friends. The friends of his & his father-in-law's family are invited, to participate in the funeral ceremonies, at McKendree Chapel, this afternoon, at 3 o'clock.

Died: on Jan 30, Geo Kleiber, sr, in his 76th year. He was afflicted with paralysis for the last 20 years, confined to his room for 17. He was one of the oldest residents in the District, having resided her upwards of 58 years. His funeral will take place from his late residence, on Pa ave, between 8th & 9th sts, this afternoon, at 3 o'clock.

Died: on Jan 28, after a long & painful illness, Mrs Eliz Hope, wife of Jeremiah Bronaugh. The family has lost a most devoted wife & mother.

Obit-died: on Jan 20, at Havana, Chas M Clayton, son of the Hon John M Clayton, of the U S Senate, in his 24th year. He was a man of extraordinary talent, of the purest & most honorable character, a scholar, a gentleman, & a Christian.

I hereby certify that John V Piles brought before me as an estray trespassing upon his enclosures, a small sorrel Mare. –Jas Crandell, J P [Owners to prove property, pay charges & take her away. –Jno V Piles]

Burgundy at public sale: by virtue of the last will & testament of Wm Lee, deceased: sale in Rockville, Montg Co, Md, on Feb 24, the tract of land called ***Burgundy***, the property of the said Wm Lee, deceased. Comprises of about 460 acres, in the town of Rockville. Apply to Henry Harding, of Rockville, who has a plot of the land, or to Orterbidge Horsey, Atty at Law, Balt. -M D Lee, Excx of Wm Lee

In Chancery. Circuit Court of Wash Co, D C. Hu McD McElrath, cmplnt, against Betsey McIntosh, & others, dfndnts. The bill alleges that the dfndnt, Betsy McIntosh, gave the plntf a power of atty to prosecute the claim for a reservation of 640 acres of land before a Board of Cherokee Com'rs, & therein convenanted to give him for his services & expenses in prosecuting the claim the half of what should be allowed her. The plntf states that he did prosecute said claim & procure a decree from the Board for $\_\_\_$, who granted a certificate therefor to be paid at the U S Treas, according to the treaty of 1835-6. Dfndnt is not a resident of this District, but resides in the Cherokee nation west. It is now Jan 27, 1849, the day assigned for the appearance of said Betsey; & in default of said Betsey to answer said bill he may proceed to take it as confessed, & have a true copy accordingly. -W Cranch -J A Smith, Clerk

Senate: 1-The following bills from the Hse o/Reps were referred to the Cmte on Pensions: A bill for the relief of:

Wm Blake	Philip Miller	David Towle
Eliz Williamson	Henry Miller	Henry Childs
Sarah White	Eliz Kinney	Isaac Downs
Polly Aldrich	Mary G Leverett	Jos D Ward
John Wilson	Mary Buck	Geo Landon
Robt Whittett	Wm Whicher	Gardner Herring
Amos Armstrong	Francis Tribon	David Murphy
Edw Taylor	Edw Cole	
Warren Raymond	Geo S Claflin	

Also, to increase the pension of Henry Clic, of Cocke Co, Tenn; & relief of Polly Damron, widow of Chas Damron, deceased. 2-Bills referred to the Cmte of Claims: relief of: A Baudonin & A D Roberts, legal reps of Oliver Lee, deceased. Relief of:

Wm P Yonge	Jas Moorehead
Legal reps of Darius Garrison	John F Ohl
Staunton W Garr	Thos L Judge
Wm Snavely, of Indiana	Satterlee Clark
Ira T Horton	Thos H Noble
Augustus Ford	John Howe
Jas Y Smith	

3-Bills from the House referred to the Cmte on Revolutionary Claims: bill to provide for the payment of 7 years' half pay due to Sarah Ann Dye, who was the widow of Lt Jonathan Dye, an ofcr in the U S Army, & who was killed in the battle of Brandywine. Relief of Abigail Stafford; heirs & legal reps of Capt Presley Thornton, deceased. Relief of the heirs of Capt Nehemiah Stokely, deceased. Relief of the heirs of Lt Bartlett Hinds, deceased. 4-Bills referred to the Cmte on Indian Affairs: relief of Israel Johnson; of E B Cogswell; of Jesse Sutton; of Lowry Williams; of Robt B Mitchell; of the legal reps of Abraham Hogeboom, deceased. 5-Bills referred to the Cmte on Naval Affairs: Relief of Edw Myers; of Wm Gove; of Saml Graves; of the legal owners of the ship **James Mitchell**. 6-Referred to the Cmte on Commerce: bill for the relief of Lewis H Bates & Wm Lacon. Bill for the relief of Wm Milford. 7-House bill for the relief of Josiah P Pilcher was referred to the Cmte on Military Affairs. 8-Communication from the Solicitor of the Treas, transmitting, in compliance with a resolution of Congress of last session, the opinion & award of Stephen R Mallory, arbitrator appointed to decide the dispute between the U S & the Catholic Church of St Augustine, Fla, & B Madeori, vicar genr'l, respecting certain property in Fla, & the evidence taken by said arbitrator in said cause. Referred to the Cmte on the Judiciary. 9-Memorial of E S Haines, asking to be released from liability as surety of Robt T Lytle, Surveyor Genr'l of the district of Ohio: referred to the Cmte on Public Lands. 10-Ptn of Emma C P Thompson, asking compensation for diplomatic services performed by her husband, the late Cmdor Chas Thompson, while in command of a U S squadron abroad: referred to the Cmte on Naval Affairs. 11-Ptn of Peter Brown, asking compensation for expenses incurred & losses sustained in attending the U S Court at Phil, as a witness, under compulsory process: referred to the Cmte of Claims. 12-Documents relating to the claims of Jos M Farrow, a soldier in the last war with Great Britain: referred to the Cmte on Pensions. 13-Bill to provide for the settlement of the claim of Henry Washington, late a deputy surveyor of the public lands in Fla: was concurred in.

Hse o/Reps 1-Memorial of Francis Grice, praying compensation for his improvement in docking ships, patented as the Keel & Bilge Support. 2-Ptn of Lydia Meacham, widow of Simeon Meacham, deceased, for a pension. 3-Ptn of the administrator of Churchill Gibbs, deceased, of Va, for half pay.

House for sale: the undersigned, being about to leave the city, offers the fine 2 story brick dwlg-house, now owned & occupied by him, on 12th st, near N Y ave. A small cash payment only will be required. –John E Norris

THU FEB 1, 1849
In Chancery: Jos Edmund Law, cmplnt, against Jas Adams, Lloyd N Rogers & others, dfndnts. By a decretal order of the Circuit Court of Wash Co, D C, passed in the above cause, on Oct 20 last, it is made the duty of the subscriber to ascertain & report to the Court the names of all the parties claiming to be creditors of Thos Law, late of Wash City, deceased, with the sums due to them, & payable out of his estate; & to give public notice to all persons claiming to be such creditors; same to apply to me, duly proved, at my ofc in the City Hall, Wash, or in Gtwn. –W Redin, Auditor

Senate: 1-Cmte of the Whole: bill for the relief of W R Campbell, Geo Meyers, & J P Clark: passed. 2-Sec of the Navy to enter into a contract, on behalf of the U S, with Wm H Aspinwall, John L Stephens, & Henry Chauncey, their associates & assigns, for the transportation, by steam, of naval & army supplies, including troops, munitions of war, army, naval, & public stores, the mails of the U S, & all persons in their employment, to & from over a railroad to be constructed by them across the Isthmus of Panama, from the Atlantic to the Pacific ocean. Annual sum for such transportation not to exceed $250,000 per annum. 3-Ptn of Wm H Topping, asking compensation for services as Sec to the Com'rs apointed to investigate the affairs of the N Y customhouse, in 1841: referred to the Cmte of Claims. 4-Ptn of Saml S Rind, asking compensation for services rendered in the ofc of the Third Auditor: referred to the Cmte of Claims. 5-Ptn of Wm C Anderson, asking to be released from a judgment against him in favor of the U S as security for John S Lamden, late postmaster at Smyrna, Delaware: referred to the Cmte on the Post Ofc & Post Roads. 6-Ptn of Jas B Moore & Co, asking the aid of Gov't in the establishment of a regular line of mail steamers from Calif to China & the East Indies: referred to the Cmte on Naval Affairs. 7-Ptn of John Mitchell, asking to be allowed an increase of his pension: referred to the Cmte on Pensions. 8-Ptn of Francis Ann Eson, widow of a volunteer in the Mexican war, asking to be allowed a pension: referred to the Cmte on pensions. 9-Cmte on Pensions: ptn of the heirs & legal reps of Jos Spencer, deceased: adverse report on the same: ordered to be printed. Same cmte: ptn of Jas H Duffer: adverse report on the same: ordered to be printed. Same cmte: ptn of Nathl Webb: adverse report on the same: ordered to be printed. Same cmte: asking to be discharged from the further consideration of John W Skiles: agreed to. 10-Cmte on Naval Affairs: House bill for the relief of Saml T Anderson: adverse report on the same: ordered to be printed.

Information wanted: of Thos Buchanan, eldest son of Judge Thos Buchanan, deceased, who left his father's residence in Wash Co, Md, in 1840. Address a letter to either Geo Schley, Jas A Dall, excs of Thos Buchanan, deceased, Hagerstown, Md.

Jas Cumming, residing near Austin, Atchison Co, Mo, a few days since, accidentally shot his wife, while repairing the lock of his rifle. She expired almost immediately.

Hse o/Reps 1-Resolution asking Congress to allow the claim of Michl Ledwith. 2-Resolution asking Congress to pass the claim of the Rev John Tucker, as chaplain for Garrason's btln, Florida militia. 3-Resolution asking Congress for the payment of the claims of Capts Thos Langford & his men, for certain services as volunteers in the Seminole war. 4-Ptn of Thos Drumond & others, citizens of Galena, praying for a reduction in the rates of postage, & the abolition of the franking privilege: referred to the Cmte on the Post Ofc & Post Roads. 5-Cmte on the Judiciary: bill for the relief of Lt John E Bispham, of the U S Navy: committed. Same cmte: bill for the relief of Francis Moreno: committed. 6-Bill for the relief of Timothy Carar: returned to the Senate. 7-Cmte on the Judiciary: Act for the relief of Wm Plummer, exc of Starkey Armistead, deceased: reported without amendment. 8-Cmte on the Judiciary: to be discharged from the further consideration of so much of the memorial of Henry O'Reilly as relates to the impeachment of Judge Monroe.

Jas Dean, L L D, formerly Prof of Math & Nat'l Philosophy in Vt Univ, died at Burlington on the 20th ult, aged 73 years.

The citizens of Alexandria have joined the throng now pressing towards Calif, & have already started for that distant region, amongst them Capt M D Corse, who commanded the Alexandria volunteers during the Mexican war.

Mrd: on Jan 9, by Rev J A McMannen, at the residence of Hon W P Mangum, of Orange, N C, Robt F Webb, of Balt city, to Miss Amanda F Mangum.

Horses at auction: by deed of trust from John M Holbrook to me, as trustee, dated Sep 25, 1848, recorded in the land records of Wash Co, D C, to secure the payment of $165, with interest, to the persons therein named. Sale on Feb 13, of 2 bay geldings: in front of the Centre Market. –B K Morsell, trustee -A Green, auct

FRI FEB 2, 1849
Reward for lost or stolen black puppy, with white feet, about 2 months old. –C Bestor, Patriotic Bank

Ho for Calif: Chas H Burgess offers his services, as a steward, to any company that may be formed in this city, or adjacent cities in Md, emigrating to the gold regions. Leave information with G C Grammar, or D W Middleton, Pa ave, near 13th st.

Wash Corp: 1-Bill for the relief of Wm B Wilson: referred to the Cmte on Improvements. 2-Ptn of Wm C Johnson, for the remission of a fine: referred to the Cmte of Claims. 3-Cmte of Claims: bill for the relief of Jas E W Thompson: passed. 4-Cmte of Claims: bill for refunding a certain amount due to C W Blackwell: passed. 5-Act for the relief of Wm Flenner: passed.

Senate: 1-Ptn of S W Aldrich, David F Wells, & N H Wyse, ofcrs of a company of mounted rangers who served at Tampico, asking compensation for their services: referred to the Cmte on Military Affairs.

Mrd: on Tue last, by Rev Mr Prettyman, Mr John Jolly to Miss Eliz A Willson, both of Wash City.

Mrd: on Jan 30, by Rev W Hodges, Geo W Spencer to Virginia Walker, of Va.

Mrd: on Feb 1, by Rev Mr Gillis, Mr Richd Lacy to Miss Eliz Kitsen.

Died: on Wed last, in her 63rd year, Mrs Lucinda Dove, relict of the late Jos Dove. Her funeral is today at 3 o'clock, from her late residence on F st, between 11th & 12th sts.

Died: on Jan 29, in Balt, Capt Jas M Hill, U S Army, of the Quartermaster Dept, an ofcr of high professional merit, & much beloved in his private relations. His interment took place on Wed last, under an escort of regulars & volunteers, commanded by Brvt Brig Gen Childs, of the Army; service by Rev Mr Trapnel, of St Andrew's Church.

Died: on Jan 31, in Wash City, Joseph, youngest son of Thos & Eliza Baker, aged 2 years & 6 months. His funeral is today at 3 o'clock, from the corner of D & 8th sts.

Cornelius S Bogardus has been reappointed by the Pres, & confirmed by the Senate, as Naval Ofcr for the port of N Y.

SAT FEB 3. 1849
Thos Turner, editor of the Fred'k [Md] Herald, died quite suddenly on Wed. He was Collector of the port of Gtwn, D C, some 12 years since, at which time he was the editor of the Potomac Advocate. He has left a large family of children to mourn the loss of their only parent.

Senate: 1-Bill for the relief of Levi H Corson: passed. 2-Bill for the relief of John Hutchinson: referred to the Cmte on Military Affairs. 3-Memorial of Thos H Holt & other ofcrs of a regt of Missoui volunteers, asking to be allowed extra pay: referred to the Cmte on Military Affairs. 4-Ptn of Wm Byrd Page, a clerk in the Treasurer's ofc, asking compensation for extra services: referred to the Cmte of Claims. 5-Cmte of Claims: House bill for the relief of Isaac Shepherd, reported back the same without amendment. 6-Cmte of Claims: bill for the relief of Manual X Harmony, reported back the same with amendments.

Hse o/Reps 1-Leave granted to withdraw the ptn & papers of Col Geo Brent, deceased, now on file in the Clerk's ofc of the Hse o/Reps. 2-Bill for relief of Eliz S Cobbs: Mr Tuck moved to amend it by increasing the amount of the pension from $15 per month to $25 per month: bill was laid over. 3-Bills reported with amendments: bill for relief of B O Payne, of Albany, N Y; bill granting a pension to Bethiah Healey, widow of Geo Healey, deceased; bill for relief of the personal rep of Wm A Slacum, deceased. The bill granting the right of pre-emption to Joshua Holden: sent to the Senate for concurrence. 3-Bill to authorize the issue of Treas scrip for $100 to Eliz Johnson, widow of Francis Johnson, late a soldier in the army in Mexico: to be engrossed. 4-Ptn of Wm D Jones, for bounty land warrants. 5-Ptn of Wm Ellis, for a pension. 5-Ptn of Wm G Bucknor et al, guardians of Chas W & John J Bulow, for confirmation of private land claim in the State of Florida. 6-Following bills were reported without amendment & passed: relief of:

Thos T Gammage
Jacob Boston
Jos Dana
Susannah Prentiss
Thos R Saunders
Sylvanus Blodget
Aaron Stafford
Hector Perkins
Peter Myers
Capt Alex McEwen
Mary Ann Pollard
Camfield Averll

John Gawney
Horatio Felch
Wm Lynch
Rebecca Freeman
Wm Kingsbury
John McIntosh
Levi M Roberts
Saml Perry
Jas Frame
Eve Boggs, widow of John Boggs
Amelia Covillon, of Louisiana

Martha Dameron, widow of Christopher Tompkins; Hannah Kinney, widow of Amos Kinney, late of the State of N Y; Sidney Flower, of Louisiana, & for other purposes

Mr Richd Mosher, of Dutchess Co, N Y, has been confined to his bed for 25 years, a victim to disease & intense suffering. The only joints which he is now able to move are the extreme of his index fingers, & one or two joints of his toes. –Albany Argus

Cmdor Gen C De Kay, whose death is announced in this day's paper, was once a midshipman in the naval service of the Argentine Confederation, & won his way to the rank & position of its commander-in-chief. He served in 18 naval engagements, & was distinguished for his desperate courage. His last battle, victorious against a much superior force, has placed his name in a proud position amongst American naval heroes. -H
+
Died: on Jan 31, in Wash City, Cmdor Geo C De Kay, aged 47 years, formerly cmder-in-chief of the naval service of the Argentine Conf, & late of N Y C. His funeral is this day at 1 o'clock, from his late residence on 17th st.

Died: on Jan 18, aged 20, Annie W, wife of Edgar Howland, of N Y, & daughter of Rev Dr Cogswell, of New Brunswick, N J.

Died: on Jan 18, at his residence near Paris, Ky, Joel R Lyle, [father of the editor of the Western Citizen,] at the advanced age of 74 years & 1 month. The deceased was a native of Rockbridge Co, Va, removed to Ky in 1800, where he established the Western Citizen, & continued as its editor & publisher until 1833, since which time he devoted himself to agricultural pursuits.

Died: on Jan 31, of scarlet fever, after an illness of 4 days, Thos Claudius, youngest son of Thos A Hawks, aged 5 years & 11 months.

Mr John J Johnson, who was shot in an affray at Alexandria last Sat week, died from the wound then inflicted last Thu. He died from a pistol shot by Jas Stewart, without malicious intention. [Feb 9th newspaper: In the case of the Commonwealth vs Jas Stewart, at Alexandria, for shooting John T Jefferson, has been concluded. Mr Stewart was discharged, the Court being of opinion that the act was in self defence.] Note: John J Johnson is now John T Jefferson.

MON FEB 5, 1849
Ex-Govn'r David L Morrell, died in Concord, N H, on Sun last, at the advanced age of 77. He was formerly a Congregational minister in Goffstown, N H, but was much in political & public life. He was in 1816 elected U S Senator for 6 years. He was Govn'r of N H in 1824, 35, & 26.

A new post ofc has been established at Governor's Bridge, Anne Arundel Co, Md, to be supplied 3 times a week from Millersville, on the Annapolis railroad, & Saml Anderson appointed Postmaster. The following P M appointments have been made by the Postmaster Genr'l: John A Stephenson, P M, Dover, Kent Co, Dela, vice Henry Cole, resigned. Geo W Davis, P M, Shawsville, Harford Co, Md, vice C D Stockman, declined.

Mrs Rose, wife of Hon Robt L Rose, Rep in Congres from the 29th district of N Y, died of consumption on Sat night week. Mr Rose reached home from Wash on Sat morning.

For Calif: the barque **Hebe**, Capt Stetson, sailed from Balt on Sat for San Francisco direct. She takes out a Calif cargo, with a manifest 12 feet long. The ship **Xylon**, Capt J Brown, sailed the same time for the same destination: manifest being 25 feet. She takes out 150 passengers.

Geo Bostwick, at Port Stanley, Canada, on Jan 19, murdered his wife, attempted to murder his child, & afterwards cut his own throat. He was under the influence of delirium tremens.

Fatal affray: from the New Orleans Delta: tragedy there on Jan 25. Affray was in the bar-room of the St Louis Hotel between 2 young men, J E Johnson & Thos D Harper, well known in the city. Johnson advanced on Harper with his cane; Harper drew a knife & killed Johnson. Mr Harper made no attempt to escape. He belongs to the firm of Harper & Caskin. Mr Johnson was a commission merchant.

Tragedy on board the British schnr **Amelia**. 3 Spanish Americans, who constituted part of the crew, killed Capt Alva, Spanish capt, Mr McNally, English master, Kilano, the mate, & Mr Cook, a passenger, & took possession of the vessel. This occurred on Oct 3. The next night, the residue of the crew recaptured the vessel & killed the murderers. The females on board escaped injury. They had left Mazatlan for China.

Hse o/Reps 1-Bill for the relief of the widow & heirs-at-law of Silas Duncan, late commandant in the U S Navy: sent to the Senate for concurrence. 2-Bill for the relief of the legal reps of Col Francis Vigo: sent to the Senate for concurrence. 3-Bill for the relief of Jeannette C Huntington, widow & sole excx of Wm D Cheever, deceased: passed. 4-The papers in the case of Geo Hix be withdrawn from the files & referred to the Com'r of Indian Affairs. 5-Bill for the relief of Stoughton A Fletcher: to be engrossed.

Died: on Feb 1, at Alexandria, Wm Mills, sr, in his 74th year.

Railroad accident near Lancaster, on Jan 31, when the engine was thrown from the track. The engineer & fireman lost their lives. Henry Murray & Chas Wolf, sober & discreet men, leave behind them families dependant upon them for support.
–Phil Bulletin

Died: on Jan 23, suddenly, at Oden's Hotel, Martinsburg, Va, Theodore M V Kennedy, son of the late Cmder Kennedy. Mr Kennedy was an artist who had passed years of diligent study in Italy. But a few hours before he enjoyed his society at an evening party.

Died: on Feb 3, in Gtwn, D C, Jas Brindley, aged 2 years & 11 months, son of Lt Col L Thomas, U S Army.

Died: on Feb 2, in Anne Arundel Co, Md, Margaret Rogers, daughter of Benj E & Jane Gantt, in her 16th year.

Died: on Feb 3, at *Greenwood*, Montg Co, Md, Thomas, eldest child of Allen Bowie & Hester Ann Davis, in his 9th year.

Gen Taylor's retirement from the Army. Assist Adj Genrl's Ofc, Western Division, Baton Rouge, La, Jan 25, 1849. Official notice of the acceptance of the resignation of Maj Gen Taylor: who relinquishes his command of the Western Division, which will be assumed by Maj Gen Gaines.

TUE FEB 6, 1849
Senate: 1-Ptn of Peter H Morgan & Geo G Bishop, administrators of John Arnold, deceased, asking the extension of a patent for an imprvement in the mode of manufacturing cloth: referred to the Cmte on Patents. 2-Memorial of Wm S Coodey & John Drew, reps of that portion of the Cherokee nation known as the "Old Settlers," asking that provision be made for paying out of the moneys appropriated for their benefit all debts which on examination shall be found justly due by them: referred to the Cmte on Indian Affairs. 3-Memorial of Nathl Lewis, asking compensation for forage & subsistence furnished to a company of Texas rangers: referred to the Cmte of Claims. 4-Mr Underwood submitted additional documents in favor of the claim of Geo W Norton & E P Norton, claimants on the late republic of Texas. 4-Cmte on Military Affairs: bill from the house for the relief of the heirs & legal reps of Antonio Pacheco: ordered to be printed. Same cmte: ptn of the heirs of Truman Cross, asking compensation for extra services, reported a bill for their relief: ordered to be printed.

Col Richd M Johnson, ex-Vice Pres of the U S, arrived in Wash City last evening.

Singing Class: Mr O B Bullard, recently from Massachusetts. He can be seen at Mrs Walker's, Missouri ave, east of 4½ st.

Explosion last Thu on the Providence railroad: Mr Cummings, the engineer, had his head blown off. None of the passengers were injured.

Copy of the last will of Comm Stephen Decatur. I, Stephen Decatur, of the U S Navy, now residing in the city of Washington, do make this my last Will & Testament as follows: I give & devise to my beloved wife, Susan Decatur, and her Heirs, all my estate, real, personal, & mixed, wheresoever situated; and I appoint my friends, Littleton Waller Tazewell, of Norfolk, Robert G Harper, of Balt, & Geo Bomford, of the city of Washington, together with Mrs Decatur, my wife, to be Executors of this my Will. In witness whereof, I have hereunto set my hand and seal, this twenty-second of March, one thousand eight hundred and twenty. Stephen Decatur, [L S] Signed, sealed, published, and delivered, on the day and year aforesaid, by the Testator, as his last Will and Testament, in presence of us, who, at his request, and in his presence, and in the presence of each other, have hereunto subscribed our names as witnesses. Jno Rodgers, Thos Sim, Sam'l R Trevitt

National Theatre, Boston, on Tue, Herr Driesbach, in quelling a fight in the lion cage, was attacked by the lion. He made his escape from the cage. Last accounts of his condition: painful but not serious.

A Female M D. Miss Eliz Blackwell, of Phil, who has been pursuing her studies for 3 years past at the Geneva Medical College, received the degree of M D at the annual comencement on Jan 23. –Albany Express

The Richmond papers announce the death of the Hon Benj Watkins Leigh, a most eminent citizen of Va. He died on Fri last, after a protracted illness, in his 68th year. He leaves a widow & family to mourn their loss.

Mrd: on Feb 1, by Rev Stephen Gassaway, at the residence of Mr Bodisco, Richd S Cox, of Gtwn, to Eliza, daughter of the late Brooke Williams, of Gtwn.

Mrd: on Feb 1, by Rev Mr Foley, Mr Edmund Clements to Miss Hester Ann Downing.

Died: on Feb 4, Mrs Mary Frederick, in her 82nd year. Her funeral is today, at 2 o'clock, from her son-in-law's residence on Missouri ave.

Died: on Feb 4, in her 52nd year, Cornelia H, wife of Cmdr John J Young, U S Navy. Her funeral is on Wed, at 11 o'clock, from the residence of Lt McArthur.

Died: on Jan 24, in Wash City, Capt Jas Saxton, in his 47th year. He was a resident of Chas Co, Md.

WED FEB 7, 1849
Senate: 1-Ptn of Chas Taylor, asking a pension on account of wounds received in the late war with Great Britain: referred to the Cmte on Pensions. 2-Ptn of Alex Y P Garnett, asking compensation for extra services: referred to the Cmte of Claims. 3-Ptn of Alex Montgomery, capt & assist quartermaster in the army, asking to be allowed a commission on disbursements made during the operations of the army in Mexico: referred to the Cmte on Military Affairs. 4-Ptn of Allen G Johnson, a volunteer ofcr in the Seminole war, asking the payment of a balance due him on the settlement of his accounts: referred to the Cmte on Military Affairs. 5-Memorial of Christian Shaops, asking that an improvement invented by him in the construction of the rifle may be adopted in the military service, & that he may be authorized to furnish the same for the use of the U S: referred to the Cmte on Military Affairs. 6-Ptn of Robt M Martin be taken from the files & referred to the Cmte on Pensions. 7-Cmte of Claims: bill for the relief of Jas McAvoy: reported the same without amendment. 8-Cmte of Claims: ptn of John A Rogers, with a bill for his relief: ordered to be printed. 9-Cmte for the District of Columbia: to which was referred the House bill to incorporate the Oak Hill Cemetery, in the District of Columbia, reported the same without amendment. 10-Bills from the Hse o/Reps were referred to the Cmte on Pensions: relief of:

B O Payne	John McIntosh
Wm Kingsbury	Rebecca Freeman
Jas Frame	Wm Lynch
Lewis M Roberts	Horatio Fitch

John Gawney
Camfield Averll
Mary Ann Pollard
Eliz S Cobbs
Capt Alex McEwen
Peter Myers
Hector Perkins
Martha Dameron, widow of Christopher Tompkins
Hannah Kinney, widow of Amos Kinney, late of the State of N Y.

Aaron Stafford
Sylvanus Blodget
Thos R Saunders
Susannah Prentiss
Jos Dana
Eve Boggs

11-House bills referred to the Cmte on Private Land Claims: bill granting right of pre-emption to Joshua Holden. Relief of Amelia Couvillion, of La. Relief of Sidney Flower, of La, & other purposes. 12-House bill referred to the Cmte on Naval Affairs: relief of the widow & heirs of Silas Duncas, late Commandant in the U S Navy. Relief of Jacob Boston. 13-House bill for the relief of Wm Kingsbury: referred to the Cmte on the Public Lands.

Hse o/Reps 1-Ptn of L C Churchill, Uri Manly, & J B King, & others, asking for cheap postage.

The estate of Stephen Girard, deceased, known as the *Girard Estates*, now in possession of the city, comprises in real property 177 houses in the city & county, of which 39 are small houses, 77 large, & 61 stores. The taxes & water rents on the property amount to about $25,000 yearly; to which an additional sum of $15,000 has been applied for repairs & in making improvement, annually, for several years. The income of the estate was last year $106,000.

Died: yesterday, Tue, Feb 6, after a short illness, Danl Sheffey Weightman, son of Roger C Weightman, of Wash City, in his 20th year. His funeral is at 12 o'clock today, from Miss Hanson's residence, on Louisiana ave.

Orphans Court of Wash Co, D C. Letters of administration be granted to Saml Redfern, [a creditor,] on personal estate of Sarah Voorhees, unless cause to the contrary be shown by Feb 27. —Ed N Roach, Reg/o wills

The Paris papers announce the death of Mrs Niles, wife of the American Charge d'Affaires at Turin. This lady was born in France, & married for her first husband Dr Sue, formerly physician to King Louis XVIII, & father of the celebrated Eugene Sue. The funeral of this lady was attended at Turin with every mark of respect from the diplomatic corps & others. She has left twin daughters about 14 years old.

Wash City Ordinances: 1-Act for the relief of Jas E W Thompson: fine imposed on Thompson, for a violation of the law relative to the harboring of dogs, is hereby remitted, provided he pay the cost of prosecution. 2-Act refunding amount found to be due C W Blackwell: sum of $29.16, being the amount overpaid the Corp upon payment of a license for a tavern. 3-The sum of $77.53 for the payment of the claims of Jas Williams, Garret & Davis, & D Clagett & Co, for furniture, carpets, & work done for the use of the Council chamber.

THU FEB 8, 1849
Wm Marshall, having returned from Europe, informs that he has taken the store lately occupied by Messrs Clark & Briscoe, on Pa ave, at 7th st, with a supply of fashionable styles winter clothing.

Senate: 1-Bill for the relief of the heirs & legal reps of Wm Grayson, of Louisiana; House bill for the relief of Geo Newton; act for the relief of Wm Blackford, late Charge de'Affaires at new Grenada: placed on the calendar. 2-Ptn of Alex'r R McKee & Johnson Rice, asking that money paid by them for land to which the Gov't had no title may be refunded. It appears that Mr Gillet, the Solicitor of the Treas, sold large quantities of land, said to belong to Mr Swartwout, lying in Texas. These lands were surrendered to the U S by Mr Swartwout to secure the payment of debts due them, & the petitioners purchased under the belief that he had a valid title: referred to the Cmte of Claims. 3-Documents relating to the claim of John Millikin & others: referred to the Cmte on Public Lands. 4-Ptn of A Rencher, late Charges d'Affaires of the U S at Portugal, asking remuneration for lost time & expenses incurrd by his detention abroad in consequence of the failure of the Gov't to relieve him at the time when he solicited his recall: referred to the Cmte on Foreign Affairs. 5-Ptn of John Spencer, late receiver of public moneys at *Fort Wayne*, Indiana, asking indemnity for losses sustained in consequence of a suit against him as a defaulter. [Spencer was receiver at *Fort Wayne* for several years, all of which time the receipts of the ofc were unusually large, particularly in 1835 & 1836. Within only 8 months he received $1,620,000, which was equal to the maximum salaried business of his ofc for 6 years & 6 months.] 6-Cmte on Pensions: ptn of Saml D Davis, asking an increase of pension, made an unfavorable report on the same: ordered to be printed. Same cmte: ptn of Mary Hassell, asking an increase of pension, made an adverse report on the same: ordered to be printed. Same cmte: ptn of Charity Chatfield, widow of a Revolutionary soldier, made an adverse report: ordered to be printed. Same cmte: House bills, without amendment: relief of Isaac Downs; of Francis Tribore; of Robt Whittett; & of Polly Aldrich. Act to increase the pension of Henry Click, of Cocke Co, Tenn. 7-Cmte of Pensions: ptn of Wm Miller, for a pension, reported a bill for his relief: passed. 8-Bill granting a pension to Bethiah Healy, widow of Geo Healy, deceased: referred to the Cmte on Pensions. 9-Bill for the relief of the legal reps of Wm A Slacum was returned with amendments: which were concurred in.

Hse o/Reps 1-Leave was granted to withdraw from the files the ptn & papers of Farley D Thompson.

Orphans Court of Wash Co, D C. Sale by order of the Court, on the premises, between E & F & 12th & 13th sts, on Feb 10: one horse, cart & harness, 1 wheelbarrow, blder's sand, lot of manure, 1 plough, cutting box & knife, & 1 lamp. Also, a stable, subject to ground rent. Being the property of the late John Landrick. –E C & G F Dyer, aucts

Montg Journal: the Lady of the Pres Elect, accompanied by Col Bliss & his Lady, arrived in that place the day before, on their way to Washington, & left it on Feb 2 in the cars for the East; Gen Taylor himself, as we already known, having taken the Western route with the same destination.

St Louis Republican: Capt Augustus L Sheppard, 8th Infty, U S Army, died suddenly on Jan 22, at Jefferson barracks. He was a native of Washington, where his parents & relatives now reside.

Post Ofc established at Anacostia, Wash Co, D C, & John Lloyd appointed Postmaster.

Mr Henry Milbourn, a planter residing in the parish of Avoyelles, on the Bayou Boeuf, La, was killed a few days since, at his gin house, when he got caught in the machinery. He was about 50 years of age, a hard working man, & the father of a large family.

Liberal reward for return or information on strayed sorrel mare. –Jos Radcliff, corner of F & 6th sts, Wash

$25 reward for the recovery of the goods stolen from my store on Feb 6: fine sewed & pegged boots & shoes, ladies black Congress & fancy gaiters, with a variety of small shoes. –E Edmonston

FRI FEB 9, 1849
Senate: 1-Cmte on Indian Affairs, referred the following House bills, viz: act for the relief of Jesse Sutton, & an act for the relief of Robt B Mitchell: reported back without amendment. 2-Cmte on Indian Affairs: House bill for the relief of Lowry Williams, made an adverse report on the same. 3-Cmte on Military Affairs: ptn of Jas Foy & others, asking to be allowed bounty land, made an unfavorable report on the same: ordered to be printed.

P W Browning, Merchant Tailor, under the U S Hotel, Pa ave, between 4½ & 3rd sts: beautiful, fashionable, good, & cheap clothes.

Mrs Taylor the Lady of Gen Taylor arrived in the Southern mail-boat last evening, & proceeded on to Balt, where, we believe, Gen & Mrs Taylor have 1 or 2 children at school The Telegraph announces the arrival of Gen Taylor at Nashville on Feb 7. He was received with every demonstration of public joy & enthusiasm.

Death of the oldest inhabitant. Lt Thos Mills died in Dunbarton, N H, on Dec 15, aged 90 years. He was the first child born in Dunbarton, & the first native of the place who joined the Orthodox Church. He was the first person in town who enlisted to join Gen Stark at Bennington, in 1777, & was among the first who mounted the enemy's breastworks He was of very abstemiouus habits, never drank ardent spirit, & was never ill a day in his life

Late robberies & daring attempt at robbery. The boot & shoe store of Mr Elijah Edmonston, on 7th st, was broke open & robbed. Last night Mr Knott, shoemaker, was knocked down & robbed, by 2 men, near Mr Hill's residence, north of 15th st, of all the money he had about him. A few nights ago, Mr Duff was walking near the Capitol, & was attacked by a fellow who set a dog on Mr Duff & tried to rob him, but Mr Duff struck the assailant & knocked the fellow down, & made his escape.

Small farms for sale: portions of the land on which she now resides, called *Woodley*, on the heights of Gtwn & Wash. –Eliz A Kervand, *Woodley*

Teacher wanted: by the Trustees of District School #7, in the First Election District of Chas Co, Md. –Jas L Brawner, Sec: Port Tobacco, Md

SAT FEB 10, 1849
Wash Corp: 1-Cmte of Claims: ptn for relief of John W Elliott: passed. Same cmte: act for the relief of Jas M Wright: passed. 3-Jonas B Ellis, member elect from the 6th Ward, to supply the vacancy occasioned by the resignation of G H Fulmer. 4-Cmte of Claims: bill for the relief of Wm Rupp, recommended that the bill do not pass: bill laid on the table. 5-Ptn of Edw Smith, praying to be reimbursed a certain amount erroneously paid the Corp: referred to the Cmte of Claims.

Hse o/Reps 1-Ptn of J W Nye, praying for payment for the services rendered under a contract with the Postmaster of the Hse o/Reps. Resolved, to pay him the sum of $525 on his executing a release under his hand & seal to the U S. The resolution was laid on the table. 2-Cmte on Revolutionary Claims: discharged from the further consideration of the ptn of Cornelius Bates: referred to the Cmte on Revolutionary Pensions. 3-Cmte on Revolutionary Claims: discharged from the further consideration of the ptn of Dempsey Nash, & leave granted to withdraw the said ptn & papers. Same cmte: bill for the relief of Jno Moore White: committed. Same cmte: bill for the relief of the legal reps of Jas Bell, deceased, with a report: committed. 4-Cmte on Private Land Claims: bill for the relief of Chas McLane, of Missouri: sent to the Senate for concurrence. Same cmte: resolution for the relief of John B Nevitt, of Adams Co, Miss: sent to the Senate for concurrence. 5-Leave was granted to the heirs of Gaetano Carusi to withdraw their papers from the files of the House. 6-Cmte on Private Land Claims: adverse report on the ptn of Jno F Faris: laid on the table. Same cmte: act for the relief of Sarah D Caldwell, wife of Jas H Brigham: reported the same back without amendment. Same cmte: discharged from the further consideration of the ptn of Wm S Ross: referred to the Cmte on Public Lands. Same cmte: bill for the issuing of a land patent to Thos B Clarke: committed. Same cmte: ptn of Richd H Barrett, to authorize the confirmation of his claim to a quarter section of land in East Florida, under the act of Aug 4, 1842, to provide for the military occupation & settlement of the peninsula of East Florida: committed. Same cmte: act for the relief of Jas P Sexton: without amendment. Same cmte: act for the relief of Shadrack Gillett & others: without amendment. 7-Cmte on Indian Affairs: adverse reports upon the memorial of the half & quarter breeds of the Sioux Indians & Nancy Agnew: laid on the table. Same cmte: act for the relief of Henry D Garrison: committed. Same cmte: act for the relief of P Choteau, sr, & Co: committed. 8-Cmte on Military Affairs: ptn of Giles N Ellis, for his relief: committed. Same cmte: discharged from the further consideration of ptn of Passed Assist Surgeon Richd McSherry, U S Navy: referred to the Cmte on Naval Affairs. Same cmte: relief of Maj R L Baker, of the ordnance corps: committed. Same cmte: ptn of Marvin W W Fisher for his relief: committed. Same cmte: adverse report on the ptn of Augustus Moore: laid on the table. 9-Bill for the benefit of Wm R Campbell, Geo Myers, & Jno Kincart: laid before the House.

House of Delegates of Va on Thu was brought to a close by an awful dispensation of providence. Col John W Thompson, of Botetourt, was on the floor when suddenly, after speaking a few minutes, sunk in his chair. He could not swallow. An ineffectual effort was made by Dr Yerby to bleed him. His spirit took flight.

The Railroad Journal has passed from the editorial charge of D K Minor, its late editor, who we hear is going to Calif, into the hands of H V Poor, late of Bangor, Maine.

Senate: 1-Ptn of O B Hill, late receiver of public moneys at New Orleans, asking to be allowed a charge for ofc rent in the settlement of his accounts: referred to the Cmte on Public Lands. 2-Ptn of the heirs of Robt Libbey, on the files of the Senate: referred to the Cmte on Pensions. 3-Cmte on Revolutionary Claims: ptn of the heirs of Benj Harrison, adverse report on the same: ordered to be printed. Same cmte: bill for the relief of Chas A Barnitz, husband of Margaret Barnitz, the only surviving heir of Lt Col David Grier, made an adverse report thereon: ordered to be printed. 4-Cmte on Military Affairs: memorial of W W Loring & others, ofcrs of the army, praying compensation for horses lost in the service: ordered to a scond reading. 5-Cmte on Patents: memorial of John B Emerson, asking compensation by the Gov't for the use of his patent in the improvement of the steam-engine: ordered to be filed. 6-Cmte of Claims: bill for the relief of Augustus Ford: reported back without amendment, with a recommendation that it do not pass. Same cmte: ptn of John J Simpson, asking remuneration for damages sustained from troops in the service of the U S, while encamped on his farm: adverse report upon the same: ordered to be laid on the table.

Hse o/Reps 1-Ptn of Rhoda Huson, of Wisconsin, for a pension on account of the services rendered & an injury received by her late husband, while employed in the service of his country in the late war with Great Britian. 2-Ptn of John P Worwick, praying for relief as contractor on mail route from West Point, Georgia, to Wetumpka, Alabama.

Obit-died: Mr Danl S Weightman, of Wash. He was a member of the present senior class at Nassau Hall, Princeton, & graduated in June wih honor to himself & friends. Peace to thy ashes, dear departed friend.

Mrd: on Jan 16, at N Y C, by Rev Saml Seabury, Chas C Keeney, M D U S A to Miss Mary, only daughter of the late Col Jas S McIntosh, 5th Infty, U S A.

Mrd: on Feb 7, in St Paul's Church, by Rev Dr Wyatt, Wm S Slack, U S Marine Corps, to Rachel Ann, daughter of Richd Henry Hall, of Balt. [Feb 12th newspaper: Mrd: on Feb 7, at Balt, by Rev Dr Wyatt, Capt Wm B Slack, of the U S Marine Corps, to Rachel Ann, daughter of Richd Henry Hall, of Balt.

Mrd: on Jan 25, at West Chester, Pa, by Rev Alfred S Patton, Mr Richd S James, of Phil, to Mary H Dexter, formerly of Providence, R I, & late of Wash City.

Died: on Feb 9, Mrs Mary Fraler, wife of Mr Chas Fraler, sen, in her 48th year, after a long & painful illness. Her funeral is from her late residence, corner of 6th & Md ave, this day, at 2 o'clock.

Orphans Court of Wash Co, D C. Letters testamentary on the personal estate of Alex Hunter, late of Wash Co, deceased. –Wm D Nutt, exc

John Ward, of Wash Co, brought before me a sorrel mare, which he alleges was fastened to his stable door by a rope on Mon last. –J W Beck, J P
Owners is to come forward, prove property, pay charges, & take her away.
-John Ward

Education. Jos E Nourse, Rittenhouse Academy, informs that he has taken as an associate in his Academy, Mr Otis C Wright, late Principal of the Rockville Academy, & long & favorably known as an instructor.

Fairfax land for sale: 325 acres in Fairfax Co, Va. 100 acres is now occupied by Mr Moses Foster, whose lease will expire on Apr 1, 1850, & will be sold subject to his lease. Apply to Cassius F Lee, in Alexandria, or to the subscriber, by letter, directed to Shepherdstown, Jefferson Co, Va. –E I Lee

For sale or rent: brick dwlg owned by the subscriber on Indiana ave, near 3rd st, & now under rent to Mr John R Nourse. The house contains 10 rooms.
–J B Nourse

For sale, a small farm [19 acres,] in Va, on the Columbian Turnpike, adjoining the farm of Mr Williams. –N Mullikin

MON FEB 12, 1849
On Jan 27, Mr Otis Dimock, of Genesee Co, N Yk, was killed by the falling of a tree. He was found lengthwise under a large dry tree, which he had chopped down, & had fallen upon him & killed him..

Alex McRae, belonging to a schnr lying at Boston, was found on Tue last in the forcastle dead. The vessel had been smoked on Mon to destroy rats. Capt McRae ventured into the cabin, & was overcome by the impure air.

Westminster [Md] Carrolltonian: explosion at a limestone quarry in that county on Sat last, by which Mr Wm Warner had both his eyes blown out & his face & body otherwise injured.

Mr John Soule, of Errol, Coos Co, N H, was killed a few days ago by 2 catamounts while visiting his traps near Umbagag lake; his body was found torn to pieces. He had not discharged his rifle at them, but retreated backwards, when he fell over a log, & the beasts dispatched him.

Died: on Fri last, in Wash City, after an illness of not more than 15 minutes, [though previously in delicate health,] Thos P Vial, in his 37th year, leaving a wife & 2 small children to mourn his loss. Mr Vial was formerly a resident of Richmond, Va, but for the last 3 years a resident of Wash City.

Died: on Jan 30, in Schenectady, Gen Isaac M Schermerhorn, in his 60th year. He was a former Mayor of that city, & held other public trusts.

The N J Legislature on Thu presented swords to several Jerseymen, ofcrs in the army who distinguished themselves in the late war with Mexico. The ofcrs honored were Lt Col Wm R Montgomery, Bvt Maj N Beakes Rossell, Capt S C French, & Maj Fowler Hamilton. The swords were presented by Gov Haines, on behalf of the State. Col Montgomery & Maj Rossell received theirs in person, & those for the other ofcrs, who were not present, were received for them by Gen S R Hamilton & R P Thompson.

On Fri week, as 4 persons, named Dickson, Stevenson, McMurray,& Eckbert, were attempting to cross the Niagara river from Allen's Store, in Black Rock Dam, in a yawl, the boat was upset, & all on board were drowned. It is said they were engaged in smuggling across a cargo of molasses & some other articles.

Furniture for sale: at my Warerooms on 7th st. –N M McGregor

Cmte of Reception of Gen Taylor upon his anticipated arrived in Wash City:

Dr J B H Frye	Richd H Laskey	Robt M Coombs
Saml E Douglass	Maxwell Woodhull	Chas Gordon
J L Henshaw	Geo M Phillips	Thos Fitnam
R Farnham	Chas McNamee	Benj E Kinsey
Geo Sweeny	Jos Follansbee	

Obit-died: on Dec 28 last, at Turin, after an illness of 8 months, Mrs Rosella Niles, wife of the Hon Nathl Niles, Charge d'Affaires of the U S at Sardinia. Mrs Niles was descended from one of the most ancient, respectable, & noble families in the South of France. Her more immediate ancestors had taken up their residence in the West Indies, from whence they fled to the U S on the occurrence of the revolution in San Domingo. She was born in Wilmington, Delaware, from whence her father, Mr De Milhau, soon afer removed to Balt. A part of her family went to France many years ago, where she married the late Prof Sue, father of Eugene Sue. She was married to Mr Niles in Jul, 1831. She leaves a disconsolate husband, her twin daughters, & 2 sons to mourn their irreparable & premature loss.

Mr W W De Maine was elected an Assist Teacher in the 2nd Dist [Dr Watkins'] School. –Local Item

A young man by the name of Hopkins was arrested on Fri under the charge of robbing the shoe store of Mr Elijah Edmonston, on 7th st.

Geo Lautner, a journey baker, in the employment of Messrs Thos Havenner & Son, on Sat, while going to his dwlg, was suddenly knocked down & severely beaten; attempt was made to rob him. He had concealed his week's earning in a secret pocket, which the villains did not discover. Dr Eliot does not consider his condition as dangerous.

Gone to Calif: One of the best organized companies that has yet started for the gold diggings left N Y C on Thu last. Among them are a son & a brother of Col Webb, of the Courier & Enquirer, & 2 sons of Col John Lorimer Graham.

Orphans Court of Wash Co, D C. Letters of administration, de bonis non with the will annexed, on the personal estate of Jos Dove, late of Wash Co, deceased. –Simeon Matlock, adm D B N W A

TUE FEB 13, 1849
Senate: 1-Joint resolution from the House for the relief of John B Nevitte: it proposes to allow Nevitte to enter a little spot of land at $1.25 per acre, he & his ancestors having had the same in possession for nearly 60 years. It adjoins the land of Barnard. Resolution passed. 2-Ptn of John McDuell, asking compensation for the use by the Gov't of his mode of scaffolding in painting the Capitol: referred to the Cmte of Claims. 3-Memorial of Robt P Kingsbury, asking to be indemnified against loss by the refusal of the Mexican authorities to allow him to dispose of a quantity of tobacco imported into the port of Matamoros while in posession of the U S forces: referred to the Cmte on Foreign Relations. 4-Ptn of Mary Saunders, widow of a Revolutionay soldier, asking to be allowed an increase of pension: referred to the Cmte on Pensions. 5-Ptn of the widow & heirs of Dr Henry Perine, asking an extension of time allowed by law for the occupation & settlement of a township of land granted to said Henry Perine for the cultivation of tropical plants: referred to the Cmte on Public Lands. 6-Cmte of Claims: Act for the relief of Wm Snavely, of Indiana, & an act for the relief of the legal reps of Oliver Lee, deceased, reported back the same without amendment. 7-Cmte on Private Land Claims: act for the relief of Amelia Couvillon, of La; act for the relief of Sydney Flower, of La, & for other purposes; act granting the right of pre-emption to Joshua Holden, reported back the same without amendment, recommending their passage. Also, asking to be discharged from the further consideration of House bill for the relief of Joshua Holden: which was agreed to. 8-Cmte on Military Affairs: House bill for the relief of Josiah P Pilcher: recommended its passaage. Same cmte: memorial of Saml Colt, made an elaborate report on the same: ordered to be printed. 9-Cmte on Territories: ptn of John P Duvall, a bill for his relief: passed to a second reading. 10-Cmte on Pensions: House bill for the relief of Mary B Dix: reported back the same without amendment. 11-Mr Davis, of Mass, said he had a letter from Andrew J Marsh, a soldier in the war with Mexico, complaining that injustice had been done him & others. He would submit a resolution & ask its immediate consideration. Resolved, that the Cmte on Military Affairs inquire whether the laws granting bounty lands require amendment in order to do justice to all persons engaged in the service. 12-Resolved, to compensate R M Johnson for the erection of certain bldgs for the use of the Choctaw academy; also, the evidence of the cost of said bldgs.

Died: on Jan 28 last, at his residence, in Tenn, Isaac Dortch, the father-in-law of the Postmaster Genr'l, in his 85th year. He was a native of Nash Co, N C, from which he removed to Tenn 53 years ago. He will be long remembered by a large circle of relatives & friends as the best of husbands, the most effectionate of parents, the kindest & most liberal of neighbors.

Died: on Feb 11, in Wash City, Rosina Sargent, infant daughter of D H Dustin, & grandchild of N Sargent.

Valentines! Large assortment. –J Shillington Odeon Bldgs, 4½ st & Pa ave

Louisville, Feb 12, 1849. Gen Taylor, accompanied by his friends, arrived here yesterday morning. He came up in a steamboat, which was literally crowded with passengers. There was also another steamer in company, also crowded. A procession was formed, headed with music, & the honored guest was conducted to the Galt House, where apartments were prepared for him. The scene was utterly indescribable. While the salute was being fired on the arrival of Gen Taylor, Mr John Anderson & Henry Nicholson, 2 gentlemen who were assisting at the cannon, had each an arm blown off by the explosion of one of the guns. This cast a gloom over the scene.

WED FEB 14, 1849
Senate: 1-Cmte of Claims: ptn of Saml F Read, asking payment for a horse surrendered to the U S during the Florida war, reported a bill for his relief: to be printed. Same cmte: ptn of the heirs of Jas Maglenen, asking compensation for a horse lost in the service of the U S during the late war, made an adverse report on the same: ordered to be printed. Same cmte: House bill for the relief of Jas Y Smith: recommended that the bill do not pass. Same cmte: ptn of Saml Simonton, asking payment of $800 allowed Isaac P Simonton, deceased, in a treaty between the U S & the Saginaw tribe of Chippewa Indians in 1837, asked to be discharged from the further consideration of the same: referred to the Cmte on Public Lands. 2-Cmte on Public Lands: resolution to make an equitable settlement with the sureties of Robt T Lytle, late surveyor general of the district of Ohio: passed. 3-Cmte on Pensions: ptn of Rosanna Maury, widow of John B Maury, asking a pension: adverse report on the same: ordered to be printed. Same cmte: ptn of Ruth Kerr, asking a pension: adverse report on the same: ordered to be printed. Same cmte: bill for the relief of B O Payne: reported the same without amendment. 3-Cmte of Claims: House bill for the relief of Noah A Phelps: recomending that it do not pass: ordered to lie on the table. Same cmte: House bill for the relief of John F Ohl: reported back without amendment. Same cmte: House bills: act for the relief of Thos H Noble & an act for the relief of Richd Young: recommended their passage.

Died: yesterday, Thomas, youngest child of Lemuel & Cornelia F Towers, aged 2 years & 8 months. His funeral is tomorrow at 10 o'clock.

Wash City Ordinances: 1-Act for the relief of John Davidson: the sum of $2.62 be payable to Davidson, being the amount of taxes on a frame house on 5th st, for certain improvements erroneously returned. 2-Act for the relief of Wm B Wilson: sum of $14.89 be paid to Wilson, a balance due him for laying a flag footway across 11th st, at C st. 3-Act authorizing the purchase of a fame for the portrait of Henry Clay.

Double Elopement: on the 13th a couple of soldiers, enlisted for the Calif regt, at Indianapolis, named Washingon Baldwin & Wm Wiseman, eloped with 2 young ladies of that place, Misses Eliza J Ray, daughter of the late Govn'r Ray, & Charity Ann Cunningham. They are supposed to have gone to Missouri. -Phil Bulletin

Hse o/Reps 1-Cmte on Revolutionary Pensions: bill for the relief of Mary Ward, widow of Chas Ward: committed. Same cmte: adverse report upon the ptn of the heirs of Noah Wiseman, Catharine O'Neal, Matilda W Beard, & Valentine Miller: which were laid on the table. Same cmte: discharged from the further consideration of the ptns of Benj Goodson, Richd Patterson, & Polly Thomas, widow of Caleb Thomas: ptns were laid on the table. Same cmte: bill for the relief of Eady Tuck: committed. Same cmte: adverse report on the ptn of John Waresch: laid on the table. Same cmte: discharged from the further consideration of ptns of Edw Evans & Jas Davis, administrators of Levi Davis: laid on the table. 2-Cmte on Invalid Pensions: discharged from tne further consideration of ptns of Jacob Sagathy, Peter Frost, Washington Denham, Eliz Haughery, Jesse W Hollister, Abijah King, John Morrison, Jas L Loyd, Levin Leachy, Chas Lynam, Jas Wright, jr, John Worle, Amos Knapp, Danl Guerrant: said ptns laid on the table. 3-Cmte on Invalid Pensions: joint resolution authorizing a settlement of the accounts of Thos M Howe, late pension agent at Pittsburg, upon equitable principles: sent to the Senate for concurrence. Same cmte: act continuing the pension granted to Patrick Walker: passed. Same cmte: bill for the relief of Sutherland Mayfield: committed. Same cmte: bill for the relief of Jonathan Naif: committed. Same cmte: act for the relief of Nehemiah Brush: returned to the Senate without an amendment. Same cmte: bill for the relief of John Kerbaugh: committed. Same cmte: bill for the relief of Jacob Zimmerman: to be engrossed for a 3rd reading. Same cmte: bill for the relief of Maj Chas Larrabee: to be engrossed for a 3rd reading. Same cmte: discharged from the further consideration of Francis Ritman: laid on the table. Same cmte: adverse reports on the ptns of A Ansman, Jas Cochran, Israel Griffin, Henry Sliver, Richd Reynolds, John Hartley, Saml Spalding, Rhoda Huson, & Sarah Jane West: laid on the table. Same cmte: ptns of John Stewart, Richd D Jones, John Gordon, Benj P Smith, & Wm Ellis, for their relief: committed. Same cmte: bill for the relief of Jas Norris: committed. Same cmte: bill for the relief of David Wilson & for the relief of Palmer Branch: committed. Same cmte: adverse report on the ptn of Saml Page: laid on the table. Same cmte: discharged from the further consideration of the ptn of Henry R Wendell: laid on the table. Same cmte: adverse reports on the ptns of Abijah T Bolton, Paul de Garno, & Robt Rose: laid on the table. Same cmte: bills for the relief of Cornelius Hughes & Saml Butler: committed. 3-Cmte on Patents: bill for the relief of Peter W Morgan, administrator of John Arnold & Geo G Bishop: committed. Same cmte: bill authorizing a patent to be issued to Wm Green, jr: postponed for the present. 4-Ptn of G W Tonants, asking pay for military services rendered in the late war with Mexico. 5-Ptn from Jas M Hughes & others, praying for the stationing of troops on the land route from Missouri to Calif.

Mrd: on Feb 8, at **Prospect Hill**, PG Co, Md, by Rev Saml Mullady, of Gtwn College, Solomon G Chaney, of Anne Arundel Co, to Mrs Jannette R Boarman, of the former place.

Post Ofcs established & Postmasters appointed: 1-New Hope, Caroline Co, Md: Wm Corkran. 2-Massey's X Roads, Kent Co, Md: J M Curtis

Appointments by the Postmaster Gen: 1-Abraham Wats, P M at Lippon's Cross Roads, Wash Co, Md, vice A B Wingerd, resigned. 2-Howard M Duvall, P M at South River, Anne Arundel Co, Md, vice W A Stockett, resigned.

THU FEB 15, 1849
The Fred'k [Md] Citizen announces the death of the Hon Jas McSherry, of Pa, at his residence in Littlestown, on Feb 3. For 20 odd years he had served in the Legislature of his native State.

Gen Gaines has resumed the command of the Western Division of the Army: headquarters at New Orleans. His staff: Col Braxton Bragg, 3rd Artl, Acting Adj Gen; Maj J H Eaton, 3rd Infty, Acting Judge Advocate; 1st Lt Patrick Calhoun, 2nd Dragoons, Aid-de-camp.

Peter Miller, of Easton, Pa, died leaving about $300,000 worth of property, which by Will he directed to be loaned to mechanics & farmers, & as it accumulated interest, this too should be loaned out. No part was ever to be sold, but the loaning to be continued perpetually. Should there be no one to loan, an asylum was to be built with the unemployed money. Last week the Court of Northampton decided against the validity of the Wll, & a nephew of the deceased falls heir to the property, as his nearest surviving relative.

Senate: 1-Cmte on Pensions: House bills without amendment: act for the relief of:
Eliz Williamson	John Wilson	David Towle
John Campbell	Amos Armstrong	Geo S Claflin
Henry Miller	Edw Cole	
Edw Taylor	Eliz Kinney	

& Polly Dameron, widow of Chas Dameron, deceased 2-Cmte on Pensions: House bill for the relief of Jos D Ward, with an amendment. Same cmte: discharged from the further consideration of the House bill for the relief of Martha Dameron, wife of Christopher Tompkins: referred to the Cmte on Naval Affairs.

Mr Jos J Couch, of Boston, has recently invented a machine for drilling rocks by steam. With 2 men to operate the machine, it is capable of doing the work of from 75 to 80 hands.

Harrisburg: on Feb 12, the body of David Miller was found upon the Railroad near the depot, having been run over by the train from the city, & completely severed in two. The deceased is supposed to have been intoxicated.

Mrd: on Feb 14, by Rev J B Donelan, Albert Ellery, of Balt, to Julia Wingate, daughter of the late Gen John Davis, of Wash.

Died: on Feb 13, after a lingering illness, John Williams, a native of Stockholm, Sweden, in his 33rd year.

Died: on Feb 13, suddenly of hemorrhage of the lungs, Miss Catharine Cecelia McArann, in her 19th year. Her funeral is on Feb 15, at 3 o'clock, from the residence of her father, John McArann, 18th st, between I & K sts.

For sale or rent: large & extensive house, with all necessary outbldgs, near Gtwn, recently occupied by M Pageot, French Minister. Information given by Mr Hyde, at Messrs Corcoran & Rigg's, or at his residence in Gtwn.

Votes of the Electors for Pres & V Pres of the U S:
For Pres: [Whole number of votes given: 290. Necessary to a choice: 146.]
Zachary Taylor, of La, received 163 votes
Lewis Cass, of Mich, received 127 votes
For V Pres:
Millard Fillmore, of N Y, received 163 votes
Wm O Butler, of Ky, received 127 votes

Hse o/Reps 1-Cmte on Naval Affairs: ptn of Priscilla Decatur Twiggs, a niece & one of the adopted daughters of the late Cmdor Stephen Decatur, made a report thereon, recommending the passage of the bill from the Senate entitled "An Act for the relief of the captors of the frig **Philadephia**: ordered to be printed.

From Calif & the Isthmus of Panama: on Tue Lt Jos Lanman, of the U S Navy, arrived in this city as bearer of despatches from the Pacific squadron. He confirms the report in regard to the extent & productiveness of the gold mines, but says that many of the letter-writers in that region who are holders of land have colored their facts to some extent, with a view of promoting their individual interests. For a year past Lt Lanman has been performing the duties of collector of the port of Monterey.

City News: fire last night in a 3 story house, on 7th st, near Pa ave, occupied by Mr Seybold as a grocery store: all destroyed. It communicated to the adjoining house, occupied by Mr Wm H Harrover as a tin, sheet-iron, & stove manufactory, & as his family residence. Bldg & contents destroyed.

On Tue in 12th st, nearly opposite the Smithsonian Institution, Mr Sewall Brintnall, a clerk in the War Dept, while going to his dwlg on 12th st, was knocked down by some unknown assailant, with a leaden colt, which left a severe wound upon the back of his head. His pockets were rifled & his purse, containing about $100, was abstracted by the villain, who also stole a penknife inscribed with the owner's name. Dr Morgan said that Mr B is in a very precarious situation, & doubtful whether he will recover.

FRI FEB 16, 1849
House for sale or rent: property of Mrs M C Meade: on F st west, square 143. For terms apply to J Mason, jr, corner of G & 12th sts.

Mrs Garret Anderson will from this date sell at a reduced price her stock of Music. Music & Stationery Store, between 11th & 12th sts, Pa ave

The Pres of the U S [Pres Polk,] will vacate the Executive mansion on or about Mar 1. He has engaged rooms at the Irving Hotel, where he will remain with his family until after the Inauguration of Gen Taylor; after which they will take their departure from Wash City.

Oats for sale, on board the schnr **Way**. Apply to Peter Berry, Water st, Gtwn.

Senate: 1-Ptn of Martin Dubois, a Revolutionary pensioner, asking an increase of pension: referred to the Cmte on Pensions. 2-Cmte on Public Lands: additional documents in relation to the claim of John Millikin & others, asked to be discharged from the further consideration of the same: to lie on the table. 3-Cmte on Public Lands: bill from the house for the relief of Wm Kingsbury, made an adverse report on the same: ordered to be printed. 4-Cmte on Commerce: bill for the relief of Wm Milford: reported back without amendment. 5-Cmte on Public Lands: ptn of Saml Simonton, asking payment of $800 allowed J P Simonton deceased, in a treaty with the Saginaw tribe in 1837, asked to be discharged from the further consideration of the same: referred to the Cmte on Indian Affairs. 6-Cmte of Claims: ptn of John S Devlin, administrator of Elijah J Weed, late quartermaster of marines, asking that the accounts of Weed be settled: recommended its passage. Same cmte: ptn of Wm Caton, of Anne Arundel Co, Md, for remuneration for services rendered during the late war with Great Britain, made an adverse report thereon: ordered to be printed. 7-Bill granting a pension to Mrs Dix, widow of the late Col Dix, of the U S Army. [Col Dix died in the service of his country, in the war with Mexico, just as clearly as if he had been struck down by disease contracted within the boundaries of that country, or slain upon the battlefield. This brings to mind the case of John Bowyer, a private soldier, a volunteer, who fought in every battles from Vera Cruz to Mexico; was discharged at the close of the war, but on his way home became sick from a disease contracted during the war; in wandering here to obtain his bounty land he fell down exhausted & was killed by a locomotive. He left a widow & children, but no man would think of giving a pension to John Bowyer's widow. He had no rich & powerful connexions, & he was a poor soldier.] Col Dix had not been discharged prior to his death: bill laid on the table. 8-Bill introduced for the relief of Moss Meeker & David G Bates: referred to the Cmte of Claims. 9-Bill for the relief of Wm A Slacum: a purser in the Navy, was directed by Mr Forsyth, the then Sec of Navy, to proceed to Oregon & examine & report the state of things there, the nature of the country, & the condition of the inhabitants. Slacum did so & filed his report. The bill proposes to give him, in lieu of his purser's pay, $6 a day during the time he was so employed. It also gives him certain expenses to which he was subjected, to the amount of over $300. This latter the House agreed; the former they dissented. 10-Cmte of the Whole: bill for the renewal of a patent for the benefit of the widow & heirs-at-law of Timothy P Anderson, deceased: amended to read & their assignees: laid on the table. 11-Bill for the relief of John A Bryan: laid on the table. 12-Cmte of the Whole: consideration of the joint resolution from the Hse o/Reps for the relief of J M Gillis & others: passed without division. 13-Bill for the relief of John P Baldwin: laid on the table. 14-Cmte of the Whole: bill for the relief of the heirs & legal reps of Col Wm Grayson, deceased: who was in the early part of the Revolutionary war as an ofcr of the army; but long before the resolution of Oct, 1818, was passed. [Col Grayson never resigned his commission.] Bill laid on the table. 15-Bill from the House for the relief of Geo Newton & the bill for the relief of Jesse Gungs: passed. 16-Bill for the relief of Nancy Tompkins: passed. 17-Cmte of the Whole: bill for the relief of Jas Glynn & others: laid upon the table. 18-Settlement of the accounts of Wm Speiden, purser in the U S Navy: passed.

The Hon John M Clayton has been called home for the purpose of discharging the last sad offices to the remains of a son who recently died in Havana.

Col Wm R Johnson died in New Orleans. He was well known as the "Napoleon of the Turf." A telegraphic despatch reached Petersburg on Mon.
[No date-current news item.]

There is a picture, entitled **Devotion**, painted by Robt W Weir, now hanging in the Congressional Library, which is a production of great merit & beauty.
The coloring is perhaps a little too cold or leaden, but the design & sentiment are truly exquisite. It is the property of Gen Jos G Totten, & was painted for him as a companion to a picture entitled **Mercy**, by Danl Huntington.

Mrd: on Feb 15, at St Paul's Lutheran Church, by Rev J E Graeff, John H Buthmann to Miss A E Desaules.

Died: on Feb 14, in Wash City, of scarlet fever, after an illness of 6 days, Mary Louisa, aged 2 year & 6 months, daughter of the Hon Abram Rencher, late Charge d'Affaires to Portugal.

Colonization Rooms. The packet **Liberia** will sail from Balt on Feb 20 for Monrovia & other ports in Liveria. Letters or parcels to be sent child of Jas Hill, Colonization Ofc, Balt, post-paid. –W McLain

SAT FEB 17, 1849

Suicide of a Communist. New Orleans Picayune: account of the death by suicide of Dr Juan Rovira, a member of the Communist Society attempted to be established at Icaria, in Texas, by Mr Cabet, but which was recently dissolved. Rovira was a native of Catalonia, in Old Spain, when he went at an early age to Paris. He wrote his Will the evening he committed the dreadful act, which left a young & beautiful wife & a fine little boy without a protector.

Darius Alberts, a fireman on the ferry-boat **Hoboken**, was struck by a crank & killed. He was a young married man of good industrious habits.

Mrd: on Feb 15, by Rev O B Brown, Mr Geo Frazier, of Florida, to Miss Isabella C Sutherland, of Washington.

Wash Corp: 1-Proposition from T W & R C Smith, to submit a plan & contract for bldg an iron bridge over Rock Creek: referred to the Cmte on Improvements. 2-Cmte of Claims: bill for the relief of W C Johnson: laid on the table. 3-Bill for the relief of John W Elliott: referred to the Cmte of Claims. 4-Ptn of Wm M Rodgers, asking remission of a fine: referred to the Cmte of Claims. 5-Cmte of Claims: asked to be discharged from the further consideration of the ptns of Jas Fitzgerald & Susan J Weedon. 6-Cmte on Police: ptn of Jas Dearborn & others: entitled an act in relation to fish stands in the Centre Market: passed.

Hse o/Reps 1-Bill for the relief of the legal reps of Col Francis Vigo: laid on the table. 2-Ptn of Scott Campbell, praying that Congress would make good to him a certain annuity & grant of land from the Sioux Indians treaty of 1837, which were stricken out by the Senate on ratification of the treaty. 3-Ptn of Richd Stadden, of Lasalle Co, Ill, for additional compensation to the volunteers in the late Mexican war.

Marshall's sale: in virtue of a writ of fieri facias under the lien law: public sale of the following property: all the right & title of John Rynex of, in & to the following: certain bldgs erected on lots 2 & 3 in Peter's Beatty's Threlkeld's, & Deaken's Addition to Gtwn, on Water st; on the piece of ground lying in front of lot 4, in said Addition; & part of property on Water st purchased by Rynex from Miller & Duvall, consisting of a large brick moulding house; seized & levied upon as the property of John Rynex, & sold to satisfy Judicials 68, to Mar term, 1849, in favor of Wm C & Simon J Temple. –Robt Wallace, Marshal of the District of Columbia.

Died: on Thu last, at Annapolis, Md, Mr Saml Peaco, aged 80 years. He filled an ofc in the Senate of Md for 27 years consecutively, & with fidelity, being only removed at the last session on account of his advanced age.

Aid to build a Sailors' Home in Norfolk, Va: agent, Mr Jas D Johnson, of the Norfolk Seamen's Friend Society. Signed:

Rev Wm Matthews
Rev John C Smith
Rev G W Samson
Rev Jos H Allen
Rev Smith Pyn
Rev E Ballantine
Rev L F Morgan
Rev Wm McLain
Rev John Lanahan
Rev J W French

Rev Wm Hamilton
Rev H Slicer
Rev R R Gurley
Rev O B Brown
Rev Jas Laurie
Rev Levi R Reese
Rev Jas R Eckard
Rev T M Reese
Wash, Feb 14, 1849

Geo Miller, convicted in Boston of forgery, has been sentenced to 9 years hard labor in the State prison.

Senate: 1-Ordered that executor of Geo Evans, deceased, have leave to withdraw his ptn & papers. 2-Cmte of Claims: ptn of Guier & McLaughlin, asking compensation for carrying the mail: ordered to lie on the table.

Public sale of Lands by Act of Assembly: for the relief of the devisees & heirs of Wm H Foote, deceased, passed Dec 14, 1848: sale of tract of land in Fairfax Co, Va, called **Hayfield**: about 1,260 acres; with a brick dwlg house of large dimensions & well built, & the necessary out-houses. Sale on Jun 2, 1849. -F L Smith, H W Davis, L B Taylor, Com'rs

MON FEB 19, 1849
Gen Robt Desha, for some years past a distinguished mechant of Mobile, & formerly a Rep in Congress from Tenn, died at Mobile on Feb 8.

Senate: 1-Ptn of Wm Greer, asking the patronage of Gov't to a work entitled "The Mirror of the Patent Ofc,: of which he is the publisher: referred to the Cmte on Patents & the Patent Ofc. 2-Ptn of Wm Chapman, a soldier in the last war with Great Britain, asking to be allowed a pension: referred to the Cmte on Pensions. 3-Memorial of Evelina Porter, a widow of the late Cmdor Porter, asking that a bill may be passed for her relief, granting a pension for 5 years in consequence of the death of her husband from the effects of wounds & sickness received & contracted while in the line of his duty in the naval service of the U S: referred to the Cmte on Naval Affairs. 4-Memorial of Jesse E Dow, for himself & associates, proposing to open a route to the Pacific ocean by means of a road over the Isthmus of Tehuantepec, on condition that the U S will authorize them, for a valuable consideration, to transport the mails & other property of the Gov't over said road. 5-Cmte of Claims: House bill for the relief of Staunton W Gaar: recommended its passage. 6-Cmte on Private Land Claims: bill for the relief of Mrs Maria Taylor: ordered to a 2nd reading. 7-Cmte of Claims: House bill for the relief of Christopher H Pix, of Texas, reported back the same without amendment. Same cmte: House bill for the relief of Thos T Gammage, reported the same without amendment.

Hse o/Reps 1-Leave granted to withdraw from the files of the House the ptn & papers of F Coberly. 2-Leave was granted to withdraw from the files of the House the papers relating to the application of Maj Jas Green, of the Revolutionary army, for a pension.

The Rev Wm Stoddert, a graduate of Hampden & Sidney College & of Union Seminary, a teacher of several years' experience, proposes, on Mar 1, to open a School for 12 boys, at the residence of his mother, Mrs Eliz Ewell, Prince Wm Co, Va; 35 miles from Wash & Fredericksburg.

Teachers. A vacancy has occurred in the Male Public High School of Balt, by the resignation of the Principal. Salary is fixed at $1,200 per annum. By order of the Com'rs of Public Schools of Balt City. –J W Tilyard, Clerk Com of Public Schools

The Brooklyn Daily Advertiser of Thus give account of a loss of life at the farm house of Mr Miller, about 2 miles from Hempstead, Long Island. The wife of Mr Miller & his 3 children were sleeping in the house at the time, & were burnt up. Mr Miller started the day previous for this city with a load of hay, & took his departure from Brooklyn this morning, before daylight. He arrived at the place where his house stood when he left. He became a maniac, & it took a dozen sympathizing neighbors to prevent him from doing something violent to himself.

Saml Lawrence, as he was returning from the city of Lawrence to Lowell, on Tue, was thrown from his sleigh, & so badly injured that his recovery is doubtful.

Richd D Doran, a merchant of Harper's Ferry, whose mysterious disappearance some few years since has been a matter of newspaper comment, returned to his former home on Sat week. He has been spending most of his time in Glasgow, Scotland. It is a singular case. Supposing he had died, his estate passed into the hands of administrators, & settled so far as the agents of the court were concerned, leaving a large surplus just in process of distribution among his legal reps.

Mrd: on Feb 15, by Rev Mr Foley, Mr Wm Brown, of Montg Co, Md, to Miss Ellen J Robinson, daughter of Col E W Robinson, of Wash City.

Died: on Feb 18, at Sidney, of croup, Richd Ross, youngest son of Erasmus J & Ellen R Middleton, aged 2 years & 11 months. His funeral is on Tue at 11 o'clock.

Correspondence of the Balt Patriot-by Telegraph. Robt M N Smyth was found in his bed at Boston on Sat with his throat cut. He committed suicide-cause unknown.

Hon John L Wilson, Ex-Govn'r of S C, died a few days ago, at his residence in Charleston, after a lingering illness. He was a native of Gtwn, & at an early period of his life rose to distinction at the Bar. In 1832 he was elected Govn'r of the State. –Mercury

TUE FEB 20, 1849
$100 reward. On Feb 14 I received intelligence that my brother Wm Ingle, residing on his farm, near the mouth of Aquia creek, Va, had set out on foot about daybreak Tue, Jan 30, to get a small iron bar belonging to a grain machine repaired, which he carried in his hand, intending to call on Mr Adams', living at the head of Acokuk creek, & then probably take the railroad cars for Fredericksburg, & that he had not been heard from since, everything about his premises indicating that he had not intended to remain from home longer than the day. He never reached Mr Adams, nor did he go to Fredericksburg. He is small in stature, not more than 5 ft 2 inches high, & about 55 years old. Address me or Jas L Taliaferro, Stafford Court-house, Va. –John P Ingle, Wash, D C

Senate: 1-Ptn of Duncan Bradford & J Sydney Henshaw, late professors of mathematics in Navy, asking to be allowed arrears of pay & the benefits of the act of Mar 3, 1801, granting 4 months' extra pay to discharged ofcrs: referred to the Cmte on Naval Affairs. 2-Memorial of A B Ralph & other citizens of the U S, asking that the military escorts may be place on the route between the valley of the Mississippi & Calif, & a permanent military post established at some point convenient to the gold region in that territory: referred to the Cmte on Military Affairs. 3-Memorial of John C Riddle, D H Carter, & E Simmonds, proposing to construct a turnpike road across the Isthmus of Panama: referred to the Cmte on Military Affairs. 4-The ptn of Thos P Harrison & A T H Duvall, on the files of the Senate, be referred to the Cmte on Private Land Claims. 5-Cmte on the Post Ofc & Post Roads: additional documents in the case of S F Butterworth, reported back the bill for the relief of Saml F Butterworth, without amendment. 6-Cmte on Private Land Claims: House bill for the relief of Chas McLane, of Missouri: recommended its passage. 7-Cmte on Pensions: House bill for the relief of Mary G Leverett: recommended its passage. 8-Cmte on Indian Affairs: ptn of Thos Snodgrass, asking remuneration for his services in removing certain Cherokee Indians, asked to be discharged from the further consideration of the same: referred to the Cmte of Claims. 9-Cmte on Naval Affairs: ptn of John Collins, asking the difference of pay between boatswain & boatswain's mate, asked to be discharged from the further consideration of the same: which was agreed to. Same cmte: ptn of Julia Martin, asking a pension for her brother, Luther Martin, late a midshipman in the

Navy, asked to be discharged from the further consideration of the same, & that the petitioner have leave to withdraw her papers: which was agreed to. 10-The bill for the relief of Henry Vincent, administrator of the estate of Jas Le Cage, was rejected.

WED FEB 21, 1849
Mrs Farnham is about to go to Calif to look after her husband's estate, & her company is principally composed of Female passengers. Thos J Farnham died at San Francisco, in Sept last.

Died: on Feb 17, Eliz Rachel Robertson, wife of Danl Robertson, aged 22 years & 5 months, after an affliction of about 3 months of consumption.

Died: on Feb 20, near the city of Washington, at the residence of his father, after a short & painful illness, Thos Notley Fenwick, son of Edw & Mary C Fenwick. His funeral is this morning, at 10 o'clock.

Died: on Feb 14, at his residence in Fairfax Co, Va, Gen John Chapman Hunter, at the advanced age of 87 years. By the purity of his life he commanded the respect of all who knew him.

Deaths on the Isthmus. Mr Myers, of N Y, formerly of Poughkeepsie, at Cruces. The death of Mr Horne is announced. Capt Elliott, Mr Birch, Mr Hayden, Mr Luckett, & Mr Myers, are all buried side by side. Mr Taylor, of Rhode Island, was buried in one of the cross paths of Pizarro's banditti.

Senate: 1-Ptn of Oliver Tucker, a Revolutionary soldier, asking to be allowed a pension: referred to the Cmte on Pensions. 2-Cmte on Claims: ptn of Alex'r Y P Garnet, asking compensation for extra services as an assist surgeon in the Navy, made a report, accompanied by a bill for his relief: passed to a second reading. 3-Cmte on Naval Affairs: House bill for the relief of Lot Davis: recommended its passage. Same cmte: House bill for the relief of Wm Gove: recommended its passage. Same cmte: memorial of John B More & Co, in relation to a line of steamers from Calif to China, & the ptn of Gen G West & Chas S Ritchie for the extension of the bounds of the Navy Yard at Phil, asked to be discharged from the further consideration of the same: which was agreed to. Same cmte: House bill for the relief of Wm Butler: recommendation that it do not pass. Same cmte: House bill for the relief of Saml Graves: reported back without amendment. Same cmte: House bill for the relief of the legal owners of the ship **James Mitchell**, asked to be discharged from the further consideration of the same: referred to the Cmte of Claims. 4-Cmte on Pensions: ptn of Sarah Crandall, widow of Jas Coon, a soldier in the Revolutionary war with Great Britain, asking a pension, made a report, with a bill for her relief. 5-Cmte on Naval Affairs: House bill for the relief of Jno J Young, a cmder in the U S Navy, reported back the same without amendment. 6-Cmte on Military Affairs: ptn of Alexander Montgomery, assist quartermaster in the U S Army, asking a commission on disbursements made by him in Mexico in order to cover losses sustained by him, made a report with a bill for his relief. 7-Cmte of the Whole: bill authorizing a patent to be issued to Wm Green, jr: passed.

Horses for sale at Franklin Livery Stables, on 8th st. –Thos Baker

By virtue of a writ of fieri facias, I have seized 2 feather beds, 2 straw beds, 3 pillows & cases, 4 sheets, 2 quilts, & 1 spread, the property of Patrick Luby, taken to satisfy a judgment in favor of Murray & Semmes, & will be sold on Feb 22, opposite the Centre Market. –John Magar, constable

On Fri a locomotive ran off the track some 2 miles south of Elkton, Md, injuring Mr Justus Benjamin so severely that he died the same night.

On Sun last, as a party of persons were coming from meeting at Havre de Grace, on a small car driven by hand on the railroad, part of the dress of Mrs Moore, wife of Mr Philip Moore, became entangled in the machinery of the car, & she was drawn off beneath the wheels. The car passed over her, breaking an arm so badly that it had to be amputated, & injuring her otherwise so seriously that doubts of her recovery are entertained. -Cecil Whig

THU FEB 22, 1849
Senate: 1-Cmte on Pensions: bills-recommending their passage: relief of:

Sylvanus Blodget	Eve Boggs	Peter Myers
Susannah Prentiss	Jas France	Hector Perkins
David Murphy	Levi M Roberts	Aaron Stafford
Philip Miller	Camfield Averill	
Warren Raymond	Eliz S Cobbs	

Hanna Kinney, widow of Amos Kinney, of the State of N Y. 2-Cmte on Pensions: bills-with a recommendation that they do not pass: relief of Gardner Herring, & of Wm Blake. 3-Cmte on Pensions: ptn of Robt M Martin, made a written report, with a bill for his relief: passed to a second reading. 4-Cmte of Claims: ptn of Alex'r McKee & Johnson Price, for their relief: passed to a second reading. Same cmte: ptn of Nathl Lewis, asking payment of a balance due him for supplies furnished a company of Texas rangers, made an adverse report on the same: ordered to be printed. 5-Resolved, that the Sec of War be directed to furnish the Senate a copy of the official journal of the march of Lt Col Philip St George Cooke from Santa Fe, in New Mexico, to San Diego, in Upper Calif, which was communicated to that Dept by Brig Gen Stephen W Kearny, deceased. 6-Act for the relief of Maj Chas Larrabee; & act for the relief of Jacob Zimmerman: referred to the Cmte on Pensions.

Hse o/Reps 1-Cmte of Claims: act for the relief of the owners of the schnr **Laconic**: committed to the Cmte of the Whole. Same cmte: bill for the relief of Geo Mowry, of Pa: committed. Same cmte: bill for the relief of Chas Stuart: committed. Same cmte: adverse reports on the ptns of Jos D Ward, John B Cooper, Jacob Moore, Jeremiah Carpenter, & of Capt Thos Duer: ordered to be printed.

Chas Eames, recently appointed Com'r to the Sandwich Islands, left N Y on Tue for Boston, to embark on board the U S frig **Savannah** for the Pacific ocean. Capt Voorhees, who is in command of the Savannah, will, on reaching the Ohio, it is supposed, at once take the command of the frig, & return by way of China to the U S, touching on his way at the Sandwich Islands to leave Mr Eames.

The 6 companies of the 3rd Infty, now at San Antonio, Texas, under command of Maj Van Horne, will leave for El Paso del Norte about Apr 10. Gen Worth, who arrived at San Antonio towards the end of Jan, will accompany this command. The companies of the 1st Infty, stationed at Austin, Fredericksburg, & Arroyo Saco, will proceed to the Rio Grande & occupy Loredo & Presidio del Norte. The 8th Infty, which reached their camp on the headwaters of the San Antonio the latter end of Jan, will take the places now occupied by the companies of the 1st Infty mentioned. The 8th lost about 130 men by cholera, but were in fine health Feb 1.

Robt M N Smythe, well known in N Y & New England as a land speculator & broker, committed suicide at Boston on Sat last. The apprehension of poverty, it is supposed, led him to commit the fatal act.

The Supreme Court in the case of Dinsman vs Wilkes settled questions of great moment to the Naval service. It not only entirely exonerates Capt Wilkes, but compliments him for his moderation & firmness towards his crew.

The British ship **Cambria**, from Londonderry for N Y, after having been out 13 weeks, put into Delaware Breakwater on Mon in distress, having become short of provisions & water. During her voyage a fatal disease broke out among the passengers, & 55 of them died at sea; 7 more died after coming into the Breakwater, & were buried.

FRI FEB 23, 1849
Wash Corp: 1-Cmte on Police: bill for the relief of Jas M Wright: passed. 2-Ptn from W W Davis & others, for the erection of a lock-up house, in the 1st Ward: referred to Cmte on Police. 3-Ptn of Elias Barnes for the payment of balance due for grading 16th st: referred to Cmte of Claims. 4-Ptn of C H Payne, praying remission of a fine: referred to Cmte of Claims. 5-Communication was received from the Register in reference to the letter of Peter Gorman: referred to Cmte of Ways & Means. 6-Ptn of Timothy O'Neale, praying the payment of certain claims against the Corp due to him as the assignee of John Fletcher: referred to Cmte of Claims. 7-Ptn of G W Harvey, on behalf of the Nightingale Ethiopians, asking that a license may be granted them on the same terms as the managers of the Adelphi Theatre: referred to Cmte on Police. [Same to include Mr Collins, the Irish songster.] Passed. 8-Cmte of Claims: bill for the relief of Wm Rupp: passed.

Wash City Ordinance: 1-Act for the relief of Jas M Wright, police ofcr of the 4th Ward, to pay him $70.46, being the balance due him on the settlement of his police accounts up to Jul 1, 1848. 2-Act for the relief of Wm Rupp: that the fine imposed for an alleged violation of the law relative to selling liquor on the Sabbath, is remitted, provided Rupp pay the cost of prosecution.

In Chancery. Circuit Court of Wash Co, D C. Esau Pickrell et al vs Stanislaus Murray, adm, et al. The Trustee in this cause reported that he has sold the following real estate of Hannah G Corcoran, deceased, lying in Wash City: part of lot 10 in square 218, to Stanislaus Murray for $710. –Jno A Smith, clk

Senate: 1-Memorial of Perry E Brochus, in behalf of certain ofcrs & noncommissioned ofcrs, musicians, & privates of the Marine Corps, who served in the late war with Mexico, asking that they may be allowed extra pay & bounty land: referred to the Cmte on Naval Affairs. 2-Ordered that Mary B Wade have leave to withdraw her ptn & papers from the files of the Senate. 3-Cmte on Public Lands: ptn of the widow & heirs of Dr Perrine, asking an extension of time for the occupation & settlement of land granted said Perrine, reported a bill for the relief of the widow & heirs of Dr Perrine: ordered to be placed on the calendar. Same cmte: bill for the relief of Saml J Bayard, late receiver of public moneys at Fairfield, Iowa: recommended that it do not pass. Same cmte: ptn of S Woods, of Missouri, asking certain mining privileges in Calif & New Mexico: recommended that it do not pass. Same cmte: bill for the relief of Elisha Hampton & others: reported back without amendment. 4-Cmte on Pensions: bill for the relief of Capt Alex'r McEwen: recommended its passage. Same cmte: bill for the relief of Mary Buck: reported back without amendment. 5-Cmte on Naval Affairs: ptns of Mary Wilkinson & of the heirs of Wm Flanigan & Wm Parsons, & also adverse report on House bill for the relief of Wm Tee, of Portsmouth, Va.
6-Cmte of the Whole: bill for the relief of Manuel X Harmony, which had been reported from the Cmte of Claims, with an amendment, proposing to insert, after the word <u>wagons</u>, the words <u>& other property</u>. The petitioner was engaged in a trading expedition to Santa Fe & the northern provinces of Mexico, having a number of wagons, mules, & merchandise. He was a citizen of the State of N Y, & had never engaged in an expedition of this kind before. After travelling some 300 miles they were overtaken by a detachment of U S troops; ordered to the rear of that detachment to Santa Fe; detained there for awhile; permitted to depart for northern New Mexico. Near the Rio Grande they were halted again. They were overtaken by Col Doniphan & his command, & ordered to go with him to Chihuahua. Doniphan wished to have the advantage of their wagons, which would be used as fortifications on the plain if they were attacked. The petitioner protested against being thus impressed & forced to accompany the troops. Under this protest he was compelled to join the command of Col Doniphan, & proceeded to make them a part of his armed force. [Harmony & others, & his wagons, mules, & merchandise, were used for the benefit of Col Doniphan.] The full value of the whole stock of goods said to have been lost, was estimated at some $80,000. Passage of the bill resulted in 25 yeas, & 19 nays. 7-Bill granting a pension to the widow of the late Col Dix: results to pass it: ayes 14, noes 21. 8-Renewal of the patent for the benefit of the widow & heirs-at-law of Timothy P Anderson, deceased: passed. 9-Bill for the relief of John Hibert: passed. 9-Bill for the relief of the heirs & legal reps of Jos McAffee, deceased: who in his time purchased from the College of Trustees a large amount of land which had been previously granted by Congress. After he paid for the land at the rate of $15 per acre, it wa ascertained that 160 acres of it were covered by a claim under a former grant, & it turned out to be legitimate, by which means this individual was deprived of his land. The Cmte of Claims concluded to allow him for the land he was dispossed of, $1.25 per acre. Read a 3rd time & passed. 10-Bill for the relief of John M Macintosh was considered in Cmte of the Whole: passed. Same cmte: bill for the relief of A H Cole: the evidence shows that various sums of money were charged in favor of this sutler on the pay-roll for soldiers who had deserted & others who had died. The paymaster is to with-hold, for the benefit of the sutlers, such sums as appear to be due to them from soldiers who have deserted or died. This claim was refused at the War Dept, because it had not been

passed by the board of administration. It took place during the Florida war. Bill was passed. 11-Cmte of the Whole: bill for the final settlement of the accounts of Thos C Sheldon, late receiver of public moneys at Kalamazoo, Mich: passed. 12-Cmte of the Whole: bill for the relief of Robt C Rodgers: he belonged to the brig **Somers**, & ordered by his superior ofcr, to make an examination of the castle of San Juan de Ulua, which service he performed. There was no great gallantry in that. He was captured by the Mexicans, held 8 months, & escaped, & he now comes here. What had he done? There are numerous individuals who have been imprisoned in the course of war, not only ofcrs but soldiers. Further consideration of the bill was postponed. 13-Cmte of the Whole: bill for the settlement of the accounts of Abraham Edwards, Register of the Land Ofc at Kalamazoo, Mich: passed. Same cmte: bill for the relief of Wm Lee: bill was rejected. Same cmte: bill for the relief of the heirs & legal reps of Regnald, alias Nick Hillary: adverse report in this case. Same cmte: bill for the relief of Eugene Van Ness & John M Brush, excs of Nehemiah Brush: passed. Same cmte: bill for the relief of Gad Humphreys: was the destruction of the property in this case necessary to prevent it from falling into the hands of the enemy to be used against us? The property was destroyed by order of an ofcr of the U S: bill indefinitely postponed.

Naval: the U S storeship **Supply** was expected to sail on Tue for the Mediterranean & Brazil. List of her ofcrs: Lt commanding, Arthur Sinclair; acting master, Geo H Cooper; passed assist surgeon, E R Kane; acting purser, John D Ghiselin, jr; passed midshipmen, W F Jones, John D Langhorne, C W Woodley, & Geo H Beir. Passengers: Lt Washington Gwaltney & passed midshipman Leonard Paulding, to join the U S frig **Lawrence**; Walter Gould, artist, for Italy; Wm H Talbot, Geo Newton & A Sinclair, jr, for the cruise.

Mrd: on Feb 19, by Rev J B Donelan, Mr John Eberhart to Marsallend L, eldest daughter of John Gould, all of Wash City.

Died: on Feb 20, in Wash City, Mary, eldest daughter of John P & Catherine Frazer, in her 6th year.

Died: on Feb 22, after a long & painful illness, Mr Ezer Ellis, in his 73rd year. His funeral is today, at 3 o'clock, from his late residence on 9th st.

The post ofc at Patuxent, Anne Arundel Co, Md, is re-establshed, & R Lemmon, jr, appointed postmaster. Appointments by the Postmaster Gen:
1-David Reindollar, P M, Taneytown, Carroll Co, Md, vice N Buffington, resigned. 2-Jas Gillett, P M, Guilford, Accomac Co, Va, vice S J Marshall, resigned. 3-Thos H Fletcher, P M, Wagram, Accomac Co, Va, vice John H Dennis, resigned. 4-Thos C McDowell, P M, Safe Harbor, Lancaster Co, Pa, vice J C Herr, resigned.

The gold digging at Stockton & Heiss' location in Va, is still very successful. The amount raised in Jan, with 15 or 20 hands, was about $26,000. The deposite of 800 ounces has just been made at the Mint.

For sale, in the village of Bladensburg, **Ross Tavern**: contains 20 rooms; extensive stabling, servants' bldg, with 2 or 3 acres of ground. For information apply to Robt T Ross, at the Counting-room of John H Duvall & Co, 231 Balt st, Balt, Md.

Washington's Birthday: yesterday being the anniversary of the birth of Gen Washington, 3 of our volunteer companies paraded in full uniform: the Washington Light Infty, Capt Tate, & the Walker Sharpshooters, Capt Bryant, marched together. The Nat'l Greys had a separate parade.

In Chancery. Circuit Court of Wash Co, D C. Murray Barker et al vs David Riley, the only heir-at-law of Catharine Campbell, deceased. Danl Ratcliffe, trustee in the above cause, reported the sale of the real estate to be sold. Sold to Jas H Holtzman, who became the purchaser of the same, to wit: lot 8 in square 16 in Wash City, for $225. —John A Smith, clerk

In Chancery. Circuit Court of Wash Co, D C. Saml Smoot, et al, cmplnts, vs Mary Jane Smoot, Saml C Smoot, Luther Smoot, John Wagerman & Lydia his wife, Jos Pleasants & Rosa his wife, & Aramenta Smoot. Danl Ratcliffe, the trustee in the above cause, reported the sale of the real estate decreed to be sold, Wm Bosher became the purchaser of the undivided 3rd part of the 2 story brick house & lot, being lot 2 in square 4, in Wash City, for $400; & also of 2 small tenements & lot, being part of the west part of lot 2 in square 4, in Wash City, for $400; & that Saml Smoot became the purchaser of the lot in Gtwn, mentioned in said decree, being lot 11, in Deakins' Lee & Cazenove's addition, for $100; & the terms of the sales have been complied with. —Jno A Smith, clerk

SAT FEB 24, 1849
Senate: 1-Memorial from Wm A Campbell, surviving partner of Jas C Watson, deceased, asking indemnity for loss sustained by the refusal of the ofcrs of Gov't to surrender certain slaves purchased by them from the Creek nation of Indians: referred to the Cmte on Indian Affairs. 2-Ptn of Jas Hamilton, asking that an appropriation may be made for testing a machine he invented for sawing timber into curves & levels suitable for ship-bldg: referred to the Cmte on Naval Affairs. 3-Cmte on Naval Affairs: ptn of Chas Colburn, asking pay for the full term of his enlistment, made an adverse report on the same: ordered to be printed. Same cmte: asking to be discharged from the further consideration of the ptn of Calvin Blythe, exc of Capt Jesse D Elliot: which was agreed to. Same cmte: bill for the relief of Martha Damerson, widow of Christopher Tompkins, asked to be discharged from the further consideration of the same: referred to the Cmte on Revolutionary Claims. Same cmte: bill for the relief of Edw Myers, reported the same without amendment. 4-Cmte on Contingent Expenses of the Senate: place the names of Noah Hanson & Jos Hedrick on the roll of messengers, with a recommendation that it be adopted. 5-Cmte on Revolutionary Claims: bill for the relief of the grandchildren of Maj Gen Baron DeKalb: recommendation that it pass as amended. 6-Cmte of Claims: ptn of the heirs & reps of the late Robt Sewall: passed to a 2nd reading. 7-Bill for the relief of Noah Phelps be recommitted to the Cmte of Claims: agreed to. 8-Bill for the relief of A C Bryan & others: passed.

After a very long & tedious journey, Gen Taylor has finally reached the metropolis. He arrived at 4 o'clock yesterday afternoon. He & his suite arrived at the Relay House in an extra train from Cumberland. His suite consists of: Maj R S Garnett, U S Army; Col J T Van Alen, of N Y; Judge Winchester, of La; J P Benjamin, of New Orleans; Col Bali Peyton & daughter, of New Orleans; A C Bullitt, of New Orleans; Dr McCormick, U S Army, & lady; Col Jas Taylor, of N Y, & daughter; Howard Christy, of Ky & lady; Miss Johnston & Miss Wickliffe, of Ky. Among the gentlemen who came from Balt to meet Gen Taylor was his brother Col J P Taylor & Maj Dusenbury, U S Army. Gen Taylor arrived in Washington after nightfall. An immense multitude accompanied the Gen's cortege to his lodgings at Willard's Hotel, where he stepped out on the balcony & returned thanks to the people for their enthusiastic welcome, which were received by deafening huzzas from the immense crowd.

Distinguished visiters to Wash at this time: Hon Jacob Burnett & John C Wright, of Ohio, both many years ago members of Congress, & Hon Jas G King, of N J, & John A King, of N Y, members elect to the next Congress.

Lewis Cass, jr, newly appointed Charge d'Affaires of the U S to Rome, was one of the passengers on the European steamer **Niagara**, which sailed from Boston on Wed last.

On Nov 26 Col Fremont commenced the ascent of the Snowy Mountains. He intends to go to the Pacific by an entire new route.

A sad accident on the Phil railroad, Tue, by which a passenger named Finley or Lindley, coming to Balt, fell under the cars & had both legs cut off.

Trustee's sale of valuable property: by deed of trust from Archibald Ludlow to the subscriber, date Dec 16, 1847: sale on Mar 3, of the eastern & western parts of lot 5 in square 229, in Wash City. –Nicholas Callan, trustee -E C & G F Dyer, aucts

H B M surveying ship **Herald** & brig **Pandora** were at Panama. The **Herald** had been to the north to endeavor to gain intelligence of Sir John Franklin, but returned withou hearing anything of him.

Furniture at auction: on Feb 26, at the residence of Danl Robinson, corner of 9th & L sts, his household & kitchen furniture. –Martin & Wright, aucts

Rochester [N Y] Democrat. The elegant Mansion of Wm R Rensselaer, in Renssalaer Co, about 1 mile from Albany, is for sale. The house is one of the most extensive ever erected in the America: its whole cost was $140,000. The walls & ceilings are painted in pieces by Bragaldi, & the whole house is warmed by Perkins' hot water pipes. The whole estate contains 500 acres. The house stands on the bank of the Hudson, 200 feet above the river. The grounds can be kept up for $2,500 per annum, & the whole establishment be supported in the true style for $20,000 per annum. It is a great pity that such a superior seat so long remained untenanted; especially when it is considered that the price asked is only $50,000.

On Sat, Justice McGrath united in the holy bonds of wedlock, on the stage of the American Museum, N Y, Robt Hales, the English giant, to Eliza Simpson, the Irish giantess, both of whom have been exhibited there for some time.

In Chancery. Jos Edmund Law, cmplnt, & Jas Adams, Lloyd N Rogers, Edmund L Rogers, Eleanor A Rogers, & other, dfndnts. Final examination of the claims against the estate of the late Thos Law, will be at my ofc on Mar 9. –W Redin, auditor

Died: Feb 22, in Gtwn, D C, after a short illness, Mrs Henrietta M Osborn, relict of the late Saml G Osborn, of Millington, Md. Her funeral is on Sat, at 3 o'clock, from the residence of her son, Wm McK Osborn, Beall st, Gtwn.

Died: on Feb 21, Lt Jas P Oellers, U S Navy, aged 67 years.

MON FEB 26, 1849
Senate: 1-Ptn of Parkerson Hocker, a volunteer in the Seminole war, asking to be allowed a pension: referred to the Cmte on Pensions. 2-Memorial of Jas C Watson, asking compensation for losses sustained when ofcrs of the Gov't failed to surrender certain negroes purchased by him from the Creek Indians: referred to the Cmte on Indian Affairs. Additional documents relating to the memorial of John C Riddle, D A Carter, & E Simonds, in relation to a macadamized road across the Isthmus of Tehuantepec: referred to the Cmte on Military Affairs.

The schnr **Flirt**, E Farren, Lt Commanding, arrived on Feb 7 at Pensacola, from a cruise in the Gulf. The sloop-of-war **Germantown**, Cmder Lowndes, was at Aux Cayes 27th ult, having arrived on the 25th from Jacmel, & was to sail in a few days for St Thomas.

Annual meeting of the Washington Nat'l Monument Society, on Feb 22, the following ofcrs & members of the Board of Managers were elected: Ofcrs:

Pres of the U S, ex-officio Pres	Thos Carbery, 3rd V Pres
Gen A Henderson, 1st V Pres	J B H Smith, Treasurer
Mayor of Washington, 2nd V Pres	Geo Watterston, Sec

Board of Managers:

Maj Gen W Scott	
Gen N Towson	P R Fendall
Col J J Abert	M F Maury
Gen Walter Jones	Thos Blagden
Thos Munro	Walter Lenox
Peter Force	T H Crawford
Wm A Bradley	B O Taylor

Elisha Whittlesey, Genr'l Agent
Bldg Cmte consists of Messrs Carbery, Watterston, Abert, & Bradley

All ofcrs of the War of 1812 now sojourning in or on a visit to Washington, are requested to meet at the rooms of Maj John G Camp, on Pa ave, on Feb 28, to make arrangements preparatory to the Inauguration on Mar 5.

The Hon Millard Fillmore, the Vice Pres Elect of the U S arrived in Washington City on Sat last, & has taken rooms at Coleman's Hotel.

Mrd: on Feb 20, in Gtwn, by Rev Mr Gassaway, Mr Albert F Yerby, of Wash, to Miss Fannie, daughter of Jos Radcliffe, of the former place.

Inaugural Procession, Mar 5, 1849.
Marshals:
Dr Wm B Magruder
J H McBlair
Dr Thos Miller
Jonas B Ellis
Assist Marshals:
Saml E Douglass
Alex H Mechlin
Dr T B J Frye
Wm F Anderson
Lem J Middleton
J L Henshaw
Alex H Clements
Chas F Lowrey*
Robt W Bates
Robt J Roche
John Alexander
Richd Abbott
Jos Bryan, jr
R W Laskey
Jos J May
E F Queen
Dr R Finley Hunt
John A Linton
Alfred B Claxton
John H Gibbs
J W Morehead
John T Towers
D Bevans
Cuthbert P Wallach
A W Fletcher
Jas B Dodson
W Nailor
Andrew Coyle, jr
Wm H Gunnell
J R Green
M Delaney
F A Klopfer
B F Burche
Wm T Porter
Chas W Boteler, jr

Stephen P Franklin
Dr Noble Young
Wm H Winter
Dr J E Morgan

Geo M Phillips
Marshal Brown
John England
Alex'r Lee
N Henning
Wm Douglass
J A Donohoo
R E Simms
Benj F Middleton
Wm H Birch
H B Sweeny
Chas B Maury
P H Hooe
Wm A Bushnell
Saml C Espey
Wm B Sasser
Edw C Dyer
Lemuel Towers
John F Coyle
John Carroll Brent
R H Williamson
Dr Geo M Dove
Wm A Kennedy
Danl Campbell
P H Brooks
Jacob G Crowley
L C Ball
Thos P Tench
John O'Donnell
Chas Gordon
B S Kinsey
Richd H Stewart
Chas R Queen
J W Martin
Wm Wise

Isaac Hall   Jas A Williams
Thos Fitnam   Wm Thompson
J L Marceron   Andree J Larner

The Marshals will be designated by pink scarfs, white rossettes, & blue cloth covers, trimmed with one row of red about 1 inch deep, & carry a baton 2 feet 3 inches long, of blue color, with gilt end 2 inches deep. The Assist Marshals will wear blue scarfs, & red rosettes, saddle covers white, trimmed with red, batons white, with red ends, same length as Marshals. Messrs Walter Lenox, J H Clay Mudd, Chas H Winder, & Geo S Gideon will act as Aids to the Marshal-in-Chief. –Richd Wallach, Marshal-in-Chief

Our city is full of distinguished visiters: Govn'r Johnston, of Pa; Ex-Govn'r Vance, of Ohio; Ex-Govn'r Young, of N Y; Ex-Senator the Hon N P Tallmadge; the Hon John Taliaferro & John P Barbour, Ex-Reps from Va; the Hon M H Grinnell, Wm Starr Miller & Henry Vail, Ex-Reps from N Y, & the Hon Jos R Chandler, Rep Elect from Phil.

TUE FEB 27, 1849
Hon Garret D Wall has been appointed a Judge of the Court of Appeals by the Legislature of the State of N J.

The name of Col Wm L Hodge, of New Orleans, was omitted from the list of gentlemen who accompanied Gen Taylor from his home to Wash City.

Situation wanted. A practical Florist & Vegetable Gardener, who thoroughly understand his business. Apply to Henry Douglas, Florist & Seedsman, opposite the State Dept.

The Hon Timothy Farrar, who was the oldest surviving graduate of Harvard Univ, died at his residence in Hollis, N H, on Tue last. He was born on Jul 11, 1747, & graduated in 1767. He was 101 years, 7 months & 10 days old. He has attained a greater age than any other graduate of Harvard. The oldest graduate now living is Jas Lovell, who resides in Orangeburg, S C, & was born in Boston, Jul 5, 1758, being in his 91st year.

Senate: 1-Memorial of Edwin Williams, praying the patronage of Gov't for a work prepared by him, containing a compilation of the messages of the Presidents of the U S & other public documents, from the formation of the Genr'l Gov't in 1789 to the present time: referred to the Cmte on the Library. 2-Memorial of Wm K Ashard, asking compensation for the use by the U S of his invention of a cannon lock & primer: referred to the Cmte on Naval Affairs. 3-Ptn from Capt Chas Wilkes, praying to be indemnified for expenses incurred in defending suits instituted against him on account of certain official acts while in command of the Exploring Expedition, & to be allowed extra pay for superintending the scientific works of said Expedition: referred to the Cmte on Naval Affairs. 4-Cmte on Public Lands: ptn of O B Hill & others, asking additional compensation for services as late receiver of public moneys at New Orleans: passed. 5-Cmte on Pensions: House bills for the relief of John McIntosh; Wm Lynch; Horatio Fitch; Jno Gawney; & Wm Whitaker: recommended their passage.

College of St James, Wash Co, Md: second term opens on Mar 5. Apply to John B Kerfoot, Rector.

Local Items: An artist by the name of Brady has recently arrived in Washington from N Y, for the purpose of obtaining daguerreotype portraits of all the distinguished men who may be present at the approaching Inauguration. His object is to form a gallery of every distinguished American now living.

Died: on Feb 26, in Wash City, John Jefferson, son of John & Susan Sessford, aged 3 months & 23 days. His funeral is today at 3 o'clock, from the residence of his parents, on C st.

Female Education. Rockhill Academy, Fauquier Co, Va: conducted by Misses Milligan, late of Wash, D C. Located within 7 miles of Warrenton. Rockhill is best known as the residence of J H Fitzgerald. Ladies in charge of this Seminary: the 3 Misses Milligan, aided by their sister, Mrs Fitzhugh. Communications addressed to Miss E Milligan, at Auburn, will receive prompt attention; as will any inquiry addressed to Miss S H Milligan, child of O Whittlesey.

WED FEB 28, 1849
Senate: 1-Cmte on Indian Affairs: Act for the relief of the legal reps of Abraham Hogeboon, deceased, & an act for the relief of Israel Johnson: without amendment. 2-Cmte on Revolutionary Claims: bill for the relief of the legal reps of Capt Saml Jones, deceased: recommended that it do not pass. 3-Cmte of Claims: bill for the relief of the legal reps of Bernard Todd, deceased; recommended its passage. 4-Ptn from John M Hepburn & other clerks in the ofc of the Adj Gen, asking extra compensation for additional services performed in that ofc owing to the war with Mexico: referred to the Cmte of Claims. 5-Ptn from Jos Treatler, citizen of Ohio, for the immediate dissolution of the American Union: ordered to lie on the table. 6-Memorial from Alex'r Brown & Sons & others, merchants of Balt, Md, in favor of a reciprocal free trade in agricultural products between the U S & Canada: ordered to lie on the table. 7-Bill for the relief of Geo Poindexter: passed.

At N Y, on Sat, as the ship **J M Ryerson** was about weighing anchor for San Francisco, Mr Chas Wetherbee, a member of the Excelsior Mining Assoc, was blown overboard by the premature discharge of a cannon which he was in the act of loading. He was rescued from death by the heroic bravery of Mr T Gardiner, of N Y, who instantly sprang into the river, & supported Mr W until they were both rescued by those on board the vessel. His hands were fearly mangled, & we fear will have to be amputated.

Hse o/Reps 1-Cmte on Public Lands: bill for the relief of David A Ely, Jas & Isham B Dodson, & C W Hardin: committed. Same cmte: act for the relief of Cadwalader Wallace: ordered to be printed. Same cmte: bill for the relief of Solomon Davis: passed. Same cmte: ptn of Wm C Jones, of Jefferson Co, Iowa, praying for a grant of land in consideration of the money he has expended & the service he has renderd the Democratic party: adverse report on the same: laid on the table.

A few days ago Mr J P Dukes, of South Ottowa, Ill, aged 26, shot himself. He had expected to start for Calif soon, but something occurred to prevent his going.

Mrd: on Feb 26, in Wash City, by Rev G W Samson, Mr Uriah Inscow to Miss Susan Jane Chrismond, both of King Geo Co, Va.

Died: on Feb 24, Sarah Catharine, youngest daughter of Michl & Sarah Ann S Rearden, aged 9 years, 5 months & 14 days.

Died: on Feb 27, Mary Eliz, only child of John H & Mgt E Smoot, aged 2 years, 6 months & 20 days. Her funeral is today at 4 o'clock, from the residence of her parents on 1st st, Gtwn.

Died: on Feb 27, Catharine Elenora, youngest daughter of Geo W Phelps, of Wash City, aged 5 years & 18 days. Her funeral is today, at 2 o'clock, from the residence of her father, on Pa ave, near 17th st.

THU MAR 1, 1849
Orem & Hopkins, [late John M Orem & Co] n w corner of Market & Chas st, Balt, Md: sale by the piece of Cloths, Cashmeres, Vestings, & Tailor's Trimmings. New Cloth Room will be open on Mar 1, entrance on Chas st.

Trustee's sale of valuable real estate. Circuit Court of Wash Co, D C, in Chancery. Chas Wallace vs Geo C Washington, Lewis W Washington, et al. The trustee will sell at public auction on Mar 24, all that lot of parcel of ground in Gtwn, in Wash Co, D C, bounded on the north by Road st, on the east by Green st, on the south by Stoddert st, & on the west by Washington st. Also all the entire lot of woodland, 15½ acres, more or less, in said county, north of & binding on said Road st. –J M Carlisle, trustee

For rent: 2 large new 3 story brick dwlg houses, on P ave, nearly opposite the residence of Robt Beale. –F Mohun, agent, upper part of 6th st west

Marble bust of the late John Quincy Adams, executed by J C King, at the Congressional Library. The Bust is in very high order. We regret to learn that the artist received a serious personal injury by exerting himself too much while removing the bust from the Railroad Depot to the Capitol.

Gen Taylor visited Gtwn yesterday. About noon Henry Addison, Mayor, accompanied by Robt Ould, Recorder, of that town, arrived at Willard's Hotel, & escorted the Pres Elect & suite to Gtwn. They were met at the bridge by the entire population. A sumptious & elegant dinner was prepared by Tilley in best style.

On exhibition at Washington Hall 2 paintings by the accomplished Rossitter: Return of the Dove, or the Triumph of Faith, & the other Miriam Exulting over the destruction of Pharaoh's Host. Ruthe & Naomi was exhibited last year.

Mrd: on Feb 20, in Wash City, by Rev J Van Horsigh, Geo B Wallis to Barbara Victoria, eldest daughter of the last John P Latruitte.

Among the 80 passengers by the ship **Europa** was Com Foxall A Parker, U S Navy, who recently went to Europe on a mission connected with the organization of the German Navy. Since then the American & the Cunard steamers **United States, Acadia, & Britannia** have been purchased for that purpose.

Mr Dielman, the eminent Prof of Music at Mount St Mary's College, Md, has composed a grand March for the Inauguration, which has been accepted by Gen Taylor, & will be performed by the Marine Band on that occasion.

For sale: first rate Rosewood Grand Piano, of the latest finish, & with all the improvements, warranted, & made by Knabe & Gaehle, of Balt. Apply to S Carusi, Music Saloon, Pa ave, above 12th st.

The trial of Mr Olcott, late cashier of the Canal Bank of Albany, for perjury, in connexion with affairs of that institution, resulted in a verdict of acquittal.

Senate: 1-Ptn of Smith & Hersey, asking a remission of duties on molasses destroyed by fire while in the public warehouse: referred to the Cmte on Finance. 2-Cmte of Pensions: act for the relief of Mary Ann Pollard, & act for the relief of Henry Childs: recommended they do not pass. Same cmte: ptns of Wm C Sterrett & Mary Wilkinson, & the ptn of Mary Hall, asked to be discharged from the further consideration of same: which was agreed to. Same cmte: House bill for the relief of Jos Dana: reported the same with an amendment. Same cmte: act for the relief of Jacob Zimmerman, & act for the relief of Rebecca Freeman, & an act for the relief of Giles Landon: recommended their passage. 3-Resolved, that the Cmte on Naval Affairs inquire into an adjustment by the Sec of the Navy, upon the principles of justice & equity, of the claims of A S & A W Benton, arising out of contracts made with the Navy Dept in 1841 for the transportation of naval stores to the Pacific. 4-House bill for the relief of Solomon Davis: passed. 5-Bill for the relief of the Hon Geo Poindexter: for payment of a claim for the use of & injury done to his splendid estate near Louisville, Ky, by the troops of the U S, which had been ascertained & agreed to by the commanding ofcr of the troops, & acknowledged to be just by the War Dept: postponed. 6-Additional documents submitted in relation to the claim of Villeneuve le Blank, to the confirmation of his title to certain lands: referred to the Cmte on Private Land Claims.

The Procession for the Inauguration will move along F st to 15th; down 15th to Pa ave, to Willard's Hotel, where the Pres Elect & Suite & the Foreign Ministers will take their places in the line; & from thence along Pa ave to the east front of the Capitol, entering the enclosure by the south gate. –Richd Wallach, Marshal-in-Chief

$50 reward for runaway servant girl Clarissa, a dark mulatto, 17 years of age. She has been living in Wash with Mr Selden, on 13th st, for some months, & 2 years ago at the Navy Yard. I will pay any reasonable expenses for her delivery to me at Rockville, Montg Co, Md. –Reuben Summers

FRI MAR 2, 1849
Senate: 1-Items for the judiciary. To Robt Beale, for his services & expenses incurred in a journey to Va, to notify Pres Tyler of his accession to the Presidency, $300. Compensation to S R Hobbie, Assist Postmaster Gen, for his services as special agent to Bremen & England, to make arrangements in respect to the mails of the U S, from May to Nov, 1847, the sum of $2,250. 2-Cmte on Indian Affairs: memorial of Susan Coody & other Cherokees, asking indemnity for property destroyed by the U S soldiers, [certain disorderly soldiers stationed at *Fort Gibson*, on Mar 12 1845.] Read a 3rd time & passed. 3-Cmte on Revolutionary Claims: bill for the relief of the legal reps of Col Francis Vigo: indefinitely postponed. 4-Bill for the relief of Jas Hotchkiss: passed.

Hse o/Reps: 1-Cmte on the Judiciary: discharged from the further consideration of the memorial of S F B Morse, Alfred Vail, & Amos Kendall, & the memorial of Henry O'Reilly, in reference to the impeachment of Judge Monroe: laid on the table. 2-Cmte on Revolutionary Claims: discharged from the further consideration of the ptn of Jos Hardaway & others: referred to the Cmte on Revolutionary Pensions. 3-Cmte on the Judiciary: discharged from the further consideration of the ptn of R W Jeffrey, John H Randall, & others, praying for the re-establishment of the U S district court for the western district of Louisiana: laid on the table. 4-Cmte on Revolutionary Claims: discharged from the further consideration of the ptn of Churchill Gibbs, administrator, & leave was granted him to withdraw his papers. Same cmte: bill for the relief of Capt Thos Beall: committed. 5-Cmte on Indian Affairs: ptn of Arba Heald: ordered to be printed. Same cmte: adverse report on the ptn of R B Mitchell: ordered to be printed. 6-Cmte on Public Lands: bill for the relief of Peter M Grant: passed, & sent to the Senate for concurrence Same cmte: resolution to make an equitable settlement with the sureties of Robt T Lytle, late Surveyor Gen of Ohio: reported back without amendment. Same cmte: ptns of Hannah Cole & of Danl Millikin: laid on the table & ordered to be printed. 7-Cmte on Post Ofc & Post Roads: discharged from the further consideration of the ptns of Arthur E Hall, postmaster at South Quay, Va; of John P Warnock, & of Robt G Ward & Co: ptns laid on the table. Same cmte: claim of David Shaw & Solomon T Corser: laid on the table. 8-Cmte on Invalid Pensions: discharged from the further consideration of the ptns of: Mary Langley, Saml Crapen, Geo Whitten; citizens in behalf of David Montgomery; Nathl Harrison, Wm Cook, Alex'r McDonald, & Hanson Poor: ptns laid on the table. 9-Cmte on Patents: ptn of S R Emerson: laid on the table. 10-Cmte on Printing: memorial of Edwin Williams, of N Y: referred to the Cmte on the Library. 11-Select Cmte: memorial of W T G Morton: laid on the table. 12-Cmte of Claims: bill for the relief of Capt Cassius M Clay: committed. Same cmte: bill for the relief of Pierson Cogswell: committed. Same cmte: discharged from the further consideration of the ptn of John T Ball: laid on the table. Same cmte: adverse reports on the ptns of Geo W Kidd, Alex'r Watson, Isaac Cook, Peletiah Shepard, & Benj A Napier: ordered to be printed. Same cmte: discharged from the further consideration of the ptn of Robt Kirkham: laid on the table. Same cmte: adverse report on the ptn of Saml B Spencer: ordered to be printed. 13-Cmte on Commerce: report on the ptn of Jas B Clarke, of N Y C,for passage of a law to protect importing merchants against the payment of illegal duties: ordered to be printed. 14-Leave was granted to withdraw from the files of the House the memorial of citizens of Jackson Co for release of judgment in favor of the U S against the estate

of Chas Matthews & Isaac L Battle, deceased. 15-Act to provide for the final settlement of the accounts of Thos C Sheldon, late receiver of public moneys at Kalamazoo, Mich: passed. Act for the final settlement of the accounts of Abraham Edwards, register of the land ofc at Kalamazoo, Mich: passed. Bills referred-relief of:
A H Cole   John M McIntosh
Wm Greer   John Crawford
Manel X Harmony
Renewal of a patent for benefit of the widow & heirs of Timothy P Anderson, deceased
Eugene Van Ness & John M Brush, excs of Nehemiah Brush
Heirs & legal reps of Jos McAfee, deceased
Renewal of a patent for the benefit of the widow & heirs of Timothy P Anderson, deceased 16-Bill for the relief of Stoughton A Fletcher: passed.

The ship **Architect**, from New Orleans, has made an unpropitious commencement of her long voyage to Calif. A letter from Capt Grey to his father states that 6 of those on board have died of cholera. She had 62 passengers.

Died: on Jan 18, suddenly of an affection of the heart, at New Lisbon, Ohio, Eliz H, wife of Jacob Janny, formerly of Wash City, in her 60th year.

SAT MAR 3, 1849
Law Notice: Andrew Wylie, jr, late of Pittsburg, Atty & Counsellow at Law. Ofc on Lousiana ave, 2nd door from the ofc of the Wash & N Y Telegraph.

Lost at the Capitol, my Memorandum Book. Suitable reward for the finder returning it to me at Brown's Hotel or the Post Ofc. –C C Battle

Hse o/Reps 1-Leave was granted to withdraw from the files of the House the ptn & papers of H K Hughes.

The new Cabinet Ministers: [These gentlemen designated by public rumor.]
Sec of State: John M Clayton   Sec of the Navy: Abbott Lawrence
Sec of the Treas: Wm Meredith   Postmaster Gen: Thos Ewing
Sec of War: G W Crawford   Atty Gen: Wm B Preston
[See Mar 7 newspaper.]

Orphans Court of Wash Co, D C. Letters of administration on the personal estate of Jas Marshall, late of said county, deceased. –Eleanora Marshall, admx

On Thu last, as 2 colored lads were scuffling in play at Lenox's wharf with a loaded gun, it went off & the entire load lodged in the stomach of one of the parties named Cole, who survived only 2 hours.

Mrd: on Jan 28 last, in London, Anthony Sampayo, late Sec of Legation of the French Mission to the U S, to Miss Virginia Timberlake, of Wash City.

Mrd: on Mar 1, by Rev Levi Reese, Mr David P Marll to Miss Mady C Poole, all of Wash City.

Mrd: on Feb 27, in Wash City, by Rev Mr Morgan, Mr Robt Reed, of Fairfax Co, Va, to Miss Sarah Anna Harrover, of the same place.

Died: yesterday, March 2, Virginia Y Mason Brown, aged 19 months, youngest daughter of Jas W & Susan Ann Brown. Her funeral is today at 4:30 o'clock, at H & 9th sts.

Capt Spencer, late of the Navy, has purchased Mr Penniman's house, in Union Square, for $72,000, the Morning Star makes a text from which to preach a very pretty sermon against the architectural extravagance & display some of our wealthy citizens are making up town. –N Y Express

Senate: 1-Bill granting a pension to Joel Thatcher: passed. 2-Cmte on the Judiciary: ptn of ___ Tunstell, in behalf of the heirs of Jaques Clamorgan, submitted a report: act passed May 26, 1824, & re-enacted on Jun 17, 1844, entitled An act enabling claimants to lands within the limits of the State of Missouri & State of Arkansas to institute proceedings to try the validity of their claims: passed to a 2nd reading. 3-Cmte of Claims: discharged from the further consideration of the ptn of Maria L Nourse: agreed to. 4-Cmte on Public Lands: bill for the relief of Chas G Gunter: recommended its passage. 5-Cmte of the Whole: bill for the relief of Mary G Leverett: passed.

Dissolution of the partnership existing under the firm of D Clagett & Co, by mutual consent. D Clagett, Jas B Dodson
+
Copartnership entered into for the transaction of the dry goods business.
-D Clagett, Jno B Clagett, A L Newton, & Jos J May

MON MAR 5, 1849
Senate: 1-Purchase of Geo Catlin's collecion of paintings & curiosities of the North American Indians, $5,000: provided the price not exceed $50,000, payable in 10 annual instalments. Mr Catlin is an American. His subject is also American. He has expended $20,000 in the prosecution of his work.

Acts passed [originating in the Hse o/Reps]-30th Congress. Relief of:
Joshua Barney, U S agent
B O Payne, of Albany, N Y
Joel Thacker
Mary G Leverett
Jas Morehead
Maj ChasLarrabee
Capt Alex'r McEwen
David Thomas, of Phil
Dr Adolphus Wislizenus
Wm Gott
Edw Quinn
Geo Newton
Robt Ramsay
Eliz S Cobbs
Danl Robinson
Jesse Washington Jackson
Mrs Anne W Angue
Eliz Mays
Nancy Tompkins
Jas H Conley
Jesse Young
Anthony Reese

Zilpha White
Hugh Riddle
Thos Badger
Noah A Phelps
Chas Waldron
Jas B Davenport
Elisha Thomason
Simon Rodriguez
Marcus Fulton Johnson
Jos Bryan
John Morrison
John Hibbart
Wm Harding
A C Bryan & others
Capt Dan Drake Henrie
Eliza A Mellon
Philip J Fontane
Levi H Carson
E B Cogswell
Jas Y Smith
Thos T Gamage
Chas Wilson
Chas Benes
Jas Norris
Jas Fugate
John Campbell
John Savage
Wm H Wilson
Andrew Flanagan
Wm P Yonge
Lowry Williams
Mary Buck
John W Hockett
Peter Shaffer
Polly Aldrich
Eve Boggs
John B Nevitt, of Adams Co, Miss
Polly Dameron, widow of Chas Dameron, deceased
John J Young, a cmder in the U S N
Saley Darby, of Randolph Co, Ga
Legal reps of Capt Geo R Shoemaker
Sarah D Caldwell, wife of Jas H Brigham
Wm Fuller & Chas Savage
John B Smith & Simeon Darden
H Carrington, exc of Paulin Le Grand, deceased
Jas P Sexton & Joshua Holden
Wm Plummer, exc of Starkey Armistead, deceased
Col Rob Wallace, aid de camp to Gen Wm Hull

Jas H Noble
Hervey Jones
Satterlee Clark
Danl Wilson
Geo Center
H M Barny
Geo R Smith
John T Ohl
Maurice R Simmons
Saml A Grier
Catharine Clark
J Melville Gilliss & others
Thos W Chinn & others
Jas F Sothoron
Jas G Carson
Henry D Garrison
P Chouteau, jr & Co
Nehemiah Brush
Jas M Scantland
Jas Hotchkiss
Timothy Cavan
Thos Talbot & others
John M Moore
Sidney Flower, of La
Amelie Couvillier, of La
Solomon Davis
Peter M Grant
Sizur B Canfield
Heirs of Wm Evans
Esther Russell
Creed Taylor
Jos F Caldwell
Stephen Champlin
Jas Glynn & others
Chas McLane, of Mo

John Percival, capt in the Navy of the U S
Archibald Bell & L S Finch
G F de la Roche & Wm P S Sanger
Wm Fuller & Orlando Saltmarsh
Thos Douglas, late U S Atty for East Fla
Reben Perry & Thos P Ligen
Wm De Buys, late postmaster at New Orleans
John P Skinner & legal reps of Isaac Green
Heirs of Jean F Perry, Josiah Bleakley, Nicholas Garrot, & Robt Morrison.
Mary Macrea, widow of Lt Col Wm Macres, late of the U S Army, deceased
Jeannette C Huntington, widow of & sole excx of Wm D Cheever, deceased
Alex'r Mongtomery, Capt & Assist Quartermaster of the army
Peter Capella, adm of Andrew Capella, deceased, & for the relief of John Caho, & for the relief of Elijah Petty & Hannah Petty, his wife, heirs of John Beardon, deceased.
And the following:
Settle accounts of Thos C Sheldon
Pension granted to Patrick Walker
Settlement of claim of Henry Washington, late a deputy surveyor of public lands in Fla
Pension to Bethiah Healy, widow of Geo Healy, deceased
Resolution respecting the claims of A S & A W Benson
Confirm Eliz Burries, her heirs or assigns, in their title to a tract of land

The Swords voted by Congress to Maj Generals Butler, Twiggs, Quitman, Worth, Henderson, & the heirs of the late Gen Hamer, have just been finished, & forwarded from the manufactory of Ames, of Springfield. They are really magnificent: cost $9,000. On Fri, Gen Towson received from the Pres of the U S the Sword intended for Gen Worth, [as desired by that ofce, he being now stationed in New Mexico.] The others will be sent by private conveyance to their respective owners.

Mrd: on Thu, by Rev Smith Pyne, D D, Rector of St John's Church, Lt Richd Wainwright, U S Navy, to Sally Frank_n, daughter of the late Richd Bache, of Phil.

Died: on Thu, at her residence in the neighborhood of Gtwn, Mrs Mariamne *Frech, in her 61st year. Wife, mother, & neighbor, & in death, she has left her memory embalmed in the affections of all who knew her. [*Paper was folded & only FRECH could be read.]

Died: on Mar 3, at her residence in Gtwn, Jane Macomb, relict of Alex'r Macomb. Her funeral is on Mar 6, at 3:30 p m.

TUE MAR 6, 1849
Household & kitchen furniture at auction, on Mar 7, at the residence of Rev J Poisel, on I st. Flag will designate the house. –A Green, auct

For rent: 3 story brick dwlg house at F & 15th sts, lately occupied by Maj Gen Scott. Apply to Richd Smith, Cashier of the Bank of the Metropolis.

On Mar 5: Inauguaral of Gen Zachary Taylor. Rev H Slicer, Chaplain to the Senate performed the devotional services. At half past 12 o'clock the Pres elect, Gen Taylor, supported by the ex-Pres, the Hon Jas K Polk, & preceded by the Cmte of Arrangements, entered the Senate the Chamber. The Inauguration of Gen Taylor, as Pres of the U S, took place in front of the great Portico of the Capitol The oath of office was administered by Chief Justice Taney. The weather was, upon the whole, though cloudy, as pleasant as could have been looked for in this season of the year. Gen Taylor was dressed in a plain suit of black, & he appeared to be in his usual good health. The Procession took up its line of march at half past 11 o'clock. The Military Escort which formed so imposing a part of the Inaugural Procession, consisted of the following companies:
Jr Artillerists of Balt, Capt Marshall
Independent Blues of Balt, Capt Shutt
Wash Guards of Balt, Capt Kalkman
Wash Light Infty, Capt Tate
Nat'l Greys, Capt Bacon
Walker Sharpshooters, Capt Bryant
Independent Greys of Gtwn: Capt Wilson
First Balt Sharpshooters, Capt Lilly
German Yagers of Balt, Capt Elterman
Jr Artillerists, Lt McNamee
Laurel Troop, Capt Capron
In its rear marched a body of the Balt Defenders, being a portion of the survivors of those patriotic citizen soldiers who took part in the defence of that city in 1814.

Died: on Mar 5, R H L Villard. His funeral is on Mar 7, at 4 o'clock, from his late residence, Bridge st, Gtwn.

Died: on Mar 4, Henry, infant son of Albert H & Evelina B Beach, aged 6 months & 6 days.

WED MAR 7, 1849
Valuable dwlg house & grounds for sale: owned by the late Gen Van Ness. As it is desirable to settle the estate of Gen Van Ness, a great bargain will be given in this property. Apply to Rd Smith.

New spring goods: Wm Egan & Son's, south side of Pa ave, near 7th st.

Nominations for high ofcs in the Gov't were made to the Senate by the Pres of the U S, as follows:
Sec of State: John M Clayton, of Delaware
Sec of the Treas: Wm Meredith, of Pa
Sec of War: Geo W Crawford, of Ga
Sec of the Navy: Wm B Preston, of Va
Sec of Home Dept: Thos Ewing, of Ohio
Postmaster Gen: Jacob Collamer, of Vt
Atty Gen: Reverdy Johnson, of Md
[See Mar 3 newspaper.]

Caution all persons from receiving a due-bill of mine dated Oct 4, 1848, payable on demand on Geo M Sothoron, for $19; as having a sufficient legal offset to the said due-bill, it will not be paid by me. –Jos F Birch, Gtwn

Mrd: on Feb 27, at **Fort Hamilton**, by Rev Francis Vinton, D D, Lt Lucien Loeser, U S Army, to Miss Sarah, daughter of Dr Jos Eaton, U S Army.

Died: on Mar 2, at Phil, where he had gone for medical aid, Dr Geo R Clarke, formerly a resident of this District, aged 38 years.

Died: on Mar 6, John Williamson, infant son of John & *Eden Paggett. Her funeral is today at 3 o'clock. [*Elen/Eden: print very light.]

Election held in Gtwn, D C, on Monday week, the vote for Mayor of the town stood thus: for Henry Addison-314; for Col John L Scull-180. Mr Addison was re-elected by a majority of 134 votes.

THU MAR 8, 1849
Gadsby's New Hotel, corner of Pa ave & 3rd st, near the Railroad Depot, Wash, D C.

The ship **Franklin**, Capt Smith, of & for Boston, from London, which left Deal about Jan 25, was totally lost on the Eastern Shore of Cape Cod, on Thu. Capt Smith, his first ofcr, & 10 persons were drowned in attempting to get on shore in the boats. Other passengers & crew were saved after the tide had fallen.

Several Balls took place in Wash City on the evening of the Inauguration day. Pres Taylor & V P Fillmore attended eash of these balls; the Pres being accompanied by Mr Speaker Winthrop & the Mayor of the City; the V P by the Hon Mr Schenck & Mr W A Bradley, 2 of the Managers of the Grand Inauguration Ball. They first proceeded to Carusi's, then to Jackson Hall, & then to the Grand Inauguration Ball in the City Hall.

Private letters received in Newark [N J] from the Pacific by the ship **Crescent City**, mentions a painful rumor that Messrs Newman & Pomeroy, clergymen of the Methodist & Baptist churches, had been murdered in the Gold Region. It gives no particulars. –Newark Daily Adv

Mrd: on Mar 1, in Phil, by Rt Rev Bishop Potter, Maj Archibald H Gillespie, of the U S Marine Corps, to Eliz, youngest daughter of Wm J Duane, of Phil.

Died: yesterday, in Wash City, of erysipelas, Col E W Robinson, a clerk in the Pension Ofc, in his 45th year. His funeral is today from his late residence on 8th st, at 4 o'clock.

Died: on Mar 6, in Gtwn, Lucy, infant daughter of Emily & the late Thos Corcoran, aged 21 mos & 27 days. Funeral today at 4 P M, from the residence of her mother, West st.

Died: on Feb 23, at Mount Morris, Livingston Co, N Y, Saml H Fitzhugh, aged 53, son of the late Col Wm Fitzhugh.

Died: on Mar 2, in Wash City, Rev Jas M Kimball, a graduate of Union Theological Seminary, N Y, & late pastor of the Presbyterian Church in Portsmouth, Va, aged 26 years.

Appointments by the late Pres: 1-Edw A Hannegan, of Indiana, to be Envoy Extra & Minister Pleni of the U S to the Kingdom of Prussia. 2-Wm Greer & Wm Easby to be Justices of the Peace for the District of Columbia.

For rent: the house on I st north, between 17 & 18th sts, & now occupied by Maj Poussin, Minister from France, & formerly by Hon John Y Mason, Sec of the Navy, is now offered for rent, together with the furniture therein. Apply to Nicholas Callan, Notary Public

For sale or rent: residence on H st, adjoining the dwlg of Dr Heiskell, U S A. Possession immediately. Inquire of H M Morfit, 4½ st, near Pa ave.

For rent or sale: the house & grounds on I st, near St John's Church, the residence of the late Col Geo Bomford. Inquire of J B H Smith, ofc on F st.

FRI MAR 9, 1849
Gentlemen & Ladies who took away articles through mistake from the Grand Inauguration Hall at the City Hall, will be good enough to return them to the room adjoining the Mayor's ofc, & get their own in return. -Cmte

Bracelet lost at the Ball in Judiciary Square, gold set with Turquoise. $5 reward for returning it to Brown's Hotel. —W T Lawrence

Reward will be paid for the return of lost spectacles, by applying at the Stationery store of W F Bayly, Pa ave, between 11th & 12th sts.

Bracelet found at the Grand Inauguration Ball, which the owner can have by applying at Robt L Patterson's Drug Store.

Found, in front of the Pres' House, on Mar 6, a carpet bag containing sundry articles of wearing apparel, which owner can have by describing property & paying for this ad. —Rinlaugh De Neale, 8th st, opposite Marine Barracks

The Mobile Advertiser of Mar 1 announces the death of the Hon Wm Crawford, District Judge of the U S for the district of Alabama. [No date-current news.]

On Tue last Isaac Buckingham was elected Mayor of Alexandria for the ensuing year:
Isaac Buckingham: 181 [L F]   T E Baird: 64 [Whig]
Jos Eaches: 172 [Whig]   Jesse T Ramsey: 17 [Whig]
A D Harmon: 149 [Whig]

G Goebel, ladies' hairdresser, from 304 Chestnut st, & H G Stuebgen, dealer in ladies fancy & dress trimmings, from 301 Arch st, Phil, have today opened today branches of their establishment on Pa ave, between 9th & 10th sts. —G Goebel

Sale of land in Loudoun Co, Va, under a deed of trust, dated Jun 30, 18_6, recorded in the Clerk's ofc of said county, executed by Wm B Chittenden to the undersigned, to secure the debt therein mentioned, due to Wm Selden: sale on Sep 9, 1849, in front of the Court House, in Leesburg, a public auction, 2,132 acres of land, more or less, lying in Loudoun Co, Va, adjoining the lands of Col John McCarty on the north, of the heirs of Landon Carter on the east, & of Mr Benj Bridges on the south. –Loftin N Ellett, W Goddin, Wm D Nutt, Trustees

List of Cadet appointments for 1849
Maine: Davis Tillson: 4th Dist, Jos Stevens: 6th Dist
N H: John P Sherburn: 1st Dist
Mass: Wm Dwight, j: 6th Dist; Thos W Clapp: 7th Dist
Conn: Robt O Tyler: 1st Dist; Thos J English: 4th Dist
R I: no vacancy
Vt: Danl A Chipman, 3rd Dist
N Y:
Thos P Hewitt: 12th Dist
La Rhett Livingston: 14th Dist
Jas Wright: 15th Dist
John Davenport: 18th Dist
Jos Spratt: 19th Dist
John R Brown: 20th Dist
Oliver D Greene: 25th Dist
Benj F Chamberlain: 28th Dist
Alex Chambers: 31st Dist
N J:
Geo B Dandy: 1st Dist
Benj F Smith: 3rd Dist
Mark F Leavenworth: 5th Dist
Pa:
Lewis H Pelouze: 3rd Dist
Augustus H Plummer: 7th Dist
David P Hancock: 11th Dist
Nelson B Switzer: 18th Dist
Milo R Adams: 20th Dist
Dela: no vacancy; Md: no vacancy
Va:
Henry H Walker, 1st Dist
John R Chambliss, jr: 2nd Dist
Ferdinand C Hutter: 4th Dist
Thos M Jones: 7th Dist
Geo A Handley: 8th Dist
Wm Craighill: 10th Dist
Wm R Terrill: 12th Dist
Connolly F Litchfield: 13th Dist
Wm Dent: 15th Dist
N C: Jos P Jones: 3rd Dist
Ga:
Henry T Latham: 4th Dist
Owen F Solomon: 5th Dist
Jas H Bowen: 7th Dist
Wm R Boggs: 8th Dist
Ky: Wm K Peyton: 2nd Dist; John Hood: 9th Dist
Tenn:
___ Willis: 1st Dist
Jas D McFarland: 2nd Dist
Reuben R Ross: 9th Dist
Ohio:
Wm J Sawyer: 5th Dist
Jas B McPherson: 6th Dist
Joshua W Sill: 8th Dist
Robt F Hunter: 9th Dist
Wm McIntire Dye: 11th Dist
Thos W Vincent: 15th Dist
Elmer Otis: 21st Dist

La: no vacancy
Indiana:
Edmund C Jones: 5th Dist   Wm Craig: 7th Dist
Thos Hight: 6th Dist
Ill:
Jas D Burns: 1st Dist   John Schofield: 6th Dist
Jos A Crain: 3rd Dist
Miss:
John Mullins: 1st Dist   Nathl G Robards: 3rd Dist
Sampaen H Harris: 2nd Dist
Ala:
Chester C Du Bose: 2nd Dist   Silas P Higgins: 6th Dist
John F de Graffenreid: 4th Dist
Missouri: Geo R Bissell, 1st Dist; Jesse Cravens: 5th Dist
Mich: Thos W Wells: 2nd Dist
Ark: no vacancy
Florida: Jas L White
Texas: Horace Randall: 1st Dist; Jas B McIntyre: 2nd Dist
Iowa: Wm W Lowe: 2nd Dist
Wisc: Alex S Hooe: 2nd Dist
District of Columbia: no vacancy
At Large:
Wm Kearny, son of Gen Kearny
Francis John Shunk, of Pa
Robt B Campbell, of Tenn
Thos M Stuart, of S C
Walworth Jenkins, of N Y
Thos Wilson, of D C
Danl J Boyle, of Md
Jas B Polk, of Ga
Robt W Keyworth, of D C
Peyton H Colquitt, of Ga

The Vice Pres named Jas Alfred Pearce a Regent of the Smithsonian Institution.

Randolph Robinson was yesterday found guilty of maiming Mr Tilley, of Gtwn. The commission of this offence subjects the prisoner to imprisonment in the penitentiary.

For sale: farm near the Wash Race Course: about 200 acres, with a new 2 story farm house, a dwlg for farm hands, stable & coach house, & other outbldgs. Inquire of Thos Carbery, of Wash, or Lewis Carbery, of Gtwn.

Small tract of land for sale in Fairfax Co, Va: 92 acres, more or less, within 2½ miles of Occoquan. I can be seen at any time in Wash, 1st Ward, Pa ave, near the War Dept. –John M McIntosh, Tailor

Household & kitchen furniture at auction: on Mar 12, on L st, between 8th & 9th sts, near Doughty's Row. –A Green, auct

SAT MAR 10, 1849
Lost, by the subscriber, near the White House, this morning, the papers relating to the application of Mrs Ann B Reese, of Galveston, Texas, for the pay & bounty of her 2 sons, Francis M & David H Robinson. Reasonable compensation will be given to the finder by Robt Hughes, U S Hotel.

J Knox Walker will practice law in the U S Supreme Court, & attend to the prosecution of claims against the Gov't. Address Wash, D C.

$20 reward for return of a pocket book containing papers valuable to no one but the owner, Mr John Lindsey. Lost on the way from Richmond to Wash. Deliver to H Langtry, 1st Comptroller's Ofc, Treas Dept, Wash, & no questions asked.

Household & kitchen furniture at auction on Mar 14, at the house formerly occupied by Mrs McDaniel, on 4½ st. -E C & G F Dyer, aucts

The Hon David R Atchison, of Missouri, Pres of the Senate, was on Sunday last, by virtue of his ofc, President of the U S-for one day!

Capt Wm H Hunter, of the U S Navy, died on Mon, at his residence in Phil, from a violent attack of inflammation of the lungs, fatal after but a few days' illness. He was in his 57th year, 38 of which had been passed in the naval service, having entered it as a midshipman on Jan 16, 1809. He stood #21 on the list of Post Capts, his commission bearing date Feb 9, 1837. He leaves a large family & a numerous circle of friends to lament his loss.

Died: Mar 8, Mrs Martha Wheeler, wife of Mr Geo W Wheeler, aged 28 years. Her funeral is this morning, at 10 o'clock, from the Union Chapel, 20th st.

The frig **Raritan**, Capt Benj Pagen will sail with the first favorable wind. After cruising off the coast for a short time, will touch at N Y, where the successor to Cmdor Wilkinson in the command of the Home Squadron will join the ship. She will then proceed to her destination in the Gulf. List of her ofcrs: Capt, Benj Page
Lts: Benj J Totten, Wm T Muse, Wm A Parker, Thos B Huger, Jas S Ridgely
Chaplain: John Blake; Fleet Surgeon: Davis D Edwards; Purser: John A Bates
Lts of Marines: Josiah Watson & Jas H Jones; Master: Francis Alexander
Assist Surgeons: Alex'r J Rice & Ashton Miles
Passed Midshipmen: Washington H Davidson, Greenleaf Cilley, J P H DeKrafft, Francis Gregory, Jonathan Young
Midshipmen: Jos D Blake, Chas W Flusser, John W Riddell, Wm P McCann, Jas H Gillis, Trevett Abbot, Carlos Bratt
Boatswain: Jos Lewis   Sailmaker: Jacob Stephens
Gunner: Andrew A Randall   Capt's Clerk: John B Forney
Carpenter: Wm Lee   Purser's Clerk: John P Gregson

Mrd: on Sun, in St Paul's English Lutheran Church, by Rev J E Graeff, Jos W Pifer to Sarah Jane Rollins.

Mrd: on Mar 5, at Montevideo, Montg Co, Md, by Rev Randolph A Smith, Rev Chas H Nourse to Mrs Eliz J Peter, all of Montg Co.

Mrd: on Feb 22, by Rev Mr Lenahan, John C Campbell, of N J, to Miss Martha A Burman, daughter of the late Henry Burman, formerly of PG Co, Md.

Mrd: on Mar 6, at Ebenezer Church, Wash, Mr Danl G Rollin to Miss Sarah E Adams, daughter of the late Geo Adams, formerly of Vergennes, Vt.

MON MAR 12, 1849
Nathl Silsbee, jr, has been chosen Mayor of Salem, Mass.

Mr Robt Wickliffe, of Ky, late U S Charge d'Affaires at Turin, & wife, arrived at N Y last Tue in the packet ship **Admiral**, from Havre.

We learn that Col J B Wallach, 4th Regt U S Artl, has been promoted to the rank of Brig Gen by brevet. Col W entered the army as Lt of Cavalry, Jan 10, 1799, & has been over half a century in the service. He was twice brevetted during the war of 1812, as Maj & Lt Col. –Balt Am

One of the last acts of the late Postmaster Gen was the appointment of Mrs Maria J Hornbeck to be Postmistress of Allentown, in place of E R Newhard, resigned. Mrs H is the widow of the late Hon John W Hornbeck, & has a large family dependant upon her for support.

Mrd: on Mar 6, in Ebenezer Church, Wash, by Rev Wm Prettyman, Mr Danl G Rollin, formerly of Vergennes, Vt, to Miss Sarah E Adams, daughter of the late Geo Adams, of Wash City. [2nd notice: includes Rev Wm Prettyman.]

Died: on Mar 3, of a lingering illness, Abraham Hill, a native of Georgia, aged 43 years. He was the colored servant of Maj Gen Worth, & following him through the conflict at Montery, thence to the city of Mexico, & died as a faithful a follower of the Cross as he had been a humble & devoted servant & a brave soldier.

Died: on Mar 9, in Wash City, of water on the brain, Mr Edw Green, in his 35th year, formerly of Alexandria.

TUE MAR 13, 1849
Geo H Sands, of Middletown, Delaware Co, N Y, committed suicide on Sat last by drowning himself in the river near his house. There was a hole in the frozen river, in which he was seen to plunge, after taking his hat off & laying it down. His body was recovered some 45 minutes later, & of course, life was extinct. He was about 45 to 50 years of age. He was the wealthiest man in Middletown, & one of the wealthiest in the county. He married his second wife just a few months since.

Household & kitchen furniture at auction on Mar 21, at the residence of the Hon Wm J Brown, on Capitol Hill. –A C Green, auct

Sale of splendid paintings, advertised by the Solicitor of the Treasury, resulted as follows:
Andrea Del Sarto: Virgin, Child, & St John. Awarded to Peter Gorman, of this city: $250.51.
Christ Bound: Guido Rene. J C Maguire, of Wash: $105.
Titian: The Martyrdom of St Sebastian. Mary Ann Irvine, of Phil: $500.
Martin De Vos: Dead Christ. J C Maguire: $105.
Rubens: The Nativity. J C Maguire: $125.
Francis Snyders: The Vegetable Market. Mary Ann Irvine: $2,500.
Hobbim_: Landscape & Figures. J C Maguire: $105.
Claude Lorraine: Architecture & Marine. J C Maguire: $105.
Philip Wovermans: Hat at an Inn. John B Morris, of Balt: $135.50.
Philip Wovermans: Traveller's Rest. John B Morris, of Balt: $135.50.
David Teneirs: Landscape & Figures. Mary Ann Irvine, of Phil: $750.
Carlo Dolci: Christ on the Mount. J C Maguire: $105.
Cavalere Benedetto Luti: Magdalen in a swoon. J C Maguire: $105.
St Sebastian. J C Maguire: $176.
Albert Van Everdingen: Snow Piece J C Maguire: $236.

Recent session of the Westcheser circuit [N Y] an action for breach of promise excited considerable interest. The plntf, Isaac L Tompkins, a young unmarried man, claimed $3,000 damages of Mary Jane Hammond, a widow lady, for breach of promise of marriage, alleged to have been made during her widowhood, after the decease of her late husband, Mr John Hatfield. The jury rendered a verdict for the dfndnt.

Mr H N Hudson, the distinguished lecturer on Shakespeare, on Sunday last, was ordained a deacon of the Episcopal Church, by Bishop Whittingham, of Md, in Trinity Church, N Y.

On Feb 16, a passenger on the steamer **Charles Carroll**, named John Farrell, after having eaten Osage oranges, died of a disease resembling Asiatic cholera, leaving 4 children on the boat. He is said to have a wife somewhere near Cincinnati. He was buried near the Widow Franklin's, above the mouth of the Red River.

Died: on Mar 9, in Wash City, suddenly, Mr Jas E Given, in his 33rd year.

WED MAR 14, 1849
The dead body recently discovered near Gtwn has been recognised as that of Thos W Hoyes, of Nottingham, PG Co, Md. He was about 40 years of age, & has left a wife & several children. He was decoyed out of his path, & cruelly murdered, there appears to be but little doubt. [Mar 16th newspaper: The body is not Mr Hoye. Mr Hoye is at home & well, per Mr Allen, who just returned from Nottingham. Alexandria Gaz]

Official: Edw Francis Sweetser has been appointed Consul of the Republic of Ecuador for the port of Phil. Mar 9, 1849, Wash City.

Mrd: on Mon, by Rev John C Smith, Mr John W Glover to Miss Eliza Rowan, all of Wash City.

Mrd: on Mar 13, in Wash City, by Rev Thos M Reese, Thos Palmer, Publisher of the Jackson [Miss] Southron, to Miss Julia D, youngest daughter of the late John Terrett, of Fairfax Co, Va.

Died: on Mar 9, in Wash City, at the residence of his brother-in-law, Aaron Dawson, after a painful illness, Edw Green, of Alexandria, in his 35th year.

Died: on Mar 10, John Slidell, infant son of Julia & Lt C R P Rodgers, U S N.

Wash Corp: 1-Bill for the relief of Henry Burdick: passed. 2-Ptn from A Lehman, praying remission of a fine: referred to the Cmte of Claims. 3-Ptn of John Tenant, for remission of a fine: referred to the Cmte of Claims. 4-Ptn of E Barnes & McHenry, praying the payment of a certain claim against the Corp: referred to the Cmte of Claims. 5-Cmte of Claims: bill for the relief of John Dulany: passed.

Boy wanted to run errands. –Wm B Todd, Hat Store, west of Brown's Hotel

Pianos for sale: at the Piano Store, 12th & F st. –F C Reichenbach

Lost, a check drawn by J W Simington on the Bank of Wash, payable to the order of Louis Rasch, for $110. Finder will please return it, as payment has been stopped. –Louis Rasch

Annual meeting of the Md Historical Society, in Balt, on Feb 1, the following were elected as ofcrs for the ensuing year: Pres, Gen J Spear Smith; V P, Hon John P Kennedy; Corr Sec, J Morrison Harris; Rec Sec, S F Streeter; Treasurer, John I Donaldson; Librarian, J Louis Smith.

Trustees sale: by deed of trust from Wm Wheatley, recorded in Liber W B 128, folios 9 & 10, of the land records of Wash Co: sale on Mar 20, of lots 23 & 25 in square 497, on 4½ st south, between G & H sts. –John Carroll Brent, trustee -A Green, auct

The Nat'l Greys announce their Ball will be held on Easter Mon, Apr 9, at the Odd Fellows' Hall. Managers: on the part of the-

Military of D C:

Maj Gen R C Weightman	Brig Gen John Mason, jr
Col W W Seaton	Col Henry Naylor
Col Wm Hickey	Maj Thos Donoho
Maj John H Riley	Capt Jos B Tate
Capt John Y Bryant	Capt Caleb Buckingham
Capt P Wilson	

Military of Balt:

Col John Pickell	Lt Col Geo P Kane
Capt Robt Hall	Capt Augustus P Shutt
Capt R Lilley	Capt Marshall
Capt Dashiell	

Citizens of Washington:
John W Maury
Silas H Hill
S P Franklin
John Boyle
J B Ellis
C W Blackwell
R W Carter
Joel W Jones
Jas F Haliday
M Delany
John F Coule
Dr T B Frye
F B Lord, jr

Walter Lenox
Richd Wallach
F W Naylor
H B Sweeny
John R Queen
Jas L White
John H Semmes
M H Stevens
P Henry Brooks
Danl B Clarke
Wm H Winter
Wm Fitzpatrick
S W Walker

Exec Cmte:
Lt M P Mohun
Cpl W W Tucker
Pvt John E Buckingham

Lt S M Tucker
Ensign Jas Sutton
–Mar 14, 1849

Trustees sale: by deed of trust from Wm Wheatley, recorded in Liber W B 128, folios 9 & 10, of the land records of Wash Co: sale on Mar 20, of lots 23 & 25 in square 497, on 4½ st south, between G & H sts. –John Carroll Brent, trustee -A Green, auct

THU MAR 15, 1849
Public sale in the village of Bladensburg, on Mar 28, a Stone House & lot of ground attached, adjoining the Tobacco Warehouse. Also a small farm about 75 acres, near Addison's Chapel, about 5 miles from Wash. For the heirs: Benj O Lowndes.

Dyer et al vs Stewart el al. By virtue of a decree of the Circuit Court of Wash Co, D C, I will offer for sale, on Apr 4, lot 3 in square 370. Also, part of lot 10 in square 348. –W S Cox, trustee -E C & G F Dyer, aucts

Household & kitchen furniture at auction on Mar 20, at the residence of the Hon Cave Johnson, on G st, between 10th & 11th sts: superior furniture. -E C & G F Dyer, aucts

From Calif. On Dec 16 a trial was held at San Jose, before Judge Kimball H Dimmick, Alcalde of the District, & a jury empanelled for the case of 3 men, Davis, Campbell, & Freer, for murder. They were pronounced guilty, & sentenced to be hanged. The sentence was carried into execution on Dec 18 in presence of a large concourse of citizens. The convicts confessed their guilt & embraced the Catholic faith. Three other men were tried for participation in the same crime: Cotton, Woolard, & Lee: each found guilty. Cotton was sentenced to 15, the 2 others 18 lashes, & Woolard & Lee, on the additional charge of perjury, 40 lashes each, & one month in the stocks. C E Picket, tried at **Fort Sacramento**, on a charge of the murder of Mr Alderman, was acquitted.

Orphans Court of Wash Co, D C. Letters of administration on the personal estate of Sarah Vorhees, late of said county, deceased. –Saml Redfern, adm

The 6 dead bodies found near Sag Harbor, Long Island, have been identified as the master [Henry Rider] & crew of the schnr **William Henry**, of Provincetown, bound from Norfolk to Portland, which is supposed to have sunk off Block Island on Feb 25.

Died: on Mar 13, of scarlet fever, after an illness of 3 days, Richd M Johnson, son of Isaac & Augusta Clarke, aged 6 years & 10 months.

Appointments by the Pres: [By & with the consent & approval of the Senate.]
John Gayle, of Ala, to be Judge of the U S Dist Court for the northern & southern districts of Ala, in place of Wm Crawford, deceased.
Archibald Williams, of Ill, to be U S Atty for the district of Ill, in place of David L Gregg: commission is about to expire.
Palmer V Kellogg, of N Y, to be U S Marshal for the northern district of N Y, in place of Jacob Gould: commission is about to expire.
John Pettes, of Vt, to be U S Marshal for the district of Vt, in place of Jacob Kent: commission is about to expire.
Saml D King & Wm Thompson, of Washington, to be Justices of the Peace for Wash Co, D C.
Collectors of the Customs:
Jos T Nye, Saco, Maine, vice Ichabod Jordon: commission expired.
Thos Hedge, Plymouth, Mass, vice Wm Morton Jackson: commission expired.
Jas Donaghe, New Haven, Conn, vice Norris Wilcox: commission expired.
Naval Ofcr: Chas Hudson, Boston, Mass, vice Wm Parmenter: commission expired.
Surveyors of the Customs:
Geo Howland, Tiverton, R I, vice Asa Gray: commission expired.
Wm P Greene, Providence, R I, vice D G Seamans: commission expired.

Furnished rooms for rent: at present occupied by the Judges of the Supreme Court [consisting of one large parlor & 4 chambers,] will be for rent after Mar 15. Call at P Brenner's, Pa ave, near the corner of 4 ½ st.

Patapsco Hotel, at *Ellicott's Mills*, for lease or rent: attached is a well laid out garden lot of about 2 acres. Possession given on May 1 next. Apply to Thos Wilson & Co.

Hon John Blanchard, of Centre Co, died at Columbia, Lancaster Co, Pa, on Thu last. He was a member of the late Congress, & was on his way home from Washington at the time of his decease. His delicate health prevented him from taking an active part in the business of Congress. –Lancaster Tribune

Miss Paulin Dewey recovered $1,573 of Mr Horace B Dewey at the present session of our County Court, for a breach of promise of marriage.
-Berkshire [Mass] Courier

FRI MAR 16, 1849
Ladies with letters in the Wash Post Ofc as of Mar 15, 1849.

Addison, Mrs Ann E
Bouvier, Miss J-2
Baggett, Ann M
Baxter, Miss Blan'a
Bridwell, Miss A
Berry, Miss E C
Bolton, Miss Eliz
Bruswick, Miss Eliz
Brooks, Miss Emily
Brooks, Mrs Henry
Boys, Helen C
Burch, Hillary
Bloomfield, Mrs I
Boyd, Mrs Jane
Bates, Miss Mary
Byrne, Mrs Mark
Bowyer, Miss Mat
Bush, Miss Julia
Burch, Miss Cordelia
Burgevin, Miss Julia
Bronough, Miss M E
Bulger, Miss Margt
Bryant, Mrs Susan J
Burch, Miss Valin'a
Carroll, Miss Ann
Cox, Mrs A M-2
Collison, Mrs Cath
Casey, Miss H-3
Cox, Mrs Mary
Cameron, Mrs M B
Cobb, Mrs Nat R
Coates, Mrs Rich S
Cutting, Mrs R L
Crooks, Sarah A
Cain, Miss Sarah
Chapman, Mrs S P
Crier, Susan
Christy, Mrs H F
Dogins, Mrs Cath
Dyer, Mis Eliza E
Davis, Miss Eliz
Davis, Miss Frank
Debaugn, Helen L
Dwight, Mrs A
Delano, Miss
Davis, Martha
Denear, Miss M
Duvall, Miss M

Diny, Mrs Mary
Dougherty, Susan
Duncan, Miss Sarah
Davies, Miss F M
Derham, Mrs Flora
Davis, Miss M D W
Fagan, Mrs Mary
Featherston, Mrs M
Fishe, Miss Rosallie
Grimes, Miss C A
Germon, Miss E
Goslin, Anne
Garner, Mary A
Gray, Mrs Martha
Gantt, Mrs Rose D
Henson, Ann
Hansel, Miss Annie
Halerman, Mrs A S
Hetricks, Mrs Barb
Hall, Mrs D W
Hollen, Mrs Eliz
Hickey, Esther C
Hall, Miss Hetty B
Hauptman, Miss H
Hanson, Mrs Jas G
Hill, Miss Mar'ta
Hoffman, Miss
Hailstock, Miss M J
Harrison, Mrs M M-2
Hestley, Mrs
Harford, Mrs S A
Ingle, Mrs M H
Johnson, Mrs Cath
Jones, Miss E C
Johnson, Eliz
Jackson, Miss Henry
James, Miss Mary F
Jones, Miss Sarah-2
Kepler, Miss Ann E
Kennedy, Miss C
Klack, Miss Lucy A
King, Miss Mgt
Keech, Mrs F M
Keech, Mrs C Smith
Lansdale, Mrs E M
Loeby, Mrs Ellen
Lee, Miss Fanny
Locke, Mrs John

Lodge, Miss K H S-2
Louis, Mgt
Lloyd, Miss Mariana
Lee, Miss S S
Lovejoy, Mrs Susan
Lynde, Mrs W P H
Lea, Miss Cathrine T
Litchfield, Miss Eliza
Leitch, Miss Virginia
Mills, Miss A V C
Morris, Mrs Anne
Morgan, Miss Ann
Murphy, Miss A M
Morton, Mrs M-3
Mills, Miss Caroline
Mudd, Miss E B
Marshall, Mrs Eliza
Morse, Mrs J E
Mason, Mrs J L
Miller, Miss Maria
Manders, Mrs M A
Murray, Mrs M T
Mead, Mrs Francis
Mickham, Miss Eliz S M-2
Morris, Miss Mary A
Monroe, Mrs Martha
Marshall, Mrs Sophia
McNew, Miss M S
McHenry, Mrs R W
McLaughlin, Mrs A
Nelson, Miss A C
Newman, Jane-2
Philips, Mrs Cecelia
Parish, Mrs Danl
Patterson, Mrs H
Polk, Miss Julia A
Parker, Miss Louisa
Paule, Miss Martha
Potter, Miss Sarah L
Rich, Mrs Anna-2
Robinson, Mrs E
Robinson, Mrs M J
Rose, Mrs
Rogers, Mrs Lucretia
Reed, Mrs Catharine
Reader, Mrs Eliz
Richards, Mrs Eliza
Rabbitt, Mrs Mary A

Robertson, Mrs M P
Smith, Mrs Ann W
Shepherd, Miss A J
Scanlan, Anne
Shorter, Mrs A E
Sewall, Caroline
Skidmore, Miss M
Smith, Mrs Mary R
Simpson, Mrs Mary
Sibley, Mrs Sarah J
Smith, Mrs Sarah P
Stevenson, Miss Sallie
Smith, Mrs Mgt
Smith, Mrs Henrietta
Stone, Miss Eliz
Shriver, Miss Amelia
Selden, Miss Virginia
Swann, Mrs Rosana
Thornton, Ann
Tarver, Mrs C M
Tabler, Mrs C E

Travis, Miss G
Tyler, Miss Jane C
Thompson, Mrs M H
Thomson, Miss M S
Thompson, Rebecca
Thompson, Rahaeha'l
VanBuskirk, Mrs O M
Wallar, Mrs Ann A
Wood, Mrs Chas
Williams, Eliz
Wright, Mrs Julia
Whitney, Mrs J B-2
Wilson, Miss M
Ware, Mrs Dr R A-2
Wise, Miss Sally E
Wager, Mrs Sarah
Worsley, Miss F
Walker, Mrs Wm
Young, Miss M E
-C K Gardner, P M

By Telegraph. St John's [N B] was visited with a disastrous conflagration on Wed, which consumed, in all, about 100 bldgs. The property destroyed was on Geo, Union, Mill, & Smith sts, & Drury lane.

Hon Danl P King, our Rep in Congress, arrived home, to a scene of domestic affliction. His eldest daughter, Mrs Loring, at Andover, was suddenly & dangerously ill. She died before his arrival. –Danvers Courier

Ofcr Bowyer, of N Y, on Mon, arrested Jas Webb, supposed to be implicated in stealing the gov't jewels from the Patent Ofc in this city. This man [the N Y Post says] is a notorious offender.

At Montreal, on Wed last, below the town, a little boy named Narcisse St Jean picked up an unexploded shot & carried it home to his mother. It exploded and Narcisse lost 3 fingers & had fearful wounds of his legs; his mother was wounded in the leg. So far he is doing well. –Montreal Herald

Senate: [Mar 15] 1-Memorial of Wm P Ross & Wm S Coodey, in behalf of the Old Settlers or Western Cherokess, complaining that they have been deprived of certain rights accruing under treaty stipulations: referred to the Cmte on Indian Affairs. 2-Peter Brown to have leave to withdraw his ptn papers from the files of the Senate. 3-Ordered that 2,000 additional copies of the military reconnoissance of Col P St George Cook be printed for the use of the Senate. 4-Bills passed in the Cmte of the Whole: passed: relief of B O Payne, Joshua Barney, & Lizur B Canfield.

Jas O Sargent & Jos Otis Sargent, Counsellors & Attys at Law, ofc on Pa ave & 14th st. [Ad]

Criminal Court: 1-U S vs Francis Hopkins, indicted for burglariously entering the dwlg-house of Catharine Langton, with intent to steal the goods & chattels of Elijah Edmonston: jury found him not guilty. 2-Randolph Robinson convicted of mayhem on the person of Mr Tilley, of Gtwn; to suffer 2 years in the penitentiary, being the shortest term the law allows, to commence on Mar 17. 3-In the case of the U S vs Henry Johnson, charged with committing an assault with intent to kill: jury found him guilty of aggravated assault, & the Court sentenced him to pay a fine of $50.

Adelphi Theatre has been well attended since last Mon night, when Miss Julia Dean announced her new engagement.

Sale of household furniture, on Mar 21, at the dwlg over the exchange ofc of J W Maury. –C W Boteler, auct

Household & kitchen furniture at auction on Mar 26, at the residence lately occupied by Hom R C Winthrop, on C st, near 3rd st. –A Green, auct

Valuable Farm for sale: formerly belonging to Mr Webb, deceased, but now occupied by & belonging to Mr J H Knott, on the Turnpike road, leading from Washington to Rockville, Montg Co, Md: contains 373½ acres: bldg improvements consist of a good dwlg house & all necessary out-bldgs. Apply to the subscriber on the premises, J H Knott. For information of the place call on the Miss Webbs, G & 11th sts, Wash.

SAT MAR 17, 1849
Admx sale, Mar 23, 1849. At auction the celebrated Kain Marble Quarry, in Westchester Co, N Y. Will be sold by order of the Surrogate of Westchester Co. The Quarry is in Tuckahoe, 16 miles from N Y C. Apply to Saml E Lyon, Counsellor at Law, White Plains, or Jas M Miller, Auctioneer, Store 85 Maiden La, N Y.

The copartnership between Morell & Miller has been dissolved by mutual consent. –Royal E Miller

Orphans Court of Wash Co, D C. Letters testamentary on the personal estate of Mary Chapman, late of said county, deceased. –Ed Chapman, exc

The late Sec of War, previous to his retiring from ofc, gave the following names to the new fortifications now being erected by Gov't:
The fort at the narrows of the Penobscot river, Me, *Fort Knox*;
fort on Govnr's Island, Boston Harbor, Mass, *Fort Winthrop*;
fort on Rouse's Point, N Y, *Fort Montgomery*;
fort at Black Rock, N Y, *Fort Porter;*
fort at Spring Wells, near Detroit, Mich, *Fort Wayne*;
fort at Grand Island, Platte River, Oregon route, *Fort Kearny.*

Furnished house to let: 2 story brick dwlg on 3rd st, near C, occupied by Lt Blunt, U S Navy. Inquire on the premises.

On Feb 24, a two-horse sleigh, containing 5 persons, broke through the ice upon Rock river, Ill, & but 2 were saved. Saml Tindall, his sister Mgt, about 19 years of age, & Miss Sarah Brasher, daughter of Wm T Brasher, were lost.

Official: appointments by the Pres, by & with the consent of the Senate.
Navy Agents: Geo Loyall, Navy Agent at Norfolk, from Mar 14, 1849, reappointed. Wm Sloanaker, Navy Agent at Phil, from Mar 15, 1849, vice S D Patterson: whose commission will then expire.
Promotions in the Navy: John C Long, now a Cmder, to be a Capt in the Navy from Mar 6, 1849, to fill a vacancy occasioned by the death of Capt W M Hunter.
Theodorus Bailey, now a Lt, to be Cmder in the Navy from Mar 6, 1849, to fill the vacancy created by the promotion of John C Long.
Chas Deas, now a Master, to be a Lt in the Navy from Mar 6, 1849, to fill the vacancy occasioned by the promotion of Lt Theodorus Bailey.
Land Ofcrs: Alfred Cowles, to be Reg of the Land Ofc at Chicago, Ill, in place of Wm Jackson, whose term of ofc has expired.
Jesse K Dubois, to the Receiver of Public Moneys at Palestine, Ill, in place of Wm Wilson, whose term of ofc will expire on Mar 18.
Mathew Gillespie, to be Register of the Land Ofc at Edwardsville, Ill, in place of Jacob Judy, whose term of ofc has expired.
Harry F Brown, to be Reg of the Land Ofc at Green Bay, Wisc, in place of Joel S Fisk, removed.
Ofcrs of the Customs: Joshua Tayloe, Collector at Ocracoke, N C, vice Thos J Pasteur, whose commission expired.
Willis H Arnold, Collector at Pearl River, Miss, vice Rufus O Pray, resigned.
John N Frost, Surveyor at Portsmouth, N H, vice Winthrop Pikering, whose commission expired.
Jas Hunter, Appraiser of Merchandise, at Savannah, Ga, vice Chas Stephens, deceased.

Bayou Sara Ledger: we record the sudden & untimely deaths of the wife & 2nd son of Mr John Sulser, of this place. Last Sun, the eldest son & the 2nd son were on a frail barque, when both the boys fell into the water. Mrs Sulser, seeing the 2nd son could not swim, plunged into the stream, & immediately sunk. Mrs Sulser leaves a bereaved husband & 2 children.

Pendleton [S C] Messenger: Carrol & Thos Henderson, convicted at the last Court of Sessions for Pickens District of the murder of Robt Wilson, were executed on last Fri at Pickens Court House. Thos, under the gallows, denied having anything to do with the transaction, & was sustained in his statement by his brother Carrol.

Jas Cooper, a negro man, the property of the late John Packete, of Jefferson Co, Va, died on Tue last, at the venerable age of 91 years. He was quite intelligent, being able to read fluently. In 1843 his eyesight failed him; & though blind, made brooms to the time of his death. –Free Press

The stable & carriage house attached to the residence of Rev O B Brown were destroyed by fire last night. None of the adjacent bldgs suffered damage.

MON MAR 19, 1849
Andrew Hall & Barney O'Donnell were executed at Troy, N Y, on Thu for the murder of Noah & Amy Smith. Both confessed their guilt, & Hall avowed that he had previously committed 2 murders, besides participating in several arsons, robberies, & other crimes. He was a hardened wretch.

Appointments by the Pres:
Chas W Rockwell, of Conn, to be Com'r of Customs
Allen A Hall, of Tenn, to be Register of the U S Treasury, in place of Danl Graham, resigned.
Custom-house ofcrs:
Collector: Jas E Norfleet, Edenton, N C, vice Zizop Rawls, resigned
Surveyors:
John H Cross, Pawcatuck, R I, vice Geo Brown, whose commission will expire Mar 19, 1849
Zebedee Rind, N Y, vice Elijah F Purdy, whose commission expired
Mrs Mary Christie, P M, Rock Run, Harford Co, Md, vice John S Christie, resigned

Mrs Col Fremont, the daughter of Senator Benton, sailed on Thu in the ship **Crescent City** for Chagres, to join her husband in Calif. Mr Jacobs, of Louisville, Ky, her brother-in-law, also went out to settle.

Rev Flavel S Mines went out in the ship **Crescent City** for Chagres, on his way to San Francisco, to establish an Episcopal Church, by means of funds recently contributed by several of the churches in N Y C.

The estate of the late Matthew France, of Charleston, Jefferson Co, Va, containing 41 acres, sold recently at auction for #21,018.20-$61.03 an acre.

At Martinsburg, Va, on Mar 12, the hotel owned by Mr Ezekiel Showers & kept by Mr John Long was destroyed by fire. Loss $2,300.

Mr Wm B Astor, of N Y, recently received certain threatening letters, stating that unless he paid over $50,000 his life & property were to suffer. A similar letter was received by Mrs Astor. Franklin G Bragg, #6, & Isaac A Biggs, #21, Morton st, were both arrested & committed for examination.

Died: at the residence of her son, Dr Wm Hardy, on Capitol Hill, Mrs Julia Brown, in her 68th year. She was a kind & affectionate parent, & a warm & sincere friend. [No death date given-current item.]

Died: on Mar 17, of acute pleurisy, Stanislaus Tench, aged 55 years. His funeral is today, at 2 o'clock, from his late residence on 10th st, near the Navy Yard.

Died: on Jan 31, 1849, in New Orleans, in his 25th year, Danl Baker Lewis, 2nd son of Saml W & Mary Ann Winslow Lewis. The deceased was for the last 5 years sergeant in Company D, 2nd Regt U S Dragoons; served through the Mexican war, was wounded at the battle of Buena Vista, which, in connexion with fever contracted in the country, caused his death. He was loved & respected by his ofcrs & companions.
+
Died: on Mar 16, at **Bella Vista**, the residence of Thos E Getting, in Balt Co, Md, in her 42nd year, Mary Jane Lewis, sister of the above mentioned. Those who knew her will require no eulogy.

The Phil newspapers mention the death, at 92, of David C Claypoole, one of the Proprietors of the first Daily Newspaper published in the U S. It was established as early, we believe, in 1776, & published many years by John Dunlap & the gentleman just mentioned, by the title of the Pennsylvania Packet & Daily Advertiser, the title of it being changed to that of Dunlap & Claypoole's Daily Advertiser. On the retirement of John Dunlap from the concern, it continued to be published by the firm of David C & Septimus Claypoole, &, soon after the death of the latter, passed into the hands of Zachariah Poulson, by whom, & afterwards by his son, it was published for many years, until it was eventaully merged in some younger but more ambitious & enterprising establishment. Mr Claypoole is reported by the papers to have been a lineal descendant from Oliver Cromwell.

Wanted to hire, in the country, about 8 miles from the city, a white man & woman; the man to work on a farm, the woman to cook, milk, etc. Apply to E Simms, corner of F & 13th sts.

TUE MAR 20, 1849
Post Ofcs in Md: New P O & appointments made: 1-Rock Creek, Somerset Co, Md, David Webster, Postmaster. 2-Zion, Cecil Co, Md, John Carhart, Postmaster. Appointment by the Postmaster Gen: 1-Robt R Robertson, Postmaster Cambridge, Dorchester Co, Md, vice E A Marshall, resigned. 2-The site of the post ofc at Principio, Cecil Co, Md, has been changed to College Green, & Benj F Kirk appointed Postmaster.

Balt Conference of the Methodist Episcopal Church was held in Staunton, Va, & just closed. Appointments for this District.
Potomac District-Wm Hamilton, P E
Alexandria: J M Jones, E F Busey
Foundry: J Lanahan, J Guest
Wesley Chapel: L F Morgan
McKendree Chapel: S A Roszell
Ebenezer: G W Israel, M A Turner, sup
Ryland Chapel: W H Pitcher, J M Hanson, sup
Union Chapel: G A Coffey
Gtwn: H Slicer, C McElfresh
Baldensburg: Thos McGee, O P Wirgman
Wm Taylor transferred to Oregon & Calif Conference. R S McClay, Missionary to China.

It will be recollected that the ship **Franklin**, Capt Smith, from London bound to Boston, was wrecked recently on Welfleet beach, & Capt Smith & several of the crew & passengers were drowned. The bodies of the Capt & others were picked up. A valise belonging to the Capt was found on the beach, & among the letters to Capt Smith, was one instructing him to destroy the ship, as she was well insured. The letter was written by a man named Wilson, of Charlestown, who was joint owner of the ship with Mr Chas W Crafts, of South Boston. Wilson has absconded. Mr Crafts has been arrested, & held to bail in the sum of $20,000.

Mr Bodisco, the Minister from the Emperor of Russia to the U S, with his 2 Secretaries-not having been able to attend at the general reception of the Diplomatic Corps-was received by the Pres of the U S, yesterday.

Promotion: Col Geo Talcott, of the Ordnance Dept, promoted to the rank of Brig Gen in the U S Army. Col Talcott entered the army, we believe, in 1814. –Albany Argus

Died: yesterday, in Wash City, after a short but severe illness, Edw Holland, in his 66th year. His funeral is tomorrow at 3 o'clock, from his late residence on 11th st.

Died: on Mar 18, at her residence, in Gtwn, D C, in her 81st year, Matilda, relict of the late Thos Wilson, of Scotland. This estimable lady, born in Ireland on Jun 17, 1768, was first married to the illustrious patriot Theobold Wolfe Tone, well know in Irish history as the friend & companion of the martyred Emmet, &, as such, her memory should be dear to every friend of liberty. Mrs Tone resided in France at the time of her husband's death. Lucien Bonaparte bestowed on her, in recommending her case, & that of her children, to the attention of the French Chambers; the effect of which was manifested by the unanimous grant of an annual pension. She preserved, in her 81st year, the energy of intellect that made her the companion of her husband, & the warmth of heart, that even her cruel sorrows could not chill. The natives & friends of Ireland, the country for which Wolfe Tone died, & particularly requested to attend her funeral from her late residence on 1st st, Gtwn, on Mar 21, at 4 o'clock.

Died: on Mar 19, of scarlet fever, Mary Eliza, daughter of Geo W & Mary Ann Robinson, aged 8 years. Her funeral is this evening, at 4 o'clock.

Ofcs for rent: in the house occupied by Mrs T P Jones, on F st, between 6th & 7th sts. Inquire on the premises.

Gardener, well qualified to attend all the branches in his line, wishes a situation. He speaks the English & German languages, & is well recommended. Among others he permitted to refer to Baron Alex'r de Bodisco, Russian Ambassador, by whom he has been engaged for the last 2 years as gardener.

Boarding: pleasant apartments in #2, ***Dowson's Row***, on the brow of Capitol Hill.
–A S Clements

Lost, yesterday, a check of C De Selding on the Bank of Wash for $73.63, payable to order of C W Pairo. Payment has been stopped. A reward of $1.00 will be paid on its return. –C W Pairo

For sale: one-half of the vein known as the Vaucluse Vein, with 150 to 200 acres of heavily timbered land: believed to be one of the richest deposites of gold in the State. A part of this vein was sold a few years ago to Capt Smith, & is now in possession of Mr Carter. Address me at Orange Courthouse, Va, or to Dr K D Taliaferro, who resides at *Vaucluse*, & will show the property. -Peyton Grimes

WED MAR 21, 1849
The Hon Rudolphus Dickinson, a Rep in the late Congress, & a Rep elect to the next Congress, from Ohio, died in Wash City yesterday. His disease, as we understand, was congestion of the brain; & he had been confined to his bed for about 5 weeks. Some members of his family were with him in his last illness. His funeral service is today, at 12:30 p m, in the Hall of the Hse o/Reps, & the procession will move to the Congressional Burial-ground. The following have been appointed to act as Pall-Bearers:

Mr Brown, of Miss
Mr Hubbard, of Conn
Mr Marsh, of Vt
Mr Marvin, of N Y

Mr Bowlin, of Mo
Mr Bowdon, of Ala
Mr Barrow, of Tenn
Mr Irvin, of Pa

Appointments by the Pres. By & with the advice & consent of the Senate:
Geo Evans, of Maine, Caleb B Smith, of Indiana, & Robt T Paine, of N C, to the Com'rs, to carry into effect certain stipulations of the treaty between the U S of A & the Republic of Mexico of Feb 2, 1848.
Wm Carey Jones, of Louisiana, to be Sec of Board of Com'rs appointed with above.
Chas K Smith, of Ohio, to be Sec of the Territory of Minnesota.
Aaron Goodrich, of Tenn, to be Chief Justice, & David Cooper, of Pa, & Benj B Meeker, of Ky, to be Associate Justices of the U S Supreme Court for said Territory.
Henry L Moss, of Minesota, to be U S Atty for said Territory.
Joshua L Taylor, of Minesota, to be U S Marshal for said Territory.
Jas G Campbell, of Louisiana, to be Judge of the U S District Court for the western district of Louisiana.
Henry Boyce, of Louisiana, to be U S Atty for said district.
John E King, of Louisiana, to be U S Marshal for said district.
Wm B Scott, of Louisiana, to be U S Marshal for the eastern district of Louisiana.
Thos C Perkins, of Conn, to be U S Atty for the district of Connecticut, in place of Jonathan Stoddard.
Gales Seaton, of the District of Columbia, to be Sec of the U S Legation to the Fed Gov't of Germany.
Custom-House Ofcrs. Collectors:
Richd C Holmes, Great Egg Harbor, N J, vice Robt B Risley, whose commission expired.
John S Rhea, Brasos Santiago, Texas: new ofc.
Edwin Rose, Sag Harbor, N Y, vice Abel Huntington, whose commission expired.
Jas Collier, San Francisco, Calif: new ofc.

Surveyors:
Wm B Norris, Phil, vice John Davis, whose commission expired.
Gordon Forbes, Yeocomico, Va, reappointed.
Robt Butler, Smithfield, Va, reappointed.
Postmasters:
Timothy Coggshall, Newport, R I
Ephraim Hutchins, Concord, N H
Jos J Pitman, Huntsville, Ala
Saml C Cook, New Brunswick, N J
Thos B Bigger, Richmond, Va: reappointed
Edwin Boyle, Annapolis, Md
Appointments by the Postmaster Gen:
Jas McDermot, Postmaster, Wash Co, Pa, vice J D Leet.
Wm R Hammond, Postmaster, Berlin, Worcester Co, Md, vice C M Williams

The Nat'l Hotel, formerly kept by Mr Coleman & recently by Mr Blackwell, has been suddenly closed, & its halls are now as desolate as those of Ossian's Balclutha.

Md Annual Conference of the Methodist Protestant Church, at Alexandria, closed yesterday. Preachers appointed for this District & neighborhood:
Gtwn, John W Everist; Alexandria, Thos M Wilson; 9th st, Wash, Wm Collier; First Methodist Protestant Church, Wash, to be supplied; Potomac, Jesse Shreeve.

Cmdor Downs has been appointed to the command of the Navy yard at Boston.

Thu last closed the career of another of the defenders of Balt. The roll of the brave is lessened by the death of Ebenezer Hubball: a native of Birmingham, England, but in his early youth became identified with the country of his adoption. He resided about half a century under our institutions, being about 65 years of age. In the defence of D C & of Balt Co, during the war of 1812, he took a very prominent part. He was an active & intrepid fireman. His own prosperity arising from his untiring industry, made him universally respected & beloved. –Balt American

Laws of the U S passed at the 2nd Session of the 30th Congress. 1-To the Choctaws. Life annuity to chief, [Bob Cole,] stipulated in the 10th article of the treaty of Jan 20, 1825, $150..

For rent: my dwlg house in Wash City. –John C Rives

Copartnership formed between B F Morsell & Jesse B Wilson, under the firm of Morsell & Wilson: retail Grocery, Wine, & Liquor Business, in the stand formerly occupied by Messrs B L Jackson & Bro, on Pa ave.

Sale by order of the Orphans Court of Wash Co, D C, on Mar 22, the personal effects of the late J Collins, on 10th st, between E & F sts: furniture & utensils.
-E C & G F Dyer, aucts

Orphans Court of Wash Co, D C. The case of Saml Redfern & John C Harkness, adms, with the will annexed, of John Williams, deceased, the administrators & Court have appointed Apr 6 for the settlement of said estate. –Ed N Roach, Reg/o wills

Mrd: on Mar 1, at Dumfries, Pr Wm Co, Va, by Rev J E Weems, Robt A Calvert to Miss Mgt Frances, daughter of John Tansill.

Mrd: on Mar 6, near Halifax, N C, Lt G W Grant, U S N, to Miss Frances J, daughter of Rice B Pierce.

Died: on Mar 19, at *Clermont*, his estate in Fairfax Co, Va, in his 83rd year, Gen John Mason. This venerable gentleman was the last surviving son of Col Geo Mason, of *Gunston Hall*, in the same county, who was distinguished in Va, as was said by Mr Jefferson, as "one of the wisest statesmen that Va ever bred, & an incorruptible patriot." Gen Mason excelled in the domestic & social relations. His numerous offspring, trained by his example & the precepts of an incomparable mother, adorn many distant circles, & have in some instances reached the highest stations of public confidence & dignity. We are informed that the remains of the deceased will be removed form Christ Church, at Alexandria, to the place of interment, this day at 1 o'clock.

Died: on Mar 20, after a protracted & painful sickness, James Stacy, son of C T Gardner, aged 5 years & 5 months, formerly of Fayetteville, N C.

Died: on Mar 11, at the Naval Hospital, Pensacola, Dr Alex'r Robinson, Assist Surgeon U S Navy.

The copartnership existing between John E Addison & Beverley Tucker has been dissolved. Beverley Tucker will continue to attend to all business before Congress & the Depts, as heretofore.

To let: one of those handsomely finished houses in the block of 5, on Massachusetts ave, between 6th & 7th sts. It is at present occupied by Col Barnard, who will vacate it about Apr 1, in order to depart for the Land of Promise, Calif. Apply to E Owens, near Willard's Hotel, or to the subscriber, next door. –Jas B Phillips

For rent: nearly new arranged Dwlg & Store on the corner of 4th & L sts: $12 per month. –C H Van Patten, Dentist, near Brown's Hotel

Elegant furnished rooms for rent: apply to J F Kahl, Manufacturer & Importer of Piano Fortes & Guitars, Pa ave, between 10th & 11th sts. Single gentlemen will be preferred.

THU MAR 22, 1849
Died: on Mar 7, at Newark, Delaware, Dr Jos Chamberlain, aged 61 years.

Died: on Mar 21, of scarlet fever, Augusta Everett, daughter of Isaac & Augusta Clarke, aged 8 years & 8 months. Her funeral is at her father's residence, this day, at 12 o'clock.

Died: on Mar 11, Mary Louisa, daughter of Wm A Rawlings, aged 11 months & 25 days.

The New Orleans Bee says that on Mar 11, Monsieur Victor Verdaile made a balloon ascension from Pydras & St Chas st. He ascended about a mile, & the balloon exploded, precipitating him to the earth from a distance of 7,000 feet! & what is astonishing, he was not the least injured. He owes his escape of death from a rose bush in the garden of F F Lerrion, in Moreau st, where he landed. The wind being very strong, the balloon was in a measure kept up in such a manner as to break the fall.

Attys at Law: Associated themselves in the practice of their profession: Richd H Hagner, Prince Fred'k, Calvert Co, Md. Alex B Hagner, Annapolis, Md.

Wash Corp: 1-Ptn from John H Semmes & Co & others: referred to the Cmte on Improvements. 2-Ptn from A C Huguenin: referred to the Cme of Claims. 3-Cmte of Claims: asking to be discharged from the further consideration of the ptns of Thos B Scott, Wm Bergman, & John Hitz: discharged accordingly. 4-Ptn of Francis Lamb, praying payment of a balance due him for the frame of a painting in the City Hall: referred to the Cmte of Claims. 5-Cmte of Claims: ptn of Wm Bayman, reported a bill for his relief: which was read. 6-Bills for the relief of A F Wilcox & for the relief of W C Johnson: referred to the Cmte of Claims.

FRI MAR 23, 1849
Mr Ira Dubois, Librarian of the House of Assembly of the State of N Y, has prepared, by authority, a most novel chapter of statistics upon the physical condition & troy weight of the honorable legislators of said State. The differenct occupations & professions to which they belong are:

Farmers 53   Mariner 1
Lawyers 25   Iron founder 1
Merchants 16   Miller 1
Physicians 7   Accountant 1
Gentlemen 6   Blacksmith 1
Manufaturers 5   Teacher 1
Mechanics 2   Hotel keeper 1
Engineer 1   Lumber merchant 1
Farmer & lawyer 1   Tanner 1

Of their condition in life, we find that 104 are married, 18 are bachelors, & 6 are widowers. Their ages vary from 20 years to 70, largest proportion varying from 40 to 50. Native of: N Y 95; Vt 8; Conn 8; Mass 7, N H 3; R I 2; Md 1; Maine 1; N J; & D C 1. Their weights range from 272 pounds to 110 pounds.

Titus Bishop, age 70 years, hung himself in his barn at Madison, Conn, on Wed last. He wrote on a board, "I am an apostate angel, whom mercy never reached, & never can." He was insane, of course.

Mrs Ann Gerry died at New Haven on Mar 17, aged 86. She was the relict of Elbridge Gerry, one of the signers of the Declaration of Independence.

Died: on Mar 10, at Postsmouth, N H, Saml Larkin, in his 76th year, for many years an extensive merchant, & always an upright & valuable citizen.

Died: on Mar 22, of scarlet fever, Emily Jane, aged 4 years & 9 months, youngest daughter of Isaac & Augusta Clarke. Her funeral is this day, at 10 o'clock.

For sale: that valuable stand for business & dwlg, corner of 7th & G sts, now occupied by Mr Thos MacGill. The stock of Groceries are also offered, with the store fixtures.

Furnished rooms to let: Pa ave & 15th st. Apply at the premises, E Robinson.

For rent: large 3 story brick house, 16th & K sts, with all necessary outbldgs. Presently occupied by Mr Jewett, who will vacate on Apr 1. The house is new. Apply to Mrs Alexander, 12th st, between C & D sts.

Trustee's sale of valuable bldg lot at auction: on Apr 23, by deed of trust from Hugh A Goldsborough, dated Mar 13, 1847, recorded in Liber W B 134, folios 12, 13, & 14, one of the land records for Wash Co, D C: sale of lot 2 in square 79, fronting on north G between 22nd & 23rd sts west, containing 9,245 square feet. –Chas De Selding, trustee -A Green, auct

$5 reward for return of the pay accounts of Capt J E G Chase & Pvt Robt Butler, of the Louisiana Volunteers, whch were lost a day or two ago, on Pa ave, in Wash City. To the first, is a power of atty authorizing the payment of a claim to Mr Judson, of New Orleans, & to the other a power of atty in favor of Jos Bryan. The above reward will be paid for the return of the papers to Madam Visser's Fancy Store, Pa ave.

Criminal Court-Wash. Trial of Benj Fowler, Joshua Batemen, John Knight, Jos Goddard, Wm Dawson, & Simon Bissell, indicted for a riot at the Union Hotel, in Gtwn, came up yesterday. The riot occurred in Jan last, during the delivery of lecture by Mr Leary. Verdict will be made known today. [Mar 26th newspaper: the jury found a verdict of guilty against all the persons indicted.]

SAT MAR 24, 1849
Appointments by the Pres, By & with the consent & advice of the Senate.
Thos Ewing, jr, to be Sec to the Pres to sign land patents.
Andrew M Tutt, of Missouri, to be Register of the land ofc at Clinton, Mo, in place of Wilkins Watson, resigned.
Richd B Dallam, of St Louis, Missouri, to be Receiver of Public Moneys at St Louis, in place of Edw Dobyus, whose term has expired.
Septimus Caldwell, of Grenada, Miss, to be Receiver of Public Moneys at Grenada, Miss, in place of Geo S Gollady, whose term expired.
John T Brooks, of Chickasaw Co, Miss, to be Register of the Land Ofc a Pontotoc, Miss, in place of Andrew J Edmondson, whose term expired.
Wm Lyon, of Demopolis, Ala, to be Receiver of Public Moneys at Demopolis, in place of David E Moore, whose term of ofc expired.
John Shelby, Postmaster at Nashville, Tenn, vice L B Sheatham, whose commission expired.

A suit which has been 10 years in contest in Boston, in which Mrs Lucretia Boss claimed the title to a large portion of Pine st, under deed from Gov Leverett in 1675, down to the present claimants, was decided on Mon in favor of the city of Boston, which was the other party to the suit.

Died: yesterday, after a short illness, John Boyle, at the age of 72, & for the last 40 years a resident of Wash City. His funeral is Mar 25, at 3 o'clock, from his late residence.

Died: on Mar 22, Jas H Chezum, in his 37th year. His funeral is this day, at 3 o'clock, from his late residence, on C st, near 12th, in the 7th Ward.

Died: on Fri, after an illness of 8 weeks, borne with great patience, Mrs Eliz, wife of Mr Henry Thorn, & daughter of the late Warner Welsh, of Anne Arundel Co, Md, leaving a husband & 6 small children. Her funeral is tomorrow, at 3 o'clock, from the residence of her husband, on 8th st, between D & E sts.

Died: on Mar 5, of consumption, in his 30th year, at the residence of his mother, Mrs P Segar, Middlesex Co, Va, Mr Richd B Segar. [The Southern Churchman please copy.]

The Rev Wm Collier, Pastor of the 9th st Methodist Protestant Church, will commence the duties of said station Sunday morning at 11 o'clock.

MON MAR 26, 1849
Senate-Mar 3, 1849: 1-Cmte on Private Land Claims: ordered to be discharged from the further consideration of the ptn of Jos Regnes & documents relating to the land claim of Jas A Lindday. 2-John Baldwin to have leave to withdraw his ptn & papers. Same for Saml Walker. 3-Act to incorporate the Oak Hill Cemetery in D C: passed.

Official: Army General Order. Gen Orders #14. War Dept, Adj Gen's Ofc, Wash, Mar 15, 1849. promotions & appointments in the U S Army made by the Pres, by & with the advice & consent of the Senate, since publication of the Army Register, Jan, 1849.
I-Promotions: Medical Dept:
Assist Surgeon Jos H Bailey, to be Surgeon, Aug 8, 1848, vice Craig, deceased.
2nd Regt of Dragoons:
Brevet 2nd Lt John Buford, jr, of 1st Dragoons, to be 2nd Lt, Feb 17, 1849, vice Armstrong, deceased.
Regt of Mounted Riflemen:
2nd Lt Julian May, to be 1st Lt, Oct 31, 1848, vice Taylor, resigned.
Brevet 2nd Lt Wm B Lane, to be 2nd Lt, Oct 31, 1848, vice May, promoted.
2nd Regt of Artl:
1st Lt John Sedgwick, to be Capt, Jan 26, 1849, vice Duncan, appointed Inspec Gen.
1st Lt Arnold Elzey, to be Capt, Feb 14, 1849, vice Merchant, promoted.
2nd Lt Julius A d'Lagnel, to be 1st Lt, Jan 26, 1849, vice Sedgwick, promoted.
2nd Lt Danl T Van Buren, to be 1st Lt, Feb 14, 1849, vice Elzey, promoted.
Brevet 2nd Lt Henry Benson, to be 2nd Lt, Jan 26, 1849, vice d'Lagnel, promoted.
Brevet 2nd Lt John C Tidball, of the 3rd Artl, to be 2nd Lt, Feb 14, 1849, vice Van Buren, promoted.

3rd Regt of Artl:
Capt Chas S Merchant, of 2nd Artl, to be Major, Feb 14, 1849, vice Van Ness, deceased.
4th Regt of Artl:
Brevet 2nd Lt Jos C Clark, jr, of the 3rd Artl, to be 2nd Lt, Jan 6, 1849, vice Crittenden, resigned.
2nd Regt of Infty:
1st Lt Delozier Davidson, to be Capt, Jan 1, 1849, vice Penrose, deceased.
2nd Lt Hermann Thorn, to be 1st Lt, Jan 1, 1849, vice Davidson, promoted.
Brevet 2nd Lt Jas McGill, to be 2nd Lt, Sep 11, 1848, vice Butler, resigned.
Brevet 2nd Lt Robt M Russell, 5th Infty, to be 2nd Lt, Jan 1, 1849, vice Thorn, promoted.
4th Regt of Infty:
Brevet 2nd Lt Wm A Slaughter, 2nd Infty, to 2nd Lt, Nov 6, 1848, vice Howard, resigned.
5th Regt of Infty: Brevet 2nd Lt Saml Archer, to 2nd Lt, Jan 30, 1849, vice Long, deceased.
8th Regt of Infty:
1st Lt Robt P Maclay, to be Capt, Jan 22, 1849, vice Sheppard, deceased.
2nd Lt Chas G Merchant, to be 1st Lt, Aug 2, 1848, vice Clark, deceased.
2nd Lt Jas G S Snelling, to be 1st Lt, Jan 22, 1849, vice Maclay, promoted.
*2nd Lt Richd J Dodge, from the 4th Infty, to be 2nd Lt, Dec 24, 1848, vice Deany, deceased.
Brevet 2nd Lt Thos K Jackson, of the 5th Infty, to be 2nd Lt, Jan 22, 1849, vice Snelling, promoted.
Brevets: for gallant & meritorious conduct in the battles of Palo Alto & Resaca de la Palma, in Texas, on May 8 & 9, 1846.
To date from May 9, 1846.
Capt Pitcairn Morrison, 4th Infty, [now Major 8th Infty.]
Capt Gouverneur Morris, 4th Infty
Capt Abraham C Myers, Assist Quartermaster, [in place of the brevet of like grade conferred for Contreras & Churubusco-cancelled]
Capt Chas H Larned, 4th Infty.
Brevet Capt Ripley A Arnold, 2nd Dragoons, [now Capt.]
Capts by Brevet:
1st Lt John F Roland, 2nd Artl, [now Capt,] in place of the brevet of like grade conferred for Monterey-canceled.]
1st Lt John A Whitall, 5th Infty, [now Capt.]
1st Lt Oscar F Winship, 2nd Dragoons, [now Assist Adj Gen.]
Brevets-for gallant & meritorious conduct in the battle of Monterey, Mexico, on Sep 21, 22, & 23, of Sep, 1846.
To date from Sep 23, 1846.
Colonel by Brvt: Brvt Lt Colonel Thos Staniford, Lt Col 8th Infty
Majors by Brevet:
Capt Richd B Screven, 8th Infty, [in place of the brevet of like grade conferred for Molino del Rey-cancelled.]
Brevet John F Roland, 2nd Artl, [now Capt.]
Capt Danl T Chandler, 3rd Infty, [in place of the brevet of like grade conferred for Contreras & Churubusco-cancelled.]

Capt by Brevet: 1ˢᵗ Lt Henry Little, 7ᵗʰ Infty, [now Capt.]
Col Henry Stanton, Assist Quartermaster Gen, to be Brig Gen by Brevet, to date from Jan 1, 1847-when he was acting as Quartermaster Gen in Washington.
Maj Jas D Graham, Corps of Topographical Engineers, to be Lt Col by Brevet, for valuable & highly distinguished services, particularly on the boundary between the U S & the provinces of Canada & New Brunswick, to date from Jan 1, 1847.
Maj Philip St Geo Cooke, 2ⁿᵈ Dragoons, to be Lt Col by Brevet, for meritorious conduct in Calif, to date from Feb 20, 1847.
Brevets: for gallant & meritorious conduct in the battle of Buena Vista, Mexico, Feb 22 & 23, 1847.
To date from Feb 23, 1847.
Lt Cols by Brevet: Brevet Maj Jos H Eaton, Capt 3ʳᵈ Infty
Maj Andrew J Coffee, Paymaster
Capt Albert Lowry, Assist Quartermaster, to be Major by Brevet, for gallant & meritorious conduct in the affair at Medelin, Mexico, to date from Mar 25, 1847.
Col Newman S Clarke, 6ᵗʰ Infty, to be Brig Gen by Brevet, for gallant & meritorious conduct the seige of Vera Cruz, Mexico, to date from Mar 29, 1847, [in place of the brevet of like grade conferred for Churubusco-cancelled.]
Capt Jos E Johnston, Topographical Engineers, to be Major by Brevet, for gallant & meritorious conduct, to date from Apr 12, 1847, when he was severely wounded under the enemy's works at Cerro Gordo, Mexico, whilst in reconnoitering duty.

Brevets-for gallant & meritorious conduct in the battle of Cerro Gordo, Mexico.
To date from Apr 18, 1847. Majors by Brevet:
Capt Geo Nauman, 1ˢᵗ Artl, [in place of the brevet of like grade conferred for Contreras & Churubusco-cancelled.]
Capt Jos R Smith, 2ⁿᵈ Infty, [in place of the brevet of like grade conferred for Contreras & Churubusco-cancelled.]
Capt Wm P Bainbridge, 4ᵗʰ Artl.
Capts by Brevet:
1ˢᵗ Lt Wm H French, 1ˢᵗ Artl, [now Capt,] [in place of the brevet of like grade conferred for Contreras & Churubusco-cancelled.]
1ˢᵗ Lt Wm B Blair, 2ⁿᵈ Artl
1ˢᵗ Lt Richd P Hammond, 3ʳᵈ Artl, [in place of the brevet of like grade conferred for Contreras & Churubusco-cancelled.]
1ˢᵗ Lt Geo Sykes, 3ʳᵈ Infty
1ˢᵗ Lt Seth Williams, 1ˢᵗ Artl
*Note-The date of Dec 24, 1848, vice Deaney, is given to 2ⁿᵈ Lt Dodge, instead of Nov 6, 1848, in the 4ᵗʰ Infty, as born on the Army Register for 1849-he having declined promotion out of the 8ᵗʰ Infty.
1ˢᵗ Lt by Brevet: 2ⁿᵈ Lt Barnard E Bee, 3ʳᵈ Infty, [in place of like grade conferred for Chapultepec-cancelled.]

Maj Albert G Bennett, Paymaster, to be Lt Col by Brevet, for gallant & meritorious conduct in an affair with the Guerillas at the Nat'l Bridge, Mexico, to date from Jun 11, 1847.

Brevets-for gallant & meritorious conduct in the affair at San Juan de los Llanos, Mexico. To date from Aug 1, 1847.
Capt Chas F Ruff, Mounted Riflemen, to be Major by Brevet.
1st Lt John G Walker, Mounted Riflemen, to be Capt by Brevet.
2nd Lt Jas M Hawes, 2nd Dragoons, to be 1st Lt by Brevet.
Capt A H Blake, 2nd Dragoons, to be Major by Brevet, for gallant & meritorious conduct in the affair a San Augustine, Mexico, to date from Aug 17, 1848.

Brevet Capt Jos Hooker, Assist Adj Gen, to be Major by Brevet, for gallant & meritorious conduct in the affair at the Nat'l Bridge, Mexico, to date from Jun 11, 1847, [in place of the brevet of like grade conferred for Chapultepec-cancelled.]

Brevets-for gallant & meritorious conduct in the battles of Contreras & Churubusco, Mexico. To date from Aug 20, 1847.
Lt Cols by Brevet: Brevet Maj Danl T Chandler, Capt 3rd Infty.
Brevet Maj Thompson Morris, Capt 2nd Infty, [now Major 1st Infty,] [in place of the brevet of like grade conferred for Chapultepec-cancelled.]
Brevet Maj Geo Nauman, Capt 1st Artl.
Brefet Maj Jos R Smith, Capt 2nd Infty
Majors by Brevet: Capt Saml C Ridgely, 4th Artl.
Capt John C Henshaw, 7th Infty
Capt Andrew Porter, Mounted Riflemen, [in place of the brevet of like grade conferred for Chapultepec-cancelled.]
Brevet Capt Wm H French, 1st Artl, [now Capt.]
Brevet Capt Richd P Hammond, 3rd Artl.
Capts by Brevet: 1st Lt Francis Woodbridge, 2nd Artl, [now Capt.]
1st Lt Zealous B Tower, Engineers, [in place of the brevet of like grade conferred for Chapultepec-cancelled.]
Brevet 1st Lt Truman Seymour, 1st Artl, [now 1st Lt.]
1st Lts by Brevet: 2nd Lt Wm K Van Bokkelen, 7th Infty
2nd Lt Jas Stuart, Mounted Riflemen, [in place of the brevet of like grade conferred for Chapultepec-cancelled.]

Brevets-for gallant & meritorious conduct in the battle of Contreras, Mexico. To date from Aug 20, 1847.
Brevet 1st Lt Gustavus W Smith, 2nd Lt, Engineers, to be Capt by Brevet, [in place of the brevet of like grade conferred for Chapultepec-cancelled.]
2nd Lt Fred'k Steele, 2nd Infty, [now 1st Lt,] to be 1st Lt by Brevet, [in place of the brevet of like grade conferred for Chapultepec-cancelled.]
2nd Lt Robt M Morris, Mounted Riflemen, now 1st Lt, to be 1st Lt by Brevet, [in place of the brevet of like grade conferred for Chapultepec-cancelled.]
2nd Lt Herman Thorn, 2nd Infty, to be 1st Lt by Brevet, for gallant & meritorious conduct in the battle of Cherubusco, Mexico, to date from Aug 20, 1847.

Brevets-for gallant & meritorious conduct in the battle of Molino del Rey, Mexico. To date from Sep 8, 1847.
Colonel by Brevet: Brevet Lt Col Francis Lee, major 4th Infty.

Lt Cols by Brevet: Brevet Maj Richd D A Wade, Capt 3rd Artl
Brevet Maj Richd B Screven, Capt 8th Infty
Brevet Maj Benj Huger, Capt Ordnance, [in place of the brevet of like grade conferred for Contreras & Churubusco-cancelled.]
Brevet Maj Wm Chapman, Capt 5th Infty
Brevet Maj Horace Brooks, Capt 2nd Artl.
Majors by Brevet: Capt Hamilton W Merrill, 2nd Dragoons
Capt Geo H Talcott, Ordnance
Brevet Capt Francis Woodbridge, 1st Lt, 2nd Artl, [now Capt.]
Capts by Brevet: 1st Lt John Beardsley, 8th Infty
Brevet 1st Lt Fred'k T Dent, 5th Infty, [now 1st Lt.]
Brevet 1st Lt Jas G S Snelling, 8th Infty, [now 1st Lt.]
Brevet 1st Lt Hermann Thorn, 2nd Lt, 2nd Infty.
1st Lts by Brevet. 2nd Lt Ulysses S Grant, 4th Infty, [now 1s Lt.]
2nd Lt Edwin Howe, 6th Infty.
2nd Lt Edmund Russell, 4th Infty

Brevets-for gallant & meritorious conduct in the battle of Chapultepec, Mexico. To date from Sep 13, 1847.
Colonels by Brevet. Brevet Lt Col Justin Dimick, Capt 1st Artl.
Brevet Lt Col Wm Turnbull, Major Topographical Engineers.
Lt Colonels by Brevet: Brevet Maj Jos Hooker, Assist Adj Gen
Brevet Maj Jos E Johnston, Capt Topographical Engineers
Brevet Maj John B Grayson, Commissary of Subsistence.
Brevet Maj Jacob B Backenstos, Capt Mounted Riflemen
Brevet Maj Danl Ruggles, Capt 5th Infty.
Brevet Maj Henry L Scott, Capt 4th Infty.
Brevet Maj Andrew Porter, Capt Mounted Riflemen
Majors by Brevet: Capt Saml Woods, 6th Infty.
Brevet Capt Roswell S Ripley, 1st Lt, 2nd Artl
Brevet Capt John Sedwick, 1st Lt, 2nd Artl, [now Capt.]
Brevet Capt Thos Williams, 1st Lt, 4th Artl.
Brevet Capt Oliver L Shepherd, 3rd Infty, [now Capt.]
Brevet Capt Pinkney Lugenbeel, 1st Lt, 5th Infty.
Brevet Capt Zealous B Tower, 1st Lt, Engineers
Brevet Capt Thos J Jackson, 1st Lt, 1st Artl.
Brevet Capt Granville O Haller, 4th Infty, [now Capt.]
Brevet Capt Fitz John Porter, 1st Lt, 4th Artl.
Captains by Brevet: Brevet 1st Lt Barnard E Bee, 2nd Lt, 3rd Infty.
Brevet 1st Lt Ralph W Kirkham, 2nd Lt, 6th Infty.
Brevet 1st Lt Fred'k Steele, 2nd Lt, 2nd Infty, [now 1st Lt.]
Brevet 1st Lt Robt M Morris, Mounted Riflemen, [now 1st Lt.]
Brevet 1st Lt John P Hatch, 2nd Lt, Mounted Riflemen.
Brevet 1st Lt Gordon Granger, 2nd Lt, Mounted Riflemen.
Brevet 1st Lt Jas Stuart, 2nd Lt, Mounted Riflemen.
Brevet 1st Lt Geo B McClellan, 2nd Lt, Engineers.
Brevet 1st Lt Marcus D L Simpson, 2nd Artl, [now 1st Lt.]
Brevet 1st Lt Henry M Judah, 4th Infty, [now 1st Lt.]

Brevet 1ˢᵗ Lt Chas G Merchant, 8ᵗʰ Infty, [now 1ˢᵗ Lt.]
Brevet 1ˢᵗ Lt Chas P Stone, 2ⁿᵈ Lt Ordnance.
Brevet 1ˢᵗ Lt Maurice Maloney 4ᵗʰ Infty, [now 1ˢᵗ Lt.]
Brevet Capt Theodore T S Laidley, 1ˢᵗ Lt Ordnace, tobe Major by Brevet, for gallant & meritorious conduct in the defence of Puebla, Mexico, to date from Oct 12, 1847.

Brevet Major Benj S Roberts, Capt Mounted Riflemen, to be Lt Col by Brevet, for gallant & meritorious conduct in the actions with the enemy at Matamoros, Nov 23, 1847, & at the Pass of Galaxara, Mexico, Nov 24, 1847, to date from Nov 24, 1847.

Brevets-for gallant & meritorious conduct in the battle of Santa Cruze de Rosales, Mexico. To date from Mar 16, 1848.
Lt Colonel by Brevet: Brevet Maj Benj L Beall, Major 1ˢᵗ Dragoons.
Major by Brevet: Capt Wm N Grier, 1ˢᵗ Dragoons.
Captains by Brevet: 1ˢᵗ Lt Wm E Prince, 1ˢᵗ Infty.
1ˢᵗ Lt John Love, 1ˢᵗ Dragoons.
1ˢᵗ Lt Alex'r B Dyer, Ordnance.
1ˢᵗ Lts by Brevet: 2ⁿᵈ Lt John Adams, 1ˢᵗ Dragoons.
Brevets for meritorious conduct while serving in the enemy's country:
To date from May 30, 1848.
Lt Colonels: Maj Adam D Steuart, Paymaster.
Maj Chas Thomas, Quartermaster.
Maj Saml McRee, Quartermaster.
Brevet Maj Geo W Hughes, Capt Topographical Engineers.
Maj Thos Swords, Quartermaster.
Majors by Brevet: Capt Edwin B Babbitt, Assist Quartermaster.
Capt Jonathan G Barnard, Engineers.
Capt Wm D Fraser, Engineers.
Capt Marsena R Patrick, 2ⁿᵈ Infty.
1ˢᵗ Lt by Brevet: 2ⁿᵈ Lt Martin L Smith, Topographical Engineers.

Brevets-for meritorious conduct particularly in the performance of their duties in the prosecution of the war with Mexico. To date from May 30, 1848.
Major Generals by Brevet: Brevet Brig Gen Geo M Brooke, Colonel 5ᵗʰ Infty.
Brevet Brig Gen Geo Gibson, Colonel & Commissary Gen.
Brevet Brig Gen Roger Jones, Colonel & Adj Gen.
Brevet Brig Gen Nathan Towson, Colonel & Paymaster Gen.
Brig Gen by Brevet: Col Geo Talcott, Ordnance.
Colonels by Brevet: Lt Col Thos F Hunt, Deputy Quartermaster Gen
Lt Col Jos P Taylor, Assist Commissary Gen.
Lt Col Aeneas Mackay, Deputy Quartermaster Gen.
Lt Col Saml Cooper, Assist Adj Gen.
Lt Colonels by Brevet: Maj Rufus L Baker, Ordnance.
Maj Jas W Ripley, Ordnance.
Maj Danl D Tompkins, Quartermaster.
Brevet Maj Wm G Freeman, Assist Adj Gen.
Majors by Brevet: Capt Alfred Mordecai, Ordnance
Capt Jas Belgar, Assist Quartermaster.

Brevets-for meritorious conduct. To date from May 30, 1848.
Major Gen by Brevet: Brevet Brig Gen Hugh Brady, Colonel 2nd Infty.
Brig Generals by Brevet: Brevet Col John B Walbach, 4th Artl, [now Colonel.] Col Richd B Mason, 1st Dragoons.
Col & Surgeon Gen Thos Lawson.
Majors by Brevet: Capt Wm A Thornton, Ordnance. Capt Edmund A Ogden, Assist Quartermaster. Capt John T Sprague, 8th Infty.

Correction of Dates, [by & with the advice & consent of the Senate.]
Maj & Brevet Lt Col Danl D Tompkins, Quartermaster, to date from Jul 22, 1842, instead of Apr 21, 1846.
2nd Lt Geo D Willard, 8th Infty, to date from Aug 2, 1848, instead of Dec 24, 1848.
II-It having been determined that the brevet commissions conferred on the ofcrs of the late "Ten Regts," who have been restored to their former commissions, regts, & corps, in the peace establishment, pursuant to the act of Jul 19, 1848, ceased to be effective when they ceased to be ofcrs of these regts by reason of the expiration of the term for which they were commissioned, the said brevet commissions, accordingly, were not recognised.

III-Appointments:
Capt John F Lee, of the Ordnance Dept, to be Judge Advocate, Mar 2, 1849, [with the Brevet rank of Major of Cavalry.]

Inspector General's Dept:
Capt Jas Duncan, of the 2nd Artl, to be Inspector Gen, Jan 26, 1849, vice Croghan, deceased.

Medical Dept: to be Assist Surgeon, Mar 2, 1849.
Henry S Hewit, of Conn.
Thas A McParlin, of Md.
John Bryne, of Missouri.
Lafayette Guild, of Alabama.
Wm F Edgar, of Missouri.
Thos H Williams, of Md.

Pay Dept: to be Paymaster, Mar 2, 1849:
Abram Van Buren, of N Y.
Robt A Forsyth, of Mich.
Robt B Reynolds, of Tenn.
Jermiah Dashiell, of Louisiana.
Sacfield Maclin, of Akansas.
Augustus W Gaines, of Ky.
Albert G Bennett, of Miss.
Hiram Leonard, of N Y.
Francis A Cunningham, of Ohio.
Geo C Hutter, of Va.

IV-Casulaties: Resignations, [4]
Maj Gen Zachary Taylor, Jan 31, 1849.
Capt Sewall L Fremont, 3rd Artl, as Assist Quartermaster, [only,] Feb 19, 1849.
2nd Lt Wm L Crittenden, 1st Infty, Mar 1, 1849.
2nd Lt Henry A Ehninger, 4th Srtl, Jan 6, 1849.

Deaths, [11]
Col Geo Croghan, Inspec Gen, at New Orleans, La, Jan 8, 1849.
Brevet Lt Col Roger S Dix, Paymaster, at Hillsborough, Pa, Jan 7, 1849.

Maj David Van Ness, 3rd Artl, at Portland, Me, Feb 14, 1849.
Capt Jas M Hill, Assist Quartermaster, at Balt, Md, Jan 29, 1849.
Capt E M D McKissack, Assist Quartermaster, at Pittsburg, Pa, Jan 27, 1849.
Brevet Maj Jas W Penrose, Capt 2nd Infty, at Plattsburg, N Y, Jan 1, 1849.
Capt Augustus L Sheppard, 8th Infty, at Jefferson Barracks, Jan 22, 1849.
Capt Edw G Elliott, Assist Quartermaster, at Curces, Isthmus of Darien, Jan __, 1849.
[Note: the "day" was blank.]
Brevet Capt John D Clark, 1st Lt, 8th Infty, near Helena, Ark, Aug 2, 1848.
2nd Lt Bezaleel W Armstrong, 2nd Dragoons, at New Lisbon, Ohio, Feb 17, 1849.
2nd Lt Richd H Long, 5th Infty, at *Fort Gibson*, Jan 30, 1849.

War Dept, Wash, Mar 15, 1849. The Senate of the U S having decided that the trial & conviction of Maj Geo B Crittenden, of the Regt of Mounted Riflemen, were illegal & contrary to the directions of law, & that no vacancy arose therefrom; & the subject having been afterwards referred by the then Executive to the late Sec of War, without any decision having been made thereon, the Pres, therefore, directs that Maj Geo B Crittenden, of the Regt of Mounted Riflemen, be restored to his commission & former rank in the Army. The Adj Gen will give the necessary instructions for the due execution of this order. –Geo W Crawford, Sec of War.

V-Ofcrs will join their proper regts, companies, & stations without delay.

VI-Acceptances or non-acceptances of appointment will be promptly reported to the Adj Gen of the Army; & in case of acceptance, the birthplace of the person appointed will be stated.

VII-Commissions noted as cancelled in this Order, will be returned to the War Dept.

VIII-Maj Crittenden will proceed to join his Regt & report for duty to the Commanding Ofcr withou unnecessary delay.

IX-The restoration of Maj Crittenden, & the promotion & subsequent resignation of Capt Taylor, cause the following change in the grades & dates of the commissions of certain ofcrs in the Regt of Mounted Riflemen, from those born on the Army Register published in Jan, 1849, to wit:
Capt John S Simonson, Mar 27, 1846. Commission of Major of Aug 19, 1847, expired Mar 3, 1849-the Senate having declared that there was no vacancy.
1st Lt Andrew J Lindsay, May 27, 1846. Commission of Capt of Oct 31, 1848, expired Mar 3, 1849- the Senate having declared that there was no vacancy.
1st Lt Julian May, Oct 31, 1848, [promotion to same grade, dated Aug 19, 1848, cancelled.]
2nd Lt Danl M Frost, Feb 16, 1847. Commission of 1st Lt of Oct 31, 1848, expired Mar 3, 1849-the Senate having declared that there was no vacancy.
2nd Lt Wm B Lane, Oct 31, 1848, [promotion to same grade, dated Aug 19, 1848, cancelled.]
Brevet 2nd Lt Caleb E Irvine, Jun 28, 1848. Commission of 2nd Lt Oct 31, 1848, expired Mar 3, 1849- the Senate having declared that there was no vacancy. By order: R Jones, Adj Gen

Memoranda: Re-appointments: Adam D Steuart, re-appointed Paymaster in the Army, from Jan 14, 1849, when his former appointment expired. Christopher Andrews, re-appointed paymaster in the Army, from Oct 24, 1848, when his former appointment expired.

General Orders, #16. War Dept, Adj General's Ofc, Wash, Mar 19, 1849.
1-Ten additional Chaplains & Schoolmasters being authorized to be employed by the act of Mar 2, 1849, the list of Military Posts designated in 'Genr'l Orders" #66 is revised as follows:
1-*Fort Mackinac*, Mich.
2-*Fort Gaines*, upper Mississippi, 160 miles above *Fort Snelling*.
3-*Fort Snelling*, Falls St Anthony, Iowa.
4-New post at or near *Fort Laramie*, on the Oregon route, 300 miles west of Fort Kearny.
5-*Fort Kearny*, Grand Island, Platte River, 220 miles west of *Fort Leavenworth*.
6-*Fort Leavenworth*, Mo.
7-*Fort Scott*, Missouri Frontier.
8-*Fort Gibson*, Cherokee Nation.
9-*Fort Townson*, Red River.
10-*Fort Washita*, Red River.
11-*Fort Pickens*, Pensacola, Fla.
12-*Fort Morgan*, Ala.
13-*Fort Brooke*, Fla.
14-*Fort Moultrie*, Charleston Harbor, S C.
15-*Fort Monroe*, Va.
16-Principal Recruiting Depot, N Y Harbor.
17-San Francisco, Calif.
18-Monterey, Calif.
19-*Fort Marcy*, Santa Fe, New Mexico.
20-Fort [blank,] El Paso, New Mexico.

2-Three Chaplains are allowed to the posts to be established in Oregon, one in Calif, one in New Mexico, & 4 in Texas, to be designated by the Commanding Ofcr of the 3rd Division, & the Depts # 8 & 9 respectively, & to be reported for the approval of the Sec of War.
The monthly pay of a Chaplain will not exceed $40, in addition to which he will be allowed 4 rations per day, & quarters & fuel provided for a captain.
The duties of Schoolmaster of the post will be performed under such regulations as may be established by the Council of Administration, approved by the Commanding Ofcr. He will teach the children of enlisted men as well as those of ofcrs. –R Jones, Adj Gen Mar 19, 1849.

Died: on Mar 24, in Wash City, Mr John White, in his 52nd year. His funeral is this afternoon, at 3 o'clock, from his late residence on Vt ave, between H & I sts.

Died: on Wed last, in the city of Annapolis, after a short but painful illness, Mrs Eliz Ann, wife of Philip Poultney, of Balt, & eldest daughter of Wm McNeir, in her 27th year.

Died: yesterday, after a short illness, Mrs Frances M, wife of Chester A Colt, of Wash City, & daughter of the late Nathl Manning, of Loudoun Co, Va. A husband & 4 children are left to mourn. The latter are all too young to feel that keen sensation of grief & sorrow that swells the breasts of those whose maturer judgments enable them to appreciate the virtues of her whose soul now rests in the bosom of her Saviour. A professing christian of the Roman Catholic Church, most faithfully did she attend to the precepts that should govern the christian's life. Her funeral is this day, at 4 o'clock, at her husband's residence, on 12th st.

Criminal Court: 1-A free negro named Sims, was tried for an assault with intent to kill Robt Burns. He was found guilty of an aggravated assault, & sentenced to be imprisoned 3 months in the county jail.

City Ordinances-Wash. 1-Act for the relief of Henry Burdick: fine imposed for selling domestic silks, is hereby remitted, provided Burdick pay the cost.
2-Act to provide for the payment of a balance due Chas Stewart, jr, for laying flag footways: sum of $18.75 to be paid Stewart.

For sale: dwlg house on G st, near 12th st. Apply to John D Clark, Magistrate & Genr'l Agent, Pa ave, near 11th st.

Appointments by the Pres: by & with the advice & consent of the Senate:
Wm Pennington, of N J, to be Govn'r of Minnesota.
Wm S Scott, of Louisiana, to be U S Marshal for the Eastern District of Louisiana.
Geo M Dewey, of Flint, Mich, to be Receiver of Public Moneys at Genesee, Mich, in place of Chas C Hascall, whose term has expired.
Appointments in the Navy:
Francis M Gunnell to be an Assist Surgeon in the Navy, vice Alex'r Robinson, deceased.
1st Assist Engineer Jesse Gay to be a Chief Engineer in the Navy from Oct 31, 1848, to fill a vacancy occasioned by the resignation of John Faron, jr.

Wreck of an emigrant ship on our coast, off Harwick. The barque **Floridian**, of 500 tons, E D Whitmore, Master, from Antwerp, for N Y, chartered by a German company to comvey emigrants, was wholly lost on Feb 28, & all on board perished, with the exception of 3 individuals. The master & crew, except the 3 men, together with 126 passengers were drowned.

TUE MAR 27, 1849
Wm Carey Jones, Atty & Counsellor a Law, will practice in th U S Supreme Court: special attention to cases concerning Lands, & to cases arising under the Revenue Laws. Residence at Senator Benton's, on C st.

Boarding, on moderate terms, can be obtained at Mrs Carter's, Capitol Hill, in the house formerly known as ***Dowson' Row*** #1.

Hon Benj A Bidlack, U S Charge d'Affaires near the Gov't of New Grenada, died at Bogota on Jan 6, 1849.

Calif Emigrants. The brig **Perfect** arrived at New Orleans on Mar 14 from Chagres, which port she left on Mar 1. Amongst her passengers is Lt Henry Lewis, U S Navy, late of the U S frig **Independence**, bearer of despatches to Washington from J Randolph Clay, our Charge d'Affaires to the Peruvian Gov't, & from Com Shubrick, commanding the squadron in the Pacific.

Police Intelligence. We learn that the land warrant 34, 104, dated Oct 30, 1848, issued to Augustus Goetz, of Co M, 3rd Artl, has been obtained upon forged papers, & will be cancelled. Goetz, being now in Wash City, will obtain his warrant again. Any person who has purchased such a warrant, will please leave information at the ofc of Justice Smith today, if practical.

Lt John Elton Bishpam, U S Navy, died at Phil, on Sat last. He was the cmder of the U S brig of war **Boxer** on her last cruise on the coast of Africa, enforcing the treaty of our Gov't for the suppression of the slave trade. After 2 years of great suffering, from the effects of a fever contracted on the African coast, he died at his residence on Mar 24. He was an ornament to the naval service of our country, a gallant ofcr, & an estimable man.

Jacob Shuster alias Tom Hand was arrested on Wed by Messrs Blany & Kline, of the Recorder's ofc, as one of the robbers of the Gov't jewels. Anonymous letters sent at various time to Pres Polk were in the handwriting of the dfndnt. –Phil Ledger

We are requested to announce Jeremiah Morton, of Culpeper Co, Va, as a candidate to rep the 9th district of the Comonwealth of Va in the next Congress of the U S.

Trustee's sale of 2 magnificent plantations in the forest of PG Co, Md: by decree of the High Court of Chancery of Md, the undersigned, will sell at the court-house, in Upper Marlboro, on Apr 13, the entire real estate of Notley Young, late of said county, deceased, consisting of: 1-Farm known as **Poplar Ridge**, consisting of part of a tract of land called **Essington**; a tract of land called **Bowdell's Choice**, & a tract called **Padsworth Farm**, & other lands adjoining, contiguous to each other, containing about 730 acres, more or less. It adjoins the plantations of Col Wm T Wootton, Thos Duckett, Jos E Cowman, Wm Clarke, & Dr B O Mullikin. 2-The estate on which the said Notley Young resided, being a tract of land called **Piano Grove**, containing 578 acres, more or less. This estate adjoins the lands of John Contee, John B Mullikin, & Wm D Bowie, & has upon it a most elegant mansion house & all the necessary out houses. –Thos F Bowie, C C Magruder, trustees, Upper Marlboro, Md.

Official: appointment by the Pres: Adam Sprice, Postmaster at Dayton, Montg Co, Ohio, vice Jos W McCorkle, resigned.
Appointments by the Postmaster Gen: Geo W McCullon, Postmaster at Frostburg, Alleghany Co, Md, vice John J Keller.
A new Post Ofc is established at WoodLawn, Cecil Co, Md, & Theodore H Knight appointed postmaster. The Post Ofc at Palmer's Tavern, P G Co, Md, is discontinued.

Turk's Island Salt at auction: on Mar 28, the cargo of brig **Belle**, at Messrs Casenove & Co's wharf, by A J Fleming, Alexandria.

$4 reward for return of strayed Red Buffalo Cow. —B S Bayly, 6th & H sts.

Household & kitchen furniture at auction on Apr 3, at the residence of Gen Dix, on C st, between 3rd & 4½ sts. —A Green, auct

The steamship **Galveston**, Capt Crane, which left New Orleans on Feb 15 for Chagres, with 162 passengers, on their way to Calif, met with a serious accident & put into Belize, Honduras, where she arrived on Mar 3. Most of the passengers engaged passage in other vessels for Chagres.

Mrd: on Sabbath evening last, by Rev John C Smith, Lt Robt J H Handy, of the U S Revenue Service, to Miss Virginia Rowan, all of Wash City.

Died: on Mar 24, Mrs Priscilla Hardy, wife of Dr Wm G Hardy. Her funeral is this morning at 9 o'clock, from her late residence on N J ave.

We want a young man who is well acquainted with the city trade; none but a good salesman need apply. —W M Shuster

WED MAR 28, 1849
In Galignani's Messenger of Mar 8 we find a letter from Genoa, dated Feb 29, which announces the sudden decease of Capt Bolton, of the U S sloop of war **Jamestown**. It is alleged that he was lying dangerously ill at Hotel Feder, in Genoa, on Feb 23, when a mob broke into the hotel to seize the person of the royal commissary, Signor Buffa. He was buried on Feb 25, in the English burial ground, being followed to the grave by the ofcrs of the **Jamestown**, & of the English 74, **Vesuvius**. The letter is credited by Galignani to the London news, but we do not find it in any of our London papers. —N Y Commercian Advertiser

Mrd: on Mar 27, at St Matthew's Church, by Rev Jas B Donelan, Chas Berault, jr, of N Y C, to Mary Agnes Anderson, of Wash.

Obit-died: on Mar 23, at age 72 years, John Boyle, a native of the County Antrim, Ireland, & for more than 40 years a resident of Wash, where for a long period he filled the station of Chief Clerk in the Navy Dept. Revering, as he did, the free institutions of his adopted country, to which he had transferred his allegiance, he forgot not the wrongs & oppression of the land of his nativity. To redress these he in early life, in the fruitless effort of 1798, had freely spilt his blood, & braved the terrors of the dungeons & the courts of a despotic Gov't. He survived but for a few days the widow of the memorable Irish patriot, Theobold Wolfe Tone. Thus link afer link is broken of the chain which connects the Rebel of '98 with the Felon of '48.

The great Telescope used by the famous Philosopher & Astronomer De Vico, in his discoveries in Europe, has been received at Gtwn College. The object glass alone is valued at $1,000. —Advocate

Died: on Mar 27, Miss Ann McKaraher, in her 72nd year. Her life was an ornament to her Christian profession which she held for many years in the First Baptist Church in Wash City. Her funeral is on Thu, at the house of Mr B F Dyer, N J ave, at 2 o'clock.

Died: on Feb 14, suddenly, on his passage from N Y to London, Jas Batchelor, aged 17 years, youngest son of John Batchelor, of London, England, & brother-in-law of John H Gibbs, of Wash City.

Orphans Court of Wash Co, D C. Letters of administration on the personal estate of Capt Edw G Elliott, late of the U S Army, deceased. –Thos Fillebrown, adm

The brick stable occupied by Mr McIlhaney, of the Exchange Hotel, in C st, was set on fire last Fri, by an incendiary, & it is believed, the villain against set fire to the bldg yesterday.

Last night, Jos Dockhard, formerly a U S soldier, was committed for trial at the present term of the Criminal Court, upon the oath of Augustus Goetz, charged with having sworn to a paper before J P Van Tyne, to the identity of the identical Augustus Goetz, at the same time knowing that he was committing perjury; also, for having forged the name of Augustus Goetz to an oath of identitly, representing himself as Augustus Goetz, & thereby obtaining a land warrant, valued at $106, in Wash Co.

Hyer's trial for an assault & battery upon Sullivan in the late barbarous prize fitht, took place last week before the Kent [Md] County Court, & resulted in a verdict against him. The court imposed a fine of $700 & costs.

THU MAR 29, 1849
$200 reward will be paid by the subscriber for any information which will lead to the apprehension & conviction of the individual who entered my printing ofc in my absence from the city on Sun last & set fire to my bldg, therfore destroying the same & the whole contents therein. –C Alexander
[All orders for printing can be left at the agency ofc of Messrs Mechlen & Winder, 17th st, or at my dwlg house, on 14th st, between G & N Y ave.]

Photography. The discoveries which have been made in this art are wonderful. According to the Revue des deux Mondes, Jos Nicephoire Niepce was the first who found the means of fixing, by chemical action of light, the image of external objects; but Louis Mandi Daguerre perfected the photogaphic process of Niepce, & discovered the method now in use. Niepce made his first discovery in 1814. Daguerre was a skilful painter in Paris, & the inventor of the Diorama. It was in 1826 that he first received the news of Niepce's discoveries. Niepce died in 1833 at age 63 years. He died in poverty & obscurity.

Mr Moreton, an American printer, died lately in Paris. He has bequeathed L40,000 to be given as a premium to anybody who shall succeed in constructing a machine capable of striking off 10,000 copies of a newspaper within an hour. –Paris paper

Died: on Mar 28, in Wash City, Mr Chas Blaksler, in his 49th year. He was formerly from the State of Connecticut, where he was universally esteemed for the uprightness of his conduct in social life. His funeral is this day at 2 o'clock, at his residence on 7th st, opposite the Patent Ofc.

Died: on Mar 28, of consumption, Mr Edw Sweeny, a native of Ireland, aged 45 years. His funeral is from his late residence on 8th st, between D & E sts, at 4 o'clock this afternoon.

Died: on Tue last, of scarlet fever, Lucretia Maria, daughter of J S & Ann Laura Reed, aged 2 years, 3 months & 15 days.

Died: on Mar 24, in Wash City, of congestion of the brain, Willson Fauble, son of C W Boteler, jr, aged 1 year & 4 months.

Mrd: on Mar 7, in Petersburg, Va, by Rev Mr Smith, Edw R Turnbull, clerk, of Brunswick Co, to Miss Eliz Harrison, daughter of the late Dr Nathl Harrison, of Prince George, Va.

Loss of the American brig **Floridian** on the Long Sands, coast of England, with the loss of nearly 200 passengers. The **Floridian** was owned by Mr E D Hurlburt, of N Y, under the command of Capt Whitmore, chartered to bring emigrants from Antwerp by a German company. She had on board from 176 to 200 young & respectable German mechanics, with their wives & children, & set sail on the 27th ult, having cleared the Flemish Banks, steered westward for the Straits of Dover. The chief mate had scarcely left the deck when the vessel struck with such terrific violence & fatal effect that her bottom planks & false keel immediately floated up alongside of her. The emigrants rushed in dismay upon the deck, &, as the waves dashed in the side of the vessel, every surge swept away one or more of them into eternity. As the second boat was lowered, Capt Whitmore leaped into it with his wife in his arms, & this being the signal for a general & desperate rush from the foundering ship, the frail boat was almost instantly overloaded & sunk committing all in her to a watery grave. The then survivors, about 12 in number, continued in the rigging of the foremast; when Thu morning broke, it was discovered that 6 of the poor fellows had died during the night; frozen to death. Only 4 survived, 3 of the crew & 1 passenger. The arrival of the British revenue cutter **Petrel** saved them, but their suffering had been so great that one of the poor fellows was deranged. A boat containing 5 noble-hearted men, who set out from Wivanhoe, a fishing village, to rescue some of the suffers after the quarter deck was swept away, was capsized, & they all perished.

At auction: large & spacious house in Alexandria, fitted for a Tavern & Restaurant. Possession to commence from the day of renting. -R B Lloyd

FRI MAR 30, 1849
For rent, the western House of Gadsby's row, corner of Pa ave & 21st st, & for the last 6 years occupied by Mrs Cmdor Patterson. The rent is $300. -J H McBlair, Agent

The Hartford Times charges the Hon Jos Trumbull, whom the Whigs are supporting for Govn'r of Connecticut, with having given $50 to the Catholics of Harford to aid them in enlarging their church! For this offence the Locofocos of Conn are called upon & expected to vote against him. The publication of this charge, howeve, has disclosed the fact that Mr Trumbull has been guilty of contributing in like cases for the benefit of other denominations.

Coal & wood for sale: at Potomac Bridge & corner of E & 10th sts. -J S Harvey & Co

The Hagerstown Herald states that a man named Miller was on Wed last committed for stealing a gallon measure filled with whiskey from the distillery of Jos Gabby. He had twice before stolen the identical measure, filled from the same whiskey barrel, & had just served 2 years in the penitentary for the last offence. [Apr 16th newspaper: Miller has been discharged by the Grand Jury on the ground of insanity.]

At auction: horses, cows, hogs, ploughs, harrows, & corn-fodder: on Apr 16, at the residence & dairy establishment of Messrs Genzenbach & Schaub, on the Corporation line, near North Captiol st & Esling's brick-yard, adjoining the residence of Mr Gilman. –A Green, auct

Calif emigration: 1-The Charlestown Mining Co of Va departed from there on Tue last. They number about 75, embracing some of the best & worthiest citizens of that town. Ofcrs of the company:
Pres: Benj F Washington, of Jefferson
1st cmder: Robt H Keeling, of Richmond
2nd cmder: Smith Crane, of Jefferson
3rd cmder: Jos E N Lewis, of Jefferson
Treas: E M Aisquith, of Jefferson
Quartermaster: Nathl Seevers, of Jefferson
Sec: J Harrison Kelly, of Jefferson
Surgeon, Dr Bryarly, of Balt
2-The Calif company organized in Shepherdstown, in the same county, destined for Calif, departed on last Wed week. Dr Richd Parran, a most estimable & worthy gentleman, was selected as president of the company.

Hurricane in Ky: in Shelby, in a brief period, immense damage was done. The house belonging to the heirs of Henry Crittenden, deceased, occupied by Mr O'Niell, has damage; Mr T Oliver's house slightly injured; Mr Coot's shop much injured; the blacksmith shop of Messrs Willis & McCampbell was razed to the ground; Mrs Marshall's kitchen was demolished; Miss Abby Mills' dwlg, Mr A Smith's, & those occupied by Mr Rosebury, Mr Demaree, Mr J W Hickman, Mr J F Chinn, & Mr W McCampbell, were greatly damaged. In Bardstown, the house of Mr Newbold, was blown down & Mr Newbold was killed, & one or two of his children badly injured. The roof of Thos Aud's house was blown down. Several houses in Elizabethtown, Hardin Co, were blown down. Mr Sanford Leslie's store in Big Spring was blown down. [No date-current news item.]

Household & kitchen furniture at auction on Apr 4, at the residence of Mr Frost, on Capitol Hill, near the East Capitol gate, *Gen Green's Row*. -A Green, auct

Orphans Court of Wash Co, D C. Letters of administration, with the will annexed, on the personal estate of Jane Macomb, late of Wash Co, deceased.
-Walter S Cox, adm c t a

Died: on Mar 28, in Wash City, in her 19th year, Sarah Adelaide, 3rd daughter of John & Jane Thomas.

Washington City & Calif Mining Association: expedition for the purpose of trying their fortunes in the gold regions of Calif. Their uniform is a short gray frock coat, single-breasted, with gilt eagle buttons; pantaloons the same color, with black stripe; glazed forage-cap, with the intitials in front, W C C M A. Each member will be armed with a rifle, pair of pistols, bowie knife, & belt hatchet, with accoutrements. The Assoc will leave here on Mon next in the cars, under an escort through the city by our volunteer companies. We heartily wish them all success, & a safe return. List of the members:
*J Goldsborough Bruff, Pres & Cmder, 43, Wash
*Gideon Brooke, V P, 29, Wash
*Benj Brooke Edmonston, Treas, 27, Wash
*Asaph H Parish, Sec, 28, Wash
*Henry Austin, 32, physician, Md
Board of Dirs: *Wm H Dietz, 43, Wash; *Geo A Young, 28, N J; John Camron, of Gtwn; *Wm Jewell, jr, director & cmte, 27, Gtwn; & *Edwin D Slye, director & cmte, 33, Wash.
*Alex'r Garratt, Ensign, 23, Wash
*Jas Foy, Blacksmith, 21, Wash
*Thos Williams, 25, Wash
*John M Farrar, director, aged 59, Wash
*John Cameron, director & cmte, 50, Gtwn
*Henry J Queen, 22, Wash
*Geo Byington, 15, Wash
*John T Coumbs, 24, Wash
*John Young Donn, 19, Wash
Washington Lewis
*Saml D Lewis, 20, Wash
*Wm Barker, 27, Wash
*David Fowble, 32, Wash
*J W Marden,21, PG Co, Md
*Stephen S Culverwell, 22, Wash
*Jos Murphy, 22, Wash
*Wm W Lloyd, 22, Wash
*Robt Slight, 31, Wash
*Thos J Griffeth, 25, Wash
*Oscar B Queen, 25, Wash
*Richd I A Culverwell, 48, Wash
*L A Iardella, 26, Wash

*Henry Vermillion, 31, Wash Co, Md
*C Columbus McLeod, 32, Wash
*Thos P Kingsbury, 24, Wash
*John Bates, 34, Wash
*Wm Truman, 20, Wash
*Gregory J Ennis, 22, Wash
*Wm Pope, 40, Wash
*Jas H Barker, 18, Wash
*Wm P Hilleary, 22, Wash
*Chas Bishop, 25, Wash
*Fielder M Magruder, 21, Wash
*John V Ennis, 25, Wash
*Jas A Ennis, 17, Wash
*Jos Thaw, 31, Wash
*Josiah B Hills, Josias B Hills, 40, Wash
*Thos B Scott, 26, Wash
*Isaac E Owen, 19, Wash
*Danl R Wall, 24, Wash
*Chas Fenderich, lithographer, 43, Wash
*Jas Wardell, 48, Gtwn
*Wm Franklin, 48, Wash
*Chas Reed, 26, Boston
*Josiah C Willis, 31, Balt
*B Franklin Burche, 24, Wash
*Jos C Riley, 25, Wash
*Matthew M Treppnell, __, Boston
*H Carter Dorsey, artist, 25, Alexandria, Va
*F R Windsor, 20, Alexandria, Va
*Wm J Stoops, 41, Gtwn
*Stephen J Cassin, 30, Gtwn, D C
*Chas G Alexander, 24, King Geo Co, Va
Chas G Morely, Laurel, PG Co, Md
*C G Moxley, 21, Anne Arundel Co, Md
*Augustus S Capron, 25, Laurel, PG Co, Md
*Richd Washington, 22, Westmoreland Co, Va
[Apr 2 newspaper additions & corrections applied in the above. 64 members, consisting of 12 carpenters & mechanics of different kinds. It appears that those without an * are not to be included.]

Criminal Court-Wash: 1-Fred'k Billings, aged 16 years, was tried on an indictment charging him with forging a check in the name of J C Lewis: found guilty; recommended to the mercy of the court. [Apr 6 newspaper: Sentenced to suffer 18 months' imprisonment in the penitentiary.]

SAT MAR 31, 1849
Appointment by the Pres: Jos Bates to be U S Marshal for the Dist of Texas.

Col Fremont arrived at Santa Fe, on his way to Calif, intending to take Cooke's route. He lost 11 men in the mountains, the names of only 3 of whom are given, viz: Mr Wise, of St Louis, & Messrs King & Preuss, the latter from this city. [Telegraphic despatch, dated at St Louis on Thu last.]

Rev Mr Burroughs, of the Phil Methodist Episcopal Conf, prior to his departure for Conference, paid a visit to his wife's relatives, near Sandy Hill, Worcester Co, Md, where he met with Mr Jas B Bishop, between whom & the minister an old grudge existed. An altercation ensued, Burroughs killed Bishop with a pistol, on the spot. Burroughs made no attempt to escape.

West Point, N Y, Mar 21, 1849. Meeting of the Fourth Class of the U S Corps of Cadets, held at West Point Mar 19, 1849: our painful task to follow to the grave the remains of our late friend & classmate, Clement Carrington, of Arkansas: we tender our deepest sympathy to the family & relatives of the deceased. Cmte: Jos C Ives, Jas W Robinson, Geo H Mendall, Geo B Anderson, Thos L Casey.

Mrd: on Mar 29, by Rev Mr Reese, Jas W Fowler, of Wash, to Margaret E Wilson, of Alexandria, Va.

Died: on Mar 30, in Wash City, Henry Walker, after a painful illness of 3 weeks, aged 30 years. His funeral is from his mother's residence, on 18th st, between I & 16th sts, Apr 1, at 3 o'clock.

Died: on Mar 2, at the residence of his son, Merriwether Co, Ga, Mr Wm H Jack, in his 78th year. His life has been eminently characteristic of true & humble piety.

N Y papers announce the death of Danl Appleton, the senior partner of the publishing house of Appleton & Co, who died in that city on Mar 28. Having been apprized of his approaching dissolution for some months, he had accordingly closed up his worldly affairs & awaited the hour of his departure with the composure of a Christian.

Wash Corp: 1-Act to authorize payment of Matthew Waite's account for repairs to the roof of the City Hall: read. 2-Ptn of F Stutz, representing the condition of the gutter at E & 11th st: referred to the Cmte on the Health of the City. 3-Communication from W W De Maen, asking an increase of compensation as assist teacher in the 2nd Dist School: referred to the Cmte on Public Schools. 4-Communication from John Jones & P Gorman, in relaton to their proposals for repairing the Wash Canal: asking to be discharged from its further consideration, & that it be referred to the Board of Control of the Canal. 5-Cmte of Claims: act of relief of Jas Williams: read. Same cmte: bill for the relief of A F Wilcox: reported the same without amendment. Same cmte: bill for the relief of W E Johnson: indefinitely postponed.

Dog lost, a black & white Newfoundland dog, about 8 months old. Suitable reward for returning him to J M Chubb, F & 15th sts.

Private sale of *Enfield Chase*, one of the most desirable estates in Md: in PG Co, adjoining the Messrs Ogle & others: about 600 acres. Apply to the subscriber on the premises, or by letter to him at Queen Anne. –N H Shipley

MON APR 2, 1849
The Albany papers chronicle the death of Jonathan Kidney, for more than 70 years a resident of that place, & who was a soldier of the Revolution, & with Gen Gates at the surrender of Burgoyne, at Saratoga.

Died: yesterday, in Wash City, Mr Thos H Stone, in his 30th year. His funeral is this afternoon at 4 o'clock, from his late residence on 7th st, between L & M sts north.

Mexican boundary survey: John B Weller is the U S Com'r & Andrew B Gay, [civil engineer] the U S Surveyor, appointed & confirmed by the Senate under the 5th article of the treaty. Ofcs attached to the survey, to aid & assist in the demarcation of the line: Maj W H Emory, Capt Hardcastle, Lt Whipple: Topographical Engineers. ____ Nooney, Assist to Maj Emory & 1st computor. ____ ____, Assist to Maj Emory 2nd computor. Chas S Whiting, principal Assist to Mr Gray. John H Forster, G W Hooper, Fred'k Emory, & ___ Taylor, Sub-assistants. [Blanks as copied ____.]

Died: on Mar 29, of scarlet fever, Saml Edward, youngest son of Jas F & Mary Wollard, aged 1 year, 5 months & 20 days.

Simpsonville for sale: the estate of the late Joel Simpson, situated near the residence of Francis P Blair on the 7th st road, 6 miles from Wash City: comprises 2 farms, & contains 450 acres. One farm has a large brick dwlg, built in the modern style, as likewise out-bldgs of the most spacious kind. Apply on E st, between 10th & 11th sts, at the residence of Mrs A Simpson, admx. N B: Also for sale, 2 frame dwlgs & 2 vacant lots, being part of square 321, on the corner of E & 11th sts, only 1 square from the avenue.

Household & kitchen furniture at auction on Apr 3, at the dwlg of Dr Hardy, adjoining the residence of Maj Barker, on N J ave, Capitol Hill. All his furniture.
-E C & G F Dyer, aucts

Criminal Court-Wash. 1-On Fri, in the case of the U S vs John P Stone, for passing counterfeit notes on V Harbaugh & H H McPherson, jr: verdict of not guilty of passing counterfeit notes on Valentine Harbaugh, & guilty in the case of H H McPherson, jr.

Fri night the stable belonging to Mr W Grupe, confectioner, on Pa ave, was wilfully set fire. The stable behind Mr Grupe's dwlg was destroyed.

Thos Whitmore, Thos Goddard, & Lawrence Conroy, arrested on Fri by Ofcr Milburn on the charge of setting Mr Alexander's printing ofc on fire, were committed for trial the same day. [Apr 9th newspaper: Thos Goddard, aged 14, found not guilty.]

Boarding: Mrs Ann H Scott, opposite Jackson Hall, by month, week or day.

TUE APR 3, 1849
Sale of valuable property: by a decree made by the Orphans Court of Wash Co, D C, in the matter of John R Hendley, guardian to Sophia J Hendley, the undersigned will sell, on Apr 18, viz: part of lot 13 in square 431; also the eastern most equal half of lot 12, in square 431, fronting on E st north 25 feet: property is on the corner of 7th & E sts, occupied at present by J R Hendley as a hotel & refectory. Apply to the undersigned, or to W Lenox, atty at Law. –J R Hendley, Guardian -A Green, auct

For rent: the store-room on Pa ave, between 12th & 13th sts, occupied by as a Lace Store. Possession on Apr 19. Apply to Elias Travers

Orphans Court of Wash Co, D C. Letters of administration on the personal estate of Matilda W Wilson, late of said county, deceased. –Catharine A Tone, admx N B. Persons who have claims against the estate of Mrs Wilson will please present them to the subscriber. –John Marbury, Gtwn

Annual Commencement of the Nat'l Medical College of Wash City took place yesterday, at the new Baptist Church on E st. The degree of M D was confered on the following young gentlemen: Elijah D Everhart, of Md; Washington Miller, Francis H Hill, Geo Latimer, Jas S Gunnell, jr, & Wm J H White, of D C; Marmaduke C Johnson & Thos Adam, of Va.

A bldg attached to the powder-mill of Mr Marshfield Parsons, at Allen's Creek, in Brighton, was blown up on Thu last, probably fatally, injuring a young man named Archibald Ross, who was at work in the bldg.

For rent: a brick bldg, occupied by F Grice, on 13th st, between G & H sts; possession on May 5. Apply to Geo Parker, or the subscriber. –Geo Cover

Died: on Mar 3, at the residence of John W Patterson, in Fauquier Co, Va, Thos Whiting, aged 84 years. He was a native of Gloucester Co, Va, but at an early period of his life removed to Fauquier Co, where he continued to reside until his death, greatly respected by his friends & neighbors.

WED APR 4, 1849
Wash Corp: 1-Ptn of Edw Kersey, praying remission of a fine: referred to the Cmte of Claims. 2-Ptn from Jos Mason & Wm J Bates, for themselves & in behalf of the free people of color of the city, praying some aid in the establishment of a system of free education for their children: referred to the Cmte on Public Schools. 3-Ptn of McClintock Young & others, for construction of a cistern at F & 13th sts: referred to the Cmte on Improvements. 4-Ptn of T B Brown & others, for the improvement of 7th st west: referred to the Cmte on Improvements. 5-Ptn of Ann McDaniel & Blair & Rives, asking that the alley between 3rd & 4½ sts, in the rear of their bldgs, may be repaired: referred to the Cmte on Improvements. 6-Bill to authorize the payment of Matthe Waite's account for repairing the roof of the City Hall: passed.

Alex'r Ramsey, of Pa, to be Govn'r of the Territory of Minesota, in place of Wm Pennington, declined.

Ephraim G Squier, of N Y, to be Charge d'Affaires of the U S to the Republic of Guatemala.

Henry King, an assist surveyor, of Gtwn, Mr Preuss, artist, of this city, & Henry J Wise, of St Louis, are the names of 3 of Col Fremont's party who are known to have perished in the Rocky Mountains.

The Donna Augustina Ferrando, of Tlaliscoyan, in Mexico, died early in Jan. The residence of this lady was on the route from Vera Cruz to Orizaba; she had frequent occasion of showing kindness to American prisoners during the late war. She prevented a Lt of the American army, who was made a prisoner, from being shot. Cmdor Perry, hearing of this heroic humanity, gave orders that all person & property belonging to the family of this lady should pass the blockading squadron off the Alvarado river free of all search. –N Y Courier

In Chancery: Circuit Court of Wash Co, D C., Mar Term, 1849. Thos Kinneraly, Augustus D Clemens, & others, vs John L Hammond & wife, Edwin Jessop & wife, Francis Forsyth & wife, & Jas Wm Bryden. Bill is to obtain a decree for the conveyance of the legal title in a certain square of ground in Wash City from the dfndnts, John L Hammond & wife & Edw Jessop & wife, & to obtain a decree for partition & sale of the same as to the other dfndnts. The bill states that, on Sep 14, 1801, a certain Geo Walker conveyed the square of ground in said city, & distinguished on the plan of said city by the number 862, unto Jas Bryden, of N Y, in fee simple; that, afterwards, on Feb 21, 1816, Jas Bryden assigned his interest & estate in said square to Wm Bryden, of Balt, by deed, which has never been recorded; that Jas Bryden is dead intestate, without a widow, having 2 children, his heirs-at-law, Jane, who intermarried with John L Hammond, of Balt, & Mary Ann, who intermarried with Edwin Jessop, of the State of Wisconsin; that, since the execution of said deed of assignment, the said Wm Bryden, the assignee, has died intestate, without a widow, leaving 5 children, his heirs-at-law, Jas Wm Bryden, Therese, who intermarried with Francis Forsyth, of Balt, Ann, who intermarried with the cmplnt, Alex'r Tait, Henrietta M, who intermarried with the cmplnt, Augustus D Clemens, & Eliz, who, having intermarried with the cmplnt, Thos Kinneraly, died leaving 3 children, her heirs-at-law, to wit, Wm Thos, Jas B, & Chas Henry, who are all infants, under 21 years of age; that, on Jan 1, 1849, the dfndnts, Jas Wm Bryden & Francis Forsyth & Theresa his wife, conveyed by deed two undivided fifth parts of the said square unto the cmplnt, Augustus D Clemens, in fee simple; & that all the dfndnts are non-residents; that the said square would be injured by a partition, & a sale be greatly for the advantage of the infants cmplnts; & that neither partition nor sale could be effected without the interposition of the Court of Chancery, in consequence of the infancy of some of the cmplnts. Cmplnts to appear in this Court, in person or by solicitor, on or before the third Mon of Oct next. –Test: John A Smith, clerk

For Calif: On Mar 26, two companies, under Capt Edwin Bryant & Jas B Huie, &, together, numbering about 90, set off for St Louis.

Cmdor Chas W Morgan to take command of the U S naval force of the Mediterranean, vice Cmdor Bolton, deceased.

Dr Valentine Mott, of N Y, performed a surgical operation last week on a patient while under the influence of chloroform. He cut off his leg without the patient feeling the least pain, or even knowing, until it was off, that the operation had commenced.

Mrd: on Apr 1, by Rev J B Donellan, Geo Hodgkins to Mary C Newton, both of Wash City.

Mrd: on Mar 29, by Rev F S Evans, Andrew Jackson, formerly of Va, to Miss Rebecca M Jones, of Wash City.

Mrd: on Mar 25, in Cincinnati, by Rev Mr Cavenaugh, John H Armstrong, of Vevay, Indiana, to Theodosia G Russell, of Wash City.

Mrd: on Apr 1, by Rev S A H Marks, Mr Andrew Burgess to Miss Eliz Frost, all of Wash City.

Died: on Apr 2, Wm O Sawyer, in his 23rd year, of pulmonary consumption. His funeral is this morning from the residence of his step-father, Mr Jas Lowry, on I st, near 17th st. [Note: no time for the funeral is given.]

Died: on Thu last, in Wash City, of scarlet fever, after an illness of 36 hours, Annie Eliz, aged 7 years & 1 month, eldest daughter of Albert Greenleaf, of Wash City.

Fine horse for sale: owner desirous of going to Calif. Apply to P W Dorsey's, corner of 7th & I sts, this day.

For rent: 3 story house on N J ave, adjoining the residence of Col Gardner, south of the Capitol gate. Inquire at Mr Jos Ingle's store, at the corner.

Saw-mill machinery for sale: nearly new. Apply to Peter Naylor or M M Bonnell, 13 Stone st, N Y.

For sale: 2 sotry brick house with lot, on 14th st, between F & G sts. Title indisputable. –Wm Serrin, 1st Ward, or Wm Durr, 2nd Ward.

THU APR 5, 1849
The Southern Literary Gaz, published at Athens, Ga, is edited by Wm C Richards.

Died: on Mar 28, in Edenton, N C, Lt Thos M Whedbee, at the age of 25. He was graduated at West Point in Jun, 1846, with the honor of a place in the first division of his class, & at the time of his death held the rank of 2nd Lt of Ordnance. During our late war with Mexico he rendered important service to his country, no less honorable nor less to be valued because no blood was on his sword & the smoke of the battle field never shrouded his form. Every shell used in the bombardment of Vera Cruz passed his inspection. The confinement & suffering he had to endure called for the exercise of greater patience than most men have or can acquire. As life waned came relief; his end was peaceful & pain unfelt in death.

For sale or rent, my Billiard & Bowling Saloon, on 14th st, fronting Williard's Hotel. Suitable for a bookbindery or printing ofc. –F Burche

Two boys killed by lightning: on Tue, over this region of country, 2 sons of Leeds Dougherty, who were fishing in East Ford, Clermont Co, ran to a large sycamore tree when the storm commenced, & sat down at its root. Another lad, son of Collins Dougherty, was also with them. While they were sitting there, the lightning struck the sycamore, &, running down its trunk, killed the 2 brothers instantly. The other lad was so stunned that he could not stir hand or foot for several hours -Cin Chronicle

The New Orleans Picayune announces the death, on Mar 26, of Jas Porter, brother of the late Judge Porter; also, of Mr Geo Cooke, the artist, & proprietor of the gallery in that city known by his name.

For sale, at the Capitol Stables, a fine Young Sorrel Horse. I have also a cheap buggy & a double & single set of Harness, which I will sell cheap, as I am going West in a few days, & want the money. Apply to Jas Henry, in the Post Ofc of the Hse o/Reps.

FRI APR 6, 1849
Appointments by the Pres: Custom-house Ofcrs:
John J Walker, Collector, Mobile, Ala, vice Jas E Saunders.
Isaiah D Hart, Collector, District of St Johns, Fla, vice Chas Byrne.
Wm R Watson, Collector, Providence, R I, vice Benj Cowell.
Moses Richardson, Naval Ofcr, Providence, R I, vice Silas A Comstock.
Land Ofcrs: Peter J Walker, of Ala, to be Receiver of Public Moneys at Lebanon, Ala.
Edgar Conklin, of Wisc, to be Receiver of Public Moneys at Green Bay, Wisc.
Thos E Birch, of Missouri, to be Register of the Land Ofc at Plattsburg, Missouri.
Wm W Adams, of Ark, to be Register of the Land Ofc at Little Rock, Ark.
Indian Agents:
David D Mitchell, fo Missouri, to be Superintendent of Indian Affairs at St Louis, Missouri.
Chas N Handy, of Missouri, to be Indian Agent at Osage river Agency.
John Wilson, of Missouri, to be Indian Agent at Salt Lake Agency, Calif.
Jas S Calhoun, of Ga, to be Indian Agent at Santa Fe, New Mexico.
Thos Wistar, jr, of Pa, to be the Com'r authorized by the second claims of the fourth article of the treaty concluded with the Menomonie tribe of Indians on Oct 18, 1848.
Marshals: Jos Bates, of Texas, to be U S Marshal for the District of Texas.
Solomon Meredith, of Indiana, to be U S Marshal for the District of Indiana.
Chas H Knox, of Michigan, to be U S Marshal for the District of Michigan.
Postmaster: Alpheus S Williams, Postmaster, Detroit, Michigan.
Inspectors of Penitentiary:
John T Towers& Thos Donoho, of Wash, & Wm H Edes, of Gtwn, to be Inspectors of the Penitentiary of the Dist of Columbia.
Appointments by the Sec of the Interior:
Andrew J Dorn, of Missouri, to be Indian Sub-Agent at Neosho Sub-Agency.
Wm H Bruce, of Wisc, to be Indian Sub-Agent at Green Bay, Wisc.
Wm Prentiss, of Ill, to be Indian Sub-Agent on Sacramento & San Joachin rivers, Calif.

Ebenezer Childs, of Wisc, to be Agent to accompany the Exploring delegation of the Menomonie Indians, under treaty of Oct 18, 1849.
Geo J Thompson, of Va, to be Pension Agent at Wheeling, Va.
John Cocke, jr, of Tenn, to be Pension Agent at Knoxville, Tenn.
Appointments by the Postmaster Gen: to be Postmasters:
S H McPherson, Pomonky, Chas Co, Md, vice J Harris, resigned.
Stephen B Ford, Northeast, Cecil Co, Md, vice Richd L Thomas.
Jas S Jones, Snow Hill, Worcester Co, Md, vice R T Walters.
John P Brown, Charlestown, Jefferson Co, Va, vice J Harris.
John Poole, Rockville, Montg Co, Md, vice H F Viers, resigned.

The New Orleans papers of Mar 29 do not confirm the intelligence of the breaking up of Col Webb's Calif Co. It is true that 18 of the adventurers had returned to New Orleans, & 8 had died of cholera on the Rio Grande. They are: Hamilton J Boden, Saml L Liscomb, J T Hall, J Sherwood, of N Y; Wm H Harrison, of Cincinnati; Edw W Whittlesey, of Buffalo; J Howard Bakewell, of New Orleans; & John Lambert. The company had consisted of more than 100 persons. Mr Audubon had been robbed of $11,000 by a hotel keeper, but had recovered $4,000 of the amount, & was endeavoring to get the remainder. Col Webb had absented himself from the party, with a view to the purchase of mules for the prosecution of their journey, & was still absent at the time of departure of that portion of the company who have returned.

Letters from Wilkesbarre, Pa, to the family of Mr Bidlack, the American Charge d'Affaires at Bogota, have letters dated from him dated Jan 12, in which he speaks of his health as being excellent. The Bogota papers contain no reference to his death, which was reported to have taken place on Jan 6.

The Boston papers announce the death of the Hon Edmund Dwight, a worthy merchant of that city. He was for several years a member of the Massachusetts House & of the Senate, & was one of the Taylor Electors at large in the last Presidential election.

Wanted to hire: a woman, as cook & washer in a small family. A slave will be preferred. Apply to Mrs Fischer, C st, near 4½ st.

Prospect Hill for sale; lies on Long Green, Balt Co, 16 miles from the city, & adjoins the lands of the late Jas C Gettings, Chas Wilson, & others, & contains 475 acres: the bldgs consist of a brick dwlg, 40 by 45. Address the subscriber, care of the editors of the American, Balt, Md. –Thos Hunter

Mrd: on Apr 2, by Rev J Morgan, Mr J W Dick to Miss Eliza E Caho, all of Wash City.

Died: on Apr 5, of consumption of the lungs, Mr John Nelson Waters, son of Wm Waters, in his 50th year. His funeral is on Fri at 4 o'clock, from his late residence on L st, near 18th st.

Died: on Apr 4, in Phil, Eliz Shepperd Heston, in her 28th year, consort of the Rev Newton Heston, of the Phil Conf, Methodist Episcopal Church, & daughter of Jos W Beck, of Wash City. Her funeral is from her father's residence, today at 4 o'clock.

SAT APR 7, 1849
N Y, Apr 5. Henry B Jones, of Phil, & T Jones, were arrested today, in this city, charged with robbing the U S Patent Ofc of the Gov't jewels. They were found buried in the cellar of Jones' house 120 diamonds, 143 jewels, $300 worth of gold in bars, [supposed to be from the scabbard of the sword presented by the Emperor of Russia to Cmdor Biddle,] a gold snuff box, & a pint bottle of the attar of roses. The parties are in prison, & will leave for Washington tomorrow, in charge of police ofcrs.

N Y Commercial Adv, Richmond, Mar 29, 1849: John Marshall's Tomb. This has been a land of first-rate men; their dust is scattered all over the state; [Virginia,] Washington, Jefferson, Madison, & Monroe. The resting place of Marshall is coverd with a respectable tabular stone. John Marshall was a devoted father & a very tender husband, as well as an upright judge. His hand inscribed the following on the tomb of his wife:
Sacred to the memory of
Mrs Mary W Marshall,
Consort of John Marshall.
Born 13th March, 1766,
Departed this life on the 28th December, 1831.
This stone is devoted to her memory, by him
Who best knew her worth, & most deplores her loss.
On the tablet that covers his remains this inscription:
JOHN MARSHALL,
Son of Thomas & Mary Marshall,
Was born the 24th Sept, 1755;
Intermarried with Mary Willis Ambler the 3rd of Jan, 1783.
Departed this life the 6th day of July, 1835.
Virginia holds no more illustrious dust.

Maj Andrews, who served in Mexico with the Massachusetts regt of volunteers, died at Boston on Tue last.

From Santa Fe: Col Fremont lost his whole outfit, his mules, instruments, baggage, & every thing else of value. Mr King, of the Dist of Col, was represented to have died of the exposure & of hunger. Capt Cathcart, of the English army, was among the survivors. Lt Beale, U S Navy, was more fortunate than Col Fremont. He prosecuted his journey to Santa Fe & reached there without much dificulty. We learn that L F Thruston, who has filled several ofcs under the American Gov't in New Mexico, died in Santa Fe during the winter.

Letter from Olmutz: the new Emperor of Austria has discarded from his Court the severe old Spanish etiquette which formerly resigned in the household of that proud monarchy. After dinner the Emperor smokes his cigar, a habit which he adopted in the camps in Italy. No member of the Imperial family of Austria was ever known to smoke. This appears to be regarded as a portentous sign of the times.

MON APR 9, 1849
Appointments by the Pres. Official:
Land Ofcrs:
Danl Sigler, of Indiana, to be Register of the Land Ofc at Winamac, Indiana.
Saml Brenton, of Indiana, to be Register of the Land Ofc at **Fort Wayne**, Indiana.
John H Thompson, of Indiana, to be Receiver of Public Moneys at Indianapolis, Indiana.
Noel Smallwood, of Indiana, to be Receiver of Public Moneys at **Fort Wayne**, Indiana.
David E Moore, of Alabama, to be Receiver of Public Moneys at Demopolis, Ala.
Marshals:
Alex'r Irvine, of Pa, to be U S Marshal for the Western District of Pa.
Geo Little, of N C, to be U S Marshal for the District of N C.
Champion J Hutchison, of Wisc, to be U S Marshal for the District of Wisc.
Saml Barr, of Delaware, to be U S Marshal for the District of Delaware.
Atty:
Bowen Sweitzer, of Pa, to be U S Atty for the Western District of Pa.
Com'r of Public Bldgs:
Ignatius Mudd, of D C, to be Com'r of Public Bldgs.
Warden:
Thos Fitnam, of D C, to be Warden of the Penitentiary.
Indian Agents:
Philip Raiford, of Alabama, to be Indian Agent for the Creek Indians.
Appointment by the Sec of the Interior:
John C Hays, of Texas, to be Indian Sub-Agent on the Rio Gila, New Mexico.

As one of C Gantt's stages was passing through Mount Holly, N J, on Wed last, it received a lurch in crossing a gutter in the seat, which unseated the driver, who fell to the ground, the vehicle passing over him & injuring him severely. Passengers who were hurt: Miss Jane Davison's collar-bone was broken; Miss Sarah Shiras' collar-bone, arm, & ribs were broken; Mrs Joanna Shiras' head & side were cut & bruised severely; Mr Bowers & Mrs Craumer, of Phil, each had an arm broken; Mr Johnson, a young man from Phil, had his thigh broken.

Mrd: in Rickville, Montg Co, Md, by Rev Basil Barry, Otho Z Muncaster, of Gtwn, D C, to Harriet Eliz, daughter of the late Zadoc Magruder. [No date-current item.]

Died: on Sat, Jos A Van Zandt, of the U S Navy, in his 21st year. His funeral is at the house of his father, at 12th & Mass ave, this afternoon, at 4 o'clock.

Died: on Apr 8, of consumption, in his 58th year, Philip Cronin, a native of Killarney, Ireland, but for the last 31 years a resident of Wash City. His funeral is from his late residence on 1st st, near Md ave, today at 3 o'clock.

Valuable 3 story brick house & lot at auction: on Apr 24, the house is now in the occupancy of Mr Thos Macgill, 7th & G sts. Title indisputable.
-A Green, aucts

Orphans Court of Wash Co, D C. Letters of administration, with the will annexed, on the personal estate of Saterlee Clark, late of said county, deceased.
-Frances E Clark, J B H Smith, adms, W A

Adelphi Theatre: Miss Kate Horn takes her benefit tonight, & announces an excellent bill of fare. She is an actress of great merit.

The house now occupied by Lt McArthur, on G st, between 11th & 12th sts, will be for rent after May 1, to a good tenant. Inquire of B Willet, 13th st.

School for Civil & Military Enginering. City Academy, 10th st: established in 1832. –J Fill, Principal

Marshal's Sale: in virtue of a writ of venditioni exponas, on judgement of condemnation, on a writ of attachment issued from the Circuit Court of Wash Co, D C. Sale on May 9, all the right, title, & interest of Richd Butler Price in & to the following property: lot 6 in square 325, in Wash City, fronting on 12th st west & Va ave, seized & levied upon as the property of Richd Butler Price, & sold to satisfy judicials 146 to Mar term, 1849, in favor of Jos Lindsay. –Robt Wallace, Marshal of D C

Health Report: ofc of the Board of Health: Apr 2, 1849. Interments during the month ending Feb 28: white males-32; white females-26; colored males [1 slave]-14; colored females [1 slave]-8. Thos Miller, M D, Pres

Mrs Kehoe has several neatly furnished front & back rooms which she will let on reasonable terms. North side of Pa av, between 4½ & 6th sts, over Lee's Exchange Ofc.

TUE APR 10, 1849
Accident on the Hudson River railroad: on Wed, Patrick Flemmins, Michl Kennek, & John *Lafferty, workmen on the line, were seriously injured by the accidental discharge of a blast in the rock which they were blasting. John Rafferty was thrown some 25 feet in the air & landed on his back. He is not expected to live. The other 2 men were not so badly injured. [*Note: Lafferty/Rafferty. Copied as written.]

Appointment by the Pres: Philip Clayton, of Georgia, to be 2nd Auditor of the U S Treasury.

Appointments by the Postmaster Genr'l. 1-Benj N Payne, Postmaster, Towson Town, Balt Co, Md, vice Geo H Cathcart, resigned. 2-Armon W Davis, Postmaster, Havre-de-Grace, Harford Co, Md, vice Henry L Cole, removed. [The post ofc at Hermitage, Montg Co, Md, is discontinued.]

Persons having claims against a balance due from the Navy Dept to the estate of Thos McVey, deceased, late an ordinary seaman in the U S service, are notified to present them at the ofc of the 4th Auditor of the Treas within 2 months from this date.

For sale or rent: 3 story brick house, H & 17th sts, now occupied by the Chief Clerk of the Navy Dept. Apply to J L Cathcart, 18th st, between G & H.

Sale of valuable property: by deed of trust from John B Coddington & Camilla his wife, dated Aug 31, 1842, recorded in liber W B 95, folio 49, a land record of Wash Co, D C: sale on May 12, of lot 5 in reservation 11, fronting on B st, on which is a 2 story brick dwlg-house. —Wm M Morrison, auct -P R Fendall, trustee

Furnished rooms for rent; at present occupied by the Sardinian Minister: on F st, near 14th st. Available on Apr 15. —S L Cole

In Chancery: Eliz Ford, cmplnt, & Peter Brady & John Ford, dfndnts. By an interlocutory order of the Court I am directed to state an account of the personal estate of the late Wm Ford, his real estate, its value, rental, & condition, & the debts owing by him at the time of his death. Execution of this order on Apr 20, at my ofc, City Hall, Wash. —W Redin, auditor

Died: in his 45th year, Danl Cannon, a native of the county of Galway, Ireland. His funeral is from his late residence, near Gtwn, today at 3 o'clock. [No death date given- current item.]

Died: on Apr 8, Francis Graham, infant daughter of Lt Alfred Taylor, U S Navy.

WED APR 11, 1849
A company of emigrants to Texas from Monroe Co, Georgia, were attacked with cholera after leaving New Orleans, & at the last accounts 18 of them have been buried, 7 servants in one grave. Some of them died in 3 hours after they were attacked. The party was comprised of 6 families with their servants, in all 77 persons.

Es-Pres Polk arrived at Nashville, Tenn, on Apr 2, & was publicly welcomed home by its citizens, without distinction of party.

Cincinnati Civilian: Jas Shaw, a miner, a Scotchman, was killed on Apr 4, in the coal mines of the Mount Savage Iron Co, by the falling down of part of the roof.

Wash Corp: 1-Ptn from W A Griffith for the remission of a fine: referred to the Cmte of Claims. 2-Ptn of Wm J Johnson, praying the refunding of a certain amount paid for a fish stand: referred to the Cmte on Police. 3-Ptn from Grafton Powell, concerning the conveyance of water in the 2nd Ward: referred to the Cmte on Improvements. 4-Ptn of Wm Mullen, praying the remission of a fine: referred to the Cmte of Claims. 5-Cmte on Police: asking to be discharged from the further consideration of the ptn of Washington Rollins & others: concurred in. 6-Cmte on Improvements: asking to be discharged from the further consideration of the ptn of Wm B Wilson: concurred in. Same cmte: asking to be discharged from the further consideration of the ptn of J S Cunningham & others: concurred in. 7-Cmte of Claims: asking to be discharged from the further consideration of the ptn of L Callan: referred to the delegation from the 5th Ward. 8-Cmte of Claims: asking to be discharged from the further consideration of the ptn of Susan Maryman: concurred in. 9-Bill for the relief of Emily G Jones, excx of the late Thos P Jones: passed with an amendment.

Appointment by the Pres: 1-Danl M Haskell, to be Postmaster at Cleveland, Ohio.

Cmder Irvine Shubrick, U S Navy, died suddenly at Wilmington, Del, on Thu last. He was a native of S C & entered the service in 1814.

Mrd: on Apr 9, by Rev Mr Foley, Mr Jas Stone to Miss Josephine Grant, both of Wash City.

Died: yesterday, at the residence of Jos Gales, [his son-in-law,] adjoining Wash City, Theodorick Lee, aged 83 years. His funeral is this afternoon at 4:30 p m. Carriages will be waiting at Mrs Walker's dwlg, on 6th st, from half past three to four o'clock, for the convenience of those who attend.

Died: on Mar 22, at Western Missouri, of cholera, Mr JohnY B Dietz, son of Wm H Dietz, late of the Gen Land Ofc, aged 19 years. On the day the news of his death reached his afflicted mother in this city, his father, on his way to Calif, expected to reach St Louis to meet him there & bid him a long adieu. -J E D

Died: on Apr 8, at Enfield, Halifax Co, N C, Mary Catharine, infant daughter of L C & A H Wheat, aged 15 months & 24 days.

For sale, on the Heights of Gtwn, a beautiful residence, recently occupied by Senator Foote, finished in the best manner. Apply to M Duffey, near the premises.

Gentlemen, with or without families, wishing good board & pleasant rooms, can be suited at J T McDuffie's Pa ave, between the Capitol & Railroad Depot.

THU APR 12, 1849
Boarding & Day School, corner of Vt ave & L st, will be resumed on Apr 16.
–G F Morison

For sale: 2 fine bay Horses. Inquire of Mr Jameson, at the Senate Post Ofc.

In Chancery: Wm Dowling & John Maguire, vs John F Ennis & the heirs at law of Bernard Kelly. The creditors of the late Bernard Kelly, deceased, who have not exhibited their claims against his estate are notified to do so on or before Apr 21, at my ofc, in the City Hall, Wash. –W Redin, auditor

The Magistrates of Wash Co yesterday paid their respects to the President, agreeable to previous arrangement. They assembled at Willard's Hotel, & proceded thence in a body. After remaining about half an hour with the President, they took their leave. They were:

B K Morsell	S Grubb	Lund Washington
C H Wiltberger	F S Myer	Jos W Beck
J L Smith	B Milburn	W Easby
W Thompson	Lewis Carbery	N B Van Zandt
D Saunders	R White	J N Fearson
J Lawrenson	C Ashford	S Stettinius

The last steamer brought to Boston intelligence of the death of the Rev Wm J Popham, missionary of the American Board at Amoy. He was lost at sea Jan 5, in attempting to leave a schnr in which had taken passage for Hong Kong, & which was wrecked 2 days from the point of his destination.

Dr H J Crosson tender his professional services to the citizens of Wash. Ofc on 10th st, between F & G sts.

Balt American: steamship **Crescent City**, off Chagres, Mar 24, 1849. Arrived this morning: among the passengers are Mrs J C Fremont with her daughter, about 7 years of age, & her brother-in-law, Mr Jacob. His lady would have accompanied him, but was too sick to leave N Y, where she was left with her father, Col Benton, to return to Mississippi. Mrs S C Gray, recently a resident of your city, accompanies her husband to San Francisco, where they will reside. Mrs Robinson, from Balt, accompanies Mrs Fremont as an attendant. Her husband is with her, & is one of a class of men much wanted in Calif, viz. carpenters. Col Hughes, from Anne Arundel Co, is with us, & will join in the survey of a route for a railroad across the Isthmus to Panama, on account of Messrs Aspinwall & Co. A brother of Capt Tucker also came passenger with us, & will remain on the Isthmus in the employ of the same company. -G

The British Admiralty have been apprised, by the last letters received from Sir Jas Ross, that he was about to send the vessel **Investigator**, to England, leaving the ship **Enterprise** alone to pursue the search for the ill-fated expedition of Sir John Franklin. Believing that such a separation would be fatal to the objects of the expedition, the Admiralty is sending out a fresh supply of provisions for both ships by the vessel **North Star**. The British Gov't has offered a reward of 20,000 pounds sterling, to be given to such private ship, or ships, who have rendered efficient service, in the judgment of the Board of Admiralty, to Sir John Franklin, his ships, or his crews, & may have contributed directly to extricate them from the ice in the Artic region. Such is the advertisement issued from the British Consulate at N Y on Apr 9.

The following missionaries embarked at Boston on Sat last for South Africa, to join the mission of the American Board in that country, viz: Rev Andrew Abraham & wife, Rev Hyman A Wilder & wife, & Rev Josiah Tyler & wife.

Mrd: on Apr 11, by Rev Jas B Donelan, J Lawrence Nelson, of Md, to Miss Eliza, daughter of the late Wm Worthington, of Wash City.

New Granite Works: foot of 17th st, on the Canal wharf. –Gardner Green

FRI APR 13, 1849
Trustee's sale: by virtue of a deed of trust from Wm Wheatly, recorded in Liber W B 128, folios 9 & 10, a land record for Wash Co: sale on Apr 17, of lots 23 & 25 in square 497, on 4½ st, between G & H sts. –John Carroll Brent, trustee -A Green, auct

Appointments by the Pres: to be Postmasters: Aaron P Hughes, Nashua, N H; Robt A Barnard, Hudson, N Y; Darius Perrin, Rochester, N Y

Mrd: on Apr 10, in Balt, by Rev Thos Atkinson, Wm Darby to Mary, daughter of the late Benj Tanner, of Phil.

Died: on Apr 12, after a painful illness of 10 months, of pulmonary consumption, about 20 years of age, Norman Willard Nye. His funeral is from his late residence on M st, between 6th & 7th sts, on Apr 14, at 2 p m.

Died: on Apr 11, after a protracted illness of consumption, Mrs Mary McDonald, wife of Chas McDonald, aged 39 years. Her funeral is this afternoon at 3 o'clock, from her late residence on 4th st, between F & H sts.

Died: on Wed last, in Gtwn, Miss Jane C Stith, of Balt. Her friends & those of Mr Hepburn are invited to attend her funeral this afternoon, at 4 o'clock, from the residence of Mr Hepburn, West st, Gtwn.

SAT APR 14, 1849
Official: appointments by the Pres: U S District Attys:
Bowen Sweitzer, of Pa, for the Western District of Pa.
Stephen Whicher, of Iowa, for the District of Iowa.
Peter Hamilton, of Ala, for the Southern District of Alabama.
Land Ofcrs:
Benj A Putnam, of Fla, to be Surveyor Gen of the Public Lands in Fla.
Smallwood Noel, of Indiana, to be Receiver of Public Moneys at *Fort Wayne*, Indiana, & not Noel Smallwood as published on Apr 9.
John Dade, of Mo, to be Register of the Land Ofc at Springfield, Mo.
Horace Mower, of Mich, to be Receiver of Public Moneys at Kalamazoo, Mich.
Isaac Moffatt, of Mich, to be Register of the Land Ofc at Kalamazoo, Mich.
Francis P Catlin, of Wisc, to be Register of the Land Ofc at Willow River, Wisc.
John G Floyd, of Iowa, to be Receiver of Public Moneys at Willow River, Wisc.
John H Kinzie, of Ill, to be Receiver of Public Moneys at Chicago, Ill.
Robt Griffiths, of Mo, to be Receiver of Public Moneys at Palmyra, Mo.
Indian Agent:
Chas P Babcock, of Mich, to be Superintendent of Indian Affairs at Detroit, Mich.
Appointments by the Sec of the Interior:
Indian Sub-Agents:
Saml C Spencer, of Fla, for the Seminole Indians at Fla.
Wm Hatten, of Tenn, at the Upper Missouri Sub-Agency.
Washington Barrow, of Tenn, at Council Bluffs Sub-Agency.
Adam Johnston, of Ohio, on the Sacramento & San Joachim Rivers.
Pension Agents:
Jas Swan, of Md, at Balt, Md.
Thos Reed, of Vt, at Montpelier, Vt.
John H Peck, of Vt, at Burlington, Vt, to which place the Pension Agency heretofore at Poultney has been removed.
Jas Hall, of Ohio, at Cincinnati, Ohio
Architect:
Robt Mills, of D C, to be Architect of the erection of the Wings of the Patent Ofc Bldg.

N J Elections. Henry J Taylor was elected Mayor of Jersey City, by 136 majority over C F Durant, both being Whigs. In Trenton, Wm C Howell, Whig, is elected Mayor.

The Liverpool papers announce that on Mar 18, in the workhouse of St George, in the east, died Louis Christopher, the soi disant Prince of Hayti.

Died: on Apr 4, of pneumonia, after a painful illness of 6 days, Geo Wallace, of Brandywine Mills, Summit Co, Ohio. 51 years have elapsed since he settled in Youngstown, then in Trumbull Co, in that part of the State known as the Connecticut Western Reserve. During the war of 1812 with Great Britain, he kept the principal hotel at Cleveland. He survived all his family but 2 sons. He had no bad neighbors. He held the ofc of deputy postmaster at Brandywine Mills from the first establishment of the ofc on Dec 26, 1825, & in all the contentions of party none thought of removing so good as man as Geo Wallace.

Message from the Govn'r of Pa, W F Johnston, to the Senate & House of Reps: of the Commonwealth of Pa, with a list of the Ofcrs of the U S army, natives of Pa, who distinguished themselves in the late war with Mexico: Col: Persifer F Smith
Lt Col: H Wilson; Majors: F Lee, G A McCall, J S Simonton
Capts:

C F Smith	A Porter	J P J O'Brien
J McClellan	G Nauman	G Deas
S P Heintzelman	J F Roland	G W F Wood
T B Linnard	J H Miller	Ed H Fitzgerald
J B Backenstos	G O Haller	J Van Horne.

1st Lts:

L Sitgreaves	W A Nichols	A W Bowman
P W McDonald	H F Clarke	P Farelly
S K Dawson	J F Reynolds	T Hendrickson
J B Gibson	J C Pemberton	Chas S Kilburn

2nd Lts:

Geo McClellan	S Oaks	W T Hancock
W B Franklin	A D Tree	

Steamboat casualties on the Western Rivers in 1848:
A W Johnson: burst her boilers above Maysville, on the Ohio River; 50 or 60 lives lost; boat & cargo total loss; new boat built at Wheeling, Va; 1st trip.
Admiral: owned in St Louis: bound from New Orleans to Ouachita; came in contact with the **Clarksville**.
Alert: snagged & sunk near Little Rock, Ark, in Apr: total loss; insured in Pittsburg & Cincinnati for $5,000.
Atlantis: cabin burnt at Portland, Ohio river, in Dec.
Algoma: struck a rock in the Missouri river, near Lexington, Apr 5; raised & repaired.
American: burst connecting pipe near Madison, Ohio river, Dec 20: 10 persons scalded, several fatally.
American Eagle: burst steam pipe near Marietta, Ohio river, in Mar; 4 passengers badly scalded.
Amelia: Capt Sully, snagged & lost on upper Red river, in June: insured.

Anglo Saxon: ran on a log & sunk near St Mary's landing, Mississippi river, in Feb: cargo saved.
Arkansas Mail: collided with the **Robert Fulton**, near Westport, Ohio river, Jun 8. Damaged by fire at Louisville, Dec 29.
Avalanche: burnt to the water's edge, at St Louis, on Mar 10; worth $10,000; partly insured at Pittsburg; machinery now in the new **Avalanche**.
Batesville: sunk & lost near Batesville, Ark, in Jun.
Bay State: struck a bluff bar at Sliding Island, Nov 22: sprung a leak, & threw overboard 30 tons of freight.
Beardstown: sunk in 5 feet water, below the mouth of the Ill river, in Jan: raised & repaired.
Ben Rush: burnt to water's edge, at Pittsburg; no freight on board; boat a total loss; one life lost.
Blue Ridge: burst her boilers 3 miles from Gallipolis: 20 or 30 lives lost. Boat & cargo a total loss.
Belle Hatchee: struck a snag near St Francis, Ark, & sunk, drowning 4 deck hands. The cabin floated off to within a few miles of Helena. 25 of the crew & passengers were saved by the Pike No 8. When the boat struck, a deck hand had seized the yawl & escaped, leaving all on board to the mercy of the stream.
Brunswick: run into at New Orleans on the night of Jul 5, by 2 ships in tow of a boat. On Oct 31, lost, by running into a bluff bank, during a thick fog, 7 miles from Vicksburg. Went down in 50 feet water. Insurance of $10,000 on the boat.
Caledonia: struck a snag below New Orleans, about Jan 1, & was lost.
Champlain: struck a snag & sunk in the Mississippi, near Sublette's Landing, Mar 11. Boat raised & cargo saved.
Cora: snagged, Mar 19, on the Missouri, near Hermann. On Aug 22, snagged & sunk in 2 feet water near Liberty Landing: raised & repaired.
Cambria: injured by a gale, & snagged, on Mar 19, near Cairo: repaired.
Charter Oak: fire on Mar 10 while lying at the St Louis landing. Totally destroyed by fire at Baley's landing, on the Mississippi, on Apr 12. She was freighted with grain & hemp for New Orleans. 8 persons, including the 1st engineer, were lost, & many others injured. Boat was new, valued at $30,000. Insured.
C Connor: struck a snag & sunk in 20 feet water, in Bayou Catalpha: boat & cargo a total loss: no lives lost.
Connecticut: injured by snagging in the Lower Mississippi.
Car of Commerce: sunk on the rocks at Louisville, in Dec.
Chalmette: fired by an explosion on the schnr **Maria Thomas**, at New Orleans, Jul 31: damage inconsiderable.
Confidence: sunk by collision with the **Edward Bates**, at Hamburg, on the Mississippi river, Sep 11. Raised.
Concordia: boilers exploded, opposite Plaquimine, Mississippi river, Sep 17. 30 persons scalded & missing. Capt Pease & Mr Mosely, 2nd clerk, mortally injured.
Circassian: burnt at Cincinnati Feb 27.
Defiance: lost at Liberty, Mississippi river, Feb 27, by running into the shore & sinking.
De Kalb-steamer: sunk on the Ohio near Paducah, in Nov, by being run into by the Clipper.

Edward Bates; boiler exploded, as was alleged, by the carelessness of the 1st engineer, on Aug 12, below Hamburgh, Mississippi river. 30 persons were killed or missing, & 30 more badly scalded, many of whom died.
Gray Eagle: on the Mississippi river below Randolph, on Jun 10, came in collision with the **Sultana**, ascending, by which the steampipe of the **Gray Eagle** was broken & the hull of the boat much injured. A number of persons were scalded, & some drowned by jumping overboard.
Greenwood: lost cabin by running into shore, Ky river, Dec. Negro man drowned.
Gondolier: sunk at Apple Creek bar, in Nov, by collision with the **Josiah Lawrence**: one life lost: only machinery was saved; boat insured for $12,000.
Homer: crippled by collision with the **Childe Harold**, at twelve Mile Point, Mississippi river, Feb 11.
Herald: injured by collision with the **Die Vernon**, above St Louis, Feb 22.
Hobolochitto: struck a snag about 30 miles from Springfield, Miss, & sunk in 8 feet water: boat & cargo supposed to be a total loss.
Hendrick Hudson: burnt at Cincinnati, Feb 27: 5 lives lost.
Hibernian: burnt at St Louis on Mar 10: owned in Nashville, Tenn: no insurance; valued at $3,800. One life lost.
Highland Mary: collapsed a flue at Coal Port, Ohio river, May 27. One person scalded. Burst steampipe at St Louis, Jul 26. The 2nd & assist engineers & several others were scalded.
Iron City: sunk at Hennepin, Ill river, Aug: raised. Sunk by ice, & totally lost at St Louis, Dec 31. Several lives lost.
J J Hardin: burnt at St Louis, Mar 10. Valued at $10,000: insured.
Kinney: blew up, on the Tombigbee, Mary 26. 7 persons killed & 18 wounded.
Lightfoot: burnt at St Louis, May 9. Insured for $5,800.
Laclede: burnt at St Louis, Mar 10. Valued at $15,000; insured for $5,000.
Little Missouri: struck a snag at Gwinn's bar, Missouri river, Mar 25, & sunk. Valued at $18,000; insured for $12,000. Machinery & furniture saved.
Lady Madison: injured by snagging at Manchester, Ohio river, in May.
Laurel: sunk by collision with the **Anthony Wayne**, in Sep, on the Ill river: raised.
Mendota: sunk in 7 feet water, near St Genevieve, Jan. Los.
Monona: sunk in the Mississippi river.
Major Barbour: run into & sunk by the **Paul Jones** on Feb 3, near Troy, Indiana. The 2nd clerk, Mr Allison, & 7 passengers were drowned. Boat then caught fire & sunk. The boat was new, & insured for $10,000.
Missouri: injured by fire at Memphis, on Mar 6. Was saved by the use of the "doctor."
Milwaukie: sunk on the Falls of the Ohio, Jul 14: raised.
Marengo: burst one of her boilers, in Apr, at Tunica Bend in the Mississippi. Capt, engineer, & 5 firemen scalded. A negro man jumped overboard & was drowned. Sunk in the Lower Mississippi by collision with the steamer **Harry Hill**: boat & cargo a total loss.
Mantaluke: injured by fire at St Louis, May 9.
Mail: burnt at St Louis, May 9; valued at $5,000; no insurance.
Missouri Mail: burnt at St Louis, May 9: insured for $5,000.
Mary: partially burnt at St Louis, May 9: insured for $5,000: repaired.
Monterey: snagged & lost in the Ky river, near Paint creek, Dec.

Metero: cut in 2 & sunk by the Paris on Aug 23, opposite Cloverport, Ohio. The accident occurred in a fog. 6 or 8 lives were reported to be lost.
Mogul: struck a snag, & sunk immediately, at Cloverport, Sep 30. Insured for $10,000. Machinery & furniture saved. The boat was new.
Nathan Hale: snagged at St Mary's Landing in Feb: repaired.
North Alabama: injured by ice at Hanging Dog bar, in Dec.
North America: injured by collision with the **Josiah Lawrence**, near Cairo, Apr 10.
Oliver: burst one of her boilers near Mobile, on Sep 2. Capt Miller, her cmder, had one of his legs broken & was badly scalded. A passenger & 1 negro man were killed & 8 negroes scalded. Capt Miller was cmder of the **Kinney** also at the time of the explosion, & had one leg broken.
Odd Fellow: injured by snagging 16 miles above St Louis, Feb 9: repaired. Ran into the woods at Diamond Island, Ill river, in Dec: lost chimneys & a large part of her cargo.
Oella No 2: collapsed a flue on the Arkansas in Nov. Several persons killed & scalded.
Planter: burst a boiler at twelve Mile Island, Ill river, in Jan. Boat appeared to be a perfect wreck. Several persons, including the engineer, the chamber-maid, & 3 cabin passengers, were killed, & several others scalded. Repaired. Sprung a leak at Pratt's Landing Aug 23, & returned to St Louis for repairs.
Paul Jones: struck a snag at Grand Chain, Mar 16, sunk & broke in two.
Prairie Bird: injured by coming in contact with the Beardstown, at the mouth of the Ill river, Aug 6: repaired.
Palestine: burst a cylinder head at Island No 40, in Aug.
Pelican: burnt at Biloxi, Aug 23: no insurance.
Plough Boy: sunk in the Missouri on Oct 6 near Providence, by running a snag. She was entirely new. One passenger drowned.
Pekin: sunk in the Mississippi, above Chouteau's Island, Dec 28.
Piney Woods: burnt on Lake Pontchartrain on Oct 6; 15 persons were known to have been lost.
Pilot: sunk in the Arkansas river: boat & cargo a total loss.
Ringgold: lost on Feb 11, by sinking, at Pine Bluff, Arkansas river.
Rambler: sunk & destroyed on Mar 20 near North Bend, Ohio river, by the falling a tree across her bow.
Robert Fulton: ran on the rocks & sunk, at Brown's Island, Ohio river, Apr 19: raised & repaired.
Ridgely: collapsed a flue on Black river, opposite Trinity, Jun 21: one person killed & some 20 dangerously scalded.
Robert Weightman: burst starboard boiler on Aug 12, at Fishing Creek bar, Ohio river. One person killed & 3 scalded.
Rio Grande: sunk at Golconda, Ohio river, on Oct 26, from Cincinnati bound for St Louis. Boat badly broken.
Sea Bird: while lying at Capt Girardeau, on the night of Jan 5, bound from New Orleans for St Louis, with 1,200 kegs of powder on board, caught fire, & in a few minutes after blew up & sunk. No person was killed, all on board having fled to the shore as soon as the fire was discovered. The concussion caused considerable injury to the town of Cape Girardeau.

Swatara: sunk by collision with the **Yazoo**, on Mar 10, in the Mississippi, 12 miles above the mouth of the Ohio. New boat, & a total loss.
Sultana: injured by snagging, on Aug 2, 15 miles above Cairo, on her way from New Orleans to St Louis. 3 privates of the 2nd Infty were knocked overboard in their sleep & drowned. The snag was 90 feet long, & passed up through the starboard guards of the **Sultana**, in front of the wheel-house, knocking down a platform amidships, on which the soldiers slept.
St Louis Oak: snagged opposite Providence, Missouri river, Mar 18. Saved from sinking by bulk heading.
Swan: sunk & lost in the Ohio, near Marietta, Nov 10: bound from Pittsburg to St Louis: no insurance.
Suwanee: struck on the Grand Chain, in the Ohio river, & sunk. A total loss.
Sea Gull: injured by striking an abutment in Ky river.
Trenton: burnt at Cincinnati, Feb 27.
Tributary: burnt at Louisville, Dec 29.
Talma: sunk in March, near new Madrid: raised.
Time and Tide: struck a snag near Claiborne Island, in the Mississippi, Feb 16, & sunk in 8 feet water: raised.
Telegraph: burst a pipe at Louisville, Apr 3, by which one of her engineers was injured.
Uncle Ben: injured by collision with the **Martha Washington**, on Jun 14, near Rome, Ohio river.
Uncle Sam: injured at Bayou Sara on Jul 18, by running on the wreck of the **Old Clipper**.
W H Day: sunk in Arkansas river; boat & cargo a total loss.
Wyandotte: sunk to her hurricane roof, & lost, at Paw Paw island, on Nov 21, by striking a snag as she was rounding to put on shore some deck passengers who were quarrelling. From 25 to 30 persons were drowned, principally deck passengers.
White Rose: destroyed by fire at Cairo, Ill: boat & cargo a total loss.
Westwood: burst her boilers 12 miles below New Orleans. 12 to 15 lives lost, & several persons severally injured.
Yazoo: sunk & totally lost near New Orleans by running on a raft, Mar 31.
Yallabusha: burst her boilers opposite Donaldsonville, La. 30 or 40 lives lost; boat burnt; cargo a total loss.
Zachary Taylor: ran into the wood, on the Ohio river, & lost chimneys.

New Hat & Shoe Store: on Pa ave, near 4½ st. –John Maguire, Fashionable Hatter

Furniture at auction: on Apr 16, at the residence of Mr Kap, corner of Bridge & Green sts, Gtwn, his stock of furniture. –Edw S Wright, auct

The steamboat **Champion**, plying on the Mississippi river burst her boiler on Apr 7 opposite New Orleans, killing the engineer & 3 firemen, besides injuring some others. [Apr 18th newspaper: Capt Brown was at the wheel at the time of the accident, & was blown with the wheel & a portion of one of the boilers nearly 50 feet into the air, & came down in the hold of the boat, miraculously escaping death. He was slightly scalded & bruised one leg.]

Mrd: on Apr 12, in PG Co, Md, by Rev Mr Richardson, Mr Wm McLean, of Wash City, to Miss Caroline Amelia Locker, of the former place.

Died: on Apr 13, at Dunbarton, [Heights of Gtwn,] after a protracted illness, Miss Eleanor Ann, only daughter of Geo C & Ann T Washington. Her funeral is at half-past 4 o'clock on Sun, Apr 15.

Died: on Apr 12, after a painful illness, of consumption, about 42 years of age, Martin King. His funeral is this afternoon, at 3 o'clock, from the residence of Mr Hughes, on the corner of 2nd & G sts.

MON APR 16, 1849
Col Fremont & his party: New Mexico, Feb 6, 1849. Mr Vincent Haler came in last night, having the night before reached the Little Colorado settlement, with 3 or 4 others, including Mr King & Mr Proulin. Manuel, [a Christian Indian of the Cosumne tribe, in the valley of San Joaquin,] gave way to a feeling of despair, & begged Vincent Haler to shoot him. Failing to find death in that form, he made his way back to camp. Carver raved during the night: in the morning he wandered off, & probably died. He was not seen again. Sorrel laid down to die. They built him a fire, & Morin, who was in a dying condition, & snow-blind, remained with him. These two did not probably last till the next morning. Rohrer became despondent. Haler, Scott, Hubbard, & Martin agreed if any one of them should give out the others were not to wait for him to die, but to push on. At night Kerne's party encamped a few hundred yards from Haler's. With this party, were the 3 brothers, Kerne, Capt Cathcart, McKie, Andrews, Stepperfeldt, & Talpin. Ferguson & Beadle remained behind. Haler learnt that Rohrer & Andrews wandered off & died. They say they saw their bodies. Hubbard gave out, & was left to die. They built him a fire & then left him. Scott gave out. He too was built a fire & then left behind. Godey & Haler turned back in search of the living & the dead. Scott was yet alive, & is saved! Hubbard was dead, but still warm. From Kerne's party, next met, they learnt the deaths of Andrews & Rohrer; they they met Ferguson, who told them that Beadle died the night before. Manuel was found alive. Vincent Haler, with Martin & Bacon, all on foot, & bringing Scott on horseback, arrived at the outside Pueblo on the Little Colorado. Santa Fe, Feb 17, 1849: I will leave Santa Fe this evening. I dine this evening with the Govn'r, Col Washington, before I follow my party. –From Col Fremont's Letters [Letters to the N Y papers mention the safe arrival of Mrs Fremont at Panama on the 27th ult, on her way to Calif.]

Appointment by the Sec of the Interior: John E Barrow, [& not Washington Barrow,] of Tenn, to be Indian Sub-Agent at Council Bluffs.

Mrd: on Apr 11, in N Y C, by Rev Mr Shaw, Chas J Nourse, jr, to Margarette T, daughter of Wm Kemble.

Mrd: on Apr 11, in Manville, R I, by Rev Mr Penny, Gen Leslie Combs, of Lexington, Ky, & Mary E Man, of Cumberland, R I.

Wm H Harrison, a grandson of Pres Harrison, & well known in Cincinnati as a highly promising young man, who accompanied Col Webb's Calif party on their way to the gold region, was of the number who died of the cholera on the Rio Grande.

Mr Eugene Grousset, one of the most eminent merchants of N Y died at New Orleans on Apr 3. He had gone thither in a declining state of health in the hope that the change of climate would be beneficial.

Orphans Court of Wash Co, D C. Letters of administration on the personal estate of Rachael M Thrift, late of Wash Co, deceased. –Edw Swann, adm

City Ordinance-Wash. Act for the relief of M Butler: fine imposed for an alleged violation relative to bread, is hereby remitted, proved he pay the costs of prosecution.

TUE APR 17, 1849
The great case of Morgan Hinchman, who sued his mother & others to recover damages for conspiracy, in confining him in the insane hospital on the pretense he was a lunatic, in order that his relatives might get possession of his property, was brought to a close at Phil on Fri, after pending for 5 weeks, by the jury rendering a verdict against Saml S Richie, Edw Richie, John M White, John Lippincott, John L Kite, Geo M Elkinton, & Eliz R Shoemaker, & assessing the damages at $10,000. The jury acquitted Anna W Hinchman, Philip Garrett, Joshua M Worthington, Benj H Warder, Wm Biddle, Thos Wister, jr, & Dr Griscom.

Mrd: on Apr 10, in Raleigh, by Rev Dr Mason, Dr Chas E Johnson to Miss Frances L, daughter of Gov Jas Iredell.

Died: yesterday, in Wash City, Wm S Coody, of the Cherokee nation-one of the reps of the old Western Cherokees. His funeral is from his late lodgings at Mr Shackelford's, opposite Willard's Hotel, at 3:30 o'clock, today.
[Masonic obsequies notice: interring with Masonic rites, the remains of our late sojourning brother, Wm S Coody. –G A Schwarzman, sec]

The undersigned will offer for sale at public auction: on Apr 25, at his residence, about 2 miles west of Poolesville, Montg Co, Md: all his personal property, consisting of 18 valuable negroes; large stock of valuable yoke of oxen, sheep, hogs, & all his household & kitchen furniture. Also all his real estate: his home farm containing 600 acres of land, with a large brick mansion. Second, a farm adjoining the lands of John Young & others: 360 acres. Third, 2 valuable wood lots: 63 & 43 acres, respectively. –Hezekiah Trundle

Furnished rooms to rent: Mrs Garret Anderson: rooms over the Book, Stationery, & Music store on Pa ave, between 11th & 12th sts.

In Chancery: Esau Pickrell & others against the heirs of Hannah G Corcoran & Stanislaus Murray, her administrator. The creditors of the late Hannah G Corcoran, deceased, who have not exhibited their claims against her estate, are to do so on or before Apr 27. –W Redin, auditor

Official: appointments by the Pres:
J Prescott Hall, of N Y, to be U S Atty for the southern district of N Y.
Chas Bingham, of Ala, to be U S Marshal for the southern district of Ala.
Jas Scott, of Indiana, to be Register of the Land Ofc at Jeffersonville, Ind.
Ofcrs of the Customs: Collectors: Philip Greely, jr, for the district of Boston.
Saml J Peters, for the district of New Orleans.
Benj S Hawley, for the district of Apalachicola, Fla.
Naval Ofcrs: Philip Hone, for the district of N Y.
Robt B Stille, for the district of New Orleans.
Manuel J Garcia, for the district of New Orleans.
Appointment by the Sec of the Interior:
John W Crockett, to be Com'r to superintend bldg the new Custom House, New Orleans. [See Apr 23rd newspaper for corrections to the above.]

$10 reward for delivery of a bay horse that strayed from the subscriber.
-John S Suit, Bladensburg

From the Delaware Republican: Obit-died: Cmder Irvine Shubrick: on Thu last. He was a native of S C, & had been in the Navy 35 years. During the war with England he served under Cmdor Decatur, & was with him in the severe action of the President with the British squadron & with Decatur in the frig **Guerriere**, & was in the Algerine squadron in 1816. In 1832, while 1st Lt of the frig **Potomac**, bearing the flag of Cmdor Downes, he commanded the expedition of sailors & marines who landed on the island of Sumatra, & after a short conflict with the Malays, took possession of the town of Qualla Batoo, & broke up a horde of pirates who had recently murdered the crew & capt of an American ship. In 1846 Cmder Shubrick returned from a cruise in the Gulf of Mexico & on the coast of Brazil with his health much shattered. A firm faith in Christ his Redeemer gave the crowning grace to his character. -F

Farm for sale: 5 miles from Gtwn: adjoining the farm of the late Danl Kurtz: contains about 240 acres, with a small dwlg-house. Apply to Mrs E Cartwight, on the premises, or to Wm H Godey, Gtwn.

Cook wanted: a colored woman, as a good plain cook, a slave. Apply to Geo W Phillips, Exchange Ofc.

For sale: a pair of bay horses. Sold because the owner has no use for them. Inquire at John Sheet's stables, on the Island.

WED APR 18, 1849
John R Bleecker, a venerable citizen, whose name more than half a century was identified with business interests in Albany, died on Apr 12, full of years. He had accumulated a large fortune, but retained the utmost simplicity in his mode of living.
–Albany Atlas

The Roman republic, in order to raise the springs of war, propose to sell the painting & other objects of art that decorate the Vatican. Pope Pius IX protests against it as sacrilege, & declares in advance he will recognize no such sale.

In PG Co Court, sitting as a Court of Equity. Apr Term, 1849. Jas H M Dunlop, by S S Williams, guardian, vs Richd Estep, adm de bonis non of Henderson Magruder. Ordered that the sale made & reported by Saml S Williams, trustee appointed to make the sale of the real estate of Jas H M Dunlop, infant, be ratified & confirmed. The report states the amount of sale to be $5,151.36. –A C Magruder, C J -John B Brooke, Clerk PG Co Court

New Piano, the manufacture & invention of J J Wise, of Balt, Md, contains important improvements upon any heretofore made. –N Y Tribune

Appointments by the Pres: to be Postmaster:
Abraham Goodwin, Paterson, N J
Wm F Pope, Little Rock, Ark
Henry Rhoads, Reading, Pa
F S Latham, Memphis, Tenn
Thos H Sill, Erie, Pa

R T Morsell, Atty at Law: practices in the Courts of D C & Md & Va.

For sale, a small farm in PG Co, belonging to the estate of Jas Moore, deceased, about 2 miles east of Bladensburg, adjoining the lands of Mr Ferrall & Judge Dorsey, containing 50 acres: land has some improvements. –Jos Ingle, agent

A new Post Ofc has been established at Lewisville, Chester Co, Pa, & it is daily supplied by way of Newark, Delaware.

Mrd: on Apr 10, at Oakland, near Pittsburg, by Rev D H Riddle, D D, Alex'r Gordon to Miss Catharine Edwards, both of Pittsburg.

Died: on Apr 16, Mrs Margaret Williams, after a lingering illness, leaving 2 dutiful sons to mourn the loss of an affectionate mother. Her funeral will take place from the residence of her son, Wm Patterson, on A st south, between 3rd & 4th sts, at 3 o'clock, on this day, Apr 18.

Information wanted: of Wm B Robertson, who left his father's residence, in Wash, D C, about 4 years past. He is a carpenter by trade, dark hair, stout made, & about 5 feet 6 or 8 inches high. Confer a favor by addressing a letter to his father in Washington. –Henry B Robertson

Beautiful country seat for sale: the subscriber will sell his dwlg-house & farm, consisting of 80 acres, on the road leading from Gtwn to Fairfax Courthouse, adjoining the plantation of Cmdor Jones, & opposite the *Salona Farm*, owned by Mr Sherman. The house is 2 story, nearly new. Inquire of Mr E Sherman, opposite the premises. –S S Randall

Died: on Apr 14, at the Patapsico Institute, Md, Hon John Phelps, formerly of Vt, aged 73 years.

THU APR 19, 1849

Orphans Court of Wash Co, D C. Letters of administration on the personal estate of John Boyle, late of said county, deceased. –Catherine Boyle, Cornelius Boyle, adms

On Mar 21 last, Mr T B Macaulay was installed as Lord Rector of the Univ of Glasgow.

Appointment by the Pres: Michel Musson to be Postmaster, at New Orleans, La.

Whig candidate, Hon Philip Ripley, was chosen Mayor of Hartford, Conn, by a large majority.

A few days ago Field Marshal Sir George Nugent, Bart, K C B, expired at his residence, Westhorpe, Little Marlow, England, at the advanced age of 92 years. He was the oldest genr'l ofcr in the army. Sir George entered the service on Jul 5, 1773, which is the date of his ensign's commission. He served throughout the first American war, having gone out when a Lt, & was employed in the expedition up Hudson's river, for the relief of Gen Burgoyne's army; & was present at the capture of *Fort Montgomery* & *Fort Clinton*. He returned in 1783 a Lt Colonel. During the whole of the Irish rebellion, Maj Gen Nugent commanded the northern district of Ireland. In Jun, 1846, he became one of the nine Field Marshals of England. Since 1796 he has been Captain or Keeper of St Mawe's Castle. –London Daily News

Wash Corp: 1-Bill for the relief of Emily Jones, excx of the late Thos P Jones: agreed to. 2-Ptn from Jos Borrows & others: referred to the Cmte on Improvements. 3-Duly elected police magistrates: John D Clark, Wm Thompson, & Peter M Pearson. 4-Cmte of Claims: asked to be discharged from the further consideration of the ptn of C Shedd. Same cmte: asked to be discharged from the further consideration of the ptn of Timothy O'Neale.

Hagley for sale: the farm on which it is, contains 1,100 acres: in King Geo Co, about 1 mile from a good landing place on the Rappahannock river. Improvements consist of a comfortable though plain mansion, sufficiently large to accommodate a family. Besides the mansion, there is a school-house. –J G Taliaferro

$100 reward for the recovery of my man Richard, about 20 years of age, mottled complexion, features being more like that of a white man than the negro race.
–John Taylor, jr, Port Royal, Caroline Co, Va

The Republic, a daily Whig Administration paper, will be published in Wash City, on Jun 13 next, committed to the exclusive care of Alex'r C Bullitt & John O Sargent.
–Gideon & Co

Orphans Court of Wash Co, D C. Letters of administration on the personal estate of Jas H Chezum, late of said county, deceased. –Catherine Chezum, admx N B: All claims to be left with W Lenox, Atty at Law.

Mrd: on Apr 17, by Rev Wm H Pitcher, Mr John Wm McElfresh to Miss Eliza Jane Langley, all of Wash City.

Mrd: on Apr 17, by Rev Jas B Donelan, Jas W Stewart to Mary Ann Smith, both of Wash City.

N Y, Apr 16, 1849: The wife of Jas Monahun stepped from the South Brooklyn ferry boat with her 2 children, & said, "I cannot find their father."
Monahun, her husband, allured by the many inducements to emigrate to the U S, left the county of Waterford, Ireland, about 3 years ago, & came to N Y, leaving her & 2 little ones in the care of his father. The last letter received from him was about a year ago, dated Wmsburg, opposite N Y, where he worked for a gentleman on 10th st. The children are now ages 4 & 6 years. She has not found her husband. The N Y Correspondent tells this story in the hopes it will find Jas Monahun.

Died: on Apr 5, in Winchester, Va, at the residence of his son, Wm L Bent, Capt Lemuel Bent, aged about 83 years, & a resident of that town for almost half a century.

Died: on Apr 9, at his residence in Loudoun Co, Va, Joshua Osburn, aged 71 years. He represented his fellow citizens in both branches of the Legislature & in the Convention which amended the State constitution

FRI APR 20, 1849
From the Custis recollections & private memoirs of the life & character of Washington. Wherever Washington established a home, whether temporary or fixed, whether the log huts of Morristown or the Valley Forge, the Pres' Mansions in N Y or Phil, or his own beloved *Mount Vernon*-every where order, method, punctuality, & economy reigned. The expenses of the Pres' Mansion were settled weekly; Washington was remarkably fond of fish; Francis was the first Steward of Washington; the chief cook was Hercules, familiarly termed Uncle Harkless, a dark brown man; the Coachman, was John Fagan, by birth a Hessian, tall & burly in person, an accomplished coachman in every respect. John Krause succeeded Fagan: bred in the Austrian cavalry, was an excessive smoker, his meersbaum [a tobacco pipe,] never being out of his mouth, excepting at meals or on the coach-box. The stables consisted of 10 coach & saddle horses, & 2 white chargers, a coachman & 2 grooms. Of the charger, the Pres usually rode the horse named Prescott. The other charger was named Jackson, from having run away with Maj Jackson, aid-de-camp to the Pres, when coming into Princeton, en route from N Y to Phil, in 1790. Private dinner was served at 3 o'clock, the public one at 4 o'clock.

Appointment by the Pres: Nathl Young, to be Collector of the Customs at Wilmington, District of Delaware.

Fred'k Billings, the youth convicted of forgery at the present term of the Criminal Court, was released from prison last Tue, & given up to his relatives. [Jun 13th newspaper: Fred'k Billings, of Wash, & Geo Northerman, of Balt, convicted in N Y of robbery at the Irving House, have been sentenced to the State Prison-the former for 2 years, & the latter for 3.]

New mode of treating Epilepsy: obliterating the caliber of one or both common carotid arteries by means of ligature. The artery is tied at the upper margin of the omobyoid muscle. After 14 days the ligature came away. It is now a month since this procedure was performed on a young man, & he has not experienced any return of his complaint.

Mrd: on Apr 17, by Rev Smith Pyne, D D, Rector of St John's Church, Robt King Stone, M D, to Margaret F, daughter of Thos Ritchie, all of Wash City.

From an address by Rev Dr Sutton, of the North Church, in New Haven, Conn, at the funeral of the late Deacon Nathan Beers, who died on Feb 10 last, lacking 14 days of 96 years of age. He was a captain in the army of the Revolution, & enjoyed the intimate acquaintance of Washington & Lafayette. He was one of the ofcrs who had charge of Maj Andre during the short time between his sentence & execution, & received from him a remarkable likeness of himself drawn with a pen the night before his death, now deposited in the Trumbull Gallery of Yale College.

$5 reward for runaway mulatto boy Dudly Wilson, 10 years of age. He ran away from the residence of Mr A Ray, north of Wash City, where he was hired.
-H R Maryman, Capitol Hill

Obit-died: on Mar 26, in New Orleans, Mr Geo Cooke, late of New Orleans, of a sudden & brief attack of Asiatic cholera. He was an artist, especially a portrait & historical painter. He spent 5 years in Europe, & studied in the schools of Italy, France, Flanders, & England. He was a man of genius in the strictest sense.

Lost or stolen in the Market yesterday, a green silk & steal bead purse, containing a two $10 notes of the Bank of Washington, & other moneys. Reward of $50 for recovery of the money & information that will lead to the conviction of the thief.
—Mrs E H Brawner, Pa ave, near 3rd st.

I hereby caution merchants & others not to trust any person or persons on my account, as I will pay no debts unless contracted by me in person. -H Harvey

Orphans Court of Wash Co, D C. Letters of administration on the personal estate of Stanislaus Tench, late of said county, deceased. —Ann Tench, admx
-Thos B Tench, Adm

SAT APR 21, 1849
Miss H McCormick & sister, having returned to the city, will open school on Apr 23, at their former place of residence, on 4½ st, south side of the ave, in the 4th house in the row belonging to Mr Ulysses Ward.

Servant at auction: by order of the Orphans Court of Wash Co, D C, sale on Apr 24, in front of the Centre Market, negro man John Thomas, belonging to the estate of Simon Frazier, deceased. By order of the administrator. -A Green auct

Rev Dr Southward, of N Y, issued an edict to his parish-which he calls a pastoral-forbidding them to marry any one to whom they may be related nearer than 5th degree.

The emigration to Calif: the steamship **Falcon**, Capt Thompson, with the mails for the Pacific, will leave North River this afternoon for Chagres. Maj Allen, a passenger, goes to Calif as postofc agent, with the power to appoint postmasters in Calif & Oregon. Since the gold excitement commenced, up to Apr 17, there have left the different ports in the U S for San Francisco, etc, 309 vessels, 226 of which intended proceeding round the Horn & through the Straits of Magellan; about 50 for Chagres, & the remainder to Vera Cruz, Brasos, etc. These vessels took out nearly 20,000 passengers.

I certify that Robt Isherwood brought before me as an estray, trespassing on his enclosures, a black cow. –Jas Crandell, J P [Owner to prove property, pay charges, & take her away. –Robt Isherwood, living 1 miles east of the Capitol.]

MON APR 23, 1849
Fire broke out at midnight last Sat in a stable attached to the tavern occupied by Mr J H Clarvoe, on 7th st. The houses occupied by Mr Clarvoe & Mrs Luskey as taverns were destroyed. Mr Sinclair's house was also on fire, & suffered damage, to the amount of $300. Mr West's brick stable & the grocery warehouse of Messrs Morsell & Wilson were saved by the firemen. The 2 infant children of Mr Geo Sinclair were rescued from the flames by Mr Wm Feeny, who, while the room in which the children slept was on fire, rushed in & snatched them from impending destruction.

From Vt: part of an address by Mr Geo Fred'k Houghton, respecting his hero: 'In memory of
Col Seth Warner, Esquire
Who departed this life December 26, A. D 1784,
In the 42d year of his age.
Triumphant at our armies' head,
Whose martial glory struck a panic dread;
Thy warlike deeds engraven on this stone,
Tell future ages what a hero's done.
Full sixteen battles he did fight.
For to procure his country's right;
Oh, this brave hero, he did fall
By Death, who ever conquers all.
When this you see,
Remember me."

Household & kitchen furniture at auction: on Apr 25, at the residence of the late Sarah Voorhees, deceased, on 17th st, between H & I sts. –Jabez Travers, adm -Martin & Wright, aucts

Hon Thos J Henley, of Indian, has decided not to be a candidate for re-election.

Dr R Young, Chief Clerk of the Navy Dept, has resigned, his resignation to take effect Jun 1. –Nat Whig

City Ordinance-Wash: 1-Act for the relief of Emily G Jones, excx of the late Thos P Jones: the Mayor is authorized to pay her the sum of $212.10, being the balance due Fred'k Crowley, contractor, for work done on 11th st west per act approved May 29, 1845, as per certificates of Surveyor & Com'r, assigned to the said Thos P Jones.

Casualty in Carroll Co, Md, on Wed last: Mr Jacob Schriner, of that county, with his family, were seated at the dinner table, when one of his sons, who previously at time had given indications of insanity, left the room, & returned with a double-barrelled pistol in his hand, with which he shot his brother, who was at the time, with the rest of the family, sitting at the table, killing him almost instantly. There was no difficulty between the brothers. He was taken to Balt on Fri & placed in a hospital.
–Balt Republican

On Mon last, Miss Emeline Newton, aged 20 years, daughter of Mr O S Newton, in a fit of somnambulism left her room at Mr Willard Weeks', where she had been staying for some months past, & wandered from the house. Her body was found in the river under the dam near the foundry of Messrs Brown & Gage on Tue afternoon.
–East Bennington Vt Advertiser

Capt Martin, of the schnr **Abby Hammond**, lost at sea, on the passage from Aux Cayes for Boston, reports that the schnr sunk so rapidly that $15,000 in specie which was on board went down with her.

In announcing the appointment of Revenue Ofcrs for the District of New Orleans, on Apr 17, the ofcs in 2 cases were transposed. They should read:
Robt B Stille to be Surveyor & Manuel J Garcia to be Naval Ofcr.

Mr Philip Dougherty, of Harrisburg, Pa, was robbed, a few days ago, of $30,000, in scrip & cash. A colored man & his wife were arrested, the whole of it found in their possession.

Died: on Apr 15, in Smithville, N C, Capt Leslie Chase, Assist Quartermaster U S Army. He graduated at the Military Academy in Jun, 1838, & was assigned to the 2nd Regt of Artl. He served with distinction in the early part of the war with Mexico, receiving a brevet for Capt for gallant conduct in the battles of May 8 & 9. In 1847 he was placed on duty in the War Dept, as acting Judge Advocate of the army. Soon after, in 1847, he received the appointment of Assist Quartermaster, & proceeded to New Orleans, where he was employed in erecting a commodious hospital for the wounded & disabled soldiers of the Mexican war.

Died: on Apr 20, of scarlet fever, Eliz C, youngest daughter of Capt A V & Mary Frazer, aged 1 year & 9 months.

TUE APR 24, 1849
From the Lowell Journal of Apr 18. By publication of a letter from a Lowell emigrant at Panama, a singular circumstance has been brought to light. 20 years ago a young man, a son of Mrs Mary Wellington, of this city, [afterwards Mrs Bailey,] then only about 20, left the city to better his condition. He had not been heard from until this week. Changes have been going on in his family relations: his mother has died, & an only brother has gone to the gold regions of Calif. Intelligence was brought to us that he is Capt Wellington, cmder of the schnr **Constellation**. Capt Wellington has a sister & other relatives in this city. The letter below is highly characteristic of the spirit he cherished at the time he left home, & alludes to the brother who has just left for Calif. "N Y, May 28, 1829. Mother, tomorrow I shall sail on board the ship **Henry Kneeland**, bound for Savannah & Liverpool. Going to see old England. Nothing more in particular to say, only if you cannot get a place in a store, or any place for John better than the machine shop-hang him. Yours, T L Wellington"

Trustee's sale: by 2 deed of trust, executed by Ahrend Ahrens & wife, to the undersigned, one for the use of John Gibson's excx, & the other for the use of Knabe & Gachle, & both dated Sep 23, 1846, recorded in the ofc of the County Court of Pr Wm Co, Va: sale on May 7, the following real estate: 2 tracts of land in said county one of which is called *Gilead*-395 acres, more or less, & the other is called *Gray's tract*-184 acres & 5 poles, more or less. Mr Ahrens now occupies the premises & will show the same. -John Williams, trustee

We announce the decease of Mrs Maria Smith, wife of Hon Truman Smith, of Conn, at the residence of Chas Treichel. –Phil Evening Bulletn

Official: Appointments by the Pres:
Collectors of the Customs:
Bela B Haskell, Waldoborough, Maine
Danl Remick, Kennebunk, Maine
Wm B Smith, Machias, Maine
Surveyors of the Customs:
John B Abell, Town Creek, Md
Wm Coad, St Mary's River, Md
Postmasters:
Richd L Wilson, Chicago, Ill
Abner Austin, Lynn, Mass
Nathl Wilson, Lawrence, Mass
Abraham Jonas, Quincy, Ill
Julius M Ackley, Ithaca, N Y

Wm K Stiles, known in this community as incumbent of the ofc of Collector of State Taxes for the 4th Rep District, has been accused of having embezzled $28,049. –New Orleans Picayune

Died: on Apr 23, in Wash City, Jane Gordon, relict of the late Geo Gordon, aged 82 years. Her funeral is today at 3 o'clock, from the residence of her son, Jas Gordon, near the Navy Yard.

Died: on Apr 21, of scarlet fever, Gertrude, only daughter of Lt Geo M Totten, U S Navy, aged 5 years & 5 months.

Died: on Mar 28, at Lexington, Mo, Dr Wm D Digges, in his 35th year. He was graduated with credit at the Univ of Balt, practiced his profession for several years in his native county of PG, in Md, & emigrated some years ago to Missouri. His early death is a severe blow to his bereaved widow & afflicted relatives.

Household & kitchen furniture at auction: on Apr 27, by order of the Orphans Court of Wash Co, D C: at the late residence of Jas H Chezum, deceased, on C st south, between 12th & 13th sts. –C W Boteler, auct

Clermont for sale: the residence of the late Gen John Mason, in Fairfax Co, Va, is offered for sale by his excs. The estate is about 4 miles from Alexandria, comprising about 320 acres. The mansion & its appurtenances are of the most ample & commodious description. The premises will be shown by Mr Butler, the overseer. For terms apply to Maynadier Mason, at Gtwn, D C, or to the subscriber, the acting exc, by letter at Winchester, Va. -Jas M Mason

For rent: comfortable house in the Seven Bldgs, recently in occupied by Lt Col Freeman. Possession give on May 1. –F Forrest

WED APR 25, 1849
On Sat, at Ripks' cotton factory, Manayunk, near Phil, Alexander Russell, aged 17 years, had his right arm torn off at the elbow when he caught it in some machingery.

Public sale of valuable improved property in Wash City: by deed of trust, dated Jan 2, 1840, recorded in Liber W B 87, pages 27, 27, & 29, of the land records of Wash Co: sale on May 18, all that south half of lot 19 in square 289, on 12th st west, with a 2 story frame dwgl. –C H Wiltberger, trustee
-A Green, auctioneer

Spring & Summer Clothing: J Galligan & Son, Pa ave, 1 door east of 7th st.

From Balt, Apr 24. Dr Ducatel, long known as State Geologist for Md, & until of recent years acting in that capacity, died suddenly yesterday.

Died: on Apr 24, in Wash City, Rev Gamaliel Bailey, aged 84 years. His funeral is this morning at 11 o'clock, from the residence of his son, corner of E & 8th sts.

Died: on Apr 24, Geo W Clarke, aged 30 years. His funeral is tomorrow, at 2 o'clock, from his late residence, near the Navy Yard.

Died: on Apr 17, in Lexington, Va, Mrs Susan Preston Taylor, relict of the late Hon Wm Taylor, & sister of Gov McDowell & Mrs Senator Benton. Mrs Taylor was one of the kindest & most generous of her sex. Her death will be severely felt, especially by her grandchildren, whose father, Col Weller, is now far away. -Union

Died: on Apr 24, in Wash City, after an illness of 14 years, Miss Wilhelmina Ann Rogers, formerly of King Geo Co, Va, in her 19th year.

Teacher wanted for District school #7, in First Election District in Chas Co, Md: salary of $300 or upwards. –Jas L Brawner, Sec, Port Tobacco, Md

Splendid new style Buffalo Tuck Combs, for sale. –T Bastianelli & Co, under Brown's Hotel.

For sale: 3 houses & lots: on 12 st, on 10th st, & on 9th st. Inquire of T B Griffin, Shoe Dealer, Pa ave, between 9th & 10th sts. N B: the above property wil be sold at a bargain, as the person to whom it belongs wishes to leave the city. -News

Wash Corp: 1-Cmte of Claims: bill for the relief of Jas C Crusor: passed. Same cmte: payment of Matthew Waite's claim: passed. Same cmte: bill for the relief of John Delaney: passed. 2-Bill for the relief of Wm Rupp: passed. 4-Ptn of Selby Parker & others: passed to the Cmte on Improvements. 5-Bill for the relief of Jas Crutchett: ordered to lie on the table. 6-Ptn of Henry Smith, praying remission of a fine: referred to the Cmte of Claims. 7-Ptn of Lawrence Callan, reported a bill for his relief: read. 8-Bill for the relief of J Lucchesi: passed. 9-Bill for the relief of Henry Turner: passed.

The following named gentlemen have been invited by the Sec of War to attend the examination of the Cadets of the Military Academy at West Point on the 1st Mon in Jun next:

1-John S Abbott, of Maine
2-Hon Horace Mann, of Mass
3-Capt Danl Tyler, of Conn
4-Jerome Fuller, of N Y
5-John L Gow, of Pa
6-Capt John H B Latrobe, of Md
7-Capt Patrick M Henry, of N C
8-Gen J McCaleb Wiley, of Ala
9-Col R W Burnet, of Ohio
10-Gen J McCaleb Wiley, of Ala
11-Henry J Ballard, of Louisiana
12-Hon Jefferson Davis, of Miss
13-Col Wm T Stockton, of Fla
14-Dr H Houghton, of Iowa
15-Gen Rufus King, of Wisc

These appointments have been made on the recommendation of the Reps & Delegates from their respective Congressional districts. In addition to these, the Executive has the appointment of 10 Cadets at large, irrespective of residence in any Congressional district.

Yesterday, the Sword voted by the Legislature of Va to Maj Gen Taylor, [now Pres of the U S,] in honor of the distinguished courage & conduct displayed in his victorious achievements in Mexico, was presented to him at the Presidential Mansion.

Thos A Cooper died on Sat, at the residence, in Bristol, Pa, of his son-in-law, Mr Robt Tyler. He was for many years the leading American tragedian, having retired some 10 or 15 years ago, since which time he has filled several political offices of trust & honor.

Mrs Hess has moved to Delaware ave, & is prepared to wit on her friends. Her name is on the door.

Congressional Burying Ground: The Vestry of Washington Parish, which body had charge of this city of the dead, have purchased the square of ground south of the old grave yard, & both grounds are embraced with one enclosure. My attention was arrested by the superb monument erected by filial affection in the memory of our late fellow-citizen, Peter Lenox. It stands upon the eastern avenue.

New invention by Thos J Lovegrove, in Balt City, for the casting of iron pipes, to supersede the ordinary sand mould.

N Y Courier & Enquirer: J Watson Webb advertises that he will sell out his share in the N Y Courier & Enquirer for $20,000, as he is going to Calif. This ridiculous paragraph is going the rounds of the press. We have not offered any portion of it, for sale, & do not intend to sell any of it.

THU APR 26, 1849
The Colony of Connecticut. The colony comprehends what were originally the colony of Connecticut, or Hartford, & that of New Haven, being incorporated into one in 1692, still retaining, by a charter granted to them, all the privileges of their ancient charters. This Colony is bounded by the Massachusetts on the north, N Y on the west, southerly by the Sound, & easterly by RI & a part of Mass. It contains about 210,000 inhabitants.

A young man by the name of Grimes, a clerk in the post ofc at Waterford, N Y, was arrested on a charge of having purloined letters & packages from that ofc, & from the U S mails. –N Y Herald

Appointments by the Pres:
Postmasters:
John S McCully, Trenton, N J
Philo S Johnson, Watertown, N Y
Saml Ware, Kensington, Pa
Thos L Tullock, Portsmouth, N H

Eathen A Warden, Auburn, N Y
Benj T Cook, Binghampton, N Y
Solomon Parmelee, Lockport, N Y
Abner Y Ellis, Springfield, Ill

Citizens of Fayette Co, opposed to the perpetuation of slavery in Ky, held a meeting at Lexington, on Sat,& appointed the following delegation to the Franklin Emancipation Convention:

Edw Oldham	Geo R Trotter	S D McCullough
Saml Shy	Wm Rodes	John T Bruce
M C Johnson	Jas Turner	J J Hunter
R J Breckenridge	W Pullen	Wm K Wallace
H P Lewis	John W Clark	R Pindell
A Vanmeter	Carter R Harrison	Jacob Ashton
C H Barkley	O D Winn	Geo P Jounett
John C Hull	Geo W Sutton	Matthew T Scott
John Curd	John Steele	T Dolan
E A Dudley	Warren Outton	B Kerr

Columbus Enq: Col J S Calhoun left that place Sun last for Santa Fe, to assume the duties of Indian Agent for New Mexico. He will take the route by Nashville, St Louisk, *Fort Independence*, etc. [etc as written.

Salem Register: letters received at Marblehead bring the intelligence of the sudden death, by cholera, of Mr Nathl R Blaney, the leader of the expedition, which is therefore broken up, & the survivors, 7 in number, are on their return to New England. The company sailed from N Y early in Mar.

Mr Jacob B Moore, who was dismissed from a clerkship under Pres Polk, has been appointed Postmaster at San Franciso, Calif, & Agent of the Gen Post Ofc Dept for the Territory of Oregon. He was formerly a Whig editor in Concord, N H, but has resided for some years in this city, & is now Librarian of the Historical Society. An able, upright & most estimable gentleman. –N Y Courier

The U S prize brig **Susan**, under charge of Lt Hunter, of the U S Navy, with whom is associated Passed Midshipman Brodhead, arrived at N Y on Tue, in 76 days from Rio Janeiro. The **Susan** was captured off the harbor of Rio Janeiro, by the U S brig **Perry**, on Feb 6, on suspicion of being engaged in the slave trade.

The Charleston papers announce the death of Mr John Strohecker, in his 74th year, & for 60 years a resident of that city. He was for many years a member of the Municipal Council & of the State Legislature.

Mrs Farnham has succeeded in obtaining 58 female emigrants in the Eastern cities, who are to sail from N Y for Calif this week in the ship **Angelique**.

Official: Dept of State, Apr 24, 1849. Information received from the Consul of the U S at Batavia of the death, on board the English schnr **Bandicott**, of Hobart Town, of Wm L Fulton, on or about Jul 8 last. Mr Fulton was represented to have been a married man, with 2 children, the son of a clergyman. He left America in a whaler- name unknown; the capt's name said to have been Wicks or Weeks. He ran away from the ship at Geography Bay. The ship belonged to New Bedford. He is stated to have been of appearance & language indicating that he "had seen better days." His father is supposed to have been a resident of Maine.

Mrd: on Apr 24, at Pittsburg, Pa, by Rev Dr Herron, Benj Rush, of Phil, son of Hon Richd Rush, to Eliz, daughter & only child of W A Simpson.

Mrd: on Apr 7, at Troy, N Y, by Rev Mr Van Kleeck, Rector of St Paul's Church, Benj Ogle Tayloe, of Wash City, to Phebe, daughter of the late Esaias Warren, of Troy.

Died: on Apr 15, after a very long & distressing illness, Eliz, son of Mr Isaac Holland, of Wash City. Her funeral is this evening, at 4 o'clock, from the residence of her husband, on 17th st.

Died: on Wed, Hugh Galigo, native of Ireland, & for the last 20 years a resident of Wash City. His funeral is today at 4 o'clock, from his residence on 6th st, near H st.

$15 reward for return of a horse stolen on Apr 23, from the farm of the subscriber, near Upper Marlborough. –Chas Clagett

FRI APR 27, 1849
There is an apple tree on the estate of Mr Jos Briggs, on Federal Hill, in Dedham, Mass, supposed to be 10 years old. The tree is second only to that in Duxbury, which is over 100 years old. –Boston Traveller

Some 15 years now past the senior editor of "The Plough, the Loom, & the Anvil," sojourned some days, at *Old Brandon*, on the James river-the venerable residence then of the late Geo E Harrison, a man of refined manners, & for hospitality at once sumptuous, easy, & elegant. Of the recreation provided for his guests, there was laid upon the hall table the celebrated Byrd Manuscript, as it was called. The author, Col Byrd, had been appointed by the British Gov't, long before the Revolution, com'r to run the boundary line between the Old Dominion & the Old North State, & this manuscript was the record of his daily proceedings. Among the items in the manuscript, we find a prescription by Col Byrd for the preparation of "portable food." It ought to find its way into the knapsacks of those who design to wend their way 2,000 miles across to the great diggings in Calif.

National Institute: this Society held a meeting at its Hall in the Patent Ofc some days ago, & the following were elected ofcrs for 1849:
Pres: Peter Force
Vice Presidents: P M F Maury, J G Totten, & Jos Henry
Corr Sec: Walter R Johnson
Rec Sec: Chas F Stansbury
Librarian: J H Causten, jr
Treas: Wm Easby

Charleston, Apr 18: Coast Survey. Arrived in the schnr **Morris**, attached to the U S Coast Survey: her ofcrs:
John N Maffit, Lt Commanding
Ed C Anderson, Lt Geo W Rodgers, Acting Master
R W Shufeldt, Passed Midshipman
Allan McLane, Passed Midshipman
J L Gamble, Draughtsman

Mrs S Masi has several large rooms, 2 fronting on the avenue, with which she would be pleased to accommodate those wishing board. Gentlemen wishing only their meals can also be accommodated.

Wm H Ainsworth, 18 years old, was run over by the railroad cars at Worcester, Mass, on Mon, & had both of his legs taken off, causing his death in a short time.

Appointments by the Pres: Collectors of the Customs:
Wm M Gallagher, Presque Isle, Pa.
Cornelius L Russell, Cuyahoga, Ohio
Chas E Avery, Michilimackinac, Mich

On Apr 20 the steamer **New Orleans** sailed from New Orleans for Port Lavaca, with Gov't stores & the following passengers, viz: Maj Gen Worth & family, Maj Deas, Maj Longstreet, Maj Dashiell, Paymaster, & Capt Sprague, of the U S Army.

$10 reward for return of strayed or stolen Bay Mare. –John Pettibone, at his Coal Yard, or Ice Depot, near the Long Bridge.

Abraham Wilkinson, one of the founders of Pawtucket, has breathed his last, in his 83rd year. Mr W, with his brothers, & Saml Slater, introduced & put into operation the cotton manufacturing business.

United States of America. Circuit Court of Wash Co, D C-in Chancery. John Baldwin, cmplnt, vs Wm E Allen, Moses Allen, Dennie Sayre, & others, dfndnts. The bill states that the cmplnt was the rightful proprietor of various certificates, for $1,000 each, issued to him by the U S, under the act of Congress, approved Sep 1, 1841, directing certificates to be issued in favor of U S citizens upon awards made in pursuance of the convention with the Republic of Mexico, concluded at Wash Apr 11, 1839, entitled: "An act to carry into effect a convention between the U S & the Mexican Republic," approved Jun 12, 1840-, that the cmplnt, to raise money, induced dfndnt, Dennie Sayre, to accept a bill at 60 days for about $500, drawn upon said Sayre by the cmplnt, for his accommodation, he, the said John Baldwin, to pay the said bill; &, as collateral security to the said Dennie Sayre that said Baldwin would pay the bill, he deposited with Sayre's five of the said certificate, whereof 3, the subjects of this bill, were numbered 983, 992; that the cmplnt did pay & take up the said bill; that Sayre never paid or advanced to the cmplnt any money for the certificates; that when the cmplnt demanded of Sayre the return of said certificate, Sayre said they were locked up for safe-keeping in the strong box of a friend then out of N Y C & when he returned he, said Sayre, would get them & return them to the cmplnt, which he has failed to do. The bill further alleges that the cmplnt never did assign the said certificates, or either of them, to the dfndnts, or either of them, & never received any value for them; that the certificates 983, 984, & 992, have by some means passed out of the possession of said Dennie Sayre, & been deposited in the ofc of the First Comptroller of the U S Treasury, Wash City, & that the dfndnts, Moses Allen & Wm E Allen, or one or both, claim an interest in them, have received thereon from the U S Treas the interest thereon up to Apr 30, 1843, & also the 5 first instalments, & are endeavoring to have & receive the residue due thereon. The bill alleges that the writings on the back, purporting to be assignments made by the cmplnt, & attested by Thos W Harvey, as false, feigned, & forged. The said dfndnts, Wm E Allen, Moses Allen, & Dennie Sayre, not having appeared, nor answered to said bill, it appearing to the Court that the said dfndnts, Wm, Moses, & Dennie, are absent from D C, residing elsewhere, it is, on motion of cmplnt, that the 3rd Mon of Oct next be assigned for the appearance of said absentees. –John A Smith, clerk -Geo M Bibb, of Counsel for cmplnt

Mrd: on Apr 23, at Balt, by Rev Mr Backus, Mr Andrew J Larner, of Wash City, to Miss Mary Laura Morrow, of Balt.

Died: on Apr 17, at Huntsvulle, Ala, of consumption, in her 22nd year, Miss M Virginia Wilson, daughter of H G Wilson, of Gtwn, D C.

Died: on Apr 25, Mary Catharine, eldest daughter of Thos C & Olivia Magruder, in her 5th year.

Circuit Court of Wash District. Wm Kirkpatrick against Fred'k Grieb, adm of Henry Grieb. The administrator is notified to attend at my ofc in City Hall, Wash, on May 5 next, when the examination & report will be made in the above case.
—W Redin, Auditor

SAT APR 28, 1849
Naval: Comdor Chas W Morgan will go out in the steam frig **Mississippi** to take command of the squadron in the Mediterranean. —Norfolk Herald

Trustee's sale of valuable Wash City property: pursuant to a decree of the Circuit Court of Wash Co, D C., sitting as a Court of Chancery, in the case of Jos Edmund Law vs Jas Adams, exc, Lloyd N Rogers, & others: sale on May 18 of lots & premises belonging to the estate of Thos Law, deceased: various lots in squares: 228, 229, 260, 295, 324, 382, 575, 633, 637, 685, 689, 690, 692, 693, 694, 705, 732, 742, 743, 744, 766, 770, & 878. On lots 1, 2, & 19, are 3 three story brick houses, at present occupied by the U S Coast Survey. On part of lot 3 in square 690 is a 3 story brick house. Title believed to be indisputable. —Jas Adams, trustee
-E C & G F Dyer, aucts

To let: 3 story brick house on Mass ave, between 6th & 7th sts, just vacated by Col Barnard. Rent $225 per year. Inquire next door of Jas B Phillips, or E Owens, near Willard's Hotel.

New & Fashionable Fancy Goods: prices shall always be low.
-Mrs H Clitch, Pa ave, between 9th & 10th sts.

For sale: large 2 story frame house & 2 lots on First & C sts, Capitol Hill. Apply to the subscriber residing on the premises. —E Elliot

MON APR 30, 1849
Hon John T H Worthington, formerly a Rep in Congress, died on Fri at his residence in Balt Co, Md.

Alleghany Co [Md] Court, on Thu, Jesse D E Quantril, convicted of an assault with intent to kill Mrs Mary E Cowton, of Cumberland, was sentenced to 5 years' imprisonment & to pay a fine of $500.

Duel: An affair of honor came off at Old Point on Thu, between J P Jones & J B Hope, of Hampton, in which both the combatants were wounded, but not mortally.
—Norfolk Beacon

City Ordinances-Wash: 1-Act for the relief of Maria A Queen: fine imposed for an alleged violation of an ordinance relative to hog pens, is remitted: provided she pay the cost of prosecution. 2-Act for the relief of John Delany: to be refunded $5, being the amount paid by him to this Corp for exhibiting a hog. 3-Act to authorize the payment of $32.85 to Matthew Waite's for repairs of the roof of the City Hall, in Apr, 1848.

More returning Californians: the brig **Leander** arrived at Boston from Bermuda, bringing as passengers Chas Jones, Jas Rogers, Benj Dart, & John Harris, who left N Y in the steam propeller **Hartford** for Calif, which vessel put into Bermuda in distress after experiencing several severe hurricanes. -Boston Traveller

From one of Col Fremont's men: from the St Jos Gaz: to Mr A Robidoux, of this place, we are indebted for the following letter from Mr Kern, who was with Col Fremont on his way to Calif. Taos, New Mexico, Feb 11, 1849. On the 26th King was sent ahead with old Bill to Abaque to bring us relief. On Jan 11, he not arriving, the Col started with his mess & Godey in hopes of meeting the relief party. Our provisions had given out & we were living on pare-fleshes & tug-ropes. Already Proulx had perished from hunger & exposure. On the 16th, here commenced our greatest suffering. The company had for its head Vincent Haler, his own lack of courage quickly diffused itself among the men. Up to the 27th we had lost 9 men. I had closed my affairs, & felt that a day or two more would end my troubles, when, about the 28th, we heard a shout, & Godey entered camp. We learned the fate of King's party, who had been found by him on his way down on the 16th. Poor King had died from exhaustion somewhere about the 9th; the rest were in miserable condition, frozen & partly crazed. The loss in dollars has amounted to over $10,000. Adios, Ned Kern

In the last war, whilst the British fleet was in the Chesapeake, & an attack upon Annapolis was dreaded, the keeper of the State House was entrusted with the State records, & removed them to a safe place. The records were later returned, but the roll of the names of persons belonging to the State of Md who had served in the Revolutionary war, & were entitled to a pension, had been purloined. Lately, the Atty Gen put the matter in the hands of Mr Snyder, & on Wed he found the long lost book in the house of Michl Dunn, on south Paca st. The inmates of the house offered considerable resistance to the ofcr taking possession of the book. It was found to be complete & in pretty good condition, though the binding had been removed & the leaves kept together in the form of a roll. –Balt American

Mrd: on Apr 25, in N Y, at the residence of the Hon John J Morgan, by Rt Rev John Hughes, Bishop of N Y, B Jos Semmes, jr, of Gtwn, D C, to Iorantha, daughter of the late Lawrence P Jordan, of the former city.

Died: on Apr 29, after 2 weeks' illness, William Pinkney, infant son of Baruch & Virginia Hall, aged 4 months & 2 weeks. His funeral is this morning, at 10 o'clock, from the residence of Mr Wm H Gunnell, C st.

The fine steamer **General Pike**, on her trip down from Cincinnati to New Orleans, while stopping at Points Coupee to discharge cargo, took fire & burnt to the water's edge on Apr 18. All the passengers & crew were saved, except Col Anthony Butler, of Independence, Texas, who was missing. The boat & cargo are a total loss.

Radetzky, the Austrian general, who commenced & has just completed the campaign in northern Italy, is 82 years of age.

Among the eminent travellers to Calif is Jas Arago, a brother of the astronomer, & a blind person. He has a large fortune in France, but goes out to ascertain the physical character of the country.

TUE MAY 1, 1849

The John Franklin's voyage of discovery: the British Gov't has offered L20,000 as a reward, & Lady Franklin has previously promised L3,000 sterling to the cmder & crew of a vessel that shall succeed in finding the expedition of 1845. [The expedition was sent out by Her Majesty's Gov't for the purpose of discovering a northwest passage between the Atlantic & Pacific Oceans, along the coast of North America, or between Davis' & Behring's Straits.] The expedition consisted of two ships, the ship **Erebus** & the ship **Terror**, commanded by Sir John Franklin & Capt Crozier; the complement of ofcrs & men in the 2 ships being about 138. They were victualled for 3 years. The ships sailed from England on May 19, 1845, & were last seen on Jul 26, 1845, fastened to an iceberg, waiting for the opening of the ice to cross into Lancaster Sound. The third portion of the expedition of search consists of 2 ships, the ship **Enterprise** & the ship **Investigator**, under command of Capt Sir Jas Ross & Capt Bird, which sailed in May, 1848, for Lancaster Sound. They were last heard of on Aug 28, at the entrance of this Sound.

Washington's Public Baths will commence on May 1 & end Sep 30. $10 in advance for one bath per day for himself, lady, or son, or daughter. Single bath .25. The Baths are on C, between 4½ & 6th sts. –P Aiken

Jenks' Patent Rifles & Carbines: for sale at reduced priced. –Jno W Baden & Bro, Sign of the Golden Saw, Pa ave near 6th st. [Union]

Appointments by the Pres: Collectors of the Customs:
Hooper C Hicks, Vienna, Md   Elias Pone, Genesee, N Y
Robt Mitchell, Pensacola, Fla   Ezra Smith, Champlain, N Y
Jas R Sanchez, St Augustine, Fla   Wm S Mallicotte, Yorktown, Va

A few weeks ago Mrs John Quincy Adams suffered a paralytic attack of such severity as at the time to occasion her family great anxiety. Though not yet able to rise, she is gradually improving in strength.

A Naval Court Martial will be held on board the U S ship **Pennsylvania**, to commence on May 7, for the trial of Cmdor Read, Capt Smoot, Lt Prentiss, & others who may be brought before it. –Portsmouth Trans

N Y, Apr 26, 1849. Sale of the French Consul's Gallery of Paintings. On account of the return to France of Chas de la Forest, the French Consul Gen, who has resided many years in this city, his furniture, library, & painting have been disposed of during the present week at public sale. The Consul's house was in 15th st, between 5th & 6th avenues. The catalogue numbered about 250 pieces, among them were works of Raphael, Guido, Salvator Ross, Michael Angelo, Van Dyke, Rubens, Murillo, Morales, & others. The sale of paintings amounted to about $4,000. The most valuable work was by Louis Morales, who was born at Badajos, Spain, in 1509. Two most noted works of this master are in the possession of the Queen of Spain: one is the head of "the Virgin in Sorrow," the other a head of "the Saviour wearing the Crown of Thorns." The painting in the present collection was a kneeling figure of "St Francis in ecstasy:" the owner had refused $10,000 for it, heretofore offered by the late King of France. It was now put up at a limit of $3,000-there being no bid beyond it was withdrawn. "Cleopatra killing herself by the bite of the asp after bathing," by Cavalier Carlo Cignani, born in Bologna 1628, was offered at a limit of $500, & withdrawn for want of a higher bid. It was painted when Cignani was about 37 years of age. It was among the military spoils taken at Bologna by the French. "Cecilia preluding for one of her divine concerts; an angel near her listening in ecstasy," by Sir Anthony Van Dyke. To obtain this work the proprietor made 2 journeys to Canada: it was valued at $600, & sold today for $360. "The Repose in Egypt," by Carlo Maratti: valued at $300, sold at $140. "A Masquerade scene," by Claude Gillot, sold at $27.50. "Interior of a Corps de Garde," by Teniers: valued at $25, sold at $75. "St John Preaching to the Multitude," by Francis Frank, sold at $100. "Snow Scene," by Gignoux, sold at $62.50. 'A Winter Scene," by Cuyp, sold at $37.50. 'A Flower piece," by Jan Van Os, $30. "A Canal scene in Holland," by Van Goyen, $27.50. "The Bath of Venus," by Vallambrosano: this work belonged to the Medici family: it sold for $25. "Portrait of Pope Alex'r VIII," by Tintoretto, $27. An original by Salvator Rosa sold at $80. "Monk & St Francis in ecstasy, before a manifestation of the Saviour," by Francesco Zurbaran: valued at $250, sold at $60. Portrait of the celebrated Nell Gwynne, by Gaspar Netcher, sold for $40. Our native artists were as well appreciated & sustained in this sale: 'Social enjoyments after dinner," by W S Mount, sold for $62.50. "St Peter & St Paul healing the lame man at the beautiful gate of the Temple," by Weir, sold at $40. "St Paul preaching at Athens," by Weir, $40. "A Freshet scene," by J E Chapman, $47.50. 'Boy resting on a fence, with his hat in his hand, looking rather sad, a storm rising in the distance," by W S Mount, sold at $62.50.

Wm S Campbell, recently appointed Judge of the U S District Court for the Western District of Lousiana, has declined the appointment. It is presumed that the emoluments of the ofc are too inconsiderable to justify Mr Campbell in relinquishing his practice at the bar. –Picayune

Died: on Apr 30, Saml Tinkler, aged 48 years, a native of Crowland parish, Lincolnshire, Eng, & for the last 14 years a resident of Wash City. His funeral is tomorrow at 4 p m, from his late residence, on 16th st.

Died: on Apr 29, Harriet, wife of Benj Baker, in her 62nd year. Her funeral is this afternoon at 4 o'clock, from the residence of her husband.

The death of the Hon John Phelps at the Patapsco Institute, Md, on Apr 14, was mentioned in the Howard Gaz: Judge Phelps was a native of Vt, an emiment lawyer & statesman: at age 34, was elected a member of the Convention for revising the State constitution; at 35, received from the Pres of the U S a commission for the collection of direct taxes & internal revenues for the 2nd district of Vt; at 40, elected a member of the State Council of Censors; a 50, was elected a member of the College of Electors of Pres & V P of the U S. In 1837 he left his native State to aid his wife, Mrs Lincoln Phelps, in those plans for female education which have been carried out so successfully in the Patapsco Female Institution.

Died: on Apr 29, Morgan Lewis, only son of Robt & Rose Greenhow, of Wash City, aged 18 months.

Female teacher wanted for the Everittsville Female Academy. Address the subscriber, post paid, at Waynesboro, Wayne Co, N C. –J C Slocumb

Teacher wanted: in his family to teach a few small children. An elderly gentleman would be preferred. Address J Waring, Chaptico, St Mary's Co, Md.

Trustee's sale of Stock of Groceries, Crockery, Boots & Shoes: on May 4, at the store of Louis J Knight, on Market Space, by order of the Trustees. -Edw S Wright, auctioneer

WED MAY 2, 1849
Within the last day or two, we have heard of the arrival in Wash City of: Col Hayne, of S C, on a visit to his daughter. Judge Banks, of Pa, formerly for several years a Rep in Congress from Pa. Col Todd, late U S Minister to Russia. Hon E H Allen, of Boston, formerly a Rep in Congress from Maine. Hon Jas Brooks, Rep in Congress from the State of N Y.

Savannah Republican of Apr 27: death of Capt Hunter. Capt Wyche Hunter, of the U S Dragoons, died on Wed last, in Charleston. He left this place on Mon, with his lady, to visit friends in Athens; but became dangerously ill after reaching Charleston & died the succeeding day.

Brevet Maj Gen Brooke, at present stationed at New Orleans, has been ordered to assume the command of the army in New Mexico lately detached from Gen Worth's command.

Letitia Blaisdell, who poisoned her foster mother & an infant at New Boston, N H, plead guilty, & has been sentenced to be hung on Aug 30th. Motive is unknown.

Mrd: on Apr 30, by Rev J B Donelan, Wm Francis Columbus to Miss Julia Amanda Pageet, all of Wash City.

Died: in Wash City, at the residence of her uncle, Mr J P Gannon, Mary A Benton, aged 4 years, only daughter of Jas & Virginia Benton. [No date-current.]

Died: on May 1, William, infant son of John W & Raina M Easby. His funeral is today, at 3:30 p m. from the residence of his parents, on D, near 26th st.

Target shooting: Private Luxen, of the Wash Light Infty, made the best shot, & won a handsome silver cup, manufactured by Mr S Lewis, of Wash City. Private Morsell, of the Walker Sharpshooters, made the best shot in that company, & won the Daguerrean portrait of the late Capt S Walker. Private Maguire, of the Nat'l Greys, made the best shot in that company, & won the silver cup manufactured for the premium.

The First Lecture at the Smithsonian Institute was delivered on Mon night by Edw Hitchcock, L L D, Pres of Amherst College, in the east wing of the bldgs. It was very crowded. The lecture room was brilliantly lighted by Mr Whittlesey.

Private sale of a bldg lot on E st, between 6th & 7th sts, adjoining the residence of A H Saunders & Noah Fletcher. Apply to John H Saunders.

THU MAY 3, 1849
$15 reward for return of runaway, my man Joe, about 25 years of age: copper color, & wears his hair usually long. Address at the subscriber, at Alexandria, Va.
–Jno H Bayne

Appointments by the Pres: Postmasters:
Isaac Dillon, Zanesville, Ohio   Andrew Mortimer, Pottsville, Pa
Aaron F Perry, Columbus, Ohio   Jos T Dunning, Brunswick, Maine
Wm Oliver, Cincinnati, Ohio   Caleb Clark, Ann Arbor, Mich
Gold S Silliman, Brooklyn, N Y

Hon Albert G Hawes, formerly a Jackson member of Congress from Ky, died at his residence in Daviess Co on Mar 14.

Mrd: on Tue last, by Rev C A Davis, Jos Linkins to Susan Coxen, all of Wash City.

Mrd: on May 1, by Rev G W Israel, Mr John N Minnix to Miss Catherine Danford, all of Wash City.

Mrd: on May 1, by Rev R A Smith, Dr Saml C Busey, of Wash, to Miss Kate A M, daughter of P D Posey, of Montg Co, Md.

Died: on May 2, in Gtwn, D C, Mrs Mary Coolidge, relict of the late Saml J Coolidge, in her 69th year. Her funeral is today, at 4:30 p m, from her late residence on Beall st.

Died: on Apr 25, at Detroit, Mich, Dr Justin Rice.

Caution: I herby forewarn all persons from hiring or harboring my servant, Nace Snowden, with or withou a line from me, as the law will be rigidly enforced against all such offenders. –Mary Ann MacPherson

The U S steam frig **Mississippi** is now being fitted out at Gosport Navy Yard, for the Mediterranean station, as the flag ship of Cmdor Morgan. The Norfolk Herald gives the following list of her ofcrs: J C Long, Capt. Lts: W C Chaplin 1st, Percival Drayton 2nd, J P Sanford 3rd, Jas D Johnston 4th, John Rutledge 5th, Thos M Crossan 6th; Master, E L Winder, Surgeon, G Blacknall; Assist Surgeon, Jas Hamilton; Purser, Henry Etting; Marine Ofcr, 2nd Lt Chas A Henderson; Passed Midshipmen: J Van Ness Phillips, P G Watmough, Jos B Smtih, Chas C Bayard, Thos Young; Boatswain, Robt Simpson; Gunner, Asa Curtis; Carpenter, F M Cecil. The ofcrs are directed to report for duty on May 15.

Mathew Wood, who was convicted a few days since in the Criminal Court of N Y of murdering his wife by administering poison to her in buckwheat cakes, was on Mon sentenced to be hung on Jun 22, by Judge Edmonds.

FRI MAY 4, 1849
Wash Corp: 1-Ptn from Henry Naylor & others in relation to the Eastern Branch bridges: referred to the Cmte on Finance. 2-Bill for the relief of Henry Turner: referred to the Cmte of Claims. 3-Bill for the relief of J Suechesi: referred to the Cme of Claims. 4-Bill for the relief of Francis Lamb: referred to the Cmte of Claims. 5-Ptn of Joel Downer & others, for a footway across D st: referred to the Cmte on Improvements. 6-Communication by Wm H Gates, on behalf of the free people, in relation to their application for aid in establishing a free school: laid on the table. 7-Ptn of John Crome, praying remission of a fine: referred to the Cmte of Claims. 8-Ptn from A Noerr & others, in relation to a culvert at 11th & E sts: referred to the Cmte on Improvements. 9-Act for the relief of Henry Smith: laid on the table.

The Colony of Rhode Island comprehends what were originally the Colonies or Plantations of R I & Providence, being incorporated into one, by a new charter, about the same time as the Colony of Connecticut. R I is bounded north & east by Mass bay, southerly the ocean, & westerly by Conn. The number of inhabitants in this Colony computed at 70,000. The principal commodities exported from hence are horses, sheep, cheese, & produce.

Private Boarding School for Boys: ages from 4 to 10 years. –M A W & S A Quincy, *Franklin Row*, corner of K & 13th sts, Wash.

Appointments by the Pres:
Collectors of Customs:
Jacob Russell, Chicago, Ill
Danl Kilby, Passamaquoddy, Maine
Chas Peters, Frenchman's Bay, Maine
Bushrod W Hinckley, Penobscot, Maine
Wm C Hammett, Bangor, Maine
Jeremiah Bailey, Wiscasset, Maine
Benj Randall, Bath, Maine
Surveyors of Customs:
Jos Gunnison, Eastport, Maine
Bazalleel Cushman, Portland, Maine

Independence [Mo] Expositor: letter from Mr T McClellen, a gentleman of intelligence & veracity, who with his family, went to Calif about a year ago. He made the trip overland in 5 months & 5 days, with the loss of only 1 animal. My average income this winter will be about $150 per day, & if I strike a good lead, it will be a great deal more. I expect to ship at this port for Jackson Co, Mo, where I expect to spend the remainder of my days in peace & quiet, in the enjoyment of my family & friends.

Wilmington [Dela] Journal: Ex-Govn'r Wm B Cooper, of Dela, died suddenly at his residence near Laurel on Apr 27.

Mrd: on May 3, by Rev Littleton Morgan, Mr Guy Carlton Humphreys to Miss Ann Rebecca Piggott, all of Wash City.

Mrd: on May 1, by Rev Mr Morgan, Mr C Perry Brown to Miss Mary Ellen Earpe, all of Wash City.

SAT MAY 5, 1849
Kitanning Free Press: a young man named Boutch drank a glass of wine, as he thought, but it happened to be laudanum. He died during the night.

Appointment by the Pres: Wm P Brobson, to be Collector of the Customs, for the District of Delaware.

Dr Jas Donovan begs leave to offer his professional services to the citizens of Wash. Ofc & residence west side of 9th st, between D & E sts.

Cows & calves for sale at the Market-house yard, on Tue morn. –L Bailey

For rent: large dwlg house & store on corner of 13th & F sts, lately occupied by B W Reed, as a grocery store. Apply to Mr John Wilson, 17th st, between H & I sts, at the residence of Mrs S M Burche, or to C H Wiltberger, City. Possession immediately.

N Y Tribune: announce the decease of Alvan Stewart, a man extensively known as a lawyer, a politician, & a philanthropist. He was a native of Vt, but his reputation as an atty was mainly won at the bar of the State of N Y.
[No death date given: current item.]

Loss of life on the Lakes: on Apr 26, the schnr **John Lillie**, Capt Keaho, was capsized during a recent blow, between Great Traverse & the North Manitou, & it is feared all on board are lost. The Indians reported they found 8 dead bodies. The **Lillie** had 12 or 15 on board.

The magnificent mansion at Silver Lake, Susquehanna Co, Pa, the residence of Dr Ross, has been destroyed by fire. It was one of the most beautiful edifices in the State. The bldg cost $30,000, & there is no insurance.

Gale at Rochester on Mon: loss of life. The severe winds blew down the tent of the Welch, Delavan & Nathan circus: injuries to Wm H Crowell were fatal. He left a wife & 4 children. Mr Geo Ives, a printer, was injured.

$100 reward for runaway negro man John Tasset, abour 28 years old. He left my farm, in Montgo Co, Md, about Feb 1st last. He has a wife living in PG Co, Md, near Bladensburg. –Allison Nailor, Wash, D C.

Mrd: on May 3, by Rev D Henshaw, Mr Robt R Fitzhugh to Miss Anna E Hyde, all of Wash City.

Died: on May 4, in Wash City, Mr Wm P Green, formerly of Alexandria, Va, in his 43rd year. His funeral is this afternoon at 4 o'clock, from his late residence, on 4½ st.

Died: on Apr 18, Lucinda P, wife of John S Talbott, of St Louis, Missouri, aged 28 years & 2 months. [Alexandria Gaz please copy.]

MON MAY 7, 1849
The success of Mr Mathew Brady in taking Daguerreotype Portraits is truly remarkable. On Sat last he was honored with a visit from Pres Taylor,
3 pictures were taken, each one was a triumph of art.

Last evening as the Houston st ferry-boat was leaving her dock a man named Francis Bates attempted to leap on board, but fell into the river, & was drowned. He was a ship carpenter, & has left a wife & 5 children. –N Y Sun

Accounts from Bermuda state that Mr John Mitchell, the Irish convict for a political offence, sailed for the Cape of Good Hope about Apr 20 with 289 other prisoners. He goes with what is called a free ticket-entitling him to liberty when he arrived at the Cape, only subject to the condition that he must settle there. His wife & children have sailed or about to sail direct fom Ireland to join him in his place of exile.

At Charleston, on Wed last, Michel Vergnol, the Chancellor to the French Consulate in that city, committed suicide by shooting himself in the head with a pistol. He arrived there about 2 months since. He appeared to be under morbid excitement.

A most nefarious attempt was made at N Y on Fri last to destroy the lives of Mr Thos Warner & his family. He was delivered a box with his name on it.
Very carefully he opened the box, & slowly drew the sliding lid from the box about half-way, when he saw a blue & yellowish flame arise from it, & quickly called to his wife & son to leave the room, & then ran out himself. The explosion took place, shook the whole bldg, & did much damage to the house. The authorities offer an ample reward in addition to the $500 offered by Mr Warner, for the detection & conviction of the scoundrel

A W Dougherty, of Ky, jumped from the steamer **Buffalo** on Wed, on the passage from Albany to N Y, in a fit of insanity, & was drowned. He had considerable money, & left a gold watch with the captain.

Appointments by the Pres:
Postmasters:
Edw W Lincoln, Worcester, Mass
Joshua Dunn, Portland, Maine
Henry H Matthews, Elmira, N Y

Elisha Starr, Milwaukie, Wisc
John F Bodley, Vicksburg, Miss
Isaac Platt, Poughkeepsie, N Y

State Ofcrs of Conn-Thu:
Hon Jos Trumbull chosen Govn'r
Hon Thos Backus, Lt Govn'r
Henry D Smith, State Treas

Roger H Mills, Sec of State
Abijah Catlin, Comptroller

Lt Henry Casper, formerly of the Dragoon service, committed suicide at St Louis on Apr 24.

Mr Balcomb, baggage-master upon the Stonybrook railroad, was killed on Tue by coming in contact with the bridge near the Groton junction.

Extract of a letter dated Hagerstown, May 3, 1849: Young Mr Hale, who was married a short time since in this city, killed himself by cutting his throat.

$10 reward for return of a red pocket-book that was lost, on Sat last, at the Centre Market. –Geo Seitz, on 10th st, near N Y ave.

New Orleans, Apr 27. Respite of Sibilich by the President. A telegraphic despath was received in town on Wed, granting a respite to Antonio Sibilich, who is under sentence of death in the parish prison for murder. This is the first instance known of a respite being sent by telegraph. He was to have been hung today. -Bulletin

Rittenhouse Academy, corner of 3rd & Indiana ave, Wash. Otis C Wight, A M, Principal. Aaron Day, A B, Assist. L Dovilliers, Prof of Modern Languages & Drawing. Next quarter will commence on May 9. -C H Nourse, Jos E Nourse

TUE MAY 8, 1849
By virtue of a decree of the Orphans Court of Wash Co, D C, the subscriber, guardian for the children of Wm Radcliff, late of said county, deceased, will sell at pivate sale, for cash, the following real property, of which the said Wm Radcliff died seized, to wit: lots 5 thru 9 in square 538, fronting on F st south, in Wash City. The title is indisputable. –Matilda Radcliff, Guardian

For rent, Tiber Mill: being within the limits of Wash City. Apply to N W Worthington, at Brentwood, adjoining the Mill.

Register's Ofc, Wash, Apr 30, 1849. List of the persons who have taken out licenses under the laws of the Corp during Jan, Feb, & Mar, 1849.
Agent Ins Co license: McKean, S M

Agent Insurance License: Morfit, H M; Webb, Pollard

Animal license: How, Willis

Auction license: Green, A; Morrison, Wm W

Cart license:
Baldwin, J A	Hyde, R A	Rawlins, Wash'n
Carroll, Jas	Jackson, P	Richardson, E
Dumnor, S	Miller, John	Tomlinson, Thos
Gess, J G	Raub, J P	

Commission license: Shanks & Wall

Concert license:
Collins, J, by W W Dennison-2	Ethiopean Serenad's-3
Distin, C	Fedesco, Signor
Distin, John	Nightingale Seren's-2

Dog license:
Adams, Jemina	Bronough, J W
Arnold, Ann E	Boyle, John
Aigler, J	Boyle, J F
Ailer & Thyson-3	Byrne, T
Adams, Washington	Brooks, F I
Anderson, Garret-2	Burgess, J
Abbot, Jos	Beche, E D
Alexander, C	Brooks, Basil
Adams, Jas	Bigman, G-2
Acton, O	Butt, Saml
Anderson, W	Brown, A
Byrne, C R	Brent, Eliz-2
Brady, P	Bogan, B L
Bock, M	Buete, H
Barcroft, Maria	Boylayer, John
Bates, F	Brashears, W B
Buckley, J S	Butler, A
Bowling, Thos	Boarman, S B
Briel, C	Bayly, W T
Brown, Wm	Burr, Thos S
Blake, J B	Barron, Mrs
Bartlett, J	Benter, Wm
Bully, A F	Brown, J E
Burr, Henry	Bestor, W C
Blair, Wm	Browning, P W
Butle, Jos	Beale, Robt
Bowen, Jos	Brent, Elton
Bestor, C	Bogus, Thos
Brady, Chas	Briscoe, Wm
Brown, Chas	Brown, T P

Butler, John
Beasley, Jas
Brooks, H
Brown, Jas
Branson, B
Donoho, W J
Douglass, H
Douglass, W
Dunwell, Saml
Dyson, Chas
Duvall, Washington
Dunnington, C W C
Downs, Solomon
Dermott, Ann R
DeSaules, P A
Dove, Wm
Devaughn, S
Deent, Bruce
David, of Abel, Jno
Dement, Richd
Downer, Joel
Dankworth, P
Dewdney, J
Dooley, M
Dillow, Wm
Day, S
Dyer, B F
Davis, G M
Dosier, Jos
Elliot, Wm P
Evans, F S
Ennis, P
Earl, Robt
Edelin, Jas-2
Eichhorn, R
Edwards, Geo
Emert, H
Evans, J D
Fitton, W H
Ford, Jas
Follansbee, Jos
Finkman, C
Ford, Wm
Farrar, J M
Frisse, J
Fearson, J C
Forrest, S-2
Fraeler, Chas

Fitzgerald, Jas
Feeney, Wm
Force, Peter-3
Fitzgerald, J
Fleming, John
Fitnam, Thos
Fister, John
Frisby, Wm
Fink, Jasper
Gray, S
Green, M
Gladmon, A
Goddard, Thos-2
Gardner, J B
Goldsmith, Thos
Goldsborough, Thos
Grupe, Wm
Gordon, Jas
Grant, Thos
Graham, Mrs John
Greason, Wm
Grimes, H
Gautier, C-2
Guyer, B-2
Griffith, w T
Greaves, J
Gannon, J P
Glick, J H
Gibson, Saml
Garner, G W
Griffith, W A
Graham, H
Goodrich, J
Hickman, A
Howe, Ignatius
Hanson, G D
Hobbie, S R
Hanly, Jane
Harrison, J H
Hitz, J
Herold, A G
Hicks, Chas
Hawkins, M
Hart, A
Howard, John
Heitmiller, A
Howle, P G
Harris, W

Holyrod, John
Hiss, J
Hiss, Paul
Horsthamp, H
Horning, G D
Hollidge, J
Henning, S
Hoffman, H
Hancock, A
Harkness, T F
Harauh, V
Handy, S W
Hagne, J R
Hamersley, E
Hess, Paul
Homas, D
Handy, W-transfer
Hill, J H
Hickman
Ingle, John P
Isaacs, Hester
Johnson, Richd
Jost, B
Jones, Raphael
Jones, A02
Jackson & Bro, B L
Johnson, Richmond-3
Jardine, H
Jamieson, J M
Jennifer, Robt
Jackson, Susan
Johnson, L
Johnson, Jos
Jesup, Thos J-2
Jones, J B
Killian, J
Kloffer, C G
Kaufman, Geo-2
Kendall, J E
Kuhl, Henry
Kingman, E
Keyworth, Robt-2
Kirby, Saml-2
Kealey, D E
Keefe, W M
Krafft, J M
King, Martin
Knott, G A

Keppler, H
Larned, Jas
Landrick, F
Law, J Geo-2
Lambell, K H
Lewis, J E
Laub, J Y
Lawson, Thos
Lusby, Saml
Litle, Jos F
Little, Peter
Lepreux, L
Lewis, Saml
Lavender, J
Lord, Wm
Laurie, Jas
Liomin, E
Lindsley, M S
Lederer, C
Lauxman, M
Lehman, A
Mustin, Thos
Magruder, R
McIntire, A
Marks, S A H
Miller, J S
Mure, L
Mechlin, J P
Mankin, Jas
Mount, Jas
McClery, J
McNorton, Geo
Mechem, C W H
Morris, W
Mason, Jos
Miller, John
Meigley, J
Morgan, Richd
Malone, L
Miller, Chas-2
Mullin, Basil
Mauns, Jas
Middleton & Beall
McGaun, J
Masi, S
McDermott, M-2
Murray, S
Masi & Co, F

Murphy, John
Mohin, F
Munck, C H
McQuay, B
Miller, Jos
McPherson, Jno
Maguire, Jas
Milburn, J M
McCoy, B
McKim, J F
Nugent, E
Nokes, Jas-2
Noerr, A
Nugent, E E
Nourse, John
Noble, Matilda-2
Nalley, John
Nepp, Danl
Newton, B
Nicholls, John M
O'Neale, H G
Orr, S L
O'Neale, J H
O'donoghue, P
Owens, Benj
Otterback, P-2
Owner, J
Peel, Rezin
Powell, J
Page, Y P
Peterson, W
Pleasanton, S
Pettit, Chas
Parker, G & T
Pettibone, Wm
Perkins, Saml
Purcell, Thos
Peck, Jos
Powell, L M
Parris, S B
Plant, Nathl
Pettibone, J
Prentiss, W H
Pumphrey, Jackson
Peake, John
Prather, A
Pulizzi, V
Pumphrey, L

Rosenstock, L
Rose, A L
Roach, R
Richardson, L
Riordan, J
Redfern, S
Roberts, J M
Ross, Augustus
Rupp, W
Ross, J W
Retter, H G
Reed, B W
Randall, H K
Richardson, C F E
Robinson, T J
Ramsey, Douglass
Rawlings, D
Reiss, A
Raub, John P
Riley, P C-2
Rappitti, Jos
Rhodes, J
Ross, Danl
Robertson, H B
Shorter, B
Saur, L
Smoot, J H
Schweitzer, Adam-2
Stanley, J T
Seufferle, F J
Shaw, Alex'r
Sullivan, Robt
Saunders, H
Stubbs, W E
Simms, Basil
Spriggs, W B
Stewart, Geo
Stalings, J S
Shaw, Richd-2
Sioussa, F
Sewall, Richd
Scott, Stephenson
Scott, S E
Sioussa, John
Stock, Geo
Stepper, A
Spignall, W
Springman, J

187

Shadd, B-2
Seitz, Geo
Smith, Thos-2
Sheckell, B O
Sleight, Jas
Sawyer, H B
Smith, Rev J C
Schwartze, A J
Stuart, F D
Simms, Ann
Tastet, N
Thomas, Geo
Thompson, G W
Tarlton, L A
Tschiffely, Fred
Tench, S
Turton, John B
Travers, E
Tucker, John F
Todtschinder, T
Tanner, Lethe
Taylor, R A
Topham, Geo
Thoma, Cha-2
Tucker, Jas
Todd, Wm B
Tilghman, R

Tenney, Pompey
Thompson, J R
Tilghman, H H
Van Zandt, N B
Visser, J
Venable, W S
Wilson, J D
Whaley, Martha
Wanderlish, J
Wilcox, A F
Whitwell, J C
Washington, jr, L
Walker, Wm
Willickman, John
Werner, J H T
Warner, H
Wallis, Wm
Whitlocke, W D
Williams, T J
Willet, V
Wirt, J L
Weber, C
Wollard, J T
Winchester, Robt
Wilkerson, E
Young, Noble
Young, A H

Exchange license: Latham & Co, R W; Maury, Jourdan W

Hack:
Beasley, Jos
Brown, A
Beckett, W H
Bush, Jas
Colvin, L
Clark, Cornelius
Dumphy, Thos
Hickman, W
Harshorn, G W

Key, G
Mullin, Wm S
Mullin, B
Nailor, W
Smith, Wm
Shorter, C W
Walker & Kimmell
Wells, Philip

Hats, Caps, etc. license:
Brown, Jas
Cash, Leonard
Closkey, J E
Cripps, W McL
Castee, J
Clements, A H

Colt, C A
Casparis, J
Casanave, P
Calvert, Betsey
Cross, T B
Coyle, Fitzhugh

Combs, R M
Crutchett, J-2
Cook, Abm
Charley, J N
Casteel, John
Clark, Wm
Chubb, J M
Corson, Saml
Caldwell, J T
Collins, Chas

Clarke, H A
Cook, Jas
Connolly, O
Cissell, Jesse
Cook, J F
Conlan, P
Johnson & Co, T W
Marshall, W
Maguire, John
Young & Orem

Huckster license:
Bicksler, John
Brown, Reuben
Brown, C
Bradley, J T
Banks, J
Baylies & Skidmore
Crampsey, W D
Cruit, R
Campbell, W W
Crump, J T
Collins, Sarah
Dyson, Chas
Delany, A
Dulany, Caleb
Dobbin, G W
Davis, J
Eichhorn, R
Eichhorn, Geo
Fearson, J C
Frank, Jacob
Golding, R B
Gordon, D S
Garrett, Milton-3
Gross, J
Henry, C F
Hawkins, P
Howell, John
Hawkins, E
Haines, Wash
Harris, Morgan
Hough, W W
Jones, A

Johnson, W C
James, John S
Moore, H W
Martin, W
Mankins, G W
Mullikin, J W
Murray, W A
McQuay, B
Miller, David
Oyster, John
Oyster, D W
Paxton, John
Peddicord, J
Payne, C H
Richardson, C F
Spignall, W
Shreve, Saml
Shreve, John
Sherwood, S
Shreve, C
Springman & Kale
Sherwood, Temp's-transfer
Tompkins, Richd
Tippett, T J
Tenant, John
Thumb, Tom
Williams, H
Wilson & Co, J L
Wallace, Jas
Wollard, H
Yeatman, J H
Young, A H

Lectures license: Williams, B D

Liquors, etc:
Birth, W W
Brown, R W
Corrigan, Bernard
Hall, J J
Leffler, John
Lavender, J
Leddy, O
Lowe, M
Leixear & Lasky
Lane, John

Ledgwick, R H
Malon, L
Mills, R T
Morsell & Wilson
Magnus, F
Parker, G & T
Riggles, W
Storm, Leonard
Shadd, J C
Sheckells, jr, Theo

Merchandise:
Borremains, Chas
Bishop & Co, D J-transfer
Beackley, J W
Devaughn, T S
Drury, S T
Davis, Jas N-transfer
Eckhardt, Thos & H
Goggin, Robt-transfer
Garner, Cath C W
Garrettson, N
Hall, E W
Hyde, Richd
Hines, C & M
Hamersley, M T
Lucas, Bennet

Lindsley, M S
Lammond & Co-transfer
Miller, R
Morley, Hannah S
McGregor, N M
Moore, Jos B-transfer
Owen & Son, E
Phillips, Ann
Radcliff, J R
Raimy, S A
Saur, L
Stevens & Peaco
Stoops, Richd
Taylor, J H
Thompson & Brodb't

Shop license:
Hassler, John
Lewis, Wm B
Morse, J E

Swearing, Fred'k
Williams, F H

Slut:
Birch, Thos
Dyvernois, G E
Gunton, Thos
Jackson, Pompey

Mckean, E
Pumphrey, L
Shaw, Richd

Stage license: Elliot, J W

Theatrical license: Brown & Nichols-12

Wagon license:
Buckley, T K
Conroy, Dominic
Edelin, C

Kibble, A
Parker, A

Persons fine for not having license required:
Black, Jane: dog
Bede, Geo: huckster
Burdick, Henry: dry goods
Creutzfelt: slut & dog
Chubb & Schenck: exchange
Dunnington, John: huckster
France, John : exchange
Griffith, Wm A: dog
Hall, Edw: dog
Heisler, John: liquor
Heisler: slut
Johnson, Wm: dog
-W J McCormick, Register

McNier, W W: huckster
Oyster, D: huckster
Pairo, C W: exchange
Plant, G H: dog
Rowland, Danl: exchange
Steger, Wm T: dog
Smallwood, R T: huckster
Sedgwick, R H: huckster
Sutton, Bobert: dog
Sheckels, B O: dog
Tenent, John: huckster
Weyrick, Jos: dog

Appointments by the Pres:
To be Marshal:
Henry F Talmadge, of the Southern District of N Y, in place of Eli Moore, removed.
Fred'k G Smith, of the Western District of Louisiana, in place of John E King, who declines the appointment.
Goshom A Jones, of the District of Ohio, in place of Danl A Robertson, removed.
Wm Paine, of Maine, for the District of Maine, in place of Rufus McIntyre, removed.
Stephen B Shelladay, of Iowa, for the District of Iowa, in place of Gideon S Bailey, resigned.
Benj Bond, of Ill, for the District of Ill, in place of Stinson H Anderson, removed.
Attys:
Octavius H Ogden, for the Western District of Louisiana, in place of Henry Boyce, who declines the appointment.
Samson Mason, for the District of Ohio, in place of Thos W Bartley, removed.
Absalom Fowler, of Ark, for the District of Ark, in place of Saml H Hempstead, removed.
Collector of Customs: Luther Jewett, Portland, Maine
Land Ofcrs:
John M Hughes, Receiver of Public Moneys at Plattsburg, Mo, in place of Bela M Hughes, resigned.
John L Green, Receiver of Public Moneys at Chillicothe, Ohio, in place of John Hough, removed.
Cyrus W Wilson, of Ark, Receiver of Public Moneys at Little Rock, Ark, in place of Lemuel R Lincoln, removed.
Lorenzo Gibson, of Ark, to be Surveyor Gen of the Public Lands in Ark, in place of Wm Pelham, removed.
Silas Noble, of Ill, to be Register of the Land Ofc at Dixon, Ill, in place of John Dement, removed.
Saml Merriwether, of Indiana, to be Receiver of Public Moneys at Jeffersonville, Ind, in place of David G Bright, resigned.
Henry F Mooney, of Ark, to be Register of the Land Ofc at Helena, Ark, in place of Henry L Biscoe, removed.

Lorenzo D Maddox, of Ark, to be Receiver of Public Moneys at Helena, Ark, in place of Geo Jefferies, removed.
Wm E Powell, of Ark, to be Register of the Land Ofc at Champagnole*, Ark, in place of Hiram Smith, removed.
Ezra Hill, of Ark, to be Receiver of Public Moneys at Champagnole, Ark, in place of Mathew F Rainey, removed.
Wm H Etter, of Ark, to be Register of the Land Ofc at Washington, Ark, in place of Benj P Jett, removed.
Bernard F Hempstead, of Ark, to be Receiver of Public Moneys at Washington, Ark, in place Danl T Witter, removed.
Jas H Stirman, of Ark, to be Register of the Land Ofc at Fayetteville, Ark, in place of Ephraim D Dickson, removed.
Richd M Thruston, of Ark, to be Receiver of Public Moneys at Fayetteville, Ark, in place of Matthew Leeper, removed.
Jas H Patterson, of Ark, to be Register of the Land Ofc at Batesville, Ark, in place of John Miller, removed.
Wm S Hynson, of Ark, to be Receiver of Public Moneys at Batesville, Ark, in place of D J Chapman, removed.
John E Manly, of Ark, to be Register of the Land Ofc at Clarksville, Ark, in place of John Bruton, removed.
Wm Goodrick, of Ark, to be Receiver of Public Moneys at Clarksville, Ark, in place of Wm Adams, removed.

The Navy Court Martial to be held on May 7 at the Gosport Navy Yard, for the trial of Cmdor Geo C Read, Capt Jos Smoot, & Lt Prentiss & others, will consist of the following members: Cmdors Chas Stewart, Chas Morris, John Downes, Lawrence Kearney, Danl Turner, M C Perry; Capts Chas S McCauley, Elis A F Lavalette, Silas H Stringham, Isaac Mayo, Jas Armstrong, Saml L Breese, & French Forrest. R S Coxe, of Washington, Judge Advocate. –Norfolk Beacon

Deed of East Boston: deed was granted to Saml Maverick, from whom it descended to the heirs of his brother, the Rev John Maverick, of Dorchester.
A Court holden at Boston, Apr 1, 1633. *Noddles's Island* is granted to Mr Samuel Maveracke, to enjoy to him & his heirs forever, yielding & paying yearly at the general court, to the Governor for the time being, either a fatt weather, a fat hog, or ten pounds in maney." A true extract from the records of the general court. Attest: John Avery, Secretary

The Pres appoints the following Justices of the Peace to be members of the Levy Court for Wash Co, D C: for the term of one year, viz: Henry Naylor, Alfred Ray, Chas R Belt, & Joshua Pierce. Lewis Carbery, John Cox, & Robt White, for Gtwn. Saml Drury, Benj K Morsell, John F Cox, & Jas Crandell, for Wash City.

For sale or rent: the Bertram Botanic Garden & Farm, on the west side of the Schuylkill river, containing 48 acres: improvements consist of a large stone mansion house, fronting on the river, with several out-bldgs. Apply to R Carr, on the premises. –Richd Smethurst, 72 South 4th st, Phil

Fauquier Land for sale: on Aug 1, a tract of land in said county, adjoining the lands of Jos Morgan & of the heirs of Wm Skinker, deceased: belongs to the estate of Col John Stuart, late of King Geo Co, & will be sold in pursuance of the directions of his will. The tract contains 427 acres. Wm Horner, of Warrenton, will give information . –J R Stith, Agent for M L Stuart, Admx, with the will annexed, of John Stuart, deceased.

Valuable Iron Works for sale: the *Caroline Furnace*, in Shenandoah Co, Va: consists of 3,250 acres of land. Persons may write to Green B Samuels, of Woodstock, or to A Goodwin, Cashier of the Ofc of Farmers' Bank of Va, Fred'g, or Wm K Gordon, Cashier of the Ofc of the Bank of Va, Fred'g.

Gen Orders #22: War Dept, Adj Genrl's Ofc, Wash, Apr 21, 1849. Four additional companies to be organized & equipped as light artl:
1st Regt of Artl, Co, I, Capt Magruder
2nd Regt of Artl, Co M, Capt Roland
3rd Regt of Artl, Co B, Capt Shover
4th Regt of Artl, Co G, Capt Freeman
Four pieces & 44 horses will be allowed each company. Co B, 3rd Artl, will proceed, without unneccessary delay, to take post at West Point for the purpose of aiding in the practical instruction of the cadets in this important branch of the military service, under its captain, Brevet Maj Shover, the present instructor of artillery at the Academy. By order : R Jones, Adj Gen

Mrd: on Apr 26, by Rev Barnet Grimsly, Mr John T Ball to Miss Rosalie J, daughter of J D Latham, all of Rappahannock, Va.

Mrd: on May 1, at White Hall, PG Co, Md, by Rev N D Young, Dr Edw Hurtt to Mary M Young, daughter of the late Edw D Young.

Died: on May 6, Mrs Eliz B Laurie, wife of the Rev Dr Laurie, of Wash City. The members of F st church, the friends of the family, & the managers of the different benevolent societies of which she was so efficient a member, are invited, to attend her funeral, which will proceed from the church at 3:30 o'clock precisely, this afternoon.

Died: on Apr 26, at Aldie, Va, after a life of christian piety & benevolence, Catherine, consort of Maj Wm Noland.

WED MAY 9, 1849
Desirable little farm in the vicinity of Brookville, Md, for sale, highly improved with bone dust, on which is a mill for crushing bones, with water power sufficient for manufacturing purposes. Improvements are a convenient frame dwlg-house, wagon-house, & barn. It adjoins the lands of Messrs Remus Riggs, A B Davis, E W Owen, & others. –B B Pleasants

Fire in Charleston, S C, last Mon, destroyed some 150 bldgs. There region of the fire is bounded by Meeting st on the west, Charleston st on the north, Elizabeth st east, & Boundary on the south.

For sale, on *Staten Island*, a beautiful country seat. The house was recently built, having numerous airy bed-rooms; & full complement of out-bldgs. Inquire of Wm L Morris, Counsellor at Law, 6 Broad st, N Y.

Balt American: Col Geo W Whistler, Chief Engineer of the Petersburgh & Moscow Railroad, & for many years past a resident at St Petersburgh, died recently at St Petersburgh, leaving behind many sorrowing friends. Col Whistler was a graduate of West Point; left the army to devote himself to civil engineering; was in the service on the Balt & Ohio Railroad Co; for a season on the Susquehanna Railroad; moved Eastward and was very active in various companies, & became the Chief Engineer of the Western Railroad, between Boston & Albany. The Emperor of Russia sent a commission to the U S to obtain a suitable person to construct the railroad between St Petersburgh & Moscow: Col Whistler was selected. [No death date given -current news.]

In Chancery: Circuit Court of D C. Wm S Herriman, on behalf of himself & the creditors of the late Thos J Davis, against Wm Winn & Isabella Davis, adms of the said Thos J Davis, & Ignatius T Davis & others, his heirs at law. By an interlocutory order of the said Court, passed in the cause above named, on May 5, the subscriber is directed to state an account of the personal estate of Thos J Davis, late of Gtwn, in said District, miller, of the disbursements & payments by his administrators, & of the several claims upon his estate; to report the value of the real estate of which the said Thos J Davis died seized; & the amount of incumbrances, if any. On Jul 2, I will attend at my ofc, in the City Hall, Washington, for the pupose of executing the order of the Court. -W Redin, auditor

Died: on May 7, Mrs Martha Ann Lee, consort of Ruland Lee. Her funeral is today at 10 o'clock, from her brother's, Wm H Richards, 7th & Md ave.

Great Row at the Astor Opera House, N Y, on May 7. The house was filled, & when the curtain rose & Mr Macready appeared, a portion of the audience commenced hissing. Chairs & missiles were hurled at him on the stage, & loud cries ensued of "Down with the English Hog!" "Off with the English bull!" Then eggs were pelted upon him. The ladies became frightened & left the house, & Macready was eventually compelled to leave the stage. Macready made his escape in a closed carriage.

Died: on May 2, at Bryantown, Md, aged 1 year, 10 months & 14 days, Mary Virginia, daughter of Danl & the late Eliz Rachel Robertson, of Wash City.

Household & kitchen furniture at auction on May 18, by virtue of a deed of trust given on Feb 3, 1849, & filed for record in the Clerk's ofc in Wash Co, D C: sale at the residence of Mr Saml Harkness, on K st, between 8th & 9th sts. The furniture is of a superior quality. –A Green, auct

Members of the Board of Health:
Dr Thos Miller, Pres
John Y Bryant, Sec
Dr Richmond Johnson
Hampton C Williams
Jas Larned
Dr Jas C Hall
Dr Wm H Saunders

G C Grammer
Dr J B Gardner
John P Ingle
Dr Noble Young
Jas Crandell
Dr Jas E Morgan
Wm B Randolph

Vaccine Physicians:
Dr T B J Frye, Seven Bldgs
Dr R King Stone, E & 14th st
Dr J M Wilson, 9th st between H & I sts
Dr Wm H Saunders, 4 ½ st & La ave
Dr Noble Young, Navy Yard
Dr Jas E Morgan, 11th st, south of Md ave
Dr W C Busey, Pa ave, south side of the Capitol
The Vaccine Physician of the several Districts are prepared to vaccinate the poor, free of charge, when called on. Physicians of the city can at all times be supplied with vaccine on application to the Pres of the Board of Health, provided they will make return of *fresh* good virus. –T M

THU MAY 10, 1849
Record of weather: the most unseasonable weather ever heard of in Va was a snow nearly a foot deep in Jun, 1774. The coldest morning ever known in Va, since its first settlement by the English, was Jan 14, 1780: the mercury sunk into the bulbs of thermometers. The ice upon our rivers was 3 feet 2 inches thick. Chesapeake bay was frozen quite over, & hundreds of people walked across it from Annapolis to Kent Island & other places. On May 9, 1780, Col Chas Dabney's regt of Va Infty marched from Falmouth to Fredericksburg upon the ice in the Rappahannock, which had been formed there the preceding Nov.

Japan Sea, Tee Shee Island, Jun 18, 1848. Ranald McDonald shipped on board the vessel **Plymouth** when she sailed from the U S. After 2 years, while at Lahaina, in 1847, he requested his discharge unless Capt Edwards would consent to leave him upon the coast of Japan. Young McDonald is the son of Archibald McDonald, formerly in the employ of the Hudson Bay Co at **Fort Collville**, Columbia. Capt Edwards allowed him to make choice of the best boat belonging to the ship. All hands gathered to see the last of the bold adventurer. –E P F [Some days after his embarkation, while the whale ship **Uncas** was cruising that region, she picked up the rudder of the tiny craft, which we will venture to name the **Young Plymouth**. Whether she reached the shore or was swamped in the surf remains a profound mysery.]

Chas A Whittlesey, cmder or sailing-master of the pilot boat **William G Hackstaff**, which sailed from N Y on Feb 7 for Calif, was lost overboard during a gale on the 7th day after leaving N Y.

Official: Appointments by the Pres:
Thos Ewbank, of N Y, to be Com'r of Patents, vice Edmund Burke, removed.
John W Ashmead, of Pa, to be U S Atty for the Eastern District of Pa, vice Thos M Pettit, removed.
Anthony E Roberts, of Pa, to be U S Marshal for the Eastern District of Pa, vice Geo M Keim, removed.
John S Myrick, of Fla, to be U S Marshal for the Northern District of Fla, vice Robt Myers, resigned.
Land Ofcrs:
Receivers of Public Moneys:
Chas L Stevenson, of Wisc, at Mineral Point, Wisc, vice Pascal Bequette, removed.
Gideon Fitch, of Miss, at Jackson, Miss, vice David C Glenn, removed.
Jas W Drake, of Miss, at Pontotoc, Miss, vice Wm W Leland, removed.
Danl Hicks, of Mich, at Saut Ste Marie, Mich, vice Michl A Patterson, removed.
Register of the Land Ofc:
Austin Morgan, of Miss, at Jackson, Miss, vice Benj R Cowherd, removed.
Henry Acker, of Mich, at Saut Ste Marie, Mich, vice Jas B Hunt, removed.
Robt W Boyd, of La, to be Surveyor Gen of the Public Lands in La, vice Pierre T Landry, removed.
Ofcrs of the Customs:
Wm D Lewis, Collector of the Customs, Phil, vice Jas Page, removed.
Peter G Ellmaker, Naval Ofcr, Phil, vice Henry Welsh, removed.
Danl McCulloch, Collector, Sackett's Harbor, vice Otis N Cole, removed.
Postmasters:
John C McAllister, Jackson, Miss   Jas C Magraw, Cumberland, Md
Ezra S Hamilton, Hartford, Conn   Henry L Bowen, Providence, R I
Barzilia Slosson, Geneva, N Y   Wm J P White, Phil, Pa
Benj F Arndt, Easton, Pa   Richd B Alexander, Tuscumbia, Ala

Marshal's sale: 2 writs of fieri facias, or scire facias under the lien law, issued from the Clerk's Ofc of the D C for Wash Co: sale on Jun 2, of the following property, viz: five 2 story frame dwlg houses on parts of lot 4 & 5, in square 369, in Wash City, seized & levied upon as the property of Sylvanus Holmes, & sold to satisfy Judicials 34, to Mar term, 1849, in favor of Ulysses Ward; also, Judicials 64, to Mar term, 1849, in favor of Waters & Zimmerman, against said Sylvanus Holmes. –Robt Wallace, Marshal-D C

Mrd: on May 8, by Rev W Hodges, Jas H Meade to Miss Julia Anne Bailey, all of Wash City.

Mrd: on May 8, by Rev M Bury, Francis B Lord, of Wash, to Miss C M Hubbard, of Balt.

Died: last evening, in his 85th year, Danl Carroll, of Duddington. His funeral is on Fri next at 3 o'clock.

Died: on May 9, of scarlet fever, Alice, daughter of Benj & Susan A Beall, in her 3rd year. Her funeral is this afternoon, from the residence of B J Middleton, at 4 o'clock, where the friends of the family are requested to attend.

Wash Corp: 1-Cmte of Claims: bill for the relief of Francis Lamb: passed. 2-Ptn from John S Cunningham & others for removal of a nuisance: referred to the members of the 3rd Ward. 3-Ptn from Jas Laurie, praying the repeal of a law passed for grading & paving the alley in square 226: referred to the Cmte on Improvements. 4-Ptn from J W Jones, respecting a nuisance in square 03: referred to the Cmte on the Health of the City. 5-Cmte of Ways & Means: asking to be discharged from the further consideration of the communication from Richd Shields, in relation to coating the City Hall with mastic. Same cmte: ptn of Timothy O'Neale: asking to be discharged from its further consideration: recommended it be referred to the Mayor for payment. 6-Ptn of Grafton Powell & others, to convey water to D st, on the 14th st line: read twice. 7-Cmte of Claims: asked to be discharged from the further consideration of the ptn of Wm Mullen. Same cmte: act for the relief of John Crome: read twice. 8-Cmte on Improvements: ptn from T B Brown & others, for the repair of 7th st: read twice.

Household & kitchen furniture at auction on May 16, at the residence & boarding-house of Mrs Turpin, on Pa ave, between 3rd & 4½ sts. Entire stock of good Furniture. –A Green, auctioneer

Ezra S Corning, of Chicopee Falls, Mass, recovered $9,045 of the Conn River Railroad Co, in the Supreme Judicial Court, at Springfield, on Sat last, for injuries received by him on his head, hip, & in his spine, while passing over the defendant's road, the effects of a collision on Feb 11, 1848.

FRI MAY 11, 1849
John A Matson, of Franklin Co, nominated by a Whig State Convention as their candidate for the ofc of Govn'r of Indiana at the ensuing election.

Norfolk papers: there are no charges against Capt Smoot, whose name was on the lst of ofcrs under trial by the Navy Court-martial now sitting.

Corpus Christi Star of Apr 21: Col Hardee, with 2 companies of the 2nd Dragoons, arrived at San Antonio on Apr 2, from the Rio Grande City, viz Laredo. He lost some 18 or 20 of his command on the road by cholera.

The Late Danl Carroll, of Duddington: venerable survivor of the original proprietors; christian, a well-bred & perfect gentleman; a good & useful citizen. With him has gone the last living link which connects us with out past. He has descended to the tomb in the fullness of years, after a well-spent life. His weeping family may well believe that their loss is his gain. -B

SAT MAY 12, 1849
Notice to the Ladies & Gentlemen. The drawing for watches & fancy articles advertised will take place at Apollo Hall on May 19. Examine the articles at my store, Pa ave, between 12th & 13th sts. -Wm Voss

Since 1810 1,400 persons have been executed in England for crimes which are no longer capital by the English law.

Mrs McAndrew, who lately murdered her sister-in-law in Madison Co, Miss, has been tried in Jackson & convicted of murder in the first degree.

Obit-died: on May 6, Mrs Eliz Bell Laurie, wife of the Rev Jas Laurie, of Wash City. After a wasting illness of several weeks & the most anxious solicitude & untiring attention on the part of her family & friends, this estimable lady passed from our midst. For many years she was the presiding spirit of the Female Union Benevolent Society, the Dorcas Society, & connected with the City Orphan Asylum. To her bereaved partner, advanced in years, we can but offer the sincerest sympathies. The funeral services were conducted on May 8 in F st church, the Rev Mr Berry, of Gtwn, delivering a beautiful discourse, followed by prayer by Rev Mr Gurley. The sobs of the little orphans who came to take a last fond look at the placid countenance of her who had been to them a mother, melted all hearts. -A Friend

Mrd: on May 8, by Rev Mr Vanhorsigh, Mr Jas W Peake to Miss Mary Eliza Griffin, all of Wash City.

Mrd: on May 10, by Rev Wm H Pitcher, Mr A W Martin to Miss Mary E Cook, all of Wash City.

MON MAY 14, 1849
$30 reward for the apprehension of negro servant Nealy Leigh, long a resident of Wash City, & having a wife belonging to Mr Benedict Raleigh, either he or his son James would be able to indentify him. –Maria Leigh
Call on C Coombs for the reward, *Great Mills*, St Mary's Co, Md.

Appropriations made during the 2nd Session of the 13th Congress:
To Philip J Fontane, balance due for mason work: $1,000.
Chas Waldron, for his payment: $198.50
Archibald Bull & Lemuel S Finch, for services as judge & sheriff: $63.38.
Col Robt Wallace, aid-de-camp to Gen Wm Hull, for services & a horse: $914.
Jos Bryan, for certain disbursements: $282,
Jas H Conley, for his payment: $222.80
Stephen Champlin: indefinite
Capt Dan Drake Henrie, for gallant services: $2,000.
Wm Harding, refund part of a penalty: $1,00.
Henry Washington, late deputy surveyor, for damages for the abrogation of a contract: indefinite.
John M Moore, for compensation as acting Com'r of the Gen Land Ofc: indefinite.
Jos F Caldwell, for carrying the mail: $1,167.
Owners of the Spanish brig **Restaurador**: indefinite.
Thos Douglas, late U S Atty for East Fla, for services in certain suits: indefinite.
Wm Fuller & Chas Savage, for services in carrying the mail: $1,229.17.
Jeanette C Huntington, widow & sole excx of Wm D Cheever, deceased, for losses sustained by payments in treasury notes: $2, 231.18
Jas Glynn & others, for certain surveys & charts: indefinite.
Thos T Gammage, for articles taken for U S volunteers: $994.
Jas Y Smith, for use of a steamboat: $3,064.

E B Cogswell, for coal & iron, & for services as blacksmith to Indians in Texas: $1,200.
Abraham Edwards, register of the Land Ofc at Kalamazoo, Mich: indefinite.
Joshua Barney, U S Agent, for services, this sum, with interest: $104.50.
A C Bryan & others, for horses captured in Mexico, to the person specified: $420.
Mary McRea, wife of Lt Col Wm McRae, late of the U S army, deceased: indefinite.
Henry D Garrison, for his pay as assignee of an indian claim under treaty: $800.
Geo Center, for property destroyed in the Fla war: indefinite.
Jas S Sothoron, for property destroyed by British troops: indefinite.
John P Skinner & the legal reps of Isaac Green: to reimburse a sum recovered against Skinner & Green, as sureties of Emerson: $8,313.
John F Ohl, to reimburse a sum paid as duties on merchandise destroyed: $420.
Jas Morehead: to make compensation for losses for the suspension by the Govn't of the erection of a dam in the Ohio river: indefinite.
Dr Adolphus Wizlizenus, for medicines & pay: indefinite.
Saml A Grier, for an amount collected from him as surety: $462.10
David Thomas, of Phil, for an amount illegally exacted as duties: $141.54.
Alex'r Montgomery, Capt & Assist Quartermaster of the army, to indemnify losses sustained as disbursing ofcr: $6,000.
Capt Geo R Shoemaker, for services under a contract: indefinite.
Danl Robinson, for damages for the violation of a contract: indefinite.
Noah A Phelps, for the amount of an award in his favor: $416.13.
Satterlee Clark, this amount to be paid: $15,632.61.
Wm P Yonge, for this sum to be paid: $214.96.
John W Hockett, for an amount due for work: $303.52.
Lowry Williams, for the amount of an outstanding certificate, under a treaty with the Cherokees: $960.50.
Thos H Noble, for charcoal furnished: $284.62½.
Peter Shaffer, for work performed: $372.46.
Chas Benns, for an amount paid into the treasury for duties: $387.20.
Thos Talbot & others, for horses & other property taken by Pawnee Indians: $4,155.
Payment to the widow of Jas McDonald, deceased, said McDonald's share of the sum granted by Congress for distribution as prize money among the captors of the British brig **Detroit**, during the last war with Great Britain: $37.50.
To pay A J Glossbrenner for work done in re-arranging & classifying the volumes in the copyright room in the Dept of State, in 1848: $250.
To Robt Beale, for his services & expenses incurred in a journey to Virginia to notify the President Tyler of his accession to the Presidency: $300.
Payment to Wm C Reddall & Wm C Zantzinger, equally to be divided between them: $771.43.
For the purchase of the remaining manuscript books & papers of Geo Washington: $20,000.
For the purchase of the remaining manuscript books & papers of Jas Monroe: $20,000.

Trustee's sale: by deed of trust, made on Apr 29, 1844, recorded in liber W B 108, folio 313, of the land records of Wash Co: sale on May 22, at public auction, part of a lot 2 in square 353, in Wash City, a corner lot. Sale on the premises. –Johnson Hellen, Trustee -A Green, auctioneer

Appointments by the Pres:
Collectors of the Customs:
Geo P Kane, Balt, Md, vice Wm H Marriott, removed.
Thos Ireland, Annapolis, Md, vice Richd Sands, who did not qualify.
John H Allen, Oxford, Md, vice Nicholas Willis, removed.
Surveyors of the Customs:
Elias T Griffin, Balt, Md, vice Wm H Cole, jr, removed.
John Blackistone, Llewellensburg, Md, vice Aloysius Thomson, removed.
John T Stamp, Nottingham, Md, vice Thos W Hoye, removed.
Geo W P Smith, Snow Hill, Md, vice Chas Parker, removed.
Robt C Coleman, Louisville, Ky, vice Nathl P Porter, removed.
Naval Ofcr:
Thos K Carroll, Balt, Md, vice Jas Polk, removed.
Land Ofcrs:
Receiver of Public Moneys:
Robt N Carnan, of Indiana, at Vincennes, Ind, vice Saml Wise, removed.
John Baird, of Indiana, at Crawfordsville, Ind, vice Bennett W Engle, removed.
Register of the Land Ofc:
John C Clark, of Indiana, at Vincennes, Ind, vice Jas S Mayes, removed.
John Ewing, of Indiana, at Crawfordsville, Ind, vice John W Rusk, removed.
Marshals:
Jas H Kent, of Md, to be U S Marshal for the District of Md, vice Moreau Forrest, removed.
Appointment by the Sec of the Interior:
Maunsel White, of Louisiana, to be Pension Agent at New Orleans, La, vice Greenbury Dorsey, removed.

Hardware & cutlery at auction, on May 14, at the hardware store of Messrs T G Russell & Co, Pa ave. –A Green, auctioneer

Casualties from the late riots on Thu night at one of the Theatres in N Y:
Gen Sanford was felled to the earth
Lt W R Harrison was badly wounded
Capt Shumway, Lt Clark, & Capt Pond were badly hurt
Edw McCormick residing at 135 First ave, aged about 19, severely wounded in the groin; employed in the press room of the Methodist Book Concern.
John Dalzel, a native of Edinburgh, aged 22, residing opposite Washington Market, wounded: was a hand on board the steamboat **Empire**.
Thos Aylward, 19, clerk, residing at East Broadway & Clinton st: wounded. [Since dead.]
Conrad Becker, residing at 27 Hudson st, employed by Mahoney & Thompson, upholsterers: flesh wound in the thigh.
Jas Boulton, shot in the left eye, eye entirely destroyed.
Jas McDonald, 28, residing at 189 Walker st: wounded. [Since dead.]
Geo McKay, 28, boarding at 107 Chambers st, a merchant: wounded in the right lung.
Henry Bluff, gave his name as Burghest, residing 510 Pearl st, received a singular wound, by no means dangerous.
Geo A Curtis, printer, shot through the right lung. [Since dead.]

Geo Lincoln, 30, residing 1t 189 Walker st: was a shoemaker. [Since dead.] Bridget Fagan, 30, residing in 11th st between avenues 1 & 2: ball entered just below the knee and the limb will be amputated. She is in a precarious situation. She & her husband were returning home, & were nearly 2 blocks from the scene. From the hospital we passed to the 15th Ward station house, in Mercer st, where 8 bodies presented itself. Geo W Gedney, formerly a dry goods merchant, son-in-law of Mr Wm B Shipman; Timothy Burns, of 472 Pearl st, shot through the head; Mathew Carhart, 1st & 12th st; Henry Otten, grocer, residing at Hester & Orchard sts, shot through the stomach; & Thos *Kiernan, 12th st. At the 17th Ward station house were 3 dead bodies: Niel Gray Willis, or Millis, residing at 119 Grand st; Timothy McGuire, 107 east 13th st; & Wm Butler, 23 Thompson st.
At Jones', corner of 9th st & Broadway, we found a printer, Andrew McKinley, aged 25, shot through the lungs, the ball entering the chest & coming out of the back. [Since dead.]
We have authentic information of the death of Geo W Brown, 42 Crosby st, who died in 2 hours after he was wounded. Also dead, Geo W Taylor, residing at 115 Varick st, & ___ Kelly, residing at 104 East 13th st; John S Jones, 219 Sullivan st; Jas McDonald, 189 Walker st; & H Mansfield. An aged gentleman, Mr Jas Stewart, a retired merchant, while stepping from the railway cars was struck by a ball. Though in danger, he was alive & doing as well, this morning, as could be hoped. Capt Saml C Reid, attached to the U S naval rendezvous, is reported dangerously wounded. Additional accounts of wounded: Fred'k Gillespie, 16, residing in Second ave, between 25th & 26th sts, shot in the foot; John Smith, 96 Perry st, shot in the thigh, not dangerously; Mr Romaine, butcher, a young man residing in 1st st, severely wounded; a son of Mr J Irwin, of 243 10th st, shot in the leg; B M Seixas, jr, wounded; Jas Riley, a cartman, living in Attorney st, shot in the hand; Stephen Cahoe, 24, wounded in the eye; Mrs Brennan, Jos Eaton, Philip Livingston, Geo McKay, W C Russell, & Thos B Stone: wounded. Attached to the military companie: Capt Pond, Capt Peck, Capt Shumway, Capt Underbill, Sgt Morton, Sgt Weller, Isaac Devoe, W H Harrison, John Mortimer, T W Todd, W Sellick, Mr Braisted, Mr Bogart, Mr Lefferts, Mr Ruckle, Mr Spafford, & Mr Tuthill: wounded. The Mayor of the city reminds all the citizens that the peace of the city must be maintained. -C S Woodhull, Mayor [*May 16th newspaper: Thos Kearnin, 21, born in Ireland, a waiter, was supposed to be the first person killed; he was shot in the right cheek, the ball passing into the brain.]

The steamer **Crescent City** arrived at N Y on Sat, bringing intelligence from Panama to the 28th, & from Chagres to the 30th ult. On Apr 30, as the signal gun was about to be fired, Mr Jas Moncrieff, the 1st ofcr, inadvertently stepped near the muzzle, unseen by the person who applied the match, &, before Mr Moncrieff could be warned of his danger, the gun exploded, killing him instantly. Deaths which have occurred at Panama since the sailing of the steamer **Crescent City**: Capt S Carmichael, of Gloversville Minng Co, N Y; Mr Haggatt, of the same company; Mr T C Clough, of Enfield, Conn, of hernia; Mr Wilson, of Vt, of fever; Mr J H Poiser, of Canada, typhoid fever; & Mr Wm Dezeny, of Geneva, congestion of the brain.

Died: on May 13, Mrs Maria A Thompson, formerly of Culpeper Co, Va, in her 52nd year. Her funeral is at the residence of her son-in-law, John R Murray, on 4½ st, at 4 o'clock this afternoon.

Died: on May 9, in St Louis, of the cholera, Mr Wm Hill, aged 25 years, formerly a resident of Wash City.

TUE MAY 15, 1849
Appointments by the Pres:
Geo Lunt, of Mass, to be U S Atty for the district of Massachusetts, vice Robt Rantoul, jr, removed.
Chas Devens, jr, of Massachusetts, to be U S Marshal for the district of Massachusetts, vice Isaac O Barnes, removed.
Gideon Fitz, of Miss, to be Receiver of Public Moneys at Jackson, Miss, & not Gideon Fitch, as heretofore published.
Thos H Kent, of Md, to be U S Marshal for the district of Md, & not Jas H Kent, as heretofore published.

E H Howard, of Sheboygan, Wisc, has started for Calif in a boat-wagon of his own construction. Upon reaching a river the running-gear of the wagon can be unshipped in a few minutes, & taken aboard the boat while crossing.

City Ordinance-Wash. 1-Act for the relief of Francis Lamb: the sum of $35 be paid to him, being a balance due for making a gilt frame for a portrait now in the Council Chamber, including irons, & hanging.

Died: on Tue last, at Langollen, Loudoun Co, Va, Cuthbert Powell, in his 72nd year. He was formerly a resident of Alexandria, where he was Mayor; &, after his removal to Loudoun, was honored with a seat in the Legislature of his native State, & afterwards represented the district in which he lived in the U S Congress. He was for many years a magistrate in Loudoun Co.

Died: on May 13, in Balt, of paralysis, Mr Clement T Coote, a native of England, but for the last 32 years a resident of Wash City. His funeral is from the residence of Purser Wm Speiden, on F st, near the Navy Dept, this afternoon, at 4 o'clock. [He was Past Grand Master of the Grand Lodge of D C. Masons in good standing to attend his funeral. –Chas S Frailey, G Sec]

Died: on May 10, at his father's residence, in Seneca, Montg Co, Md, Chas Vinson, jr, in his 33rd year.

Died: on May 14, in Wash City, Eliz Parsons, in her 13th year. Her funeral is this day at 4 o'clock, from the residence of her mother, near the Navy Yard Bridge.

Died: on May 9, in Wash City, Noble Eugene, son of Mr Thos Bayne, aged 2 years, 1 month & 8 days. His untimely death has cast a pall of gloom over the hearts of a family circle whose affections centered in him.

Mrd: on May 13, in Wash City, by Rev L I Gilliss, Mr Theodore P Stallings to Miss Honora Anne Day, of Alexandria, Va.

From St Louis, May 9. 1-Gov Boggs writes from Sonora, Calif, that he has acquired great wealth. He says that nothing would induce him to live in the States. He was formerly of Missouri. 2-Capt Howard, the husband of the woman recently tried at Cincinnati for the murder of her husband's paramour, killed a Mr Freeman at Independence, Mo, on May 6, & also shot Capt Steward.

Calif emigrants: authentic information to May 2, that the East Tennessee & Calif Mining Co was to leave Knoxville for El Dorado on May 3. Members of this company, which we are requested to publish. Gen A Anderson, conductor; Maj Jas M Anderson, assist conductor; Rev R G Williams, chaplain; David A Deaderick, treas; B M Knight, assist treas; Byron Ford, Commissary; E F De Selding, sec; J A Anderson, quartermaster; J Crozier Deaderick, Cyrus Englis, W W Ramsey, Alex Ramsey, S White, Robt Deaderick, J King, Andrew King, Madison Ross, Wm Lowry, Kelsey Powers, Fred Kemp, Jos Bailey, Dr J P Garvin, surgeon; Dr J B Anderson, physician; J C Brown, F F Keller, A P Henley, Jacob S Stuart, Jas V Anderson, John Englis, Saml G McClellan, Wm King, Chas Ford, Matthew Knox, Burdett Hatch, A L Bohrer, Jos Q Wilbur, Geo Russell, Newton Reynolds, B M McCulloch, celebrated Texan ranger, Mr McCulloch, his brother, & Mr McNutt.

Sale of horses, cattle, & corn at auction, on May 18, at *Abingdon*, the farm of the late Gen Alex Hunter; also wagons, carts, & household furniture.
—Wm D Nutt, exc of Alex Hunter, deceased.

Official: Gen Orders, #27: War Dept, Adj Gen Ofc, Wash, May 10, 1849.
In purusance of the orders of the Pres of the U S, Maj Gen Scott will resume the command of the Army & the duties in all that regards its discipline & military control, according to the regulations prescribed for the guidance of the Gen Commanding-in-Chief.

Obit- of Danl Carroll, of Duddington; none enjoyed more of the confidence & esteem of its founder, Geo Washington, than Danl Carroll, of Duddington. He made every exertion for the accommodations of the first Congress in Washington, by the erection of numerous bldgs. He was a friend to the poor. The infirmities of age & disease had deprived him of the ability to leave his own mansion for a considerable period of time. He died as a Christian & as a parent should die, blessed with the full vigor of his intellectual faculties.

Wm A Richardson announces that he has commenced the Tailoring Business again on 15th st, & is prepared to make the most fashionable styles, for cash.

To let, an Ofc on Pa ave, at 14th st. Apply on the premises to J O Sargent.

WED MAY 16, 1849
Appointments by the Pres: 1-Hugh Maxwell, [to take effect Jun 30 next.] to be Collector of N Y, vice Cornelius W Lawrence, resigned. 2-John Young, to be Assist Treas, vice Wm C Bouck, removed.

Explosion on Lake Erie, on May 6, on board the steamer **Michigan**. The following were killed: Richd Williams, Seymour, Apperwolm, Martin Fitz, firemen, & Louis Keiffer, a young man who was working his passage to Erie. Geo Merritt, deck-hand, was badly scalded, but not mortally. It was doubtless the effect of racing.

At the Franklin Institute of Phil, a medal & premium were awarded to B Franklin Palmer, of Meredith, N H, for his invention of an artificial leg.

May-day at the Academy of the Visitation, Gtwn, on May 7. Participants: Miss Mary, daughter of Saml Adams, of Wash; Miss Mary Ellen, daughter of Peter Brady, of Wash; Miss Mary Ann, daughter of G Ennis, of Wash; Miss White, of Charleston, S C; & Misses Deveraux, Broscoe, Ford, & P Roach, of Wash. Directress: Sr Mary Bernard, aided by Misses Marion Ramsey & Amanda Clare, of Wash.

The corner-stone of the new St Vincent's Female Orphan Asylum was laid on Mon last by Rev Fr Mathews; address was delivered by Rev J P Donelan, of Balt. The new asylum is at the corner of G & 10th sts.

Household & kitchen furniture at auction on May 21, by order of the Orphan's Court, at the late residence of Gen Alex'r Hunter, deceased, at the corner of 3rd & C sts. –Wm D Nutt, exc -A Green, auctioneer

Died: on May 14, in Wash City, Isaac Canfield Smith, formerly of Duchess Co, N Y, & for the last 12 years a resident of Wash City. His funeral is this evening, at 4 o'clock, from his late residence, in 12th, near F st.

Died: on May 15, in Gtwn, Chas A Burnett, in his 81st year. His funeral is today, at 5 o'clock, from his late residence, on Bridge st.

Died: on May 12, Catherine Batista, infant daughter of Abraham & Sarah Butler, aged 10 months & 18 days.

Trustee's sale of valuable Mill property: by deed of trust from Edw W Beatty to Clement Cox, dated Aug 26, 1840, recorded in liber W B 83, folios 27, of the land records of Wash Co, D C, by order of the Circuit Court of D C, in the cause of Beatty vs the Farmers & Mechanics' Bank of Gtwn, in Chancery. For sale on Jun 15 next: the mill property with the apurtenances, now in the occupancy of Beatty, in said county, on the Chesapeake & Ohio Canal: includes 1 acre, 3 rods, & 34 perches of land: 3 story stone-mill, with modern machinery. –Walter S Cox, Trustee -Ed S Wright, auctioneer

THU MAY 17, 1849
For rent: upper part of the house on Pa ave, near 9th, over J M Peerce's grocery, & now occupied by Miss Jane Biscoe as a millinery establishment. Possession given Jun 1, 1849. Apply to J M Peerce below.

Appointment by the Pres: Chas T Maddox to be Postmaster for the city of Balt, to take effect on Jul 1, vice Jas M Buchanan, who resigned the ofc on Apr 17, his resignation to take effect on Jul 1.

Mrs Charles, a prominent actress, who has been announced to appear at New Orleans on May 4, died suddenly the same afternoon.

Wash Corp: 1-Ptn from Edw Chapman: referred to the Cmte on Improvements. 2-Ptn of W H Ward & others, for flag footways across H & I sts: referred to the Cmte on Improvements. 3-Cmte on Improvements: ptn of Z M P King & others, for a flag footway across H st north: passed. 4-Ptn of Joel Downer & others: for a flag footway across D st: passed.

For rent: 2 story frame cottage, on Capitol Hill, adjoining the residence of B B French: rented at $150 per annum. Inquire of John C Brent, 4½ & C sts, or at his residence, Capitol Hill.

Mrd: on May 15, at *Rosedale*, near Gtwn, D C, by Rev Mr Ten Broeck, Nicholas Quesenberry, of King Geo, Va, to Eliz Rousby, daughter John Green.

Died: on May 14, in Wash City, accidentally, in consequence of a fall, John Stark, of N H, a descendant of the late Gen Stark, of Revolutionary memory.

FRI MAY 18, 1849
The descendants of Franklin. Footnote on page 7, part one, of the Authbiography of Franklin, just published by the Harpers: there is not a male descendant of Dr Franklin's grandfather now living, who bears the name of Franklin, the reader is informed that his daughter, Sarah, married Richd Bache in 1767, & their descendants are numerous, 6 out of 7 marrying, viz: Benj Franklin Bache, who married Margaret Marcoe/Markoe; Wm, who married Catharine Wistar; Deborah, Wm J Duane; Richd, a daughter of Alex'r J Dallas; Sarah, Thos Sergeant. This statement is imperfect & inaccurate. Below is the list of the children of Richd & Sarah Bache:
Benj F Bache married Mgt Hartman Markoe
Wm Bache married Catharine Wistar
Sarah Bache died in infancy
Eliz Franklin Bache married John E Harwood
Louis Bache married, first, Mary Ann Swift; second, Hester Agee
Deborah Bache married Wm John Duane
Richd Bache married Sophia B Dallas
Sarah Bache married Thos Sergeant.
-Veritas

Terrible destitution: within 4 days last week inquests were held by P Mannion, coroner, on the bodies of John Hart, Thos Glynn, Mary Forde, Patt Walsh, Jas Walsh, & T Gibbons: death was caused by destitution & starvation. In Ruskmuck, a woman died from want of food & was found by the side of a ditch -Tuam Herald. On Thu John Denahy & his wife were found dead at Upper Ahane, in the parish of Cullon, near Millstreet. Denahy was a farmer, & tenant ot Mr Thos G French, of Marino. –Cork Examiner. On Monday Michl Corcoran & his wife Mary Corcoran died of starvation at Curryquin. -Neagh Guardian

Willis Hall, for some time past counsel of the Corp of N Y, had tendered his resignation of said ofc, which has been accepted by the authorities.

Sickness at the West: Mr Ricketts, a contractor on the railroad, & 7 of his men, have died of cholera at Floydsburgh, Ky. The Cincinnati steamboat **Chas Hammond**, arrived from New Orleans at Louisville on May 11, had 30 cases of cholera & 9 deaths. The steamer **St Joseph**, down from Council Bluffs, report having met the steamer **Mary** at Glasgow, bound up, with a number of Mormon emigrants on board. Capt Scott, of the **Mary**, informed the ofcrs that there had been 21 deaths on board since she left this city. Mortality was confined to the Mormon emigrants on deck.

Personal damages. John Flagg has recovered $800 damages against the town of Millbury, for injuries sustained through a bad road in the town. Wm Cushman & wife have recovered $400 at Worcester, of the Western Railroad Corp, for injury sustained by Mrs Cushman, in consequence of the train having been too soon set in motion from the station at East Brookfield, where she was to stop. Wm W Boyington has recovered $950 at Springfield, of the Western Railroad Co, for the burning of his shop, through a spark from one of the Company's engines. The Conn Railroad Co have filed a motion for a new trial in the case in which Ezra H Corning obtained a verdict of $9,040, on the ground of excessive damages. –Boston Courier

Household & kitchen furniture at auction on May 25, by order of the Orphans Court of Wash Co, D C, at the late residence of Mrs Eliz Ross, deceased, on 7th st. –R L Ross, exc -A Green, auctioneer

Criminal Court: U S vs Danl Drayton: found not guilty of stealing the 2 slaves belonging to Andrew Hoover.

Mrd: on May 15, in Wash City, by Rev Mr Rozell, W H Walker to Miss Sarah L Murphy, all of Wash City.

SAT MAY 19, 1849
Principal of the Cumberland Academy having become vacant by the appointment of Mr Magraw to an ofc under the Gov't, the trustees are desirous of filling the vacancy without unnecessary delay: salary of $700 over & above all tuition fees. Address The Trustees of the Cumberland Academy, Cumberland, Md. –Wm Price, Pres of the Board of Trustees.

Criminal Court: 1-Yesterday, Danl Drayton was convicted of transporting upwards of 70 slaves belonging to different owners from the District of Columbia. The Court sentenced the prisoner to pay a fine of $140 & costs in each case, & to be imprisoned until the said fines were all paid. 2-Edw Sayres, convicted of the same offence in the like number of cases, was sentenced to pay a fine of $100 & costs in each case, & to be imprisoned until the said fines were all paid. 3-Thos Hand, alias Shuster, found guilty of stealing the Gov't jewels from the Patent Ofc, was sentenced to suffer 3 years imprisonment in the Penitentiary.

Appointments by the Pres: Logan Hunter, of New Orleans, to be U S Atty for the Eastern District of Louisiana, vice Thos J Durant, removed.
Land Ofcrs:
Receiver of Public Moneys:
John Corkery, of La, at Greensburg, La, vice Theodore Gillespie, removed.
Wm H Wallace, of Iowa, at Fairfield, Iowa, vice Verplanck Van Antwerp, removed.
Easton Morris, of Iowa, at Iowa City, Iowa, vice Enos Lowe, removed.
Mordecai Morly, of Iowa, at Dubuque, Iowa, vice Geo McHenry, removed.
Register of the Land Ofc:
Thos Webb, of Louisiana, at Greensburg, La, vice C D Strickland, removed.
Geo Wilson, of Iowa, at Fairfield, Iowa, vice Bernhart Henn, removed.
Jesse Bowen, of Iowa, at Iowa City, Iowa, vice Chas Neally, removed.
Thos McKnight, of Iowa, at Dubuque, Iowa, vice Warner Lewis, removed.

Mr Senator Rusk, on his return from this city to Texas, presented, on the part of the ex-Pres Polk, the sword voted by Congress to Gen J P Henderson, for his conduct at Monterey. Gen Henderson declined receiving the honor in public.

Mrs Brooks & her niece, while crossing the railroad at Cheshire, Conn, on Fri, in a wagon, it came in contact with the engines attached to the cars. The ladies were violently thrown out, & the latter killed.

On Apr 20 Louis Napoleon entered upon his 42nd year. The President opened the grand ball at Elysee with the Princess Callimaki, the wife of the Turkish Ambassador. He was most particular in his attentions to the marchioness of Londonderry.

Colt's improved repeating pistols. Expecting to be absent in Europe for some months, all inquiries to said arms may be addressed to J Knox Walker, Washington, who is empowered as my atty & general agent to contract & receive orders for the delivery of said Pistols. –Saml Colt

Died: on May 18, Saml Lewis, of Wash City, in his 70th year. His funeral is on Sun next, at 4 o'clock, from his late residence on 17th st.

Died: on May 18, Dr John L Hawkins, formerly of Chas Co, Md, but for the last 12 months in Wash City, in his 58th year. His funeral is today, at half past 4 o'clock, from his late residence on L st, between 8th & 9th sts.

Died: on May 17, after a short illness, Michl Kehrer. His funeral is this morning at 10 o'clock, from his late residence on Pa ave, between 14th & 15th sts.

Died: on May 7, at his residence, in Culpeper Co, Va, Maj Yancey, in his 75th year; a participant in the closing events of the Revolutionary war, & as a private citizen remarkable for simpicity & integrity of character.

Handsome brick house for rent: lately occupied by Mr S Harkness: located between 8th & 9th st, fronting on K st. Apply to Mr J T Walker, 2 doors east of the premises.

In Chancery: Dyer et al vs Stewart et al. Trustee in this cause has sold: part of lot 10 in square 348, to Chas Cluskey, for $396; the western part of lot 3 in square 370, on L st, to Jas H Smith, for $375; & the residue of said lot 3 to Thos Bowman for $674.18. Ratify same. –Jno A Smith

MON MAY 21, 1849
The steamer **Empire**, Capt Tupper, which left N Y on Thu for Albany & Troy, was run into at night, near Newburgh, by a schnr heavily laden with lumber. The steamer was struck near the forward gangway, & as soon as struck, began to sink rapidly. The steamer **Rip Van Winkle**, nearby, got alongside & relieved many of the passengers from their perilous situation. It is ascertained that about 10 persons are known missing. Among the bodies found are, Miss Delia Avery; 4 brothers named Ladd; a child of Mrs Smith; 2 children of Mr Carson; & 2 children of Mr Hayes. Among the most afflicted of the sufferers was Mr Noyes Ladd, last from Stonington, Conn, who was one of the party of 14, himself, wife, 3 children; mother, sister, brothers; his wife's sister, Miss Eliz Williams; Miss Delia Avery, of Preston, Conn; Miss Celia Gallop, of Ledyard, Conn, all on their way to Springfield, Ill, to reside.

Lt Woodhull S Schenck, U S Navy, died of cholera on Fri last, at St Louis. He had proceeded there with the party of Gen Collier, on the way to Calif. He was the son of Gen W S Schenck, of Ohio, & brother of Robt C Schenck, Rep in Congress from the Dayton district, & of Lt J F Schenck, of the Navy; he was also a nephew of Com Rodgers, of the Navy. He left a very interesting family, having married a fair daughter of one of the most estimable families of this city, to whom & to all his family & friends we tender our sincere condolence. –Cin Chron [May 31st newspaper: see correction.]

Catharine Murphy, aged 9 years, & Hermoa Murphy, aged 6 months, daughters of John Murphy, of Albany, were found drowned in a cistern on Wed last. It is presumed that the elder child dropped the infant into the cistern, & in attempting its rescue was herself drowned. A 3rd child also fell in, but was rescued. –Evening Journal

The Hon Danl Duncan, late a member of the Hse o/Reps from the State of Ohio, died in Wash City on May 18. His funeral will take place from Mrs Harrison's, his late residence, between 4½ & 6th sts, Pa ave, on May 22, at 12 o'clock. –Thos J Campbell, Clerk of the Hse o/Reps. [Jun 18th newspaper:Mr Duncan died of a pulmonary affection, in his 43rd year. He was born in Shippensburg, Pa, Jul 22, 1806. He lost his father when he was but 6 years old. At age 9, he accompanied Gen Saml F McCracken, of Lancaster, to Ohio, on horseback. He was employed in the McCracken's store about 6 years, & returned to Pa & went to school. He entered the College at Canonsburg & spent some years there. His mother died in 1822. In 1827 he returned to Ohio, & established himself in the mercantile business in Newark. On Oct 18, 1832, he was married to the daughter of the late Col Danl Convers, of Zanesville. He was elected to the Hse o/Reps in 1844 & 1846. During a protracted illness of about 5 months no murmur of complaint escaped his lips.]

J D Learned, formerly a resident of Balt, & for a few years a resident & editor of a paper in this city, died at St Louis on May 8.

Suicide of a murderer: Boston, May 19. Dr Coolidge, the murderer of Mathews, committed suicide in consequence of having been detected in a plot with a prisoner, who was about to be liberated, to kill Flint, his former student. Coolidge was found on the floor expiring, & soon died. [May 24th newspaper: Dr Valorus P Coolidge committed suicide in the State prison at Thomaston; letters in his handwriting contained confessions of the murder of Edw Matthews. –Boston Cour]

Lt Hartslein, U S Navy, has received orders from the Navy Dept to take command of the U S mail-steamer **Falcon**. She leaves N Y on May 26 with the mails for the Pacific.

Mr Jas O Oliver, of Chas Co, Md, has a white crow which was recently taken from the nest of its black parent crows.

Mrd: on May 8, by Rev Mr Hodges, Mrs Jas H Mead to Miss Julia Ann Bayley, all of Wash City.

Mrd: on May 15, by Rev Mr Dieson, Stephen J Ober, of Wash City, to Hannah, youngest daughter of Chas Kettlewell, of Adams Co, Pa.

Died: on May 19, Henry Ann Queen. Her funeral is this day at 4 o'clock, from the residence of John R Queen, Garrison st.

Nat'l Institute: meeting this evening, at 7:30. –C F Stansbury, Rec Sec

Boarding: Mrs Eliza Robinson can accommodate with room & board. Situated in Mechanic's Row, free from the dust of the avenue.

Santa Fe: St Louis, May 17. By the arrival of Mr Skinner in this city today we have intelligence from Santa Fe to Apr 30. Two of the party that went out with Col Fremont, Bill Williams & *Ned Kerne, were killed by the Utahs in Mar last while on an expedition in search of the philosophical instruments & other property lost by Col F during his unfortunate journey. Mr Aubry & 3 others are reported to have been killed by Indians near El Paso. A band of American robbers were recently captured & taken to Santa Fe. [*See May 29th newspaper.]

Horses & carriages for hire & sale: T M Milburn, at his residence next door to McKendree Chapel, Mass. I forewarn the public against buying or trading for a conditional due bill for $27.12½ given by me to Geo Barber, [horse doctor,] as I, for good & sufficient reasons, will not pay said due bill. -T M Milburn

For rent: 2 story brick house on Capitol Hill, near the old Capitol, on A st. Apply to Mrs Mary Sweeny, on East Capitol st.

TUE MAY 22, 1849
Mrd: on May 9, in Caswell, N C, by Rev J H Pickara, Maj Thos S Slade, of Lincoln, to Miss Emeline H Cobb, only daughter of John Cobb.

Mrd: on May 15, in Boston, Mr Wm C Rives, jr, son of Hon Wm C Rives, of Va, & Miss Grace Winthrop Sears.

Black Walnut Island for sale: on Jul 9, at the Court-house in Leesburg, Loudoun Co, Va: formerly owned by Washington Bowie, situated in the Potomac river, in Montg Co, Md: contains 470 acres of arable land; improvements are a large octagon stone barn, with extensive sheds. Mr Lamb, on the premises, will show the same; & Wm H Gray, of Leesburg, Va, will make known the terms. –Wilson C Swann

Cotton Factory for sale: on Jun 20, on the premises, at Elysville, Howard district, Md: improvements consist of a new 3 story granite factory bldg; a 2 story stone mill or factory bldg; a 1 story granite bldg, intended for a dye-house; a saw-mill; smith shop; store house; 6 brick & 2 stone dwlgs; & 2 smaller stone tenements. Dr Moore, residing on the premises, or the Messrs Ely, residing in the neighborhood, will show the property. By order of the Board: L W Gosnell, Pres Okisko Co.

The Buffalo Daily Courier of Tue says: A telegraphic despatch was received yesterday from Louisville, stating that our fellow citizen, Danforth Marble, had died of cholera on the day pervious in that city. He was widely known in this country as an actor of the first talent, & here, where he had long been a resident, he was universally admired & beloved.

Mrd: on May 15, in Norwich, Conn, by Rev Mr Morgan, Thos A Hubbard & Sarah Coit Lanman, daughter of Chas Jas Lanman.

Died: on May 20, in Wash City, in his 48th year, after a tedious illness, John Reitz, a native of the State of N Y, but for many years a resident of Wash City.

Died: May 18, Mrs Margaretta, consort of Zachariah Chaney, aged 27 years.

Died: on May 8, at Mantua, Northumberland Co, Va, in her 42nd year, Mrs Agnes A Smith, wife of Col Jas M Smith.

WED MAY 23, 1849
The funeral of the Hon Danl Duncan, late a Member of the Hse o/Reps, took place yesterday from his late residence in Wash City. The following gentlemen acted as pall-bearers:

Mr Cabell, of Fla	Mr I E Holmes, of S C
Mr Pendleton, of Va	Mr Bowdon, of Ala
Mr Marsh, of Vt	Mr Barrow, of Tenn
Mr Marvin, of N Y	Mr C B Smith, of Indiana

Maj Gen W J Worth died of cholera, on May 7, at San Antonio de Bexar, in Texas. There was not a braver spirit in all the ranks of his chivalric profession than his. [May 25th newspaper: Gen Worth entered the army a Lt in 1813, & served with distinguished credit during the war with Great Britain; rewarded by promotion to the 2 highest grades in the army for his brilliant & successful conduct in the campaigns in Fla & Mexico.]

Appointments by the Pres:
Register of the Land Ofc:
Turner R King, at Springfield, Ill, vice Jas W Barrett, removed.
Cornelius Rosevelt, at Genesee, Mich, vice John Barton, removed.
Receiver of the Land Ofc:
Walter Davis, at Springfield, Ill, vice Archer G Herndon, removed.
Geo H Smith, at Newnansville, Fla, vice John Parsons, removed.
Andrew Guthrie to be Marshal of the western district of Tenn, vice Robt J Chester, removed.
Collectors of the Customs:
Wm R Easton, Nantucket, Mass, vice Chas W Rand, removed.
Ebenezer Bacon, Barnstable, Mass, vice S B Phinney, removed.
Saml L Thaxter, Fall River, Mass, vice Phineas B Leland, removed.
Wm T Russell, New Bedford, Mass, vice Jos T Adams, removed.
Jacob Richardson, Oswego, N Y, vice Geo H McWhorter, removed.
Levi Allen, Buffalo, N Y, vice Henry W Rogers, removed.
Wm Bowden, Petersburg, Va, vice J Travis Rosser, removed.
Surveyors of the Customs:
Wm T Averill, Ipswich, Mass, vice A H Wildes, removed.
Philip J Gray, Camden, N J, vice Chas S Garrett, removed.
Henry Woods, Pittsburg, Pa, vice John B Guthrie, removed.
Wm K Bond, Cincinnati, Ohio, vice Patrick Collins, removed.
By the Sec of the Interior:
Wm J Howard to be Pension Agent at Pittsburg, Pa, vice John B Guthrie, removed.

Mrs Farnham has had to leave for Calif with a very small number of ladies accompanying. These are the ladies who sailed in the ship **Angelique** for Calif from N Y on Sat, there being also 15 gentlemen: Miss Sampson, Mrs Barker, Mrs Griswold, Mrs Farnham, 2 children & servant.

Meridian Hill, an elegant mansion, will be sold with the valuable farm of 110 acres. Title indisputable. Situated on the height directly in front, 1¼ miles from the Pres' House. –J Florentius Cox

Lynch Law: at Mills' Point, Ky, Dr Jas S Douglass suspected Wiley E Brinkley of stealing $3,000 from him, & had him flogged in a most cruel manner to make him confess. Several days later, after partially recovering, Brinkley shot & killed Dr Douglass.

Ofcrs of the Bible Society of Wash City for the ensuing year:
Pres: Matthew St Clair Clarke
Vice Presidents:
Rev Jas Laurie, D D   Rev L F Morgan
Rev C M Butler, D D   Rev O B Brown
Rev J C Smith   Rev S D Finckel
Sec: Mitchel H Miller
Treas: Michl Nourse

Directors:
Rev C A Davis
Jas Adams
Wm H Campbell
John P Ingle
Wm Lloyd
Presley Simpson

Rev Ulysses Ward
Thos Blagden
Jas L Edwards
Dr R Johnson
A Rothwell
A N Zevely

For rent: 3 story brick dwlg on Md ave & 10th st. Inquire of W G Emery, Granite Cutter, near Railroad Depot.

Land for sale: the undersigned is authorized by the proprietor, Thos Berry, of **Oxen Hill**, to make sale of that desirable little farm called *Spring Valley*, containing about 145 to 150 acres. I have resided very near the place for a number of years, have known it well upwards of 40 years, & have never known a death there, although large families have resided upon it, to wit: Saml Hanson, the Rev Mr Mackenheimer, & others. –Zach Walker

Died: on May 22, in Wash City, Mrs Martha Boone, relict of the late Ignatius Boone, in her 78th year. Her funeral will take place today, at 4 o'clock, from the residence of Mr John F Boone, on 8th st.

Wrecking of the steamer **Empire**, in Orange Co, on May 17: inquest before the Coroner at Newburgh concluded on Sat, & resulted in a verdict attributing the collision to the carelessness or want of judgment of the pilot of the **Empire**. Deaths by drowning: Eliza Noble, Geo L Buckland, & Isabella Carson. Additional dead bodies have been found: Eliza Carson, her son, aged 8, Geo Buckland, a boy named Duncan, aged 10, 3 females, aged from 18 to 30, a man aged about 25, a boy aged about 14, without money, who had leave to work his fare to Albany, 3 of the brothers Ladd, & one other not identified. [May 25th newspaper; Levi Smith, the pilot of the steamer **Empire**, has been arrested at N Y, & to be tried for alleged misconduct in not preventing the collision which caused the wreck of the boat & the loss of so many lives.]

For rent: large & beautiful residence at the intersection of Md & Va aves, recently occupied by Wm A Bradley. Possession given immediately. -Marshall Brown

Marshal's sale: by writ of fieri facias under the lien law, issued from the Clerk's Ofc of the Circuit Court of Wash Co, D C., to me directed: public sale, for cash, on Jun 18: all the right & title of John Rynex of, in, & to the following property: certain bldgs erected on lots 2 & 3 in Peter's Beatty's Threlkeld's & Deaken's Addition to Gtwn; on the piece of ground lying in front of lot 4 in said Addition; & on the western half of all that part of Fayette st which lies between Water st & the C & O Canal; & on that part of Water st, 20 feet wide, north of the southern line of Water st, purchased by said Rynex from Miller & Duvall, consisting of a large brick moulding house, 2 stone stacks for melting iron ore, 1 large brick wheel-house & connecting shed: seized & levied upon as the property of John Rynex, & sold to satisfy Judicials 68, to Mar term, 1849, in favor of Wm C & Simon J Temple. –Robt Wallace, Marshal of D C

Died: on May 21, Jacob Payne, in his 69th year, leaving a large family & numerous friends to mourn his loss. His funeral is today at 2 o'clock, at his late residence, near the Little Falls Bridge.

Balt, May 22. From *Snow Hill* we learn that the trial of Rev Thos J Burroughs for shooting Jas Baird Bishop was concluded on Sat, when the jury brought in a verdict of acquittal, on the ground that Burroughs had acted altogether in self-defence.

THU MAY 24, 1849
Wash Corp: 1-Election of the com'rs to superintend the annual election on the first Mon in Jun next: duly elected:

Chas A Davis	Valentine Harbaugh	Chas Munroe
Saml Duvall	Jas C McGuire	Jas Crandell
Jas W Sheahan	Peter F Bacon	Michl Carroll
Willard Drake	Savid Saunders	Chas Newton
Elexius Simms	E H Metcalf	J W Martin
Robt Farnham	J T Van Resick	Craven Ashford
Geo Crandell	Cornelius Tims	Wm Wise

2-Ptn of Patrick McGee, praying remission of a fine: referred to the Cmte of Claims. 3-Ptn of Jos Thompson & others, in regard to the grade of K st, between 12th & 14th sts: referred to the Cmte on Improvements. 4-Ptn of John E Neale, praying the remission of a fine: referred to the Cmte of Claims. 5-Ptn of Alfred Prather & several other butchers of the city, praying remission of fines: referred to the Cmte of Claims.

The beautiful residence of Mrs Freme, near Brattleboro, Vt, was destroyed by fire on Mon. The inmates of the house were all females, consisting of Mrs Freme, her 2 sisters & 2 domestics. All escaped except the lady of the mansion, who perished in the flames. There is every reason to suppose she was suffocated by the heat & smoke, so that her end was not as painful as might as first appear. Mrs F was an opulent widow lady, of English origin. Her brother, Capt Eben Wells, & his family, lived near by.

Wanted immediately, a good journeyman Barber. –L Saur, Hair-dresser, 2nd door above Odd Fellows' Hall, 7th st.

Mr Geo C Longacre, of Reading, Pa, was jammed between 2 cars on Sat last, at the depot in that placed, & so seriously injured that he died the following day. He leaves a wife & 4 children.

Danl Cummings, who was seriously beaten in Balt about 2 weeks since by a number of men who undertook to administer Lynch law to him for the offence of stealing some shirts, died on Sat from the effect of his injuries. All the parties were arrested except Luke Flynn, who is said to be the man who inflicted the fatal blow, with a pair of tongs, crushing his skull.

$3 reward for return of a red horned cow, that strayed from my premises, in Wash, on Fri. –John Foy

Mrd: on May 22, by Rev J B Donelan, Mr John S Finch to Miss Ellen Eliza Ridgway, eldest daughter of Mr E Ridgway, all of Wash City.

Died: on May 13, in St Louis city, of cholera, Miss Helen Augustine, daughter of Smith Minor, late of Fairfax Co, Va, in her 18th year. Her father & mother, with a family of 6 daughters, had just arrived in St Louis from the Old Dominion, full of hopes, but in a few short hours the scene was changed.

N Y Courier & Enquirer: the obit notices record the death, on May 14, in her 83rd year, that of Mrs Hannah Gallatin: born in this city, where her maternal ancstors were established, in 1766. She was the daughter of Jas Nicholson, the first on the list of American post capts, a distinguished ofcr in the war of the Revolution, & the elder of the family which, through 3 generations, has sustained the honor of the naval service. Cmdor Nicholson was also connected with the public men of the Union by the marriage of 3 of his daughters, besides Mrs Gallatin, to members of Congress, two of whom [Mr Seney & Mr Montgomery] represented Md, the State of his origin: & the third, the Hon Wm Few, was a member of the Fed Convention & a Senator from Georgia. In 1793, the subject of this notice married the Hon Albert Gallatin, who had then been elected a Senator of the U S from Pa. During the eventlful career of this eminent statesman-who still survives, on the brink of eternity, this greatest of human bereavement-Mrs Gallatin was his constant friend & adviser. To Mrs Gallatin was mainly owing the establishment of that American Church or Congregation in Paris, the first minister of which was our townsman, the late Rev Mr Bruen, whose premature death a few years since the whole community had so much reason to lament. For the last 20 years Mrs Gallatin resided in this city of her nativity, in the full enjoyment of her children & her children's children.

Shad fisheries for rent: on the Potomac river, well known as the Gut & Bar Landings, in Pomonkey Neck, Chas Co, Md, midway between Craney Island & the White House. Address Edmund J Plowden, at Miles Town P O, St Mary's Co, Md.

Valuable tract of land at auction: Jun 4, adjoining the District line, near Rock Creek Church road, it being a part of the farm occupied by Mr Wm Markwood, contains 60 acres, with a comfortable dwlg house. –A Green, auct

FRI MAY 25, 1849
Foreign Items: 1-Miss O'Neil, the celebrated actress, has recently married Wm Becher. 2-Lord Ashburton has bought the **Stowe MSS**, for $32,000. 3-Chas Whitney, well known in N Y, having recently married a lady of Halifax, proceed with her to England. At the last accounts he was giving his imitations of American orators at Willis' rooms, London. 4-Horace Twiss, author of the Life of Lord Eldon, died suddenly on May 4, under most painful circumstances.

A sad accident at Harper's Ferry on May 17. Mr Beckham, the agent, & Jacob Greenholtze, *or Greenwood, one of the hands in the employment of the B & O Railroad Co, were engaged in the road, when a train suddenly came upon them, scarcely giving Mr Beckham time to escape, & crushing Greenholtze to death. He was an honest, industrious, & worthy man. [*Copied as written.]

Jackson Mississippian announces the death of Hon Chas Fisher, of N C, at Hillsborough, Miss, May 7, in his 59th year. He was long a member of the Legislature of N C, of which he was several times chosen Speaker, & elected to Congress.

Appointments by the Pres:
District Attys:
Wm Halsted, of N Y, for the district of N J, vice Jas S Green, removed.
Henry W Miller, of N C, for the district of N C, vice Duncan K McRae, removed.
Land Ofcrs:
Receiver of Public Moneys:
Chas H Williams, of Wisc, at Milwaukie, Wisc, vice J Albert Helfenstein, removed.
Seneca W Ely, of Ohio, at Chillicothe, Ohio, vice John L Green, who declines the ofc.
Geo H Slaughter, of Wisc, to be Register of the Land Ofc at Mineral Point, Wisc, vice Albert W Parris, removed.
Naval Ofcrs:
John McClintock, Portsmouth, N H, vice Danl Vaughan, removed.
Adam S Coe, Newport, R I, vice Geo C Shaw, removed.
Surveyors:
Asa B Waite, North Kingston, R I, vice Geo T Nichols, removed.
Jos Paddock, jr, Newport, R I, vice A Atkins, removed.
John G Needham, Pautuxet, R I, vice Jas Fisher, removed.
Appraiser:
John H Withers, Phil, from May 31, vice ___ Carpenter, removed.
Justice of the Peace:
Thos Donoho in Wash Co, D C.

Norfolk Beacon: the U S razee **Independence**, bearing the broad pennant of Cmdor Wm Brandford Shubrick, arrived in Hampton Roads on Tue. She comes direct from Valparaiso, & made the passage in 63 days. List of her ofcrs: Cmdor, Wm Brandford Shubrick. Lt Commanding, Richd L Page. Fleet Surgeon, Baily Washington. Lts, Chas Heywood, Montgomery Lewis, Wm Taylor Smith, Isaac N Brown, Henry A Wise, Saml Marcy. Purser, Hugh W Green. Chaplain, Chester Newell. Master, Wm Downes Austin. 1st Lt Marines, W W Russell. Passed Assist Surgeon, Saml Jackson. Passed Midshipmen, Alex'r F Warley, G V Denniston, F X Conover, Geo A Stevens, Earl English. Purser's Clerk, Wm W Simons, Midshipmen, John R Hamilton, Wm Henry Smith, Ralph Chandler. Boatswain, John Mills. Gunner, Benj Bunker. Carpenter's Mate, Wm Morgan. Sailmaker's Mate, ___ Hutchins.

John C Shafer has a Flour Store at the west end of Market Space, corner of C & La ave, where he will keep a general stock of Baker's & Family Flour.

Piano for sale: second-hand fine toned; reasonable terms. Apply at Mr Moenster's, on 13th st, between E & F sts.

Charleston Courier: John Robinson, died on Sat last, the oldest member of the mercantile fraternity of that city. He was in his 74th year; commenced business in this city, 53 years ago, was active up to the recent attack of disease, which terminated fatally.

Household & kitchen furniture at auction on May 28, at the residence of Mr Ferguson in Mechanics' Row, D st, near 4½ st. —A Green, auctioneer

Died: on May 24, in Wash City, at the residence of her father, Mr Andrew Smith, on G st, between 12th & 13th sts, Mrs Isabella Graham Weaver, in her 46th year. Her funeral is Fri, at half past 3 o'clock.

Orphans Court of Wash Co, D C. In the case of Rosanna Brown, Edw C Dale, & Tillotson Brown, excs of Jesse Brown, deceased, the execs & Court have appointed Jun 12th next for payment & distribution of the assests in the hands of the excs.
—Ed N Roach, Reg/o wills

Meeting of the pew-holders & members of the Central Presbyterian Church on May 26, for the purpose of electing a Pastor to said Church. —Lund Washington, sr, one of the trustees.

Marshal's sale: in virtue of a writ of fieri facias, issued in Wash Co, D C: sale of the following property: lot 10 in square 501, in Wash City, with two 2 story frame bldgs upon it. Seized & levied upon as the property of Jas Gill, & sold to satisfy judicials 148 to Mar term, 1849, in favor of Robt Brown, use of Hall & Co.
—Robt Wallace, Marshal of D C

SAT MAY 26, 1849
On May 9, a daughter of Wm & Temperance Rohrbaugh, residing a few miles from this place, aged 2 years, was killed when Mr & Mrs Rohrbaugh went to a field near the house to work a horse not accustomed to a shovel plough. The horse took afright, & the plough line, as he passed the little daughter at play, lashed around the neck of the child, killing her. —Weston [Va] Sentinel

Arrest of hotel thieves: Ofcr Norris, assisted by Ofcr Calraw, of the chief's ofc, arrested Geo Northerman & Fred'k Bilings, alias Chas F Stone, charged with stealing $45- in gold coin from Saml L Wells, of Alexandria, La, while putting up in the Irving House prior to his departure for Europe. A large portion of the money was recovered.
—N Y Journal of Commerce

Note lost or mislaid: a promissory note for $40 drawn by John Hands, endorsed by A Nailor, dated Feb 17, 1849, at 90 days, now past maturity. Reward of $1 if left at the ofc of C W Pairo, F & 15th sts.

Died: on Fri, after a lingering illness, in his 44th year, Alfred B Thruston, son of the late Judge Thruston, leaving a family & a numerous circle of relatives to mourn his death. His funeral is today at 4:30 o'clock, from his late residence on Capitol Hill.

Died: on May 22, in Gtwn, D C, of consumption, Susannah Sheppard, consort of Lodowick Sheppard, in her 60th year, leaving a family of children & grand-children, & a large circle of friends & relatives to mourn her loss.

MON MAY 28, 1849

Gerrit Smith, of N Y, offers to give lands to 1,000 white men who now have no land, & he apportions the recipients among the several counties. He excludes Madison Co, in which he lives, having already given lands to 250 persons, & he names only white persons, because he has already given deeds of lands to 3,000 colored persons. Judge Peter Smith, from whom a vast landed estate was inherited by his sons, Gen Peter Sken Smith, now in Phil, & Gerrit, who resides at Peterboro, N Y, began life a poor man, of Dutch origin, but, possessing great shrewdness & energy, became a millionaire in the little country village of Peterboro. –Kennebec Journal

Bob Moore, the thief who robbed the Quincy Stone Bank of $5,100 on Tue last, has been arrested at N Y. A part of the money was recovered.

Sir Benj D'Urban, cmder of the British forces in Canada, died suddenly at Montreal on Fri. He was struck with apoplexy.

Executions in New England. 1-Elder Enos G Dudley, who was recently convicted at Plymouth, N H, of the murder of his wife, was executed on Wed at Haverhill. He asserted his entire innocence of the crime. 2-Washington Goode, convicted of the murder of a sailor in Ann st, Boston, early last winter, was executed on Fri. He attempted to commit suicide the previous evening in his cell, with a piece of glass, but failed. He denied his guilt.

Wash Corp: 1-Act for the relief of Henry Turner: passed. 2-Act for the relief of J Succhesi: passed. 3-Cmte of Claims: asking to be discharged from the further consideration of the ptn of Jas Fitzgerald.

Household & kitchen furniture at auction on Jun 6, at the residence of Gen Herran, Minister from New Grenada, on Pa ave, near 23rd st. –A Green, auct

St Louis: fire commenced on May 17, on board the steamer **White Cloud**, lying near the head of the levee; flames carried across to the ship **Edward Bates**; to the ship **Eudora**; & to the ship **Belle Isle**. The **Edward Bates**, being half burnt up, was cast loose & fired & consumed the following **steamers**:

Taglioni	Acadia	**Martha**
Alice	**Mamluke**	**Eliza Sewart**
American Eagle	**Prairie State**	**Mandan**
Sarah	White Cloud	**Alex Hamilton**
Boreas #3	Edward Bates	**Belle Isle**
Montauk	Eudora	**Gen Brooke**
Kit Carson	**St Peters**	**Frolic**
Timour	**Red Wing**	

Estimated loss of these steamers is $318,000; value of cargoes destroyed on board or on the wharf: $200,000. The steamers **Autocrat, De Witt Clinton, Danube, Embassy, South America, New Uncle Sam, Julia, Old Uncle Sam, & Marshal Ney** were saved.

Republican of Mar 31. Dr Kearns & Bill Williams, the well known guide & trapper, were recently murdered by a band of Utahs.

Mrd: on May 24, in Wash City, by Rev G W Samson, Mr Geo Beasely to Miss America M Smith, all of Wash City.

Died: on May 22, at his home, in Phil, Victor L Godon, M D, late Assist Surgeon in the U S Navy. He bore the pains of tedious illness with cheerful fortitude, & died with the merited comfort of Christian hope.

Died: after a brief illness, at Bladensburg, PG Co, Md, at the residence of her son, Robt Wright, Mrs Harriet Wright, consort of the late Danl Wright, of Alexandria, Va, in her 78th year. [No death date given-current item.]

Suitable reward for return of lost dog, a white Spaniel Puppy. –J C Burche, C st, between 2nd & 3rd sts.

For rent: the house & premises corner of I & 13th sts: a 3 story brick, with basement. Apply to the undersigned at the Second Comptroller's Ofc, or at Mrs Willis', corner F & 13th sts. –W A Evans

Orphans Court of Wash Co, D C. Letters testamentary on the personal estate of Danl Carroll, of Duddington, late of Wash Co, deceased. –Maria Fitzhugh, Ann C Carroll, excs

By an order of distrain against the good & chattels of J W Beakley, I shall expose to sale, on Jun 2, the following goods, to satisfy rent due in arrears to Walter Lenox: 1 carved Indian sign, 1 refrigerator, 1 glass showcase, 6 arm chairs, lamps & carpet. –E G Handy, Bailiff

TUE MAY 29, 1849
Despatch from St Louis announced that Edw Kern, of Col Fremont's expedition, was killed by the Indians of the Plains. The name of Mr Kern, however, who has thus fallen, was Benj J Kern, M D, the physician of the expedition, who had relations & many friends in Phil The object of Dr Kern was to recover his own property & his brother's property lost in the expedition, as well as that of the corps. The Kern brothers were: Benj, Edw, & Richd. –Phil Bulletin

From Calif: telegraphic despatch from New Orleans, dated May 22, mentions the arrival there of the barque **Florida**, from Chagres. Mr Beall, of the U S Navy, came passenger in this vessel, & it is stated that he has a lump of gold in his possession worth $2,000. The **Florida** brings the intelligence that Col Fremont had arrived in Calif.

A young man named Wm R Griffith, at N Y, got a verdict of $5,000 for injuries sustained by being struck by a truck belonging to a hook & ladder company. His leg was broken by the concussion, &, after it had been set, erysipalitic inflammation set in that threated his life. By care & medical skill he survived.

Appointments by the Pres:
Marshals:
Geo W Jackson, of R I, for the district of R I, vice Burrington Anthony, removed.
Saml Garfield, of N H, for the district of N H, vice Cyrus Barton, removed.
Attys:
Jas M Clarke, of R I, for the district of R I, vice Walter S Burges, removed.
Wm W Stickney, of N H, for the district of N H, vice Josiah Minot, removed.
Jas R Lawrence, of N Y, for the Northern district of N Y, vice Geo W Clinton, removed.
Land Ofcrs
Register of the Land Ofc:
Jas F Mahan, of Missouri, at Palmyra, Mo, vice Benj Davies, resigned, to take effect Jun 30 next.
Isaac Leffler, of Iowa, at Stillwater, Minesota, vice Cornelius S Whitney, resigned, to take effect Jun 30 next.
Indian Agents:
Wm Butler, of S C, for the Cherokee Indians, vice Richd C S Brown, removed.
John Drennen, of Ark, for the Choctaw Indians, vice Saml M Rutherford, removed.
Thos Mosely, jr, of Missouri, for the Wyandot Indians, vice Richd Hewett, removed.
By the Sec of the Interior:
Pension Agent:
John Kelley, of N H, at Portsmouth, N H, vice Richd Jenness, removed.
Israel W Kelley, of N H, at Concord, N H, vice Isaac Hill, removed.

Mrd: on May 27, in Wash City, by Rev Jas B Donelan, Mr Wm E Morcoe to Miss Teresa Ann Culverwell, all of Wash City.

Mrd: on May 27, by Rev J B Donelan, Mr Thos Croggon to Miss Jane McCarty, all of Wash City.

Died: yesterday, Mary Kyle, infant child of Jas A & Annie E McLaughlin, aged 13 months. Her funeral is this evening, at 4 o'clock, from the residence of her grandfather, Mr Jas Caden, corner of G & 10th sts.

Died: yesterday, Miss E Harry, daughter of Mr John Harry, of the Heights of Gtwn. Her funeral will take place from her father's residence this day at 2 p m.

Information wanted of Mr Wm Frochlick, a German, [engineer & machinist,] left the Navy Yard on May 24, laboring under an aberration of mind from injuries received. He has not been heard of since, & we are apprehensive that he has destroyed himself. If found dead I will give a reward of $5 to any one who will inform me of the fact as soon as possible. –Chas H Gordon

Sale today at the residence of W G Snethen, on Missouri ave, of splendid Rosewood, Mahogany, Oak, & Ebony furniture. -E C & G F Dyer, aucts

Household & kitchen furniture at auction on Jun 1, at the residence of Capt Powell, on 3rd st, north of Gadsby's Hotel. –A Green, auctioneer

Waterloo for sale: the undersigned, the excs of Josiah Tidball, deceased, offer the farm on which he resided, near Upperville, Fauquier Co, Va, containing 800 acres: with a handsome & comfortable dwlg house, & all necessary out bldgs suitable to a gentleman's residence. –J A Tidball, Jas Marshall, excs
[Sep 27th newspaper: *Waterloo* is again advertised for sale.]

WED MAY 30, 1849
On Thu, as the train of the Rensselaer & Saratoga Railway Co was near Ballston, the engine & tender were thrown off the track & upset. The engineer, Mr Todd, was killed on the spot, & the fireman mortally wounded.

Wm Froehlich, a draughtsman, employed at the Wash Navy Yard, was found drowned in the Potomac on Mon. It appeared from testimony that Froehlich had been severely beaten, & Mr R H Harrington, & Chas Finnegan, a hackdriver in his employment, have been charged with assaulting the deceased on Thu last, in Mr Harrington's hotel, at the Navy Yard, where the deceased boarded. Finnegan was committed to jail & Mr Harrington was held to bail yesterday, in the sum of $500.

A letter received from Mr Jos Scholfield, of this city, who was at the city of Durango, State of Durango, Mexico, on Mar 29, says he left the cholera & the Rio Grande at Camargo, by detaching himself in company with 8 others from the Independent Yankee Mining Assoc, of 85 men, who embarked from N Y on Jan 29 last. Amongst his companions he names Wake Watson, Mr Buckingham, Mr Richards, [an aged man,] Fr Loverage, Noble Morehouse, Mr Bennett, & an intelligent Irishman, their interpreter, whom he does not name.

Six cents reward for runaway mulatto girl Susan Stewart, about 9 years of age.
–Maria Barcroft

Mrd: on May 27, by Rev Jas B Donelan, Mr Geo Hilbus to Miss Mary Earl, both of Wash City.

Mrd: on May 26, in Wash City, by Rev L J Gilliss, Mr Benj B Chambers to Miss Mary F Suit, of PG Co, Md.

Died: on Sat last, in Wash City, in his 32nd year, of consumption, Walter Stoops, a native of Alexandria, Va, but for several years a resident of Wash City.

Died: on May 25, at St Inigoes, St Mary's Co, Md, the Rev Jos Carbery, S J, aged about 65 years. For 30 years or more he has been the faithful & kind pastor of that & adjacent congregations.
+
Rev Jos Carbery, the amiable & esteemed Superior of *St Inigoes*, in St Mary's Co, Md, died suddenly on May 25.

THU MAY 31, 1849
Quebec papers report loss of the ship **Maria** from *Limerick*, with 111 emigrants. She foundered among the ice in the Gulf of St Lawrence, & only 5 of the crew were saved.

Lt J F Schenck, of the U S Navy, corrects one part of the obit notice of his brother which we lately copied from the Cincinnati Chronicle, by stating that their maternal grandfather was not Cmdor Rodgers, but Capt Wm Rodgers, of Long Island, who comanded the private armed ship **General Montgomerie**, during the Revolutionary war, under a commission granted him by the Congress of N Y. [See May 21st newspaper: first death notice.]

Among the passengers which embarked from Liverpool in the steamship **Caledonia** for Boston were the Abbot of Mount Millery, & 3 brothers of the Cisterian order of Trappists. They are accompanied by Brother Macarius, & design to make all arrangements for the founding of 2 monasteries of their Order somewhere in North America. The Abbott, after arranging matters here, will return ot Ireland, from whence in Aug, 40 or 50 brothers, including 4 or 5 priests, will embark for this country.

Mr Jas Cassidy, on Sun, while standing on the lower step of the front of the ladies' car attached to the Wash train of the B & O railroad, was struck by the post to which the gate is hung & knocked off. The wheel of the car severed his head from his body.

The robber of the Quincy Bank has not been caught after all. Bob Moore, who was supposed to be guilty, is now ascertained to be the robber of the Matapan Calif Co of Boston of a box containing $1,200. This money had 2 $100 notes upon the Quincy Bank, which led to the mistake.

Dr Silas Holmes, an Assist Surgeon of the U S Navy, was accidentally drowned in Mobile Bay on May 21. He was at the time the surgeon of the U S steamer **Walker**, engaged in the coast survey, & was returning to that vessel from Mobile in a sailboat when she was capsized by a sudden squall of wind. Two were lost, & 4 who clung to the boat were saved.

Berkeley Springs is now ready for company: valuable medicinal properties in the water. –John Strother

Valuable house & lot at auction: on Jul 2, by decree of the Circuit Court of Wash Co, D C, sitting in Chancery, passed in a cause wherein Jas Redfern is cmplnt & Barbara Parker & others are dfndnts. Sale of parcel of lot 4 in square 41, with a 2 story frame house, nearly new. Property is on north G, between 18th & 19th sts. –John F Ennis, trustee -A Green, auctioneer [Oct 24th newspaper: Property is resold on account of the noncompliance of the purchaser with the terms of the sale made on Jul 2, 1849.]

Mrd: on May 30, in Wash City, by Rev S A Roszel, John T Halleck, of Key West, Fla, to Mary Jane Howard, of Wash City.

Mrd: on May 22, by Rev Jas B Donelan, Mr Bernard Zell, of Balt, to Miss Julia M Byrne, of Wash City.

FRI JUN 1, 1849
Madame Rothschild, widow of the founder of the banking house, died at Frankfort-on-the-Maine, on the 7th ult, aged 99.

Appointments by the Pres: Lawrence P Crane, of Louisiana, to be U S Atty for the Western District of La, vice Octavius N Ogden, who declines the ofc.
Lawrence P Crane, of Louisiana, to be U S Atty for the Western District of La, vice Octavius N Ogden, who declines the ofc.
Orlando Brown, of Ky, to be Com'r of Indian Affairs, from & after Jun 30th next, vice Wm Medill, removed.
Lansing B Mizner, of Mich, to be Register of the Land Ofc at Detroit, Mich, vice Elisha Taylor, removed.
Robt S Kennedy, of N J, to be U S Marshal for Dist of N J, vice Saml McClurg, removed.
By the Sec of the Interior:
Wm S Wallace, of Springfield, Ill, to be Pension Agent at that place from & after Jun 30th next, vice Chas R Hurst, resigned.

Brownsville [Texas] Flag of May 16. The Camanche Indians murdered Doroteo Zamora, a most estimable citizen. He had just decided under the treaty to become an American citizen. One of his sons was killed at the same time, another badly wounded, & his daughter, a girl about 14 years of age, was carried into captivity. At the rancho de los Indios Mrs Willsey, the wife of Capt Benj Willsey, his brother, & sister-in-law, were carried off captives. The aged mother of Mrs Willsey persisted in following her children, & did so for some distance, when the Indians, seizing her, tied her hands behind her, pierced her with their lances & arrows, & left her for dead. This poor woman succeeded in reaching a neighboring rancho, in a most shocking condition, & is now, we understand, a maniac. Mr Bangs & his companion escaped from captivity.

Wash Corp: 1-Cmte of Claims: bills for the relief of Wm Baynam; of Patrick Twomy; of John H Mullen; of Owen McGee; of John E Neale; of Jas Williams, & of M Rosenstock: passed. 2-Cmte of Claims: recommend the rejection of the bills for the relief of Wm Rupp, & of E Fuller: rejected. Same cmte: discharged from the further consideration of the ptns of Edw Kersey, of Wm M Rodgers, of Susan J Werden, of Philip Eames, of John Fitzgerald, of C Shedd, & of Jas Fitzgerald.

Wash City Ordinances: 1-Act for the relief of A F Wilcox: fine for alleged violation in taking earth from the public street, is hereby remitted: provided Wilcox pay the costs of prosecution. 2-Act for the relief of Richd Harrison: fine imposed for violation of law relative to harboring of dogs, is remitted: provided Harrison pay the costs of prosecution. 3-Act for the relief of Jas C Crusor: fine imposed for an alleged violation of the law relative to hucksters, is remitted: provided he pay the costs of prosecution.

A Boston Notion: Goode, the colored man convicted & hung for murder, has been honored with a public funeral in Boston, the expenses of which, $100, were raised by subscription. –Phil Ledger

From Calif: 1-The sloop-of-war **Dale**, which sailed from San Francisco for the U S on Mar 20, has $200,000 in gold dust on board. 2-Fears are entertained at San Francisco that the brig **Lola**, from San Blas, with 55 passengers & a crew of 7, for San Francisco, had been lost at sea. The brig **Volaute** reports having passed at sea 18 dead bodies & pieces of a wreck.

Copartnership. I have this day associated with me Mr Saml Hamilton. The business will be conducted under the firm of Stans Murray & Co. –Stans Murray

Household & kitchen furniture at auction on Jun 5, at the residence of Mr J E Fowler, corner of 11th & F Sts. –A Green, auctioneer

For rent: 2 story house on 13th st, late in the occupancy of Geo W Emerson. Inquire of Henry Janney, 8th st, or to the subscriber, Alexandria, Va. –Wm Yeates

$5 reward for a horse that strayed away from Washington, F st, between 2nd & 3rd sts –David Fitzgerald

Dissolution of partnership existing between the late Raphael Semmes & B I Semmes, jr, under the name of Raphael Semmes & Co. B I Semmes, jr, will settle up the affairs of the firm. The business wil hereafter be conducted by B I Semmes, jr, & Thos I Semmes, under the name of B I Semmes & Brother. B I Semmes, jr, Thos I Semmes

The Springfield [Mass[Republican of Mon says that 3 Irish brothers of the name of Donnohan were carried over the Rapids on Sun, while fishing in the Connecticut river, & all drowned.

Died: on May 31, Clara Catharine, youngest daughter of Saml C & Mary Ann Davison, in her 2nd year. Her funeral is today at 3 o'clock, from the residence of her parents, on H st, between 18th & 19th sts.

The present surveyor, Mr Chas B Cluskey, who has discharged the duties of the ofc since the resignation of Mr Randolph Coyle, on Jun 14 last, is now before the people of Wash City for their suffrages.

SAT JUN 2, 1849
Geo Buckhart, living in Harlan Co, Ky, is perhaps the oldest man now known to be living. He is 114 years old: was born in Germantown, Pa, & has lived for several years in a hollow sycamore tree, of such dimensions as to contain his family, consisting of a wife & 5 or 6 children. The exploring agent of the American Bible Society, in his travels in Ky, recently found him. He professes to hold the Lutheran faith, being of a German family. –Bible Society Record for May

Appointments by the Pres: Collectors of the Custom:
Maurice C Black, Belfast, Maine, vice Alfred Marshall, removed.
Oliver M Hyde, Detroit, Mich, vice Chas G Hammond, removed.
E Whittlesey, to be First Comptroller, vice J W McCulloh, resigned.

Unofficialy we learn that the Hon Geo P Marsh, of Vt, has been appointed by the Pres, Minister Resident at Constantinople, vice D S Carr, recalled.
Also, that Dr Thos M Foote, of Buffalo, N Y, has been appointed Charge d'Affaires at Bogota, vice B A Bidlack, deceased.

We had yesterday the satisfaction of welcoming back to the home of his youth, for a season at least, Lt Edw F Beall, U S Navy, who lately arrived in this country, after a most expeditious journey, direct from San Francisco. We saw, in his hands, a lump of virgin gold, weighing 80 ounces, found in Calif.

One of the two statues of Adoring Angels, sculptured at Florence under the superintendence of Powers, for the sanctuary of the cathedral at Cincinnati, has arrived, & is now at the house of Bishop Purcell, in that city.

Mrd: on May 31, at Alexandria, Va, by Rev Mr Briggs, E Worthington Hall, of Wash, to Miss Louisa H Ball, of the former place.

Died: yesterday, in Wash City, in his 37th year, of consumption, Jas P Gannon, a native of county Westmeath, Ire, but for many years a resident of this District. His funeral is from his late residence on Md ave, on Sunday, at 2 o'clock.

Died: yesterday, at his residence, 1 miles east of the Capitol, Robt Isherwood. His funeral is this afternoon, at 5 o'clock.

MON JUN 4, 1849
Mr Geo Porter, Associate Editor of the Picayune, died on May 24th, after a brief illness. –New Orleans Delta

Dr Hardenbrook, who was tried last week at Rochester, N Y, on a charge of criminal practice in the line of his profession by poisoning Mr Nott, has been acquitted.

Etienne Mazureau, the distinguished jurist, was found dead in his bed at New Orleans, early on May 25. It is probable that he died of asthma. He was a native of Rochelle, France, & served some time in the French Navy. He emigrated to this country in 1804. At age 24, he settled in Louisiana.

Orphans Court of Wash Co, D C. Letters testamentary on personal estate of Saml Lewis, late of Wash Co, deceased. –Mary A Lewis, Saml J E Lewis, excs

TUE JUN 5, 1849
Teacher wanted, at Primary School, #1, in the 7th Election District of PG Co, Md: liberal salary. W W Bowie, Wm Clarke, Henry Jones, trustees

For rent: my late residence on Monument Square, Balt, for a term of not less than 4 years. Apply to Wm H Garchell, Balt. –Reverdy Johnson, Wash

The Hull of the steamer **Empire** has not been entirely raised. On Sat last, in the ladies' saloon, the body of Miss Delia Avery was found. She was from Conn, & was in company with the Ladd family. Her's is the 23rd body recovered.

John Lowry died in Stokes Co, N C, on Apr 17, aged 100 years. He was in the service against the Indians before the Revolutionary war.

Appointments by the Pres:
Wm McQuiston, of Miss, to be U S Marshal for the northern District of Miss, vice John Rayburn, removed.
Woodson L Ligon, of Miss, to be U S Atty for the northern District of Miss, vice Andrew K Blythe, removed.
H W Evans, Appraiser, Balt, Md, vice Philip Poultney, removed.
John Cowan, Surveyor, Wilmington, N C, vice Jos S Murphy, removed.
Land Ofcrs:
Receiver of Public Moneys:
Geo M Clayton, of Miss, at Columbus, Miss, vice Has H Westbrook, removed.
John W Morton, of Ill, at Shawneetown, Ill, vice Braxton Parrish, removed.
Register of the Land Ofc:
Andrew McCollum, of Ill, at Shawneetown, Ill, vice J C Sloo, removed.
Henry O McEnery, of La, at Monroe, La, vice Danl B Richardson, removed.
Evariste de Baillou, of Louisiana, at Opelousas, La, vice Murdock McIntire, removed.

Lost, a check drawn by us on the Bank of the Metropolis for $85.16, payable to A B or bearer, dated Jun 4, 1849. Payment has been stopped. The finder is requested to leave it at our store. —Geo & Thos Parker

Norfolk Beacon: a new court-martial was ordered to convene at Gosport Navy Yard yesterday, composed of the following members:

Cmdor Morris, Pres	French Forrest
Capt E A Lavallette	CmderW H Gardner
Silas H Stringham	Cmder T Aloysius Dornin
Isaac Mayo	Lt Jas H Ward
Jas Armstrong	Lt C H A H Kennedy
Saml L Breeze	Judge Advocate, Purser L T Waller

Cmdor Kearney has been ordered to Annapolis, as one of the Board for the examination of Midshipmen.

Mrd: on Jun 3, by Rev Mr Morgan, Mr Saml Handy to Miss Mary Ann Bright, all of Wash City.

Mrd: on May 31, in PG Co, Md, by Rev G W Samson, Mr Heman L Chapin, of D C, to Miss Catharine V Dement, of PG Co, Md.

Mrd: on Jun 2, in St Mary's Church, by Rev Mathias Alig, Mr Danl Shannehar to Miss Mary Ragan, both of Wash City.

Died: on Jun 4, in N Y C, Miss Mary Ellen Fitzpatrick, one of the pupils of the Mount St Vincent Academy, near Harlem. Her funeral is today at 5 o'clock, from the residence of her father, John C Fitzpatrick, Capitol Hill.

Died: on Jun 3, Mrs Catherine, wife of Michl Nash, in her 41st year. May she rest in peace!

Died: on May 14, at the *Gaines Plantation*, Wash Co, Ala, Capt Erasmus Darwin Bullock, formerly of the U S Army.

Died: on May 25, at Jefferson Barracks, Mo, Indiana B, wife of Bvt Maj D P Whiting, 7th Infty U S A, & daughter of Alfred Sandford, formerly of Covington, Ky.

Died: on May 31, Gen Geo W Tucker, of N J, in his 57th year. He had filled many offices of honor & trust under the State & Genr'l Gov't, & enjoyed the confidence of all who knew him.

Wash City Election was held yesterday: following votes from every ward but the 5th:

For Collector:
Andrew Rothwell: 857
John Hands: 577
Jas F Halliday: 376

For Register:
W J McCormick: 1247
J D Hoover: 312
C H Wiltberger: 131
Jos Radcliff: 81

For Surveyor:
C B Cluskey: 1253
W W De Main: 413

WED JUN 6, 1849
Phil Co, Pa, on Sat, two persons were killed by railroad cars, Henry Robinson, who fell from one of the cars of the passenger train from Balt, & was instantly killed. He was a Marine recently discharged from the U S ship **Independence**, at Norfolk, & on his way to Phil, where is it supposed he has friends residing. He had a considerable sum of money about him, which, with his body, was taken charge of by the Coroner. The second was an old lady named Mary McCully, aged 72 years, who was knocked down & run over by a locomotive on the Willow st railroad. The deceased was deaf.

Lost on Jun 5, a pair of heavy gold spectacles. Finder will be liberally rewarded by leaving them at Mr Albert J Webb's grocery store, near the Market, corner of 9th st & Pa ave.

Horses for sale at the stables of Jos A Williams, 8th st, between D & E sts.

Orphans Court of Wash Co, D C. Letters testamentary on the personal estate of John Reitz, late of said county, deceased. –A H Lawrence, exc

Boarding: Mrs Willis, corner of F & 13th sts.

Mrd: on May 24, by Rev Mr Chisholm, R A Williams, of Richmond, to Eliz, daughter of Col Edw Colston, of Honeywood, Berkeley Co, Va.

Died: on Jun 5, after a long & protracted illness, Mr Michl Ward, a native of the county Monaghan, Ireland, but for the last 30 years a resident of Wash City. His funeral is this evening at 4 o'clock, from his late residence.

Died: yesterday, Mr Porter Robinson, a native of King Wm Co, Va, aged 32 years, leaving a wife & one child. His funeral is from his late rsidence, on F, between 17th & 18th sts, this afternoon, at half past 4 o'clock.

City Council, Mayor's Ofc, Wash, Jun5, 1849. Duly elected for members of the Board of Aldermen & Board of Common Council:

Aldermen:
Wm B Magruder	John W Maury	Peter M Pearson
John Wilson	Jos W Beck	
S P Franklin	Jas A Gordon	

Common Council:
Wm T Dove	Jos Bryan	John L Wirt
Saml E Douglass	J A M Duncanson	Aaron W Miller
Jas L Cathcart	Hugh B Sweeny	Jonas B Ellis
Jesse E Dow	Wm H Winter	John R Queen
Nicholas Callan	Geo S Gideon	Joeel W Jones
Wm F Bayly	Geo M Dove	Dearborn Johnson
Silas H Hill	John Johnson	Wm Lloyd
-W W Seaton, Mayor		

Wash, May 29, 1849. We the undersigned do hereby agree to close our stores at the ringing of the bell, at sunset, from Jun 4 to Sep 4.

Grocery Merchants:
Saml Bacon & Co	Jno T Kilmon
G & T Parker	Jno T Ryon
B S Jackson & Bro	Edw Hall
Morsell & Wilson	J T Radcliff
Middleton & Beall	J M Peerce
S Pumphrey	John Ball
Murray & Semmes	J H Semmes & Co
Simms & Son	A Holmead
D W Ferrall	A J Webb
Wm H Upperman	

My rule is always 8 o'clock, not including Sat night: John A Donohoo

Dry Goods Merchants:
Clagett, Newton, May & Co	Perry & Bro
Clagett & Dodson	R W Carter & Co
Maxwell & Sears	Henry Carter
Walter Harper & Co	Pim, Nevins & Co
Wall & Donn	J B & A Tate
Hyatt & Frazier	

The bell will be rung by our Porter, Nicholas Warner.

THU JUN 7, 1849
Furnished rooms for rent. Has a Restaurant attached. –J Boulanger, G & 17th sts, near the War Ofc.

An old gentleman, by the name of Miley, residing in the lower end of Rockingham Co, died recently from grief, caused by the burning of his barn. He seemed to have been perfectly overwhelmed by the loss of his barn. -Rockingham Register

Rev J W Douglass, a graduate of Yale College, & recently from N Y as passenger in the steamer **California**, has received & accepted an invitation from the people of Pueblo de San Jose to take up his residence there as a preacher of the Gospel, & the sum of $2,500 has been promptly raised for his support the coming year.

From Texas: the Indians have carried off large quantities of stock belonging to Col Kinney & Mr Mann, & killed a number of Mexicans.

Orphans Court of Wash Co, D C. Letters testamentary on the personal estate of Jas P Gannon, late of said county, deceased. –Peter Vonnessen, Walter Lenox, excs. Persons with claims to present them to W Lenox, Atty-at-Law.

Mrd: on Jun 5, by Rev G W Israel, Mr John E Bates to Julia, daughter of the late Israel Little, all of Wash City.

Died: on May 29, at New Orleans, Mrs Susan Olroyd, wife of Mr Francis Olroyd, aged 29 years, formerly of Wash City.

A young man committed suicide at Cincinnati on May 31 by drowning himself in the Little Miami canal. Papers found stated his name to be Wm Plater, that he was the support of a widowed mother, & had come from England to New Orleans. 'On tomorrow I shall be 25 years of age, & in an hour after I shall be in eternity.'

FRI JUN 8, 1849
Appointments by the Pres:
Collector of Customs:
Saml Cooper, Middletown, Conn, vice Wm D Starr, removed.
Surveyors of the Customs:
Penfield B Goodsell, Hartford, Conn, vice Seth Belden, removed.
Allen Putnam, Salem, Mass, vice Nathl Hawthorne, removed.
Appraiser of Merchandise:
Mathias B Edgar, N Y, N Y, vice Geo F Thomson, removed.
Marshals:
Alex's M Mitchell, of Ohio, for the Territory of Minnesota.
John W Twichell, of Mo, for the district of Mo, vice Robt C Ewing, removed.
By the Sec of the Interior:
Pension Agents:
Cahs Fitz, of New Orleans, La, at that place, vice Maunsel White, who declines the ofc.
Jas Huske, of Fayetteville, N C, at that place, vice Geo McNeill, removed.

$100 reward for runaway colored man Richd Edwards, left on Jun 3, to see his sick mother, who lives at Mr Waters', near Brookville, Montg Co, Md. He is about 27 years of age. –Alex'r Suter, Gtwn

The Legislature, judges, & citizens, in the State Council Chamber at Richmond, on Mon, Gov Floyd presented to Gen Garland the sword voted to him two years since for his gallantry in Mexico. The sword is set with pearl, topaz, & solid gold mountings, & in the head of the grip an exquisite gold eagle. It cost $600. On the scabbard is the Va coat of arms, with the following inscription: "Presented by Virginia to her distinguished son, Lt Col John Garland, for his gallantry & conduct at Palo Alto, Resaca de la Palma, and Monterey." [Lt Col Garland has since become Brig Gen by Brevet.] -Richmond Enquirer

Orphans Court of Wash Co, D C. Letters of administration on the personal estate of Wm Froehlich, late of said county, deceased. –Jas Casparis, adm

For sale: the undersigned, excx & excs of the late Gen John Mason, offer for sale the following property in Gtwn, D C, belonging to the estate of their testator: A large brick dwlg house on Bridge st west, with extensive backbldgs & stabling. Adjoining this property is a vacant lot belonging to it. Also, a large brick warehouse on Water st. Adjoining this property, at Fred'k st, is a lot 60 feet fronting on Water st, with a small house. For terms, apply to Maynadier Mason, in Gtwn, D C, or by letter to Jas M Mason, at Winchester, Va. –A M Mason, excx, Jas M Mason & Eilbeck Mason, excs of John Mason, deceased.

Loudoun Lands of the best quality for sale: on behalf of the heirs we offer for sale *Llangollen*, the residence of the late Cuthbert Powell. It is in Loudoun Co, Va, & contains 762½ acres: dwlg is of brick, rough cast. We offer also 4 other farms in the same neighborhood, one containing about 275 acres, one about 300 acres, one of 200 acres, & one of 262 acres. –Wm H Gray, Chas L Powell, Leesburg, Loudoun Co, Va.

Mrd: Jun 6, by Rev V Palen, Mr Geo H Loveless to Miss Franes Greggs, of Wash City.

Mrd: on Jun 6, by Rev Mr Colyer, Mr Wm H Bangs, of Balt, to Miss Eliz G Drake, daughter of Mr Willard Drake, of Wash City.

Mrd: on May 29, by Rev French S Evans, Mr Reuben R Brown to Miss Rosina Bowen, all of Wash City.

Died: in PG Co, Md, while on a visit, Miss Julia Ann Vinton, daughter of Thos N Wilson, of Montg Co, aged 16 years. [No date: current item.]

SAT JUN 9, 1849
Examination at West Point commenced on Mon. The following gentlemen, comprising the Board of Visiters had arrived there:

Hon Horace Mann, of Mass	Col R N Burnett, of Ohio
Capt Danl Tyler, of Conn	Gen Wiley, of Ala
Jerome Fuller, of N Y	Judge Ballard, of La
John L Gor, of Pa	Col W Stockton, of Fla
John H B Latrobe, of Md	Dr H Boughton, of Iowa
Capt P M Henry, of N C	Gen Rufus King, of Wisc

Mr Latrobe was elected Pres, & Gen King Sec.

Official Telegraphic Despatch was received at the War Dept yesterday, communicating the sad intelligence of the death of Brevet Maj Gen Edmund Pendleton Gaines, of the U S Army. He died on Jun 6 in New Orleans. It was said to be of cholera. He was in command of the Western Division of the Army of the U S. The particular exploit that **Fort Erie** gave Gen Gaines his distinguished reputation was his conduct at in 1813, which he defended with great ability from the night attack of a powerful British force, under the command of Gen Drummond-the loss of the British amounting to 962, while that of the Americans was only 84. Gen Gaines entered the service as Ensign in Jan, 1799. [Jun 11th newspaper: Col Walback, of the 4th Artl, entered the Army on the same day with Gen Gaines, Jan 10, 1799, & that the venerable Col Many, of the 3rd Infty, entered it Jun 4, 1798, 6 months earlier than either of these gentlemen.]

Died: on Jun 8, in her 89th year, Mrs Mary Ramsay, relict of the late Edw Ramsay, formerly of Alexandria, Va. Her funeral is this evening, at 5 o'clock, from the residence of her son-in-law, R H Clements, Capitol Hill, ***Dowson's Row***, #2.

Liberal reward for return of strayed large buffalo cow. –Mrs Cronin, 6th st.

MON JUN 11, 1849
The death of Mrs Ann Maria Pinkney is announced in the Balt papers. This venerable Lady was sister of the late veteran Cmdor Rodgers, & relict of the Hon Wm Pinkney, one of our most distinguished statesman of our country.
[No death date give -current item.]

The trial of Thos A Walker, for murder, in N Y C, has resulted in a verdict of acquittal. –N Y Express

The Telegraphic report of the murder of Col Kinney, which was circulated about a week ago, had no other foundation than the misapprehension of some Telegraphist.

Antoni Sibellich, convicted of murder upon the high seas, was executed in New Orleans, in the Parish prison, on Jun 1, by the U S Marshal.

A little girl, daughter of Mr Wm Hubbard, residing in East Wheeling, lost her life in a most painful manner. After dinner she was washing her face at a rain barrel, her feet slipped, & she was precipitated head first into the barrel. She was preparing to start for school.

Mrd: on May 30, by Rev Wm Matthews, Mr Adams Foster, of Boston, Mass, to Sarah Jane Burch, of Wash City.

Mrd: on Jun 7, by Rev Wm H Pitcher, Mr Andrew Ferguson to Miss Catherine Baily, all of Wash City.

Mrd: on Jun 7, by Rev Jas Donelan, Mr John T Jarboe, of PG Co, Md, to Miss Mary H Soper, of Wash.

Died: yesterday, in Gtwn, Mr Jos Gross, in his 20th year. His funeral is tomorrow at 8 o'clock a m, from the residence of his father.

Died: on Jun 6, Mr Dennis O'Driscoll, aged 65 years, a native of Clonakilty, County Cork, Ire, formerly of Phil, & for the last 15 years a resident of Wash City.

Died: on Jun 10, Mrs Anna Maria Dent, wife of Henry H Dent, & daughter of the late Maj John Adlum. Her funeral is at *Springland*, the residence of Mr Dent, near Wash City, on Jun 12, at 4 o'clock p m.

$5 reward for strayed or stolen from the subscriber's residence, near the Marine Hospital, on Jun 5, 4 cows. –H Gildemeister

Stone cutters & stone masons wanted: wages $2 per day. –Gilbert Cameron

TUE JUN 12, 1849
The steamboat **Emily** exploded at the wharf at Apalachicola on May 28. The passengers escaped without injury. Capt Vanveghton had one rib broken-doing well. W Mahappy, engineer, scalded, doing well; Simon Hudson, engineer, dead; W Magner, hand, dead; 2 colored boys were scalded to death, & one white boy & 2 colored boys drowned. John Moore, of Liverpool, legs broken & otherwise injured.

Appointments by the Pres:
Attys:
Robt Hughes, of Texas, for the District of Texas, vice Franklin H Merriman, removed.
Francis T Bartow, of Ga, for the District of Ga, vice Henry R Jackson, removed.
P Sherward Johnson, of Delaware, for the District of Delaware, vice Wm H Rogers, removed.
Land Ofcrs:
Thos T Russell, of Fla, Receiver of Public Moneys at St Augustine, Fla, vice John M Fontaine, resigned.
Hercules R W Andrews, of Fla, to be Register of the Land Ofc at Tallahassee, Fla, vice Thos J Hodson, removed.
Ofcrs of the Customs:
Robt W Allston, Collector at St Marks, Fla, vice Nathl W Walker, removed.
John C Martin, Appraiser of Merchandise at Phil, vice Thos Stewart, removed.
Appointments by the Sec of the Treas:
Redwood Fisher, Assist Appraiser of Merchandise at Phil, vice Reuben Hanse, removed.
Edw M Donaldson, Assist Appraiser of Merchandise at Phil, vice Wm Little, removed.

Desirable stock of groceries for sale: the undersigned, in consequence of ill health, is disposing of his Groceries, with the privilege of the stand, which he has the right to occupy until Apr 1 next. Information will be given at the store, on La ave, between 6th & 7th sts. –Wm Allen

Balt, Jun 11. Ex-Pres Polk is lying dangerously ill with cholera at Nashville.

N Y, Jun 11. 1-Hon Augustus Porter died at Niagara Falls last night. 2-Benedict Schmit, proprietor of the Fort Washington Hotel, near Harlem, was yesterday committed to prison, charged with the murder of Patrick Boylan, by shooting.

Mrd: on Tues, in Wash City, by Rev G W Samson, at the E st Baptist Church, W H Spangler, son of the late Col M H Spangler, of York, Pa, & Miss Abbie B Smith, daughter of Wm Smith, of West Durfield, N H.

Died: on Jun 11, Mrs Sarah Summers, relict of the late Jas Summers, in her 66th year. Her funeral is from her late residence, on I between 7th & 8th sts, on Wed at 10 o'clock.

Died: Jun 2, at Leesburg, Loudoun Co, Va, Robt P Swann, in his 37th year.

Died: on Jun 5, in Loudoun Co, Va, at the residence of her father, Miss Temple Anna Mason.

Died: on Jun 2, in the village of Upper Marlborough, Md, Mrs Catharine, wife of Thos F Bowie, aged 42, & daughter of the late Col Henry Waring.

Died: on Fri, in Richmond, Va, Peter Cottom, an old & respectable citizen of that city.

WED JUN 13, 1849
The arrival at N Y of the U S store-ship **Lexington** has been announced. The following are the ofcrs of the **Lexington**: F Chatard, Lt Commanding; Wm H Macomb, Lt; Jos Wilson, Purser; John J Abernethy, Passed Assist Surgeon; J H Spotts, Acting Master; J Blakeley Creighton & J D Bullock, Passed Midshipmen. Passengers: Lt Saml S Hazard, from Rio Janeiro; Thos H Stevens, U S Navy, & family, from San Francisco; Midshipman F W Robinson, from San Francisco.

Mrd: on Mon, by Rev John C Smith, Mr Thos Cooke to Miss Louisa Slatford, all of Wash City.

Died: on Jun 11, at her residence, near the Navy Yard, Miss Eliz Greenwell. Her funeral is this afternoon, at 3 o'clock.

Among the trunks, carpet bags, & valises found in the steamer **Empire** was one that bore the name of Chas J Fithian, Brighton, N J. In one of the coats the captain found a receipt for medical attendance by a physician of Schenectady, made out in the name of I Skerrett. One body was found in the cabins, the remaining brother of the Ladd family from Conn. Four young brothers of this family were lost, & their sister, a little girl, was saved by cutting a hole through the deck & taking her out.

Shuster alias Hand & Stone, both convicted at the last term of the Criminal Court, were on Sun last removed from the jail to the Penitentiary, pursuant to their sentences. A ptn to the Pres for the pardon of Shuster was presented by his wife a few days ago.

Desirable property for sale or exchange: the dwlg near the Marine Barracks, Navy Yard, Wash, well known as the residence of the late Timothy Winn. Apply to Mrs Rebecca Winn, at Mrs Peyton's, on Pa ave.

House wanted for a small family, convenient to the Capitol & Depts. Address Mr Silas H Hill, 8th st, near Pa ave.

THU JUN 14, 1849
Williammsburg Academy to establish Male & Female Schools of the highest grade. Schools to be opened on Oct 1. –Ron McCandlish, Pres of the Board of Trustees, Williamsburg, Va.

The Whig, the first number of a new Whig paper, edited by Messrs Alex'r Bullitt & John O Sargent, made its appearance yesterday.

Appointments by the Pres: To fill vacancies:
Thos M Foote, of N Y, to be Charge de'Affaires to New Granada, in lieu of Benj A Bidlack, deceased.
Alex'r K McClung, of Miss, to be Charge d'Affaires to Boliva, in lieu of John Appleton, resigned.
Chas L Fleishchmann, of D C, to be Consul at Stuttgard, Wurtemberg, in lieu of Tobias Beehler, resigned.
Stephen D Poole, of N C, to be Consul at Turk's Island, in lieu of J T Pickett, resigned.
Geo F Usher, of R I, to be Cmmercial Agent at Port au Prince, in lieu of Jos C Luther, resigned.

Removals:
Geo P Marsh, of Vt, to be Minister Resident at Constantinople, in lieu of Dabney S Carr, recalled.
Thos W Chinn, of La, to be Charge d'Affaires to the Kingdom of the Two Sicilies.
John Trumbull Van Alen, of N Y, to be Charge d'Affaires to the Republic of Ecuador, in lieu of Van Brugh Livingston, recalled.
John C B Davis, of Mass, to be Sec of Legation of England.
Lorenzo Draper, of N Y, to be Consul at Havre de Grace, in lieu of Wm J Staples, recalled.
Edw Kent, of Maine, to be Consul at Rio Janeiro, in lieu of Gorham Parks, recalled.
Rev Thos Sewall, of Md, to be Consul at St Jago de Cuba, in lieu of John W Holding, recalled.
Wm R Hayes, of Conn, to be Consul at Barbadoes, in lieu of Noble Towner, recalled.
Elijah Payne, of N Y, to be Consul at Panama, in lieu of Wm Nelson, recalled.
Chas Benjamin, of Conn, to be Consul at Demerara, in lieu of Saml J Masters, recalled.
Israel D Andrews, of Maine, to be Consul for News Brunswick & Canada, in lieu of Collins Whittaker, recalled.
Bailey M Edney, of N C, to be Consul at Pernambuco, in lieu of C G Salinas, [a foreigner,] removed.

The Whig, the first number of a new Whig paper, edited by Messrs Alex'r Bullitt & John O Sargent, made its appearance yesterday.

The last steam-packet from Liverpool brought the news of Miss Maria Edgeworth's death. She died on May 21, at Edgeworthstown, county of Longford, Ire, above 82 years old. She died on the spot which was always her home, surrounded by those she entirely loved & trusted, after only a few hours of illness. Our pleasures in literature do decrease with age. I think that from my books I had as much enjoyment last year [her 82nd birthday,] as I ever had in any year of my life. —Boston Daily Adv, Jun 9

Brick house for sale: 2 story with basement, on D st, between 2nd & 3rd st, in what is now called *Pollard's Row*. Apply at the Housefurnishing Warerooms of J M Donn & Bro, between 10th & 11th sts, Pa ave.

Pres Zachary Taylor, Pres of the U S, recognizes Fernando Moreno appointed Vice Consul of Russia for the port of Key West, Fla. Also: W Shaer appointed Vice Consul of Russia for the port of Balt, Md.

Military movements of the West: *Fort Leavenworth*, May 25, 1849. On May 16, the command of Brevet Col Alexander, 3rd Infty, composed of 4 companies of his regt & 2 companies of artillery, [the 3rd regt,] under command of Brevet Maj Kendrick, left this post for New Mexico. Under the protection of this escort, Col Calhoun, Indian Agent for New Mexico, [with his family,] was placed. On May 17, Capt Ker, 2nd Dragoons, with his company, left as escort to Col Collier, collector for San Francisco. This entire command made about 35 miles, when an express was despatched with an order for it to there await the arrival Gen Brooke & staff, under orders for New Mexico. The Rifle Regt left on May 10 on the Oregon route: the following disposition has been made of the companies, as far as I have been able to ascertain: Maj Sanderson stops at the first post on the route, viz *Fort Laramie*; his command will be companies C & E, mounted rifleman, & Co G, 6th Infty: Ofcrs: Brevet Lt Col Roberts, Capt Duncan, Lt Elliot, Brevet Capt McLane, of the riflemen, Capt Ketchum, Brevet Capt Hendrickson, Lt Bootes, & Lt Tubbs, 6th Infty. Capt Vanvliet, a Q M, & Lt Woodbury will also be at that post. Brevet Maj Simonson, with his company, G, & that of Capt Newton, B, garrisons the 2nd post, to be established at or in the vicinity of Bear river. On or about Jun 1, Brevet Lt Col Roberts, with his company, C, rifles, & company G, 6th Infty, leaves with the supply train of about 400 wagons. Lt Elliott accompanies this command as Commissary & A Quartermaster. After the departure of these trains, *Fort Leavenworth* will consist of company K, 1st Dragoons, & companies B & F, 5th Infty, Brevet Capt Morris, mounted riflemen, with 30 men, awaits the arrival of Gen John Wilson, Indian Agent, for Calif, as his escort via Salt Lake.

Notice: W Peterson has lately removed his Tailoring shop to 8th st & Pa ave.

Mrd: on Jun 12, at Christ Church, Gtwn, by Rev S G Gassaway, Allen Dodge to Mary Ellen Berry, Chas Lanman to Adeline Dodge, & Ben Perley Poore, of Boston, to Virginia Dodge; & on the same day, by Rev R T Berry, Chas Dodge to Eliz G Davidson.

Mrd: on Apr 30th last, at *Fort Snelling*, Minnesota Territory, by Rev Mr Ravoux, Capt Jas Monae, jr, U S Army, of Va, to Virginia M, daughter of Dr J Martin, U S Army, of Norfolk, Va.

Madame Gallot has been committed for trial on charge of forging a note for $10,000, with the name of Mr Michoud, a merchant of New Orleans, attached to it. This is the lady whose marriage a short time since was noted in New Orleans, attended with the presentation of this note to the groom as her marriage dowry.

FRI JUN 15, 1849
Wash Corp: 1-<u>Board of Aldermen</u>: Walter Lenox elected Pres; John Wilson, Vice Pres; Erasmus J Middleton was duly elected Sec; Jacob Kleiber appointed Messenger.
2-Vote Returns:
Register:
*Wm J McCormick 1, 443 votes   Jos Radcliff, 88
J D Hoover, 338
C H Wiltberger, 148
Collector:
*Andrew Rothwell, 1,002   Nicholas Callan, 1
John Hands, 628   David A Hall, 1
Jas F Halliday, 405
Surveyor:
*Chas B Clusky, 1,456   Randolph Coyle, 3
Wm D DeMaine, 464   Thos Scrivener, 2
*Duly elected.

3-<u>Board of Aldermen-following gentlemen appeared</u>:

Saml Drury	Walter Lenox	Jas A Gordon
Wm Orme	John W Maury	Saml Byington
John Wilson	Benj B French	Peter M Pearson
John T Towers	Jos W Beck	
Stephen P Franklin	Thos Thornely	

4-<u>Board of Common Council members</u>:

Wm T Dove	Jos Bryan	John L Wirt
Saml E Douglass	J A M Duncanson	Aaron W Miller
Jas L Cathcart	Hugh B Sweeny	Jonas B Ellis
Jesse E Dow	Wm H Winter	John R Queen
Nicholas Callan	Geo S Gideon	Joel W Jones
Wm F Bayly	Geo M Dove	Dearborn B Johnson
Silas H Hill	John Johnson	Wm Lloyd

5-Silas H Hill elected Pres of the Board; Richd Barry-Sec; Jacob Kleiber-Messenger.

Capt Robinson, of Washington, & a party under him, who left **Fort Smith** for Calif this spring, returned to that post on May 19, having lost their oxen, provisions, & entire outfit by an overflow of Sleepy Creek, in Creek Nation, which raised 50 feet during 1 night, compelling them to seek safety by climbing into trees. They will probably go another route. -Balt Sun

Brownsville Flag: Capt Edw Deas, 4th U S Artl, stationed at Camp Ringgold, was drowned from on board the steamer **Yazoo**, near Rio Grande city, on the 6th ult. Capt Deas served on both lines during the Mexican war, & was taken prisoner shortly before the battles of May 8 & 9, & carried into Matamoros. -Picayune

Appointments by the Pres: A A Pettingall, of Conn, to be U S Marshal for the district of Conn, vice Benning Mann, resigned.
Geo W Lakin, of Wisc, to be U S Atty for the district of Wisc, vice A Hyatt Smith, removed.
Land Ofcrs: Register of the Land Ofc:
Paraclete Potter, of Wisc, at Milwaukie, Wisc, vice Geo H Walker, removed.
Samson Clayton, of Ala, at Lebanon, Ala, vice Hugh P Caperton, removed.
Receiver of Public Moneys:
Moses Gibson, of Wisc, at Willow River, Wisc, vice John G Floyd, who declines the ofc.
Stephen F Page, of Mich, at Ionia, Mich, vice Fred'k Hall, removed.
Merriwether Lewis Clarke, of Mo, to be Surveyor Genr'l for Ill & Mo, vice Fred'k R Conway, removed.
Ofcrs of the Customs:
L A Trigg, Collector of the Customs at Richmond, Va, vice Thos Nelson, removed.
Ezra Hotchkiss, Surveyor of the Customs at New Haven, Conn, vice Chas S A Davis, removed.
Franklin Haven, to be Assist Treasurer at Boston, Mass, vice Henry Hubbard, removed.

The firm of D H Branch & Co, [proprietors of the U S Hotel, Wash, D C,] was dissolved on Jun 9, by mutual consent. Those indebted to make payment to Mr Robt Morrow, who will continue at the Hotel. –D H Branch, Scott & Haw

Poisoned by Root Beer: in Blairsville, Pa, 5 persons had died, & some 16 or 18 were still suffering severely. Mr Ginter, who prepared the beer, was one of the first victims, & one of his sons also died. The rest of the family were dangerously ill. It is said to have been caused by drinking beer in which the root of the wild parsnip had been boiled by accident.

The Master Masons of New Jerusalem Lodge 9 are notified to attend the funeral of our late brother, M W Fisher, who died on Jun 14. His funeral is at Trinity Church, on Sunday, at 2 o'clock. –Urias Hurst, Sec
+
Died: on Jun 14, of consumption, Marvin W Fisher, in his 49th year. His funeral is on Jun 17, at 3½ p m, at Trinity Church, on 5th st.

Died: on Jun 6, at Dayton, Ohio, Nelly Woodhull Schenck, aged 10 months, daughter of Hon R C & Rennelche Woodhull Schenck.

Died: on Jun 13, Thomas, youngest son of Thos & Emily S Blagden, of Wash City.

Farm for sale, 8 miles from Wash, adjoining the farms of Mr Robt V Brent, Miss Ann Carroll, Mr R L Ross, & Capt J C Jones, containing 160 acres: with a new 2 story frame dwlg, a new Switzer barn, & necessary outbldgs. Property will be sold with or without the crop, stock, farming utensils, & household furniture.
–Benj J Perry, *Edgewood*

We regret to have a revival of the report that Ex-Pres Polk is dangerously ill. His malady is now represented to be of a bilious type.

SAT JUN 16, 1849
Official-Appointments by the Pres. 1-Chas H Delavan to be Commerical Agent to St Thomas. 2-Wm Henry Peet, to be Collector of the Customs at Fairfield, Conn, vice Wm S Pomeroy, removed.

Relic copied from the Ky Gaz, the first newspaper published west of the Alleghanies, edited by the venerable John Bradford, of Lexington. Copy of Advertisement dated Sep 6, 1778. Notice: the subscribers, being proprietors of a tract of land opposite the mouth of the Licking river, on the n w side of the Ohio, have determined to lay off a town upon that land; inlots to be half an acre, out lots 4 acres, 30 of which to be given settlers upon paying $1.50 for the survey & deed of each lot. Sep 15 is appointed for a large company to meet in Lexington, & mark a road from there to the mouth of Licking, provided Judge Symmes arrives, being daily expected. When the town is laid off lots will be given to such as may become residents before Apr 1 next.
–Matthias Denman, Robt Patterson, John Filson. Lexington, Ky

The last tribute of respect to the remains of Gen Gaines was paid by the citizens of New Orleans on Jun 7. The body to be removed to Mobile, by the Pontchartrain Railroad, & thence to the lake, were it will be placed on board a steamer. The ceremonies were highly imposing.

Trustee's sale of valuable site in Gtwn: on Jun 18, being authorized by the Circuit Court of D C. Public sale of lot 80, in the original plan of Gtwn, in D C, adjoining *Messrs Ray's Mill* & the Cotton Factory. –John Marbury, trustee
-E S Wright, auctioneer

Trustee's sale of valuable real estate: by decree of the Circuit Court of D C, sitting in Chancery, in the cause of Mary King et al vs Chas King's heirs et al: sale on Jul 11, ground in Gtwn, part of the estate of the late Chas King. All that part of Peter, Beatty, Threldkeld & Deakins' addition to Gtwn, of the real estate of the late Chas King, improved by a double 2 story brick house. Also, part of lot 72, in old Gtwn, beginning on the south side of Cherry alley: improved by two 2 story brick tenements. Two parts of lot 62, in old Gtwn, fronting each 20 feet on Jefferson st, improved by a small 2 story brick house. –Walter S Cox, trustee -Edw S Wright, auctioneer

Trustees' sale of a valuable dwlg house & eligible bldg lots, in Gtwn. Sale on Jul 17, by decree of the Circuit Court of D C. Public auction of that valuable property in Gtwn aforesaid, many years the residence of Thos Turner, deceased. It fronts 120 feet on Dunbarton st, the same on Gay st, & extends from the one street to the other, having a front line of 240 feet on Congress st. The boundaries of the property embrace lots 159, 160, 166, & 167, in Beall's addition. The dwlg is a large 2 story brick house, occupies lot 167, & fronts on Dunbarton st. Lot 66 to be sold in one lot. –John Marbury, trustee
-E S Wright, auctioneer

Unofficially, we believe that the Hon Danl M Barringer, of N C, has been offered by the Pres the appointment of Minister to Spain.

MON JUN 18, 1849
Norfolk Herald: by way of reducing the enormous expenses of the Revenue dept of the Gov't, 8 of the revenue cutters employed in that service have been dispensed with & their ofcrs discharged, conformably to a law of the last Congress. List of her ofcrs:

Captains:
Wm W Polk	J J Nimmo	Wm A Howard
Andrew Matthew	____ Kapp	Levi C Howard
Wm B Whitehead	Caleb Currier	Winslow Foster

1st Lts:
Chas Grover	Osmond Peters	Nicholas Austin
Thos Stodard	Jos Amazeen	J G Breshwood
Caleb Prouty	H N Tracy	

2nd Lts:
Geo Berryman	John B Hendren	E T Hyatt
John M Jones	Richd S Jones	W H Albertson
John T Stoneall	Benj J Kellum	

3rd Lts:
Henry Wilkinson	J B Yates	Alex'r Murray
Eugene W Watson	F G Mayson	J A Underwood
Wm C Dunnavant	J Ross Brown	

Gen Robt McCoy, formerly of Carlisle, Pa, died at Wheeling on Jun 7. He was formerly Prothonatary of Cumberland Co, Brig Gen, Rep in Congress, & Canal Commissioner.

The Winchester [Va] Republican, published by John S Gallaher, is offered for sale.

Col Jacob G Davies, formerly Mayor of Balt, has been elected Pres of the Md Marine Ins Co.

Mr Jos Buffington has been appointed by the Govn'r of Pa to be President Judge of the 18th judicial district of Pa, composed of the counties of Clarion, Venango, Jefferson, Elk, & McKean.

Wm C Bryant, editor of the N Y Evening Post, has left that city for Europe.

Geo N Kay, aged 28 years, a native of New Brunswick, N J, who was shot during the Theatre riot at N Y, died on Thursday last. He was a merchant in N J, being in N Y on business, unfortunate as to be there at the time of the riot.

Washington G Tuck appointed as Inspector of the Customs for the port of Annapolis, vice Jas H Inglehart, removed. –Annapolis Republican

Summer Boarding: Mrs Col Brooks has very commodious summer accommodations at her residence, 3 miles from Wash, on the old Bladensburg road, where she will be happy to entertain a few families during the approaching warm season.

Superior sugar-cured hams: Milton Garrett, #99 Centre Market, outside.

S T Rowe was shot at Hoeyville, La, on Jun 5, by Jos Miller, barkeeper at the hotel at that place. Rowe was jealous of Miller's attenion to the former's wife & had threatened Miller's life. Miller shot & killed Rowe. He was taken to the jail at Lafayette.

Augustus Porter, of Niagara Falls, who died lately, at age 80 years, was a native of Salisbury, Conn, & located himself at Niagara Falls in Jun, 1806, where he ever after lived. His dwlg & mills were burnt to ashes at the time of the destruction of Buffalo & the whole frontier by the British in 1813. Narrative written by the deceased: During the winter past [of 1797] Gideon King & Zadock Granger, 2 of the proprietors of the tract of 20,000 acres in the north part of the township, [which included the land on which Rochester now stands,] & 2 other families from Suffield, commenced thereon a settlement. Mr Phelps, my brother Peter B, & myself, were also proprietors. This 20,000 acre tract was sold originally by Phelps & Gorham, in 1790, to a company of gentlemen of Springfield & Northampton, Mass, among whom was Ebenezer Hunt, Quartus Pomeroy, & Justin Ely. The 20,000 acres had previously been sold to Ebenezer Allen, to erect a mill. The line of this 20,000 acres had been run by Fred'k Saxon in the summer of 1790. [I omitted to mention in the proper place, that in returning to Canandaigua, after completing the survey for Robt Morris, in company with Jos Ellicott, we traveled down the lake to Buffalo, no road, just an Indian trail from Buffalo to Canawagus, [now Avon.] There was then, 1797, one dwlg house between the 2 places, which was owned by a Mr Wilbur. It as at the point where Mr John Ganson afterwards built a large house & kept a taven for many years.]
-Rochester Advertiser

Heinrich Bornstein, who was reported to have died of the cholera in the West, is still alive & in good health at Highland, Ill, where he is about to establish a hydropathic institution.

Mrd: on Jun 14, by Rev John Lanahan, John Gordon to Miss Rachel Taylor, both of Wash City.

Mrd: on Jun 14, by Rev Mr Steele, Jos W Cheney to Mary Antoinette Magee, both of Wash City.

Mrd: on Jun 14, by Rev J B Donelan, Mr Adolphus Eckloff to Miss Sarah Eliz Ridgway, both of Wash City.

Mrd: on Jun 12, at St Peter's Church, Wash City, by Rev J Van Horsigh, John Dunbar Brandt, of Charleston, S C, to Miss Rosannah E Cole, of Wash City.

Died: on Jun 17, after a protracted illness, John Ward, a native of the county of Monahan, Ire, but for the last 30 years a resident of Wash City. His funeral is today, at 4 o'clock, from his late residence, corner of 12th & C sts.

Died: on Jun 13, at West Point, N Y, Isabel, daughter of Thos B Coleman, late of Lebanon Co, Pa, deceased.

Died: on Jun 2, at his residence, near New Baltimore, Va, of pneumonia, in his 56th year, Elder John Ogilvie. He was one of Nature's noblemen; a self-made man, of superior capacity & high attainments. As a friend, husband, & father, he was universally admired & beloved.

Telegraphic despatch from Louisville states that at a public discussion in Madison Co, Ky, on Fri last, a rencoutre took place between Cassius M Clay & Jos Turner, which resulted in the death of both parties. Having first snapped pistols at each other, they came into close quarters with bowie knives. Mr Clay was stabbed through the heart, after having mortally wounded Mr Turner in the abdomen & groin. The latter is since dead.

Household & kitchen furniture at auction: on Jun 21, at the residence of Mr Parrot, on G st west, between 17th & 18th sts. –Martin & Wright, auctioneers

House & lot on Pa ave, & whole squares on 4½ st: for sale. Inquire at my ofc near Brown's Hotel, D A Hall.

TUE JUN 19, 1849
New Bedford Mercury: capture of the schnr **Zenobia**, of Balt. On Mar 23, 1849, arrived at St Helena, the **Zenobia**, [for adjudication in the Vice Admiralty Court,] which vessel had been captured by H B M sloop **Philomel**, on the west coast of Africa, with a cargo of 550 slaves, 33 of whom were females, the vessel not being over 100 tons burden. She was 11 days on her passage to St Helena, & lost 10 or eleven of them. These poor creatures were in a perfect state of nudity, & many of them [the women in particular] bearing the brands of a hot iron recently impressed on their breasts

On Wed in Balt, a fine little son of Mr Edw Larrabee, aged 5 years, was shot by the ball from a pistol in the hands of Mr J K Jones, of St Mary's Co, who was in the act of packing his trunk preparatory to start for Calif, when the weapon went off. He suffered about 12 hours & died on Thursday.

A Telegraphic despatch was received in Wash City last evening announcing the melancholy news of the decease of Ex-Pres Polk, at Nashville, on Jun 15th.

Col Upshaw, U S Indian Agent for the Chickasaws, writes to the editor of the Ark Intelligencer, on May 15, he heard of the murder of a party of 26 persons who left Texas some 2 weeks previous for Calif. Two others of the party made their escape. They were killed by the Indians. –St Louis Republican

Mrd: on Jun 7, Brevet Lt Col Braxton Bragg, U S Army to Eliza B, daughter of Mary Jane & the late Richd G Ellis. The ceremony was performed in the family residence, in the parish of Terrebonne, La, by Rev John Sandel.

Died: on Jun 12, at Chilton's Cross Roads, Westmoreland Co, Va, Kitty M Reed, consort of John Reed, leaving a large family to mourn their loss.

Died: on May 11, at sea, on board the U S frig **Raritan**, flag-ship of the West India squadron, of bilious fever, Lt Francis Alexander, of Mississippi, in his 30th year.

By virtue of 3 writs of fieri facias, to me directed, I shall expose to public sale, on Jun 23, in Wash City, the following property: one bay horse, seized & taken as the property of David S Waters, & will be sold to satisfy 3 judgments due to Lewis Rosenstock. –Wm Cox, constable

Farmers' Hotel, Rockville, Montg Co, Md: can accommodate 30 or 40 boarders, at reasonable prices. –F Kidwell

By an order of distrain, I shall expose at public sale, on Jun 20, all the household & kitchen furniture, seized & taken as the property of M Karar, deceased, to satisfy rent due in arrear to Thos Carbery. –Jos H Hitton, Bailiff

Caldwell Institute, Hillsborough, N C, will resume on Jul 18. –J W Norwood, Sec of the Trustees

WED JUN 20, 1849
Overland emigration to Calif: letter from Capt Stewart Van Vleit, of the U S Army, dated at *Fort Kearny*, Nebraska Territory, 220 miles west of *Fort Leavenworth*, Mo, on May 21. On May 6 the first party bound for Calif passed this post, & since that date 1,203 wagons have gone by; on an average there are 4 men & 8 to 10 animals to a wagon. Over 5,000 wagons & 25,000 men will attempt to reach Calif this season by this route. Postscript: yesterday 232 wagons passed, making 1,435 in all.

Schnectady Court: Recently Dores Brand, a German woman, obtained a verdict of $2,000 against the Troy & Schnectady Railroad Co, for injuries sustained by being run over by the locomotive & tender, while crossing Maiden Lane, in the city of Albany.

The steamer **Memphis** encountered a hurricane at New Madrid last week. The following persons were drowned: Jas L Morton, of Cincinnati; W W Johnson, family in Cincinnati; Albert Boyd, pilot, of Cincinnati; W Wilcox, barkeeper, of Cincinnati; also, the pastry cook, 3 cabin boys, & 4 or 5 passengers. None of the ladies were lost.

Mrs Van Wormer, wife of Danl Van Wormer, of Poughkeepsie, while on her way to Rochester, on board a canal boat, to join her husband there, was fataly injured in passing under the Brighton lock, being struck by one of the string-pieces of the bridge, which, having been broken, hung below the level. She died before reaching Rochester.

Mrd: on Jun 14, by Rev Mr Israel, Mr Lewis H Pool to Miss Eliz A Jones, both of Wash City.

Cincinnati Times: Mr Wm De Groff, a contractor on the Little Miami Railroad, made a leap of 50 feet down an excavation, to save himself from a land slide, &, alighting on his feet, escaped without injury.

Official: appointment by the Pres: Hon Danl M Barringer, of N C, to be Envoy Extra & Minister Pleni to the Court of Madrid, in lieu of Hon Wm A Graham, who declined the office. Mr Saunders, our present Minister, having been recalled at his own request.

Died: on Jun 18, after a short illness of bilious pleurisy, Mrs Jane Cook, consort of Rev J F Cook, in her 35th year. Her funeral is today at 2 o'clock.

Died: on Jun 18, Wm Millar, aged 44, a resident of Wash City for 14 years. His funeral is from his late residence on 4th st, near L st, today at 2 o'clock.

Died: on Tue, in Wash City, Margaret Jane, aged 10 months & 10 days, infant daughter of David A & Mary M Baird. Her funeral is this afternoon, at 5 o'clock, from the residence of her father, on 8th st, near Pa ave.

Passengers brought from Chagres in the steamer **Crescent City**, lately arrived at New Orleans: For New Orleans: Col Mason, U S A; Mrs Persifer F Smith, Mrs Ogden, J West & lady; Mr Duther, lady, & 3 children; Capt Thomas, P J Treadway & lady, W W Boyden & servant, A L Loring, Messrs C L Weller & servant, J LeFevre, O K Smith, Aldridge, W Garr, C Taylor, R Jacobs; Morsman,& Williams. For N Y-Engineer Corps of Panama Survey: Col Hughes, chief; Gen Morris, commanding general; Capt Tilghman, Dr M B Halstead; Messrs W H Sidell, J L O Baldwin, J J Williams, W W Riddley, Wm G Norris, W J Gary, Griffiths, J J Mapes, G W Brown, C B Hall, John May, E W Sewell, W J Corcoran, Geo Wolcott, Jas Armstrong, H D Stone, Dr G Burr, J W Stump, W S Ogden, H M Milnor, J Wright, R Petherbridge, Wm Hindes, H H O'Callahan, W Hopper, R B Jarvis, C H Sherman, J O'Brien, W Gordon, J W O'Brien, B Burns, D Facsi, F Z Cole, G Deffner, & 4 servants. Capt Wachten, H Wark, 1st Ofcr, & 12 of the crew of Bremen ship **Humboldt**, sold at Panama; Lt Porter, U S N, late Com steamer **Panama**; Capt Forbes, late Com steamer **California**; Lt Chandler, U S N, Lt Hall, U S N, Dr Rendenstein, U S N, Lt Bonnycastle, U S A; Mr Sinclair & 3 ladies & 2 servants, Mr Ludlum, Capt Thomas; Capt Tucker, late Com steamer **Orus**; Mr Odborn, Mr Harris, Mr Stevenson, Mr Paredes, Master Vellerino, Miss Denike & Valentine, Mr Raymond, & 23 in steerage.

Explosion of the steamer **Embassy**, at Evansville, Indiana, mentioned a few days ago by telegraph. Killed: Jeremiah Miller, cook, of Wheeling, Va; 2 firemen, Irishmen, names not known; Mr Watts, wife, & 2 children, of Bainbrook, N J; Mr Willer, a German emigrant; John Myers, engineer, of Steubenville, O; Mrs Isley & 4 children, of Tuscarawas Co, O; L Merton, a lad, from England; Thos Brogon, fireman-family in Cincinnati; Catherine Folly, of Ireland. 12 persons scalded, but likely to recover, are at Evansville.

Orphans Court of Wash Co, D C. Letters testamentary on the personal estate of Maria W Fisher, late of said county, deceased. –Harriet F Fisher, excx

Criminal Court-Wash: The following freeholders were summoned to serve on the Grand Inquest for the present term:

Saml McKenney, foreman	Stanislaus Murray	Geo McCeney
	Wm H Gunnell	Phil T Berry
Jesse E Dow	Michl Schanks	Wm H Edes
Robt S Patterson	Wm T Dove	Robt White
Isaac Clarke	W Bird	John P Ingle
Benj F Middleton	Franklin S Myer	Ch R Belt
Wm Wilson	Wm Cockrell	Francis Dodge, jr
Andrew Coyle	Zachriah Walker	
Gregory Ennis	Henry Haw	

Following citizens summoned to serve on the Petit Jury:

Watkins Tolson	Robt Brooke	Geo W Hopkins
Jas Middleton	Saml Hanson	Robt W Bates
Geo McNeir	Jas Crump	John Suter
Wm Parsons	David Shoemaker	Edw H Edelen
Archibald White	H T Weightman	Wm H Craig
Ephraim Wheeler	Lewis J Knight	John W Martin
Eben G Brown	Gabriel Barnhill	W Clark
Josh T Clarke	Bennett Sewall	W S Venable
Leml J Middleton	Geo Mantz	
Peter Magruder	Caleb Buckingham	

Orphans Court of Wash Co, D C. Letters of administration on the personal estate of Azariah Fuller, late of said county, deceased. –Geo Lowry, adm

THU JUN 21, 1849
Four men were killed at Phil on Mon by the caving in of a heavy bank of earth, where they were working: the deceased are Jas Colegan, Jas Wiley, Thos Linton, & Jas Cogswell.

Capt Henry C Pope, of Louisville, Ky, was killed in a duel on Jun 14.

At Hartford [Md] Co Court, on Fri last, Jas Lynch plead guilty to the robbery of Mr Mirkem, & was sentenced to the penitentiary for 6 years. Bill Hill, a negro boy about 20 years old, was convicted of violence upon a white girl 14 years of age, & sentenced to the penitentiary for 21 years.

Mrs Bagley, of Milo, Maine, shot a large gray eagle last week, which was pouncing upon her child at play in the yard.

$200 reward for delivery to B O Shekells, in Wash, of runaway slave named Chas, belonging to the estate of J P Gannon, deceased. He is of mulatto color, aged about 17. –W Lenox, Peter Vonnessin, Excs of J P Gannon, deceased.

FRI JUN 22, 1849
Van Buren [Ark] Intelligencer of May 26 states that Bishop Freeman has preferred charges against Gen Belknap, the commanding ofcr at *Fort Gibson*. Specifications: irreligious conduct, in not permitting the chaplain at that post to preach longer than an hour. Congress has sanctioned the one hour rule.

A man named Batemen, whose dwlg is not far from Gtwn College, last Wed, assaulted his wife & daughter & afterwards another female. A colored man, who was also assaulted by Batemen, retaliated by knocking him down with a stone.

Mrd: on Jun 5, by Rev Mr Collier, Mr Cyrus E Perry, of Montg Co, Md, to Miss Sarah Ann Summers, of Wash.

Appointments by the Pres:
Justin Butterfield, of Ill, to be Com'r of the Gen Land Ofc, from & after Jun 30, vice Richd M Young, resigned.
Thos A Deblois, of Portland, to be U S Atty for the District of Maine, vice Geo F Shepley, removed.
Luther Chase, of Ark, to be U S Marshal for the District of Ark, vice Elias Rector, removed.
Albert L Catlin, Collector of the Customs, for the District of Vt, vice R G Hopkinson, removed.

Fatal duel: Louisville Journal of Jun 16. Duel took place on Jun 15, on the Indiana shore, between 2 well-known citizens of Louisville, Mr John T Grey & Capt Henry C Pope. Shot guns were fired nearly simultaneously, & Capt Pope fell, the ball passing through the upper part of the body. A bed was procured & placed in a small boat, & the wounded man was brought down the river, but he expired before reaching Louisville.

Rev Wm B Tappan, General Agent of the American Sunday School Union, died of cholera on Monday, in the vicinity of Boston.

On Sat last, a young man named Davis Burns went in to Antietam river, 2 miles above Waynesboro, Pa, for the purpose of bathing, & being seized with a cramp, he suddenly sunk & drowned. He was of Greencastle, Pa, & a very worthy estimable young man.

Alfred Bishop, recently deceased, in New Haven, disposed by will of an estate valued at $1,000,000. He gave liberally to his near relations, as well as to others who had been unfortunate in business. An annuity of $100 is to be paid by his wife during her life, to the Rev Dr Hewitt. The residue of his estate he gave to his wife & children, to be divided according to the statute of Connecticut.

Mrs McAdams was a few weeks since convicted of the crime of murder before the Circuit Court of Madison Co, Miss. Her husband was allowed to visit her in prison, & at last dressed her in a suit of his own clothes, by means of which she escaped from prison. She was traced as far as Vicksburg, & has not yet been arrested.

The Providence Journal announces the death of the Rt Rev Wm Tyler, Bishop of the Catholic Church for that Diocese. He died at his residence in Providence on Monday.

U S Patent Ofc, Jun 19, 1849. Ptn of Chas Davenport, of Campridgeport, Mass, praying for extension of a patent granted to him for an improvement in draw springs for railway carriages for 7 years from the expiration of said patent, which is Sep 9, 1849. –Thos Ewbank, Com'r of Patents

Died: on May 13, in Arkansas, Mrs Mary Craighead Preston, wife of Thos W Preston, in her 23rd year. She had endeared to her a wide circle of relatives & admiring friends.

Died: on Jun 14, in PG Co, Md, of a protracted & painful disease, Mrs Hecatissa Wade, widow of Benoi H Wade, at the advanced age of 83 years. The last quarter of a century a kind Providence granted her a fit companion of equal worth in the person of her sister, Mrs Julia Lanham, a few years her junior, with whom she resided. They were both natives of Nanjemoy, Chas Co, Md.

Died: on Jun 9, in Concord, N H, in his 80th year, Rev Sylvester Dana. He was born at Ashford, Conn, but passed the earlier years chiefly at Wilkesbarre, Pa. His father & brother-in-law were among those slain by the British & Indians in their cruel attack upon many places in the valley of Wyoming in 1778. He with many other survivors fled through the wilderness, & reached Conn. In 1786, with 2 brothers, he returned to Wilkesbarre, which was desolated by the Indians, & successfully began to cultivate his father's land. In 1793 he entered Yale College, & graduated in 1797. He studied theology with Dr Backus, & in 1801 was settled as a Minister of a parish in Oxford, N H, where he remained about 35 years. During the later years he resided in Concord, where his wife died in 1846.

SAT JUN 23, 1849
The Court House at Concord, Mass, was burnt on Tue, together with a dwlg-house which stood adjoining, owned by John S Keyes. The records were nearly all saved, & also the papers in the County Treasurer's ofc.

The Weverton Manufacturing Co [Weverton, Md,] meeting is on Jul 2, for the election of Directors. –John G Chapman, Pres.

Ship timber for sale: to be delivered at his residence, **Bluff Point**, Northumberland Co, Va. Address Kilmarnock, Lancaster Co, Va. –Cyrus Haynie

For rent: 2 story brick dwlg at 7th & I sts, adjoining the residence of A Rothwell. Inquire of E C & G F Dyer, aucts, or subscriber. –Jane M Dyer

MON JUN 25, 1849
On Mon last, as Hugh Walker, of Cumberland, Md, was running before a burden car, which was detached from the locomotive, for the pupose of checking it, he stepped in a small ditch & fell upon his back, when the car came upon him, crushing him to death almost instantly.

The telegraph announces that Miss De Forrest, daughter of one of the most respectable citizens of Buffalo, fell into the stream at the Hog's Back on Thus. Mr Chas C Addington, a young merchant of Buffalo, plunged in to save her, but both were carried over the Falls. –Commercial Advertiser

Miss Sallie Ann Elliott, daughter of the late Com Elliott, died of cholera at Wheeling a few days since, being on her return from Cincinnati to Westchester, having been on a visit of a few weeks to some friends in the former city.

Geo W Hoffman, a clerk in the house of Messrs Jaffray & Sons, N Y, committed suicide on Wed by jumping from the 3rd story window of a house, during a delirium caused by fever.

Mr Kell, an Irish laborer, in the employment of Mr Wise, was taken sick on Sat, while working at a sand bank. He was taken home to his lodgings on East Capitol st, & there died that evening.

Criminal Court: 1-Negro Geo Bowen convicted of stealing 2 loads of wood, the property of Louisa Devaughn. Sentenced to 4 months in the county jail, & fined $1. 2-Geo Harry convicted of an assault on Kesiah Long. Sentenced to 2 weeks in the county jail. 3-The case of grand larceny: U S vs Milly Davis, verdict of guilty. Sentence: 1 year at labor in the penitentiary. 4-Thos Hogan found guilty of keeping a disorderly house: fined $10. 5-John Dewdney, charged with assault & battery on John Mullikin: acquitted. 6-Negro Lewis Lee was found guilty of stealing 5 chickens, the property of Stevenson Scott. Sentenced to 6 weeks in the county jail.

Mrd: on Jun 20, in Wash City, by Rev C M Butler, Henry Oelrichs, of Balt, to Julia M McRa, daughter of the late Dr F May, of Wash City.

Mrd: on Jun 19, by Rev Mr Vanhorsigh, Mr Wm Quigley to Miss Mary Harrington, both of Wash City.

Died: on Jun 23, suddenly, of congestion of the brain, Mrs Cecilia Smith, aged 66 years, after an illness of 3½ hours.

TUE JUN 26, 1849
Appointments by the Pres: Attys:
Henry Williams, of Ga, for district of Ga, vice Francis T Bartow, who declines the ofc.
Wm H Haigh, of N C, for district of N C, vice Henry W Miller, who declines the ofc.
Land Ofcrs: Receiver of Public Moneys:
Wm Sheffield, of Ohio, at Defiance, Ohio, vice Wm L Henderson, removed.
N Green Willcox, at Stillwater, Minesota Territory, vice Saml Leech, removed.
J T B Stapp, of Ill, at Vandalia, Ill, vice Danl Gregory, removed.
Register of the Land Ofc:
Abner Root, of Ohio, at Defiance, Ohio, vice John Taylor, removed.
Hugh Y Waddell, of La, at Natchitoches, La, vice John F Payne, deceased.

Near the Navy Yard at Pensacola, on Jun 9, the wife of Michl Cracton, & a Mr Mansfield were unfortunately drowned. Mrs Cracton & a young woman were bathing, when the former was seized by a shark & drawn into deep water. Mr Mansfield went to her assistance, but lost his own life. The body of Mrs Cracton drifted ashore much mulitated. Mr Mansfield's clothing drifted on the beach, leaving little doubt that he was devoured by sharks.

Poughkeepsie, N Y: on Jun 22, the earth in Maine st gave way & buried a number of workmen, Christo Punis & John Shepard were taken out dead.

Rev John D Moriarty, long known to the traveling community as the host of the Congress Spring House, at Saratoga Springs, died on Jun 18, of apoplexy. The business of the hotel will be conducted by his widow & one of his sons.

For sale or rent: *Woodlands*, the Farm on which I have resided for the last 6 years, exclusive of the quarries. It is in D C, & contains about 400 acres. Apply to Timothy O'Neale, Gtwn, or the subscriber, at *Friendship*, the adjacent farm. —Wm D C Murdock

Valuable farm, crop, & stock at auction: on Jul 10: within the District limits, contains 108 acres, 2 roods, & 22 perches; large dwlg-house & all necessary out-bldgs. It is surrounded with the best society, being in the neighborhood of Maj Walker, Mrs Saunders, Messrs Clagett, Blair, Carbery, Causin, & other respectable gentleman. Title indisputable. —A Green, auctioneer

Trustee's sale of valuable city property: by deed of trust from Thornton F Hickey, recorded in Liber W B 127, folios 206 through 209, among the land records of Wash Co, D C: sale on Jul 17, of lot 2 in square 688, fronts on B st, on which is a 2 story brick house & back bldg. —Wm Gunton, trustee -E C & G F Dyer, aucts

For sale or rent: 2 story brick house, on First st, Gtwn, at present occupied by Wm A Gordon. Possession on or about Jul 1. Apply to Mr John Marbury, jr, in Gtwn, or to the subscriber in Wash. —Jos Reynolds

$50 reward for recovery of stolen horse & buggy: stolen on Jun 22, by a young man who came to my stable & hired a horse & buggy, to be absent one hour, & has not returned. —Levi Pumphrey, Wash, Stable-keeper, C st

WED JUN 27, 1849
Appointments by the Pres: Collectors of Customs:
Geo W Charles, Camden, N C, vice Wm D Pritchard, removed.
John D Whitford, Newbern, N C, vice Thos S Singleton, resigned.
Oliver York, Stonington, Conn, vice Benj Pomeroy, removed.
Appraisers of Merchandise: Robt F Canfield, New Orleans, La, vice John Duncan, removed.
Surveyors of the Customs: 1-John C O'Grady, Madisonville, La, vice Thos W Kellum, removed. 2-Giles Blague, Saybrook, Conn, vice Wm Willard, removed.
The Mint: A W Redding to be Superintendent of the Branch Mint at Dahlonega, Ga.

Fatal rencontre in which Wm E Blackburne, of Lake Providence, La was killed by Mr Steele, Sat last, at a temperance meeting, at Harmony, near Frankfort. Blackburn assaulted Steele with a whip, & Steele drew a pistol & shot him through, killing him almost instantly. Mr Blackburne is the son of Col Edw Blackburne, of this State. —Louisville Courier

The expedition to El Paso del Norte started from San Antonio about Jun 1st. It consists of 6 companies of the 3rd Regt U S Infty, as follows: Co A, Light Infty, under command of Lt Thos J Mason; Co B, Grenadiers, under Brevet Maj O L Shepherd & Lt John Trevitt; Co C, under Capt Wm B Johns & Lt Wm H Wood; Co E, mounted Howitzer Battery, under Brevet Maj Richardson & Lt L W O'Bannot; Co I, under Lts J C McFerray & J N S Whistler; Co K, under Brevet Maj W S Henry. 15 mounted men under command of Lt W J Mechlin. Assist Surgeons P G S Ten Broeck & Lyman H Stone. Lt John D Wilkins, acting Adj of the Btln; Brevet Capt A W Bowman, Regimental Quartermaster & Commissary Subsistence; Brevet Capt Wm G French, Quartermaster in charge of train; Brevet Maj Jefferson Van Horn, 3rd Infty, in command of the expedition. Mrs Maj Henry & family, Mrs McFerrin & family, Mrs Whistler, & Mrs Wilkins also accompanied the 3rd Regt. Col S E Johnson, Lts Wm E Smith, Francis F Bryan, & N Michler, Topographical Engineers, were also proceeding with the command.

Niagara Falls, Jun 22. Last evening a party was visiting the Luna island, among whom were the lady & little daughter of Mr De Forest & young Chas C Addington, & others. While standing on the brink of the river, holding the hand of a young gentleman, young Addington came up & playfully said, "I'm going to throw you in," when she sprang forward & slipped from the hand of the gentleman who held her. They fell into the water, & in an instant young Addington & the little girl were swept over the falls. Miss Annette De Forest was a very interesting child, about 9 years of age. Mr Addington was 21; son of S H Addington, for many years a resident of Buffalo.

Stolen or strayed from the subscriber on Sat last, a large white cow. Handsome reward for restoring said cow to my residence. —G F Morison, corner of Vt av & L st.

Fatal affray a few days ago at a land sale at Otumna, Iowa, a small town on the Des Moines river, between Dr White & Mr Ross, in which Dr White was killed & Mr Ross dangerously, if not mortally, wounded.

At New Orleans, on Jun 15, a young man named Robt Lintell was tried for the murder of his wife, Susan Jane, age 17, on Apr 7. They had been married but a few months, when they parted & she went to live with her young widowed sister. Lintell came to the house, & after talking 2 hours or more, stabbed Susan Jane in the abdomen. She died the next day. The jury found Lintell guilty of murder, without capital punishment.

One cent reward: Alfred Singleton Soper, bound apprentice to the Butchering Business, left my residence on Jun 24. I forbid all persons trusting or harboring said Soper on my account; & I will also hold any person responsible who may employ him within the District. —Jas J Shedd

Notice: was committed to the jail of Wash Co, D C, on May 10, 1849, as a runaway, a negro man calling himself Edw Brooks, about 30 years old. He says he is free, & was born in Wash City. He has been absent from this city 15 or 16 years, & before he left he was known by Saml Redfern, Jas Eslin, & Richd Butt; & in Richmond, Va, by Jas Evans & Mr D W Carter, clerk in the Bank of Va, & has a pass purporting to be from him, stating that he is free & has lost his papers. Owner is to prove him, & take him away. –Thos A Hawke, for R Wallace, Marshal D C

Marshal's sale: by writ of fieri facias: sale on Jul 5, all the right, title, & interest of Mary Callnan & Ellen Collins in & to lot 12 in square 377, in Wash City, with four 2 story frame houses, fronting on 10th st, seized & levied upon as the property of the said Callnan & Collins, & sold to satisfy judicials 86, to March term, 1849, in favor of Jas O'Conner, use of Danl Ratcliffe. –Robt Wallace, Marshal of D C

Criminal Court: Joshua Bateman was arrested on Mon last & placed on trial for 3 assaults committed on Mary Ann Dickens, Lawrence Leary, & John Johnson, a colored man. The dfndnt was found guilty & fined $20 for assaulting Dickens, $10 for the assault on Leary, & $5 for the assault on Johnson. The Court & Jury yesterday tried the case of the U S vs R H Harrington, charged with an assault & battery at the Navy Yard on Wm Fraelig. This trial will probably continue for 2 or 3 days. [Jun 28th newspaper: Harrington found not guilty-acquitted.]

THU JUN 28, 1849
The Augusta [Ga] Republic has the following, dated Oxford, Jun 17, 1849: "I regret to inform you that the nephew of Rev Dr Geo F Pierce has been severely burnt by the explosion of phosgene, & he died shortly afterward." Rev Pierce was severely burnt on his right hand.

Appointment by the Pres: Wm Y Leitch, Surveyor of the Customs, Charleston, S C, vice Myer Jacobs, removed.

On May 20, Capt John Hargraves, of this county, returning home, riding a mule, during a severe thunder storm, fell into chasm some 8 feet deep, with the mule on top of him. He cut the mule until he died, but still could not get from under the animal. His calls for help were heard by Mr Swearingen, a neighbor, who extricated him, by cutting up the mule with an axe. Capt Hargraves is fast recovering.
–Van Buren [Ark] Intelligence

An affray on Sun last occurred at Boyleston, Mass, between 2 brothers named Wm & Marshal Flagg, in which the former was killed by a wound from a jack-knife, inflicted by the latter.

A letter dated Wallingford, Conn, on Sat last says: Jane Andrews-18, & Juliet Miller-13, both of this town, went to bathe in a pond near the residence of Miss Miller, when Miss Miller got beyond her depth. Miss Andrews rushed forward to succor her young friend, but perished in the effort. Jane was the daughter of Col Ira Andrews; Juliet was the daughter of Saml Miller.

Household & kitchen furniture at auction on Jul 2, at the residence of A F Patrick, on L st, between 9th & 10th sts. –T C Donn, trustee -Martin & Wright, auctioneers

Household & kitchen furniture at auction on Jul 2, at the residence of Mrs Ladd, on 12th st, between E st & Pa ave. --Edw C & G F Dyer, aucts

In Chancery: Robt W Dyer & others against Sarah G Stewart, admx, & Chas A Stewart & Wm H Stewart, heirs of Wm H Stewart. The creditors of the late Wm H Stewart who may not have exhibited their claims against the estate are to do so on or before July 10. –W Redin, auditor

Balt: fire broke out on Jun 27, which destroyed the work-shop attached to the extensive house-furnishing establishment of Jas Cortlan & Son. The loss is $8,000 to $10,000.

Mormons: Elder Addison Pratt arrived in company with a part of the btln, on Sep 28, 1848, & found his family in health, from whom he had been absent about 5 years, on a mission to the Society Islands, where he has baptised about 1,200 souls. On Jan 1 John Smith, uncle to the Prophet Jos Smith, was ordained Patriarch to the Church, holding the keys & powers thereof, same as Fr Jos Smith & Hiram. Newell K Whitney, Pres of the Bishops' Quorum, presiding, is instructed to set in order all the lesser officers.

Criminal Court-Wash. Chas Finnegan, charged with an assault on Wm Froehlig, will be tried today. [Jun 29th newspaper: Finnegan was acquitted.]

Mrd: on May 30, in San Antonio, Texas, by Rev Mr Smith, Lt J D Wilkins, 3rd U S Infty, to Miss Caroline Howard, of Wash City.

Mrd: Jun 19, at New Orleans, by Rev E R Bradle, Lt Col D D Tompkins, U S Army, to Miss Ellen H Cornell, daughter of the late Dr J S Cornell, of Natchez, Miss.

Died: on Jun 27, in Gtwn, Mrs Ann S Simpson, aged 70 years & 20 days, consort of Jas Simpson. Her funeral is this morning, at 8 o'clock, from her late residence, corner of High & West sts.

Died: on Sun, Ann Eliza Neilson, eldest daughter of Hall Neilson, of Richmond, Va.

FRI JUN 29, 1849
Wash Corp: communication from the Mayor making the following nominations, viz:
Jos Radcliff, 1st Clerk   Jos H Bradley, Atty
Wm E Howard, 2nd Clerk   Jacob Kleiber, Messenger
Com'r of the Wash Asylum:
Chas A Davis   Geo H Fulmer   Theodore Wheeler
Benj E Gittings, Intendant of the Asylum
Alex McWilliams, Physician of the Asylum
Geo Bean, Inspector of Tobacco
Wm M McCauley, Sealer of Weights & Measures
Jacob Kleiber, Inspector of Flour & Provisions

Jas A Tait, Com'r of the Western section of the Wash Canal.
Jos Cross, Com'r of the Eastern section of the Wash Canal
Caleb Buckingham, Inspector of Fire Apparatus

City Com'rs:
Geo W Harkness	F B Lord	John Magar
John Sessford	W A Mulloy	
C P Wannell	Ignatius Howe	

Police Constables:
F B Posten	E G Handy	Ignatius Howe
John Dewdney	R R Butt	John Magar
O E P Hazard	J M Wright	John Waters-declining
Wm H Barneclo	Wm A Mulloy	
J F Wollard	Hanson Brown	

Com'r of the Centre Market:
Ignatius Mudd	Wm Orme	John H Goddard

Clerks of Markets
Wm Serrin	H B Robertson	Wm B Wilson
John Waters	Peter Little	

Inspectors & Measurers of Lumber:
Wm G Deale	Benj Bean	John G Robinson
John W Ferguson	Wm Douglass	H S Davis

Wood Corders & Coal Measurers:
Nathl Plant	John B Ferguson	
Richd Wimsatt	John P Hilton	

Gaugers & Inspectors:
Elexius Simms	Florian Hitz

Measurers of Bran, Shorts, & Shipstuff:
Jas Gaither	John B Ferguson

Com'rs of the West Burial Ground:
Wm Wilson	John C Harkness
John Wilson	Guy Graham-Sexton

Com'rs of the East Burial Ground:
John P Ingle	F Y Naylor	Thos J Barrett-Sexton

Superintendents of Chimney Sweeps:
John Lewis	Roger Moffitt	N B Wilkerson
Geo B Bowen	Wm M Robinson	

Scavengers:
G T McGlue	Wm Johnson	Thos Greeves
Luke Richardson	Jas Hollige	John Cox
Jas Hollige	Saml Curson	Jas B Lockey

Which communication was ordered to lie on the table.

Mr Alex'r de Bodisco, the highly esteemed Envoy Extra & Minister Pleni from Russia to the U S, sailed on Wed from N Y on his route to St Petersburgh, on a visit to his own country, which will probably occupy him for several months. He leaves his family with us, the surest pledge of his intention to return to this country. In his absence, M Edw de Stoeckly, First Sec of the Russian Legation, is Charge d'Affaires of the Russian Empire to this Republic.

Appointments by the Pres:
Alfred Mitchell, of N J, to be Consul at Cork, in lieu of John Murphy, deceased.
Jas Heuderbert, of Miss, to be Consul at Lyons, in lieu of Jas A Jones, resigned.
Philip Richd Fendall, to the U S Atty for the Dist of Columbia.
Richd Wallach, of D C, to be U S Marshal for D C, vice Robt Wallace, removed.
Appointments by the Sec of the Interior:
Wm R Vance, to be Pension Agent at Louisville, Ky, vice Newton Lane, removed.
Stephen P Mead, of N Y, to be Indian Sub-Agent for the New York Indians, vice Robt H Shankland, removed.

We learn, officially, that Wm A Bradley, has been appointed Postmaster of Wash City.

Wm H Delany was on Monday last elected, by a large majority, to be Mayor of the city of Norfolk, Va.

On Jun 21, Mr Geo Webb, of the steamer **Globe**, died on the boat on her passage from Chicago to Milwaukie. For several weeks he had taken brandy & laudanum freely, through fear of cholera. It is feared excessive drugging was the cause of his sad & sudden death. He was found dead in his berth.

The cholera at Nashville: Dr McCall writes, under date of Jun 18: Prof Hamilton of our University is dying; his 3 sisters are dead; & 9 persons dead at the Blind Asylum. Only my son, now sick with typhus fever, & my wife & little daughter are at home. Our cook & boy have the cholera. Many streets are deserted, & death stalks around.

On Monday a hat containing a paper on which was written "Look in the water," was found on Taylors wharf, foot of Poplar st, Boston. A rope was attached to a stick of wood, & upon drawing in the rope the body of Mr Richd Witherell came up with it. The deceased was a well known mason & builder, & leaves a wife & several children.

Fatal accidents from the careless use of the Gun. In Concord, on Jun 11, 2 sons of Mr H C Shephard, one 12, the other about 10, were in the field hunting chipmunks. The older boy accidentally shot & killed the younger brother. In the town of Burnett, Dodge Co, on May 31: 2 sons of Mr Duell, aged 9 & 12 years, were shooting blackbirds in the cornfield, the gun exploded & caused the death of one of the boys. –Watertown [Wis] Chron

Death of a pioneer editor: Wm F Legg, of this city, late foreman in C Scott's printing room, & publisher of the Panama Star, died on May 5, after 4 days' illness. He fell victim to the insalubrity of the climate on the Isthmus.

A Silver shilling of the reign of Queen Elizabeth, dated 1579, was found in the garden of W P Fessenden, on State st, in Portland, a few days ago.

John Sessford, a young man, who was at work on the Nat'l Monument, fell from the top of it last Tuesday, & was internally very much injured. He fell a distance of 30 feet.

Balt, Jun 28. Dr P Macaulay, an old & highly esteemed citizen, who for some time has been residing a short distance out of Balt, in the county, died this morning of heart disease. He had been sick but a few days.

Mrd: on Jun 28, at the Church of the Epiphany, by Rev Mr French, Mr David H Hanlon, of Balt, to Miss Lydia J Halliday, of Wash City.

Mrd: on Jun 27, at Chester, Pa, by Rev Mortimer Talbot, Edw F Beale, U S Navy, to Miss Mary, daughter of Saml Edwards.

Mrd: on Jun 28, in Trinity Church, by Rev Dr Butler, John P Hubbard, of Boston, to Adelaide, daughter of Jas W McCulloh, of Wash City.

Died: on Jun 26, suddenly, of apoplexy, at his residence in Middleburg, Va, Maj Geo Cuthbert Powell, in his 42nd year.

Stray cow came to my house about May 1st; about a week since she had a calf. Owner is to come forward, prove property, pay charges, & take her away.
-Jas Fraser, Square 663, Wash

Marshal's sale: by writ of fieri facias, Circuit Court of Wash Co, D C: sale on Jul 23, of all the right, title, & interest of John Young in & to all that piece or part of lot 9 in square 290, in Wash City, with a dwlg house, partly of brick & partly of frame-work, on 13th st. Also, part of lot 9 in square 290, on 13th st. Seized & levied upon as the property of the said John Young, & sold to satisfy judicials #22 to Mar Term, 1844, in favor of Washington Berry, against said Young. –Thos Woodward, Deputy to the late A Hunter, Marshal, deceased.

SAT JUN 30, 1849
The N Y Grand Jury of the Court of Sessions brought in 21 bills of indictment on Sat against individuals concerned in the Astor Place riots. Among those indicted were Capt Rynders, John S Austin, & other members of the Empire Club.

The Hon Calvin Blythe died on Wed last, at Fairfield, Adams Co, Pa, in his 57th year. He was a lawyer of distinguished abilities & filled many responsible stations. A few weeks since he went to Adams Co to spend a portion of the summer with the family of his brother. –Phila News

Mrd: on Jun 28, at Gtwn, D C, by Rt Rev Bishop Johns, Hon Andrew Stevenson, of Va, to Miss Mary Shaaff, 3rd daughter of the late Dr Shaaff, of Md.

Marshal's sale: 2 writs of fieri facias, issued at the Clerk's ofc of the Circuit Court of Wash Co, D C. Sale on Jul 23, all the right, title, or claim of John Lawrence in: part of lot 81 in Threlkeld's addition to Gtwn: adjoins Jas Scrivner's property. Seized & levied upon as the property of John Lawrence, & sold to satisfy judicials 19 & 20, to Oct Term, 1848, in favor of Mayor, Recorder, Aldermen, & Common Council of Gtwn. –Thos Woodward, Deputy to the late Alex'r Hunter, Marshal.

Copy of Henry King's letter from Calif, Mar 30, 1846, postmarked Independence, Mo, Sep 5. Camp on Deer Creek, Upper Calif, Mar 30, 1846.
Dear Parents: I embrace this opportunity to write you a few lines. I know not whether this will reach you, so I will write but briefly, as I shall probably reach home at least a month or so later then this will probably reach you, & can then tell you of my trip; & then I shall be apt to postpone it until the long winter nights, as I shall have some very tough yarns to tell; but true, nevertheless. I shall merely, then, state now that I have enjoyed excellent health, notwithstanding a good deal of hardship. After leaving Bent's Fort, we travelled at a pretty swift rate, & very soon the animals began to give out. [I rode down 3 horses from Westport to nearly the lower point of the Cordilleras ridge of mountains.] Our usual rate of travelling is about 3 miles an hour, our horses being kept in a pretty fast walk. We fared very well in the way of provisions, having plenty of game, as far as the Great Salt Lake, [if I except being without sugar & coffee for some 3 weeks, & also flour.] I soon fell into the habit of making a hearty meal of meat alone, which will probably surprise you; nevertheless, I always thought of the hot rolls & coffee at home. We are now camped at the head nearly of Sacramento valley, on our way to Oregon. I think it very likely that we will return yet, & go down through Calif-peacefully if we can, forcibly if we must.

Land for sale or rent: a Farm containing 150 acres, the former residence of Gen Alex'r Hunter. For terms apply to Mrs Hunter, 3rd & C sts, Wash.

Marshal's sale: writ of fieri facias, issued at the Clerk's ofc of the Circuit Court of Wash Co, D C. Sale on Jul 23: all the right, title, or claim of Jas B Philips in & to lot 7 in square 449, Wash City, fronting 80 feet on L st & 80 feet on 7th st, in Wash City. Seized & levied upon as the property of said Philips, & sold to satisfy judicials #1, to Oct Term, 1848, in favor of Owen G Cates against Enoch W Smallwood & Jas B Philips. –Thos Woodward, Deputy to the late Alex'r Hunter, Marshal.

Criminal Court-Wash. Yesterday the trial of John Henry Edwards, Henry Keenan, & Franklin Camper, charged with riot, they being the persons concerned in a prize fight a few Sundays ago. All found guilty of a riot on May 10, & of an assault & battery on Mr Tait.

MON JUL 2, 1849
Mr Skinner went out to establish a telegraphic line from Vera Cruz to the city of Mexico, has returned without accomplishing his object.

Criminal Court-Wash. 1-P R Fendall, the lately appointed Dist Atty, appear in Court on Sat, & entered on the duties of his ofc. 2-J H C Mudd charged with an assault on Mr Edw Simms, was submitted; sentence of the Court was not passed upon the traverser. 3-Elias Lomas, free negro, charged with an assault upon John Logan, with intent to kill him, was acquitted. 4-Edwards & Keenan, prize fighters, convicted of riot on Jun 17, sentenced each to 2 months in the county jail. 5-Keenan, convicted of the same offence: sentenced to 6 weeks in jail. 6-Edwards, for resisting ofcr Dewdney, sentenced to 2 weeks in imprisonment. 7-Camper, for a riot on May 10, sentenced to 2 weeks imprisonment in jail.

An ancient document, namely a Proclamation issued by Sir Edmund Andross, from *Fort Pemmaquid*, in New England, date 1688, printed at Boston by R P, which hung in one of the Reading-rooms of the N Y Society Library, was carried off last week by some individual, who took it from the frame. –N Y Tribune

Orphans Court of Wash Co, D C. Letters of administration on the personal estate of Wm Ingle, late of the State of Va, deceased. –Jos Ingle, adm

Mrd: on May 25, at Havana, Thos Sloo to Miss Maria Frances, 3rd daughter of Gen Robt B Campbell, U S Consul for the port of Havana.

Died: on May 29, at *Rose Hill*, near Rockville, Md, the Rev John Mines, D D, for many years the faithful & much loved pastor of the Presbyterian Church of Rockville & Bethesda.

Died: last evening, Susan Rowles, eldest daughter of Cornelius & Mgt C Barber, in her 7th year. Her funeral is from her father's residence, *North View*, near Gtwn, this evening, at 5 o'clock.

Died: on Jun 29, in Gtwn, D C, Thos Bolling Brooke, infant son of Walter T & Olivia C Brooke.

TUE JUL 3, 1849
Appointments by the Pres: 1-Thos S Hall, of Va, to be U S Marshal for the Eastern District of Va, vice Edmund Christian, removed. 2-Benj H Smith, of Va, to be U S Atty for the Western District of Va, vice Geo W Thompson, removed. 3-Jas Gwinn, to be Collector of Customs at Vicksburg, Miss, vice Hardy Hendrew, removed.

The Louisville papers announce the death of Thos S Forman, late Pres & business agent of the Louisville Manufacturing Co.

Prof Jas Hamilton died of cholera at Nashville on Thu week. He had been Prof of Mathematics in the Nashville Univ for 25 years. Three of Professor Hamilton's sisters also died during the same week.

On Sun last 2 negroes were brought to town, charged with the murder of Mrs Foster. They belong to Messrs John R Anderson & Jesse Hainline, of the vicinity in which the deed was done. One negro made a full confession, but the other persists in his innocence. Articles taken from the house of Mr Foster were found in the possession of one of them. One had been sentenced to be hung on Aug 12.

The Newark Advertiser says that the body of Henry Crim, aged 60 years, was on Sun last found in his house near Rockaway, Morris Co, where he lived alone, perfectly lifeless. He was found at the side of the bed, & pools of blood around him. The coroner's jury said he had been killed by some person unknown.

Mr Nathan Coy, of Oxford, Me, was drowned in the Androscoggin river a few days since, in rescuing his own son. He succeeded in saving his son, but he became so exhausted that he was unable to maintain himself above water.

On Sat last, at John Price's store, at Sassafras Neck, Md, a boy about 11 years of age, called for some goods; a barrel of rum near where he was standing exploded, enveloping him in a sheet of flames. He was so burnt that he died in 15 minutes. —Cecil Democrat

Brother Macarius & a few <u>Trappist Monks</u> have arrived in this country to make arrangements for the establishment of 2 monastaries of the order somewhere. They had better traps bears, clear woods, make settlements, & marry, as good citizens ought to do. —Home Journal

On Sat, Mr G Clark, proprietor of the Sarsaparilla establishment in Holliday st, Balt, was considerably injured by one of the cocks of the gasometer blowing off while he was repairing it. He was burnt in the face & body.

Mrs Mitchem, residing in Richmond, Jefferson Co, Ohio, was found drowned in Yellow creek a short time since, together with her 3 children. They had been reduced almost to starvation by the neglect of the husband, who was a drunkard. They left home, it is supposed, on their way to Mrs Mitchen's father's residence, in Mercer Co, Pa. Whether their drowning was accidental or designed is not known.

Geo Howell, one of the most notorious pickpockets in the country, left Boston last week in custody of Ofcr Starkweather, for Phil, where he is wanted to answer the charge of being concerned in the late robbery of the Chester County Bank. Howell was arrested at the Fitchburg depot, in Boston, on May 25, for picking the pocket of Mr Moody Morse, of Westbrook, Maine, & committed for trial, in default of bail for $2,000.

Depth of sea off *Cape Hatteras* 19,800 feet. —Coast Survey

Died: on Jun 22, at her residence near Woodgrove, Loudoun Co, Va, Mrs Massie Osborne, wife of Joel Osborne, in her 57th year, leaving a large circle of friends & relatives to mourn their irreparable loss.

Medical Dept of the Army: Medical Board convened in N Y C on May 1 last, & the following applicants for appointment in the Medical Staff of the Army were examined & approved:

Wm H Ballard, of La
Geo K Wood, of N Y
Jos B Brown, of Mich
Alex'r B Hasson, of Md
Jonathan Letherman, of Pa
Wm A Hammond, of Pa
Francis Sorrel, of Ga
Edw W Jones, of Md
Wm W Anderson, of S C

The Marshal of the Day [Jul 4th,] has selected the following gentlemen as Assistants, & report to Mr Geo S Gideon at the Capitol at 10 o'clock.

Geo S Gideon	Jesse E Dow	Wm Wiley
John B Sullivan	J Laurens Henshaw	Jas McHenry
J H Clay Mudd	Jas A Gordon	Dr Wm Saunders
John Junnicutt	Jas E Berrett	Dr Wm V H Brown
John A Linton	Isaac Hall	Geo Harrington
Miles Selden	John Mitchel	John England
Augustus E Perry	A Thos Bradley	P H Hooe
Jas W Moorhead	Marshall Brown	Chas B Maury
Jonah D Hoover	Robt S Patterson	Wm H Winter
Chas McNamee	Eugene Cummiskey	Jos J May
John F Ennis	John T Towers	Andrew Coyle
Patrick H Brooks	John F Coyle	K H Lambell
Hugh B Sweeny	Thos W Howard	Wm A Kennedy
Geo C Whiting	A S H White	J Covington Burche
Wm Jackson	Dr J B Gardiner	
Wm B Webb	J L Cathcart	

WED JUL 4, 1849
Groceries & liquors at auction, on Jul 10, in consequence of the affliction of Mr Allen. We shall sell the extensive stock of Groceries & Liquors in his store on La ave, near 7th st. –Green & Tastet, auctioneers

Winchester Republican of Jun 20. Visit to *Carter Hill*, a fine estate 2 miles west of Newtown, owned by Mr Wm A Carter. The mansion is an elegant edifice, with the all the conveniences & comforts which could be desired. Mr Carter has a capacious & well-arranged barn, with stabling, stalls, & shelters for his horses & cattle. His tract of land is 1,200 acres.

Suicide: from Tampico information received at New Orleans that, about a month since, Mr John C Henderson was found drowned in the river at that city. From the fact that a cannon ball in a handkerchief was tied to his neck it was concluded that the act was one of deliberate suicide. He was a native of Waterford, Ire, about 34 years of age, & has a respectable wife & young family residing in Victoria, Texas.

Dept of State, Wash, Jul 3, 1849. Information received from Stanhope Prevost, Consul of the U S at Lima, of the death, in Lima, of Mr Emeel Moncini, Dentist, who arrived at Callao in the Apr steamer from Panama, with upwards of 100 emigrants from the U S, seeking passage to Calif. The effects left by the deceased were taken possession of by Mr Prevost & sold at auction. From Mr Moncini's private papers it appears he was a resident of Boydton, Va, about 18 months previous to Sep, 1848.

Trustee's sale of valuable bldg lots at auction: on Jul 12, by deed of trust, dated Nov 5, 1844, recorded in Liber W B #112, folios 151, 152, & 153, of the land records of Wash Co, D C: sale of lot 19 & east half of lot 18, in square 496, fronting on F st, between 4½ & 6th sts, immediately opposite the residence of Mr Geo Mattingly.
–H Naylor, Trustee -Green & Tastet, aucts

N Y Express of Sat relates the melancholy mortality in the family circle of Mr J H Bassett, of the firm of Bassett & Aborn, of that city, but residing in Brooklyn. On Fri his son, Isaac Hodges, aged 5, & a daughter, Adaline Amanda, aged 7, died suddenly of cholera; &, hardly had their afflicted parents had time to realize their sad affliction, ere 2 others of the family, Frederick & Amy, fell victims to the destroyer, Death. The 4 bodies were interred together in *Greenwood*. The Board of Health fears they had their origin in the imprudence of the children eating green apples.

Louisville Democrat: Lt Geo Adams, U S Marines: this gallant ofcr has been in our city nearly 2 months, under the surgical care of Prof Gross. Adams was in the severe conflict which took place at Nat'l Bridge, on Aug 12, 1847, between Maj Lally's command & 1,500 Mexicans in position, Lt Adams fell, as it was then thought, with a mortal wound. Lt Adams was born in Frankfort, Ky, in 1824, & is the son of the last Judge Adams, of the U S Circuit court at Jackson, Miss, formerly a distinguished lawyer of Frankfort. He was educated at Centre College, & at 20, [3 years since,] received his commission as Lt in the Marine Corps. –A M, jr, Louisville, Apr, 1849

Orphans Court of Wash Co, D C. Letters of administration on the personal estate of Cecilia Smith, late of said county, deceased. –J L Smith, adm

Mrd: on Jul 2, at *Kalorama*, near Wash City, by Rev Smyth Pyne, Capt Arthur Breese Lansing, U S Army, to Mrs Louisa Cochran, daughter of the late Thos Lovett, of N Y.

Stage accident at Louisville as it was going out from Maysville, Ky, on Tue: the driver lost control in descending the hill at the entrance of the bridge. Prof Sherman, of the Columbia Institute had his face fractured & crushed, & he died soon after. Mr Pleasant Smith, a citizen of Nashville, so injured, that he is expected to die. A German, W Goldstein, a merchant of Phil, has his leg fractured in 2 places, with other hurts, renders his recovery doubtful.

Died: on Jun 23, at *Woodlawn*, in Pr Wm Co, Dr John W Tyler, late Surgeon to the Regt of Voltigeurs.

FRI JUL 6, 1849
The St Louis papers report the death by cholera of Capt G T M Davis-some years ago an able member of the Alton bar; a brave & active ofcr in the Mexican war under Gen Taylor, & for some months past, & at the time of his death, one of the editors of the St Louis Era. Capt Davis was a well educated, well informed man, & a graceful & forcible writer. [No death date given-current item.] [Note: correction in Jul 9th newspaper.]

Destructive fire yesterday, in a stable attached to the bakery & dwlg of Mr L A Tarlton, on 10th st: all was destroyed: dwlg was owned by Mr Martini. Mr Dufief's house was destroyed, also 3 new bldgs, 2 of which belonged to Mr Schlegel, who was insured for $800 on each. Mr Hyder owned the other.

Criminal Court-Wash: 1-Jas Higgins, charged with stealing $14, the property of John Coleman: not guilty. 2-Jas Maguire, charged with assault & battery on Edw Simms: not guilty.

Appointments by the Pres: John D Cook, of Mo, to be U S Atty for the district of Mo, vice Thos T Gantt, removed.
Abel Underwood, of Vt, to be U S Atty for the district of Vt, vice Chas Linsley, removed.
Wm H Ringo, of Ark, to be Receiver of Public Moneys at Helena, Ark, vice Lorenzo D Maddox, deceased.
Sylvester Brown, Collector of the Customs, Washington, N C, vice Jas H Hatton, removed.
Thos Gatewood, Naval Ofcr, Norfolk, Va, vice C C Robinson, removed.

Accident at Charlotte, Delaware Co, N Y, Sat last: Rev S D Ferguson, Principal of the Charlotte Seminary, was out riding with a portion of the pupils, near a mill pond. Four of the girls got into a boat on the pond. It upset and 2 of them were drowned: Hannah Ann, daughter of Thos Ferguson, & Frances, only daughter of Anthony Civill, both of N Y C. A gentleman who plunged into the water to their assistance, also drowned. He has left a wife & 8 children.

On Sun week, while returning from church at Gravel run, & crossing at the mouth of Conneaute creek, Pa, a buggy containing Mr Ash, Miss Ash, & Miss Lucinda Phelps, daughter of Mr Theodore Phelps, of Washington township, & Miss Strong, daughter of Mr C Strong, of Waterford township, was precipitated into the water, & all the ladies drowned. Miss Strong has been engaged teaching school in the neighborhood of Mr Phelps & Mr Ash. Mr Ash was saved by being washed against a boat tied below the bridge. Miss Strong's body is the only one recovered. –Erie Gaz 28th ult

Brutal murder & robbery in Alachus Co, Ky, a short time ago. Mr Cornelius Rain, a man of property, was returning to his house, when he was shot dead by 2 men. Although Mr Rain's wife & family were present, these men robbed the house of $4,000 & fled. They were not recognised.

Augusta [Ga] Sentinel, records the death in Columbia Co, Ga, on Jun 25, of Mr Philip Banks, a map peddlar. He was driving down a hill when the horse ran away; one of the wheels striking a stone, he was thrown out with such violence as to cause his death in about 4 hours.

Wash Corp: 1-Ptn from Wm McAboy: referred to the Cmte of Claims. 2-Ptn of P McGarvy, praying remission of a fine: referred to the Cmte of Claims. 3-Ptn of Z Hazel, praying that his privilege of continuing his hay-scales at 2nd st & Md ave may not be interfered with: referred to the Cmte on Police. 4-Ptn of Robt Beale, in relation to the licenses for wagons: referred to the Cmte on Police. 5-Ptn of R Triay & others, praying for curbstone & footway on south front of square 903.

Mrd: on Tue, by Rev John C Smith, Mr Manuel Lacey to Miss Eliz Deevers, all of Wash City.

Mrd: on Jun 13, in Tenn, at the residence of Gen Moore, by Rev Mr J Matthews, Mr Geo V Hebb, late of the U S Army, to Miss Jane Yell, daughter of the late Geo A Yell, of Ark.

Died: Jul 3, Wm Francis, only son of Francis H & Mgt Elwell, aged 18 months.

For rent: the store lately occupied by A Lemmons, on Pa ave, near 10th st. –S H Hill, 8th st, near Pa ave.

Information wanted of Mrs Mary Ann Drury, an elderly person, for some time a resident of Wash City, has been missing since about sundown of Sun last, when she was seen on 12th st, on her way home from the house of a friend whom she had been visiting. She was dressed in a second mourning calico. –Wm Peake, L & 8th sts

SAT JUL 7, 1849
Ofc of the Board of Health: 13 cases of Asiatic Cholera with 7 deaths, in Wash City since Jun 25. –Thos Miller, M D, Pres

The subscriber tenders to the Fire Companies, & fellow citizens, his grateful acknowledgments for their prompt & vigorous exertions in preserving his residence from destruction by fire on Thu last. –C C Jewett

Grateful thanks are tendered to his fellow citizens in particular, & the firemen in particular, for their efforts during the terrible conflagration on Thu, by which his property on 11th st was saved. –John A Blake

Rev G M Giger, of Princeton, N J, will preach in the F st Presbyterian Church tomorrow at 11 o'clock, & in the afternoon at 4 o'clock.

N Y-Jul 6: the Board of Health report 71 cases & 28 deaths of cholera for the 24 hours at noon today.

Phil, Jul 6. The Board of Health report 34 new cases & 12 deaths of cholera up to noon today.

Mrd: on Jul 5, in Wash City, at the Church of the Epiphany, by Rev Mr French, Dr HiramN Wadsworth, of Gtwn, to Sophie, youngest daughter of the late R M Whitney.

Mrd: on Jul 3, in St Mary's Church, by Rev Mr Alig, Mr Lawrence Williams to Miss Eliz Dacy, both of Wash City.

Died: on Jul 6, in Wash City, Wm B Pope, of Mobile, in his 29th year. His funeral is from the residence of Mrs Wise, 13th & E sts, today at 4 o'clock.

Died: on Jun 24, at St Louis, Mo, of hemorrhage of the lungs, Mr Chas W Johnson, aged 19 years & 11 months, son of Mr Geo Johnson, of Wash City.

Died: on Jul 5, Annie Maria, 2nd daughter of J Bayard H & Henrietta Smith, aged 3 years & 7 months. Her funeral is at 4 o'clock from the residence of Mrs Henley, **Franklin Row**.

Died: on Jun 24, in Wash City, Miss Catharine W Greenfield, formerly of St Mary's Co, Md, but a resident of Wash City for the last 9 years. Her distinguishing trait of character was that of submission to the Divine will. This led her to meek resignation when those she loved most tenderly melted one after another from the earth; & when she felt the touch of the same disease, to look to her own death with composure & calmness.

The Funeral ceremonies of Ex-Pres Polk on Jul 9: the Church bells of Wash City will toll for the space of half an hour at half-past 11 a m. At 12 the exercises will commence at the E st Baptist Church: prayer by Rev Geo W Sampson; eulogy by Gen Henry S Foote; & benediction by Rev Henry Slicer. Cmte:

B F Brown	Jno M McCalla	Thos G Galt
J E Dow	J D Hoover	Z W McKnew
Thos Ritchie	G W Phillips	

College of St James, Wash Co, Md: annual commencement on Jul 26. –John B Kerfoot, Rector

Information wanted of Wm Keough, a native of Templemore, Tipperary Co, Ire. His mother & sisters arrived in this country about one year since, are all comfortably located in Syracuse, N Y, & are very anxious to hear from him. Persons can communicate to his sister, Sarah Keough, or John Lathrop, at Syracuse.

Household & kitchen furniture at auction on Jul 12, at the residence of Dr Towle, on B st, near N J ave. –Green & Tastet, auctioneers

Sale of Farm Stock etc, on Jul 10, 4 miles from Wash, adjoining the farm of Dr Causin; it being the same farm formerly belonging to Mr Henry Ould. It is a valuable tract of land. –A Green, auctioneer [Etc as written.]

MON JUL 9, 1849
Telegraphic report: Col Jas Duncan, Inspector Genr'l of the U S Army, died at Mobile on Jul 3. He was a gallant & accomplished ofcr, & did good service in the late war with Mexico. [Jul 14th newspaper: Col Duncan was born in Orange Co, N Y, in Sep, 1810, of worthy yet undistinguished parentage; his boyhood was quietly passed upon his father's farm; he entered the Military Academy at West Point in Nov, 1830, & although prevented by an accident from commencing with his class, he attained at the very first examination a distinguished standing; in Jul, 1834, was graduated & commissioned as a brevet 2nd Lt in the 2nd Regt of Artl. His first military service was performed in Fla. Upon the anticipated breaking out of war ith Mexico, Lt Duncan's battery was ordered to Corpus Christi. Col Duncan landed in Mexico a Lt, he left its shores a Colonel by Brevet; in less than 10 months afterwards rose to the rank of a Colonel & Inspector Genr'l of the Army.]

Thos Woodward, for many years the worthy & efficient Deputy Marshal of this District, was appointed to be Naval Storekeeper at the Wash Navy Yard.

John Y Mason, late Sec of the Navy, has lost, in less than one month, both his excellent parents. They lived & died in Greensville Co, Va, on the same farm & at the same house where they had settled in 1792, soon after their marriage. Mr Edmunds Mason died on May 27 last, in his 80th year; & his wife on Jun 22, in her 76th year. They had been married 57 years. -Union

G T M Davis: the papers throughout the country are erroneously announcing the death of this gentleman. He is Editor of the St Louis New Era, & was alive & well on Tue last. Saml H Davis, formerly Editor of the Peoria [Ill] Register, died recently of cholera, which probably led to the error above noted. -Tribune

A daughter of Capt Benj F Howland died at New Bedford on Mon when someone threw a lighted firecracker among shavings, setting fire to the pile. The child was nearby & so severely burnt as to cause her death in a few hours.

Madame Cavaignac, the mother of the General, Gen Donadieu, who filled a prominent part in politics under Louis XVIII, & Gen Pont le Roy, died in Paris, of cholera.

Criminal Court-Wash. 1-Wm Donovan, guilty of keeping a disorderly house on Md ave: fined $20 & costs. 2-Francis Goodrich convicted of assault & battery in 2 cases. 3-Robt Moore, indicted for stealing $132, said notes the property of Arthur Cooper, found not guilty. 4-John Donovan, indicted for mayhen, in assaulting & beating Wm Craig, as to cause the loss of Craig's left eye, was found guilty of assault.

Mrd: on Jul 5, by Rev L F Morgan, Simpson P Moses, of Cincinnati, to Lizzie C, daughter of Enoch Tucker, of Wash City.

Died: on Jul 6, Margaret Adlum, youngest daughter of Cornelius & Margaret Barber, in her 4th year.

Died: on Jul 8, John Mackay, infant son of Capt M M Clark, U S Army, aged 2 months.

Furniture for sale at his warerooms on 7th st. –N M McGregor

Household & kitchen furniture at auction on Jul 13, by order of the trustee, at the Boarding house of Mrs Comdor Thompson, on Pa ave, between 4½ & 6th sts. –Martin & Wright, auctioneers

The undersigned, having occasion to proceed to Ky, Ohio, & the n w parts of Va, on legal business requiring an absence of some weeks, will have it in his power to attend personally to any business with which he may be entrusted.
–Chas De Selding, #11 Todd's Bldgs, Pa ave

TUE JUL 10, 1849

Past Events:
The first white child born in North America was Virginia, daughter of Annania & Eleanor Dare, & grand-daughter of Govn'r White. She was born on Aug 18, 1597, in Roanoke, N C. Her parents were of the expedition sent out by Sir Walter Raleigh in that year. There is no record of her history save that of her birth.
The first Minister who preached the Gospel in North America was Robt Hunt, of the Church of England, who came out in the same company with Capt John Smith, in 1607. There is no record of his death, or of his return to England; he died at Jamestown. His library & all his property was lost in the burning of Jamestown, the next winter after he came out.
The first females who came to Va proper were Mrs Forrest & her maid Anne Burns, in the expedition of Newport, 1608. The first marriage in Va was in the same year-John Laydon to Anne Burns.
The first intermarriage between the whites & Indians was John Rolfe to Pocahontas, in Apr, 1613. Pocahontas was also the first of the Virginia Indians that embaced christianity & was baptized.
The first Legislative Assembly in Va met in Jul, 1619, at the summons of Govn'r Geo Yeardley. One month after negroes were first brought into the colony by a Dutch man-of-war.
The first periodical in North America was the Boston News Letter, which made its appearance in Aug, 1705. The first in the Old Dominion was the Va Gaz, published at Wmsburg by Wm Parks, weekly, at 7 shillings. It appeared in 1736, & was long the only paper published in the colony.
The Blue Ridge was first crossed by whites in 1714.
The first iron furnace erected in North America was by Govn'r Spottswood, in 1730, in Spottsylvania, Va.

Pres Taylor made a visit to the village of *Laurel*, in PG Co, Md, on Fri, & returned on Sat. He was the guest of the hospitable Col Capron. Laurel is perhaps the most thriving & beautiful village in Md, & is about an hour's ride by railroad from Washington to Balt.

Among the deaths recently announced in the English papers is that of Sir Chas Richd Vaughan, who was formerly for several years Minister from Great Britain to the U S.

Hon Thos W Chinn, of La, lately appointed Charge d'Affaires of the Two Sicilies, is to leave today on the way to his place of embarkation. Mr Alex'r Barrow, his Private Sec, [son of the former & late lamented Senator from La of that name,] will accompany him in his mission.

Died: on Jun 23, at Meadville, Pa, Evalina, wife of Rev John V Reynolds, in her 29th year. Bodily sufferings, during her last illness, she viewed as a mark of Divine favor. Her last words were, "This is death!" & with a smile expired.

Died: on Jul 6, at Portsmouth, N H, of consumption, Eleanor Sophia, daughter of the late Saml Larkin.

Official: Gen Orders, #38. War Dept, Adj Gen Ofc, Wash, Jul 5, 1849. Promotions & Appointments in the U S Army made by the Pres since the publiction of Gen Orders #14, of Mar 15, 1849.
I-Promotions. Medical Dept:
Assist Surgeon Leonard C McPhail, to be Surgeon, Aug 8, 1848, vice Baily, who declines promotion.
Assist Surgeon Saml P Moore, to be Surgeon, Apr 30, 1849, vice McPhail, resigned.
2nd Regt of Dragoons:
1st Lt Wm H Saunders, to Capt, Apr 25, 1849, vice Hunter, deceased.
Brevet 2nd Lt Chas H Tyler, to 2nd Lt, Apr 25, 1849, vice [blank,] appointed adjutant.
2nd Regt of Artl:
2nd Lt Anson J Cook, to 1st Lt, Apr 15, 1849, vice Chase, deceased.
Brevet 2nd Lt Thos S Rhett, of the 4th Artl, to 2nd Lt, Apr 15, 1849, vice Cook, promoted.
4th Regt of Artl:
1st Lt John P J O'Brien, to Capt, May 16, 1849, vice Deas, deceased.
2nd Lt Albert L Magilton, to 1st Lt, Feb 28, 1849, vice Hill, resigned.
2nd Lt Gustavus a De Russey, to 1st Lt, May 16, 1849, vice O'Brien, promoted.
[2 splgs of Russey/Russy]
2nd Lt J S Garland, to 1st Lt, May 20, 1849, vice Bradford, resigned.
Brevet 2nd Lt Wm G Gill, of the 3rd Artl, to 2nd Lt, Feb 28, 1849, vice Magilton, promoted.
Bevet 2nd Lt Jas Holmes, of the 2nd Artl, to 2nd Lt, Apr 24, 1849, vice Symmes, transferred to Ordnance.
Brevet 2nd Lt Truman K Walbridge, to 2nd Lt, May 16, 1849, vice De Russy, promoted.
[2 splgs of Russy/Russey]
Brevet 2nd Lt Grier Tallmadge, of the 1st Artl, to 2nd Lt, May 20, 1849, vice Garland, promoted.
Brevet 2nd Lt John C Booth, of the 2nd Artl, to 2nd Lt, May 31, 1849, vice Gouverneur, resigned.
1st Regt of Infty:
Brevet 2nd Lt A G Miller, of the 6th Infty, to 2nd Lt, Apr 11, 1849, vice Hall, deceased.
Brevet 2nd Lt Thos D Johns, to 2nd Lt, Jun 30, 1849, vice Bradford, resigned.
2nd Regt of Infty:
1st Lt Geo C Westcott, to Capt, May 7, 1849, vice Kingsbury, promoted.
2nd Lt David R Jones, to 1st Lt, May 7, 1849, vice Westcott, promoted.
Brevet 2nd Lt Geo H Paige, of the 6th Infty, to 2nd Lt, Mar 10, 1849, vice Johnston, deceased.
Brevet 2nd Lt Nathl H McLean, of the 7th Infty, to 2nd Lt, Mar 29, 1849, vice McGill, resigned.
Brevet 2nd Lt Ferdinand Paine, of the 4th Infty, to 2nd Lt, May 7, 1849, vice Jones, promoted.
4th Regt of Infty:
Maj Benj L E Bonneville, of the 6th Infty, to Lt Col, May 7, 1849, vice Garland, promoted.
5th Regt of Infty:
1st Lt Spencer Norvell, to Capt, Apr 30, 1849, vice McPhail, resigned.
2nd Lt Clinton W Lear, to 1st Lt, Apr 30, 1849, vice Norvell, promoted.

Brevet 2nd Lt Wm N R Beall, of the 4th Infty, to 2nd Lt, Apr 30, 1849, vice Lear, promoted.
6th Regt of Infty:
Capt Julius J B Kingsbury, of the 2nd Infty, to Major, May 7, 1849, vice Bonneville, promoted.
8th Regt of Infty:
Lt Col John Garland, of the 4th Infty, to be Colonel, May 7, 1849, vice Worth, deceased.
II-Appointments: Medical Dept.
Assist Surgeons, in the order of precedence to rank from Jun 29, 1849.
Report in person at Jefferson Barracks:
Wm H Ballard, of Louisiana   Geo K Wood, of N Y
Report in person at *Fort Mackinac*: Jos P Brown, of Mich
Report in person at *Fort Leavenworth*: Alex'r B Hasson, of Md
Report in person at *Fort Monroe*: Jonathan Letherman, of Pa
Report in person at Carlisle Barracks, for duty with troops under orders to Santa Fe: Wm A Hammond, of Pa
Report in person at *Fort Johnston*, N C: Francis Sorrel, of Georgia
Report in person at *Fort Columbus*: Edw W Johns, of Md
Report in person at *Fort McHenry*: Wm W Anderson, of S C
Pay Dept:
Albert J Smith, of Va, to be Paymaster, Jun 1, 1849, vice Smith, resigned.
III-The following named Cadets, graduates of the Military Academy, attached to the Army with the Brevet of 2nd Lt, to take rank from Jul 1, 1849.
Brevet 2nd Lt attached to the Corps of Engineers.
Rank
1-Cadet Quincey A Gillmore
Brevet 2nd Lt attached to the Corps of Topographical Engineers:
2-Cadet John G Parke
Brevet 2nd Lt attached to the Ordnance:
3-Cadet Stephen V Benet
Brevet 2nd Lts attached to the Dragoon Arm
20-Cadet Horace F De Lano [Co C, 1 Drgs]
25-Cadet Beverly H Robertson [Co E, 2 Drgs]
27-Cadet Chas W Field [Co D, 2 Drgs]
Brevet 2nd Lts attached to the Regt of Mounted Riflemen.
21-Cadet Danl McClure [Co E]
24-Cadet Washington C Tevis [Co G]
Brevet 2nd Lts attached to the Artl Arm:
4-Cadet Thos J Haines [Co K, 1 Art]
6-Cadet Wm Silvey [Co C, 3 Art]
7-Cadet Beckman Du Barry [Co I, 1 Art]
8-Cadet Delavan D Perkins [Co A, 2 Art]
9-Cadet Absalom Baird [Co M, 2 Art]
10-Cadet Wm A Nimmo [Co B, 4 Art]
13-Cadet Edw R Platt [Co H, 3 Art]
14-Cadet Chauncey McKeever [Co B, 1 Art]
16-Cadet John Kellogg [Co G, 4 Art]

17-Cadet John C Moore [Co H, 4 Art]
18-Rufus Saxton, jr [Co E. 3 Art]
22-Cadet Edw M Hudson [Co I, 3 Art]
Brevet 2nd Lts attached to the Infty Arm.
11-Cadet Milton Cogswell [Co D, 4 Inf]
15-Cadet Wm H Lewis [Co G, 4 Inf]
19-Cadet Thos Wright [Co A, 7 Inf]
23-Cadet John Withers [Co G, 5 Inf]
26-Cadet Jos S Tidball [Co I, 4 Inf]
28-Cadet Seth M Barton [Co G, 3 Inf]
29-Cadet Duff C Green [Co B, 5 Inf]
30-Cadet Richd W Johnson [Co C, 6 Inf]
31-Cadet Saml B Holabid [Co D, 1 Inf]
32-Cadet Thos G Williams [Co B, 2 Inf]
33-Cadet Thornton A Washington [Co F, 6 Inf]
36-Cadet Thos C English [Co K, 5 Inf]
37-Cadet Jos H McArthur [Co G, 2 Inf]
38-Cadet Jas P Roy [Co B, 8 Inf]
39-Cadet Chas B Alvord [Co D, 8 Inf]
40-Cadet Darius D Clark [Co C, 2 Inf]
41-Cadet Louis H Marshall [Co D, 3 Inf]
42-Cadet Saml H Reynolds [Co A, 1 Inf]
43-Cadet Jas McIntosh [Co F, 1 Inf]
The following named Cadets will take rank as Brevet 2nd Lts, from Jul 2, 1849.
5-Cadet Johnson K Duncan [Co F, 2 Art]
12-Cadet Edw D Stockton [Co F, 2 Art]
34-Cadet John W Frazer [Co K, 2 Inf]
35-Cadet Alfred Cumming [Co G, 8 Inf]
IV-Casualties.
Resignations:
Brevet Maj Danl H McPhail, Capt 5th Infty, Apr 30, 1849
Brevet Maj Danl H Hill, 1st Lt 4th Artl, Feb 28, 1849
Brevet Maj Albert Lowry, 1st Lt 2nd Dragoons, as Assist Quartermaster [only] Mar 31, 1849
1st Lt Edmund Bradford, 4th Artl, May 20, 1849
Brevet 1st Lt Saml L Gouverneur, 2nd Lt 4th Artl, May 31, 1849
2nd Lt Jas Magill, 2nd Infty, Mar 29, 1849
2nd Lt Edmund G Bradford, 1st Infty, Jun 30, 1849
Brevet 2nd Lt Saml Ross, 3rd Infty, May 30, 1849
Surgeon Leonard C McPhail, Apr 30, 1849
Assist Surgeon Jos Walker, Apr 2, 1849
Paymaster Chas H Smith, May 31, 1849
Declined:
Assist Surgeon Jos H Bailey [promotion of Surgeon]
Deaths:
Brevet Maj Gen Edmund P Gaines, at New Orleans, La, Jun 6, 1849
Brevet Maj Gen Wm J Worth, Col 8th Infty, at San Antonio, Texas, May 7, 1849
Capt Nathl W Hunter, 2nd Dragoons, at Charleston, S C, Apr 25, 1849

Capt Edw Dead, 4th Artl, near Camp Ringgold, Texas, May 16, 1849
Capt Leslie Chase, Assist Quartermaster & 1st Lt 2nd Artl, at *Fort Johnson*, N C, Apr 15, 1849
2nd Lt Cyrus Hall, 1st Infty, near Victoria, Texas, Apr 11, 1849
2nd Lt Thos M Whedbee, Ordnance, at Edenton, N C, Mar 28, 1849
2nd Lt Wm W Johnston, 2nd Infty, at Gtwn, Ohio, May 10, 1849.
Transfers:
2nd Lt John C Symes, of the 4th Artl, to the Ordnance, to take place on the Army Register next below 2nd Lt McAllister
2nd Lt John De Russy, of the 2nd Infty, to the 2nd Artl, to take place on the Army Register next below 2nd Lt Adams
2nd Lt Caleb Smith, of the 2nd Artl, to the 2nd Infty, to take place on the Army Register next below 2nd Lt Sweeney.
List of Paymasters in the order of precedence in the Pay Dept of the Army.
Name & date of 1st appointment of continuous service/date of commission in the regular service.
Rank:
1-T J Leslie: Nov 27, 1815/Nov 27, 1815
2-D S Townsend: Apr 29, 1816/Apr 29, 1816
3-T P Andres: May 22, 1822/May 22, 1822
4-E Kirby: Aug 5, 1824/Aug 5, 1824
5-A D Steuart: Jan 14, 1833/Jan 14, 1833
6-C Andres: Oct 24, 1836/Oct 24, 1836
7-B Walker: Dec 17, 1839/Dec 17, 1839
8-E Van Ness: Dec 18, 1839/Dec 18, 1839
9-St Clair Denny: Oct 15, 1841/Oct 15, 1841
10-D Hunter: Mar 14, 1842/Mar 14, 1842
11-L J Beall: Sep 13, 1844/Sep 13, 1844
12-A J Coffee*: Jun 24, 1846/Feb 23, 1847
13-A Van Buren: Jun 26, 1846/Jun 26, 1846
14-J Y Dashiell*: Jul 2, 1846/Mar 2, 1849
15-S Maclin/Maelin*: Jul 2, 1846/Mar 2, 1849
16-A W Gaines*: Jul 20, 1846/Mar 2, 1849
17-G H Ringgold*: Aug 4, 1846/Jul 21, 1847
18-R A Forsyth: Aug 8, 1846/Aug 8, 1846
19-A G Bennett*: Aug 14, 1846/Mar 2, 1849
20-A Leonard*: Nov 24, 1846/Mar 2, 1849
21-R B Reynolds: Mar 3, 1847/Mar 3, 1847
22-H Hall: Nov 6, 1847/Nov 6, 1847
23-F A Cunningham*: Dec 30, 1847/Mar 2, 1849
24-G C Hutter*: May 10, 1848/Mar 2, 1849
25-A J Smith: Jun 1, 1849/Jun 1, 1849
*Volunteer service
By order of the Sec of War. -R Jones, Adj Gen

WED JUL 11, 1849
Criminal Court-Wash-Monday: 1-Wm Butler, Jas Chisley, & Wm Holland, free negroes, indicted for Sabbath breaking & playing cards in the wood at Kalorama, [Col Bomford's former residence,] each found guilty: 1 week in jail & fined $1 & costs. 2-Jas Stenant, Jas Stenant, jr, & Levin Morris, free negroes, guilty of riot: fined $1 each, 5 days in jail, & pay costs. 3-John C Peitch, guilty of keeping a disorderly house: fined $30 & costs. 4-Yesterday: Robt Williams, John Hubbard, Saml Brown, & Robt Burns, found guilty of riot: each sentenced to 10 days imprisonment in the common jail, & fined $1 each & costs. 5-Jos West, alias Snider, found guilty of perjury in falsely swearing to obtain extra-pay due to a deceased soldier: sentenced to 4 years in the penitentiary

Wash Corp: 1-Ptn of C Cammack, praying for remission of a fine: referred to the Cmte of Claims. 2-Nominations by the Mayor: John Davis, Superintendent of sweeps for the 7th Ward. H R Maryman, as police ofcr of the 4th Ward, in place of Jas M Wright, who declines re-appointment. Hanson Brown, as Superintendent for the 2nd district of the 5th Ward. Read & ordered to lie on the table. 3-Ptn of Augustus Lepreux & others, praying for the filling up of a pond in the 2nd Ward: referred to the Com'r of the 2nd Ward. 4-Act for the relief of Wm Rupp: referred to the Cmte of Claims. 5-Act for the relief of Mary Ann Baltzer: passed. 6-Ptn of Jos A Deeble & others, praying for the widening of the gutter on I st, between 9th & 10th sts: referred to the Cmte on Improvements. 7-Ptn of Wm Fensley, praying remission of a fine: referred to the Cmte of Claims. 8-Ptn from Geo H Plant & others, in relation to their proposals for finishing the exterior of the City Hall: referred to a select cmte.

The Hagerstown Torchlight announces, by authority, that the Hon J Dixon Roman, Rep in Congress from that district in Md, declines a re-election, on account of the impaired state of his health.

At Phil, Sat last, Judge Parsons sentenced Chas McVey, Hugh Greeves, & Wm Love, convicted of participating in the Moyamensing riots, to 9 months in the Eastern Penitentiary. Emanuel Snyder, convicted of a similar offence, sentenced to 1 year & 3 months in the Penitentiary.

Brevet Col Munroe, of the Artl, & Brevet Col Chas A May, left N Y last Wed, with dragoon recruits sufficient for 2 companies, en route for Santa Fe, where Col Munroe is ordered to assume command of that district of country.

St Louis Republican, of Jun 26: list of the killed & scalded by the recent explosion of the steamer **Embassy**, near Shawneetown, Ill. John Watts, wife, & 3 children, of Bainbrook, N J, all killed; John Myers, dead; Augustus Miller & wife, dead; Mrs Jacob Isley & 5 children, killed; wife of Rudolph Bekenhault; wife of Chas Rope; wife of Christian Sipher; a child of Mr Morton; Mgt Hilts; Jeremiah Miller, 1st cook; John Myers, stoker & 2 firemen, all lost. Jeremiah Miller jumped overboard, & was drowned. The largest portion injured were German emigrants, whose names could not be correctly ascertained.

Information wanted of John Roach, son of Jas & Honora Roach, who left Ireland on or about Sep 6, 1848. He took shipping at Liverpool for N Y. About 21 years of age, 5 ft 7 ins high, with brown hair. He is from Youghall, county of Cork. Will be thankful for information respecting him, by his mother & brothers, Philip & Jas Roach, Wash, D C. Address Jas Keleher, Missouri Ave, near 6th st, Wash.

Portland, Maine trial. Mrs Caroline M Swett was found guilty for a misdemeanor, when after finding her husband having a drink at Cole's shop, after imploring Cole not to let her husband have a drink, she broke windows, bottles, & glasses of the one Cole, keeper of the drinking shop. The jury added a written request that a lenient sentence might be pronounced. -N Y Com Adv

John Wilder, of Warsaw, N Y, was instantly killed on Jul 5, at Pike, Wyoming Co, by his horses running away. He was an estimable & influential citizen of Wyoming Co, & was twice elected to the ofc of Sheriff before the division of Genesee Co.
--Rochester Democrat

Dr Robt L Shaw, of Ridgebury, Orange Co, N Y, came to his death on Jul 3 by the accidental discharge of a gun in the hands of another gentleman. He was in a party on a shooting excursion, when one of the guns accidentally discharged, the contents taking effect on the left side of Dr Shaw's neck, severing the jugular vein. He survived about 24 hours.

THU JUL 12, 1849
Tatum's great paintings, The Passion, Crucifixion, & Resurrection of Jesus Christ, now at Union Chapel, 1st Ward, & will be removed to Ryland Chapel on Jul 11, for exhibition for 2 nights: admittance .25, children half price. -C J Kathrens

The copartnership existing between the subscribers having been dissolved by limitation, the business will be conducted, as formerly, by S J Ober, to whom persons indebted will please make payment. –S J Ober, R J Ryon

Tribute to the memory of Wm Wallace Gordon, late of Va, & a soldier in the war with Mexico, who died on Jul 14, 1848, at Pinol, a rancho of Gov Trias, 60 miles north of the city of Chichuahua, Mexico. For 6 long weeks he wasted beneath the slow bu fatal disease, fully apprized of its deadly aim. Tho' lost to earth he is saved in heaven.
--Gloucester Co, Va, Mar, 1849

The U S sloop of war **John Adams** sailed from Boston on Sat for Brazil. List of her ofcrs: Cmder, Levin M Powell; Lts, Guert Gansevoort, Robt B Pegram, Jas H Strong, Wm C B S Porter, & Jas C Williamson, [passenger;] Lt of Marines, J C Rich; Surgeon, Jos Beale; Purser, Edw C Doran; Acting Master, Wm W Pollock; Assist Surgeon, Jas Suddards; Passed Midshipmen, Jas Higgins, T B Wainwright; Midshipmen, Jas F Milligan, Chas H Cushman, Jas D Legare, Bushrod B Taylor, Jas W Sherk; Capt's Clerk, Cuthbert Powell; Boatswain, Saml Drew; Gunner, Geo Sirian; Carpenter, Geo Wisner; Sailmaker, David Bruce. -Traveller

Household & kitchen furniture at auction on Jul 16, at the residence of Mrs Matlock, on 4½ st, near Pa ave. –Green & Tastet

North British Review. John Pounds, the founder of Ragged Schools, was the son of a workman employed in the Royal Dockyards at Portsmouth, & was born in that town in 1766. At age 15 he met with an accident, which crippled him for life. He was a cobbler by trade, in a small workshop, in St Mary st, Portsmouth. In addition to mental instruction to the children who gathered around him, he gave them industrial training, & taught them to cook & to mend their own shoes. H died on Jan 1, 1839, aged 72.

Orange lands for sale, without reserve: on Sep 5, *Four Farms*, in said county: *The Meadows* contain 1,005 acres: dwlg house has 6 rooms. *The Winder Tract* contains 600 acres: small tenement upon it. *The Birchland Tract* contains 600 acres. The *Independent Tract* contains 468 acres. Information will be given by my brother, Jeremiah Morton, living near the premises, who is fully authorized to dispose of the property. His address is *Racoon Ford*, Culpeper Co, Va. –Jackson

$5 reward for lost cow for her delivery to Thos Young, 4½ st & Pa ave.

Land for sale: a beautiful little farm of about 68 acres, adjoining my land, on the Wash & Rockville Turnpike, 4 miles from the city. There is a good house, not quite finished inside, but it may be made comfortable at small expense. –Thos Carbery

Mrd: on Jul 9, in Wash City, by Rev G W Samson, Maj Jas Arnold, of King Geo Co, Va, to Mrs Sarah E Adams, of Chas Co, Md.

Died: on Jul 11, in Wash City, Mrs Mgt Follansbee, consort of Jos Follansbee, in her 53rd year. Her funeral is from her late residence this afternoon, at 4 o'clock.

Died: on Jun 14, in Sugar Grove, Boon Co, Ky, of cholera, Mrs Zebuline A P Hunt, wife of John Hunt, & eldest daughter of J C Symmes Harrison, deceased. The deceased was granddaughter of Generals Pike & Harrison.

Died: on Jul 11, Cecelia, infant daughter of Alex'r & Mary Rutherford, aged 2 months & 21 days. Her funeral is this morning at half past 10 o'clock, from the residence of her parents on 13th st, between C & D sts.

Died: on Jul 9, at North View, near Gtwn, Luke White, infant, aged 5 weeks; on Jul 10, Mary Virginia, in her 5th year: children of Cornelius & Mgt Barber.

FRI JUL 13, 1849
The Courrier des Etats Unis announcs that the ex-King of Sardinia died in Portugal on Jun 9.

Ex-Pres Van Buren is at present engaged in superintending the enlargement of his residence at Lindenwald. The additions are to be spacious & elegant.

Savannah Republican: on Mar 29 Mrs Lourania Thrower, died, at her residence on the Agechee, & she was at least 133 years of age. At a census taken in 1825 her age was put down 110, & some accounts made her 137 at the time of her death. She had 7 children before the Revolution; her youngest living child is between 70 & 80 years; she has great-grandchildren 30 years old, & a number of great-great-great-grand-children living in Florida. Her sight failed her for awhile, but returned about 20 years ago. Her faculties remained almost unimpaired till the time of her death. She had been a member of the Baptist church for more than 100 years.

Official: Appointments by the Pres:
Collectors of the Customs:
John L Rogers, Gloucester, Mass, vice Eli F Stacy, removed.
Gideon S Sackett, Cape Vincent, N Y, vice Peleg Burchard, removed.
Surveyors of the Customs:
Lonson Nash, Gloucester, Mass, vice John Woodbury, removed.
John A Chew, Havre de Grace, Md, vice Robt Gale, removed.
Marshals:
Wm M Brown, of Ga, for the district of Ga, vice Henry Williams, who declines the ofc.
Walter C Maloney, of Fla, for the Southern district of Fla, vice Jos B Browne, removed.
Attys:
Hiram W Husted, of N C, for the district of N C, vice Wm H Haigh, who declines the ofc.
Geo W Call, jr, of Fla, for the Northern district of Fla, vice Chandler C Younge, removed.
Land Ofcrs: Receiver of Public Moneys:
John Dinkgrave, of La, at Monroe, La, vice John B Filhiol, removed.
Registers of the Land Ofc:
Danl Clapp, of Ill, at Danville, Ill, vice Wm E Russell, removed.
Lewis S Lovell, of Mich, at Ionia, Mich, vice Benj Sherman, removed.
Thos B Thorp, of La, at New Orleans, La, vice Louis Ste Martin, removed.

In 1799 cut nails for the first time came into general use. Ten years previous the machines for cutting nails from iron hoops were invented by 2 brothers named Pierson, in N Y. They were a very coarse article at first. –From Laurie Todd's Note-Book.

Criminal Court-Wash: 1-W T Bayly, not guilty of assault on Miss Z Dodds. 2-John Ready, not guilty of keeping a disorderly house. 3-John Roberts, for the same offence, not guilty. 4-Biddly Donovan, for an assault & battery on Wm Craig: guilty: fined her $10. 5-John Herbert, alias Hubbard, free negro, tried for assaulting Uriah B Mitchell, constable: guilty: 4 weeks in prison, $1 fine & costs. 6-John Donovan found guilty of an assault on Wm Craig, who lost an eye in the affray: fine $50 & costs.

Died: on Jul 10, after a lingering illness, Henry Wright, in his 61st year.

Died: on Mar 26 last, in New Orleans, of Asiatic cholera, Roswell Wright, aged 29 years.

Wanted to hire: a small colored boy, 10 to 14 years of age, to do the errands at his shop. He must be such a boy as will "go" when he is told to go, & "come" when he is told to come. —P J Steer

SAT JUL 14, 1849
It is with saddened hearts that we announce the decease of Mrs D P Madison, widow of Jas Madison, Ex-Pres of the U S. She died a her residence in Wash City on Jul 12, aged about 82 years. She continued until within a few weeks to grace society with her presence.

The U S storeship **Erie**, Cmder M McBlair, from the Mediaterranean, via Fayal, Jun 10, arrived at N Y on Wed. Mrs Cmdor Bolton & Miss Croxall came passengers.

Trustee's public sale: by decree of the Circuit Court of Wash Co, D C, passed on Dec 1, 1848, in a cause wherein Edmund Hanley's excx are cmplnts & Susan D Shepherd, Alex R Shepherd, & others, heirs-at-law, & widow & admx of Alex Shepherd, deceased, are dfndnts: sale on Aug 6 of the following very valuable real estate, to wit: part of lot 2 in square 286, on N Y ave; lot 7 in Reservation A; lot 3 in square 328; lots 1,2,& 18 in square 761, & part of lot 3 in square 761, on B st; part of lot 9 in square 480. There are several valuable dwlg houses & other improvements on all the lots except the last. -W Redin, trustee -Martin & Wright, auctioneers

Trustee's sale: by deed of trust from John Byrne dated Jul 30, 1847, recorded in Liber W B 136, folio 23, one of the land records of Wash Co, to satisfy the debts mentioned in such deed: sale on Aug 15 next of: part of lot 20 in square 254, on F st, in Wash City, with the frame tenement thereon, now occupied by said Byrne. —Geo Cover, trustee -Martin & Wright, aucts

Lynchburg Virginian: On Jun 14, Mrs Mary Barnett, consort of Mr Robt P Barnett, of Prairieville, Pike Co, Mo, & daughter of Mr Archer Brown, of Lynchburg, Va, set out, in company with her niece & nephew, to visit the daughter of a friend who was ill. After travelling about 2 miles they discovered a cloud rising, & stopped at the house of an acquaintance. A young man rode up & informed them that the young lady was not expected to live through the ensuing night. This determined Mrs Barnett to go on with him, leaving her niece & nephew to follow on after the storm. The rain later stopped, & the niece & nephew resumed their journey, & in about a mile they came upon the bodies of their aunt & the young man, Mr Geo Wells, formerly of Albemarle Co, Va, together with their horses, all having been killed by lightning. The screams of the young lady brought to the scene of death several neighbors who were in hearing, when every effort was made to resuscitate them, but in vain. Mrs Barnett has left to mourn their loss a father, 2 sisters, a little daughter of 12 years, & an affectionate husband, now on an expedition to Calif. The work of death did not stop there. Just after dark of the same evening the sick lady referred to, Miss Maria Louisa, daughter of Mr Jos Roberts, formerly of Nelson Co, Va, who but a week before was in the bloom of youth & health, bid adieu to all that was earthly.

Mrs Laura Sophia, wife of Isaac Lawrence, of Lowell, Mass, died suddenly on Sunday, in an apoplectic fit. She was the daughter of Alex'r T Willard, of Ashby, & was 38 years of age.

On Jul, Mr Wm Wallace, son of John Wallace, in the upper end of our county, stepped out of the hotel at the Natural Bridge, & for several days was missed. On Jul 5, inquiry was made for him by his father, & after a diligent search his boy was found lying on the cliff, above the Bridge, about half-way down. His skull was fractured. The deceased was of intemperate habits, & no doubt his death is owing to his indulgence of them. –Lexington [Va] Republican

Wm Blake, son of Mr Joel N Blake, machinist, residing on North Eutaw st, Balt, was drowned on Wed while bathing in Johns' Falls. His youthful companions made every effort to rescue him, but he sunk to rise no more.

Mrd: on Jul 12, in Wash City, at Brown's Hotel, by Rev Mr Morgan, Mr Jas A Hopkins to Miss Mary Ann Kent, all of Lynchburg, Va.

Died: on Thu last, in Richmond, after a long illness, in his 71st year, Chapman Johnson, an eminent member of the Va Bar. The Whig observes that within 3 years Richmond has witnessed the death of 3 lawyers, Stanard, Leigh, & Johnson.

Died: on Jul 13, Jos Hessett, a native of Truro, Cornwall, England, 40 years of age. His funeral is tomorrow at 5 o'clock, on 16th st, at the residence of Mr Tinklers.

Chancery sale of valuable real property: by decree of the Circuit Court of Wash Co, D C, made in the matter of Janet B Phillips & Ann Phillips, against Jas Lynch, the heirs of Enoch W Smallwood, & others: sale on Sep 3 of: lot 24 in square or Reservation B, with a large 3 story brick house, on Pa ave, at present occupied by Mrs Arguellis as a boarding-house. Lot 6 in square 728, with a good 2 story brick house on East Capitol st, at present occupied by Mrs Phillips. Lot 3 in square 687, with a good 2 story brick house, on A st north, opposite the east park of the Capitol, at present occupied by Jas D Waller. –Richd Wallach, trustee -Chas W Boteler, auctioneer

MON JUL 16, 1849
The funeral of Mrs Madison will take place this afternoon, at 4 o'clock, from St John's Church. Pall bearers:

Hon J M Clayton	Gen Henderson	Gen Totten
Mr Gales	Gen Walter Jones	Com Warrington
Gen Jesup	Hon W M Meredith	Mr Pleasonton
Com Morris	Mr Ritchie	Mr Fendall

[Jul 17th newspaper: Rev Mr Pyne, Rector of the Church, delivered an eloquent eulogy; Rev Mr French aided the Rector in the funeral solemnities. The funeral procession moved from the Church to the <u>Congress Cemetery</u>, where the corpse will remain until it is removed to its final resting place at Montpelier, Va.]

The death of Pierre Chouteau, one of the founders of St Louis, took place in that city on Mon. He was in his 91st year. He was said to have been the last survivor of the La Clede party.

Gen Charlton, of the British army, died recently at age 94 years, 77 of which he spent in the military service of his country.

Died: on Apr 15 last, at New Orleans, Mr Wm W Haliday, of Wash, but for some years past a resident of Natchez, Miss.

Died: on Jul 12, at Albany, of cholera, after an illness of 24 hours, Fanny, wife of Israel Smith, jr, & daughter of Cmder Chas H & Eliza Bell, U S Navy. To her devoted husband & immediate family the loss will be irreparable.

Died: yesterday, Gideon Smith Tucker, aged 10 months & 19 days, son of Jas & Harriet Tucker. His funeral is this afternoon at 4 o'clock from the residence of his parents on I st, between 4th & 5th sts.

African newspaper: vol 6, published at Cape town, Africa, Mar 22, 1849. Mrd: on Feb 25, 1849, at Haslope Hills, by Rev Wm Shepstone, Wesleyan Minister, Saml Ka Kama, eldest son of the Kaffir Chief Wm Karna, of the House of Kwani, of the Amagunukweby tribe, to Eliz, eldest daughter of Dushani, a Chief of the House of Kouta, of the Amaxosa tribe.

TUE JUL 17, 1849
Appointments by the Pres:
Saml R Rogers, of Tenn, to be U S Atty for the eastern District of Tenn, vice Thos C Lyon, resigned.
Land Ofcrs:
Jas M McLean, of Ill, to be Register of the Land Ofc at Palestine, Ill, vice Harman Alexander, removed.
Nathan Sargent, of Pa, to be Recorder of the Gen Land Ofc, vice S H McLaughlin, removed.
Collectors of the Customs:
Nathl G Marshall, York, Maine, vice Jos P Junkins, removed.
Jos Eaches, Alexandria, Va, vice Edw Green, removed.

Died: on Jul 13, in Balt, Frances Clark, eldest daughter of the late Francis & Eliza Clark, of Wash.

Died: on Jul 11, after a short illness, John Samuel, eldest son of Richd & Sarah A White, aged 2 years & 5 months.

Gtwn College, D C: Annual Commencement to take place on Jul 24.
-Jas Ryder, Pres

Shocco Springs, Warren Co, N C: Summer Retreat is again open for the reception & accommodation of visiters. –Saml Calvert

Clark Co land for sale: the subscriber, intending to remove to the West, offers for sale the farm on which he resides, 2¼ miles from Berryville: well known as **Llewellyn** tract, & contains 416 acres: with a large stone dwlg, & all necessary outbldgs. Apply to Franklin J Kerfoot.

Balt, Jul 16. Dr John D Buck, for some time past employed as clerk by the Smelting & Mining Co on the Fort road, was shot through the head last night, while sitting at the window. His body was found this morning. He was a highly esteemed gentleman. No clue has been had of the murderer.

From English Papers: O'Keefe, the owner of the pistol with which Hamilton fired at the Queen, has been offered 40 pounds for it! It was returned to him by the court after Hamilton's trial

Dentistry: O A Dailey has opened an ofc on Pa ave, over Mr S Parker's Fancy Store: warranted to give entire satisfaction.

WED JUL 18, 1849
Valuable property for sale: by decree of Circuit Court of D C, sitting in Chancery, in a cause in which Fred'k L Keller is cmplnt, & Henreitta Keller & Chas Keller are cmplnts. Sale of property in Wash City, the the late Fred'k Keller died seized, to wit: lot 17 in square 327, with a commodious 2 story brick house & outbldgs.
–A H Lawrence, trustee -E C & G F Dyer, aucts

N Y, Jul 16, 1849. The Hon David B Ogden, long known as an eminent counsellor at law, as well as this bar as at that of the Supreme Court, died of cholera this morning. He had reached, I believe, the age of 3 score & ten.

It deserves mention as an extraordinary circumstance that, at the funeral of Mrs Madison, on Mon, were present two of her old friends who were both present at her first marriage with Mr Todd, 60 years ago, & the latter of whom was also present at her second marriage with Mr Madison. We allude to the venerale Mrs Eliz Lee, widow of Richd Bland Lee, of Va, & Anthony Morris, of Pa.

Balt: Thos Davis, a workman belonging to the copper works, was arrested Jul 17, charged with the murder of J D Buck.

Official: Dept of State, Wash, Jul 17, 1849. Information received from John B Williams, U S Commercial Agent for the Feejee Islands, of the death of Geo Barrows, of Norwich, Conn, & of Capt Thos Ellis, of Fairhaven, Mass. The latter, late of the ship **Kingston** was wrecked in schnr **Coll Castle**, of Sydney, & drowned.

Mr Higby, foreman at T F Secor & Co's foundry, N Y, was instantly killed on Sat by the giving way of a derrick by which the men were raising the bed plate for the engine of the new steamer Georgia. Beverly Parkin's thigh was broken, & Francis Miller had his skull fractured.

Richmond, Va, on Sun, Thos W Lottier, an overseer in Mr Goode's tobacco factory, suspecting the infidelity of his wife, encountered the alleged paramour, Wm Cook, & shot him, the contents of which wounded Cook severely in the abdomen. He is not expected to survive.

Died: on Jul 5, in Nashville, of cholera, Thos Chaney, aged 54 years, for many years a resident of Washington.

THU JUL 19, 1849

Fatal railroad accident on Sat, when the train ran off the track about 4½ miles east of Auburn. The tender was passed directly over the engine, crushing to death Wm Delano, the engineer, & ___ Hooper, the fireman.

Hon A W Cochran, a distinguished scholar, died at Quebec on Jul 11.

Official: Zachary Taylor, Pres of the U S of America, recognises Guillermo Robinet, who has been appointed Vice Consul of the Republic of Peru, for the port of San Francisco, Calif.

Annual Commencement of the Columbian College was held yesterday in the E st Presbyterian Church. We noticed the Pres of the U S, Col Bliss, the Postmaster Gen, the Mayor, & other distinguished citizens. Prayer by Rev Dr Bacon, the Pres of the College. Oration by John B Canada, Halifax Co, Va-excused on account of illness. Orations by A Given Carothers, Wash, D C; F H Collier, Gtwn, D C; C W Collier, Gtwn, D C; Thos Jones, Balt, Md; A J Quinche, Galena, Ill; B Stark, King Wm Co, Va; & Wm M Young, Edinburgh, Scotland. First degree in Arts & Sciences conferred on:

John J Berryman, Va   Thos Jones, Md
A J Boulware, Va   J G Nash, Miss
John B Canada, Va   C A Price, S C
A G Carothers, D C   A J Quinche, Ill
F H Collier, D C   R R Richardson, Ga
C W Collier, D C   B Stark, Va
B Z Gaulden, Ga   W M Young, Scotland
R H Griffith, Va

The following received the second degree:
Francis M Barker, Va   Jos Hammitt, Pa
W I Brookes, Ga   Geo P Nice, Pa
Robt Burton, Va   Horace Stringfellow, jr, Va

Honorary degree of A M was conferred on Rev Elijah Hutchinson, of Vt, & Rev S G Mason, of Va; also, the honorary degree of D D on Rev J B Jeter.

Mrd: on Jul 2, at *Cottage Farm*, the residence of Mr Jas Peerce, Shelby Co, Ky, Mr Abraham Alexander, of said county, to Miss Rachel P Dawes, of Montg Co, Md.

Died: on Jul 12, at St Louis, Mo, of bilious diarrhoea, Mrs Ann Louisa Lowry, in her 20th year, wife of Mr John Lowry, & youngest daughter of Edw & Mgt Deeble, all of Wash City.

Died: on Jul 13, at her residence in Piscataway, after a short but painful illness, Mrs Rebecca M Edelin, consort of Dr Philip R Edelin, & daughter of the late Dr Wm H Clagett, in her 18th year.

FRI JUL 20, 1849
Appointments by the Pres:
Collectors of the Customs:
Edw W Lawton, Newport, R I, vice Edwin Wilbur, removed.
Henry Addison, Gtwn, D C, vice Robt White, removed.
Surveyors of the Customs:
John M Spencer, East Greenwich, R I, vice Silas Weaver, removed.
Wm H S Bayley, Bristol, R I, vice Nathan Bardin, removed.
Chas Randall, Warren & Barrington, R I, vice Benj M Bosworth, removed.
Benj T Fendall, Alexandria, Va, vice Jas McGuire, removed.
Naval Ofcr: Wm Brown, Salem, Mass, vice John D Howard, removed.
Appraiser: Cornelius Savage, N Y, vice Saml J Willis, removed.
Appointment by the Sec of the Treasury;
Wm W Thomas, Assist Appraiser, N Y, vice John W Manley, removed.

The suit brought by the heirs at law of Edw B Phillips, contesting the validity of his will, by which, among other legacies, $100,000 was left to Harvard Univ, to be applied to the support of the observatory attached to that institution, has been decided. The will, according to the telegraph, has been sustained in every particular. Mr Phillips, in 1837, became a resident of Lynn, living at Nahant, & in Jun, 1848, committed suicide at the Brattleboro Water Cure establishment. The will bequeathed in usual form $100,000 to Chas Emory & Chas G Loring, in trust, the interest of the same to be paid in quarterly instalments to Chas Beck & wife during their lives, & after their decease to Abby S Beck & Theresa Phillips, his sisters; $100,000 to Harvard Univ-as detailed above; $60,000 to Chas Emery & John H Gray, or the survivor; the remainder of his property & all his personal effects to his cousin, Wm Phillips [The Will was contested on the following grounds: will was made on the Lord's day, Oct 10, 1847; E B Phillips was not of sound mind; he was unduly influenced in the making & signing of the will; will is not attested by 3 competent witnesses, nor any competent witnesses; persons whose names are attested are interested in the probate of the same; Court of Probate of Essex has not proper jurisdiction; said will is not attested by the testator in the presence of 3 or more competent witnesses.]

On Sat evening, Lewis Eddy, while bathing at the foot of Desbrosses st, N Y, in leaping from the top of the bath, struck his head against the plank at the bottom & was instantly killed. He was a wood engraver, & leaves a widow & 5 children.

Died: on Jul 16, at her residence, *Tulip Hill*, West River, Md, Mrs Mary Maxcy, relict of the late Hon Virgil Maxcy, in her 62nd year.

Died: on Jul 19, Mrs Ann H Vancoble, aged 52 years, after a long & painful illness. Her funeral is today, at 4 o'clock, from her late residence on 4½ st.

Died: on Jul 14, in Wash City, after a long & painful illness of consumption, Mr Jacob C Fulton, in his 28th year, formerly of Alexandria, Va, but for some time past a resident of Wash City. He has left a disconsolate mother & sisters & a large cirlce of friends to mourn his loss.

SAT JUL 21, 1849
Transylvania Univ, Lexington, Ky. 32nd session will open on Nov 1.
Medical Dept-Faculty:
Benj W Dudley, M D
Jas M Bush, M D
Saml Annan, M D
Ethelbert L Dudley, M C
Robt Peter, M D, Dean of the Faculty
Henry M Bullitt, M D
Wm M Boling, M D
H M Skillman, M D

Nat'l Medical College, Wash, D C. Lectures will commence on the first Mon in Nov & continue until the end of Mar. Faculty:
Thos Miller, M D
Wm P Johnston, M D
Joshua Riley, M D
John Fred May, M D
Grafton Tyler, M D
Leonard D Gale, M D
Robt King Stone, M D
-Wm P Johnston, M D-Dean, 7th st, between E & F sts

Light Infty Excursion on Aug 7 on the commodious steamer **Columbia**. Tickets $1: to be had at E J McClery's & S Butt's drug stores, at J Shillington's, & D Keally, as well as the cmte:
Joss B Tate
John W Mead
Wm E Morcoe
Andrew J Joyce
Benj F Beers
Jas H Mead
P M Dubant
Wm W S Kerr

Groceries, liquors & farming utensils at public auction, the subscriber to change his present business: sale at the store corner on 9th & Pa ave. -A J Webb
-E C & G F Dyer, aucts

Died: on May 29 last, in Richmond City, Mrs Eliz, consort of Mr Benj T C Robins, formerly of Gloucester Co, Va.

Another fatal rencounter in Ky: on Mon week, at Paducah, between the Hon Jas Campbell & Benedict Austin, resulted in the death of Mr Austin, who was instantly killed by a pistol shot from Mr Campbell. They were both candidates for the Convention to revise the State Constitution, & difficulty originated in personal remarks made upon the hustings. Mr Campbell immediately gave himself up. Four magistrates acquitted him of blame.

Mrd: Jul 19, by Rev F S Evans, Mr Alex'r Wheeler to Miss Mary Warder.

Mrd: Jul 19, by Rev F S Evans, Mr Jas R Steele to Miss Mary E Belt.

Died: yesterday, Lund Washington, jr, in his 56th year. He was favorably known in connexion with the public press of Wash City some years ago, & lately as clerk in the State Dept. His funeral is this morning at 10 o'clock, from his late residence on K, between 7th & 8th sts.

Died: on Jul 18, at Hagerstown, Md, Wm Price, son of W B & Sophia D Clarke, aged 4 years & 1 month.

Died: on Tue, at Fauquier, White Sulphur Springs, Mr Thos L Nelson, the doorkeeper of the Senate of Va.

For rent, the large dwlg house over Messrs Morsell & Wilson's store on Pa ave. Apply to B H Cheever, *Franklin Row*.

Household & kitchen furniture at auction on Jul 23, at the residence of Mr Emmonds, on H st, between 7th & 8th sts. –C W Boteler, auctioneer

By writ of fieri facias, I shall expose to public sale, for cash, on Jul 28, all the right, title, & interest of Zachariah Hazell in, of, & to the Hay Scales & fixtures at Md ave & 2nd st, Wash City. Seized & taken as the property of Hazell to satisfy a judgment in favor of Benj F Middleton & Benj Beall. -R R Burr, Constable

MON JUL 23, 1849
For rent, a nearly new brick house on the corner of 16th & K sts, with a brick stable attached. –Mary B Alexander, 12th st, between C & D sts.

In Montg Co Court, as a Court of Equity, Jul Term, 1849. Henry Harding, administrator of Thos F W Vinson, vs Jas N Allnutt, administrator of Robt Syles, Juliet Syles, widow, & Robt J Syles. The object of this suit is to procure a decree for sale of certain mortgaged premises in said county, on Jul 4, 1835, mortgaged by one Robt Syles, since deceased, to one Thos F W Vinson, since deceased, of whom the cmplnt is the administrator. The bill states that on Jul 4, 1835, Robt Syles conveyed certain real estate, which is particularly described in the bill, unto Thos F W Vinson in his lifetime, by way of mortgage, to secure the payment of $400, with interest from Nov 1, 1830, which was then due & owing from the said Robt Syles to the said Thos F W Vinson; that the said Thos F W Vinson has since died, & letters of administration on his personal estate have been granted by the orphan's court of Montg Co to the cmplnt; that the said Robt Syles has since died, leaving a widow, Juliet Syles, & Robt J Syles his heir at law, who reside in the State of Tenn; & letters of administration on his personal estate have been granted by the orphan's court of said county to said Jas N Allnutt; & that no part of the aforesaid sum of money or interest thereon hath been paid, but that the whole of said debt, with interest, is still due & owing to the cmplnt as administrator as aforeaid. The bill prays that the said mortgaged premises, or so much thereof as may be necessary, may be sold for the payment of the said claim of the cmplnt as administrator, with interest as aforesaid. Notice is given to the absent dfndnts to appear in this court, in person or by solicitor, on or before the second Mon of Nov next. –T H Wilkinson -S T Stonestreet, clerk

Washington & Alexandria Boat: the steamboat **Joseph Johnson**, leaves Alexandria at 7, 9, 11, 2, 4, & 6 o'clock. Leaves Washington at 8, 10, 12, 3, 5, & 7 o'clock. –Job Corson, Captain

House & lot at privae sale: a 2 story brick house with an adjoining 2 story brick back bldg, on square 185, fronting on 16th st, next house north of the residence of Com Morris. –Alex'r McIntire, 16th st, First Ward

Telegraphic report: 1-The news of the surrender of Rome to the army of France. 2-Terrible disaster at sea, by the sinking of an American packet-ship & the loss of 133 lives.

Matthew Wood, convicted of the murder of his wife, was executed at N Y on Fri. He made no confession of the crime for which he suffered death.

Harvard College Commencement was held in the Unitarian Church at Cambrige on Wed last: among the guests were Govn'r Briggs & suite. Pres Sparks presided. Among the class of 78 who received the degree of A B were: sons of Abbott Lawrence, Ex-Govn't John Davis, Rev Drs Lothrop, Lawson, & Peabody, deceased, & of Rev Mr Stetson; also, nephews of Ex-Pres Everett & of the Hon Rufus Choate, & a son of the late Prof Follen. The honorary degree of doctor of laws was conferred on Hon Geo Eustis, Chief Justice of the Supreme Court of La; Hon Richd Fletcher, Associate Justice of the Supreme Court of Mass; Hon Horace Mann, member of Congress from Mass; Hon Theophilus Parsons, Dane Prof of Law in the law school for Harvard College. The honorary degree of doctor of divinity was conferred on Rev Geo Washington Burnap, of Balt; Rev Levi Washburn Leonard, of Dublin, N H; & Rev Chas Kittridge True. The honorary degree of master of arts was conferred on Francis Alger, of Boston; Jonathan Ingersoll Bowditch, of Boston; Prof Arnold Guyot, of Neufchatel, Switzerland.

Albany Journal of Fri announces the death of Harmanus Bleecker, a prominent resident of that city. He was many years ago a Rep in Congress, & during Mr Van Buren's Presidential term was appointed Charge d'Affaires to the Hague, where he resided many years.

Hon Geo Tibbits, an aged & wealthy citizen of Troy, N Y, died of the prevailing epidemic on Thu last, in his 87th year. He was reputed to have been the richest man in Rensaelaer Co.

Mrd: on Jul 15, at St Peter's Church, by Rev J Van Horsign, Capt Antonio Maeulete to Saledad Ahumada, all of Mexico.

Died: on Sun, Mr Bennet Booth, aged 63 years, a native of St Mary's Co, Md, but for the last 43 years a resident of Wash City. His funeral is this evening, from his late residence, near the Navy Yard.

Died: on Jul 13, at Lafayette, Indiana, of cholera, after an illness of 10 hours, Mr Thos Underwood, formerly of the firm of Murray, Draper, Fairman & Co, Bank Engravers, Phil.

Died: on Jul 17, at Norfolk, Va, Mr Richd Vermillion, formerly of Wash City, in his 47th year. He leaves a devoted wife & interesting children to mourn his loss.

Execution: Nicholas, the slave of Mr Kelly, John, the slave of Mr Toomer, & Geo, the slave of Mr Holmes, were hung at Charleston, S C, on Fri last. They had been inmates of the work-house, & on the preceding Fri had resisted & assailed the keepers.

Wash Corp: 1-Ptn from Zachariah Hazell: referred to the Cmte on Police. 2-Act for the relief of Wm Rupp: passed. 3-Cmte of Claims: act for the relief of Wm Finsley, & an act for the relief of Thos Fitnam: passed. Same cmte: asked to be discharged from the further consideration of the ptn of Timothy O'Neal: which was agreed to. 4-Ptn of Robt Earl, for remission of a fine: referred to the Cmte of Claims.

Police Intelligence: Charge against Hall & Pleasants, free negroes, for a barbarous assault on Manuel Paralto, servant of the Mexican minister, was resumed on Sat, before Justices Grubb & Goddard, at the Court House. Edw Hall was committed; Pleasants, was recognised to appear as a witness for the prosecution.

Exhibition of the Washington Seminary, D C, held on Jul 19 & 20, 1849. Students who have distinguished themselves during the year:

John Callan	Geo Maher	Philip Ennis
Saml Savage	Eugene Crosson	Nicholas Brooks
Eugene Fleury	Richd Harvey	Columbus Eslin
Wm McCormick	Geo Murray	Albert Greenleaf
Jas Callan	Chas McColgan	David Wiber
Jas Newton	Wm Faherty	Wm Houcke
John O'Connor	Wm Ousley	Adolphus Beckert
Jos Caden	Jos Cox	Eugene Fleury
Michl Dooley	Martin Morris	John Kerby
Wm Gainor	John King	Philip Ferris
John Fitzgerald	Chas Thomas	Jos Donevan
Martin Morris	Reuben Cleary	John Johns
Jas McCarthy	Francis Cleary	Stephen Willard
Thos Boone	Francis Shekell	Andre Roth
Thos King	Jos Lindsley	Chas Melcher
Jas O'Donnell	Constantine Smith	Peter Fitzpatrick
John Dobbyn	Hugh Heany	Isaac Jones
John Fenwick	Jas Smith	Saml O'Brien
Wm Cleary	Wm Laskey	Howard Howlett
Chas McCarthy	Thaddeus Morris	Martin Morris
Philip Ferris	Edw Caton	John Franklin
Jos Donevan	John T Lowry	Jas O'Donnell
Cajeton Bastianelli	Richd Mohun	Henry Burgevin
Chas Laporte	John Ousley	John Boone

Jas Dooley	Jos Donevan	Albert Greenleaf
Jos Noyes	Adolphus Beckert	Morgan English
Chas Jesup	Stephen Ford	Richd Mohun
Jas Smith	Stephen Willard	Douglass Cleary
Wm Cleary	Lucian Linton	Jas May
John Thomas	Geo Murray	Philip Ennis
John Dobbyn	Andrew Roth	Stephen Ford
John O'Donnoghue	Wm Clure	Geo Maher
Thaddeus Morrice	Wm Harvey	Jas Hill
Jas DeKraft	Jos Cox	Richd Mohun
Thos King	Geo Coombe	Albert Greenleaf
Martin Morris	Chas McColgan	Wm Gainor
John King	Jas Leckie	Wm Waters
Isaac Beers	Theodore Orme	Chas Perrie
Edw Caton	Theodore Lay	Jas Newton
Wm Waters	Michl Quigly	Geo Caton
Marcellus Stoops	Jos Dant	John McColgan
Geo Cox	Wm O'Connor	Wm Murray
Morgan English	Wm Alsworth	Chas Murphy
Wm King	John Hurley	Augustinus Hill
Wm Gould	Wm Moenser	Jos Donevan
Eugene Fitzgerald	Edw Sweeny	John Howlett
Jas Hoban	Martin Morris	Anthony Ruppert
John O'Connor	Henry Burgwin	Lucian Linton
Jas Hill	Jas Smith	Chas Cripps
Jas Ferris	John Dobbyn	Wm Faherty
Willard Fitzgerald	Jos Noyes	Florence
John Howlett	Thaddeus Morris	O'Donnoghue
Jas Maron	Alex'r Ford	

Class of Elocution: medal/premiums to:
Alter Briscoe, John Mattingley, Lysander Trook, Thos King, Jas McCarthy, Chas Jesup, Eugene Fleury, Chas Thomas, Jos Noyes, Thos Marron, Richd Lay, Chas Laporte, A Macomb Ford, Martin Morris, Wm Cleary, Jas Smith, Jno O'Donnoghue, Jas Dooley, Chas Perrie, Thos Cox, Leonidas Smith, Jas Hoban, Morgan English, Jacob Vandelcher, Thos Lay, Marcelius Stoops, Gerald Fitzgerald. For good conduct premiums: John Thomas, Jas Marron, Thaddeus Morris, Francis Shekell, John Fenwick, Wm Laskey, Fred'k Maguire, Jas Callan, Chas Ewing, Jas DeKrafft, John Ouseley, Richd Mohun, Richd Washington, Wm Waters, Geo Caton, A Macomb Ford, Calvert Ford, Alex'r Young, Wm Faherty. [Repeated names:-more than one premium.]

Furnished room for rent: on corner of 4½ & O sts, formerly the residence of Dr Sewall, deceased. Apply to Dr Van Patten, Dentist

Notice: there are in the warehouse of the steamer **Columbia** 2 boxes marked W H Cassedy, Wash D C, shipped in Balt Apr 28, 1849, by J F Miller; also, 2 boxes marked E Everett, Wash, D C, shipped Jun 16, 1849, by J F Miller. Owners of the boxes are to call for them, or direct where they shall be sent. -Thos W Riley, Agent for the steamer **Columbia**, Wash.

Orphans Court of Wash Co, D C. Letters testamentary on the personal estate of Martha Young, late of said county, deceased. –Thos J Semmes, exc

TUE JUL 24, 1849
I B Burbbayge, the proprietor of the 10 year old established Ofc of Intelligence, Information, & Gen Agency at St Louis, Mo, is now in Wash City. Persons seeking general information, work, or employment in the large cities of North, West, or South will find it in their interest to consult with him without delay. He can be seen at Mr Gilbert's, on Pa ave, west of Gadsby's Hotel.

Late Collision on the Atlantic. Copied from the Liverpool Times. The steamship **Europa**, Capt Lott, arrived at here on Sun last, after a passage of 10 days 18 hours from Boston to this port. She had 43 persons, the survivors of the passengers & crew of the American barque **Charles Bartlett**, which vessel the **Europa** ran down at sea on the 27th ult, about 700 miles to the westward of Cape Clear, causing the loss of 134 lives. The **Charles Bartlett**, Capt Bartlett, was an American ship of 400 tons burden, chiefly loaded with lead & chalk, & having 162 steerage passengers, one cabin passenger, & a crew of 14 men, outward bound for N Y: both vessels were enveloped in dense fog. Of 40 women who were on board only one was rescued. The collision was purely accidental.

Hagerstown News: letter received from a late fellow townsman, John A Freaner, now on his way to Calif, dated at Panama, Jun 11, 1849. Death, desolation, & destruction hovered around our little band ever since we touched upon the Isthmus. The Balt & Fred'k Company have been very unfortunate. The greater part of this company have suffered from the sickness. The pres of the company died today. Another letter, dated Jun 12, has been received from Rev Wm F Mercer, of Ellicott's Mills, confiming the death of Mr Waesche, the president of the company.

The British Gov't has conferred a gold medal upon Capt Oliver Gorham, of the ship **Adelphi**, of Boston, for his humane exertions in rescuing the ofcrs & crew of the British barque **Jane Blain**, 17 in number, in Feb last, from death by drowning. To Mr Lovell & Mr Hussey, the 2 mates of the **Adelphi**, silver medals have been awarded to them. The medals were transmitted to the Sec of State in this city, through Mr Crampton, the British Charge d'Affaires.

Fatal affray on Jul 13, [says the Gerrard, Ky Banner of the 13th,] some 5 or more men went last week in the night time to the residence of Mr Edw Slaughter, in Rockcastle, for the purpose of lynching him, or taking his life. Slaughter is an old man & had no weapons; he was badly cut & mangled, but succeeded in slaying the foremost assailants-a man by the name of Lunts, with an old gunbarrel; this put an end to the battle. Slaughter is still in a precarious condition.

Land for sale: I have, within one hour's ride of Wash City, 740 acres of land, occupied by 4 tenants. Equal to any land in PG Co. Apply to Simms & Son, or Edw Simms, Pa ave, Wash.

Mrd: Jul 18, at the Ninth st Methodist Protestant Church, Wash, by Rev Wm Collins, Fred'k H Collier to Catherine, youngest daughter of Wm King, all of Gtwn, D C.

Died: on Jul 9, at St Mary's Hall, Burlington, N J, in her 13th year, of Asiatic cholera, Catharine Bowie Clarke, only daughter of the late Danl & Catharine Clarke, of PG Co, Md.

Died: on Jul 21, of cholera infantum, Clarence, aged 5 months & 28 days, infant son of Wm & Jane A Walter, of Wash City.

Died: on Jul 19, of cholera infantum, Mary Greenleaf, only daughter of Geo C & Mary Ann Jackson, aged 11 months & 12 days.

Died: on Jul 19, at Preston, Alexandria, Va, Frances Alexander, infant daughter of Wm T & Rosina M Swann.

Valuable land at public sale: the undersigned, excs of J J Gough, late of St Mary's Co, deceased, by virtue of the last will & testament of said deceased, & an order of the Orphans' Court, will offer at public sale, at Leonard Town, Aug 9, all the real estate of which the deceased died seized, consisting of: 1st: the house plantation, called part of *St John's*, or *Oakland*, containing 358 acres more or less, situated in *St Joseph's Forest*, within 4½ miles of Chaptico, near Messrs Jos Hayden's & Henry Drury's lands: bldgs consist of a comfortable dwlg house with every convenient out-houses. 2nd: a lot of land containing 49½ acres, more or less, being part of lot #1 of the division of the real estate of the late Philip Key. 3rd: a tract of land containing ___ acres, being part of lot #2 in the division of the real estate of the late Philip Key. No houses on either 2 or 3. [Acreage on 3rd tract is missing.] -Sarah C Gough, Ben't I Heard, excx

Marshal's sale: in virtue of 2 writs of fieri facias: sale on Sep 17, in front of the permises, all the right, title, or claim of John Lawrence in & to the following property, viz: all that part of lot 81, in Threlkeld's addition to Gtwn, near Jas Scrivner's property: seized & levied upon as the property of John Lawrence, & sold to satisfy judicials 19 & 20, to Oct Term, 1848, in favor of the Mayor, Recorder, Alderman, & Common Council of Gtwn. -Thos Woodward, Deputy to the late Alex'r Hunter, Marshal

WED JUL 25, 1849
Indian outbreak in Fla: Extra from the ofc of the Savannah Georgian, under date of Jul 21: Seminoles have become hostile on Indian river, in South Fla. Attack made in St Lucia Co: Mr Baker was killed & mutilated; Maj Wm F Russell, deputy collector at Indian river, was shot in the arm; his family, it is feared, have fallen into the hands of the Indians, as they have since been missing. A number of other persons, mostly females, are also missing. [Jul 27th newspaper: the Savannah Republican learns that Mr Russell, who was wounded by the Indians, at Indian river, had previously had some difficulty with the Indians, & it may have been personal revenge.] [Jul 30th newspaper: accounts differ in describing the outrage of Seminoles on Indian river. Nothing indicative of a general outbreak. Mrs Russell & others have arrived at New Smyrna.]

Charlestown [Va] Free Press: a negro man, Isham, belonging to Mr John E Boyd, of Berkeley Co, died on Jul 8. He was 21 years old at the time of Braddock's defeat, making him 115 years old at the time of his death. He was the first colored man owned by the late Gen Boyd, of Berkeley.

Mr Rathburn, son of the proprietor of the hotel bearing his name, in N Y, while oppressed by a fit of delirium tremens, attempted on Mon to cut his throat with a razor. His mother attempted to prevent it & he turned on her, cutting her throat, that no hopes are entertained of her recovery. He did not renew his attempt upon his own life. -Post

Wash Corp: 1-Permission to Jeremiah Hepburn to erect scales on the south side of East Capitol st: passed. 2-Cmte on Improvements: payment of the claim of Wm B Wilson for repair of certain paved alleys: passed. 3-Ptn of Noah Fletcher & others, praying the closing of a portion of the alley in square 456: referred to the Cmte on Improvements.

Telegraphic despatch dated Cincinnati, Jul 21: Capt Sammons, with his family of 8 or 9 persons, was poisoned by arsenic being put into the tea. A woman employed as seamstress, Mr Hanson, an engineer, & 3 others are dangerously ill. Capt Sammons is very sick. Jas Sammons, his son, has been arrested on suspicion. He was known to have purchased the poison last evening. Of late young Sammons has led a somewhat dissipated life. [Jul 29th newspaper: the family lately poisoned was that of Capt Blair Summons, an old, respected, & wealthy citizen, proprietor in the Louisville packet line of steamboats. Poisoned were J B Summons, father; Mrs Summons, mother; Mrs Reeves, acquaintance; Robt Armstrong, brother-in-law; Mrs Mary Jane Armstrong, sister; a son of do, 4 or 5 years old; Wm Summons, brother; & Paul Houston, cousin. Mrs Reeves died the next monring, & the little boy died subsequently to that time. Hopes were entertained for the recovery of the rest.]

Boston, Fri last: a number of small boys playing upon the sidewalk near Pearl place, the sign board of Mr Jas Tucker fell upon their heads, wounding 3, if not fatally, very badly.

Gtwn College, D C: Annual Commencement was held on Jul 24, 1849. Degree of Dr of Music was conferred on: Prof Henry Dielman, of St Mary's College, Emmitsburg.
Degree of A M was conferred on:
John C Brent, D C   Richd H Clarke, D C
Philip C Gooch, M D, Va   Eugene Cummiskey, D C
Degree of A B was conferred on the following students:
Edmund L Smith, Pa   J B Adrain Lepretre, La
Edmund A Deslonde, La   Louis Le Couteulx, N Y
Same degree of A B was conferred on the following students of the College of the Holy Cross, near Worcester, Mass:
John Brownson   Hugh Healy
John McCabe   Jas Healy
Honorary degree of A B was conferred on: John Reid, M D, of Md

<u>Medals were awarded to:</u> Peter D D Delacroix, La; Edmund L Smith, Pa

Accesserunt:
Edmund A Deslonde, La
J B Adrian, Lepretre, La
Medals/premiums were awarded to:
Wm H Moore, Miss
Manuel M Aldunate, Chili, S A
Frederico Aldunate, Chili, S A
Zenon Freiere, Chili, S A
Thos A Della Torre, S C
Alfred J Higgins, Va
Richd H Bryan, Md
Wm Mouton, La
Richd H Bryan
Wm Wills, Md
John B Wills, Md
John C Hamilton, D C
John L Carriel, Miss
Edwin F King, D C
Geo W Fulmer, D C
John W Graham, Va
Jules A Choppin, La
Wm J Boarman, Md
Richd Welsh, Md
Thos M Blount, Fla
Francis M Baby, Canada
John H Hall, Tenn
Wm A Rickard, Ala
Wm F Gaston, N C
Benedict I Semmes, Md
Jules D D Delacroix, La
Hugh J Gaston, N C
Chas N Morse, La
Edwin F King, D C
Thos A Della Torre, S C
Mathews F Lancaster, Md
Richd Welsh, Md
Lloyd Williams, D C
Jas Pritchard, La
Henry W Brent, Md
Eugene A Shekell, D C
John A Pizzini, Va
Thos C Jenkins, Md
Mathew F Maury, D C
Richd W Tompkins, Md
Aristide L Aubert, Ala
Geo L Smith, Pa
David Ramsay, D C
Wm A Johnson, Miss

Louis Le Couteulx, N Y
Ex aequo

Josiah T Mason, La
Edw Williams, D C
Wm S Lance, S C
Wm A Parrott, D C
Geo E Gwynn, Md
Luis de la Rosa, Mexico
Leopold L Armant, La
Chas H Mathews, D C
Abraham Shekell, D C
Miguel Torrente, Cuba, W I
Jose W Guttierez, Mexico
Edwin W Robinson, D C
Jules A Choppin, La
Edwin F King, D C
Ernest L Forstall, La
John C Hamilton, D C
Geo W Fulmer, D C
Richd Welsh, Md
Dominic A O'Byrne, Ga
Wm Wills, Md
John B Wills, Md
Jas C Middleton
Wm W Tilley, D C
David Ramsay, D C
Hugh J Gaston, N C
Wm A Rickard, Ala
John M C Duncan, Ala
Henry P Tricou, La
Alfred J Higgins, Va
John Savage, Pa
Zenon Freire, Chili, S A
Lewis F Pise, N Y
Jas E S Harvey, Md
Jas Tillman, Ala
Geo L Smith, Pa
Oscar P Tete, La
Lloyd Williams, D C
Geo King, D C
Leopold L Armant, La
Geo E Gwynn, Md
Jas F Gasquet, La
Jas R Randall, Md
Amos P Labarbe, N C
David Ramsay, D C

Josiah T Mason, La
Louis de la Rosa, Mexico
Wm A Parrott, D C
[Repeated names:-more than one premium.]

Paul Bres, La
Chas W Francis, Dela
Jos A Hebert, La

Land for sale : a portion of his land in Wash City: several lots. The distance from the Centre market, by way of 14th st, does not exceed 2 miles, & is therefore but a short walk. Apply to Lewis Carbery, in Gtwn, or to the subscriber, on the ground. –Wm Holmead

Patent Ofc: 1-Ptn of Henry Burden, of Troy, N Y, for extension of a patent granted to the said Henry Burden for an improvement in Horse-shoes, for 7 years from expiration of said patent, which takes place on Nov 23, 1849. 2-Ptn of John Elgar, of Balt, Md, for extension of a patent granted to said John Elgar, for an improvement in apparatus for transporting good on canals & railroads, for 7 years from the expiration of said patent, which takes place on Nov 7, 1849. –Thos Ewbank, Com'r of Patents

Died: on Jul 24, Bryan Morsell, son of Gerard & Clara Stith, aged 8 months. His funeral is this afternoon, at 4 o'clock, from the residence of his grandfather, B K Morsell, Pa ave, between 6th & 7th sts.

Died: on Jul 20, at the residence of C C Hyatt, Bladensburg, Md, Florence, aged 14 months, daughter of Reuben & Mary Ellen Middleton, of St Joseph's, Mo.

Information wanted of Wm Ottison, who left Wash about 1829 or 30. He is a bootmaker by trade. He left Wash to go to Charleston, S C, to get money left to his parents by his uncle Dr Carmichael. Any information of the above will be thankfully received by his sister. –Matilda Skilling, Wash, D C

L A Tarlton has taken the house of Wm Greer, on 10th st, between E & F sts, & is now fitting it up for a bakery & confectionary. As misfortunes for the last 2 months have fell thick & heavy upon me, I hope the citizens in general will continue to encourage me by a still more liberal patronage.

Died: on Jul 22, at Bladensburg, Md, Reuben, aged 9 months, child of C C & Fanny Hyatt.

Store for rent on Bridge st, Gtwn, next door to Messrs English & Son, Hardware merchants. Inquire at the store of Mrs Ann H Clarke, near the Farmers' & Mechanics' Bank, Gtwn. –Saml Clarke

Household & kitchen furniture at auction on Jul 27, at the residence of the late W H Kessler, on H st, between 17th & 18th sts. -E C & G F Dyer, aucts

I certify that Enos Berkley, of Wash Co, brought before me as an estray, a sorrel horse. -Jas Crandell, J P Owner is to call & pay the charges & take him away. [Enos Berkley, East of the Marine Garrison, Wash.]

THU JUL 26, 1849
Proposals will be received until Aug 5, for the constructing of a reservoir in the open space east of 7th st, near the intersection of La ave & C st north. -Francis B Lord, Com'r 4th Ward

$100 reward for runaway negro man Henry Duke, about 22 years old. -Young D Hance, Prince Fred'k P O Calvert Co, Md.

It appears by late accounts from Europe that Chas Albert, late King of Sardinia, is not dead: he is seriously ill, but hopes were entertained of his recovery.

The Rahway [N J] Register notices the death by cholera of Miss Mary Knight, age 90 years, sister of the brave Gen Isaac Worrell, of Revolutionary memory. The deceased was one of those most devoted women that helped to relieve the horrible sufferings of Washington's army at Valley Forge: cooking & carrying provisions to them alone, through the depth of winter, even passing through the outposts of the British army in the disguise of a market woman. When Washington was compelled to retreat before a superior force, she had the tact & courage to conceal her brother, Gen Worrell, [when the British set a price on his head for his bravery,] in a cider hogshead in the cellar for 3 days, & fed him through the bunghole; the house in the meantime being ransacked four different times at Frankfort, Pa, by the British troops in search of him, without success.

John L Lawrence, Comptroller of N Y C, died there on Mon last. He was seized with a renewed attack of chronic diarrhoea, an old complaint, & has now fallen victim to it.

At Boston, on Sat, Jos H Simmons, 12 years old, son of Wm H Simmons, was instantly killed by the accidental discharge of a gun in the hands of another boy about the same age.

O S X Peck will practice law in the Courts of the District of Columbia: letters postpaid.

To let, the residence of the late Dr Fred'k May, on Capitol Hill. Inquire of Dr J F May, on La ave.

The Lexington [Ky] Observer of Jul 18 announces the death of Robt S Todd, of Franklin Co. He has been Clerk in the Hse o/Reps of the State & a State Senator, & was a highly respected citizen.

A venerable citizen of Richmond, Mr Archibald Freeland, died on Sat last. He was a native of Scotland, & emigrated to this county nearly 70 years ago, & engaged in mercantile pursuits in Manchester, afterwards in Petersburg, & then in Richmond. He died at age 92 years.

Matamoros Flag: received from the Rio Grande city: a few days since, while in a fandango ball room, Jack Mills committed an unprovoked murder upon a respectable Mexican citizen, by shooting him down with his revolver. A cmte was formed to exterminate him. He was found & pierced with 30 bullets.

Public Schools: Annual Examination commenced on Mon last with:
Primary School #7, under charge of Miss L Sherman: located on B st south, near 1st st east: about 64 students, both sexes, from 6 to 12 years.
Primary School #8: under the charge of Miss Bradley, principal, & Miss Moss, assistant; 120 pupils, both sexes; school room is in the basement of the Methodist Radical Church, on Va ave, between 4th & 5th sts.
Primary School #9: under the charge of Mrs Martin; house on 11th st; number of pupils is 61 or 62, both sexes. Pupils of the 3 primary schools in the 3rd district assembled at Miss Bradley's school: pupils who received medals, viz: Ellen Higgins, Mary Ellen Simms, & Mary Jane Murphy.
Examination of the pupils of District School #3: Mr Hugh McCormick, principal; Mr Goldsmith, assistant. District School, #4 examined: located in the 7th Ward, under the charge of Mr Thompson, principal; Mrs Hinton, assistant. [Jul 30th newspaper: Primary schools First District under Mr Henshaw. Primary schools 2nd District under Dr Watkins.]

Pony for sale: he is young, sound, & goes well in harness or saddle, & suitable size for a lady or youth. –M H Stevens, Hatter, #1, Brown's Hotel.

Mrd: on Jul 10, by Rev Mr Marks, Mr John Gipson to Miss Ann Maddox.

Died: Jul 25, Nicholas W Worthington, M D, in his 61st year. His relatives & friends & those of his sister, Mrs Pearson, [from whose residence at **Brentwood** the funeral will take place,] are invited to attend at 3 p m, today.

Died: on Jul 18, at Norfolk, Va, after a short illness, Mrs Frances Selden Gardner, wife of Cmder Wm H Gardner, U S Navy, & daughter of Carey Selden, formerly of Wash.

Died: on Jul 25, Henry Cookman, infant son of Jas H & Anna S Boss, aged 9 months. His funeral is today at 4:30 o'clock, from the residence of his parents, on H, near 4th st.

FRI JUL 27, 1849
Appointments by the Pres: Henry Asbury, of Ill, to be Register of the Land Ofc at Quincy, Ill, vice Saml Holmes, removed.
Henry V Sullivan, of Ill, to be Receiver of Public Moneys at Quincy, Ill, vice Hiram Rogers, removed.
Jefferson F Jackson, of Ala, to be U S Atty for the northern district of Ala, vice Jos A S Acklin, removed.
Appointments by the Sec of the Interior:
Greenbury Dorsey, of New Orleans, to be Pension Agent at that place, vice Chas Fitz, who declines the ofc.
Wm H Bell, of Miss, to be Indian Sub-Agent at the Osage sub-agency, vice John M Richardson, resigned.

The N Y Common Council have appropriated $1,000 to defray the expense of bringing home the bodies of Gen Worth & Col Duncan to be suitably interred in N Y, their native State.

Pennsylvania: the following are the Major Generals of the several Divisions of Militia returned as elected recently in the State of Pa:

Robt Patterson, of Phil
ChasH Mathews, of Bucks
Geo Ford, of Lancaster
Wm H Keim, of Berks
Francis W Wynkoop, of Schuylkill
Con Shimer, of Northampton
Wm H Kase, of Northumberland
E W Sturdevant, of Luzerne
Amherst Carpenter, of Susquehanna
Wm Brindle, of Lycoming
Seth Cloon, of Clarion
Wm E Barton, of Bradford
Reuben C Hale, of Mifflin
Contested between Edw M Biddle & Henry Fitter
John Humphreys, of Cambria
Cymer P Markle, of Westmoreland
Wm Robinson, of Alleghany
Thos W Clark, of Mercer
Contested between Jas R M Clintick & Jos Douty

The St Louis papers announce the death of Col Saml MacRee, on Jun 14, in that city, in his 49th year. He was Quartermaster U S Army; was in the Florida war, & the Mexican war.

Hon Amos Tuck did not sail for Europe in the steamer **Canada**. He had engaged passage; but, 2 days before the steamer sailed, he was attacked with a bilious disorder, accompanied by a severe neuralgia, which has prostrated his strength, & rendered him entirely helpless. He has been & is dangerously sick. Confident hopes are entertained for his recovery.

Zachary Taylor, Pres of the U S of A, recognizes Augusto Lopes Baptista who has been appointed Vice Consul of Portugal, for the port of Balt & State of Md. Jul 26, 1849

Died: yesterday, Mr Wm Allen, merchant, aged 38 years, leaving a wife & several children, to mourn the loss of an upright citizen & a faithful friend. His funeral is this morning, at 12 o'clock, from his late residence, on Pa ave, between 9th & 10th sts.

Died: on Jul 26, Wm MacPherson Washington, son of Peter G Washington, Auditor for the Post Ofc Dept, in his 21st year. His funeral is this afternoon, at 4 o'clock, from the Irving House.

Died: Sat last, Mrs Mgt E Smoot, wife of John H Smoot, of Gtwn, D C, a lady much esteemed & admired for her gentle manners & benevolent character.

Groceries at auction: the remaining stock in the store at G & 7th sts, occupied by Mr Thos McGill: sale on Jul 30th. -E C & G F Dyer, aucts

SAT JUL 28, 1849
$5 reward for bay mare that strayed from the subscriber, near the Northern Liberty Market-house, Wash. –Alexius Wood, near Bryantown, Chas Co, Md, or to Richd Burch, Wash.

Academy of the Visitation, B V M, Gtwn, D C. Annual Distribution of Premiums took place on Jul 25. The premiums were distributed by his Excellency the Pres of the U S Zachary Taylor. Premiums awarded to:

Gertrude Fetterman, Pittsburg, Pa
Mary Ellen Brady, Wash, D C
Josephine Pleasonton, Phil
Glovinia Neale, Wash, D C
Mary Ann Ennis, Wash, D C
Mary Loughborough, Gtwn, D C
Mary Adams, Wash, D C
Isabel Cole, Detroit, Mich
Christiana Green, Gtwn, D C
Rosa Ford, Wash, D C
Amanda Clare, Wash
Virginia Foote, Miss
Adel Cutts, Wash
Catherine Tilgham, Eastern Shore, Md
Ellen Roach, Wash
Marion Ramsey, Wash
Matilda Devereux, Wash
Victoria Branch, Petersburg, Va
Jane Carroll, Gtwn, D C
Georgiana Hill, Wash
Julia Young, Wash
Jane Neale, Chas Co, Md
Harriet Thayer, Petersburg, Va
Anne O'Donohue, Gtwn, D C
Mary C O'Donoghue, Gtwn
Mary Jane Boarman, Martinsburg, Va
Mary Harris, Claiborne Parish, La
Rosa Queen, Wash
Josephine Clements, Gtwn
Mary Ann Borremans, Wash
Mary Jane Jones, Wash
Virginia Magruder, PG Co, Md
Mary White, Charleston, S C
Celestia Neale, Chas Co, Md
Margaret Jewett, Wash
Caroline Poe, Gtwn, D C
Georgiana Fisher, Norfolk, Va
Eliz Cissel, Wash
Ellen Rose Matthews, Chas Co, Md
E Jones, PG Co, Md
Amelia Stoops, Gtwn, D C
Arabella Foote, Jackson, Miss
Ann Foote, Jackson, Miss
Mary Spalding, Milwaukie, Wisc
Mary Peabody, Wash
Caroline Noland, Montg Co, Md
M Cammack, Gtwn, D C
Ada Semmes, Gtwn, D C
Mary Osborne, Gtwn, D C
Eltrida Holland, Nansemond Co, Va
Ellen J O'Donohue, Gtwn, D C
Mary Jane Carroll, PG Co, Md
J Cammack, Gtwn, D C
Pauline Blache, New Orleans
Mary Burke, Eastport, Maine
Maria Jane Smoot, Gtwn, D C
Mary Payne, Gtwn, D C
Frances Offutt, Gtwn, D C
Anna King, Gtwn, D C
E O'Donoghue, Gtwn, D C
Emily Morton, Chas Co, Md
Emma Magruder, PG Co, Md
Lavinia Clements, Gtwn, D C
Adelaide Goszler, Gtwn, D C
Maria Jane Briscoe, Wash
Eliz McAtee, Gtwn, D C
Victoria Brent, Chas Co, Md
Emma Woolard, Gtwn, D C
Sarah Forte, Monroe, La
Albine Montholon, Wash
R Allison, Gtwn, D C
S Allison, Gtwn, D C
Virginia Laub, Wash
Nora Bonner, Wash
Lela Bonner, Wash
Clara Mitchell, Balt
Josephine Briscoe, Wash
Eliz O'Donoghue, Wash
Catherine Edelin, Calvert Co, Md
Francinia Berry, Wilmington, N C
Amanda Lepretre, New Orleans, La
Anna Bateman, Gtwn
E Blache, New Orleans, La
Alice Semmes, PG Co, Md
Josephine Laub, Wash
Laura Trunell, Gtwn
Rose Lancaster, Chas Co, Md
Nina Fremont, Wash
Geraldin Bellinger, Charleston, S C
Mary C Montague, Fayetteville, N C

Mrd: on Jul 26, at Trinity Church, Upper Marlborough, Md, by Rev Henry Woods, Robt Montgomery Larmour, of Alexandria, Va, to Mary Eliz, daughter of H C Scott, of the former place.

Mrd: on Jul 26, by Rev Mr Hodges, Benj F Beers to Miss Susan Duvall, both of Wash City.

Died: on Thu, in Gtwn, Miss Fanny B Redin, daughter of Wm Redin. Her funeral is from her father's residence, on Gay st, Gtwn, this morning, at 10 o'clock.

Died: on Jul 26, Edmund B, youngest son of John A & Harriet Donohoo, aged 8 months & 3 days. His funeral is this afternoon at 3 o'clock.

Died: on Jul 13, at St Louis, of the prevailing epidemic, in his 32nd year, John W Carroll, late of the State of Md. His afflicted widow & helpless children have suffered an irreparable loss. His friends mourn the death of a good & worthy man.

Died: on Jul 22, in Gtwn, Mr Robt B Rust, eldest son of Gen Geo Rust, of Leesburg, Loudoun Co, Va, in his 33rd year.

Died: on Jul 20, after a short illness, in King Geo Co, Va, Catharine D, wife of Fielding Lewis.

A report circulated some weeks ago of the death of Col Jack Hays, of Texas, is contradicted. He is alive, & doing well.

Mr Cornelius Lansing, of Watervliet, N Y, was found dead in his barn, on Thu last, having been shockingly gored by an infuriated bull.

MON JUL 30, 1849
Pittsburg Gaz of Fri brings us news of the death of the Hon Thos Henry, a most worthy citizen of Beaver Co, Pa. He was a native of Ireland, but was brought to this country with his father when he was but 2 years old, the family settling in the West, in 1787. He was a sound Whig.

The late Mr Theodore Lyman bequeathed a legacy of $50,000 to the Reform School at Westborough, of which he was the founder. He has also given $10,000 to the Farm School of which he has been an active ofcr for several years, & $10,000 to the Horticultural Society, where he had a deep interest.

A handsome new brick bldg, 4 stories, has been erected for Mr Lyon, corner of F & 9th st, near the Patent Ofc. It was built by Mr G H Plant, contractor.

City Ordinances: Wash: 1-Act for the relief of Wm Rupp: to refund to him the fine of $10: fine remitted. 2-Act for payment of the claim of Wm B Wilson for repair of certain paved alleys: sum of $117.79.

Suicide: Rev Lorin Haven left his father's house, at Sangerfield Centre, yesterday, & not returning, the family became alarmed. He was found in a cornfield with his throat cut, evidently the work of his own hand. He graduated at Hamilton College a few years ago, with a good reputation for scholarship. He had been married about a week, & was visiting with his wife at his father's. –Utica Observer

Augusta, Ga, was shocked Monday with the drowning of 3 youths, from 9 to 11, sons respectively of Mrs J P Andrews, N B Moore, & Luther Roll.

Accident at Nantucket last Tues, at Madeket, at Capt Nathan Chase's. A large party of young men & women were in a boat that upset from a gust of wind. Drowned were Susan P Cleveland, a daughter of Mr Zimri Cleveland, aged 25, & Phebe Allen, a daughter of Mr Geo Allen, aged 18. –Nantucket Inquirer, 26th

Butler Divorce: case of Pierce Butler vs Fanny Kemble Butler. Mr Butler is to allow Mrs Butler $1,500 annually, he to retain possession of their children, 2 daughters, excepting 2 months each year, which they are to spend with their mother. The daughters are now with their mother in Massachusetts, where she purposes to take up her residence. –Phil News

Danl J Desmond, member of the Phil Bar, & for many years Consul at Phil for several Italian States, died at his residence in that city on Thu. He was esteemed & beloved by a wide circle of relatives & friends.

Death of a Printer: at his residence in Cambridge port, Mass, Wm Manning, in his 84th year. He was the oldest printer in the State, having been a member of the old firm of Manning & Loring, publishers in Spring Lane, Boston. He was afterwards Messenger to the Govn'r & Council at the State House. –Transcript [No death date given-current item.]

Boston Journal of Wed says that Elias Phinney, Clerk of the Supreme Court & Court of Common Pleas of Middlesex Co, died suddenly at his residence in Lexington on Jul 24. He was an enterprising & scientific agriculturist.

Mr Alexander, of Covington, Ky, is bldg in that neighborhood 25 large frame bldgs for Calif, to be transported by a steamship from New Orleans. The ship **Belle of the West**, on her last trip down, brought 55 frames of houses & cottages, ready to be set up. –New Orleans Crescent

Trustee's sale: by deed of trust from Louis J Knight & his wife to the subscriber, dated Jan 1 last, for the benefit of Alfred H Boucher, & by his directions will be exposed to sale on Aug 1, a tract of land in Gtwn, being lot 8 in Deakins' & Bailey's addition to Gtwn, fronting 60 feet on Bridge st; also 10 feet of the westerly part of lot 201 in said addition, with dwlg-house & other improvements; also, the following personal property, to wit: one blood bay Stallion, one Rockaway & harness, one carryall & harness, one cart & harness, 2 saddles & 3 bridles, one cutting box & corn sheller. –Robt White, Trustee -E S Wright, auctioner [Will be added an excellent Barouche.]

House & valuable bldg lots at auction: on Aug 2, lot 6 in square 494, on E st, between 4½ & 6th sts, square next north of the beautiful residence of Mr G Mattingly. –Green & Tastet, auctioneers

The U S ship **Independence**, Capt Conover, bound to the Mediterranean, as flag ship of Cmdor Chas W Morgan, Cmder-in-Chief of the Mediterranean Squadron, sailed from Hampton Roads on Thu. List of her ofcrs: Capt, Thos A Conover

Lts:
J Tingey Craven   John Contee   John Q Adams
Geo Minor   Francis Winslow
J Lingan Henderson   Alex'r Murray
Surgeon, Wm Whelan
Purser, Chas Murray
Brevet Maj Geo H Terrett, Commanding marines
Chaplain, Theodore B Bartow
Masters, Ed Higgins, John C Beaumont
Passed Assist Surgeon, Wm Grier
Assist Surgeon, Washington Sherman
Brevet 1st Lt marines, A S Nicholson
Passed Midshipmen
Thos S Phelps   Saml E Franklin
Jos M Bradford   Jas J Waddell
Capt's Clerk, Ferdinand Coxe
Midshipmen:
G U Morris   A McF Davis   E K Owens
Austin Pendergrast   S C Mish
E R Shubrick   C Carter
Purser's Clerk, __ Spieden
Boatswain, Edw Cavendy
Gunner, John Caulk
Sailmaker, Elec Middleton
Carpenter, Henry S Leslie

Died: on Jul 28, Martha E Tucker, consort of Saml W Tucker, in her 28th year. She leaves a disconsolate husband & 4 young children to mourn her sudden demise.

Died: yesterday, in Wash City, Isabella Virginia, daughter of David A & Mary M Baird, aged 3 years, 7 months & 20 days. Her funeral is this morning, at 10 o'clock, from the residence of her father, 8th st, near Pa ave.

Died: on Jul 17, at Guyandotte, Va, in her 61st year, Mrs Harriet Campbell, widow of the late Hon Geo W Campbell, of Nashville, Tenn, formerly Sec of the Treasury, & daughter of the late Benj Stoddert, of Md, the first Sec of the Navy. Mrs Campbell was travelling from her residence in Nashville to the Va Springs, accompanied by her son & daughter, her only children, when she was seized with cholera at Guyandotte, & survived but a few hours. Her last words spoken to her children were, "meet me in Heaven, where I have faith that I am going, through the mercy of my Redeemer."

Died: on Sat last, at Gtwn, Wm Alex'r Duer, son of the Hon Wm Duer, of N Y, aged 8 years. Thus, in the absence of the father, has death, after a few days of great suffering, deprived this family of a intelligent son, & of one of the most devoted mothers of one in whom her very life itself seem centred, & around whose bed, from the moment of sickness to its close, she clung with devotedness. -Adocate

TUE JUL 31, 1849
Wanted. I wish to purchase a Servant Girl, from 14 to 16 years of age, or a woman from 25 to 30; one from the country would be preferred. Address a letter to John Wilson, 17th st, Wash, for further particulars.

Appointments by the Pres:
Collectors of the Customs:
Jefferson Minor, Tappahannock, Va, vice J A Parker, removed.
Jas Gregory, Marblehead, Mass, vice P Dixey, removed.
Jas D Thompson, Little Egg Harbor, N J, vice S Willets, removed.
John Larzelere, Burlington, N J, vice G Mott, removed.
C M Smith, Perth Amboy, N J, vice J A Nicholls, removed.
Wm W Baldwin Newark, N J, vice H Hewson, removed.
Franklin Spalding, Niagara, N Y, vice R H Boughton, removed.
Jas C Barer, Oswegatchie, N Y, vice T Bacon, removed.
Surveyors of the Customs:
T B Bagwell, Accomack, Va, vice S Melvin, removed.
Wm W Greene, St Louis, Mo, vice Thos Gray, removed.
Assist Treasurer:
Louis A Labeaume, at St Louis, vice Geo Penn, removed.

Hon Amos Tuck, one of the Reps Elect to Congress from N H, is lying dangerously ill at Dover, N H.

The body servant of the Pres, Chas Porter, was on Sunday attacked by an apoplectic fit, from the effects of which he died in a short time. He was a worthy man, & a great favorite with Gen Taylor, having been his constant companion through his Florida & Mexican campaigns.

A victim of cholera at Buffalo, N Y, was the wife of Dr Foote, of the Commercial Advertiser. Dr Foote, who had made arrangements to leave home with his family, under his appointment as Charge d'Affaires to Bogota, thus finds himself overwhelmed by this unexpected & painful calamity.

Trustee's sale of valuable real estate: by decree passed by PG Co Court, as Court of Equity, on Jul 24, 1849, in a cause wherein Saml Phillips, adm of O C Phillips, is cmplnt, & Alvertus H Basford & wife & others are dfndnts: the trustee will expose at public sale, at Beltsville, on Aug 20, all those tracts, parts of tracts, or parcels of land, lying in said county, & formerly owned & occupied by Nicholas Knighton, deceased, called *Isaac's Park*, *Isaac's Additon*, & ***Beall's Park Enlarged***, containing 162 acres of land, more or less. Improvements consist of a dwlg house & outhouses in tolerable repair. Possession can be had at once if desired. –Danl C Digges, trustee

The Sisters of Charity of the city of St Louis have proven themselves to be the good Samaritans of this community.

$20 reward for detection of information that will lead to the diabolical wretch who besmeared the front of my store. This is the second time that this villanous act has been perpetuated. –Saml Fowler

Farm for sale: 30 acres, near the Eastern Banch, west of Benning's bridge; with a 2 story frame dwlg house, & all necessary out bldgs; the whole is surrounded by a beautiful thorn hedge-Pyracantha. The owner wishing to remove to the West is the only reason why it is for sale. –Henry Miller, on the farm

Forsyth [Ga] Bee of Jul 25 records the suicide of Mrs Sutton who came to the desperate resolution of destroying herself & children rather than move to Van Buren, where her husband had purchased a grog shop, against her wishes. On Jul 20, when herself, her 2 children, & a negro girl were in the house, she fastened the doors & set it on fire. The oldest child & the negro girl made their escape, but the mother & youngest child perished.

Died: on Mon last, in Gtwn, Col John I Stull, in his 69th year. His funeral is this evening at half-past 5 o'clock, from his residence on Bridge st. [Aug 9th newspaper: Col Stull was born at Hagerstown, Md, in 1780, from parents whose family names stood conspicuous on the catalogue of eminent civil & military characters. His father was a judge of the county court of the Hagerstown district; his mother was one of the Williams family, who distinguished themselves in the battles of the Revolutionary war. In 1812 he took up arms in defence of his country & acquired a just reputation for undaunted courage.]

Zachary Taylor, Pres of the U S of A, recognises Jose C Keef who has been appointed Consul of Venezuela for the port of Phil. Jul 30, 1849

Died: on Jul 14, at Pensacola, Dr Saml C Lawrason, M D, Surgeon U S Navy, & Surgeon of the sloop of war **Germantown**. His great devotion to his duties, his long & most efficient & arduous sea service, have brought to the early tomb, by a profuse hemorrhage from the lungs, him whom all loved. [Aug 11th newspaper: It becomes our painful duty to state that Dr Pearson, the Assist Surgeon of the same ship, is also no more. He died about 10 days since, after a short illness, at the Naval Hospital at Pensacola. –Norfolk Herald]

WED AUG 1, 1849
Jas M Summons, who is charged with having attempted to poison his Father's family at Cincinnati, has been indicted for murder in the 1st degree: for having killed by poison Mrs Reeves & Henry Armstrong.

Vacant Professorship in N C Univ, by the resignation of Rev Dr Wm M Green. Trustees will proceed to fill the vacancy: salary is $1,200 per annum, with the use of a commodious dwlg house & all convenient appurtenances. Apply to Chas L Hinton, Sec of the Board of Trustees. –Raleigh Register

Wash Corp: 1-Ptns of Thos Lewis & Thos Greeves: committed to the Cmte of Claims. 2-Cmte on Unfinished Business: an account of W H Harrover for work done at the asylum: referred to the Cmte on the Asylum. 3-Nomination of Wm Martin as police constable for the 4th Ward, in the place of J M Wright, who declined: was confirmed. 4-Ptn of David Horning, praying the remission of a fine: referred to the Cmte of Claims. 5-Ptn of Edw Hammersley, praying the remission of a fine: referred to the Cmte of Claims. 6-Cmte of Claims: asking to be discharged from the further consideration of the ptns of Wm Fleming, of Sidney Talbot, of C H Payne, & of Antoinne Lekmann.

By virtue of an order of distrain, from A Small & S Pumphrey, to me, against the goods & chattels of Brown & Nichols, I have levied on the following to satisfy the same, & give notice that on Aug 7, at the Adelphi Theatre, I shall proceed to sell, for cash, to wit: a looking glass, lounge, chairs, stove, carpet, chairs, crockery, tablecloth, lamp buckets, candlesticks, table, chandeliers, scenery, curtains, mattress, cot, step ladder, & 3 pair Baize Doors. –Wm Cox, Bailiff

Died: on Fri last, in Gtwn, Mr Richd W Redin, only son of Wm Redin. The deceased had but lately commenced the practice of law in this place in conjunction with his father. His death was unexpected. He was the only brother of a lovely sister, bursting into womanhood, who suddenly died a day or two ago. –Gtwn Advocate

Died: on Jul 19, suddenly, at Thompson, Conn, Rev Danl Dow, D D, in his 77th year, & the 53rd of his pastoral relation to the First Congregational Church in that town. For many years he was one of the trustees of Yale College, & was among the original founders & ever an efficient friend of the Theological Seminary at East Windsor. Dr Dow was the father of Jesse E Dow, of Wash City.

Fire & riot broke out on Jul 29 on board the steamer **Algoma**, just arrived from Missouri with full freight, which was destroyed, together with the steamers **Mary**, **Phenix**, **San Francisco**, & **Dubuque**. The steamer **Algoma** was commanded by Capt Geo E Young. He was seen to jump overboard with his clothes on fire, & has not been heard of since. Mr Wm Fitch, a passenger was lost, besides many others. A tremendous riot occurred between the Irish & the Firemen. John Grant, of Missouri Co, was shot in the face.

Binghampton, Jul 30. Two men drowned last evening. A young man named Geo Martin was bathing in the Chenango river, when he seemed to be drowning. Mr Lewis Seymour rushed to his assistance, but lost his own life. The bodies were soon recovered. Mr Seymour leaves a wife & 6 children

Household & kitchen furniture at auction on Aug 6, at the residence of Mrs Latimer, on 15½ st, near Pa ave. Excellent furniture. –Green & Tastet, auct

THU AUG 2, 1849
Trustee's sale of groceries & store fixtures: on Aug 6, at the store on Bridge st, by order of the trustees. –A F Offutt, trustee -E S Wright, auctioneer

From Texas: 1-Cholera is raging at Fredericksburg as an epidemic; 30 persons had died at the last accounts. Brevet Maj Collinson R Gates, 8th Regt U S Infty, died of it at that place on Jun 28. Maj Gates was a brave & gallant ofcr, & served with distinction in the Florida war, & in the Mexican war, at the Resaca de la Palma, where he was severely wounded. As soon as he recovered he joined Gen Scott's wing of the army, & bore a gallant part in the capture of the city of Mexico. 2-Lt John Broker, 8th Infty U S A, was thrown from his horse in San Antonio a few weeks since. His head coming in contact with a post, he was so severely injured that he died in 30 hours

Capt H H Truesdell, long known as a popular steamboat cmder, & formerly captain of the ship **South America**, died on Sun at Coxsackie, N Y, of bronchitis, after a few hours' illness.

Rev Mr Berry, of Gtwn, has tendered his resignation of the ofc of Pastor of the Bridge st Presbyterian Church. The cause assigned for this step is ill health; but it is understood he intends to leave the place where he has won the kindest regards of many friends.

Alexandria Gaz: on Mon last, in Fairfax Co, Va, near the residence of David Fitzhugh, 10 miles from Alexandria, horses attached to a spring wagon, in which Mrs M A Fitzhugh, Miss Dickins, & 2 other ladies were riding, took fright & ran off. The wagon dashed against a tree. Miss Dickins, about 12 years of age, daughter of Francis A Dickins, of Wash City, died in an hour or two after the accident. Mrs Fitzhugh was very much injured, but her wounds were not dangerous. The other ladies were slightly injured.

Mrd: on Aug 1, by Rev Dr Laurie, A Ferree Shriver, of Balt, to Mary Jane, youngest daughter of the late Chas Glover, of Wash City.

Sale of house & lot at auction: by decree of the Orphans Court of Wash Co, D C, made in the matter of the ptn of Sophia M Clements, guardian to Alex'r, Richd, Harriet R, & Sophia A Clements, dated Jun 5, 1849, & approved by the Circuit Court. I shall proceed to sell all the interest & estate of said infants in & to the following piece of ground in Wash City, known as lot 14 in square 493; with a large frame house, requiring considerable repair. –Sophia M Clements, Guardian -C W Boteler, auctioneer

I certify that John Lloyd, of Wash Co, brought before me as a stray trespassing upon his enclosure, a black horse. –Jas Crandell, J P
Owner is to come forward, prove property, pay charges, & take him away.
-John Lloyd, east end of the Navy Yard Bridge

Died: on Jul 31, in her 43rd year, Mrs Mgt Johnson, leaving a husband & 7 children to mourn her loss. May she rest in peace! Her funeral is today, at 3 o'clock, from her residence on south 2nd st, Capitol Hill.

Died: Jul 31, Mrs Maria Nourse Cozens, afer a short illness, in her 56th year.

Died: on Jul 28, at his late residence, in Cold Spring, Putnam Co, N Y, of bilious fever, after an illness of nearly 2 weeks, Hon Cornelius Warren, in his 60th year, a Rep in the last Congress of the U S from the counties of Dutchess & Putnam. Judge Warren lived universally respected & esteemed by all who knew him. -Tribune

The corner stone of *Carroll Chapel*, in Montg Co, Md, 8 miles from Wash, will be laid on Aug 9, by the most Rev Archbishop of Balt.

FRI AUG 3, 1849
Weyer's Cave in Augusta Co, Va: 17 miles from Staunton. In 1804 Bernard Weyer ranged these hills as a hunter. While pursuing a ground-hog, which carried off a trap set for his capture, Weyer made an assault upon the domicile of the depredator with spade & mattock. A few moments' labor brought him to the ante-chamber of this stupendous cavern, where he found his trap desposited. The Gude's house is at the northern extremity. Mr Mohler, the guide, resides at the cave, & attends to visiters with great cheerfulness.

Appointments by the Pres: Custom-house Ofcrs
Hiram Roberts, Collector, Savannah, Ga, vice Wm B Bulloch, removed.
Bryan Morel, Naval Ofcr, Savannah, Ga, vice Jacob De La Motta, removed.
Wm P White, Appraiser, Savannah, Ga, vice Wm Mackey, removed.
John C Clark, N Y, to be 1st Auditor of the Treasury, vice Wm Collins, removed.

Milledgeville "Federal Union" states that Hon Wm H Stiles, now Charge d'Affaires at the Court of Austria, has requested to be recalled, & in Oct next he will resume his residence in Cass Co.

Hon W B Maclay, of N Y, has suffered sad bereavements by the pestilence. His wife perished in Illinois, on their way to the new settlement which the family of Mr Maclay intend to make in Ill, On Mr Maclay's return to N Y he left his family in good health. His little daughter, aged 2½ years, is now in the agonies of death.

Telegraphic despatch was yesterday received at the Treasury Dept announcing the death of Jas Larned, late chief clerk in the ofc of First Comptroller of the Treasury, who died at Fred'k, Md. He had been ill for some months by consumption. He has left behind a large number of friends & acquaintances to mourn his untimely death. [No death date given-current item.]

For Liberia. The *Liberia Packet*, Capt Goodmanson, under the auspices of the Md Colonization Society, sailed from Balt for Liberia on Wed. Cabin passengers: Mrs Russworm, the wife of the Govn'r of Cape Palmas, child & servant; Rev Mr Bastion, superintendent of the Methodist Episcopal Mission in Liberia, his lady & child; Rev R R Gurley, of Wash, D C; Rev Hilleary Teague, of Liberia. There were about 24 emigrants purchased by the Society, specially to be sent out-they were Thos Gross & family. Those from S C were sent out by the American Colonization Society. -Sun

Household & kitchen furniture at auction, Aug 7, at the residence of the late Dr May, N J ave, Capitol Hill: superior furniture. -E C & G F Dyer, aucts

Phil, Aug 2. Mr Jos Tagert, aged 92 years, & for 50 years Pres of the Farmers & Merchants' Bank, died this morning at his residence in Germantown. He was among our oldest & most respected citizens.

Obit-died: on Jul 25, Dr Nicholas W Worthington: born in Gtwn, Md, now D C: son of Dr Chas Worthington: attended the Medical College at Phil: became associated with his father in the practice of medicine. In performing a surgical operation upon a diseased subject, the virus coming in contact with an unperceived wound on his hand, so thoroughly diffused itself throughout the system as to endanger his life for a considerable time, from which he never perfectly recovered. After the death of his father, Dr N W Worthington continued the practice successfully. He accumulated a property sufficient to satisfy any reasonable man. Too enfeebled, he some years since retired to **Brentwood**, the residence of his beloved & devoted sister, Mrs Pearson.

Died: yesterday, suddenly, John Williamson, a native of England, in his 36th year, but for many years a citizen of this country. His funeral is this morning, at 8 o'clock, from his late residence, 2nd & Md ave, Capitol Hill.

Died: Aug 2, Mary Griffith, the youngest child of Geo W Riggs, jr, aged 16 months. Her funeral is this afternoon, at 5 o'clock, from his residence near Wash City.

Died: on Aug 1, of scarlet fever, Mary Joseph, aged 3 years & 6 months, daughter of Abraham & Sarah Butler.

Died: on Aug 1, Kate, daughter of Wm & Jessie McDermott, aged 10 months.

Died: on Jul 30, at **Oak Hill**, the residence of Mrs R Fitzhugh, in Fairfax Co, Va, Mary Randolph, a lovely daughter of Francis A & Mgt H Dickins, aged 9 years & 5 months.

Died: on Jul 13, at Port Lavara, Texas, after a few days' illness, Lt Chas N Hagner, of the Corps of Topographical Engineers, & eldest son of Peter Hagner, Third Auditor of the Treasury.

Died: on Jul 31, at Balt, Catherine Milligan McLane, consort of the Hon Louis McLane, in her 60th year.

Died: on Jul 31, in Balt, Mrs Eliz Foyles, in her 58th year, formerly of Wash, D C.

Died: on Jul 15, at Montrose, Iowa, after a few hours' illness, of the prevailing epidemic, Richd H Whiting, of Va, aged 26 years.

$50 reward for runaway negro girl Rose, a first-rate house servant, about 15 or 16 years old. –Eliz Darne, living in Darnestown, Montg Co, Md.

Wm Beron, Painter in general, Pa ave, between 9th & 10th sts, prepared to do painting in all its branches.

MON AUG 6, 1849

The London papers announce the death of Horace Smith at Tunbridge Wells, on Jul 12, in his 70th year. His brother James, who shared with him the authorship of the Rejected Addresses, died some years ago. Horace was also the author of Brambletye House & some other novels.

Maj Jas M Scantland, of Tenn, died at the Red Sulphur Springs, Tenn, on Jul 22. He was a volunteer in the Mexican war, & fought at Monterey & Cerro Gordo. At the latter place he received a severe wound in the head, to which his death is ascribed.

Rev Worthington Smith, D D has been inaugurated Pres of the Univ of Vt.

On Tue last, the 10 year old daughter of Dr Johnson of this city, was struck by the noon Providence train, near the Tremont road crossing & her skull so badly fractured that she is not expected to survive. She stepped out of the way of the Stoughton train, in front of the Providence train. –Boston Traveller

Mrs Organ, residing at 51 Eliz St, N Y, being seized with cramps, her husband procured three cents worth each of camphor & laudanum, which she took 4 doses of at different times. She became more stupid & lost her senses, & died during the evening.

Marriage of Lola Montez, an extraordinary lady, whose connexion with the late events in Bavaria will be in the recollection of our readers. Lola Montez was married at London, Jul 19, to Geo Trafford Heald, of the 2nd life guards. The ceremony took place first at the French Catholic chapel, & subsequently at St George's church, Hanover square. Mr Heald is a very young man, stated to have about L14,000 per annum. English paper

Nathan F Dixon has received the unanimous nomination of a Whig Convention to represent the western district of R I in the next Congress. The Providence Journal confidently predicts his election by the people.

Another old citizen gone: Mr Sylvester Labadie, a native of St Louis, died at his residence there on Jul 25, after an illness of some duration. He was in his 71st year, & was the last, we believe, of the old inhabitants of St Louis. He never failed his duties as a citizen, husband, or friend. His wife yet survives him. -Republican

Train accident on Thu last near Princeton, N J, killed Wm Conover, a carpenter in the employ of the company; & a German passenger, whose name is unknown. Capt Shippen, the agent of the company, was seriously injured. Others injured: Jas Hollingsworth & his wife Sarah Ann, Matthias North, Eliza Bryan, Chas Maslbury, Wm Milkburne, Martin Merrill or Merrett, Mrs Mary Lindsay, Eliza Hand, Barbara House & child, Mary Ann Garrison, of Phil, Thos Glassup, Jos Galssup, of Frankford, Pa, Simon Griswold, of N Y, Patrick McPorril, of Wmsburg, L I, W R Waters, of Pottsville, Md.

Dr Chas H Mathews, who was recently elected Maj Gen of the division of Pa Militia, of Bucks, Montg, & Delaware Counties, died in Doylestown on Wed last.

Orphans Court of Wash Co, D C. Letters of administration on the personal estate of Wm Allen, late of Wash Co, deceased. –Letitia Allen, admx

I certify that John B McFarland, of Wash City, brought before me as an estray trespassing upon his enclosures, a small dark brindle Cow. –Jas Crandlel, J P
The owner is to prove property, pay charges, & take her away.
-John B McFarland, East of the Marine Garrison, Navy Yard

$5 reward for a strayed black Cow: reward will be given if brought to my residence on Mass ave, between 7th & 8th sts -Thos C Magruder

Ladies with letters in the Post Ofc, Wash, Aug 1, 1849:

Anderson, Mrs Chas
Adams, Miss Char
Actios, Mrs F A
Abbott, Miss M M
Bryan, Mrs Ann F
Blackwell, Miss A
Brown, Miss Ann
Brady, Miss Anna
Blackburn, Mrs A
Boyd, Miss Ann
Bailey, Miss Ann
Beard, Miss Ann C
Baker, Miss Car C
Blanche, Miss Curly
Brown, Miss Cath
Batemen, MissE A
Bowling, Miss E K
Boerum, Mrs Eliz
Braden, Miss Eliz
Berry, Miss Hester
Burrows, Mrs J S
Butler, Miss
Blackston, Miss M-2
Braxton, Miss Nancy
Burgess, Theresa
Brown, Mrs Ellen J
Bronough, Miss M J
Cramer, Mrs Eliza
Cook, Miss E C
Chevis, Mrs E W F
Campbell, Miss L-2
Callahan, Mary C
Clary, Mrs Nancy
Cain, Miss R C
Cooper, Mrs Susan
Disher, Catharine-2

Doudin, Mrs Elen'ra
Dalton, Mrs E A
Deavon, MissHar
Dick, Miss Harriet
Dyer, Ellen N
Dyson, Mrs Rosanna
Ennis, Mrs Eliza
Eyre, Miss Sarah
Fuller, Miss Eliz
Fisher, Mrs Harriet
Ford, Miss Lucinda
Finly, Mary Ann
Frank, Mary
Grigsby, Mrs E
Grimes, Mrs
Gabler, Mrs Marg
Gordon, Miss Mary
Greer, Mrs Rachael
Gunn, Rosanna
Gordon, Mrs Sarah-2
Hanfler, Mrs Ann M
Hunter, Mrs L A A
Hall, Miss Lavinia
Hough, Mrs L L
Hoban, Miss Mary
Hyde, Mrs Eliza
Jones, Miss Harriet
Johnson, Mrs L
Johnson, Miss Marg
Johnson, Miss Maria
Johnstone, Mrs R M
Kramer, Miss Em R
Kansler, Theresa
Lucas, Mrs Ann M
Lincoln, Miss M
Lee, Mrs Marg

Mason, Miss Bettie
Marshall, Miss E
Morris, Mrs Red'd
Mount, Miss S F
Mason, Miss Sophia
Nailor, Miss Saph'ia
Prentiss, Miss E
Peters, Mrs Esther
Pane, Hannah
Parker, Mrs Luc'da
Parker, Mrs M E
Purle, Miss Martha
Powers, Mrs M E
Payne, Miss Anna
Penny, Miss Mary
Pumphrey, Miss R
Queen, Miss Char
Roberts, Mrs Ang'e
Rhorch, Miss Eliz
Rodier, Mrs H A
Rediks, Mrs Jas
Rice, Mrs Maria
Ross, Mrs Mary
Riordan, Mrs M
Russell, Miss S A
Reiner, Miss T

Sanders, Mrs Nancy
Suter, Miss Ann M
Simms, Mrs D-2
Smith, Eliza Jane
Steward, Miss E
Silvers, Mrs E H
Thomas, Mrs E J A
Tucker, Miss E J
Taylor, Eliz
Townley, Mrs M
Taylor, Mrs Marg
Werner, Mrs A V
Williams, Mrs Ann
Walters, Miss A
Ward, Miss Cath
Wiesler, Miss Eliz
Williamson, Mrs M
Wellford, Miss M P
Williams, Mrs S
Walker, Mrs P-2
Ward, Susannah E
Whitcomb, Mrs S L
Ward, Miss Barbara
Weeks, Miss Mary of Jos
Woodward, Miss M L
Young, Mrs Eliza

The following letters, not being prepaid, remain in this ofc:
F G Keim, Rotterdam, Germany
Conradt, Niebergall, in Salzungen, Heozockthum, Meinengen, in Deushlant.
Edw Stryhos, Boulevard Poissonnier, Paris, France
J O Wadman & Co, Havana, Cuba
Thos Lingford, for Wm Malan or Catharine Bennett, Upper Canada West
S G Archibald, St John's, Newfoundland
Mrs Eliz Hickman, Toronto, Canada
-Wm A Bradley, P M

Died: on Aug 1, at the residence of Dr J T Johnson, near Fred'k, Md, Jas Larned, chief clerk of the ofc of the First Comptroller of the Treasury. The widespread hospitality of Mr Larned will make this announcement one of sad interest to many of the readers of the Nat'l Intell in every section of our country. To the citizens of Wash, beloved as he was for his social virtues, his decease will be felt as a common loss.

Died: on Tue, in Wash City, John Bonthron, youngest son of Wm J & Mary Ann Sangfitt, aged 1 year & 8 months.

Died: on Jun 29 last, of typhus fever, Jas Edmund Eckloff, eldest son of Edw C & Martha Eckloff, aged 4 years.

Died: on Jul 31, at the country residence of the Hon Hugh Maxwell, after a short illness, Frank Baretto Woodhull, son of Ellen F & Lt Maxwell Woodhull, U S Navy, aged 9 months.

TUE AUG 7, 1849
Appointments by the Pres:
Collectors of Customs:
Robt G Rankin, Wilmington, N C, vice Wm C Bettincourt, removed.
R H J Blount, Washington, N C, vice Sylvester Brown, declined.
Henry W Kinsman, Newburyport, Mass, vice Wm Nichols, removed.
D C Hutchinson, Natchez, Miss, vice John D Elliott, removed.
Ephraim Buck, Bridgetown, N J, vice Jas M Newell, removed.
John H Dilworth, St Mary's, Ga, vice H E W Clarke, removed.
Fred'k S Thomas, Newark, N J, vice Wm W Baldwin, deceased.
Naval Ofcr:
Thos J Clark, Newburyport, Mass, vice Enoch Fowler, removed.
Surveyors:
John Wiler, Savannah, Ga, vice Robt W Tooler, removed.
E T Carpenter, Greenport, N Y, vice Walter Havens, removed.
Isaac H Parker, Norfolk, Va, vice Dennis Dowley, removed.

Hon Joshua Mathiot, formerly a Rep in Congress from the State of Ohio, died of cholera at his residence in Newark, on Monday of last week.

Col Jacob Cramer, who commanded a regt at the battle of Bladensburg, died at Fred'k a few days ago, in his 82nd year.

The Western Texian announces that Capt G K Lewis has succeeded in obtaining from the Govn'r an order to raise a company of rangers for 3 months, to be stationed on the lower Rio Grande. They are to rendezvous at Brownsville, New Orleans Bee

Taken up, Jul 21, one dark bay mare, with a rope round her neck. Owner will prove property, pay charges, & take her away. –Richd Eaton

Proposals for meat, until Aug 17, for furnishing & delivering at the Wash Asylum. –C A Davis, Theodore Wheeler, Geo H Fulmer, Com'rs Wash Asylum

Commitment for murder was made to the county jail on last Fri: Lewis Carley, the prisoner, a seaman on board the U S steamer **Alleghany**, now lying off our Navy Yard, on the passage of that vessel from Rio Janieiro to the Mediterranean, on Dec 2, 1848, was discovered to be drunk by the ofcr of the deck, & was placed in the ship's brig for punishment, under the charge of Wm Brown, a Marine guard. He insisted upon returning to the deck: the guard refused: Carley stabbed & killed him. Carley was seized & brought to the U S for trial. He was conveyed from the steamer to the jail by Capt Goddard & Police ofcr Burr. The prisoner is about 33 years of age, & states the he is a native of Batavia, N Y. –Republic, Aug 6

City Ordinances-Wash. 1-Act for the relief of Thos Fitnam: that the Intendant of the Asylum be required to surrender to Thos Fitnam 9 hogs claimed & owned by him, the same having been taken from his hog-pen, as testified to in his petition, without any cost to said Fitnam. 2-Resolution to allow pay to Josias Adams, police ofcr of the 6th Ward, the sum of $50 per year for his services as such, to take effect from Jul last, & to be paid as other police ofcrs are now paid.

Died: on Aug 3, in Gtwn, of typhus fever, John H Oyster, in his 25th year, son of the late Geo Oyster.

Died: on Aug 6, in Wash City, after a lingering illness of 2 months, Edw Winfield, only son of C H & M E Burgess, aged 12 months & 18 days.

Died: on Jul 1, at Marmion, King Geo Co, Va, Saml D Lewis, in his 13th year; & at Claymont, Westmoreland Co, Va, on Jul 29, Jane B Lewis, in her 39th year, the son & wife of Geo W Lewis of the latter place.

Died: on Aug 1, at Phil, at the advanced age of 76 years, Col Wm Pechin, formerly of Balt.

Died: on Aug 4, at Riversdale, Jule Van Havre, youngest son of Chas B & Charlotte A Calvert, aged 9 months.

In Chancery: Balt & Ohio Railroad Co vs Saml Stettinius & Henry T Pairo. The bill states that Stettinius became indebted to cmplnts before 1847; that he was sued, & at Oct term, 1848, confessed judgment by atty for the amount claimed, on the terms that, if he should pay cmplnts $800 within 15 days from Oct 9, 1848, & $700 within one year from said date, with interest, said judgment should be released, otherwise it should remain in full force; that he paid only $600; that he has gone to Calif, or parts unknown, & a writ of fieri facias issued on said judgment has been returned nulla bona. Stettinius was seized of a lot at the n e corner of lot 18 in square 490, on La ave, with a 4 story brick house; that sundry persons have filed claims against said house under the lien law, to wit: Campbell & Coyle for $62.81; Harkness & Purdy for $94; John Purdy for $518.54; Wm Easby for $211.75; Wm Thompson for $878.76; Jas S & A S Harvey & Wm Lloyd for $130.85. It further shows that Stettinius & wife, by indenture dated Mar 20, 1845, & recorded in Liber W B 115, folios 231, of the land Records of Wash Co, D C, conveyed said lot to Henry T Pairo in trust, to secure $1,900 due from said Stettinius to Thos W Pairo; that by indenture dated Mar 15, 1847, recorded in Liber W B 18, folios 138, conveyed the same premises to said Pairo, to secure $700 due from Stettinius to Chas W Pairo; that, by indenture dated Apr 27, 1847, recorded in Liber W B 132, folios 352, which recited that Mary Ann, wife of said Stettinius, had made & might make advances out of her separate estate & earnings on account of the debts of her husband, the said Stettinius & H T Pairo conveyed said premises, subject to the above mentioned deeds, to Jas M McKnight, to reimburse said Mary Ann for said advances, said money so due & to become due to her to be her separate estate, free from the control & debts of her husband. It states that Eliza Keyworth obtained judgment against Stettinius at Oct Term, 1848, for $204, with interest from Jan 2, 1847, & costs: Wm Easby recovered a

judgment against him at Mar term, 1848, for $180, with interest from Sep 17, 1846, & costs; Wm M Perry recovered a judgment at Oct term, 1847, for $86.13, with interest from Jul 23, 1848, & costs; & Edw Hall recovered a judgment at the same term for $201, with interest from Sep 23, 1846, & costs. It charges that Mary Ann Stettinius had no separate estate, that her earnings were the means of her husband, & said last conveyance was without consideration & void as against creditors, or at least was only operative by way of mortgage, leaving an equity of redemption subject to their claims. It shows that, the legal estate being out of Stettinius, cmplnts cannot levy on the premises, but their judgment is a lien in equity, entitling them to redeem prior incumbrances, or have the property sold to pay off all liens, & their claim, according to their priorities; & it asks a sale for that purpose. It further states that Stettinius & H T Pairo reside out of D C. They are warned to appear in Court, in person or by solicitor, on or before Dec 10 next, to show cause why a decree should not pass as prayed.
–Jas Dunlop -John A Smith, clerk

In Chancery. The U S vs David Ott's heirs, at al. The bill states that D Ott was surety in the official bond of Jno Hall, a paymaster in the army; that D Ott died in 1820, leaving a large real & personal estate, after devising the same to Catherine Ott, his mother; Juliana C & Maria Ott, his sister; Eliza Mauro his sister, & wife of Philip Mauro; Catherine Riley, his sister, & the wife of Wm Riley, & Jacob & Chas B Ott, his brothers; that Catherine & Juliana C Ott have since died, & their interests in said estate have passed to the surviving children of D Ott, & to Jno W Ott, surviving child of Jno Ott, David's brother. It further states that administration of D Ott's personal estate was granted to Phineas Bradley & Andrew Way; that Jno Hall having been a defaulter to the U S in more than $20,000 in D Ott's lifetime, the bond aforesaid was put in suit against D Ott's administrators, & at Mar term, 1841, of the Circuit Court of D C, the U S had judgment for $20,000, the penalty of the bond. It further states that Phineas Bradley survived Way, & died intestate; that letters of administration on his personal estate, letters of administration de bonis non on D Ott's estate, were granted to Wm A Bradley, of Wash, who has received a large amount of D Ott's personal estate, but not enough to discharge the judgment above mentioned. I asks for an account of D Ott's personal estate & its application to the above judgment, & pray a sale of his remaining real estate, consisting of part of lot 2 in square 379, on Pa ave. It further states that all the dfndnts, except Wm A Bradley, are non-residents. Absent dfndnts are warned to appear in person or by solicitor, on or before Dec 10 next. –Jas Dunlop
Test: Jno A Smith, Clerk

WED AUG 8, 1849
Blacksmith wanted, one accustomed to Fancy Hand Railing & other house work generally. Fair wages for a good hand, & regular employment. Apply on C st, between 10th & 11th sts, Wash. –C Buckingham

A Favier gives notice that an injunction has been granted by the Circuit Court of Wash Co, D C, upon his bill of cmplnt against Julius Rother, commanding Rother, his agents & servants, from collecting & using the mineral water bottles bearing the name of A Favier, & belonging to him.

French & English Seminary for ladies, 9th & E sts, under direction of Mrs D H Burr, will re-open on Sep 17. The Principal is a native of France & has French assistants; it is the language of the family, thus affording Boarders the opportunity of hearing & conversing in it at all times.

Orphans Court of Wash Co, D C. Letters of administration on the personal estate of Thos J Beall, late of the U S Army, deceased. –Lloyd J Beall, adm

The Mayor of Fred'k, Md, M E Bartgis, died on Sun at his residence in that city. He was by profession a printer, & edited & published in Fred'k for many years.

Batesville [Ark] Eagle states that Mr Wm Berry, of Lawrence Co, who killed Jas Marshall in Apr, was shot on Jul 5, while at his plough. He was killed instantly. The murderer was not discovered.

Phil Bulletin: Chas Hanson & Levi Smith, both colored, fought a duel with knives on Fri, in which Hanson received a mortal wound in the lungs. Smith received 7 wounds, but none dangerous.

Danville [Va] Register: in Pittsylvania Co a few days ago, the wife & 2 sons of Mr Adams were sick of chills & fevers. The attending physician sent to Lynchburg for a supply of quinine, but failed to receive it. He asked the wife of a deceased physician, if there was quinine in the ofc that he might use. He brought a small vial labelled quinine. It proved to be something fatal & his 3 patients all died. Ir is supposed to have been arsenic or morphia.

Mr Green, an Aeronaut, who ascended in Cardiff, Wales, was found dead on the Flathouse Sands. His balloon was seen floating at sea.

Mrd: on Aug 6, by Rev Mr Hodges, Mr Benedict Havener to Miss Eliz Ann Anderson, both of D C.

Mrd: on Jul 11, in Balt, by Rev Mr Wolfe, Mr Chas W Patterson to Miss Mary R Dorsey, both of Wash City.

Died: on Aug 5, in the city of Phil, Mrs Catharine Coyle, relict of the late Capt John Coyle. Her funeral is this afternoon, at 4 o'clock, from the residence of her daughter, Mrs Whitwell, on 4½ st.

THU AUG 9, 1849
Mrs Mercer's School for Young Ladies, at Belmont, Loudoun Co, Va: successful for more than 20 years. Will re-open on the first Mon in Sep.

Rockhill Academy, Ellicott's Mills, Howard District, Md. –Rev John P Carter, Principal References in Md: Hon D W Naill, Carroll Co; W W Handy, Princess Ann; Dr J G Morris & Dr Wm T Plumer, Balt. In Wash, D C: Rev Jas Laurie & S A Elliot. In Alexandria, Va: Rev E Harrison & Wm Gregory.

High School for Boys in the Southwest. Ravenscroft Seminary, Columbia, Tenn. Under the control of the Bishop & Convention of the Prot Episcopal Church.
Rt Rev Jas H Oley, D D, Visiter
Rev J T Wheat, D D, Pres
Donald McLeod, A M, Univ of Glasgow, Prof of English Lit
M S Royce, Prof of Ancient Languages & Math

Cmte of Convention:
Rev J T Wheat, D C
Rev E Cressey
Lucius J Polk, Hamilton Pl
Andrew J Polk, Ashwood

Death of a Pioneer. The Cincinnati Chronicle announces the death, in Gallatin, Ky, of Capt Jacob White, one of the very earliest settlers of the Miami Valley, in his 93rd year. While a boy he left N J, with his father's family, for the Redstone settlement, on the western frontier of Pa, & was at that place when the Declaration of Independence was adopted & publshed. He commenced the village of Columbia in the fall of 1788, which was the first settlement made within the limits of Judge Symmes' purchase. He built a blockhouse, to which he removed his family. It was attacked by a strong party of Indians, who were repulsed & compelled to retreat.

The Louisville Courier of the 14th contains the notice of death of Danl Bradford, long connected with the Ky press: Danl Bradford, of Lexington, Ky, expired of cholera several days ago in that city. He was the son of John Bradford, the pioneer of printing in the West. The elder Bradford established the Ky Gaz in Lexington, when a large part of Ky was a wilderness. Upon the retirement of John Bradford from the editorship of the paper, Danl Bradford assumed it. Mr Bradford was a Magistrate of Fayette Co for many years, & was an upright & faithful citizen. [Aug 11th newspaper: the son of Danl Bradford, who resides in this city, said that the statement is incorrect. Mr Bradford suffered an attack of cholera, but it did not prove fatal.]

Family Gathering: the descendants of Richd Haven, of Lynn, Mass, were to have a great family party, at Farmingham, on Jul 30. Five years ago the family gathering had 1,500 present, & it was then voted to have another in 5 years. All the Havens, & all connected with them by marriage, or who expect to be so connected, were invited.

Among the passengers in the ship **St Denis**, from Havre, was Pearce Cranch, of N Y C, who has been 3 years in Italy improving himself as an artist.

Victim of the prevailing epidemic last week was the Press in N Y C. Mr W Bloxham, had been a general writer for 9 years, the post of Editor of the Balt Sun. -Express

Hon Stephen Longfellow died at his residence in Portland, Maine, on Aug 2, at age 73 years. He was a distinguished citizen of New England; a leader of the old Federal school in Mass before the separation of Maine from that State; a lawyer, celebrated for his nice & subtle discriminations; a Christian devout in his feelings. Mr Longfellow was the father of Prof Longfellow, of Harvard Univ, & of the Rev Mr Longfellow, of the Unitarian Church at Fall river, Mass. –N Y Tribune

The two ladies Stillman, who were charged with arson in New Orleans, were commited for trial on Aug 25.

St Andrews [N B] Standard: obit-died, on Jul 21, at St Stephen's, Mrs Eliz Dodd, aged 111 years. She was born on board a British ship of the line in the Bay of Biscay, cradled on the broad Atlantic, her father killed fighting the battles of Geo I, she was cast an orphan on the shores of N Y. Thence carried to St Augustine, her youth passed in the South. Here she married & settled on the banks of the Alabama. On the outbreak of the war between France, Spain, & England, she & other settlers were made prisoners & taken to New Orleans. After 2 years she was transferred to the Spaniards & taken to the Castle of Vera Cruz, where she remained until its capture by the British in 1761. She was then relieved & taken to N Y. During the first American war she followed her husband through the principal campaigns, & was at the hardest fought battles-at Monmouth, White Plains, & Yorktown. At the close of the American war she came with the Loyalists to this province, in 1784.

Albany Argus: death of a brother & sister, at Trenton Falls, near Utica, N Y, recorded under the telegraph head the day before yesterday. Eliza Bryan, 19, & Edwin Bryan, 22, children of Mr Bryan, of Utica, arrived at the Falls yesterday. They both were drowned this morning above the upper fall. Late last night their bodies were recovered. It appeared that they had wandered further up the stream than is usual for visitors.

Jos Bradwell, a native of Yorkshire, Eng, who had come over in the ship **Ivanhoe**, brought with him L500 worth of railroad iron, died of the cholera a few days ago in the hospital. His papers confirm his identity. He had said he had friends near Kingston & Toronto, Canada, one by the name of Jonathan, & the other Jos Bradwell, a nephew. They have been written to, but no answer is received. His wardrobe is abundant, indicating easy pecuniary circumstances. –Alb Jour

By order of distrain from Small & Pumphrey, against the goods & chattels of Brown & Nichols, I have this day distrained on the following goods to satisfy rent due & in arrears: clothing, library, guitar, sword, paint, fencing swords, foils, chains, & lot of wardrobe: sale on Aug 16 at the Adelphi Theatre. –Wm Cox, Bailiff

Died: on Wed, in Wash City, Mr Lewis Ratcliff, in his 47th year, leaving a wife & 7 children to mourn the loss of a devoted husband & affectionate father. His funeral is this afternoon, at 4 o'clock.

Died: on Aug 3, in Wash City, Mr Chas Schley, in his 50th year.

Cincinnati, Aug 7. The Cincinnati House was destroyed by fire this morning, & Mr Farley, of this city, perished in the flames, & his wife was most severely injured that no hopes are entertained of her recovery.

FRI AUG 10, 1849
Lumber & Coal: John Purdy, 1st st. [Ad]

Groceries, Old Stand, opposite Centre Market, formerly occupied by G & T Parker. –Jno B Kibbey

Bargains on Dry Goods: W M Shuster & Co, Pa ave & 7th sts.

Wash Corp: 1-Ptn of Wm Pettibone, praying remission of a fine: referred to the Cmte of Claims. 2-Ptn of Leonard Storm & others, for graveling 7th st, from N Y ave to L st: referred to the Cmte on Improvements. 3-Ptn of Luke Richardson, praying remission of a fine: referred to the Cmte of Claims; 4-Ptn of Edw H Edelen, praying remission of a fine: referred to the Cmte of Claims. 5-Ptn of Jas A Saunders & others, respecting a nuisance in Judiciary square: referred to the Cmte on Health. 6-Cmte of Claims: asked to be discharged from the further consideration of the ptn of R W Latham: to lie on the table. 7-Cmte of Claims: Act for the relief of Robt Mills; & act for the relief of Mary Ann Baltzer: recommended that they be rejected: bills were rejected. 8-Cmte of Claims: asked to be discharged from the further consideration of ptns of T J Johnson & Wm MacAboy: cmte was discharged accordingly. 9-Cmte of Claims: bill for the relief of Thos Lewis: passed.

Official: Appointments by the Pres: Collectors:
Saml J Douglas, Key West, Fla, vice S R Mallory, removed.
Leavitt Thaxter, Edgartown, Mass, vice Jos T Pease, removed.
Danl B St John, Oregon, vice John Adair, removed.
Surveyors:
Thos Foss, Marblehead, Mass, vice Nicholas Tucker, removed.
John Q Kellogg, Troy, N Y, vice Martin Russell, removed.
Appraisers:
Rudolph Groning, New Orleans, vice Ernest Morphy, resigned.
M M Beale, Assist Treasurer at New Orleans, vice J R MacMurdo, resigned.

By the Sec of the Interior: Jos J Coombs, of Ohio, to be U S Atty for the district of Oregon, vice Isaac W Bromley, removed.
Chas M Gibbs, of Tenn, to be U S Atty for the western district of Tenn, vice Henry W McCorry, removed.
David McCallum, of Tenn, to be U S Marshal for the eastern district of Tenn, vice Arthur R Crozier, removed.
Robt Smith, of Missouri, to be Receiver of Public Moneys at Springfield, Mo, from & after Aug 25, vice Nicholas R Smith, removed.
John Laplace, of La, to be Receiver of Public Moneys at Natchitoches, La, from & after Aug 25, vice Jas M B Tucker, removed.
Thos Allen, of Missouri, to be Receiver of Public Moneys at Clinton, Mo, from & after Aug 25, vice Danl Ashby, removed.
Abraham Van Vorhes, of Ohio, to be Register of the Land Ofc at Stillwater, Minnesota Territory, from & after Aug 25, vice Isaac Leiller, who declines the ofc.

Wash Corp: 1-Surveyor's ofc, Aug 4, 1849: Wash. In relation to the Wash City Canal: Mr Geo W Harkness, one of the contractors hopes to prosecute the work regarding the leakage through the walls of the canal. –C B Cluskey, Engineer, Surveyor of Wash City. 2-Cmte of Claims: asking to be discharged from the further consideration of ptns of C H Payne, of Sidney Talbot, of Antoine Lechman, of Wm Flenner, & of Geo Gibson: agreed to. 3-Cmte of Claims: act for the relief of Thos Lewis; relief of Robt Earle; & relief of Edw Hammersly: laid on the table. 4-Cmte on Improvements: ptn of J A Deeble & others, for relaying the gutter on I st, from 9th to 10th: read twice. Board adjourned.

Fine sugar-cured hams: Geo & Thos Parker & Co, opposite Brown's Hotel. [Ad]

Obit-died: on Jul 11 last, at Louisville, Ky, Frisby Freeland Chew, a resident of Yazoo Co, Miss. Accompanied by Mrs Chew, his wife, & 5 little children, he reached Louisville on his way to the Washington, where he had been called to fill a situation under the Gov't. Fate decreed it otherwise; &, in the bright prospect of soon meeting his relatives & friends in Md & D C, his progress was arrested by the hand of death. He fell a victim to cholera. He was a most devoted husband, father, master, & friend. He was about 40 years of age, highly talented, having the best collegiate education. –Nottingham [Aug 21st newspaper: Obit from the Village Recorder, at Canton, Miss. Died, at Louisville, Ky, on Jul 11, Frisby Freeland Chew, He was in his 42nd year, a native of this state; the eldest son of Wm L Chew of this county. He was on his way to Md with his family.]

Died: on Aug 9, in Wash City, Mrs Eliza W, consort of Dr R H Speake, in her 38th year. Her funeral is this afternoon at 4 o'clock, from the residence of Mrs King, F & 11th sts.

Died: on Aug 6, in Wash City, after an illness of 8 months, Miss Harriet Lavinia, daughter of the late Alex'r Scott, of Md.

Died: on Wed, in Wash City, of cholera infantum, Edward Borrows, youngest son of Thos B & Laura E Brown, aged 7 months & 14 days.

Died: on Aug 9, in Wash City, John, infant son of John & Anne Williams, aged 3 months. His funeral is this afternoon, at 4 o'clock, from the residence of his mother on Pa ave, between 4½ & 6th sts.

25 first rate stone cutters wanted: $2.25 per day, from Aug 13 up to Nov 30. None need apply but sober & industrious men. –Gilbert Cameron

Death of a Chickasaw Chief. Col Benj Love, one of the treaty com'rs of the Chickasaw nation is dead. He was waylaid several miles from his house & shot, it is supposed, by a party of Buloxies, a tribe of Indians, who, no doubt, a century since, formed a part of the Choctaw nation; but having separated & wandered through Texas, has lost many traces of their origin; yet, when the 2 people again met in the West, tradition, & affinity of language proved their origin, & they have been tolerated on the skirts of the Choctaw nation ever since, though they are in a rude & barbarous state, far below the people of their original stock. -Ark Intell, Jul 2

Died: on Aug 3, at Lexington, Ky, of the prevailing epidemic, after a short illness, the Hon Aaron K Woolley, in his 50th year. He was formerly Judge of the Circuit Court; State Senator for many years from the Fayette district; at the time of his decease, was Law Prof in Transylvania Univ, & one of the candidates for the Convention in his district. His bereaved widow & fatherless children mourn the decease of the best of husbands & kindest of parents.

Lewis Carley, committed to our county jail on the charge of murder, has been visited by Rev Mr Butler & Rev Mr Webster, who administered to him the consolations of religion.

Wanted to rent, a little dwlg house, with stable & large kitchen garden, on High st, Gtwn, D C, or its neighborhood. Apply to C A W, care of Mr A Gross, Wash, D C, Pa ave, near 14th st.

SAT AUG 11, 1849
By private letter from Namur, we learn of the death of Madame Beaulieu, wife of the Minister of Belgium, who died in that city some months ago. Madame Beaulieu left Wash last autumn, suffering under a painful malady.

Pouchkeepsie Journal gives the particulars of the death of John Vashaw, Overseer on the railroad at that place. He was in a quarrel with 3 discharged laborers, who struck him, while he was attempting to force them from the work, with a pickaxe handle & a crowbar. One has been arrested.

A daughter of Mrs Stanyon, living at Kingston, N H, lost her life last Tue by the explosion of a camphine lamp. Mrs Stanyon was filling the lamp at the time & badly burnt & not expected to live.

Camp Buffalo, at *Fort Laramie*, Jun 26, 1849. On Jun 21 Dr Gilbert McBeth, died of cholera, after a short sickness of 12 hours. On Jun 23, Mr A Hayden & H O Hayes were taken sick with cholera. Mr Hayden & Mr Hayes died on Jun 24. Col John J Fay took sick & died yesterday.

Died: on Aug 9, in Gtwn, Octavia O Woodward, daughter of Thos Woodward. Her funeral is this Sat, at 9 o'clock, from her father's residence, near the Methodist Burial Ground, in Gtwn.

Died: on Wed last, Garret Wynkoop Bishop, aged 9 months & 4 days, son of Henry & Maria Louisa Bishop, of Wash City.

In the harbor of Kingston, Canada, on Aug 3, the Wolf Island steam-ferry boat was struck by a sail boat. Messrs Alex'r McLeod & Walter MacNee, of the firm of J & W MacNee, who were in the boat at the time, were drowned.

To Contractors: proposals will be received by C Crozer, Engineer Blue Ridge Railroad, at his ofc in Brooksville, Albemarle Co, Va, until Oct 1, for the construction of the tunnel through the Blue Ridge.

Trustee's sale: by deed of trust dated Dec 14, 1848: sale on Sep 3, of valuable real estate in Wash City: 2 undivided sixth-parts in lot 16 in square 141 fronting on H st, that piece or parcel of ground distinguished on Saml Davidson's subdivision of his real estate, of lot 10 in square 166; & lot 16 in square 42. –D Ratcliff, Trustee

Zachary Taylor, Pres of the U S of A, recognizes G O Gorter who has been appointed Cousul of Belgium, for the port of Balt, Md. Aug 9, 1849

By writ of fiera, issued by J L Smith, a justice of the peace for Wash Co, to me directed, I shall expose to public sale, on Aug 14: chairs, washstand & drawer, cot, milk-cans, spades, & other articles, at the Centre Market, in Wash City; & on the same day, on *Greenleaf Point*, one red buffalo cow, seized & taken as the property of Zebulon Brundege, & will be sold to satisfy a judgment in favor of Richd Williamson -John Magar, Constable

In Montg Co Court, [Md] sitting as a Court of Equity, Jul Term, 1849. Jas B Higgins vs Jos Loyd, Ruth Loyd, Henry West & others. The bill in this case charges that Jas B Higgins, late of said county, deceased, was in his lifetime seized & possessed of real estate, in said county; &, being thereof so seized & possessed, some time in 1848 departed this life, leaving a last will & testament, devising & leaving thereby the real estate of which he died so seized & possessed to Ruth Loyd, who intermarried with Jos Loyd, Eliza West, who intermarried with Henry West, Susana Knowles, who intermarried with Geo Knowles, Mary E Higgins, John Higgins, Horatio Higgins, Chas A C Higgins, Darius M Higgins, Jas P McElfresh, John W McElfresh, John H Higgins, & Chas A C Higgins, trustees for the benefit of Mgt R Higgins, & her children. Benj F Higgins, late of Fred'k Co, Md, who has died since the original bill in this cause was filed, & his widow Eliz Higgins, & his children, viz: Mary, Eliz, Franklin, & Chas Higgins, his heirs at law, have been made parties by an amended bill, & Jas W Higgins, [the cmplnt in this bill,] all of whom reside in Montg Co aforesaid, except Jos Loyd, Ruth Loyd, Jas P McElfresh, & John W McElfresh, who do not reside in Md-the said Jas P & John W McElfresh, having appeared, by solicitor, & answered the bill in this cause. The object of this bill is to obtain a decree for a partition of the aforesaid real estate among the parties, under the direction of this Court. Jos Loyd & Ruth Loyd his wife are to appear in this Court on or before the 2nd Mon in Nov next. –T H Wilkinson -S T Stonestreet, Clerk

Christopher Grammer, Atty & Counsellor at Law, has removed to Pa ave, between 4½ & 6th sts, & will practice in the Courts of the District.

Household & kitchen furniture at auction on Aug 16, at the residence of Mr Wm Slade, 11th & I sts. –Green & Tastet, auctioneer

MON AUG 13, 1849
Ky elections: Linn Boyd, Dem, re-elected over John M Johnson, Whig.
Jas L Johnson, Whig, elected over Francis Peyton, Independent Whig. [Last represented by Beverly L Clark, Dem.]
Chas S Morehead, Whig, re-elected over S F J Trabue, Native.
John C Mason, Dem, elected over John B Houston, Whig. [Last represented by Richd French, Dem.]
Richd H Stanton, Dem, elected over John P Gaines, Whig.

Stephen Meashaw, residing in Schroeppel, in this county, was arrested last week on a charge of murdering his wife, & on examination before Mr Justice Merry, was fully committed to the jail in this city. He was drinking at the time he beat & killed her.
—Oswego Times

Harford [Md] Gaz of Fri says that Mr John R Magness, residing near this town, has lost 5 of his children within 2 weeks of dysentery; & Mr Jehu Hare has lost 4 by the same disease in the same space of time.

A man broke into the Convent of the <u>Sisters of Mercy</u>, corner of Prince & Houston sts, N Y, on Jul 21, & assaulted Mary Monica, one of the sisterhood, & has been sentenced to 10 years' service at hard labor in the State Prison.

The Corner Stone of the new <u>Catholic Church</u>, about to be erected near ***Carroll Cottage***, in Montg Co, Md, was laid last Thu, with imposing ceremonies, by Archbishop Eccleston. Rev John P Donelan, of Balt, preached an eloquent sermon.

Died: on Aug 12, after a long & painful illness, Mary Ann Bronson, the only child of Simeon D Bronson, aged 5 years & 6 months. Her funeral is at the residence of Mrs Shinner, her grandmother, 13½ st, this evening at 5 p m.

TUE AUG 14, 1849
In Chancery, at a Circuit Superior Court of Law & Chancery of Fauquier Co, held on Oct 8, 1842. The Bank of the U S & Jos Cowperthwaite, plntfs, against John B Steenbergen, Alex'r S Tidball, Robt Y Conrad, Jas Marshall, jr, Rhesa Allen, Saml Jones, jr, The Western Bank of Balt, Chas Moore, Saml Moore, & John Williams, dfndnts. Extract from decree. Court to take an account of all the individual debts due from John B Steenbergen on Jan 25, 1840, to his creditors, & for which they had no other security then the deed of trust of that date, as well the debts now expressly named in the deed of trust as those that are named, & report the same to the Court.
—Wm F Phillips, Clerk
+
Com'rs Notice: all persons interested in the decree, to meet on Sep 13, 1849, at my ofc, in Warrenton, Fauquier Co, Va, & I shall proceed to execute the same. —Jas V Brooke, Com'r, Warrenton

Mr Jas Adair, a Superintendent of the Balt & Ohio Railroad, was accidentally run over & killed by a train near Mariottsville on Fri last.

Mr Jas Bartgis, son of the late Mayor of Fred'k, Md, who died about a week since, has been elected Mayor of that city.

Died: on Aug 13, Sarah Constance, daughter of Duff & Lucretia M Green, in her 17th year. Her funeral is from the residence of her father, today, at 4 o'clock.

Died: on Aug 13, in Wash City, in his 11th year, Jas Wilson, son of Saml & Ellen A G Grubb. His funeral is this morning at 10 o'clock, from the residence of his father, on C st, between 12th & 13th sts.

Brookeville Academy will resume on the first Mon of Sept. –E J Hall, Principal, Brookville, Md.

$5 reward for return of a pocket book lost on Sat, on 9th st. –Wm Lewis, colored, residence 110 5th st, Gtwn.

WED AUG 15, 1849
Accident at Camden, N J, Sat, while workmen were plastering a new 3 storied brick house, in Stevens st, the whole tenement tumbled down. Levi Cook, colored, a laborer, was taken out dead; he leaves a large family. Richd Cheeseman, plasterer, seriously injured. Alex'r Griscom & John Lucas, plasterers, injured internally. The bldg was the property of T Newell. -Phil American

Distribution of Premiums: St Mary's Female Institution, near Bryantown, Chas Co, Md, Aug 1, 1849. Premiums awarded to:

Eliza F Dyer, of Wash
Annie Downey, Chas Co
Mary H Mitchell, Chas Co
Mary C Thompson, Chas Co
Mgt Queen, Chas Co
Mary Emily Bowling, PG Co, Md
Mary V Gardiner, Chas Co
Rosalie Boone, Chas Co
Anna F Gardiner, PG Co, Md
Henrietta M Dyer, Wash
Maria L Murray, Wash
Eleanor R Boarman, Chas Co
Mgt H Gardiner, PG Co, Md

Beatrice Gardiner, Chas Co
Emily Boarman, Chas Co
Eliz Bowling, Chas Co
Ellen Jameson, Chas Co
Mary V Hamersley, Chas Co
Marion Burch, Chas Co
Valinda Dent, Chas Co
Susan D Curry, Chas Co
Sarah Middleton, Chas Co
Susan E Kenny, Balt, Md
Martha Lawson, Chas Co
Alice Hamersley, Chas Co
Mary Sophia Du Bernard, Balt, Md

$200 reward for 2 bay horses stolen on Aug 1. –Jas Perrine, Dayton, Ohio

Strayed, or ran away, from the place where he was hired by his mother, Cloe Ann Butler, on Sat last, a boy 11 years old, yellow complexion. He was hired to Mr Edw Smith, in Wash. Information will be thankfully received of where he is.
–Cloe Ann Butler

The ship **Juniata**, of Balt, arrived at N Y on Fri, in charge of the first ofcr, Mr Seymour: from London, & had on board 294 steerage passengers. The captain, Washington Hands, of Balt, died during the voyage, of cholera, with 9 of the passengers.

Mrd: on Aug 14, by Rev L J Gilliss, Wm D Pratt, of New London, Conn, to Miss Rachel Landon, of Wash City.

Died: on Aug 13, Rev Ninian Bannatyne, jr pastor of F st Presbyterian Church, in his 34th year. His funeral is this day, at half past 4 o'clock. The services will be conducted in the church, & the interment will take place in the yard at the south end of it.

Died: yesterday, in Wash City, Wm Byrd Page, late of Fred'k Co, Va. His funeral is from his late residence, [Mrs Lanphier's, Pa ave,] today at 5 p m.

Died: on Aug 9, at Lexington, Ky, of typhoid fever, after an illness of 8 days, Saml D Woolley, in his 34th year, eldest son of Col A R Woolley, formerly of the U S Army.

Orphans Court of Wash Co, D C. Letters of administration on the personal estate of Wm Thompson, late of said county, deceased. –Jas Davis, adm

THU AUG 16, 1849
At the Tremont st crossing, Boston, on Sat, Jos Lewis, about 35, who resided at 7 Orange Lane, was run over by the train, & died in a short time after.

Petersburg Republican: Thu last, a young man named Winless, a machinist, belonging to the establishment of Mr U Wells, while attempting to open a large clasp knife, struck his elbow on some machinery, which caused the knife to fly out of his hand & inflict a severe wound in his thigh, of which he died the same evening. He was highly esteemed by all who knew him.

Farm for sale: on which I reside, adjoining the Beltsville depot: contains 100 acres of land, with a comfortable frame dwlg house & other out-houses. Also, a farm, within 1½ miles of Beltsville, containing about 188 acres. I will show the premises & make known the terms. –E G Emack

Thos G Woodward, one of the editors of the New Haven Daily Courier & Herald, died at New Haven on Sun, aged 61 years, after an illness of a week.

Household & kitchen furniture at auction on Aug 18, by order of the Orphans Court of Wash Co, D C, the effects of the late Wm Thompson. -E C & G F Dyer, aucts

Episcopal High School of Va, the Diocesan School near Alexandria, Rev E A Dalrymple, Rector, will commence on Sep 12. Address to the Rector, P O. Theological Seminary, Fairfax Co, Va.

Mrd: on Tue, in the Fourth Presbyterian Church, by Rev John C Smith, Mr Geo W McLane, of Cumberland, Md, to Miss Rosanna Boyd, of Wash City.

Mrd: on Aug 14, by Rev F S Evans, Mr Peter Hepburn to Miss Mary Ellen Young.

Mrd: on Aug 14, by Rev Littleton F Morgan, Luther L Martin, of Va, to Sarah C L, daughter of Thos C Donn, of Wash City.

Died: on Aug 14, after a few hours of severe illness, Mrs Martha Ann Gittings, consort of Benj E Gittings, [Intendent of the Wash Asylum,] in her 41st year. She was one of the best of companions & mothers, & much esteemed by all who knew her. Her funeral will take place this afternoon, at 5 o'clock, from the residence of her husband, near the Congressional burial ground. Carriages will be in attendance at the Wesley Chapel, at 4 o'clock, to convey any friends who may be disposed to attend.

Died: Aug 15, at his residence, near Wash City, Jas D Barry, aged 75 years. His funeral is today, at 3 o'clock, from St Peter's Church, Capitol Hill.

Died: on Jul 29, in Dorchester Co, Md, Julianna Carroll, consort of Ex-Govn'r Carroll of Md.

Died: on Aug 11, in Chas Co, Md, of paralysis, Thos McPherson, in his 65th year. He was a kind & affectionate father, a true & sincere friend. A large family has been suddenly called upon to mourn a father's loss.

FRI AUG 17, 1849
Unlike all the other towns of the country, **Washington City** is exempt from taxation for State & county purposes. A great part of the municipal expenses, which in other cities are paid by the inhabitants thereof, are in Washington defrayed by the General Government. Congress pays the expenses of the courts, prisons, judges, jurors, coroner, marshal, & city guard. Congress puts the city goverment to no expense.

Mrs White, an old lady who has resided in the neighborhood of the village of Rockville, Md, a great number of years, left, over 3 weeks ago, to visit her daughter, Mrs Wm Harris, who resides some 4 or 5 miles distant, & has not been heard of since. It is feared that she became lost in the woods, & perished.

Shocking affair at Bardstown. Robt Wickliffe, a young lawyer, son of Nathl Wickliffe, shot W P Grey yesterday with a double barrel shot gun, which was loaded with shot. Grey was dangersouly wounded & no hopes of his recovery. Wickliffe took one of Grey's horses, without leave, & about this the difficulty originated.
–Louisville Journal of the 10th

The Funeral of the late Albert Gallatin took place on Tue in N Y C, the obsequies were performed in Trinity Church at 4 o'clock in the afternoon. Burial service was performed by Dr Whitehouse, Rev J McVickar & G F Bedell, after which the body was deposited in the family vault. The Pall-bearers were: Cornelius W Lawrence, Dr J A Smith, Judge S Jones, Judge Ulshoeffer, Wm B Aston, Beverly Robinson, Robt Hyslop, & Dr Watson.

Wash Corp: 1-Nomination of David Westerfield as additional Police Constable for the 7th Ward: confirmed. 2-Ptn of Timothy O'Neill: passed. 3-Act for the relief of Luke Richardson: passed. 4-Cmte of Claims: bill for the relief of John E Neale: passed. Same cmte: bill for the relief of Owen McGee: passed. Same cmte: asked to be discharged from the further consideration of the bill for the relief of Wm P Shedd & others, & the ptn of E Hughes. 5-Ptn from Ezra Phelps for the remission of a fine: referred to the Cmte of Claims. 6-Following bills were referred to the Cmte of Claims- relief of: Edw Smith; M Rosenstock; Patrick Twomey; & Owen Magee. 7-Ptn of J H O'Neill, praying to be exempted from the payment of a dog tax: ordered to lie on the table. 8-Ptn of Jas Maher, praying remission of a fine for running a cart without license, & praying that his carts employed on Gov't work may be exempt from taxation: referred to the Cmte of Claims.

At the meeting of the Grand Division of the Sons of Temperance at Lewisburg, Va, on Jul 27, the Grand Worthy Patriarch, Mr Gally, was prostrated & instantly killed by the furious plunges of the horse of the chief marshal, & the Rev Mr Riley slightly injured.

Mr Stiles, the tax collector at New Orleans, who was convicted of being a defaulter to the amount of $28,000, has been sentenced to 2 years hard labor in the penitentiary, to restore the sum embezled, pay a fine of the same amount, & the costs of prosecution. He has appealed to the Supreme Court.

Zachary Taylor, Pres of the U S of A, recognizes Pedro Oueto who has been appointed Consul of the Republic of Chili, for the port of San Francisco, Calif. Aug 16, 1849

For sale: brick house on 9th st. Apply to John Davison, G & 8th sts, Wash.

$5 reward for the detection of the boy who threw purposely a stone through one of the stand-glass windows of the Church of the Epiphany on Jul 4 last. $10 reward for the detection of him or them who flung several stones on Aug 15, causing great injury. –J W French, Rector of Church of the Epiphany

SAT AUG 18, 1849
Thos G Woodward, one of the editors of the New Haven Daily Courier & Herald, died at New Haven on Sun, aged 61 years, after an illness of a week.

Dr Van Patten, Dentist, has returned to his ofc & business. He has for sale any & all of his real property: 2 acres now enclosed as a garden, on the brow of the hill in front of Mrs Tayloe's & Mr Shanks' residence; the half of square 173, now enclosed, being the same square on which Capt Carbery resides, & adjoining Gen Van Ness' mansion; quarter of square 145; lot 26 in square 534; lots 22, 23, & 24, in square 584; lot 1 in square 638; lot 28 in square 643; lots 1,5, & 7, in square 644; & 2 lots in square 732, on Capitol Hill. The title of all of the above is indisputable. –C H Van Patten, Dentist, near Brown's Hotel, Pa ave.

Culloma Mills, May 1, 1849. Since the date of my last another party has been formed to avenge the death of Jack Doyle. About 18 were gone 2 days in pursuit. Last evening they returned with a sqaw prisoner, & killed 2 out of the party they met; that the squaw promised to guide them to the Indian ranchero, where they found from 300 to 500 warriors. They came upon a party of 25 Indians who were digging gold. At first fire 17 dropped. May 2. Indian hunters have returned, having killed 30 or 40, in as far as Williams' ranche. Chief Jesus was the principal object of their search, said to be the worst Indian in the neighborhood, & the cause of all the murders. He cut the throats of all the daughters [Indian] that were from 8 to 23 or 24 years old, lest they should fall into the hands of the white. May 9-Indians killed near Daly's ranche, as they were moving across the plain. A few escaped, but the others were shot down.

Capt Dan Drake Henrie, well known here & in other places as a volunteer ofcr during the Mexican war, recently died at St Louis. So says a despatch from that city dated yesterday.

Mortality of the 8th Infty: Lt Chas G Merchant, writing from Texas, furnishes the following list of deaths within the past year.
At Brooklyn, N Y, Aug 2, 1848, Lt Geo Wainwright.
On the Mississippi river, near Helena, Ark, Sep, 1848, 1st Lt & Brvt Capt John D Clark.
At Port Lavaca, Texas, Dec 24, 1848, 2nd Lt J A Deaney.
At Jefferson Barracks, Mo, Jan 22, 1849, Capt A L Sheppard.
At San Antonio de Bexar, Texas, May 7, 1849, Col & Brvt Maj Gen Wm J Worth.
At San Antonio de Bexar, Texas, Jun 26, 1849, 1st Lt J J Booker.
At Camp Chadbourne, near Fredericksburg, Texas, Jun 28, 1849, Capt & Brvt Maj Collinson R Gates.
At & near Port Lavaca, Texas, from Dec 20, 1848, to Jan 2, 1849, of cholera, 127 non-commissioned ofcrs, musicians, & privates of the 8th Regt of Infty.

Cmder Jacob Crowninshield, of the U S Navy, died recently of apoplexy, on board the steamer **Oregon**, while on his way from San Francisco to Panama. He was a native of Massachusetts, & entered the Navy in 1815.

The ship **Sheridan**, Capt Cornish, from Liverpool, arrived at N Y quarantine ground on Wed. She sailed from Liverpool on Jul 13. Disease broke out on Aug 7. 80 cases & 31 deaths of cholera occurred on the passage. –N Y Com Adv

In Boston on Mon, 3 small girls, between 8 & 11 years old, drowned when playing on a pile of lumber on the wharf. The plank tilted projecting them into the water. Honora & Eliza McDonough & Virginia Clark's bodies were recovered the same night.

From Santa Fe: Maj Chevalie, a Texan, at the head of 25 Americans, accepted the terms offered by the Govn'r of Chihuahua to fight the Apache Indians. The contract price for the scalp of a warrior is $200; for others $50, & for prisoners $200 each. Lt Thomas encountered a band of Camanches, near Sawgre Christi Placer, & killed 17 of them.

Yorkville, Mich: Mr Ashbeil Kellogg, a respectable gentleman of that place, had a son whose reckless habits had almost turned his father's brain. On Aug 7, the son demanded money from his father, & endeavored to enforce his demand by the exhibition of a pistol. This so incensed Mr Kellogg that he seized an axe & killed the young man instantly.

Noble & daring act. One of the steamboats recently burnt at St Louis had on board 30 kegs of powder. Mr Lewis Brown, one of the pilots, at great personal hazard, threw 29 of the 30 kegs into the river. He had barely time to escape when the fire communicated to the hold. This act probably saved many lives.

Died: on Aug 16, Alex'r Suter, Cashier of the Farmer's & Mechanics' Bank of Gtwn, D C, in his 66th year. His funeral is this afternoon, at 4½ o'clock, from his late residence, corner of Congress & Bridge sts.

Obit-died: on Aug 13, in Wash City, Mrs Anne Stewart, relict of the late Hugh Stewart, & daughter of the late John Orr, of Va, in her 87th year. For more than 30 years she was a resident of Washington, & her house the abode of hospitality & kindness. As a mother she was tenderly affectionate, as a friend ardent & sincere.

MON AUG 20, 1849
Public Schools-Wash. Members of the Sub-Boards:

Mr Abbot	Mr Bacon	Mr Van Reswick
Mr Haliday	Mr Watterston	Dr Morgan
Mr Farnham	Mr Ellis	-C A Davis, Sec
Mr Donoho	Dr Roberts	
Mr Harbaugh	Mr Mudd	

Western Academy exercises will be recommenced on Sep 10, at the corner of 17th & I sts. –G J Abbott

$20 reward will be paid for information that will lead to the arrest of the vile wretch who fired a gun & shot my dog, who is not obnoxious to honest people, inside of my yard, with the gate fastened. –P O Browning

The Fred'k Citizen announces the death of Col John Thomas, [father of Ex-Govn'r Francis Thomas,] an old & highly respected resident of Fred'k Co, who died on Monday last, at his country seat, near Petersville.

Worcester, Mass: on Fri Mr Levi Chas Coes, of the firm of Bigelow & Coes, shoe & leather dealers, committed suicide by hanging himself. He was an young man of excellent character. He opened his own business lately, but within a few weeks past, he was bankrupt. -Nat'l Aegis

Fatal accident at N Y, on Fri last, as the ferry-boat **Bedford** was nearing the Fulton station, she came in sudden collision with the pier. Julia Brady, a passenger, had her arm wrenched off & she was killed on the spot. She was a chambermaid at the Astor Hotel.

The Phil papers announce the death of Gen John Mitchell, at his residence in Beaver Co, Pa, last week. He was twice elected to Congress, was the first engineer on the Erie Canal, had repeatedly represented his county in the State Legislature, & was Canal Com'r under Gov Wolf.

Private letter from Maj Gen Brooke, dated San Antonio, Jul 18, in which that veteran ofcr states that there had been no Indian disturbances for some time previously to his arrival at that city, [his headquarters,] & that nearly the whole of these depredators, it is believed, have retired to their villages. -New Orleans Picayune

The Ohio State Journal notices the death, in Columbus, on Aug 12, of Jas H Ewing, who was Senator for Hamilton Co in the last legislature.

Rev Danl E Reese, a much respected clergyman of the Methodist Episcopal Church, & one of the oldest in Balt, Md, died suddenly on Fri, at his residence in South Exeter st.

A young man, Michl Gillen, at work on a vessel on Amos st, N Y, was knocked overboard by the boom of the vessel. Christopher Cragen, aged 11 years, standing by at the time, threw a plank overboard, & jumped into the water & shoved the plank to Gillen, thereby saving him from drowning.

Last Sat, the brig **Analosta**, laden with sugar from Porto Rico, & bound for Gtwn, was struck by lightning while in the Potomac, about 10 miles this side of *Piney Point*. The chief mate of the brig [E J Marshall, of Balt,] was struck by lightning & remained perfectly insensible for an hour & 10 minutes. He was severely injured in his leg, & is entirely crippled for the present, the electric fluid having left large red streaks in the leg, which are extremely painful.

Died: on Aug 17, in Wash City, Chas Locke Rand, son of Mary J & Jas B Rand.

Died: on Aug 17, at *Mount Pleasant*, near Wash, in her 23rd year, Jane Lenthall Abert, wife of Lt J W Abert, U S Topographical Engineers, & only daughter of Wm J & Eliz J Stone.

Died: on Aug 15, at her residence *Forest Home*, Westbrook, Maine, Junia Lauretta, the wife of Hon F O J Smith. As an affectionate wife & mother she had not her superior. All who knew her, knew but to praise.

TUE AUG 21, 1849
Sudden death on board the steamboat **America**, going from Cobourg to Rochester, on Mon, Jas Anderson, a passenger, was found lying dead on he deck. He had come on board heavily in liquor. He was about 40, 5 feet 8 inches, & very stout.

The Richmond papers bring us news of the death of Philip Norborne Nicholas, stricken down by paralysis on Thu last, & died on Sat. He was a member of a popular family, & at an early age appointed Atty Gen of Va. He was afterwards for many years Pres of the Farmers' Bank, & had been 8 years Judge of a new circuit created for the city of Richmond.

A young man, Henry Frier, while bathing in Gwynn's Falls, a day or 2 since, at the Powhatan Factory dam, 7 miles from the city of Balt, was seized with the cramp & drowned. His father, hearing his cries for aid, plunged in, & was himself carried down. The bodies of both have been recovered.

Maj Thos Rowland died at Detroit on Aug 13. He had been for nearly half a century a citizen of Michigan, & honorably filled several public offices. He obtained his military rank by gallant service in the war of 1812.

Horrible ravage of cholera at Birmingham, Pa: 21 persons died yesterday, & 30 to 40 are under treatment. Dr Moy, one of the physicians, is dangerously ill; Mr Hermann, one of our best musicians, died on Thu. Whole families have been carried off.

Cholera at Saut St Marie: Capt Danl Hicks, of Adrian, who arrived there but a few weeks since, to enter upon his duties as Receiver of Public Moneys, died Thu last. He commanded one company of the Michigan volunteers in the Mexican war. Mr Edw Clark, of Worcester, Mass, Superintendent of the Marquette Iron Co, died on Tue. Maj Martell, who accompanied a delegation of Indians to Washington last winter, died the same day. 3 Indians died today.

On Tue, the only daughter of O M Spencer, of Cincinnati Ohio, while on a visit with her parents at Yellow Springs, fell from the railing around the Springs on a pile of stones beneath, & was so injured that she expired in about 8 hours.

In a letter from Calif we noticed the name of our fellow-citizen, Mr Philip T Tyson, [called Dr Tyson,] as being one of the Exploring Expedition under the direction of Gen Smith, who has left San Francisco on a tour of discovery & observation. Mr Tyson is an experienced Geologist & Chemist. -Balt Patriot, Aug 17

On Mon week, Jacob Winder, Senr, of Madison township, was committed to jail of this county charged with shooting John Dunmead on Sun at the residence of said Winder. Dunmead died that night. The shooting seems to have been in a drunken brawl. The prisoner claims the shooting was accidental. —Zanesville Gaz

Trustee's sale of real estate: by decree of PG Co Court, as Court of Equity, the subscribers will offer at public sale, at Dr Edelen's tavern, in Piscataway, on Sep 11, 2 tracts or parcels of land, of which John Bowling died seized & possessed, the one tract supposed to contain about 175 acres, more or less, being part of Piscataway Manor, & the other tract containing about 90 acres, more or less. There is a dwlg house & some out-houses on the first tract. —C C Magruder, D C Digges, trustees

Died: Aug 18, at her father's residence, in her 22nd year, Ann Serene, wife of Mr John G Smith, & eldest daughter of Leonard O & Eliz Cook, leaving an infant daughter. Very suddenly has a husband, father, mother, 2 sisters, & a large circle of friends called to mourn the loss of an affectionate wife, daughter, sister, & friend.

For sale: young bay horses, recently brought from the State of Ky. Apply to P H Leokron, I st, between 22nd & 23rd sts, 1st Ward, Wash.

Teacher wanted for the Primary School near the village of Piscataway, PG Co, Md. —John W Ward, Chas R Bealle, & Ho Edelin, trustees

For rent: fine brick dwlg house on Dunbarton st, now, & for several years occupied by the Rev Mr Berry. Also, the very large wharf property on Water st, occupied by John Dickson. —F A Dodge, Gtwn

WED AUG 22, 1849
Orphans Court of Wash Co, D C. Letters of administration on the personal estate of Wm B Page, late of Wash Co, deceased. —R L Page, adm

First election in the new Territory of Minnesota took place on Aug 1. Partial list of members elect to the Legislative Councils:
Councillors:
Jas S Norris	Jas McBoal	Martin McLeod
Saml Burkleo	D B Loomis	
Wm H Forbes	J W Rawlins	

Representatives:
Sylvanus Trask	P K Johnson	Mr Olmsted-a
Mahlon Black	Mr Setzer or	possible
M S Wilkinson	Mr Taylor	Alexis Baily
B W Bronson	Wm R Marshal	G H Pond
Henry Jackson	Wm Dugas	
John J Dewey	Mr Sturgis-a possible	

Wash Corp: 1-Ptn from Nathl Parker for remissions of a fine: referred to the Cmte of Claims. 2-Act for the relief of Thos Greeves: passed. 3-Cmte of Claims: discharged from the further consideration of the ptn of Jas Maher. 4-Act for the relief of Chas Stewart: passed. 5-Bill for the relief of Walter Lenkins: referred to the Cmte of Claims. 6-Cmte on Improvements: discharged from the further consideration of ptn of Robt Beale, respecting licenses for wagons: referred to the Cmte on Police.

The Superior of the Catholic Orphan Asylum, at Mobile, Sister Martina, died on Aug 7. She was a native of Phil, & at age 17, joined the Sisters of Charity. She first joined the sisters at Emmetsburg, Md, & then served in the asylum hospital at Balt; susequently she went to St Louis, & was one of the founders of the celebrated hospital of that city, & finally, in 1841, came to Mobile, & took charge of the orphan asylum. The world knows what gentlemess, & faith, & love, & heroic endurance are the attributes of the Sisters of Charity.

Zachary Taylor, Pres of the U S of A, recognizes Albino Barelli who has been appointed Vice Counsul of Portugal, for the port of New Orleans, in Louisiana. Aug 21, 1849

Mrs C C McLeod's Academy for young Ladies, 11th st, between F & G sts, will reopen on Sep 3.

Loudoun Co land for sale: as excs of the late Joshua Osburn, we offer all his landed estate, in said county: 560 acres 3 miles west of Hillsborough, having 2 good dwlg-houses on it, with all necessary bldgs. –Hector Osburn, Norval Osburn, Jos Worthington, excs

Mrd: on Aug 21, by Rev Mr French, Lt Chas Deas, U S Navy, to Joanna S, only daughter of Francis H Davidge, of Wash City.

Mrd: on Aug 16, at Phil, by Rev D Washburn, A M, Cmdor E W Moore, Cmder of the late Texas Navy, to Emma, daughter of the late Wm T Stockton, of Roxborough, Pa.

Died: on Jul 17, Gen Abraham Godwin, of a lingering illness, Postmaster of Paterson, N J, aged 58 years. He served as a Lt of Infty during the whole of the last war with Great Britain, & was retained on the peace establishment, but shortly after he resigned for the more active duties of civil life.

Died: at St Amie, Canada, at age 102 years, Frs Fontaine. Although blind for the last 12 years, he was able to go without help almost every where. His memory was good. His father had received from Gen Montcalm, as a reward for his services, a silver cup, with his arms & initials engraved on it. Beside his death bed stood 4 respectable looking old men with white hairs. They were his sons. He gave them his blessing before breathing his last. –Montreal Avenir [No death date given-current item.]

A lot of ground for sale: bordering on North Boundary st, outside the city limits, adjoining the farm of Mr E Gilman: lot contains about 5½ acres, more or less. Apply to Z D & W H Gilman, Druggists.

THU AUG 23, 1849
Nathl Denby, late Navy Agent, has confessed judgment in the U S Dist Court at Phil for $159,443.67, being the amount claimed by the Gov't with interest. He still remains in custody. He did not appear in court, being too debilitated to leave his bed. His health was stated to have become greatly impaired since his arrest.

Mrs Eliz Wilkins, who died in Pittsburg, a few days since, was the granddaughter of the famous Gen Morgan, of the Revolution. Her maiden name was Neville.

Augusta, Ga, Aug 20. Col Wm English, of Fla, who was reported to have been murdered by the Indians, is safe, though he was compelled to desert his plantation.

For rent: 3 story brick house adjoining the residence of Mc C Young, on F st. Inquire of Mr Davidge, now in the house, or to me. –Thos Carbery

Information wanted of Andre Byrne. When last heard from, Jul 4, 1835, he resided in Walker st, N Y. Supposed to be dead. He, or any person having possession of his papers, can hear of something to their advantage by addressing A D Cabasa, Mayaguez, Porto Rico, under cover to J Gaither, Wash, D C.

Mrd: on Aug 21, by Rev Wm Collier, Jas F Tucker to Susan E Boswell, both of Wash City.

Mrd: on Aug 22, at St Peter's Church, by Rev Jos Van Horsign, Mr John L Marceron to Miss Delia Lucchesi, all of Wash City.

Mrd: on Jul 24, at Elmwood, Roanoke Co, Va, by Rev Geo Wilmer, Mr Thos C Read to Sally A E, 2nd daughter of Col Wm M Peyton.

Household & kitchen furniture at auction on Aug 29, at the residence of Mr Cudlip, on Pa ave. –Green & Tastet, auctioneers

From the N Y Express of Tues. Another ship of death arrived at quarantine. The packet ship **Oxford**, which sailed from Liverpool on Jul 18, arrived here this forenoon. Mortality from cholera lasted from Aug 2nd to the 9th. Names & birthplaces of the dead:
Rich Coltman, 45, Camden, Eng
Hannah Chapman, 40, Leeds, Eng
Nancy Mater, 50, County King, Ire
Mary Mater, 20, County King, Ire
Pat Carey, 60, Longford, Ire
Ellen Higgins, 45, King's Co, Ire
Ann McLaughlin, infant, Tipperrary, Ire
Pat Gillroy, 22, Longford, Ire
John Carey, 40, Longford, Ire
Catherine Fitzpatrick, 18, Mount Mattuck, Ire
Pat Reynolds, 30, Mount Mattuck, Ire
Jno Reynolds, 4, Mount Mattuck, Ire
Mgt Kell, 66, Roscommon, Mount Mattuck, Ire
Mary Kinniffe, Roscommon, Ire [no age given]
Wm Mahoney, 36, Longford, Ire
Bridget Divine, 6, County King
Ann Adams, 22, West Meath, Ire
Mary Bardis, 60, Ire
Wm Mathews, King Co

Died: on Aug 15, suddenly, Archibald Robt Bogardus, in his 54th year, eldest son of the late Gen Robt Bogardus. The deceased entered the U S Navy in 1815, & resigned his commission in 1828. Since then he has held 2 responsible & arduous situations in the Navy, & fulfilled the duties to the perfect satisfaction of the commanding ofcr.

Died: a few days ago, in Detroit, Maj Thos Rowland, a much esteemed & prominent citizen. Maj Rowland was formerly Sec of State, & was post master of Detroit under Gen Harrison. Maj Rowland was among the most venerable citizens of Detroit. He was the contemporary & friend of Gov Woodbridge, Maj John Biddle, Judge Chipman, & other well known pioneers of Western civilization. [See Aug 21st newspaper.]

Died: on Aug 4, at Rutherfordton, N C, Joshua Forman, after an illness of 12 days, aged 72 years. The deceased formerly held a prominent position with the enterprising men of the State of N Y. He was early connected with the commencement & construction of the Erie Canal. He was among the first settlers of the county of Onondaga, & first judge of the county. He was the founder of Syracuse. He removed from there in 1826, & had resided for the last 21 years at the place of his death.

Died: Wm Byrd Page, the eldest son of Wm Byrd Page, of Fairfield, Va, a man whom his contemporaries justly regarded as the pattern of a Va gentleman of the old school.

FRI AUG 24, 1849
The Utica Observer mentions the death of Thos Rockwell, Cashier of the Branch Bank at Utica. He sank down as he was standing at his desk, literally died at his post. He was in his 70th year.

Westchester Village Record publishes a sketch of the trial & conviction of Amos McFarlan & Solomon Staites on the charge of kidnapping a colored boy. The outrage was committed near Downington. The boy, about 15, was an apprentice of Wm Evans. McFarlan is a young man who has been married but a few years. He was sentenced to 6 years, & Staites to 5 years in the penitentiary & $500 fine.

Rittenhouse Academy, 3rd & Indiana ave, Wash: will re-open on Set 3. Apply through Rev J E Nourse, on 13th st; or Otis C Wight, Principal. References:

Rev L S Gillis
Rev E Ballantine
*Rev Wm McLain
Rev J C Smith
Rev J E Nourse
*Col Wm P Young
*Patrons
*Prof Henry
*J P Ingle
J H Bradley
*Capt Wm W Moore
*Mr Wm M Morrison
*Capt C V Morris

By writ of fieri facias, I shall expose to public sale, for cash, on Sep 1, one Sorrel Mare, taken as the property of John Lee, & will be sold to satisfy a judgment in favor of Benj F Middleton & Benj Beall. –R R Burr, Constable

Under a resolution of the Legislature of Md, passed at a late session, Henry G S Key, of St Mary's Co, has been appointed by Govn'r Thomas to be a Com'r on the part of the State of Md, to ascertain the original site of the boundary stone at the point on Mason & Dixon Line, where the States of Pa, Dela, & Md join each other, & to re-mark & re-set a boundary stone or other proper monument.

Naval School of Annapolis: following Midshipmen have passed their examination with credit, & are now Passed Midshipmen.

Theodore Lee, of Ala
Sylvanus J Bliss, of Mass
Wm Mitchell, of D C
Robt R Lewis, of Mo
E Vanderhorst, of S C
Alex'r M DeBree, of Va
Chas P McGarry, of N C
Andrew W Johnson, of D C
N H Van Zandt, of D C
Albert Allmand, of Va
Edmund Shepard, of Va
Henry St Geo Hunter, of Va
Wm R Mercer, of Md
Robt R Carter, of Va
Hunter Davidson, of Va
Wm Van Wyck, of Md

Their position has not yet been assigned them.

Mrd: on Aug 23, by Rev Wm H Pitcher, Mr Robt Jackson to Miss Maria Hepburn, all of Alexandria, Va.

Died: Aug 17, at Alum Creek, Ohio, the residence of her husband, Mrs Julia Ann Dawes, consort of Isaac Dawes, & daughter of Aden Darby, of Montg Co, Md.

Died: on Aug 22, Alex'r Dent, aged 2 months & 25 days, son of Jas & Deborah Mankin. His funeral is this afternoon, at 4 o'clock, from his father's residence, 9th st, between H & I sts.

SAT AUG 25, 1849
Official: Appointment by the Pres: Henry Shelton Sanford, of Conn, to be Sec of the Legation of the U S at Paris.

Rochester American: Col Edmund Kirby, Paymaster in the Army, died at Avon Springs on Aug 20. He joined the army as an Ensign of the 4th Infty in Jul, 1812, & served with distinction during that war as aid to Maj Gen Brown. He joined the army under Gen [now Pres,] Taylor soon after the battles of Palo Alto & Resaca de la Palma, & acted as a volunteer aid to Gen Taylor at the battle of Montery. Two years prior to the day of his death he was in the sanguinary conflict at Churubusco. While in Mexico he contracted a disease of the liver, which some weeks since assumed a most dangerous form, & ultimately terminated in death. He reached Avon Springs on Thursday last in a state of extreme debility. Col Kirby married a daughter of Maj Gen Jacob Brown, & has left a family of 9 children. His remains, attended by his widow & several friends, reached this city on Monday, & left soon after for his late residence at Brownsville, Jefferson Co, N Y.

The U S schnr **Taney**, Lt Hunter comanding, from the Mediterranean, arrived at N Y on Wed. List of her ofcrs: Chas G Hunter, Lt Commandant; J Dorsey Read, Acting Master; Jas S Gilliam, Assist Surgeon; Alonzo C Jackson, Passed Midshipman Richd J D Prince, Passed Midshipman; Edmund T Storms, Capt's Clerk

The U S ship **Dale**, Capt Rudd, has been absent from the U S 3 years & 3 months, & has sailed 62,000 miles. She left San Francisco, on her homeward voyage, on Mar 14 last, with nearly $300,000 in Calif gold, the greater part of which was landed at Valparaiso. She arrived Aug 22, after a passage of 38 days from Rio de Janeiro, & has on board $65,000 in gold dust. List of the ofcrs of the Dale: Cmder, John Rudd
Lts: Ed M Yard, T A M Craven, Wm B Muse, acting
Purser, McKeon Buchanan; Passed Assist Surgeon, Jas McClelland
Master, Nath C Bryant; Passedmidshipmen: John Downes, jr, Robt M McArann
Cmder's clerk, E T Devans
Midshipmen: T Truxton Houston, Bancroft Gherardi, Philip C Johnson, jr, Chas B Smith, Thos M Hammer
Acting boatswain, Thos Ditson; Acting gunner, John F Erskine
Acting Carpenter, Wm Hyde; Sailmaker, Stephen Seaman
Purser's clerk, Wm E Merford
Passengers: Hon Seth Barton, [Charge d'Affaires to Chili,] lady & servant; Miss Astaburuage, of St Jago de Chili; Passed Midshipman J Posey Hall, from Pacific squadron, Woodward Knight, Augusta, Ga. The following deaths occurred during the cruise: Jos C Clark, colored, ship's cook, Oct 9, 1846. Wm Brown, seaman, Oct 23, 1846. John Curl, colored, ordinary seaman, of N Y, Dec 21, 1847, at Guaymas. Geo Theobald, sgt of marines, Jul 19, 1849, at sea.

Rev Thos Burch died at Brooklyn, N Y, on Aug 22, in his 71st year. He was connected with the Ministry of the Methodist Episcopal Church for nearly half a century, highly esteemed by all who knew him.

Mrd: on Thu, by Rev John C Smith, Mr Jos D Ward to Miss Anna E Dunnington, all of Wash City.

Died: on Aug 24, Vincent King, a native of Chas Co, Md, but for the last 45 years a resident of D C, in his 81st year. His funeral is this evening at 5 o'clock, from his late residence on E st.

Commencement at Yale College occurred on Aug 15 & 16; this is the 149th Commencement. The oldest living graduate is Dr Jos Darling, of New Haven, who graduated in the class of 1777, or 72 years since. The graduating class numbered 95.

Mr Edw Hughes, a well known citizen of Alleghany Co, Pa, of the firm of Wood & Hughes, brewers, of Pittsburg, was found drowned near the landing place of Jones' Ferry, in that city, on Aug 19. His gold watch & some $120 in money was found on his person, which precludes the suspicion that he had been robbed & thrown into the river.

Mrd: on Tue last, in Greenwich Church, Va, by Rev T B Balch, Robt Carter, of Mississippi, to Eliz M Comb, 2nd daughter of the officiating Clergyman.

During one of the recent engagements between the Austrians & Hungarians, near Comorn, a battle-painter, named Lalleman, is said to have been killed by a cannon shot while he was taking a sketch of the fight.

The Most Rev Archbishop of Balt will give Confirmation in St Mary's Church, 5th st, tomorrow, at 11 o'clock, after the Gospel, at High Mass, which will be celebrated by the Very Rev Fr Brochar, Provincial of the Jesuits.

Mondawmin for sale: the beautiful country residence of the late Dr Patrick Macaulay, near the western verge of the city of Balt, is offered for sale by the trustees in chancery. It comprises about 73 acres of land, with ornamental gardens. The dwlg is a modern structure of great elegance, 85 feet by 40 feet, 2 stories, with basement & attic, with porticos & extensive conservatory. The title is perfect, & all liens, taxes, etc, will be paid up to the day of sale. Public auction, on the premises, Sep 28, 1849.
–J J Speed, Henry Webster, trustees

MON AUG 27, 1849
Very sudden death on Sat early: a respectable female, the wife of Mr Herman, residing in D st, near 13th, died while seated on her chair. It was thought her death was caused by an affection of the heart.

Mr Barber, an embosser & diemaker of this city, died on Wed at Gowanus. In company with his brother-in-law, Mr Mucklow, he went to bathe & shortly afterwards it was discovered he was drowned. –Brooklyn Adv

On the straits of Sunda, in the ship **Channing**, of which he was cmder, & on her passage from Canton to this port, a studding-sail boom fell from aloft, striking Capt Henry Huttleson upon his shoulder & breaking the arm in 2 places, besides dislocating the elbow. After 5 days of intense suffering he was landed at Anjier, & removed thence to Serang, where amputation of the limb was immediately resorted to as the only possible hope of relief. He survived the operation but a few hours. Capt Huttleson was known & esteemed by many of our citizens, as the cmder for several years of the packet ships **Ontario** & **Ashburton**, & we believe was a native of Fairhaven, Mass. –N Y Express

Died: on Aug 25, in Wash City, after a protracted illness, in her 77th year, Mrs Mary Baird, relict of the late Andrew Baird, of Gtwn. Her funeral is from the residence of her son-in-law, David Munro, on 11th st, near Pa ave, on Mon, at 4 o'clock.

City Ordinances-Wash: 1-Act for the relief of Wm H Harrover: the sum of $78.58 be paid to him for work done at the asylum.

Household & kitchen furniture at auction on Aug 30, by order of the Orphans Court of Wash Co, D C, at the residence of the late A Suter, deceased, over the Farmers' & Mechanics' Bank. –Edw S Wright, auctioneer

Trustee's sale of improved real estate. Circuit Court of Wash Co, D C-in Chancery. Sarah E Craven et al vs Wm Craven: public auction, on Sep 25, all those parts of lots 11 & 12, in square 118, in Wash City, whereof John Craven, late of the county, died seized, saving & excepting a small portion of said property which fronts 3 feet on 19th st, & runs west with that width 40 feet along the south side of said lot 12.
–J M Carlisle, trustee

Orphans Court of Wash Co, D C. Letters of administration on the personal estate of Alex'r Suter, late of Wash Co, deceased. –Thos R Suter, adm

TUE AUG 28, 1849
The London papers announce the death, on Jul 30, of Jacob Perkins, formerly of Boston, but for many years residing & established inLondon, the inventor of engraving on steel & of the method of transferring engravings to steel plates, in his 83rd year.

A farmer named Talmadge, who was arrested some time since for laying rails on the track of the Troy & Saratoga railroad, near Ballston Spa, whereby the engine was thrown from the track, & the engineer, Mr Dodge, a valuable citizen of Watervliet, was killed, has been indicted by the Grand Jury of Saratoga Co, for murder, & committed to prison. A man who was passing along the road on foot saw him, & that on this testimony the Grand Jury found a true bill.

Md Military Academy will be re-opened on Oct 1: situated in Oxford, Talbot Co, Md. –John H Allen, Superintendent

Landon Female Seminary, Urbana, Fred'k Co, Md: will be re-opened on Sep 12. Mrs Mgt Schenck, Principal, [late Principal of the Columbus Female Seminary, Ohio.]

By virtue of 10 writs of fieri facias, against the goods & chattels of Geo H Kendrick & Ann L Kendrick, I shall expose to public sale, on Sep 6, the following property: one hack & harness & 2 horses, seized & taken as the property of said Kendricks; to be sold to satisfy sundry executions in favor of Allison Nailor.
–O E P Hazard, Constable, Wash Co.

New Post ofcs established during the week ending Aug 25, 1849.

Ofc	County, State	New Appointment
Ashley Falls	Berkshire, Mass	John Scoville
Frontier	Clinton, N Y	John McCoy
Port Leyden	Lewis, N Y	John H Williams
Niskayuna	Schenectady, N Y	A Van Hovenburgh
Lamson	Onondaga, N Y	John H Lamson
Axeville	Cataraugus, N Y	Horace W Cowley
Kensico	West Chester, N Y	Dwight Capron
Arendtsville	Adams, Pa	Jacob Kechler
New Mahoning	Carbon, Pa	Tilghman Arner
Keefer's Store	Franklin, Pa	Lewis Keefer
Huntersville	Lycoming, Pa	Jos Webster
Brooklandville	Balt, Md	Joshua A Fuller
Breckton	Somerset, Md	Thos W Dashiell
Muskingum	Muskingum, Ohio	John W P Lane
New Corwin	Highland, Ohio	J Roberts
Sylvia	Hardin, Ohio	Wm S Lewis
Hibenia	Franklin, Ohio	Wm F Armstrong
Ansonia	New Haven, Conn	Geo Bristol
Haddrell's Point	Charleston, Dis, S C	Henry S Tew
Hancock City	Hancock, Ill	Homer Brown
Kelly's Springs	Talladega, Ala	Wm H Parks
Pentress	Monongalia, Va	C Cox
Big Laurel	Yancy, N C	John Roberts
White Rock	Yancy, N C	Kneeley Weede
Ark	De Kalb, Ga	Levi H Harwell
Pleasant Grove	Madison, Miss	Thos Harton
Birmingham	Pontotoc, Miss	D Lawson
Hewellen's Cross Roads	De Soto, Miss Sol Stewart	
Green Valley	Lafayette, Miss	Wm R Wilson
Lansing	Alamakee, Iowa	W S Garrison
Freedom	Keokuck, Iowa	Geo W Drake
Mount Pleasant	Wilkinson, Miss	Wm F Dyson

Mrd: on Aug 23, at Balt, by Rev Mr Duncan, Henry Roy De Lareintrie to Mgt, daughter of the late Dr John Harper.

Mrd: on Aug 4, at St James' Church, Paddington, London, Austin Cuvillier, eldest son of the late Hon A Cuvillier, late Speaker of the House of Assembly in Canada, to Charlotte, daughter of E Erichsen, of Gloucester Rd, Hyde Park.

Died: on Aug 27, at the residence of Saml Hanson, Miss Eliz Bayly, daughter of the late Gen Mountjoy Bayly, in her 61st year. Her funeral is today at 4:30 P M.

Died: at his residence near Riseyville, Culpeper Co, Va, Jas R Risey, after a protracted illness of many weeks, in his 31st year, leaving a wife & child, & many friends, to mourn their loss. Union paper will please copy. [No death date given-current item.]

Died: on Aug 19, at Phil, after an illness of 10 days, Jos Pablo Roura, a native of Barcelona, Spain, in his 29th year.

Meeting of the Medical Profession of St Louis, held on Jul 11, Dr Meredith Martin called to the chair; Dr Chas A Pope, appointed Sec. Tribute to the memory of friend & brother, Dr Hardage Lane, who for nearly 40 years was a skilled physician.

WED AUG 29, 1849
For sale: 1,612 acres of valuable land near Sheboygan, Wisc. Apply to Henry H Conklin, of Sheboygan, or to Edw Simmes, Wash, D C. –E S

The Gtwn Classical & Scientific Academy, formed under the care of Rev Jas McVean, deceased, will be re-opened on Sep 3, by Rev T W Simpson, formerly Prof of Languages in Newark College, Dela. References: Rev Wm S Plumer, D D, the Faculty of Nassau Hall, the Profs of the Theological Seminary, Princeton, N J; Rev Jas Laurie, D D, Wash; Rev Elias Harrison, Alexandria; & Rev R T Berry, Gtwn.

A young German, 18 years old, a native of Hanover, of a good family & education, & a sound Musician on the Piano Forte & Organ, offers his services as Professor of music in a private family or school. Apply to Mr Franz Tepe, at Mrs Peyton's Boarding House, Wash.

Thos Laughrey fired from his window upon 2 men who were attacking his house about 4 o'clock in the morning. One of them died. The jury believe that Laughrey, the accused, was justified in defending his house & family. The accused was discharged from custody. –N Y Mir

Whig nominations for Congress in the 5 districts of Md which are usually contested with any chance of success. The candidates are:
Richd J Bowie, Montg Co   Alex'r Evans, Cecil Co
Thos J McKaig, Alleghany Co   John Bozman Kerr, Talbot Co
John R Kenly, Balt City

Rev John Pierce, of the Unitarian Congregational Church, Brookline, Mass, died on Friday, in his 76th year. He was one of the earliest total abstinence men in the State, & was famous as a pedestrian, to which his long life is attributed.

The First <u>Unitarian Church</u> at Worcester, Mass, was destroyed by fire on Fri. The society was under the pastoral care of the Rev Alonzo Hill. Loss estimated at $15,000.

Col Washington Cushing died at his place of residence in South Hingham, Mass, on Aug 22. He was born on Jan 8, 1776, & was in his 74th year. During the war of 1812 he was in command of the regt stationed at the Castle in Boston harbor, & was ever distinguished for his promptness, fidelity, & zeal in the discharge of his military as well as of all the other duties of life.

Luke Lea has been nominated as the whig candidate for Govn'r of the State of Mississippi, in lieu of Gen Thos G Polk, who declined the nomination. Gen Quitman is the Democratic candidate.

Judge Mellen, of the Boston Municipal Court, sentenced Robt W Brown to 2 years' confinement in the State prison, for having stolen from his own brother, $120, the hard earnings of a long voyage at sea.

Miss H McCormick & sister will resume the duties of their School on Sep 3, at their place of residence, on 4½ st south of the avenue, in the house belonging to Mr Ulysses Ward.

Valuable country residence at private sale: the residence of the late Edw Dyer, about 2 miles from the Capitol, on the Balt turnpike: about 75 acres: with a large dwlg house & all necessary out houses. -E C & G F Dyer, aucts

Pursuant to a decree of the Circuit Court of Wash Co, D C., passed on Nov 2, 1848, in the case of Henry Naylor against the heirs of Edw W Clark & others, the Trustee will offer for sale, on Sep 29, lot 11 in square 688, in Wash. –E J Middleton, trustee -Green & Tastet, auctioneers

Stray Cow. $5 reward will be paid for the delivery of the cow at the residence of Mrs Tompkins, corner of Gay & Montg sts, Gtwn, D C.

Hon Gabriel H Ford, venerable citizen of N J, died at his family residence, in Morristown, Mon last, at the advanced age of 85 years. He was a native of Morristown, read law with the late Abraham Ogden, was admitted to the Bar in May, 1789, 60 years ago, then on his 25th year. He was appointed Presiding Judge of the Court of Common Pleas for the eastern district of the State, & in Nov, 1820, was elevated to the Bench of the Supreme Court as an Assoc Judge, where he continued for 21 years. –Newark Daily Adv

Erie, N Y, Aug 27. In firing a salute from the U S steamer **Michigan** this morning, in honor of Vice Pres Fillmore, a cannon exploded, & a man named Gilbert was killed on the spot, 3 others were blown overboard, & another had both hands blown off, & is since reported to have died. [Sep 1st newspaper: Explosion on board the U S steamer **Michigan** on Aug 27. Peter Gilbert was blown overboard, & John Robinson had both arms carried away. He has since die. None others were hurt. –Buffalo Com Adv]

Died: on Aug 28, Caroline Matilda Leib, daughter of S D Leib, of the Ofc of Indian Affairs, aged 14 years, 11 months & 27 days.

Died: on Aug 24, in Gtwn, D C, Catharine Eloise Hepburn, aged 12 years, daughter of John M Hepburn.

The German Lutheran Church, having lately purchased a piece of ground near the Railroad, in the eastern part of Wash City, to be used by them as a burying place, it was on Sun last dedicated by Rev Mr Finkel, Pastor of that Church. About 150 members of the German Beneficial Society attended.

Flour for sale: barrels of extra fine flour. –J D Read, Water st, Gtwn

THU AUG 30, 1849
Mrs Chalmers' Seminary for young Ladies will be re-opened on Sep 3.

Household & kitchen furniture at auction on Sep 6, at the residence of Gov A P Bagby, on C st, between 3rd & 4½ sts, *Ashland Row*. -E C & G F Dyer, aucts

Servant & House wanted: a negro woman, competent to cook & wash for a family, [a slave would be preferred] will find a good situation by applying to J F Callan, Druggist, 7th st.

Valuable farm in Montg Co for sale at public auction: on Sep 15, the well known farm of the late C A Burnett, on Gtwn & Rockville Turnpike, containing 235½ acres; a good dwlg, large barn, negro quarters, & other convenient bldgs. Apply to W D C Murdock, near Gtwn, or to the subscriber, at Balt. –C Levering, 118 Lombard st

S S Seward, the venerable father of Hon Wm H Seward, died at his residence in Orange Co, N Y, on Sat last, after a lingering illness.

The Emperor of Russia, through the Russian Minister at Washington, has appointed Maj T S Brown, to succeed the late Maj Whistler, as Chief Engineer of the great Railroad from St Petersburgh to Moscow, & he has accepted on certain conditions. Maj Brown was educated at West Point, & is the Chief Engineer on the Erie Railroad. The St Petersburgh road is 420 miles long, & the estimated cost is $40,000,000. It is expected that the distance will be regularly travelled in 12 hours.
–Connecticut Courant

The degree of Dr of Laws has recently been conferred by Geneva College upon our townsman, Henry R Schoolcraft.

Wash Corp: 1-Cmte of Claims: bill for the relief of Saml Carson: passed. Same cmte: bill for the relief of Nathl Parker: passed. Same cmte: bill for the relief of Edw Smith: without amendment. 2-Ptn from John Dewdney: referred to the Cmte on Police. 3-Cmte of Claims: bill for the relief of Wm Becker: passed.

At the Nat'l House in Charlestown, Mass, on Mon, Lt Edw C Bowers stabbed Benj Crowninshield, Cmdor's Clerk, twice near the heart with a dirk, but not fatally. Bowers is in jail. The cause is said to have been family jealousy.

Maj R J Dunn, of Ky, died of chronic diarrhoea on Aug 19, at Princtown, N J, where he stopped on his way from Balt on Aug 11, having had a severe attack in the latter city.

Texas land for sale: 1,280 acres in Gonzales Co, Texas. Inquire of R W Latham & Co.

For sale, the house & lot occupied by the undersigned, on C st. –A P Bagby

Foreign Item: Rev Mr Hicks recently attempted to climb St Vincent's rocks at Clifton, Eng, but lost his foothold, fell, & was immediately killed.

Mrd: on Aug 19, at St Peter's Church, by Rev Jos Vanhorsign, Mr John Browers to Miss Bridget Delaney, all of Wash City.

FRI AUG 31, 1849
Richd J Ryon announces that he has taken the grocery store recently occupied by Mr Edw Hall, a few doors above Messrs Geo & Thos Parker's old stand, opposite the Centre Market. A share of public patronage is respectfully solicited.

We regret to learn that Pres Taylor became very ill at Cambridge, & it was deemed advisable to convey him privately into Erie, in advance of the cortege by which he was accompanied. Vice Pres Fillmore is in company with the Pres, & designs travelling with him through the State of N Y, after which they go to Boston.

Hon Austin E Wing, of Michigan, died at the Water-cure Establishment in Cleveland, Ohio, on Aug 25. He was a Delegate to Congress from the Territory of Michigan as far back as 1832. He resided in the city of Monroe.

Mr B F Bourne, mate of the schnr **John Allyne**, of Bedford, was taken prisoner by the Patagonians, Indians of Procession Bay, while on shore, the vessel having come to anchor in the Straits of Magellan, on her voyage to Calif. Action for his rescue: Navy Dept, Aug 23, 1849. The U S sloop of war **Vandalia** is about to sail for the Pacific, & if practicable, secure the return of Mr Bourne. –Wm Ballard, Preston [From a letter written to Hon Jos Grinnell, New Bedford, Mass.]

Mr Thos C Magruder has been appointed by the Collector of the District, with the consent of the Sec of the Treas, Collector & Inspector of the Customs for the port of Washington, in the place of Jas Towles.

Death at Sullivan's Island, S C, on Thu last, of an estimable citizen, Andrew Moffett. He had been in bad health for some time & was on a temporary visit to a daughter residing on the Island. Mr Moffett visited a bathing-house & was found by a servant, on the steps of the bathing-house in the agoinies of death, & expired in a few minutes. He was a native of Scotland, but came to this country in early life, & engaged in mercantile pursuits in Charleston, upwards of 40 years.

The large Saw Mill of T O Holmes & Co, in Jacksonville, Fla, was entirely destroyed by fire last night: loss about $8,000.

Accident on Wed week on the Hudson & Stockbridge railroad, near Chatham. The train stuck a cow that was grazing on the edge of the road, which threw the passenger train off the rails & down the embankment. The 5 year old son of Mr Wm S Murray, of N Y, was leaning out of the window & was instantly killed by the car falling upon him. He was an only child.

Died: on Aug 22, at Greenville, Green Co, N Y, where he was on a visit, after a short illness, Mr Leoline Jenkins, son of Lemuel Jenkins, of Wash City, late a clerk in the Pension Ofc at Wash, a young man of good abilities, & much esteemed by his acquaintances. He leaves a wife, to whom he was recently married, & many friends, to regret this sudden bereavement.

Died: on Aug 29, Clara Marion Moorhead, only daughter of John & Martha Wilson, aged 1 year, 1 month & 14 days. Her funeral is Fri at 10 o'clock, from the residence of her parents, N Y ave & 11th sts.

Died: on Aug 30, in Wash City, Anne, only daughter of Jos B & Susan Stanley, aged 21 months. Her funeral is on Sat, at 10 o'clock, from the residence of Mr Jack, on 4½ st, between Missouri & Pa aves.

SAT SEP 1, 1849
Appointment by the Pres: Horatio J Perry, of N H, has been appointed Sec of the U S Legation at Madrid.

City lots at private sale: the subscriber has lots in Wash City, some in the 3rd Ward, called Northern Liberties, & others in the 7th Ward. Apply at his ofc, 7th st, near the Genr'l Post Ofc. –Geo Sweeny

Rappahannock Academy, Caroline Co, Va: next session will commence on Oct 3. Geo G Butler, A M, Principal A F N Rolfe, A M, Assist in Ancient Languages; Briscoe G Baldwin, jr, Assist in Math & Tactics.
References:
*Rev H M Denison, Wmsburg, Va
*Wm W Lamb, Norfolk
*F W Seabury, Norfolk
*Capt Wm Green, U S Navy
*Wm Bloxham, Tallahassee, Fla
*John L Vickers, Columbus, Miss
Hon T Butler King, Ga
Hon Danl E Watrous, Ala
*Wm P Taylor, Caroline, Va
Rev Wm Friend, Port Royal, Va
*Geo Fitzhugh, Port Royal, Va
Col E T Tayloe, King Geo, Va
*Dr F Fairfax, King Geo, Va
*Aug Fitzhugh, King Geo, Va
*W Roy Mason, King Geo, Va
*Geo W Lewis, Westmoreland, Va

*Robt Mayo, jr, Westmoreland, Va
Hon Willoughby Newton, Westmoreland, Va
*Dr E H Henry, Fauquier, Va
Dr Wm Shutheo, Matthews C H, Va
Gen S H Lewis, Rockingham, Va
*Capt Jas Maget, Southampton, Va
Rev A Shiras, Gtwn, D C
Rev Dr May, Theo Seminary
Judge Jno T Lomax, Fredericksburg, Va
Col John W Gilliam, Dinwiddie, C H, Va
Dr E H Smith, Dinwiddie, C H, Va
*Gentlemen who either have had or now have sons or wards at the Institution.

Wm Abbott, Mayor of the city of Bangor, died at his residence there on Sat, aged 73 years. He had been sufferring for some time with typhus fever.

Trustee' sale: by deed of trust from John Mullikin to me, for the benefit of Saml Redfern, dated Dec 24, 1847, I shall sell, on Sep 10, the following real estate in Wash City, to wit: part of lot 7 in square 74, fronting on Pa ave, [to the line of a lot sold by one Wm G Williams to Thos Lundy.] -D Ratcliffe, trustee
-Martin & Wright, auctioneers

Mrd: on Aug 7, at South Strafford, by Rev John Moore, Capt O A Buck, of Raleigh, N C, to Miss Lucia Dow, of Strafford.

Boston, Aug 29. Stabbing affair at Charlestown, on Mon, Lt Edw D Bowers, U S N, armed with a large dirk knife, went into the bar-room of the Nat'l House, where Mr Benj Crowinshield, Cmdor Downes' Clerk at the Navy Yard, was sitting reading a newpaper, &, without uttering a single word, Bowers assaulted the latter with the dirk. The wounds inflicted were dangerous but not fatal. Bowers was committed for trial. He had but recently received orders to sail in the ship **Germantown**. –Courier

Farm for sale: the farm on which I reside, containing 145 acres, more or less, on the Marlboro road, adjoining the land of Messrs F L Darnell & F Magruder: with a small frame dwlg, stable, & meat house. Apply to Mr Wm Lloyd, Wash; or to subscriber, Horatio Newman

Died: on Aug 28, aged 52 years, Mrs M R Smith, daughter of the late Gen Mountjoy Bayley.

Died: yesterday, at her residence in Wash City, in her 49th year, Mrs Mary P Slye, relict of the late Thos G Slye, & daughter of Capt Aquila Johns, deceased.

Died: on Aug 28, at his residence, Bellevue, PG Co, Md, Mr Loyd M Lowe, in his 82nd year.

Died: at his residence near *Rixeyville*, Culpeper Co, Va, Jas R Rixey, after a protracted illness of many weeks, in his 31st year, leaving a wife & child, with many friends, to mourn their loss. [No date-current item.]

MON SEP 3, 1849
Rugby Academy, corner of Vt ave & L st, will be resumed on Sep 3. -G F Morrison, Principal

The Misses Rooker's Academy, for Young Ladies, Md ave, near 12th st, [Island,] will re-open on Sept 3.

The Phil papers announce the death, in that city, of Chas Chauncey, for the last 50 years one of its most respected inhabitants. [No death date given-current item.]

Marlborough [Md] Gaz: the corner stone of the Catholic chapel, to be erected in Spaulding's district, PG Co, was laid Thu of last week, ceremonies by Rev Mr Finotti, of Gtwn College, in the absence of the Rev Archbishop of Balt. This chapel is about 6 miles from Wash, & about 3 miles from the ferry opposite Alexandria.

The will of the late Cyrus Butler, of Providence, R I, was proved on Wed. The estate is estimated at $4,000,000.00, nearly all of which goes to Mr Duncan, formerly of Canandaigua, who married the testator's niece. To the eldest son of Mr Duncan, a young gentleman, of 20, $250,000 is bequeathed.

On Mon last, Jos Bradshaw, age 19 years, met with his death at Barnum's Museum Bldg, in Phil. He was sportively amusing himself upon the swinging rope, when he fell to the floor, causing death instantly.

Obit-died: on Aug 19, in Phil, Pa, in his 29th year, Mr Jos P Roura, organist of St Philip's Church, & resident of, & professor of music, in this city. A native of Barcelona, Spain. He died of the incurable disease, consumption; &, preceded for a few short weeks by an infant daughter, he sunk into an untimely grave. A widowed wife & childless mother remains.

Obit-died: the annunciation yesterday of the death of Chas H Smith, late major & Paymaster in the U S Army, although not unexpected, will smite with anguish the hearts of a widely extended circle of children, relatives, & friends. No man living in Va was more universally beloved. Maj Smith was a liberally educated & a highly intelligent man; a devoted follower of the Redeemer. –Norfolk Beacon

Died: on Sep 2, Allefanc Gautier, aged 8 months & 19 days, son of Chas & Alice Gautier. His funeral is this day at half past 4 o'clock.

TUE SEP 4, 1849
Patrick Collins, late Surveyor of the port of Cincinnati, died at his residence in that city last Tue, after an illness of several weeks.

A friend has placed in our hands a copy of "The Gtwn Weekly Ledger," published Nov 26, 1791, it being the 85th number of the publication. We notice that Geo Plater was unanimously elected Govn'r of the State of Md. The description of person born a negro who afterwards became white. A sonnet by Dr Aiken, addressed to His Excellency Geo Washington.

Orphans' Court of PG Co, Md: Aug 21, 1849. Ordered by the Court that Clement Young & C C Magruder, administrators de bonis non of Notley Young, deceased, give the notice required by law to the deceased's creditors to exhibit their claims.
–Jas Harper, Reg/o Wills for PG Co. The notice required followed the above notice: signed-Clement Young & C C Magruder. [Also, C C Magruder is alone authorized to settle the business of the estate.]

Mrd: on Sep 1, by Rev E Ballantine, Mr Owen Hobson to Miss Harriet M Badger.

Died: on Aug 31, at the residence of her son-in-law, R S Smith, U S A, at West Point, Mrs Anna R Clarke, Consort of Matthew St Clair Clarke, of Wash City. This sad information will be a shock to the large circle of the friends of this Lady in the place of her residence & elsewhere, who will first learn the news of her death from this notice. As wife, mother, & friend, her death will long be lamented in our city.

Died: on Sep 1, Wm Ryland, son of Geo R & Sarah J Ruff, aged 1 year, 6 months & 24 days.

By writ of fieri facias, I have levied & taken in execution, to wit: 1 frame house & lot in square 579, & lot 1 in square 579, on D st, so seized & taken as the property of Henry Craig: sale on Sep 8, to satisfy a judgment in favor of John Van Reswick.
–John Magar, Constable

Extensive sale of stock, & farming utensils, at auction: on Sep 26, at the residence of Mr J Williams, on the farm belonging to Mr R Clark, adjoining the farms of Messrs Digges, Jackson, Kirkwood, & Chew, near the *Adelphi Mills*, PG Co, Md.
–Green & Tastet

For rent: new 2 story frame house on 22nd & F sts. Inquire of Wm H Minnix, on the premises, or Lewis Haslup, at the Coach Factory.

WED SEP 5. 1849
By virtue of an order of distress, I shall expose to public sale, for cash, on Sep 13, at the Jail, Wash City, D C, one mulatto woman slave, Eliza Mason, & her infant boy child: seized & taken for house rent due & in arrears by the late Mary B Slye, deceased, to Walter Lenox, & will be sold by the same. -R R Burr, Bailiff

The steamship **Caledonia** brings news of the death of Rev Henry Coleman on Aug 17, near London. His purpose was to return home in the **Caledonia**, & he had actually engaged his passage, but died before the day of departure. With him Agriculture was an absorbing passion, aside from the important duties of his vocation.

New Post Ofcs established by the Postmaster General:

Ofc	County, State	New Appointments
Flag Staff	Somerset, Maine	Wm Butler
Moose River	Somerset, Maine	Chris Thompson
North Shapleigh	York, Maine	Levi Loring
West Chesterfield	Hampshire, Mass	Jas M Augell
Lapeer	Cortlandt. N Y	Royal Johnson
Pompton Plains	Morris, N J	David M Berry
Kellysville	Delaware, Pa	Chas Kelly
Rose Tree	Delaware, Pa	Matil B Cummins
New Wash	Clearfield, Pa	Saml Seabring
Maple	Delaware, Pa	E R Curtis
Quarryville	Lancaster, Pa	Geo W Hensel
Hosensack	Lehigh, Pa	David Gehman
Quinn's Mills	Clinton, Ohio	D P Quinn
Sharpe's Forke	Athens, Ohio	Chas S Dickey
Livonia Centre	Wayne, Mich	Danl P Hinson
Carlton	Barry, Mich	Jared S Rogers
Base Lake	Washtenaw, Mich	Moses Y Hood
Noble Centre	Branch, Mich	Wm Butts
Bear Branch	Ohio, Indiana	Hugh B Downey
Raysville	Henry, Indiana	Jos Wood
Montgomery	Jennings, Indiana	Allen Hill
Lick Branch	Parke, Indiana	Calvin Newlin
New Centreville	Jennings, Indiana	Wm S Rondbush
Casey	Clark, Ill	Ewing Chancellor
Liverpool	Fulton, Ill	J B Burlingham
Rapids	Whiteside, Ill	A W Worthington
Penney's Ferry	Henry, Ill	Solomon Penny
Walker's Grove	Fulton, Ill	John L Chase
Yankee Hill	Menard, Ill	Asa Cleveland
Argo	Crawford, Mo	Reuben S Bacon
Fayette	Lafayette, Wis	M W Anderson
Kewaskum	Washington, Wis	Nathan Wheeler
Baker's Corners	Walworth, Wis	Jas Baker
Elk	Crawford, Wis	Henry Bailey
Willet	Greene, Wis	Jonas Shooke
Barkersville	Marion. Iowa	Jas Barker
Monona	Clayton, Iowa	Phin P Omsted
Elkport	Clayton, Iowa	John R Blanchard
Prunty's	Patrick, Va	John Prunty
Rough & Ready Mills	Henry, Va	Wm J Clarke
Peonfield	Davidson, N C	Jeremiah Piggott
Fish Port	Rock, Ill	B Gorton
Eden	Randolph, N C	D W C Johnson
Taylorsville	Madison, Ga	Heinmon J Patton
Antioch	Pickens, Ala	Jas Eddins
Mexico	Jefferson, Ala	R R Montgomery

Fort Browder	Barbour, Ala	Saml J Smith
Blue Creek	Pike, Ala	Robt F Owen
Lamington	Russell, Ala	Abram C Philips
Caddo	Caddo, La	Wm Stucker
San Louis	Brazoira, Texas	Augustus Burr
Sugar Land	Matagorda, Texas	Thos Jamison
San Cosme	Rusk, Texas	Sol M Grigsby
Centreville	Conway, Ark	Alex'r Gordon
Oxford	McMinn, Tenn	John Goss, jr
Pigeon Forge	Sevier, Tenn	Wm J Trotter
Coffee Landing	Hardin, Tenn	John Barham
Union	McMinn, Tenn	A M Cate
Johnson's Forks	Morgan, Ky	Wm S Lykins
Glencoe	Gallatin, Ky	Philip O Turpin
Mount Hope	Clay, Ky	Reuben May
Farmers	Heming, Ky	J B Zimmerman
Corydon	Henderson, Ky	John N Dorsey
Savern	Owen, Ky	S S Rowlett

Names & sites changed:
Newburg, Boone Co, Ill, name & site changed to Cherry Valley & Jos M Riddle appointed P M.
Illinois City, Rock Island Co, Ill, name & site changed to Buffalo Prairie, & J F Whitney appointed P M.
Cold Mountain, Amherst Co, Va, name & site changed to Oronoco, & Geo Markham appointed P M.
Farley, Culpeper Co, Va, name changed to Strode.
Iron Works, Cass Co, Ga, named changed to Etowah.
Rich Hill, Itawamba Co, Miss, name changed to Cummingsville.
Lyons, Lucas Co, Ohio, site changed, & Wm Smith appointed P M

Mrd: on Sep 4, in Trinity Church, by Rev C M Butler, Edw M Spillman to Miss Eliza C Day, both of Va.

Fatal casualty: from Thomaston, Upson Co, of Aug 28. Mr H Platt, collecting agent, was killed this afternoon by the falling of a tree, about 6 miles from this place, on his way to Talbotton. He was associated with Mr Israel James, of Phil, as a general newspaper agent. –Augusta [Ga] Chron

The U S storeship **Supply** arrived at Norfolk on Mon, after a passage of 41 days from Rio Janeiro. Her ofcrs: Arthur Sinclair, Lt Commanding
Geo H Cooper, Master & ex-ofcr; E K Kane, Passed Assist Surgeon
Passed Midshipmen: Geo H Bier, Robt D Minor, & Walter F Jones
A F Gray, Midshipman; J D Ghislin, Capt's Clerk
Passengers from Rio: Mrs Eldridge, [wife of Purser Eldridge, of the brig **Perry**, & daughter of Mr Parks, U S Consul at Rio,] child, & nurse.

The sloop of war **Vandalia** has orders to touch at Possession bay, in the Straits of Magellan, for information of the mate of a New Bedford schnr, who was detained there by the natives some time ago. Ofcrs of the **Vandalia**: Cmder Wm H Gardner Lts: R E Johnson, Wm L Herndon, Reid Werner, Thos H Patterson Surgeon Jas C Palmer; Assist Surgeon Robt Carter; Purser John V B Bleecker Acting Master J P Bankhead; Passed Midshipmen: J B Stewart, A T Byrens, H St Geo Hunter, S B Luce, A W Habersham; Midshipman A R Simmons Acting Midshipman Chas H Cushman; Capt's Clerk D F Gardner Acting Boatswain Z Whitmarsh; Gunner John D Brant; Carpenter R M Bain; Sailmaker John W North

Five persons were drowned in the Susquehanna river on Wed last, a mile above Safe Harbor, while attempting to cross in a skiff. Their names are Mrs Manning, Miss Hughes, aged 19 years, another married lady, the wife of David Roland, Mr Peters, & a son of Peters, aged about 14 years.

Wash Corp: 1-Bill for the relief of Harrison Taylor: referred to the Cmte of Claims. 2-Bill for the relief of J F Wollard: laid on the table. 3-Cmte of Claims: asked to be discharged from the further consideration of the ptn of C Shad. 3-Ptns of Wm Cammack & Jas Maher, praying remission of fines: referred to the Cmte of Claims. 4-Ptn of Wm Greason, for remission of a fine: referred to the Cmte of Claims. Same for Geo W Wren; & for Jas A Wise: both for remission of a fine each: referred to the Cmte of Claims. 5-Cmte of Claims: asking to be discharged from the further consideration of the ptns of Geo Stutz & of David Horning: discharged accordingly. 6-Bill for the relief of Lawrence Callan, reported without amendment.

Died: on Sep 4, Fred'k Mohler, a native of Switzerland, & for many years a resident of Wash City, in his 52nd year. His funeral is this morning at 10 o'clock, from his late residence, on 14th st.

Died: on Sep 4, in his 7th year, of congestive fever, John, son of the late Thos R Hampton, of Wash City. His funeral is this morning, at 10 o'clock, from the residence of his mother, on 13th st south.

Died: on Aug 28, in Wash City, of scarlet fever, Mary Rosena, aged 3 years, 2 months & 19 days; on Aug 29, Louisa Virginia, aged 16 months & 21 days; on Sep 3, Wm Henry, aged 4 years & 7 months, children of Allison & Rachel D Nailor.

Farm for sale: subscriber's farm in Alexandria Co, nearly opposite the residence of Jas Roach, containing 61 acres of land. Also, a new 3 story brick dwlg & store on Pa ave, between 17th & 18th sts. Also, a frame dwlg on G st, near 22nd st. Apply to Selby Parker, Fancy Store, Pa ave, or to the subscriber on the farm. –Jos Fraser

Household & kitchen furniture at auction on Sep 10, in the 2 large houses now occupied by Mrs E H Bawner, on Pa ave, between 2nd & 3rd sts.
-E C & G F Dyer, aucts

THU SEP 6, 1849
Some time since the Rev Mr Fairbanks was committed to the penitentiary of Ky for having aided the escape of a slave. He has since been pardoned & liberated, but a correspondent of the Boston Traveller says it was not done until about $600 were paid to the owner of the slave.

Foreign item: Mehemet Ali, the Ruler of Egypt, died at Alexandria Aug 2.

Mrs Wells, residing in Nassau st, near the Navy Yard, Brooklyn, N Y, died on Sun of dysentery, after a few hours' illness; shortly after 3 children were taken ill & died, leaving Mr Wells a widower & childless. They were all buried on Monday.

Mrd: on Aug 26, by Rev J Vanhorsigh, Mr Jas W Fowle to Miss Mary E Sengstack, all of Wash City.

Mrd: on Sep 3, by Rev Mr Hodges, Mr John M Clarke to Miss M Boswell, of the Dist of Columbia.

Mrd: on Sep 4, by Rev J B Donelan, Mr John Boyle to Miss Mary Ann Sullivan, all of Wash City.

Mrd: on Sep 5, by Rev Wm A Collier, Clayton Chery to Lethe Knowles, both of Gtwn, D C.

Died: on Sep 3, at **Millwood**, the residence of his father, in PG Co, Md, William, infant son of Wm A & Mary R M Gunton, aged 10 weeks.

For rent: commodious dwgl hses at 7th & I sts. Apply to A Rothwell.

John Tointon. Whereas John Tointon, late of Kirton, Linconshire, Eng, left Eng for the U S in 1836, & resided with Mr Overton Woods, of Whirl's mill, Jorden, on the Erie canal in N Y, the said Tointon, if alive, is about 30 years of age. Notice is given that, if he be alive, will make application to Mr Jebb, Solicitor, Boston, Linconshire, Eng, he will hear of something to his advantage. If John Tointon be dead, any person who shall satisfactorily prove such fact, & communicate the particulars to the said Mr Jebb, or to Mr Pishey Thompson, 5 Bank Chambers, Lothbury, London, shall be properly remunerated for his trouble. –London, August, 1849

Valuable farm for sale: in consequence of a contract entered into with the Gov't for furnishing brick for the new Patent Ofc now erecting in Wash, requiring his whole time & attention, offers at private sale the Farm on which he resides, called **Crownsville**, lying & being in Anne Arundel Co, Md: 185 acres, more or less: with a commodious dwlg house & all other necessary out-bldgs. I also offer another Farm, containing about 125 acres, within 1 mile of the Crownsville farm: no improvements. Apply to Mr R Welch of Ben, Annapolis, or to the subscriber, Wash. The title is indisputable, & reference is made to John Glenn, of Balt, who can give all information in reference to the same. –Thos Crown

Orphans Court of Wash Co, D C. Letters testamentary on personal estate of Nicholas W Worthington, late of Wash Co, deceased. —Catherine Pearson, excx

Mrs Mary E Clark informs that her extensive home, at F & 14th sts, is now in order to receive guests. Transient boarders received at $1 per day.

For rent: two new 3 story dwlg houses on Pa ave, between 3rd & 4th sts. Terms made known by Geo Collard, at Blagden's Wharf.

FRI SEP 7, 1849
Two boys aged 5 years, were fishing when they both fell into the water & went to the bottom. The alarm was given, & John Brooks Pratt, of Charlestown, son of Danl Pratt, of Chelsea, came immediately to their rescue. -Boston Adv

Jas Evans, age about 30 years, lives at Batavia, Ohio, & educated himself in N H, & is a good printer, farmer, teacher, engineer, map maker & practical surveyor. His father died very poor, when he was young, & his mother supported the family several years by hard labor. —Cin Com

The noble packet ship **Henry Clay** took fire on Wed, while lying at her wharf at the foot of Maiden Lane, N Y. She was one of the largest & finest ships in the world. She was built in 1845, in this city, & belonged to Messrs Grinnell, Minturn & Co's, N Y & Liverpool line of packets. Her value may be set down at about $90,000. She was insured, with freight & cargo, in several ofcs in Wall st, to the amount of about $80,000.

The Pres of the U S has appointed Nathan Brown, of N Y, to be Paymaster in the U S Army, vice Col Edmund Kirby, deceased.

From Yucatan: reported battle. A passenger who arrived at New Orleans on Aug 29, states that on the 16th a diligence came into that place from Merida with a report that, in the absence of a part of the soldiers, Indians attacked the Mexicans, & drove them into the citadel at Bacalar, & retired. 600 Mexicans remained dead on the field. Capt Kelly, of the Louisiana volunteers, was reported killed in the action.

Mrd: on Sep 3, by Rev Mr Hodges, Mr John M Clarke to Miss Ann M Boswell, both of Md.

Died: on Sep 6, after a short illness, Wm Wamsley Smith, a native of Stockport, Lancashire, Eng, in his 39th year. His funeral is this morning, at 10 o'clock.

Died: on Mon last, at the residence of her father, Mr Robt Ball, of Alexandria Co, Va, after a protracted illness, of consumption, Mrs Eleanora Dyer, in her 26th year, wife of Mr Wm B Dyer, of Wash City, leaving a husband & 3 small children, & numerous relatives to mourn her decease.

Died: Sep 5, Charles W, infant son of Abel G & Mary D Davis, of Wash City.

Hogs for sale: at 15½ st & Md ave, near the Long Bridge. —Wm Thomas

Household & kitchen furniture at auction Sep 10, at the residence of Wm Mann, 6th st, between E & G sts. —John Martin & Co, aucts

Orphans Court of Wash Co, D C. Letters testamentary on the personal estate of Sarah Murray, late of said county, deceased. —Henry G Murray, adm

SAT SEP 8, 1849
Writ of fieri facias, at the suit of John E Dement, against John Gibson, I have seized 4 hogs, the property of said Gibson: will be sold on Sep 15, at the Cross Keys, 7th st, to the highest bidder. —Wm Cox, Constable

Writ of fieri facias, at the suit of Wm Hughes, against John Gibson, I have seized 6 hogs, the property of said Gibson: will be sold on Sep 13, at the Cross Keys, 7th st, to the highest bidder. —Wm Cox, Constable

By an order of distrain from Wm B Magruder, adm of E Evans, deceased, against the goods & chattels of ___ Dent, the following property has been seized to satisfy house rent due to Magruder as administrator, to wit: hair-seat sofa, 5 mahg chairs, ingrain carpet, candlesticks, & andirons: sale on Sept 14, in front of the Centre Market-house. —E G Handy, Bailiff

Wm A Wisong, 2 North Liberty st, Balt, Wholesale & Retail Dealer in window glass, paints, oil, varnishes, brushes, & artist materials. [Ad]

Subscriber has obtained letters of administration, with the will annexed on the estate of Amelia Thomas, late of Wash Co, D C. Persons having claims to exhibit the same, with vouchers, on or before Sep 7 next. —S W Williams, adm, W W A

I certify that Jacob Harshan, of Wash Co, D C, brought before me a chickasaw horse, as an estray. —Jas Crandell, J P [Owner of the above horse is to prove property, pay charges, & take him away. —Jacob Harshman, living at the east end of the Navy Yard bridge.]

Miss Anna Bird has a Select School for Young Ladies at Phil, containing between 30 & 40 pupils. Reference: while Principal of the Central High School of Phil, I was thoroughly acquainted with the female dept under Miss Bird, & recommend the school now opened by her. —A D Bache
Reference: during the 7 years that I have been Principal of the Phil High School, I have been well acquainted with Miss Bird, & she is a teacher of superior qualifications. —John S Hart, Central H S, Phil, Aug 20, 1849

The Cincinnati Chronicle memtions the sudden death, on Tue, by cholera, of Dr Harrison, one of the most eminent physicians of that city, Prof of Materia Medica & Therapeutics in the Ohio Medical College.

Extensive robbery. A package of bank notes, $3,000, had been entrusted to Mr D G McCreary, of Parkersburg, by the Bank of that place, & was discovered to be missing from the steamer **Elite** on Sun. The trunk of Mr McCreary had been unlocked & the package taken was placed in it along with another package of $2,500, which was left in the trunk.

Albany, Sep 6. Gen Taylor has just arrived here, accompanied by Dr Wood, his son-in-law & Medical Attendant. He will dine with Gov Fish, & will leave this evening in the steamer **Isaac Newton** for N Y.

Fort Laramie, Jul 10, 1849. On Sun last, one of our men, Chas Bishop, died. We buried him on Sun on the summit of a high bluff overlooking the Platte river. [Letter from a member of the Wash & Calif Mining Assoc, commanded by Capt Bruff, to his father in Washington.]

Fatal steamboat accident: St Louis, Sep 6. The steamer **Hardee**, for Council Bluffs, bursted her connexion pipe a few days since, when 30 miles above Weston, killing Capt Geo Wishback, & scalding, supposed mortally, Geo Martin, pilot, & Robt Lindsey, clerk. The two Misses Powell, of Boonsville, & Mrs Tompins, of this city, were severely scalded.

Died: on Sep 7, William Asbury, aged 2 years & 6 weeks, son of Robt A & Ellen M Connell.

Lost on Pa ave, a red silk bead purse. Suitable reward, if desired, if delivered to Wm Gunton.

For rent: 2 story brick house, now in the occupancy of Prof Jas Major, on West st, between Congress & Wash sts, Gtwn. Possession on Oct 6. Apply to Robt Read, Gtwn.

Household & kitchen furniture at auction on Sep 13, at the late residence of Isaac C Smith, deceased, on 12th between F & G sts. –Green & Tastet, aucts

MON SEP 10, 1849
The Union of yesterday announced the death, at Wheeling, Va, on Sep 8, by cholera, of Hon A Newman, one of the Reps elect to Congress from the State of Va. He was a stanch Democrat, & a worthy man.

Hon Augustus C Dodge, Senator from Iowa, arrived in Wash City on Sat, on his way to visit his father, the Senator from Wisconsin, who, we learn, is suffering under severe indisposition at Berkeley Springs, Va.

Decision of the examining court at Palmyra, Mo, in the case of John S Wise, arrested for the murder of Thos B Hart, the paramour of his wife. We think the killing of Thos B Hart is an offence against the law, amounting to murder in the first degree. We therefore commit him to prison.

Jas G Lyon, late U S Marshal for the Southern District of Ala, died at his residence in Mobile on Aug 29, after a long & painful illness.

Died: on Sun, Mrs Caroline Ousley, consort of Mr John Ousley, in her 38th year. Her funeral is at half past 4 o'clock, this day, from her late residence.

Pottsville, Pa, Sep 7. An 11 year old son of Hon Jas Cooper, U S Senator, who was standing on a train of cars drawn by horses, in attempting to jump from the cars, fell, & they passed over him, severing one of his legs from his body.

In St Louis, Sep 5, a German, Richd Kennedy, was arrested, & held to answer the charge of arson & riot, in firing the house of Madame Clemantine, last Sun week.

On Aug 24, a man named Atchison, residing in Harrison Co, Va, while under temporary derangement, went into the field of his neighbor, Saml Elder, took up a scythe, & as Mr Elder was stooping in mowing, Atchison cut the head of Elder almost entirely off the body. Both Atchison & his victim were sober & respectable men, members of churches, one a Baptist & the other a Methodist.

Tue last **Warner Hall**, the large & beautiful residence of Colin Clark, of Gloucester Co, Va, was destroyed by fire. Some furniture was saved. He was only partially insured.

For rent: commodious dwlg, just erected at the corner of 10th & F st. Apply to S M McKean, 17th st, near Navy Dept.

City Ordinances-Wash. 1-Act for the relief of Edw Smith: to be refunded $2, paid by him, in pursuance of an act concerning free negroes, passed Oct 29, 1836, said Smith being entitled to a permanent residence in the District. 2-Act for the relief of Saml Curson: to be paid $160.98, being the balance due him for grading & graveling certain streets.

Found near the City Post Ofc, a small sum of money, which the owner can receive by application. –P A Byrne

Hogs for sale at the Wash Asylum, on Sep 11, by order of the Com'rs.
-Benj E Gittings, Int W A

I have this day associated Mr Jno C Whitwell with me in the Grocery business, to be conducted under the firm of Jno B Kibbey & Co, 5 Pa ave. –Jno B Kibbey

TUE SEP 11, 1849
A 16 year old son of Mr Wm Cain, of Cleveland, Ohio, was accidentally shot on Sep. He had been hunting, & the gun went off when 2 boys were wrestling, & one threw the other against the gun, discharging it. The physician called thinks a part of the charge passed into the brain.

Chas S Fowler, Importer of China & Queensware: 7th st, Wash. [Ad]

Raleigh Register states that the beautiful residence of Henry K Burgwyn, in Northampton Co, was entirely consumed by fire last week. Little was saved out of the fine furniture, paintings, & plate that belonged to the mansion.

Sales of property in Alleghany Co, Md, belonging to the heirs of L W Stockton, deceased, sold on Sep 1 at trustee's sale: 1-U S Hotel, in Cumberland, purchased by Arthur Cowton, the present lessee, for $8,500. 2-*Highland Hall*, at Frostburg, purchased by Messrs J C Atcheson, of Wheeling, & Howard Kennedy, of Uniontown, for $5,000. 3-The house adjoining the U S Hotel, & now occupied by Mr John C Hull, was purchased by Alpheus Beall, for $3,600.

$20 reward will be given for the detection of the thief who broke into my shop on 6th st, through the back window of the Nat'l Hotel, on Sep 9, & stole sundry articles of value, amongst which were 2 diamond rings worth about $50. --John H Gibbs

Valuable farm at private sale: the handsome farm *Melrose*, containing 225 acres, on the road leading from Bladensburg to *Phillips' Mill*, PG Co, Md, adjoining the farms of Messrs Lounds, C B Calvert, & H Cross. The house is a well finished frame, nearly new. Apply to Green & Tastet, aucts.

Hon Edw J Black, for several years a Member of Congress from Ga, died on Sep 1, in Barnwell district, S C.

Hon Amos Lane, formerly a Rep in Congress from Indiana, died at his residence in Aurora a few days since.

Hon Adam Huntsman, of Tenn, died at his residence near Jackson, Tenn, on Aug 23.

The baking business which has been carried on by L A Tarlton, as agent for the undersigned, is no longer under his management; no person is authorized to receipt for moneys due to that establishment, but J Visser, or M A Lincoln, trustee. The subscriber informs the public, that she is prepared to furnish them with bread, biscuits, & confectionary, at the residence of Wm Greer, 10th st, between E & F. All orders promptly executed.

Died: on Sun last, after a short illness, Mrs Ellen Stone, wife of Mr Michl Stone, aged 49 years. Her funeral is this afternoon, at 2 o'clock, from the residence of her husband, near Gtwn.

WED SEP 12, 1849
A letter from Henderson, dated Aug 25, states that P H Bell, a Virginian by birth, is unquestionably elected Govn'r of Texas. Mr Bell is a Whig, & that will do very well for Texas. The Locos are greatly annoyed at his election.

Chas Fred'k Glasier, who was found hanging dead in Phil on Wed, after a quarrel with his wife, the coroner's jury returned a verdict of death by strangulation-a fact which the Times thinks could scarcely be disputed.

Md Whig Nominaion: election will take place on Oct 2. Candidates for the House of Delegates:
Balt City: Robt C Barry, John Watchman, Jno Coulson, Geo E Sangston, & Thos B Hambleton.
St Mary's Co: Wm J Blackiston, Geo C Morgan, & Jos F Shaw.
Anne Arundel Co: John M S Causin, Gabriel H Duvall, Jas Kent, Thos Burgess, & John Cook.
Chas Co: Richd T Merrick, Jas D Carpenter, & Geo Gardier.
Fred'k Co: Jacob Root, John Lee, B A Cunningham, Michl Siuss, & E B Baltzell.
Montg Co: Wm T Glaze, Dr S N C White, Alex'r Kilgour, & Washington Bonifant.
Wash Co: Elias Davis, Jos Garver, Andrew B Stake, Zach S Clagett, & Nelson McKinley.
Alleghany Co: Wm Fear, Wm Combs, Levin Lenton, & Saml Colhoun.
Cecil Co: Richd Bryan, Jas H Jamar, John Simpers, & Mark Brown.
PG Co: Danl C Digges, Thos I Marshall, Jos J Duvall, & D Sheriff.
Carroll Co: Benj Shunk, Henry Devries, Lewis Trumbo, & Caleb Douty.
Harford Co: Abraham Cole, H D Farnandis, H C Whiteford, & John Hawkins.
Somerset Co: Benj Lankford, John S Crockett, L H Trader, & T W Perry.
Balt Co: Wm Tagart, Wm N Hoffman, Joshua F Cockey, & Wm Hutchins.
Calvert Co: Geo W Weems, J S Dixon, & Geo W Dowell
Kent Co: Saml W Spencer, Thos Baker, & W F Smith.
Dorchester Co: Danl M Henry, Dr A C Smith, Wm Mace, & Jacob Wilson.
Queen Anne's Co: Jas Temples, Lloyd Tilghman, & Chas E Skinner.

<u>Whig Candidates for Congress:</u>

Richd I Bowie	Geo W Gray	Alex'r Evans
Thos J McKaig	John R Kenly	John B Kerr

<u>New Post ofcs: during the week ending Sep 8, 1849</u>:

Ofc	County, State	New Appointment:
East Poland	Cumberland, Maine	Gilman Martin
Braggville	Middlesex, Mass	Dennis Hartshorn
West'rmans Mills	Balt, Md	Levi Slade
Lake Drummond	Norfolk, Va	Alfred Wallace
Milford	Caroline, Va	Rich F Darracott
Crow Creek	Wood, Va	Hugh M Tygart
Shady Spring	Fayette, Va	Edgar Hemans
Silver Hill	Davidson, N C	Chas E Seidell
Green Pond	Union Dis, S C	Jehu Gregory
Hopewell	Jennings, Iowa	John S Thomas
Neet's Creek	Jefferson, Iowa	Joshua C Tibbets
Way	Riple, Iowa	Geo Conaway
Beaver	Boone, Ill	Amyi Abbe
Saint Auburt	Calloway, Md	Louis Robron
Kirkville	Wapelo, Iowa	Henry Kirkparick
Montezuma	Powesheik, Iowa	Isaac G Wilson
Cooksville	Rocks, Wis	John D Chambers
Ulster's Corners	Walworth, Wis	E B Older
Ashton	Dane, Wis	Geo Gillatt

Names & sites changed:
Durham, Cumberland Co, Maine, name changed to West Durham.
Southwest Bend, Cumberland Co, Maine, name changed to Durham.
West Gardiner, Kennebeck Co, Maine, name changed to French's Corner, & John W Herrick, appointed postmaster.
Sweden, Oxford Co, Maine, site changed, & Jacob S Powers appointed postmaster.
Rocksville, Lehigh Co, Pa, name changed to Mechanicsboro.
Orr's Corners, Mahoning Co, Ohio, name & site changed to Hanna's Mills, & David Hanna appointed postmaster.
Austin, Oakland Co, Mich, named changed to Taylorsville, & Thos Terwilliger appointed postmaster.
Long Level, Cabbell Co, Va, name & site changed to Mud Bridge, & John M Reese appointed postmaster.
Fair Grove, Davidson Co, N C, site changed, & John W Thomas appointed postmaster.
Providence, Sumter dist, S C, site changed, & I J Dinkins appointed postmaster.
Gully, Darlington dist, S C, name & site changed to Swift Creek, & C J Hind appointed postmaster.
Bellefontane, Choctaw Co, Miss, site changed, & Wm McCombs appointed postmaster.
St Joseph, Refugio Co, Texas, name changed to Aransas, & Wm H Jones appointed postmaster.
Huntersville, Madison Co, Tenn, name changed to Andrew's Chapel.
Big Foot Prairie, McHenry Co, Tenn, name changed into Walworth Co, Wisc, & Eldridge G Ayer appointed postmaster.
Martinsville, Walworth Co, Wisc, name changed to Vienna, & Winslow P Storms appointed postmaster.
Merrimack Mills, Crawford Co, Mo, name changed to Short Bend.
Border, Harrison Co, Texas, site changed, & Thos E Rives appointed postmaster.

Mrd: on Sep 10, at the 9th st Methodist Protestant Parsonage, by Rev Wm Collier, Mr Jas Cochran to Martha Cooley, all of Wash City.

Orphans Court of Wash Co, D C. Letters of administration on the personal estate of Fred'k Mohler, late of said county, deceased. –Ursula Mohler, Jacob Brodbeck, jr, adms

Wash Corp: 1-Ptn from Geo Krafft: referred to the Cmte of Claims. 2-Ptn from Chas Garner & others: referred to Cmte on Improvements. 3-Ptn of Colin Bayliss, for remission of a fine: referred to Cmte of Claims. 4-Ptn of Nathl Hofflein, for remission of a fine: referred to Cmte of Claims. 5-Account of Jas M Wright, a police ofcr, against the Corp: referred to Cmte of Claims. 6-Ptn of Nicholas Travers, in relation to his claim against the Corp: referred to Cmte on Ways & Means. 7-Cmte of Ways & Means: act for relief of Benony Jones & Jas Spurling: passed.

City Infirmary, Wash, E st, south of Wash City Hall: charges for the sick:
In the public wards, $3 per week; private rooms: $5 per week. Patients admitted by Mr R Adamson, the Steward. My address is, Washington & Gay sts, Gtwn.
–Grafton Tyler, Curator of Wash Infirmary

Balt, Sep 11. Mr Chas R Taylor, cashier of the Bank of Balt, was driving his 2 little daughters to school, when the vehicle came in contact with a dray & upset. The horse took off at top speed, with Mr Taylor & his children still being inside. The vehicle was dashed completely to pieces. Neither of them received any serious injury.

THU SEP 13, 1849
Hon John J Cummins, a Rep in the last Congress from the State of Ohio, died at Milwaukee, of cholera, on Tue last. So says a telegraphic despatch.

Register's Ofc, Wash, Aug 31, 1849. List of the persons who have taken out licenses under the laws of the Corporation during the months of April, May, June, Jul, & Aug:
Auction:
Dyer, E C & G F   McDevitt, J   Robinson, John

Birds: Spinotti, Seignr-2

Cart:
Addison & Cockrell-2   Baeschlin, Jno   Dowling, Wm-2
Adams, C   Bell, Thos J   Ennis, Philip-2
Ailer & Thyson   Baldwin, J A   Edes, Philip
Allen, Benj   Bell, Richd   Fugitt, Jos
Adams, Robt   Barnes, Jno-2   Fletcher, John-2
Butler, M-2   Buneff, John   Fletcher, J
Burghalter, B-2   Burgess, Jno   Fletcher, Wm
Boone, J B   Chew, P   Fry, Jos
Bayliss, Thos   Chew, John   Gildermeister, H
Bean, C   Cissell, W   Giveny, Bernard
Brent, Elton   Crowley, Wm-2   Green, M
Brereton, W H   Cross, A V   Gingenback, D
Beardsley, Geo   Casanave, Peter-2   Green, O
Brooks, Hanson   Conlan, P   Green, Patrick
Barnes, Wm   Cruttenden, Harvy   Goldsmith, Thos
Brown, Archer   Cockrell, G W   Gunnell, Wm H-2
Bates & Bro-2   Caho, J M   Gibson, W
Bateman, Abm   Cruttenden, H   Grinder, John-2
Brown, Robt   Chapin, H L   Hyde, R A
Brown, Jno   Downing, Jos   Haislip, H-2
Barr, W   Dick, Moses   Harvey & Co, J S-4
Bruce, Chas   Day, D G   Hertmuller, A-2
Bowie, Catharine   Dent, Bruce   Hill, Isaac
Butler, John   Davis, Henry   Hanson, Chas
Barrett, Thos J-2   Davis, Elias   Hanson, Geo
Burke, Henry   Deevers, Robt   Hugerty, W
Bridget, John   Dodd, R   Haines, John
Blagden, Thos   Devers, Wm-2   Harkness, Geo W
Barnes, Elias   Dove, John   Hughes, Wm
Bryant, E   Dunlap, G W   Holland, Moses
Barnes, John   Dyson, Chas   Hatch, Wells

Hughes, Wm
Harling, L
Hicks, W
Harohman, Jesse
Iddins, Saml
Johnson & Townley
Jones, Noch
Jolly, John
Jones, Andrew
Jones, Alfred
Jones, Thos S
Kickham, Wm
Knott, J H
Kaufman
King, E
Knight, Mary
Knight, F
Lee, Michl
Little, Peter-2
Lynch, Ambrose
Loveless, John
Latmite, A
Linkins, Walter
Lucas, Henry
Linkins, Jos-2
Lucas, O
Linkins, Danl-2
Lyons, Chas-2
Loveless, Jas
Linkins, Walter
Lewis, J E
Lambell, K H
Lokey, Jas B-2
Lewis, Thos-2
Langley, W H
Lauxman, Martin
Mason, Jos-3
Madison, C
Moore, Wm
Mohun, Philip
Misterer, Isaac
McGlue, G T-2
Mohler, F
Miller, John
McNeeney

Mills, Lydia
Magruder, Fielder
Maguire, Jas
Mills, J E
Noer, Andrew
Noble, Martha
Nepp, Danl
Neale, John E
Neale, Levi
Otterback, Philip
O'Donoghue, P & T
Peterson, Henry
Pulizzi, V
Payne, Saml
Plant, N
Prather, O J
Purdy, John
Payne, Saml
Roach, J-4
Riley, Thos W-4
Rhodes, Jas
Redfern, Saml
Richards, A-2
Riley, John
Ready, John
Richards, W
Rice, Edw
Raley, Jas
Raley, Thos
Rawlings, W
Ragan, Danl-2
Reinz, Wm
Redin, David
Resin, Chas
Richardson, E
Smith, Richd
Stewart, D W
Simmons, R A
Stevenson, Jos
Smoot, Saml-2
Stewart, jr, Chs-2
Sampson, H
Simms, J M
Selby, Thos
Stott, Saml

Simmons, A-2
Simmons, Thos
Stewart, Geo-2
Sibley, C
Sengstack, C P
Spurling, Jas
Simms, Basil
Smallwood, R T
Shacklett, W
Simms, A
Tomlinson, F
Thomas, Saml
Taylor, J H-2
Taylor, E P
Thorn, Henry-2
Tinckler, Saml-2
Travers, M W-2
Territy, Nicholas
Tench, T P
Talbot, Thos
Uniach, John
Uttermuhle, H
Williams, Thos G
Waters, Gustar
Webster, Rezin
Weaser, E
Williams, Z-2
Warder, Wm
Williamson, Thos
Wood, Edw
Warden, W
Woods, John
Woods, Dennis
Waters, E-2
Walker & Peck-2
Wilson, Marcellus
Wilson, John
Waters, Theo
Wilson, J S
Ward, Enoch-2
Wilson, H T l
Warner, Saml
Wood, Nicholas

Circus: Robinson & Co

Dancing: Madame Weiss

Dog:
Andrews, T P
Arth, Philip
Blagden, Thos
Barrett, Ths J
Barber, Geo
Butler, Nathl
Berry, John
Baltimore, Thos
Borre, W
Beschlin, J
Bell, Thos
Barnes, Hanson-2
Bowman, Chs
Bean, W
Brooks, Clement
Barnes, Mary
Brown, Jno
Brown, Hanson
Barber, Jos
Bell, Jas H
Bell, Wm H
Beckett, P
Catalano, A
Caden, Jas
Corson, Job
Chiseltyne, E
Carter, Luke
Coke, W
Conner, Thos
Cox, Clement
Chauncey, John
Crandell, Jos
Corcoran, W W
Clarke, J T C
Clark, M M
Clarke, Danl B
Clements, R H
Cornish, Harriet
Douglass, W
Drake, Willard
Daley, Jas
Dodson, J
De Saules, P A
Dulany, C
Diggs, Ann

Eckloff, C G
Eaton, J H
Elliot, J W
Edelin, E H
Fergerson, W
Fox, Grace
Freeland, Susan
Frank, Jacob
Fisher, D
Galt, M W
Goins, Patrick
Grimes, J F-2
George, Sarah
Green, O
Giveney, B
Grover, W
Grimes, J M
Hampton, Emily
Haines, L
Harris, Angelo
Holden, F
Hill, Henry
Holland, Robt
Hamilton, W M
Hamilton, Va
Joyce, Susan
Jones, Alfred
Johnson, Isaiah
Jacob, G
Johnson, Morris
Jennings, H
Jones, Eliz
Ingraham, Wash'n
Jones, Jas
Jones, Richd
King, Z M P
Kelig, Jno M
Knott, M
Knight, F
Lusby, Thos
London, W H
Leddy, O
Linkins, Wm
Lee, Josias
Lord, W

Linkins, Danl
Landrick, Isaac
Middleton & Beall
McClery, E J
Moore, J H
Morgan, W
Mason, Enoch
Mason, Jos
McNamee, Chas-2
Mills, Clarke-2
Mankin, Wm
McDonald, W J
McConnell, M
Mahar, Jas
Magar, Jno
Martin, Wm
Ofensteink, C
Parke, W P
Parton, F B
Phelps, A
Payne, G W-2
Peck, Jos
Riggs, Elisha
Ruff, J A
Reintz, Wm
Ramsey, Douglass-2
Riggs, Warren
Ryon, Richd J
Smallwood, D
Simms, A
Sengstack, C P
Shields, Thos
Speaks, Letiia
Smith, J C
Serrin, D
Sessford, J
Sweeting, Mrs
Simpson, T
Seymour, Richd
Thomas, J H
Talbert, Thos
Thomas, Henry
Thompson, J E
Taylor, Patrick
Tascoe, Thos

Talbert, W
Twine, D
Turner, H

Watson, Jas
Wilkinson, E
Wagner, Nich's

Wright, L
West, Jas-2
Wilcox, J A

Dray:
Bacon & Co, Saml
Emery, M E
Jackson & Bro, B L
Kibby, J B
Middleton & Beall
Ober & Ryon

Pullin, Jas
Parker, Geo & Ths-2
Peerce, J M
Ryon, J T
Stevenson, Jos
Wise, Chas J

Hack:
Butler, Jas
Cook, Wm

Fletcher, W A
Schwaitze

Hats & Caps:
Fisher & Co, M
Gueneman, Geo
Glick & Co, J

Marshall, Wm
Perkins & Dyer
Seldner, L

Sinsheimer & Co, I
White & Bro
Wilson, J Q

Huckster:
Biggs, J D
Brown, R W-transfer
Crown, G P
Chafee, W E-transfer
Davis, A
Elisha & Lewis

Elisha, S & W W
Humphreys, M A
Jones, Noah
Lane, Henry
Moran, Elijah
Miller, Francis-transfer

Newmyer, L
Seldner, L
Skidmore, J
Wilson, Thos K
Wagner, H
Wollard, H-2

Liquors:
Brown, Robt T-transfer
Caho, J M
Carpenter, Tim and-transfer
Gannon, Edmund
Gengenback, D

King, V E
Kibbey, J B
Keobel, Jacob
Makay, Philip
Orme, Wm
Quigley, David
Ryon, Richd J

Shutz, F
Scott, Henry T
Sengstack & Clark
Watson, B T
Whalen, Patrick

Merchandise:
Boone, J B
Bean, Geo
Crogan, John
Cockrell, G H
Casanave, P
Day, D G
Dove, Wm T
Douglass, S E
Douglass, Saml E

Ebeling, Henry
Fugitt, J
Frazier, G W
Haislep, H
Hill, Isaac
Harvey & Lloyd
Harvey & Co, J S
Hall & Co, P
Jolly, John

Lenman & Bro
Marshall, Wm
Magruder, F
Magle, Jacob
McCutchen, Jas
Murtagh, Mary E
Pegg, J R-transfer
Phillips, E A
Pearson, P M

353

Preston & Co, O J
Purdy, John
Pettibone, John
Shadd, B
Travers & Son, J

Van Reswick, J
Waters, G
Ward, John B
Wilson, John
Water, Elkanah

Warder, Wm
Williams, Z
Webb & Hatch
Wheeler & Co, W A

Opera: Italian Troupe: [3 nights]

Serenaders: Harvey, G W: [3 nights]

Shop:
Doyle, M C
Kleindienst, A

Neil, Andrew-transfer
Shadd, C

Slave:
Bell, Susan
Boyden, Fred
Beall, Ann E

Cooper, Wm
McPherson, Wm
Muncaster, Harriet

Marriott, G W
Maddox, W M

Slut: Ehrmancroutt, Jos; Magee, Owen; Parker, S; Tucker, W

Tavern:
Donovan, John
Hewison, W G-transfer

Howard, John
Ragan, Jas
Riley, John

Ridgway, H
Stutz, Geo-transfer

Theatrical: Adelphi Theatre-2

Wagon:
Addison & Cockrell
Adams & Co-2
Butler, M
Briscoe, Henry
Brady, M
Barber, Geo
Barnes, Wm
Bates & Bro
Burnett, Enoch
Brown, Robt
Brown, Thos
Bohlayer, John
Buckley, T K
Berkley, Enos
Bowen, Jas A
Blagden, Thos
Colburn, John
Caton, M & J
Donovan, Wm

Dunlap, Henry
Emery, M E
Emerson, G W
Eslin, Wm-2
Fugitt, Jos
Foshee, M
Fitzgerald, D
Fister, John
Favier, A
Glick, J H
Guyer, B
Groupe, Wm
Gillespie, Alex
Green, A
Hager, C
Howard, John
Hamersley, Edw
Harvey & Lloyd
Horning, g D

Hall, E
Havener & Son, T
Hall, Jas
Hagar, F
Jones, Alfred-3
Isaacs, Hester
Knott, Geo
Key, Saml
Krafft, Jno M-2
Lenman & Bro
Linkins, Wm
Lambell, K H
McGarvey, P
Mason, Jos
Miller, Michl
Magee, S
Mullikin, John
McDevitt
Mills, R T

Mason, Enoch
Noer, Andrew
Nugent, Henry
Otterback, Philip
O'Donoghue, P & T
Pearson, P M
Prather & Co, O J
Payne, Saml
Parker, Albert
Purdy, John-2
Roach, J-2
Rhodes, Jas
Rawlings, D
Roths, Julius
Slade, Wm

Shedd, J P
Straub, Jos
Shedd, J J
Stevenson, Jos
Sederer, C
Shaub, John
Simms, J M-2
Simms, Bazil
Sweiger, Jos
Smith, Thos
Sibley, Jas
Thomas, Chas
Thyson, P
Tyler, Washington
Todlschnider, T

Thomas, Geo-2
Thomas, G
Visser, J
Van Reswick, J
Wakeling
Wonderlick, John-2
Waggoner, John
Washington, J
Worcester, Giles
Willard, Ed & Ha
Webb, A J
Walker & Peck
Ward, W
Young, John
Young, W W

List of the persons fined during Apr through Aug, for failing to procure their licenses:

Allen, Wm: huckster
Adams, Robt; cart
Anderson, S J; dog
Bohrer, Rush: dog
Butler, Richd: dog
Brent, Jno D: dog
Berry, Jno: wagon
Boshlin, J: dog & wagon
Brown, Chas: wagon
Buck, W H: cart
Brown, Archibald: dog
Blagden, Thos: wagon
Bell, John: dog
Brown, Mary: dog
Bush, Wm: dog
Bush, Wm: cart
Buckely, P J: dog
Curry, Jas: dog & slut
Clark, Robt: dog
Conner, Thos: wagon
Cannon, Mary: liquor
Connor, Jno: wagon
Cockrell, Geo W: cart
Collins, Louisa: dog
Carnan, Chas: hacks
Coles, Mrs: dog
Conagan, Bernard: liquors
Diggs, Matthew: dog
Denham, A: dog
Duff, Jas: dog
Dowling, Wm: cart-2

Day, Spencer: liquor
Dodson, J B: dog
Davis, Mrs: dog
Easby, Wm: wagon
Emerson, Geo W: wagon
Edelen, E H: dog
Fox, G A: dog
Favier, A: wagon
Ford, Wm: cart
Fisher, Morris: 2 dogs
Fairfax, Wm M C: 2 dogs
Garnett, Milton: dog
Gallispie, Alex'r: wagon
Givney, B: dogs
Heister, Uriah: wagon
Hoover, Andrew: dog & 2 carts
Henry, John: 2 wagons
Havener & Son: wagon
Hoover, Jno: cart
Hofflin, W: hawking & ped
Hawkins, Wm: dog
Hogan, Tho: liquor
Howard, Thos: dog
Hazel, Z: 2 dogs & 2 carts
Johnson, Peter: dog
Jennings, Horace: dog
Jones, Noah: merchandise
Jones, J: dog
Kelly, Saml: dog
Kent, Dewitt: dog
Keyworth, Eliz: dog

Knight, Caleb: dog
Kedglie, Thos: dog & cart
Lyon, Chas: cart
Lenman & Bro: cart
Lewis, Benj: huckster
Lynch, Jas: dog
Lee, Jno: wagon & cart
Magee, Patrick: liquor
Maguire, Jas: wagon
Middleton: dog
Morgan, Wm E: cart
Mahar, Jas: cart
Murphy, Jno: wagon
McKelden, Jno: wagon
Miller, Jos: wagon
Masell, Chas: dog
Monroe, Mrs: dog
Murphy, Cornelius: merchandise
Magee, Owen: liquor
Norbeck: dog
Neale, Jno E: cart
Neale, Levi: dog
Owen, Jas: wagon
O'Leary, Mrs: liquor
Osborne, Eliz: dog
Phelps, E: dog
Peetsch, T C: liquor
Prather, A: wagon
Prather, Jos: wagon
Purdy, Jno: wagon
Plant, Nathl: cart
Peters, Mary: dogs
Raney, Ann: liquor
Runnells, Jesse: dog
Rix, Ellen: dog
Rollan, Alfred: dog

Ritter, Mrs: slut
Roberts, Jno: liquors
Robinson, Randolph: huckstering
Reilly, Mary: liquor & hack
Royall, Ann: dog
Riley, T B: 2 dogs
Sibly, Jas: wagon
Smith, Chas: liquor
Selden, Francis: liquor
Somerville: cart
Spicer, Fred'k: wagon
Stepper, Andrew: wagon
Seitz, Geo: wagon
Swagart, Jos: wagon
Smith, Jeremiah: dog
Shadd, C: liquor
Talbert, Mrs: dog
Thomas, Selina: dog
Tay, Parick: dog
Throop, J V N: dog
Wilson, Wm: dog
Woodeard, Jno: dog
Wright, Jas: dog
Wormley. Lynch: selling cigars
Willard, E D & A H: wagon
Wilson, Wm: wagon
Warder, Wm: cart
Waters, E: carts
Wise, Jas A: carts & dog
Wilson, Patrick: dog
Wright, C: dog
Washington, Mr: dog
Waller, Jas D: dog
Webster, Wm: dog
Wendell, A: wagon
-Wm J McCormick, Reg

Dissolution of the partnership of Martin & Wright, auctioneers, by mutual consent. Having associated his son in the business, it will hereafter conducted under the name of Martin & Co. -John Martin & Co

Hon Geo Bancroft, late Minister to Great Britain & family, have returned to Boston in the steamer **Europa**, & have just arrived there.

Hon John J Cummins, a Rep in the last Congress from the State of Ohio, died at Milwaukee, of cholera, on Tue last. So says a telegraphic despatch.

A prisoner, Geo Adams,who had been arrested at Keokuk, Iowa, on a charge of stealing money, & who was in charge of Mr Wills, on board the steamer **Visiter**, on a late trip to Louisville, jumped overboard & was drowned.

Mrd: on Sep 11, by Rev C M Butler, Mr Younger Kennady to Miss Ephilinda Cliff, both of Virginia.

Died; yesterday, after a very protracted illness, Mrs Moriah Byrne. Her funeral is tomorrow, at 1 o'clock, from her late residence on 10th & Pa ave.

FRI SEP 14, 1849
Appointment by the Pres: Hiram Lennox, Collector of the Customs for the district of Burlington, N J, vice John Larzaere, resigned.

Dr Amariah Brigham, Superintendent of the N Y Lunatic Asylum, died at Utica on Sat last. His disease was chronic diarrhoea. He was formerly a physician of high popularity in Hartford, & when called to the Utica Asylum, was Superintendent of the Conn Retreat for the Insane. He was a man of great benevolence & purity of character.

At Berkshire, Mass, last week a verdict of $7,000 was rendered against the Berkshire Railroad Co, & in favor of D B Campbell & wife, for injuries sustained by them while crossing the railroad track.

Mrd: on Sep 6, by Rev Chas A Davis, Mr Uriah Heiter to Miss Jane Kitchen, of Wash City.

Mrd: on Sep 11, by Rev Chas A Davis, Mr Jos W Cornwall to Miss Rebecca Cammack, all of Wash City.

Geo Whitcomb shot his wife & child at Rindge, N H, on Tue last, while in a fit of intoxication. The monster was arrested & lodged in jail. The wife & child are still alive.

A fire broke out in Jackson township, Pa, on Sep 3, which entirely consumed the residence of Dr J J Udegraff. He had barely time to escape with his children. He estimates the whole loss at about $8,500, part of which, $3,750 is covered by insurance.

For sale: at the Capitol Stables, one of the best ponies in the District. Also, a first rate Top Buggy for sale. Apply to Jas Henry, Capitol Hill.

SAT SEP 15, 1849
Trustee's sale of frame house & lot on 13th st: by deed of trust from Martha Morgan, dated Aug 3, 1847, recorded in Liber W B 136, folios 30 & 31, of the land records of Wash Co, D C: sale Oct 1: all that part of ground being lot 1 in square 256.
—Wm Q Force, trustee-E C & G F Dyer, aucts

On Dec 12, the annexed list of property will be sold by public auction, at the City Hall, Wash City, to satisfy the Corp of said city for taxes & fees as may have accrued at the time of payment. -A Rothwell, Collector
Adams, John: 1843-1848: $58.30
Lot 691 leased by D Carroll to Ambrose White: N J ave
Appleton, Henry: 1846-48: $2.16
Adams, Geo: improvements in name of Stepney Forrest.
Butler, Abraham: 1845-48: $259.18
Bean, Benj: 1842-48: $100.43
Borreman, Chas: 1846-48: $16.50
Barron, Eliz: 1846-48: $9.24
Brooke, Edmund: 1843-48: $7.75
Brown, John Ross: 1846-48: $20.76
Boyd, Jos K: 1845-48: $217.93
Bonthorn, John: 1846-48: $13.41
Ball, John: 1846-48: $28.98
Brodhead, Jno M & Jas Adams: 1847-48: $11.26
Barber, Jos: 1846-48: $12.93
Bank of the Metropolis: 1846-48: $138.99
Byrne, Maria: 1842-48: $1.98
Bonthorn, Mary Ann: 1847-48: $9.07
Barnes, Mary: 1846-48: $15.05
Bowen, Mary: 1845-48: $11.04
Brown, O B: 1843-38: $15.28
Burns, Patrick: 1846-48: $42.06
Briscoe, Richd G: 1843-48: $465.21
Billing, W W: 1845-48: $7.21
Bulfinch, Thos: 1846-48: $11.22
Bryden, Wm: 1846-48: $22.11
Billing, W W & others, trustees: 1842-48: $56.43
Bradley, Wm A: 1842-45: $30.80
Bulfinch, Geo S: 1844-48: $175.19
Bank of Wash: 1844-48: $193.84
Brent, Danl: 1846-48: $21.54
Bliss, Elam: 1844-48: $7.56
Bontz, Henry & Wm Kalb: 1846-48: $17.16
Bradford, Henry: 1846-48: $1.08
Baker, John: 1846-48: $10.35
Brightwell, John L: 1844-48: $2.60
Brightwell, John A: 1845 & 1848: $58.10
Clements, B H: 1846-48: $15.51
Clements, Chas A: 1846-48: $25.95
Coote, Clement: 1835-48: $358.75
Coddington, Camilla: 1846-48: $106.74
Cruttenden, Joel: 1846-48: $5.76
Campbell, Jas: 1846-48: $7.98
Clagett, Sarah E: 1846-48: $12.81
Crawford, Thos B: 1846-48: $9.03

Craven, Tunis: 1846-48: $24.36
Carroll, Danl: 1844-48: $295.57
Campbell, Eleanor & Catharine: 1846-48: $9.63
Coons, Eliz: 1846-48: $8.70
Cross, Eli: 1845-48: $62.43
Cross, Francis: 1845-48: $8.36
Coburn, John: 1939-48: $67.50
Clarke, Jos S: 1844-48: $304.68
Carbery, Janies: 1837-48: $1.25
Coxen, Jesse: 1846-48: $6.09
Costigan, Jos: 1846-48: $4.47
Cuvillier, Jos: 1845-48: $23.44
Costigan, John: 1846-48: $3.75
Clarke, Letitia: 1846-48: $91.26
Cash, Leonard: 1846-48: $5.88
Clarke, M St Clair: 1844-48: $574.45
Callan, Nicholas, jr, in trust for Jane Lynch: 1846-48: $3.63
Collins, Owen J: 1846-48: $7.65
Connolly, Owen: 1846-48: $180.75
Chapman, Pearson: 1846-48: $56.55
Clements, Rachael & Mary E: 1845-48: $23.40
Corcoran, Thos & Wm W: 1845-48: $37.03
Cookendorffer, Thos: 1846-48: $328.53
Corcoran, W W: 1846-48: $47.88
Connelly, Thos of John: 1846-48: $238.59
Dunn, Amelia: 1845-48: $26.37
Davis, Alex'r McDonald: 1846-48: $149.16
Druett, Jas jr: 1846-48: $2.28
Druett, Jas, in trust for Jas T Druett: 1846-48: $1.38
Duff, John: 1846-48: $31.71
Dove, Jos: 1846-48: $78.60
Daut, Jas: 1846-48: $11.04
Dowley, Mich: 1846-48: $8.16
Diggs, Saml J, in trust: 1846-48: $19.65
Digges, Sylvia: 1846-48: .99
Day, Sarah: 1846-48: $2.73
Daley, Thos A: 1846-48: $11.43
Deitz, Wm H: 1846-48: $21.78
Dowling, Wm: 1845-48: $196.46
Davidson, Lewis G: 1845-48: $367.74
Dunlop, Jas, trustee of Eliz Dick: 1845-48: $43.72
Dunlop, Jas: 1847-48: $4.53
Dyer, Robt W: 1845-48: $34.28
Donn, G W: 1845-48: $34.33
Dale, Richd: 1846-48: $45.84
Elzey, Arnold: 1845-48: $117.04
Eaton, Chas J M: 1846-48: $5.88
English, David: 1846-48: $20.07

Elwood, Ellen M & others: 1844-48: $5.70
Erving, Geo W: 1846-48: $87.63
Ennis, Gregory: 1846-48: $28.50
Eckhart, Henry: 1846-48: $12.75
Edwards, Jas M: 1846-48: $2.66
Edwards, Jos: 1845-48: $44.48
Elwood, Isaac T: 1845-48: $73.42
Edwards, Lewis; 1845-48: $62.80
Eckloff & Wagler: 1845-48: $98.08
English, Wm H: 1844-48: $10.95
Earle, Jas; 1846-49: .93
Ellicott, Philip: 1846-48: $65.67
Elliot, Jonathan: 1846-48: $33.61
Fenwick, Thos: 1846-48: $21.63
Furlong, Valentine D: 1846-48: $11.10
Fitzpatrick, John C: 1842-48: $108.82
Fuller, Azariah: 1846-48: $150.05
Forest, Bladen: 1845-48: $30.78
Fales, Barnabas: 1846-48: $7.91
Fisk, Chas B: 1846-48: $3.09
Freedy, Christian: 1844-45: $20.02
Fowler, Hanson: 1846-48: $19.26
Freer, Jas B: 1846-48: $62.13
Fraser, Jos: 1846-48: $55.63
Forest, Jos: 1846-48: $43.56
Fossett, Jas: 1846-48: $65.19
Foulkes, John E & others: 1846-48: $50.37
Forest, Mary Helen; 1845-48: $20.00
Forbes, Saml C: 1845-48: $7.00
Fischer, Wm & R T Mills: 1845-48: $30.03
Goldsborough, John R: 1846-48: $6.21
Gass, John G: 1846-48: $17.10
Goodrich, Josiah: 1846-48: $42.48
Gunnell, Wm H & Geo Sweeny: 1846-48: $38.91
Gunton, Wm: 1845-48: $81.35
Greenleaf & Eliot: 1845 & 1848: $192.21
Gillies, Groenvelt, & others: 1844-48: $81.08
Garnett, Henry T: 1846-48: $1.56
Gardner, Saml: 1844-48: $102.05
Gelston, Hugh: 1845-48: $101.28
Gordon, Martha: 1846-48: $7.11
Gray, Wm: 1846-48: $6.06
Gill, Jas: 1846-48: $107.07
Green, Benj E: 1845-48: $588.81
Greenleaf, Jas: 1844-48: $164.10
Higdon, Andrew F: 1846-48: $6.21
Hackney, Barton: 1846-48: $22.20
Hansell, Emerick W: 1846-48: $8.27

Hubbard, Eleanor: 1846-48: $12.60
Hoban, Francis P: 1842-48: 8: $5.01
Howard, Hamilton P: 1846-48: $22.42
Hoban, Jas: 1842-28: $25.77
Hoban, Jas & Alex'r Diamond: 1846-48: $11.88
Hamilton, Matthew: 1846-48: $20.07
Hutton, Salome R: 1846-48: $6.72
Holtzman, Saml: 1835-48: $1.41
Hyatt, Seth: 1846-48: $330.36
Hoover, Thos D: 1845-48: $24.76
Hayman, Wm: 1846-48: $29.13
Hurley, Walter G: 1846-48: $2.01
Hunt, Wm: 1842-48: $201.02
Hazle, Zachariah: 1845-48: $38.22
Hamilton, Chas B: 1845-48: $21.60
Hay, Geo: 1846-48: $39.51
Hill, Henry: 1846-48: $1.53
Hollohon, John T: 1846-48: $10.05
Hollins, Wm: 1846-48: $.57
Henley, Wm D: 1841-48: $25.10
Johnson, Catherine M: 1846-48: $1.68
Jones, Chas L: 1847-48: $21.72
Ingle, Henry: 1839-48: $.60
Indermaurer, Jeremiah: 1845-48: $41.66
Jeffers, Matthias: 1844-48: $134.09
Inch, Philip: 1846-48: $7.86
Jarboe, Thos: 1846-48: $9.93
Johnson, Joshua: 1846-48: $48.27
Jewett, Nathl: 1847-48: $121.75
Kurtz, Danl: 1845-48: $2.65
Key, Henry S: 1846-48: $5.88
Kidwell, Mary F: 1845-48: $87.40
Kerr, Alexandra: 1846-48: $9.51
King, Abigail, & Wm Wilson: 1845-48: $99.59
Kloppher, Christian G: 1845-48: $32.85
Kiernan, Chas: 1846-48: $29.79
Kane, Elias: 1846-48: $15.90
Kingman, Eliah: 1846-48: $72.75
Krafft, Geo: 1846-48: $127.53
Kendrick, Geo W: 1846-48: $24.21
Knowles, Robt O: 1846-48: $39.63
Kerr, Robt E: 1847-48: $59.76
Keyworth, Robt: 1846-48: $453.39
Kavanaugh, Thos: 1846-48: $4.44
Laidler, Eliza: 1846-48: $1.62
Lutz, John: 1846-48: $12.32
Longaere, J B: 1846-48: $5.61
Lindsay, Adam: 1835-38: $3.15

Long, Jas: 1845-48: $809.09
Logan, John: 1845-48: $64.04
Lowry, Rebecca: 1845-48: $24.09
Lee, Saml: 1845-48: $6.80
Law, Thos: 1845-48: & in name of R Patton: $97.60
Lee, Wm: 1846-49: $49.68
Lambel, Wm: 1846-48: $3.60
Lewis & Coats, in trust: 1846-48: $10.74
Lawrence, Eliz; 1846-48: $5.10
Linthicum, Edw M: 1845-48: $7.12
Lenox, Peter: 1844-48: & in T Wheeler: $1195.01
McCerren, Andrew: 1846-48: $64.27
McWilliams, Alex'r: 1846-48: $92.64
McCarty, Chas F: 1846-48: $5.34
Massey, Eliz P: 1846-48: $9.24
Meigs, Francis C: 1845-48: $52.89
Miner, Jas: 1845-48: $16.68
Martin, Jas E: 1844-48: $19.35
Miles, Jane A E: 1845-48: $2.31
Moran, Patrick: 1844-48: $18.63
Marlborough, Rachael: 1845-48: $9.52
Milburn, Thos M: 1846-48: $11.16
McCorkle, Christiana: 1842-48: $.77
Maddox, Wm R: 1844-48: $48.58
Murdick, Geo: 1846-48: $10.41
Mason, John: 1846-48: $99.64.
Mattingly, Geo: 1847-48: $357.74
Miles, Jane A E: 1846-48: $50.59
Nailor, Allison: 1846-48: $543.67
Norton, Fortuune: 1846-48: $6.03
Neale, Henry A: 1846-48: $1.86
Nourse, Jos: 1846-48: $68.07
Orr, Benj G: 1846-48: $9.66
O'Neale, Rhoda: 1846-48: $18.84
O'Neale, Wm: 1846-48: $9.33
Oyster, Geo: 1846-48: $200.49
Prather, Overton, J: 1847-48: $49.73
Pons, Anthony: 1846-48: $18.74
Peake, John: 1845-48: $26.44
Parker, Selby & Geo Savage: 1846-48: $40.43
Prout, Wm: 1844-48: $7.31
Preston, Wm: 1846-48: $60.15
Prout, Wm: 1845-48: $3.23-money o k
Price, Chandler: 1846-48: $33.39
Payne, Danl: 1846-48: $89.46
Pickrell, Esau & Adolphus: 1845-48: $1.92
Pumphrey, Thos B, Jas W, & Francis A: 1846-47: $60.59
Pearson, Jos, M Y, & A M: 1844-48: $130.05

Pollock, John: 1846-48: $1.50
Parrott, Richd: 1844-48: $.85
Pratt, Wm: 1846-48: $.60
Peake, John: 1847: $49.37
Rothwell, Andrew, & Geo Page: 1845-48: $161.74
Rose, Danl: 1846-48: $15.88
Rigdon, Eliz: 1846-48: $5.34
Robey, John: 1846-48: $7.71
Reily, John: 1846-48: $55.77
Riggs, Geo W: 1845-48: $35.88
Rice, Geo: 1845-48: $5.50
Roward, Jos, & John Moore: 1846-48: $101.46
Rabourg, Wm, & Wm Taylor: 1846-48: $6.57
Shryock, Henrietta: 1846-48: $44.10
Swartz, Jos: 1846-48: $2.16
Scrivenner, Jas: 1845-48: $20.66
Scallan, Jas: 1846-48: $11.19
Scott, Rebecca: 1845-48: $3.06
Smith, Saml H: 1840-48: $3.24
Stewart, Wm: 1847-48: $39.78
Smith, Thos L & A T Smith: 1843-48: $5.70
Simpson, Tobias: 1846-48: $14.40
Stewart, W W: 1846-48: $9.68
Scholfield, Andrew: 1846-48: $19.59
Shroeder, Henry: 1845-48: $1.28
Swift, Jonathan; 1835-48: $2.55
Scott, Jas W: 1843-48: $37.15
Sprigg, Saml: 1845-48: $244.00
Sewall, Thos: 1845-48: $202.56
Sidebotham, Wm: 1846-48: $5.02
Smith, Walter: 1835-48: $58.31
Tims, Henry: 1845-48: $110.48
Tayloe, John: 1842-48: $6.32
Thompson, John L: 1844-48: $1.50
Tayloe, B O: 1846-48: $193.84
Thompson, Jas; 1846-48: $1.05
Trock, John N: 1844-48: $23.89
Tucker, Thos: 1844-48: $11.41
Turner, Thos: 1845-48: $23.20
Van Coble, Aaron & Co: 1845-48: $17.92
Van Patten, C H: 1846-48: $93.00
Villard, R H L: 1847-48: $107.06
Withers, John: 1845-48: $50.30
Whalen, Nicholas: 1846-48: $136.59
Williams, Jas: 1845: $71.04
Wagler, F A: 1846-48: $41.31
Williams, Geo W: 1846-48: $23.76
Wright, Jas-heirs: 1841-47: $23.64

Wheatley, Ignatius: 1846-48: $14.88
Wood, Mary Ann E: 1845-48: $59.68
Wilson, Wm B: 1845-48: $56.98
Woodward, Wm: 1845-48: $44.16
Walker, Wm S: 1844-47: $.45
Ward, Wm H; 1846-48: $5.31
Walker, John: 1844-48: $161.30
Young, Henry N: 1846-48: $191.50
Young, Noble: 1846-48: $87.88
Young, Nicholas, Notley, Ignatius, Benj, & Sarah E Clagett: 1845-48: $9.81

Mrd: on Sep 10, in Wash City, by Rev Jas B Donelan, Thos Fitnam, jr, to Miss Rosalia Dant, all of Wash City.

Private tutorship wanted: a gentleman, a graduate of a German Univ, who speaks French, German, & English, desires a private tutorship in a respectable Southern family. Apply to Otto T De Hefner, Phil, Pa, P O.

For rent: 3 story brick dwlg on 9th st, between D & E sts. Inquire on the premises, or at Drury's Lace Store.

For sale or rent, the west house & lots on north side of south B st, Capitol Hill. Apply at Mrs Whitwell's, 4½ st.

Trustee's sale of frame house & lot on 13th st: by deed of trust from Martha Morgan, dated Aug 3, 1847, recorded in Liber W B 136, folios 30 & 31, of the land records of Wash Co, D C: sale Oct 1: all that part of ground being lot 1 in square 256.
–Wm Q Force, trustee-E C & G F Dyer, aucts

Orphans Court of Wash Co, D C: the subscriber, guardian for the children of Wm Radcliff, late of said county, deceased, will sell at private sale, for cash, the following real property, of which the said Radcliff died seized, to wit: lots 6 thru 9 in square 538, lot 8 in square 267, & lot 23 in square 501, in Wash City. Title is indisputable.
–Matilda Radcliff, guardian

Attack of foreigners at San Francisco: on Jul 16, upon several bodies of Chilians & other foreigners, committed by a number of lawless persons, mostly discharged volunteers, who associated together under the name of Hounds & occupied a tract of land called Tammy Hall. 17 were taken into custody: trial ensued: Saml Roberts 10 years' hard labor in the penitentiary where the Govn'r of the Territory of Calif may direct; Theodore R Saunders to 10 years' hard labor; John Curley fined $1,000 & 1 year hard labor; David Gale fined $500 & 6 months in the penitentiary; Augustus S St John fined $500 & to give bond for $5,000 to keep the peace for 12 months; John F Barker fined $250 & to give bond $2,500 to keep the peace for 12 months; Wm Mickle fined $250 & to give bond of $2,500 to keep the peace for 12 months. The prisoners, after being sentenced, were remanded on board ship until the Govn'r should be heard from. After the riot, the Chileans left the vicinity of San Francisco.

$25 reward for runaway negro John Brown, between 50 & 60 years of age. -Thos Hawkins, living on *Cleandrinking Farm*, Montg Co, Md.

Trustees sale of furniture, confectionary, birds & cages: on Sep 19, at the store & residence of Wm Feeny, on 7th st. –D Ratcliff, trustee -Martin & Co, auctioneers

MON SEP 17, 1849
Died: on Sep 15, in Gtwn, Miss Jane Threlkeld English, daughter of David English. The deceased was unsurpassed in her devotion as a daughter, sister, & friend.

Died: on Sep 13, at the residence of Dr Wallace Kirkwood, PG Co, Md, Mary E, eldest daughter of Thos Woodward, of Gtwn, D C.

The subscriber hath obtained letters of administration, with the will annexed, on the estate of Amelia Thomas, late of Wash Co, deceased. –S S Williams, adm W W A

On Sat, a frame stable in the occupancy of Mr Hammersly, confectioner, on 12th st, was set on fire & totally consumed.

Looking for bargains: stoves & grates & house furnishing articles. -C Woodward, Pa ave between 10th & 11th sts

Household & kitchen furniture at auction on Sep 20, at the residence of Mrs Newton, on C st, between 4½ & 6th sts. –Green & Tastet, auctioneers

TUE SEP 18, 1849
The extraordinary Peaches noticed in our last paper were grown in the garden of Eleazer Lindsley, near Wash City.

Election at San Francisco-from the Alta Calif extra of Aug 2. Judge of the Superior Court: *Peter H Burnett, 1,298; Kimball H Dimmick, 212.
Prefect: *Horace Howes, 913; Wm A Burrum, 444; Clarence Livingston, 118.
Alcalde: *John W Geary, 1, 516. Second Alcaldes: *Frank Turk, 1,005; *John T Vioget, 936; J Mead Huxley, 459; Wm Landers, 47; B Simmons, 51. Sub-Prefect: *Francisco Guerrero, 1,503; J R Curtis, 1, 399; Wm H Davis, 97. For Town Council: *Talbot H Green, 1, 510; *Henry A Harrison, 1,491; *Alfred J Ellis, 1,354; *Stephen Harris, 1,323; *Thos B Winston, 1,052; *John Townsend, 1,052; *Rodman M Price, 840; *Wm H Davis, 835; *Bezer Simmons, 825; *Saml Brannan, 823; *Wm M Steuart, 815; *G B Post, 691; John H Merrill, 616; Wm C Parker, 528; Thos J Agnew, 526; M L Mott, 481; F D Kohler, 471; T W Perkins, 439; J P Haven, 405; Moses G Leonard, 384; H H Booker, 303; J H Peoples, 124; J V Plume, 170; R Haley, 144; A J Grayson, 108; S A Wright, 84 Delegates to the Convention: *Edw Gilbert, 1, 512; *Myron Norton, 1, 436; *Wm M Gwin, 1,072; * Jos Hobson, 839; *Wm M Steuart, 833; John Patterson, 520; Jonathan D Stevenson, 495; E Gould Buffum, 451; A H Sibley, 1842; Wm Burgoyne, 54; A D Peachy, 35. Supernumerary Delegates: *Wm D M Howard, 876; *Francis J Lippitt, 874; *A J Ellis, 872; *Francisco Sanchez, 872; *Rodman M Price, 871; S W Haight, 489; Wm M Smith, 430; J B Bidleman, 431; A C Peachy, 40; scattering 31. *Those who were elected.

Wm Marsh was fatally wounded on the two-path of the canal, at Syracuse, last week. The boats had got into jam, when the tow-line of one of them broke, & the staple or bit struck Mr Marshal over the right eye, near the temple, causing his death in about 20 minutes.

Monterey, Calif, Aug 1, 1849. Delegates chosen yesterday in this town as delegates to a Convention, to form a Constitution, on Sep 1: Messrs Thos O Larken, H W Halleck, C T Botts, Lewis Dent, & Pariflew Ord.

Mrd: on Sep 16, by Rev O B Brown, Benj Berkley to Miss Martha A Drury, both of Wash City.

Telegraphic Despatch: Balt, Sep 17. While a sailboat, containing Messrs Devouge & Croyean, & a gentleman named Claray, was out in the basin near the city, yesterday, it was run into & upset by the steamer **Mount Vernon**, & Mr Claray unfortunately drowned. He was one of the Principals of the French & English Institute in St Paul st.

Robbing of the mails: from Cleveland to Pittsburg: Postmaster D M Haskell adopted measures for the detection of the offenders, it was done. Mr John Ickis, the Postmaster in the Fred'k ofc was arrected by P O Agent McHatton. -Cleveland Herald

Mrd: on Sun last, by Rev Chas A Davis, Mr Wm Fletcher Connell, of St Louis, Mo, to Miss Sarah A D Hopkins.

Mrd: on Sep 16, by Rev V Palen, Mr Chas F Shultze to Mrs Susan Jones, both of Wash City.

Died: on Sep 15, in Wash City, aged 62 years, Mary, the beloved wife of Wm Williams, late of Merthyr Tidvil, Glamorganshire, South Wales.

Died: on Sep 17, after a protracted illness, Gen Merritt L Covell, aged 43 years. His funeral is this afternoon at 4 o'clock, from the residence of Mrs Williams, on Pa ave, between 4½ & 6th sts. Gen Covell was formerly a resident of Ill, where he frequently discharged various public trusts. For 4 years past he has been a clerk in the Gen Land Ofc in Wash City. -P

WED SEP 19, 1849
Appointments by the Pres: Custom House Ofcrs:
Fred'k G Low, Collector, Gloucester, Mass, vice John L Rogers, deceased.
Wm R Smith, Collector, Galveston, Texas, vice Hiran G Runnels.
Jas G Green, Naval Ofcr, Wilmington, N C, vice Jas T Miller, removed.
Henry Dart, Surveyor, Pontchartrain, La, vice S H Page, removed.

Naval: Lt Chas H Poor has been ordered to the Gosport Navy Yard as Inspector of Provisions. Capt French Forrest is to be ordered to the Wash Navy Yard in place of Capt McCauley, who, it is rumored, is to have the command of a squadron.

Mail robber convicted: at Nashville, Geo Booker, a mail carrier, convicted of robbing the mail between Sparta & Monroe, & sentenced to 5 years in the State prison.

Ptn of the Navahoes & Pawnees, praying for the appointment of Maj Beal as military commandant, has been sent to Wash. Quite a difference, one would think.
–St Louis Republican

Chauncey Hunter, alias Chas W Smith, who figured so largely in Boston a few weeks ago as a Lt in the Navy, was on Sat sentenced to the State prison for 3 years.

Powder mill kept by Hamner & Forbes, in east Hartford, Conn, was blown up Sept 13, & John O'Brien, aged 27, single, one of the hands, was killed.

New Post ofcs: established, discontinued, & changed the site & names of the following ofcs, during the week ending Sep 15, 1849.

Ofc	County & State	New Appointment:
Palo Alto	Highland, Va	Decatur H Jones
Ashton's Mills	Fred'k, Va	Casper Rogers
Pleasant View	Jackson, Va	Wm H Flesher
Lively Oak	Lancaster, Va	War W C George
East Bend	Surry, N C	Richd Phillips
Airy Grove	Lenoir, N C	Jas Pridgen
Franklin Springs	Franklin, Ga	Richd W Royston
Benhaden	Wakulla, Fla	John A Barco
Mende-	Madison, Ind	M S Drury
Fall Creek	Marion, Ind	John W Combs
Sylvan Grove	Clark, Ind	John Y Weir
Lost Grove	De Kalb, Ill	Chauncey Luce
Quiver	Mason, Ill	Saml Patten
Bou Pas	Richland, Ill	Wm Higgins
Pineville	McDonald, Mo	John Holpain
Green Top	Schuyler, Mo	Dan H Wellborn
Scott	Sheboygan, Wis	Edgar Havilland
Nepenskin	Winnebago, Wis	J J Catlin
Unionville	Oppanoose, Iowa	Jas Ewing
N Brownsville	Piscataquis, Maine	Jos Gowin
West Newport	Orleans, Vt	Philander Sawyer
Waquoit	Barnstable, Mass	Francis M Boggs
South Carver	Plymouth, Mass	Thos B Griffiths
Worcester	Marquette, Mich	Amos R Harlow

Names & sites changed:
South Middletown, Orange Co, N Y, name changed to Middletown.
West Perth, Fulton, N Y, site changed, & John M Benedict appointed p m.
Langdon, Du Page, Ill, site changed, & Ira Jewel appointed p m.
White, Hancock, Ind, named & site changed to Warrington, -Jas H King appt'd p m.
Hicks' Mills, De Kalb, Ill, site changed, & Sidney P Harrington appt'd p m.
French Mills, Onslow, N C, site & name changed to Piney Green, & Isaac Marshall appointed p m.

The families of Messrs B W Macrae & W W Wallace, of Fauquier Co, & Lucien Dade, of Prince Wm, have started in company to seek new homes in Tenn. We understand that the emigrants number 140, white & colored, all told. –Alexandria Gaz

Obit-died: on Jul 21, at Old Point Comfort, Va, of consumption, Thos Jones Johnston, sen, aged 49 years. He was born at Louisville, Ky, on Jul 10, 1800, a son of one of the finest lawyers & pioneers of the dark & bloody ground that emigrated from Va. He graduated with honors in the law class of Harvard Univ, but never practiced his profession until 1838, when he removed to Natchez, Miss, where he continued the legal compeer of Quitman, Walker, Winchester, & others. In 1845 he came to this city to prosecute in several cases in the Supreme Court. He now rests in peace in the village church yard near Hampton, Va, a spot he had visited & much admired while living. –Mississippi

Wash Corp: 1-Bill for the relief of Harrison Taylor: passed. 2-Cmte of Claims: bills for the relief of Owen Magee; & for the relief of M Rosenstock: recommended they be rejected: which was agreed to. 3-Cmte of Claims: bill for the relief of Patrick Twomy: passed. Same cmte: asked to be discharged from the further consideration of the ptn of Geo Johnson & others: discharged accordingly. 4-Cmte on Improvements: asked to be discharged from the further consideration of the ptn of Chas Garner & others: which was agreed to. Same cmte: bill for the relief of Geo Fosnaught: passed. 5-Ptn of Jos Ferguson, for remission of a fine: referred to the Cmte of Claims. Ptn of John Hill, for remission of a fine: referred to the Cmte of Claims. 6-Ptn of Wm Fletcher, praying to be refunded a certain amount erroneously paid for the redemption of a lot: referred to the Cmte of Claims. 7-Ptn from John Magar, police ofcr of the 7th Ward, praying the payment of a balance due him: referred to the Cmte on Police. 8-Ptn of Grafton Powell & others, praying that certain improvements in the 2nd Ward may be placed in charge of the City Surveyor: referred to the Cmte on Improvements. 9-Cmte on Police: asked to be discharged from the further consideration of the ptn of R J Ryan. 10-Cmte of Claims: ptn of Jas Maher & Wm Pettibone: asked to be discharged from the further consideration of the same. 11-Cmte of Claims: ptns for the relief of Basil Simms; act for the relief of J M Wright; act refunding Jas C Cruser the amount of a fine remitted: severally read.

Improvements at the Capitol: we learn from Mr Cassell, superintendent of the painting, that since Apr 16, when the work commenced, there have been on an average about 17 hands constantly employed in painting the Capitol. The exterior walls have already received 4 coats of paint. Handsome repairs have been made by Mr Emery, under the direction & superintendence of Mr Mudd, the Com'r of Public Bldgs.

Died: on Sep 1;7, Mrs Sarah Pumphrey, consort of Levi Pumphey, of Wash City. Her funeral will take place this morning at 10 o'clock.

Died: on Sep 11, at **Fort Johnson**, Charleston harbor, S C, after an illness of 4 hours, Annie, only daughter of Lt John D & Jane T Kurtz, aged 3 years.

THU SEP 20, 1849
The York [Pa] Gaz: 1-Mentions the death, by drowning in a mill-race, of a son of the Hon Geo Hammond, of that place. 2-The same papers contains an account of the death of Danl Sprenkel, aged 77 years & 1 month, caused by having cut his foot with an axe while chopping wood.

N Y, Sep 17. Rathburn Allen, book-keeper at *Rathburn's Hotel*, was killed yesterday by falling from one of the upper windows of that hotel. He was a nephew of Mr Rathburn.

Public sale of negro woman Jane, age about 22 years, at the public jail, on Sep 25. –C W Boteler, auctioneer

Detroit Advertiser of Mon: Chas F Barstow, for some years a resident in this city, came to his death yesterday by jumping from the 3rd story of Gen Williams' bldg, on Jefferson ave, while in a fit of insanity. Fracturing his skull, he died immediately. He was a son of Dr Barstow, of Salem, Mass.

The Bowdoin family: Mr Winthrop, in his address before the Maine Historical Society states: Mr Winthrop's mother, Eliz Temple, was the adopted daughter of her uncle, Gov Bowdoin, the father of Jas Bowdoin, the founder of Bowdoin College. Manuscript in French interpreted as follows: To his excellency the Govn'r-in-chief of New England, humbly prays Pierre Baudouin, saying: having been obliged to depart thence with his family & having sought refuge in Dublin, Ire, your petitioner was employed in one of the bureaus; there being a change of ofcrs, he was left without employment. The petitioner & his family, 6 in number, [4 children] withdraw into this territory, in Casco, province of Maine; he requests about 100 acres at the point of Barbary Creek. –Pierre Baudouin
+
Driven out from his home & native land by the religious persecution for which Louis XIV gave the signal by the revocation of the edict of Nantz; Pierre, in 1687, presents himself a suppliant to Sir Edmund Andros, then Govn'r of New England, for land. Bowdoin was the eldest descendant, lived in affluence upon a handsome estate in the neighborhood of Rochelle, which at that time, 1685, yielded the considerable income of 700 Louis d'ors per annum. This estate was of course irrecoverably forfeited by his flight after 2 years to New England. His petition was endorsed on Aug 2, 1867, & the public records in the State Dept of Mass contain a warrant signed by Sir Edmund & directed to Mr Richd Clements, Deputy Surveyor authorizing him to lay out 100 acres of vacant land in Casco Bay for Pierre Bowdoin, as should be directed by Edw Ting, one of his Majesty's Council. The warrant bears date Oct 8, 1687. This is now the high road from Portland to Vaughan's Bridge, a few rods northerly of the house now or late of Hon Nicholas Emery. In this original dwlg place, Bowdoin remained about 2 ½ years. On May 17, 1690, the fort at Casco was attacked & destroyed, & a general massacre of the settlers was perpetrated by the Indians. On May 16, just 24 hours previously, Pierre Baudouin & his family had plucked up their stakes & departed for Boston.

Andrew Thompson, machinist, of South Trenton, N J, has received a letter from his wife's mother in England, informing him that she is about coming into the possession of two-thirds of an immense estate in England, amounting to no less than three millions of pounds of sterling, of which one million is in cash & the remaining in real estate. The property was accumulated by a brother of the old lady's grandfather, & that since the death of all the descendants of the first owner she has been contending in the English Chancery for the property with the descendants of a younger brother of the first owner. Since Christmas these descendants have died, & she & one brother-in-law are the only heirs. The right of another brother-in-law was bought out some years ago, so that she is entitled to two-thirds of the three millions. The old lady is 74 years old. She had been contesting the matter for many years, & has spent L40,000 in lawsuits. Mr Thompson is on his way to Gov Vroom, to place the matter in his charge as his legal counsel. If this is realized, it will make him the richest man in America.
—State Gaz

Returned from Calif: Mr Jas King, of Gtwn, D C, who went to Calif in 1848, has returned home. He says: Dr Craigin is at Sacramento city fitting up a hospital at the Fort. He is well & in fine spirits. Mr Peachey, formerly of Gtwn, has established himself at San Francisco, in the practice of law. At Panama I found Mr Jones, of Wash, [son-in-law of Col Benton,] Mr Robt Merrill, E Shoemaker, & my brother, Wm King, jr.

Rockville [Md] Journal: Mr John Lowe was taken ill with apoplexy on Sat last, & died in a few hours.

D B Campbell, of West Stockbridge, Conn, who with his wife was hurt some 3 years since by an accident on the Housatonic Railroad, has obtained a verdict of $7,000 damages against the said company. A motion has been made for a new trial.

Died: on Mon last, at his residence in N Y C, Dr J A Houston, formerly Official Reporter for the U S Senate.

Died: on Aug 19, at Venice, Dr Wm Sparks, U S Consul at that place.

Died: on Sep 1, at Litchfield, Conn, Maj Gen Francis Bacon, aged 38 years. He was Clerk of the Hse o/Reps of his State in 1847 & 1848, & a Senator from the 15th district in 1849. He was the last of 3 sons of Asa Bacon, of Litchfield.

Died: on Sep 17, Edwin Spencer, Cashier of the Connecticut River Bank, aged 50 years.

Jos Ackles, the lost boy, whose mother has been for the last 2 or 3 weeks seeking him, has been found, & is now at the Wash Asylum, awaiting the arrival of his parents.

Dissolution of the partnership existing under the firm of Wm Morrow & Co, by mutual consent. Persons having claims will present them to either of the parties.
—Wm Morrow, Jas H Birch, Wm P McConnell, Gtwn

FRI SEP 21, 1849
Appointments by the Pres:
W F Kecheval, of Tenn, to be U S Atty for the middle district of Tenn, vice Thos D Mosely, removed.
John H Murphy, of Ill, to be Receiver of Public Moneys at Danville, Ill, from & after Oct 10 next, vice Lunsford R Noel, removed.
Wm H L Noble, of Indiana, to be Register of the Land Ofc at Indianapolis, Ind, from & after Oct 10 next, vice Nathl Bolton, removed.
Chas Fitz, of Louisiana, to be Register of the Land Ofc at New Orleans, La, vice Thos B Thorp, who declines the ofc.

Rumor from London that Pres, Louis Napoleon Bonaparte, has demanded & secured the hand of the daughter of the King of Sweden, aged 19 years. The mother of Louis Bonaparte, the Queen Hortense, was sister of Eugene Beaubarnais, & the Queen of Sweden, mother of the affianced, is daughter of the same Eugene Beauharnais; consequently, Louis Bonaparte is cousin german to the Queen of Sweden. His marriage with her daughter had, therefore, nothing very improbable in it. The Marchioness of Douglas, daughter of the Grand Duchess of Baden, & cousin of Louis Bonaparte, has just arrived at Paris, & the Pres immediately quitted the chateau of St Cloud to come to receive his kins woman at the Elysee. Recollections: the Prince of Leuchemberg, brother of the Queen of Sweden, married a daughter of the Emperor of Russia. If Louis Bonaparte obtains the hand of the daughter of the King of Sweden, it is with the approval of Russia, & that this double alliance, conjugal & political, would give to his imperial pretensions a foundation & an importance which they have wanted until now. But is it possible to think that the Czar Nicholas, that fanatical supporter of legitimacy, would forsake that religion & take part in an imperial restoration?

Mrd: on Sep 16, by Rev Mr Van Horsigh, Mr Jas Rhodes, of Wash City, to Miss Eliz Ann Fowler, eldest daughter of Jas H Fowler, of PG Co, Md.

U S Flag ship **Plymouth**, Outer Road of Macao, Jun 20, 1849. The lower part of Shanghai is occupied by foreigners, & their residences are very much the same as our country houses at home. This place is a great station for missionaries; the prinicipal one [American] is Bishop Boone's, of South Carolina, who has a school with upwards of 80 Chinese boys attending it. We expect the ship **Ohio** here soon.
List of her ofcrs: Cmdor: David Geisinger
Cmder: Thos R Gedney
1st Lt Thos I Paige
2nd Lt Geo W Doty
3rd Lt Edw Donaldson
4th Acting Lt: Gustavus V Fox
5th Acting Flag Lt: Geo P Welsh
6th Acting Lt, Clark H Wells
Purser: Lewis Warrington, jr
Fleet Surgeon, Dr J F Brooke; Assist Surgeon, O I Wistar
Cmdor's Sec: Fred'k Schley
Midshipmen: Jas H Rowan, jr, Chas L Haralson & John I Cornwall.
Cmder's Clerk: Geo R Goldsborough

Latest from Santa Fe: we learn from *Fort Leavenworth*, by the Kansas, that John Philips & Jas M Clay, express mail carriers from Santa Fe to *Fort Leavenworth*, have reached the latter post. They left on Aug 15 & arrived on Sep 4.

From the ofc of the Santa Fe Republican, dated Aug 8. 1-Col Calhoun, agent for the different tribes of Indians in New Mexico, has established his agency at Santa Fe. 2-Robt Stanfield, who murdered Jos Kane, of Missouri, some 3 months ago, at San Miguel, was hung on Jul 27 at Los Vegas.

Troops numbering about 60 are to sail in the schnr **Empire**, now at Alexandria, for Pilatka, Fla, some time next week. Ofcrs are Capt Wm H Fowler, 1st Lt, Lewis O Morris; 2nd Lt, T S Everett, Acting Commissary of Subsistence.

Letter from Monroeville, Ala, Aug 29: suicide on that evening. Dr Geo A Wattle, who had several days been intoxicated, cut both arteries of his neck & windpipe with a razor. The frantic cries of his wife were too late. The lady is from the North, & she is alone here without a relative in the South.

Sat night, near Gray's Ferry, a passenger, who was standing on the platform, was thrown upon the track & killed. The wheels severed his head from his body. From a certificate of discharge from the frig **Raritan**, was found on his person, the name Jos W Winks.

Died: on Sep 20, of dropsy on the brain, Joshua Sands, son of Chas V & Eliza M Morris, aged 6 years & 10 months. His funeral is today at 10 o'clock, from the quarters of his father on the Navy Yard.

Died: yesterday, after a short but painful illness, Alice, only child of Wm E & Mary Goggin, aged 16 months & 20 days. Her funeral is this evening, at 4 o'clock, from the residence on Pa ave, between 6th & 7th sts.

Died: on Wed, Fanny Lear, infant daughter of J Bayard H & Henrietta Smith, aged 11 months & 10 days.

For sale, or exchange for property in Wash: a small farm 19 acres, in Alexandria Co, Va, adjoining the farm of Mr Williams. Apply on the place or by letter through the post ofc. –N Mullikin

SAT SEP 22, 1849
Washington Minute Men: meeting on Sun, 8 a m, subject of temperance, by Messrs Tipton, of Ohio, Camack, of Wash, & others. –C W Denison, Pres P Kleiss, Sec

Teacher wanted in my school, a single gentleman, to take charge of he Classical Dept. –Caleb S Hallowell, Alexandria, Va

To let: for rent a good store room & cellar, on the corner of 7th & I sts. For terms apply to Jas H Shreve, Livery Stable.

Chas W Schuermann, [formerly pupil of the celebrated L Spohr] gives instructions on the Piano, Guitar, & in Vocal Music. Residence on L st, between 9th & 10th sts.

Goldfinche, Linnets, Thrush, & handsome French Lap Dogs, will be sold cheap if applied for immediately. Also, some German Canary Birds. Apply at Mrs Greer's, on 10th st, near Pa ave.

MON SEP 24, 1845
Window Glass: having made arrangements with the Waterford Works, N Y, I am now receiving supplies of window glass-for sale. -Robt H Miller, Alexandria, Va

I certify that Chas W Fowler, of Wash Co, brought before me as an estray, trespassing upon his enclosure, one milch cow. –J L Smith, J P
Owner of the above is to come forward, prove property, pay charges, & take her away. –Chas W Fowler, Old Bladensburg rd.

Wash City Item: on Sep 27, a Sacred Concert will be given for the benefit of the Lutheran Church, 11th & H sts. The chief performers will be the young family of Mr Eberbech, whose wonderful talents & proficiency in music have excited so much attention in our city.

Wash City Ordinances: 1-Act for the relief of Harrison Taylor: sum of $5.83 be paid to him for repair of 7th st. 2-Act for the relief of Patrick Twomy: fine imposed for alleged violation of the law relative to stove-pipes, is remitted: provided Twomy pay the cost of prosecution. 3-Act for the relief of Geo Fosnaught: sum of $69.04 be paid him for the balance due for improvement of K st.

The Capitol: The circular library, provided for the use of the Senate, is erected over the small rotunda in the north part of the Senate. It is capable of holding from 15,000 to 20,000 volumes. It was executed by Mr Springle Slight, carpenter, & is a very convenient & well finished apartment.

Mr Robt Cruit, formerly of Wash City, but who removed a few years ago to his farm in Fairfax Co, Va, was seriously injured while gunning Fri last. He blew off one finger, & injured two other fingers. Dr Riley expects to save the injured fingers.

Valuable timber for sale: as agent of Eliz C Sulivane, of Dorchester Co, Md, will sell at private sale 200 acres of wood land, heavily timbered. Apply to Richd Grason, Elkton, Cecil Co, Md.

New Music received today: Mrs Garret Anderson, Pa ave, between 11th & 12th sts, Wash.

Marlboro Gaz: Thos Duckett, formerly a prominent member of the Legislature from that county, died at his residence at ***Willow Brook*** Tuesday last.

TUE SEP 25, 1849
The New Albany has an account of the operation by Dr Sloan, of New Albany, upon the eyes of Rev N Hoskins, of Crawford Co, Iowa, who had been blind from birth. He now sees his wife & children for the first time.

Official: Appointments by the Pres:
Blueford Johnson, of Ill, to be Receiver of Public Moneys at Edwardsville, Ill, from & after Oct 10 next, vice John G Cameron, removed.
Andrew Backus, of Mich, to be Receiver of Public Moneys at Saut Ste Marie, Mich, vice Danl Hicks, deceased.
Ferdinand Maxwell, of Ill, to be Register of the Land Ofc at Kaskaskia, Ill, from & after Oct 10 next, vice Jacob Feaman, removed.
Greer W Davis, of Mich, to be Register of the Land Ofc at Jackson, Mo, from & after Oct 10 next, vice Franklin Cannon, removed.

Geo W Cutter has been appointed Navy Agent, & John Rice Naval Storekeeper, at Portsmouth, N H.

Balt, Sep 22: arrest of a hotel thief: Jos K Ashby was arrested & committed to jail; stolen articles were found in his room. When his commitment was made out he was much affected at his situation & shed tears. -Patriot

Portland, Oregon, May 21, 1849. Town of Portugal. The first settlement here made was in Nov, 1845, by Capt N Crosby, master, & Mr B F Stark, supercargo, of the barque **Toulon** from N Y. Since that time Crosby has built a fine house, at $5,000 expense. It derives its name from Portland, Maine, an early settler in the town being from that State.

Valuable land for sale in Anne Arundel Co, Md: the property on which I reside: 7 miles from Annapolis; contains 300 acres: & a large 2 story brick house, with a beautiful view of the Round Bay & surrounding country. Also, I offer a tract of land containing about 250 acres, adjoining the other property: with a good dwlg for a small family. –N B Worthington, Brotherton Post Ofc, Anne Arundel Co, Md.

Mrd: on Sep 4, at Trinity Church, in Wash, by Rev C M Butler, Edw M Spilman to Miss Eliza C Day, both of Warrenton, Va.

Mrd: on Thu, at Springfield, Mass, by Rev H W Adams, Wm H Harding & Mary E, eldest daughter of the late Maj J B Clark, U S Army, both of Springfield.

Died: on Sep 24, Nicholas Travers, son of the late Nicholas Travers, of Wash City. His funeral is on Wed, at 10 o'clock, from the residence of the family.

Died: on Sep 19, at *Fort Columbus*, Govnr's Island, N Y, in his 60th year, Jos P Russell, M D, of the U S Army. Dr Russell was among the oldest of the army medical ofcrs, having been in the service since 1813.

Died: on May 24, on board of the schnr **Calista**, while on his way, as passenger, to Calif, of bilious pleurisy, Mr Saml Hugh Shryock, in his 19th year.

Died: on Sep 10, at Cincinnati, Mrs Cicily Spalding, aged 63 years, wife of John Spalding, formerly a resident of Wash.

Died: on Jul 6, in Lexington, Ky, Mr S F Bonfils, formerly the esteemed Principal of a successful Female Academy in Wash city, & lately professor of modern languages in Transylvania Univ, which place he resigned, on account of failing health, a few weeks before his death. Mr Bonfils was a native of France, & died aged 54 years.

Judge Jones, in the Court of Common Pleas of Northampton Co, Pa, has set aside the will of Peter Miller, a wealthy old bachelor, who died lately at Easton, which was affirmed by the Supreme Court. The entire estate, nearly $400,000, with the exception of a few trifling legacies, which are valid under will, goes to Peter Miller, of Ohio, the nephew & only heir at law of the deceased. The Easton Whig says: the fortunate individual who comes into possession of so large an estate is about 60 years of age, & resides in Morgan Co, Ohio, where he has worked a farm as tenant for a long time. He has a large family-a full baker's dozen of children, all poor.

City Court report of Balt on Sat: Jas Miller, 17, convicted of petit larceny, & sentenced to the penitentiary. He is one of 3 brothers whose father was killed on one of the railroads several years since, & who, left in charge of a mother unequal to the task of curbing their bad condduct, have all come to the same end. An elder brother was sent to the penitentiary some time since for larceny, & the next eldest, Jas, went there yesterday, & the youngest had been in jail for some months for larceny, being too young to imprison in the same instituion with his elder brothers. -Clipper

For rent: brick residence at I & 12th sts. Inquire at the Grocery Store at the corner of H & 12th sts. —Geo W Stewart

Received, a lot of superior finished Grates & Stoves, & Fire bricks of all sizes: for sale. —Wm H Harrover, 7th st

By virtue of a warrant of distrain from Wm W Corcoran vs Richd H Stewart for ground rent due upon lot 23 in square A, I have levied on one small frame house, on said lot; on Oct 4 next, in front of the premises, on Pa ave, I shall offer for sale the same. —O E B Hazard, Bailff, for W W Corcoran

WED SEP 26, 1849
The Vestry of the Parish of *Rock Creek*, in Wash Co, have it in contemplation to extend the ancient burial place of the Parish Church, by enclosing about 40 additional acres of the glebe, for the purpose of establishing a permanent cemetery, to be open to all denonimations of Christians. This Parish is believed to be the oldest in the Md Diocese of The Protestant Episcopal Church in the U S. The glebe had been owned & held by it for upwards of 125 years. The Parish Church, about to be thoroughtly repaired & enlarged, was built in the colonial times by imported brick. The parsonage stands hard by, upon an eminence overlooking the glebe, & is occupied by the rector, The Rev Mr Wood, who has recently been settled in the parish, with his family. The Present members of the Vestry are Mr Agg, Mr G W Riggs, Mr Carlisle, Mr Davis, Maj Walker, U S M C, Mr Harvey, Mr Wiltberger, & Mr McCeney, register.

Ofc, stable, & lumber at auction: on Sep 28, at the public space where Wm H Gunnell formerly kept his lumber yard, corner of 6th & Canal sts. -Green & Tastet

Wash Corp: 1-Bill for the relief of Jas McEllegett: referred to the Cmte of Claims. 2-Bills for the relief of Edw H Edelen, & for the relief of Wm Becket: referred to the Cmte on Claims. 3-Ptn from John Dove, praying the payment of a claim for earth deposited on 9th st: referred to the Cmte on Improvements. 4-Ptn of Wm Lord & others, for a flag footway across E st & 5th st: referred to the Cmte on Improvements. 5-Cmte on Police: bill granting to Jeremiah Hepburn permission to weigh hay in the 5th Ward, reported the same, without amendment. 6-Ptn of Mrs H B Macomb: referred to the Cmte of Claims. 7-Ptn of Grafton Powell: referred to the Cmte on Improvements.

The 3½ year old son of Dr D R Lyman, of Lynchburg, Va, fell on Mon last, from the dormer window of his father's residence, & died that day.

The Brooklyn Daily Advertiser publishes a report on the body of Mrs Kinney, of that city, who was strangled by her husband Thursday. From evidence it seems probable that Kinney labored under temporary derangements of mind. He & the deceased have always lived happily together.

Michl Gannon, in the employ of Messrs Humbird & Atkinson, railroad contractors near Cumberland, broke his leg on Friday last; mortification ensued, producing his death on Monday.

Appointment by the Pres: Nicoll Fosdick to be Collector of the Customs, New London, Conn, vice Thos Mussey, resigned.

Mr Clifford, late Minister to the Republic of Mexico, arrived at Mobile on Sep 19, in the British steamer **Severn**, from Vera Cruz. It is reported that Gen Padres lately died in the city of Mexico.

New Post ofcs: established, discontinued, & changed the site & names of the following, during the week ending Sep 15, 1849:

Ofc	County, State	New Appointment:
Cheat Bridge	Preston, Va	Jas Martin
Esteline Furn'e	Augusta, Va	Wm M Bryant
Reed Creek	Randolph, N C	Isaac H Forest
Cove	Shelby, Ala	John W Naish
Burrsville	Russell, Ala	Allen Burr
Equality	Coosa, Ala	Braddock Harris
Stateland	Choctaw, Miss	Asa A Sullivan
Mount Yancey	__mper, Miss	A G Nicholson
Matacha	__wamba, Miss	Jas C Gilstrap
Mount Pleasant	Caldwell parish, La	Thos Meredith
Toro	Sabine parish, La	Sam G Lucius
Ashland	De Soto parish, La	Wm G Davis
Alpine	Clark, Ark	Sam B Jones
New Salem	Rusk, Texas	Poindexter Payne
Lyons	Fayette, Texas	Wm B Bridges
Gilleland Creek	Travis, Texas	Stephen Boyce
Coon Hill	Santa Rosa, Fla	Wm L Williams

Consolation	Shelby, Ky	R W Hawkins
Shady	Johnson, Tenn	Wm M Tipton
Poplar Grove	Gibson, Tenn	John M Northern
Collamer	Whitley, Ind	Robt Reed
Craig	Switzerland, Ind	Peyton Wheeler
Boon Grove	Porter, Ind	Aaron Lettle
Rutledge	McDonald, Mo	Larkin McGlue
Fuller's Point	Cole, Ill	J T Johnson
Virgil	Fulton, Ill	Chandler Hollister
Olio	Sheboygan, Wis	Geo H Smith
Shawrette	Portage, Wis	John Strong
Dotyville	Fond du Lac, Wis	Thos J Davidson
Taylor	Davis, Iowa	Wm Dau
Bellmonte	Lancaster, Pa	F Brinton
Triadelphia	Morgan, Ohio	Francis Petit
Stepney Depot	Fairfield, Ct	Wm H Hoyt
West Falls	Erie, N Y	Geo H Palmer
Eastmanville	Fulton, N Y	R Eastman
East Windham	Greene, N Y	Ira Sherman
Orleans 4 Corn's	Jefferson, N Y	Henry W Joslin
Onondaga Castle	Onondaga, N Y	Albion Jackson
Rough & Ready	Steuben, N Y	Danl L Starr

Names & sites changed:
Sandy Ridge, Desmoines Co, Iowa, site & name changed to Green Bay & Robt Carpenter appointed p m.
Independence, Madison Co, Iowa, named changed to Montpelier.
Cornelius, Blount Co, Ala, named changed to Walnut Grove.
Colchester, Delaware Co, N Y, name & site changed to South Milford, & W H Coon appointed p m.
South Canton, St Lawrence Co, N Y, name changed to Craig's Mills, & Truman Hunt appointed p m.
Onondaga Hollow, Onondaga Co, N Y, named changed to Onondaga Valley.
Decatur, Van Buren Co, Mich, named changed to Porter.
Decatur Depot, Van Buren Co, Mich, named changed to Decatur.
Beemerville, Sussex Co, N Y, site changed, & J H Beemer appointed p m.
Agawam, Hampden Co, Mass, site changed, & Lyman Allen appointed postmaster.
Robinson's Store, Harford Co, Md, name changed to Mill Green.
Stony Point, Champaign Co, Ohio, named changed to Spring Hills, & Jas A Smith appointed p m.
Medina, Lenawee Co, Mich, site changed, & Saml Gregg appointed p m.

Wm Jennings died in England in 1798, leaving an estate of $40,000,000. He had no legal rep in England. The heirs there, on the maternal side instituted suit, & were defeated by the Crown upon the ground that the heirs on the paternal side were in the U S. This information came to a branch of the Jennings Family in the Northern & Eastern Staes some 15 years ago. On Sep 15, a convention of reps, 78 delegates from 8 States, took preliminary steps for the prosecution of their claims before the courts of England

House & lot for sale: his 2 story frame house & lot adjoining, on F st, between 6th & 4½ sts, Island. Enquire of Craven Ashford, at his ofc at 9th & Pa ave, who is fully authorized to sell. –John A Young

Mrd: on Sep 22, in St Mary's Church, by Rev Mr Alig, Jeremiah Ragen to Miss Catherine Quinn, both of Wash City.

Mrd; on Sep 23, at St Peter's Church, [Capitol Hill,] by Rev Mr Vanhorsigh, Armand Jardin, of France, to Honorine, eldest daughter of A Favier, of Wash City.

Died: on Sep 25, after a long & painful illness, Miss Josephine Costigan, in her 18th year. Her funeral is from the residence of her mother, on D near 9th st, this evening at 4 o'clock.

Died: on Sep 15, in Wash City, Mrs Arabella Clermorne, aged 54 years. She was a native of Lyons, France, & has been a resident of this country 22 years. She has a son, supposed to be residing in Geneva, Switzerland, whom she was anxious might see this notice.

THU SEP 27, 1849
For rent: large house in Carroll Pl, Capitol Hill. Apply to R H Clarke, next door to the Exchange Hotel, or to Dr Busey, Carroll Pl.

Edwin O Perrin has been appointed Navy Agent at Memphis, Tenn, to succeed Geo W Smith on Oct 1 next.

Divorce granted by the Court of Phil, in the case of Pierce Butler & Frances Anne Butler. Sep 22, 1849, she not appearing, the Court do order, adjudge, & decree that the said Pierce Butler, the libellant, be divorced & separated from the bond of marriage contracted with the said Frances Anne Butler: said parties be severaly at liberty to marry again, in like manner, as if they never had been married.

Saml E Atwell, of Alexandria, Va, died of cholera at Chicago on Jun 29. He had started for Calif, & got as far as Independence, Mo, but when the cholera broke out he concluded to return, & with 3 others left the company; but of them all, only D A Jones survived.

W R Henry, a West Point Cadet, a resident of Hagerstown, Ind, took passage at Buffalo for Sandusky on the steamer **Queen City**, on Tue last, & he disappeared. His baggage has been forwarded to his brother in Hagerstown. -Cin Chronicle

Jos B Abbott, formerly one of the editors of the Richmond Whig, died suddenly on Sunday of a disease of the heart.

Household & kitchen furniture at auction on Oct 1, at the residence of Mr Hands, on 11th st, between F & G sts. -E C & G F Dyer, aucts

One by one the Revolutionary Patriots are passing away. We announce the death of 2 of these heroes: Moses Perkins, aged 99 years, & Thos Brown, aged 105 years, both of Warren Co, Tenn. Murfeesborough [Tenn] Telegraph

Thos W Lottier, charged with shooting Wm P Cook, in the European House, on Jul 15, at Richmond, Va, was fully acquitted Sat last. He proved a long existing criminal intimacy between his wife & Cook, considered a justification of the shooting. -Ledger

Rockville [Md] Journal: the Burnett farm, in that county, containing over 200 acres, & highly improved, has been sold to Seth Hyatt, of Wash, at $20.12½ per acre.

Died: on Sep 26, Susanna Ophelia Beardsley, aged 4 years & 12 days. Her funeral is today 4 P M, from the residence of her mother, on E between 13th & 14th sts.

Died: on Sep 20, at Windsor, King Geo Co, Va, Sarah Mytton, wife of Wm Maury, formerly of Liverpool, the son of Jas Maury, the first Consul of the U S for that port. She was born on Nov 2, 1801, Liverpool.

Bldg lots in Wash City for sale. Apply at the ofc of Edw Swann, 5th st.

For rent: having been ordered to Phil, the subscriber offers for rent the house in which he resides; which he had leased for 4 years, from Apr 1, 1849. The house is on G st, near 10th, formerly occupied by Hon Cave Johnson. Inquire at the house, or at the ofc of Chief Naval Constructor, 49 Winder's new bldg. –Francis Grice

For rent or sale: commodious double house on H st, between 13th & 14th sts, known as the Demenou Bldg, containing 20 rooms. Apply to H L Heiskell

FRI SEP 28, 1849
Unfortunate accident on Wed to a little girl, the child of Dr S H Williams, Dentist, of Alexandria. Dr W was melting lead in a kettle in his yard, when the kettle upset & a large portion of the melted metal was thrown upon the head & face of the little girl, burning her very severely & dangerously. -Alex Gaz

The Concord & Claremont [N H] Railroad opened on Fri last: near Concord, a bolt connecting the tender with an open car broke, by which Mr Harvey Gould, of Warner, was precipitated on the track & run over. He died in 2 hours.

By deed of trust from John Williams, deceased, dated Apr 11, 1848, recorded in Liber W B 142, of the land records of this county, I shall sell on Oct 18: east half of lot 16 in reservation A, square D, in Wash City, with a well-built frame house, & outbldgs. –W Lenox, trustee -C W Boteler, auctioneer

Mary Jane Russell, wife of Franklin P Conant, aged 25 years, came to a sudden death at Williamsburg, N Y, on Sat, in consequence of injuries received by the burning of her garments, which took fire by the accidental ignition of some alcohol which she was heating.

Appointment by the Pres: Solomon F Halliday, of Fla, to be Receiver of Public Moneys at Newnansville, Fla, vice Geo H Smith, who declines the ofc.

Cincinnati, Ohio. The well known old mansion house & garden on the hill side, at the upper end of Broadway, in Cincinnati, so long the residence of Jesse Hunt, was more recently of his son-in-law, N G Pendleton, was sold out & laid off into bldg lots about 18 months since. The house has been torn down & rebuilt, not far from its old site. Now on the Pendleton ground there are now 52 elegant new brick houses, besides St Paul's Church, on the corner.

Died: on Sep 18, at Pittsburg, of cholera infantum, John Quincy Adams, son of the late Col Clifton Wharton, aged 22 months.

SAT SEP 29, 1849
Dancing Academy: Mr F R Labbe, will re-open Nov 12, at his residence on Pa ave, opposite Willard's Hotel.

F Y Naylor, Tinner & Stove Dealer, south side of Pa ave, near 3rd st. [Ad]

Dr Moffat, the great pillman, is about completing a first class dwlg on the north side of Union square, N Y, to be occupied by himself. The cost for the bldg will be about $85,000, including the lot which it occupies. Adjacent to Dr M's dwlg elegant houses are in progress & near completion for Henry Young, Ferdinand Suydam, & others.
--Journal of Commerce

Some 6 years ago Augustus Kennerly, city collector at St Louis, was discovered to be a defaulter in $8,000, & dismissed even though he claimed to be innocent. Recently it came to light, by re-examination of his accounts, that instead of being a defaulter, the city of St Louis really owes him $2,000 with interest, besides the restoration of his blighted reputation.

Supreme Court of the U S, Dec Term, 1848. #15: Peter F Kimball, owner of the steamboat **De Soto**, her tackle, apparel, & furniture, & Thos W Reed, now or lately master thereof, appellants, vs Geo H Caldwell, master & one of the owners of the steamer **Buckeye**, & Jas Smith, the other owner of the steamer **Buckeye**, her tackle, apparel, & furniture. Mr Barton, of counsel for the appellees, having suggested the death of Peter F Kimball, one of the appellants in this cause, moved the Court to dismiss this appeal under the 28th rule of Court; on consideration whereof it is now here ordered by this Court that unless the proper reps of said Kimball, deceased, shall voluntarily come in & become parties within the first 10 days of the ensuing term, then the said appellees shall be entitled to have this appeal dismissed.
--Wm Thos Carroll, C S C U S

Col Saml Bunch died at his residence in Granger Co, Tenn, on Sep 5, in his 64th year. He commanded a regt in the Indian wars under Gen Andrew Jackson, & in the charge of the battle of the Horse Shoe was the first or second man over the breast-works of the enemy. He represented his district 4 years in Congress during the administration of Pres Jackson.

Supreme Court of the U S, Dec Term, 1848. #116-Robinson Lytle & al, plntfs in error, vs The State of Arkansas, Wm Russell, & al. Mr Badger, of counsel for the plntfs, having suggested the death of Chester Ashley, one of the dfndnts, moved the Court for an order under 28th rule of Court; on consideration whereof it is now here ordered by this Court that unless the proper reps of said Ashley, deceased, shall voluntarily come in & become parties within the first 10 days of the ensuing term, than the said plntfs in error shall be entitled to open the record, &, on hearing, have the same reversed if it be erroneous. –Wm Thos Carroll, C S C U S

Persons killed by the bursting of the boilers of the steamer **Mary Kingsland**, on the coast of Fla: Jas Studley, acting master; Wm Holmes, 2nd engineer; Jos Meckins, steersman; Henry Stevens, Wm Sommers, Peter Eaton, & Geo Richards, deck hands; John Mulligan, Thos Dockerty, Cornelius Clay, Richd Town, John Simpson & Jas Henderson, firemen.

Died: on Sep 28, in Wash City, after a long & painful illness, Mariel, wife of Mr John Clapham, Pyrotechnist of the U S Navy, aged 34 years & 8 months. Her funeral is on Sun, at half past 2 o'clock, from her husband's residence on L st, near the Navy Yard.

Died: on Sep 25, at Gtwn, D C, John, son of Wm & Mgt Alexander, aged 25 years, a native of County Tyrone, Ire, but for the last 12 years a resident of this district.

Died: on Sep 17, at his late residence, near Huntingdon, Carroll Co, Tenn, in his 84th year, Gen Caleb Hawkins, formerly of Chas Co, Md.

Mrd: on Sep 25, by Rev Mr Lanahan, Jesse B Wilson to Anna A, 2nd daughter of Mr John Scrivener, all of Wash City.

Dissolution of the partnership under the firm of Locke & Tucker, by mutual consent. W W Tucker is authorized to settle up the business. –A R Locke, W W Tucker. The Cigar & Tobacco Business will hereafter be conducted at the Old Stand, in the Nat'l Hotel, 6th st, by me. –W W Tucker

For sale: the patent right of John Thruston's Fanning Mill for Va, except for certain counties. Patented 1848; re-issued 1849. Apply to Clinton, Knight & Bro. -Cincinnati, Ohio

MON OCT 1, 1849
More troops for Fla: Cos A & D, of the 1st Regt Artl, left Charleston last Tue, in the steamer **G W Coffee**, for Pilatka. Number about 120 men. Ofcrs accompanied the detachment, viz: Brevet Col Dimick, commanding Capt J Vodgers, Lt B Dubarry, of Co A, & Capt H D Grafton, & Lt A P Hill, of Co B. The steamship **Gladiator** arrived in Charleston on Tue from Smithville, N C, having on board Co E, 2nd regt Artl, comprising 50 rank & file. The ofcrs accompanying them were Capt Elgy, commanding, Lts Carlisle, Cook, & Larned, & Dr Sorrell, Surgeon. The steamer left the same afternoon for Pilatka.

Camp Washington, 25 miles east of *Fort Laramie*. Died, Jul 8, 1849, Chas Bishop, of Wash, member of the Wash City Calif Mining Assoc, of cholera, after an illness of 8 hours. The Assoc thanks Dr Austin, & the messmates of the deceased, for their unceasing efforts & kind attention during his illness. We buried him upon a small hill near the roadside, in a stone coffin. A neat head-stone marks the spot, upon which is cut this inscription:
In Memory of
CHARLES BISHOP,
of Washingon city, aged 25 years.
Died July 8, 1849, of cholera.
–J G Bruff, Capt, Geo A Young, Stephen J Cassin, Wm N Barker, & H C Dorsey, Cmte
Attest: H C Parrish, Sec

Strayed or stolen from the subscriber, on Sep 21, a large yellow Cow. All reasonable charges will be paid for her recovery. –John Hoover

Private Tutor Wanted: to take charge of 3 boys pretty well advanced, by addressing the subscriber at Good Luck P O, PG Co, Md. –G W Duvall

Cincinnati Commercial relates that a girl named Mgt T Weede, who was taken into the family of John Castle, on Sycamore st, a few years ago, from the Orphan Asylum, was lately placed in the Lunatic Asylum under false charges. Mgt was found not to be insane & is now living in the family of Mrs Turner.

The Woodbury Constitution reports the death of Jonas Cattell, who died at that place on the 19th ult, aged 91 years. He participated in the battle of Trenton, & was actively engaged through the Revolution.

Suicide: Hudson Gaz: Mr Abraham Van Allen, of Ghent, committed suicide by shooting himself on Sat last.

Henry Pitt, of Jersey City, was arrested for enticing away, abducting, & marrying Eliza Smith, who her mother swears was 13 years old in Feb last. He was held to bail in $500. –Portland Argus

Mrd: on Sep 7, by Rev Thos Owen, Mr Jas S W Caldwell to Miss Edmonia Virginia, only child of Maj Edmund Richmond; & on the evening of the same day, the parents of this young couple, Maj Edmund Richmond & Mrs Lydia E Caldwell, [sister of the late ex-Pres Jas K Polk,] were joined in marriage by Rev Arthur Davis, all of Haywood Co, Tenn.

Died: yesterday, after a short but severe illness, Mr Jas A Burch, aged 37 years. His funeral is this afternoon, at 3 o'clock, from his late residence, on 4½ st, near Md ave.

TUE OCT 2, 1849
Hon Thos W Chinn, who left this country a few weeks ago on his way to the post of Charge d'Affaires to Naples, has been compelled to turn back because of ill health, after getting as far as Paris.

From Santa Fe: a band of Cheyenne Indians a short time since surrounded & burnt Bent's fort. Wm Bent & several men who were in charge of the fort are supposed to have been massacred by the Indians, as nothing has been heard of them.

Miss Frances F Clark, of Stonington, Conn, has recovered of Capt Otis Pendleton, master of a whale ship, $1,500 for breach of promise of marriage. He went to sea deeply in love, but for some reason he cooled off before his return, when he refused to fill his contract.

Thos Davis, who has been in prison at Balt for 2 months past, on the charge of murdering John D Buck, who was shot whilst standing at his desk in the ofc of the copper smelting co, has been discharged, nothing having been proved against him sufficient to hold him for trial.

Isaac Q Underhill, an elderly & very respectable citizen of N J, has been for the last 2 or 3 days undergoing his trial, at the Hudson Co Oyer & Terminer, for the murder of Thos McGinn. McGinn suspected criminal intimacy between his wife & the prisoner. McGinn approached the prisoner with an iron bar, & Underhill shot & killed him with a pistol. Guilty of manslaughter: sentenced at hard labor for 2 years & fined $500, with costs of the prosecution. –N Y Comm Adv

Died: on Sep 31, Mrs Eliz Smoot, wife of Saml Smoot, in her 63rd year. Her funeral is today, at 2 o'clock, from her late residence on K st, near Gtwn.

Died: on Sun last, in his 41st year, Mr Cornelius Cox, late of the City Post Ofc. He leaves to a devoted widow & 3 children, a sister & a brother, the rich legacy of an umblemished character. His funeral is today at 3 o'clock, from his late residence on I st, betwee 9th & 10th sts.

Died: on Sep 10, near Port Tobacco, Md, Mary Clair, consort of Jas R Brent, & daughter of the late Geo W Neale. Twenty one days of the most agonizing suffering, was borne with almost unexampled patience. To the last moment she enjoyed the full possession of her senses. -W

Household & kitchen furniture at auction on Oct 2, at the residence of Mrs Arguelles, Pa ave, between 4½ & 6th sts. –Green & Tastet, auctioneers

WED OCT 3, 1849
Robt H Murphy, Deputy Sheriff, is not dead of his wounds received from the anti-renters, but is likely to recover. –N Y Post

A letter from Saratoga Spings mentions the death, at that place, of Mr G H Hill, the comedian. He died on Fri.

Court of Common Pleas, at N Y, on Sat, Anna Judson, wife of Ed Z C Judson, that day sentenced to the Penitentiary for leading in the Astor Place riots, obtained a decree of divorce from her husband under the new code for various acts of ill-treatment.

Wash Corp: 1-Ptn from Rev Chas M Denison & others, for an alteration in the present laws for the sale of intoxicating liquors: referred to the Cmte on Police. 2-Cmte of Claims: asked to be discharged from the further consideration of the ptns of Geo W Wren, of Jos Ferguson, & of Nathl Hofflein. 3-Ptn of John M Kraft, for remission of a fine: referred to the Cmte on Claims. 4-Ptn of Jas Dixon, respecting the grade of Pa ave, between 1st & 2nd sts: referred to the Cmte on Improvements. 5–Ptn of Chas Kerrnan, praying for the restoration of certain geese: referred to the Cmte of Claims. 6-Ptn of J W Eberbach, for remission of a fine: referred to the Cmte of Claims.

Madame de Krudener was born in 1764, & died in 1824. Her conversion took place about her 40th year. She had made a brilliant figure in the aristocratical world. Her publications in verse & prose had won her the homage of celebrated literati.

New Post Ofcs: established, discontinued, & changed the site & names of the following ofcs, during the week ending Sep 29, 1849.

Ofc	County, State	New Appointment:
West Swanzey	Cheshire, N H	Jonathan W Frink
Somerville	Tolland, Conn	Ansel Arnold
East Randolph	Cataraugus, N Y	Merrick Nutting
Worthville	Jefferson, N Y	Lorenzo P Gillet
Bellevale	Orange, N Y	Augustus J Burt
Barton Hill	Scharie, N Y	Jacob J Barton
Jeffersonville	Sullivan, N Y	Isaac Snyder
N Cambridge	Washington, N Y	Esek Brownell
Bergen Point	Hudson, N J	Joshua Van Name
Carter Camp	Porter, Pa	Hub Starkweather
Hebron	Potter, Pa	Geo C Rossiter
Mountville	Lancaster, Pa	Robt Fullerton
Saversville	Butler, Pa	Wm S Boy
Milltown	Chester, Pa	Jesse Mallock
Mount Nebo	Lancaster, Pa	Jos Engles
Kettle Creek	Potter, Pa	Francis D French
Watts' Mills	Westmoreland, Pa	Jacob Watts
Strinestown	York, Pa	Geo H Seip
Clio	Greene, Ohio	Isaac N Carman
Maybee's	Jacksen, Ohio	Wm Maybee
Brandt	Miami, Ohio	D Y Seward
Elk Run	Fauquier, Va	H B Ralls
Wesobulga	Randolph, Ala	N A Teakle
Bluff Springs	Attala, Miss	Jos K Coffey
Pleasanton	Itawamba, Miss	Nath'l B McClellan
Deep Water	Marshall, Miss	Wm H Cowan
Greenwood	Sumner, Tenn	W M Toomey
Cedar Ford	Grainger, Tenn	Anderson Acaff
Gaines' Bend	Hawkins, Tenn	Wm B Francisco
Owen Hill	Williamson, Tenn	Wm Lanier
Unity	Muhlenberg, Ky	John S Eaves
Lynnford	Jefferson, Ky	Whelon W Evans

Pl Grove Mills	Fleming, Ky	Austin R Saunders
Curry's Run	Harrison, Ky	Jas Slade
Arba	Randolph, Ind	John W Fulgham
Argyle	Jefferson, Mo	Wm G Walker
Rose Hill	Mahaska, Iowa	W M Jarvis
Allen's Grove	Walworth, Wis	Philip Allen
Helena	Iowa, Wis	Thos Pound

Names & sites changed:
Greene, Kennebeck Co, Maine, site changed-Geo H Dearborn appt'd p m
Wadley's Falls, Stafford Co, N H, name & site changed to Tuttle's Corner, & Thos Tuttle appointed p m.
Salem, Rockingham Co, N H, site changed, & Silas Hall appointed p m.
West Stockholm, St Lawrence Co, N Y, site changed, & Loren Ashley appointed p m.
Rockland, Sullivan Co, N Y, site changed, & Marvin Kimball appointed p m.
Fair Mount, Somerset Co, Md, name changed to Jamestown, & L D Handy appt'd p m
Medill, Montg Co, Ohio, name changed to New Lebanon, & Henry Grubb, appt'd p m.
Red House, Caswell Co, N C, name & site changed to Moore's Store, & Wm J Moore, appointed p m.
Gravelly Hill, Bladen Co, N C, site changed & Jas H Meredith appointed p m.
Raines' Store, Twiggs Co, Ga, name changed to Jeffersonville.
Miltonville, Wayne Co, Miss, name & site changed to Taylorton, & Wm S Linson appointed p m.
Big Eagle, Scott Co, Ky, name & site changed to Little Eagle, & John S Getty appointed p m.
Indian Prairie, Tipton Co, Ind, name & site changed to Tetersburg, & Reuben Tansey appointed p m.
Brownsville, Saline Co, Mo, name & site changed to Sweet Springs, & Putnam Hays appointed p m.

Official: Dept of State, Wash, Oct 2, 1849. Information received from Thos W Slemons, U S Consul at Matamoros, of the death of the following American citizens within his consulate, viz:

C K Gleason, from Ala	Dr Wm Fosdick, from Ind
Wm T Frazier, from Texas	John Thomas, from Texas, murdered
John Mills, from Texas, murdered	John Adams, from Texas, murdered
R Brummill, from Ala	John Snively, from Texas, murdered
R A Crumpton, from Ala	Miguel Suezineau, from Louisiana

Mrd: on Sep 25, by Rev Mathias Alig, Geo Simms to Anna Hodge, both of Wash City.

Mrd: on Sep 30, at St Mary's Church, by Rev Mathias Alig, Fred'k Klots to Miss Martha French, of Wash City.

Died: on Oct 1, at her residence in PG Co, Md, of apoplexy, Mrs Matilda Magruder, wife of the late Fielder Magruder, in her 62nd year.

Died: on Sun last, in Balt, Cecelia Jane Sweeney, aged 14 years, daughter of the late John W Sweeney, of Wash City.

Died: on Sep 31, after a few hours' illness, Mary Agnes, only daughter of Wm & Mary Wheeler, aged 7 years & 9 months.

THU OCT 4, 1849
Stolen. The person who took away a Terrier Pup from my residence this morning is requested to return him without delay, as he was seen & known. –Wm C Zantzinger

Found: a gold chain & locket, which owner can have by identifying & paying costs. Apply to Geo F Hartshorn, 22nd st, between G & H sts.

Wash City Hermann Bldg Assoc: meeting on Oct 8. –Alfred Schucking, sec

Three cows stray or stolen: suitable reward will be paid for the recovery of all or any of the above cows. –Mary A Lewis, 17th st, west

Maj John P Gaines, late Rep in Congress from Ky, has been appointed Govn'r of the Territory of Oregon.

A new paper, Cincinnatus of the West, has been started in Cincinnati, Ohio, by R F Ryan, one of the sympathizers who was imprisoned in Ireland last year.

Circuit Court of Wash Co, D C: in Chancery. Edw F Queen vs Robt W Borrows. By decree of said court, I shall sell at auction, on Oct 11, all that tract of land called *Cedar Hill*, in Wash Co, D C, containing 38 acres more or less. It adjoins the tract called *Haddock's Hills*, & also the farm owned & occupied by Arthur Scott.
–Chas H Laskey, trustee   John Martin & Co, auctioneers

Teacher wanted for the Upper Marlborough Academy: salary is $350 per annum. –Jno B Brooke, Pres of the Board of Trustees of U M A

Rose Hills estate for sale: known as the property of the late Capt Lynn, adjacent to the city of Cumberland, comprises about 1,200 acres of land. The family mansion, *Rose Hill*, is immediately on the Potomac river, on high ground. The Mountain tract will be disposed of in pasture lots. –Erastus Edgerton, trustee

B Perley Poore, of the Boston Bee, was thrown from a chaise near his residence in West Newbury, on Thu last, & considerably injured.

Gettysburg Star: Fred'k Smith, who was convicted during the Aug term of the murder of Fred'k Foster, was sentenced on Sep 25 to be hanged. On Sep 27 he committed suicide in his cell, having made a rope from a part of his bed, by which he had suspended himself from a bar running across the top of his cell. He had made a full confession of the murder.

Mrd: on Oct 2, at *Mount Pleasant, Kalorama*, by Rev Chas A Davis, S Britt Waite, of Wash, to Marie C, 2nd daughter of Louis Vivans, of the former place. And at St Patrick's church, on Oct 3, by Rev Wm Mathews, S Britt Waite, of Wash, to Marie C, 2nd daughter of Louis Vivans, of the former place.

0FRI OCT 5, 1849
Appointment by the Pres: Francis W Fitch, Surveyor, new London, Conn, vice Perry Douglass, removed.

Alexandria Gaz: Chas T Stuart has been appointed Surveyor of the port of Alexandria, Va, vice Benj T Fendall, deceased.

Vessels, with the master's name, & port from which they sailed, which have cleared for Calif during the month of Sep, so far as they have reached us:
Date: Vessel: Master: Port:
Sep 1: brig **Wellingsley**: Parsons: Boston
2: ship **Friendship**: Stott: New Bedford
3: ship **South America**: Soule: Providence
3: barque **Sarah**: Morse: Edgartown
3: brig **Andrew M Jones**: Duling: Portland
4: brig **Cybele**: Davis: Portland
5: ship **Manco**: Fish: Boston
8: ship **Hampton**: Davis: Bath
10: ship **Akbar**: Worth: Boston
10: ship **Carthage**: Ropes: Boston
10: ship **Susan Drew**: Drew: N Y
10: ship **Ambassador**: Hadley: N Y
10: barque **Chief**: Brown: Boston
10: brig **Ruth**: Stevens: Portland
11: brig **Carter Braxton**: Lane: Boston
11: brig **Herald**: Pratt: Salem
11: barque **Adario**: Burrows: N Y
12: ship **Talma**: Davis: Salem
14: ship **Byron**: Janvrin: N Y
14: ship **Oriental**: Talbot: East Machias
16: Br barque **Ada**: [blank:] Eastport
17: schnr **Eagle**: Perry: New Bedford
19: brig **Wyandot**: Ellis: Boston
19: brig **Antares**: Howe: Salen
20: ship **John Jay**: Benjamin: New Bedford
20: ship **Splendid**: Baylies: Edgartown
20: barque **Valhalla**: Howes: New Orleans
21: ship **Wm Sprague**: Chase: N Y
22: barque **Danl Webster**: Higgins: Boston
24: barque **Magnolia**: Herrick: New Haven
24: brig **Tarquina**: Moulthrop: N Y
24: schnr **Elizabeth**: Lee: N Y
25: ship **Flavio**: Jenkins: Boston

25: ship **S Baldwin**: McFarlan: Phil
25: schnr **Chesapeake**: Marvel: Fall River
26: barque **Chester**: Warren: Boston
27: ship **St Lawrence**: Brown: N Y
27: brig **Meta**: Rich: Phil
28: ship **Russell**: Hill: N Y
29: schnr **Spartacus**: Welch: Boston
-Boston Journal

Died: on Oct 4, Mrs Harriet Mattingly, after a long & painful illness. Her funeral is this evening, at half past 3 o'clock, from the residence of her son, on 5th st, between G & H sts.

Died: yesterday, in Wash City, Catherine Pauline, aged 2 years & 9 months, only daughter of Mary P & Paulus Thyson. Her funeral is today at half past 3 o'clock.

The Rev Joy H Fairchild, of the Payson Church, South Boston, has commenced an action in the Supreme Judicial court against Rev Nehemiah Adams, D D, of the Essex st Church, Boston, for libel & slander, & suing for damages in $10,000.

City Ordinances-Wash: 1-Act for the relief of Benone Jones & Jas Spurling: to pay $14.58 to Jones, & $12.58 to Spurling, for services rendered as scavengers of the 5th Ward for the year ending Jun 30, 1849. 2-Act for the relief of John Dove: to be paid $66 for removal of a nuisance in square 530.

Buffalo Commercial of Mon: rumor was current at that place that the steamer **Tecumsch**, with all on board, had been lost on Lake Huron, in the late gale.

At Norfolk, on Fri, while Mr N M Tarrall & his workmen were slating a roof, the scaffold gave way, & Mr T, with Mr Henry C Guy & a negro man belonging to Mr Todd, were precipated to the ground, about 30 feet. They were so dreadfully bruised that their recovery is yet very uncertain.

SAT OCT 6, 1849
Thos Warhurst, who was in custody in N Y on the charge of seducing Eliz Warden, of Dutchess Co, settled the matter on Sat by marrying the girl, & he was discharged.

Mrd: on Oct 4, in Wash City, by Rev O B Brown, Mr Henry C Bell to Miss Sophia Bullock, both of Orange Co, Va.

Died: on Sep 23, in Smithfield, Va, of scarlet fever, Harriet Lowndes, only daughter of Geo H & Ann L Beckwith, aged 4 years.

Rare chance for capitalists: the subscriber offers at private sale his beautiful estate, on the Potomac river, in Chas Co, Md, containing about 731 acres: house is commodious, & built at a cost of nearly $6,000, with all necessary out bldgs. The adjoining farm contains 400 acres. –Chas A Pye, near Port Tobacco, Chas Co, Md.

Household & kitchen furniture at auction on Oct 10, at the residence of Saml B Beach, on N J ave, next below the residence of Thos Blagden. –Green & Tastet

Woodley for sale: by decree of the Circuit Court for D C: in a cause wherein Gen Lowry & others are cmplnts, & Ann E Kervand, widow of Lazare Kervand, & Ann Louisa Kervand, Isabel Kervand, & J L Kervand, his heirs at law, will be exposed to sale, at public auction, on Nov 7 next, on the premises, the beautiful estate called *Woodley*, part of *Pretty Prospect*, on the heights above Gtwn, formerly the residence of Philip B Key, & now of Mrs Kervand. The mansion is spacious & has about 226 acres attached. –W Redin, trustee -E S Wright, auctioneer

For sale: private residence in Wash, on G st, near the State Dept. Inquire of D A Gardner, on the premises.

The subscriber wishes to hire a Servant to cook & wash & a man servant to do the services of the house. A good home & fair wages punctually paid is offered to persons who can be recommended for capacity, good temper, sobriety, & honesty of character. Persons from the country by the year will be preferred. I have for rent a brick stable, with 3 stalls, carriage, & food house, on the alley of my residence. –G C Grammer

MON OCT 8, 1849
By virtue of a distrain warrant from Anthony Hyde, agent for W W Corcoran & others vs Jas W Rowland, for ground rent due Sep 23, 1849, & to me directed, I have seized & levied on one frame house on Capitol Hill, on lot 19, in square 688: sale on Oct 16. –O E P Hazard, bailiff for W W Corcoran & others.

Hon Jonathan H Hubbard, one of the oldest & most esteemed citizens of Vt, died at his residence in Windsor on Sep 20, aged 81 years. He was a Rep in Congress from 1809 to 1811, & from 1813 to 1845 was Judge of the Supreme Court.

The Vergennes Vermonter of Oct 3 announces the death of Hon Silas Jenison, for several years Govn'r of that State, & one of its most esteemed & valuable citizens. He died at Shoreham on Sep 30.

The new U S steamer **Ohio** is expected at N Y on her return this week, & will sail again from there on Oct 16. Among the passengers engaged for this trip are Hon John Slidell & family of Louisiana; Hon Balie Peyton, U S Minister to Chili, & daughter; Maj Waggaman, U S A; Richd Taylor, son of the Pres of the U S.

The Phil North American of Sat announces the death of Danl Fitler, a well known citizen of Kensington, & formerly high sheriff of the city & county of Phil. [No death date given-current item.

On Thu last at the steamboat landing in Albany, Mr Nathan O Banks, jr, of Patterson, Putnam Co, who arrived in the train from the West, while attempting to pass on board the ship **Isaac Newton**, with his wife, owing to the darkness of the night, walked off the dock, his wife being on the plank, & before assistance could be rendered was drowned. He was a respectable member of the Society of Friends, 53 years of age.

Miss Catherine Crowley, [age 16 years,] daughter of Mr John Crowley, of Wash Co, Md, was drowned in the Chesapeake & Ohio Canal, about 1 mile above Harper's Ferry, on Tue last. She was attempting to cross the canal on a board, near the lock, when she fell in, & was drowned. Her body was found a short time after.
–Charlestown Free Press

Mrd: on Oct 4, by Rev Mr Johnson, Dr D M French, of Giles Co, Va, to Miss Mary E Smoot, daughter of Geo H Smoot, of Alexandria, Va.

Fort Leavenworth, Sep 19. In June last Col Mackay was ordered to *Fort Laramie*, & left, escorted by Lt Geo Evans & a company of 10 dragoons, & accompanied by his son, age 13 years, Capt E A Easton, Dr Russell, U S A, Dr Geo B Parks, of Boston, & Rev John Robertson, a Scotch gentleman, who was travelling for pleasure. Capt Easton had a box with several thousand dollars in it that he was to convey to *Fort Kearny*, & when the sgt of the company got wind of it, immediately proposed to the 9 dragoons under his charge to shoot the others, in their tents at night, & he would take care of the Col. The affair was exposed, the plot discovered, & the sgt is now under arrest.

Died: on Oct 6, in Wash City, Mrs Mary Brown, in her 97th year, relict of Geo Brown, sr, an old & respectable resident of Phil. Her funeral is this afternoon, at 4 o'clock, from her daughter's residence, [Mrs Mary Barry,] near the Navy Yard.

Died: on Oct 6, Mary Ann Robinson, youngest daughter of Chas H & Eliz E Gordon, aged 3 years, 6 months & 21 days. Her funeral is Oct 8, at 2 o'clock. Residence, Va ave, near 8th st, Navy Yard.

TUE OCT 9, 1849
The Raleigh Register completed its 50th year on Oct 3. It was established in 1799, by the Grandfather of the present Editor, [who was father to the senior Editor of the Nat'l Intell,] & during all that time it has prospered in the unfaltering support of Republican principles.

During the evening of Sep 27 the river bank at Morganza, in the parish of Point Coupee, La, caved in, carrying about 2 acres of ground. Mr Bissett, the proprietor of the hotel there, Mr Boyd, & 2 negro man belonging to the estate of Mr Chas Morgan, lost their lives by being engulphed in the fall.

By order of distrain from Wm Uttermule, sen, to me directed, I have seized some goods & chattels: wood & carpenter's tools, trunk, & other items, to be sold for cash, at public auction on Oct 16. –A E L Keese, Bailiff

For sale: 3 story brick house & lot on Pa ave, between 6th & 7th sts. Apply to Richd H Clarke, ofc on C st, next to Exchange Hotel.

For rent: commodious dwlg just erected at 12th & F sts. Apply to S M McKean, 17th st, near Navy Dept.

U S A: District of N C-Circuit Court of the U S. The U S vs Nathl M Sneed-in Equity. The U S vs Jas R Sneed-in Equity. Sale in Raleigh, on Nov 26, various tracts of land in Alabama, & in the district of Huntsville. By the decree made in the cause the purchaser will be put into possession of the property, & the sale will be made for cash. Witness, Wm H Haywood, Clerk of the Court, this 3rd of Oct, 1849.

For rent: the U S Hotel on Pa ave. Apply to Jos Fallansbee, or W Henry Upperman.

Household & kitchen furniture at auction on Oct 15, at 4½ & C sts, fromerly Dr Sewall's residence. —Green & Tastet, auctioneers

For rent or lease, the 4 story brick house, on Gravier st, New Orleans.
—Jacob Barker, 79 Baronne st, New Orleans

Balt, Oct 8. Edgar A Poe, distingusihed as a writer, & I may say widely known for his literary qualifications, died in this city yesterday morning, in his 38th year.

Mrd: on Oct 2, by Rev L F Morgan, Richd J Ryon to Miss Julia M Wheeler, all of Wash City.

Mrd: on Sep 25, at Cerro Gordo, Fiskkill Landing, by Rev Dr Robertson, Wm G Peck, U S Topographical Engineers, & Eliz, daughter of Prof Chas Davies.

Mrd: on Oct 4, at New Haven, Conn, by Rev C J Knowles, of Long Island, B W Knowles, of Richmond, Va, to Miss C H King, daughter of Roswell King, of Westfield, Conn.

Died: on Sep 25, at Bonpas, White Co, Ill, Geo Webb, aged 80 years. Mr Webb formerly resided in Winchester, Ky, & for nearly 30 years past has been a much honored & highly esteemed citizen of White Co.

Died: on Oct 4, in Harrisonburg, Rockingham Co, Va, Frances S, wife of the Hon Danl Smith, of that place.

Died: on Oct 2, at Lexington, Ky, at the residence of his brother, Capt Henry Johnson, after a protracted illness, the Hon Benj Johnson, a Judge of the Supreme Court of the State of Ark, a gentlman widely known & greatly respected.

Died: on Sep 29, in Frankfort, Ky, Henry Clay Harlan, son of the Hon Jas Harlan, in his 20th year, a very estimable & promising young man.

WED OCT 10, 1849
The British barque **St John**, from Galway, Ire, struck on Grampus Rocks on Sun last & immediately sunk. 150 passengers were drowned. The capt, crew, & 10 others were saved on pieces of the wreck. So says a Telegraphic despatch received last night.

Mr A W Babbitt, who has been elected to represent the Mormon State of Deseret in Congress, has arrived at St Louis.

Balt & Ohio Railroad Co: elected Directors on Mon last:
Moses Shepard   Columbus O'Donnel   Edw Patterson
Johns Hopkins   Wm McKim   Jas Swan
John L Donaldson   Andrew Gregg   Fielding Lucas, jr
Saml W Smith   Thos Black   Jas H Carter
Thos Swann, the Pres of the company submitted his annual report.
[Note: Jas Swan & Thos Swann, as written.]

Letters from Palermo, dated Sep 17, received at Phil, announce the decease of Capt John Gwinn, of the Mediterranean squadron, which took place on Sep 4, on board the U S flag ship **Constitution**. Capt Gwinn was a native of Md, & entered the naval service in 1809.

The late Miss Demilt has left some $80,000 to charitable institutions in this city. –N Y Com Adv

Mr Robt Evans, a slater, residing in Phil, on Sat, was shockingly burned while pouring oil into a lamp. On Sun death put an end to his sufferings. He leaves a family. –North Amer

New London Chronicle: decision in 2 divorce cases tried in that ancient town: Mr John C Holland & Mrs Frances E Holland. Each sought a divorce, Mrs Holland accusing her husband of infidelity-proved-divorce granted. Mr Holland accusing his wife of infidelity-not proved-divorce not granted.

Wash City Items: fencing has been completed on the Mall by Mr Chas F Wood. It runs 6,300 feet.

The St Chas Hotel passed into the ownership of J W Maury, & has made improvements inside & out. The iron pillars, were cast by Messrs Rider & Co, at the Wash Foundry; the carpenter's work was by Mr John G Robinson; & the iron balustrading was by Mr Buckingham.

Mrd: on Oct 9, in the Church of the Ascension, by Rev L J Gilliss, Wm Henry Lyon to Miss Eliz Brawner, both of Chas Co, Md.

Died: on Oct 8, in his 54th year, Florence S McCarthy, a native of Cork Co, Ire, but for the last 30 years a citizen of Wash. His funeral is this evening, at 4 o'clock, from his late residence on F st.

From a gentleman of Caroline Co we learn that Rev Jas Nicols, a minister of the Methodist Episcopal Church, residing in Hillsborough, of said county, on Thu, after prayers, began to talk wildly, & hearing a rap at the door, seized a gun, & deliberately shot his cousin, Miss Julia Ann Nicols, the contents entering in the front & passing down near the heart. Mr Nicols was found to be insane, & secured in jail. He is subject to fits of insanity, & had been in a Phil hospital. -Easton [Md] Gaz

A young son of Mr John Burt, of Albany, N Y, was lost 3 years ago, being then but 4 years old. A most diligent search was made for him. Lately Mr Burt saw a paragraph in a newspaper that a little boy 6 or 7 years old, had been picked up in Syracuse while finding shelter in a dry goods box. He was recognized by flesh marks, & restored to his parents.

Nurse wanted: a steady white woman, capable of taking care of a sick lady. Apply opposite to Mr Jacob Gideon's, on 7th st.

Household & kitchen furniture at auction on Oct 12, at the 3 story house on Bridge st, next adjoining C E Eckle's. –Edw S Wright, auctioner

Wash Corp: 1-Ptn from P J Steer & others: referred to the Cmte on Police. 2-Ptn from Wm Barker: referred to the Cmte on Improvements. 3-Cmte of Claims: bill for the relief of John Crome: recommended it do not pass. 4-Cmte of Claims: asked to be discharged from the further consideration of the ptns of Geo Krafft & J H McBlair: discharged accordingly. Same cmte: act for the relief of John E Neale; act for the relief of Michl H Grimes: recommended that they do not pass. Same cmte: asked to be discharged from the further consideration of the ptn of Thos Baker: discharged accordingly. 5-Ptn of Ulysses Ward: referred to the Cmte on Improvements. 6-Ptn of Thompson Nailor, praying permission to erect a stable within 24 feet of a brick bldg: referred to the Cmte on Police. 7-Ptn of Elias Barnes, praying payment for work on 16th st: referred to the Cmte on Improvements. 8-Ptn of N P Van Zandt & other citizens, praying certain alterations in the license laws for the sale of liquors: referred to the Cmte on Police. 9-Ptn of John Bohlayer, jr, praying the restoration of certain hogs belonging to him, & found going at large: referred to the Cmte of Claims.

J C Weichmann, Merchant Tailor, Pa ave, nearly opposite Brown's Hotel: latest styles will be made up in a superior manner.

By writ of fieri facias: sale on Oct 16, in Wash City, the following to wit: one carryall, seized & taken as the property of John Seitz, & will be sold to satisfy a judgment in favor of Christopher S O'Hare. –A E L Keese, Constable

THU OCT 11, 1849
Convention for framing a State Constitution for Calif assembled at Monterey Aug 31. The composition of the body, as far as known, is as follows:

District of San Francisco:

Regular	Supernumeraries
Edw Gilbert	W D M Howard
Myron Norton	Francis J Lippitt
Wm M Quin	A J Ellis
Jos Hobson	Francisco Sanchez
Wm M Steuart	Rodman M Price

District of San Jose:

Jos Aram	Pedro Sansevain
K H Dimmick	Julian Hanks

J D Hoppe
A M Pico

Antono M Pico
Elam Brown

District of San Diego:
Miguel de Pedrorena
Henry Hill

Cave J Couts
John Forster
Wm Richardson

District of Monterey:
Regular:
H Wager Halleck
Thos O Larkin
Lewis S Dent
Regular:
Joel P Walker
Robt Semple

Chas T Botts
Pacificus Ord
District of Sonoma:

L W Boggs
M G Vallejo

Appointment by the Pres: Anthony Walke to be Register of the Land Ofc at Chillicothe, Ohio, vice Thos J Winship, resigned.

Boston Courier: the late Jacob Perkins was descended from one of the oldest families of Essex Co, Mass. Matthew Perkins removed to Newburyport early in life, & here Jacob Perkins was born, Jul 9, 1766. At 12 he was put apprentice to a goldsmith of Newburyport of the name of Davis. His master died 3 years afterwards, & Perkins, at 15, was left with the management of the business. Perkins was 21 when he was employed by the Gov't, to make a die for striking coins. During the war of 1812 his ingenuity was employed in constructing machinery for boring out old honey-combed cannons, & in perfecting the science of gunnery. Perkins removed from Newburyport to Boston in 1816. After a short residence in Phil he removed to London. He continued in London during the remainder of his life.

Orphans Court of Wash Co, D C. In the case of John P Ingle & Jos Ingle, excs of Jas Moore, deceased, the excs, with the approbation of the Court, appointed Oct 30th for settlement of said estate. –Ed N Roach, Reg/o wills

Valuable property for sale: under authority from the devisees of the late John Zimmerman, property in Fairfax Co, Va:
1-*Tavern Stand* now occupied by John H Zimmerman, near Alexandria: about 21 acres of land attached: extensive bldgs.
2-*Stump Hill*, near Alexandria, in the neighborhood known as *Quaker Hill*: from 80 to 100 acres in this tract.
3-*Flag Hill*, containing 40 acres, adjoining *Stump Hill* & the land of the late Jas Atkinson.
4-2 acre lot in West End, adjoining the land of W Richards & B Rotchford.
5-An acre lot on the main road in West End, having on it 2 tenements.
Sale to take place on Nov 30.
6-Also, 2 undivided seventh parts of a tract of land in Loudoun Co, Va, adjoining Goose Creek [Friends'] Meeting-house, now in the tenure of Mrs Eliz Zimmerman for her life. This sale is on Nov 26. –R Johnston, trustee

Dr Robt Goldsborough died at Centreville, Md, on Sep 30, aged 77. For more than 40 years he was a practitioner of medicine in Queen Anne's Co. For many years he was Pres of the Medical & Chirurgical Society of Md. -Sun

Calvin, eldest son of Capt Jos Upton, jr, lost his life yesterday from the accidental discharge of a gun in his own hands. He was 16 years of age.
-Fitchburg [Mass] Sentinel of the 5th

Died: on Oct 10, Rose, infant daughter of Robt & Rose Greenhow. Her funeral is on Thu, at 5 o'clock, from their house, on F st.

New Post ofcs: established, discontinued, & changed the site & name of during the week ending Oct 6, 1849:

Ofc	County, State	New appointment:
Bensons'Landing	Rutland, Vt	Perrin W Converse
East Shelburne	Franklin, Mass	Isaac T Fisk
West Rutland	Worcester, Mass	Warren H Sibley
Seward	Schoharie, N Y	Jacob H Dufendorf
Constantia Centre	Oswego, N Y	Homer Hayes
West Anson	Somerset, Me	Thos Gray
Rochester	Beaver, Pa	R G Parks
Randolph	Crawford, Pa	Leonard Reed
Castile	Greene, Pa	John Lewis
New Columbus	Luzerne, Pa	Geo Kremer
Beech Woods	Warren, Pa	Benj Oviatt
West Windsor	Eaton, Mich	Geo P Carman
Windsor	Eaton, Mich	O D Skinner
East New Vineyard	Franklin, Me	Moses Bradbury
Blue Creek	Habersham, Geo	Young Davis
Forest Hill	Decatur, Ind	Geo Hogg
Big Woods	Du Page, Ill	John Stoep
La Salle	La Salle, Ill	Edwin R Moffatt
Olinda	Pike, Ill	Thos M Massee
Ash Grove	Greene, Mo	Jas S Cook
Roubedoux	Wright, Mo	Hobbs Burckhartt
Badger	Fond du Lac, Wis	Purley H Giltner
Hoadley	Racine, Wis	Jos B White
McGregor's Ldg	Clayton, Iowa	Henry D Evans
McKissack's Grove	Fremont, Iowa	Thos Farmer
St Anthony's Falls	St Croix, M T	A Godfrey
Santa Fe	Santa Fe, N M	Wm S McKnight
Westminster	Shelby, Ill	Washbon Wade

Names & sites changed:
Darien, Fairfield Co, Conn, site changed, & Edw Scofield appointed p m
Conshohocken, Montg Co, Pa, site changed, & Fred'k Naile, jr, appointed p m.
Polkville, Onondaga Co, N Y, name changed to Little Utica, L Dunham appointed p m.
Dallasville, Tioga Co, Pa, name changed to Daggett's Mills, & John W Joslin appointed p m.

Talbott, Fairfield Co, Ohio, named changed to Lockville, & E T Mithoff appointed p m
Hughes, Jackson Co, Ohio, name changed to Keystone, & Edwin H Griswold appointed p m.
Crow Creek, Wood Co, Va, name changed to Willow Island.
Chattahoochee, Gadsden Co, Fla, site changed to Steamboat Landing.
Bellville, Gonzales Co, Texas, name changed to Belmont, & Thos Gray appointed p m.
East Bend, Hancock Co, Ill, name & site changed to Pontoosac, & Jeremiah Smith appointed p m.
White Creek, Wankesha Co, Wisc, name changed to Genesee.
Goodlet, Walworth Co, Wisc, name & site changed to West Hebron, McHenry Co, Ill, & John Adams appointed p m.
Genesee, Wankesha Co, Wisc, name changed to Keewanee.
Fountain, Racine Co, Wisc, site changed & Ira N Miller appointed p m.

FRI OCT 12, 1849
Bennet Clements, Notary Public, Bounty Land, Pension, & Genr'l Agent, at Washington. His long service as clerk in the Treas Dept, & more recent & extensive experience as general agent, enables him to act with promptness & efficiency.

The subscriber is no longer connected with the business heretofore conducted by him, now carried on by J & J Visser, 10th beween E & F sts, & has entirely separated himself from the said firm. He has removed to the house formerly occupied by Mrs Davy, on E st. He is determined to give his customers the very best Bread, Biscuit, & other things. –L A Tarlton

A H Beach & S M Tucker have establised themselves in the Gen Auction & Commission Business in Wash City, under the firm of Beach & Tucker. Salesroom is on Pa ave.

Legislature of the State of Tenn assembled at Nashville, on Oct 1. In the Senate John F Henry, [Whig] was chosen Pres by 13 to 10; in the House Landon C Haynes [Dem] was chosen Speaker by 38 to 32 votes for Allen, [Whig.]

Balt Board of Trade: elected ofcrs recently at Balt: Pres: John C Brune
V Presidents: Wm McKim, Herman H Perry, Henry Tiffany, Nathan Rogers
Treas: E B Dallam; Sec: G U Porter
Directors:

T C Jenkins	W G Harrison	B C Buck
W P Lemmon	W R Travers	Henry S Garrett
Jos C Wilson	A Schumacher	T W Levering
P H Sullivan	Alex'r Rieman	G B Hoffman
Jas George	D S Wilson	J J Abrahams
Enoch Pratt	Josiah Lee	Hugh Jenkins
Danl Warfield	Thos Wilson	E S Courtney
G W Lurman	Wm Bose	G K Walter

Mrd: on Oct 11, by Rev Mr De Necker, Mr Chas P Woods, of Berryville, Va, to Miss Mary Anne Dillon, of Wash.

Rev Edw J Helme, formerly of this town, died suddenly yesterday, just as he was entering a pew at Trinity Church, without a struggle. His death was caused by an affection of the heart to which he has been subject. He was 26 years of age, & had for the last year been pastor of a Baptist Church at Concord, N H, & had only been in town a few days, on a short visit to his father's family. –Newport [R I] News of Monday.

Md Agricultural Fair: from the Balt American of Oct 11. 2nd Annual Cattle Show & Agricultural & Horticultural Exhibition commenced yesterday, in *Carroll's Woods*, near the western suburbs of Balt City. Pres Taylor will visit the Fair again today.
Cmte to receive & attend the Pres:

Dr J O Wharton, of Wash Co	Ramsay McHenry, of Harford
J H Bradley, of D C	Rev Mr McIntyre, of Cecil
Gen B C Howard, of Balt Co	Hon J A Pearce, of Kent
Dr S P Smith, of Alleghany	E Paca, of Queen Ann's
Capt Edw Schley, of Fred'k	J Pearson, of Caroline
A B Davis, of Montg	Gen T Tilghman, of Talbot
Augustus Shriver, of Carroll	R T Goldsborough, of Dorchester
C W Hanson, of Howard District	J Glenn, of Balt
Col W W W Bowie, of PG	Dr Wm Williams, of Somerset
Gen J G Chapman, of Chas	J S Purnell, of Worcester
Hon Richd Thomas, of St Mary's	N B Worthington, of Anne Arundel

The Phil papers give the following list of the killed & wounded during the riot of Tue night.
Killed: Chas Himmelwright, white, shot through the head, & John Griffith, a colored man.
Wounded: Mrs Smith, residing in 6th st, above South, shot through the head.
Chas Westerhood, residing at 13th & Race sts: thigh fractured by a ball.
Jeremiah McShane, shot in the temple: not expected to live. [Oct 13th newspaper: Jeremiah McShane died on Wed of a wound in the head. He had been in this country but a short time, & had made arrangements to return to Ireland.]
Wm Coleman: shot in the thigh & leg.
Geo Williams: shot in the breast.
Edw Matthews: shot in the breast & ribs: mortally wounded.
Augustus Green: shot in the hand & leg.
John Hall: wounded in the neck & arm.
R Rundal, colored: wounded in the last riot this morning.
Chas Anderson, colored: shot in the thigh & arm in the last conflict.

Boston papers. Wreck of the barque **St John**: Mr J B Munroe, alien com'r, returned to Cohasset to identify the bodies washed ashore. Mr Elliot, the British consul, reports the following as the names of those saved:

Austin Kearn	Michl Fitzpatrick	Honora Cullen
Catharine Flanagan	Michl Gibbons	Honora Burke
Betsey Higgins	Barbara Kenely	& 11 of the crew
Mary Kane	Michl Redding	

The Mail publishes the following list of the bodies which have been identified among those who have washed ashore, & also a few who were on board who have not yet been recovered.

Identified:

Mary Freeman	Sally Swaney	Bridget Burke
Mary Joice & child	Peggy Fahey	John Doland & wife
Martha Fahey	Mary Freeman	____ Lahiff-female
John Dolan & wife	Catharine Fitzpatrick	Child unknown

Peggy Miller & her sister's child
Patrick Swaney & 11 children, also his servant girl

Lost, but bodies not recovered:

Mrs Brook	Mgt Kanan	Mary Curtani
Mary Flanagan	Bridget Quinen	Bridget Kane
Ann Flanagan	Eliza Brien	Catharine Swaney
Mgt Flanagan	Catharine Henif	Mary Freeman
Mary Ann Slatery	Mary Henif	Bridget Cornelia
Bridget Slatery	Peggy Mullen	& 3 children

The Traveller says: the names of the passengers in the cabin were three Misses Flanagan, two Misses Slatterly, Bridget Quinn, & Eliza O'Brien, with several children. They were all lost. The Flanagans were the nieces of the owner of the vessel. Among the last are Bridget Kennelly & 3 children, wife of Patrick Kennelly of this city; Honora Donnelly, aged 16, who has a sister in Lynn; Honora, Mary, & Mgt Mulkennan, children of Mrs Mulkennan of 4th st, South Boston; one woman with 11 children, who has a husband in Massachusetts; Honora & Thos Lahey; 2 sisters of Mrs McDermott, of Springfield. The **St John** arrived at this port on May 1st last, from Galway, with 98 passengers. The capt stated that there were 120 souls on board. Three of the passengers said that on Sat, after they had made Providence light, the capt mustered his passengers on deck & joyfully assured them that the last night of their confinement on board had arrived. His passage had been a good one. The passengers decorated the deck & rigging with candles, & dance & song wore away the evening. [See Oct 10th newspaper.]

For rent: large 3 story brick house, with all necessary out-houses, on Pa ave, adjoining the Six Bldgs. With or without furniture. Inquire of Mrs H Worthington, or W W Davis, on the premises.

A man named Meekes, from Ohio, was lately committed to our county jail, charge with a robbery at Dorsey's Hotel, on 7th st. He is also charged with a similar robbery at McGrann's Hotel.

SAT OCT 13, 1849
Died: on Oct 12, after a lingering illness, Mrs Eliz Barry, a native of Areglan, County Cork, Ire, aged 82 years. Her funeral is tomorrow, at 2 o'clock, from her late residence on 3rd st, between E & G sts.

Died: on Oct 12, after a long & painful illness, Mrs Mary D Ferris, wife of Henry C Ferris, in her 37th year. Her funeral is today, at 11 o'clock, from her late residence, H st, between 12th & 13th sts.

Tornado swept over the upper part of Cape May Co, N J, on Thu last. A new house belonging to Willis Godfrey was blown down. Mrs Godfrey & 2 children were in the house, & escaped with slight injuries. The new house nearby belonging to Jones Carson, was entirely demolished. Mrs Carson & her sister were in it at the time. Mrs Carson was found dead some 40 yards from the house; her sister was terribly mutilated, & but slight hopes of her recovery. Another house, occupied by the widow of Danl Young, her daughter, & 3 others, was also blown down, all had slight injuries.

For rent: new brick house on 9th st, between I & N Y ave. Inquire of John Hood, next door to the premises, or to S P Franklin.

Subscriber's house on G st, between 2nd & 3rd sts, was broken open on Oct 11, & some money was stolen. Persons with notes on the Putnam Co Bank, Farmers' Mills, N Y, passed to them will leave word with Thos C Donn, Justice of the Peace. –Jos Herrity

MON OCT 15, 1849
Appointments by the Pres:
Wm M Brown, of Tenn, to be U S Marshal for the Middle District of Tenn, vice Jesse B Clements, removed.
C P Bertrand, of Ark, to be Receiver of Public Moneys at Little Rock, Ark, vice Cyrus W Wilson, deceased.
John Ford, to be Assist Treasurer at St Louis, vice L A le Beaume, resigned.

Hurricane swept over a part of Worcester Co, Md, on Sat. The Snow Hill Shield says: Messrs John H Allen & John S Jones, of *Sandy Hill*, had their granaries blown over into the creek, where both will prove a total loss. Jos Cherrix, in charge of the same, is missing. The dwlg on one of the farms of Geo Bishop, near *Sandy Hill*, was greatly damaged by a large tree blown against it, knocking the chimney down. The barn on the farm occupied by Thos Reed, near *Sandy Hill*, was destroyed. Also a kitchen at *Sandy Hill*, occupied by the servants of Mrs Catharine Selby, was blown down. On the farm of Mrs Jones, near *Girdletree Hill*, the house & bldgs were blown over.

The barque **C Devens**, Capt Bailey, arrived at Savannah on Mon last from Newport, R I, with 4 companies of the 3rd Regt of U S Artl, embracing a total of 192 men. Ofcrs attached to it: Brevet Lt Col E J Steptoe,-commanding
Brevet Maj Geo H Thomas; Lt Geo T Andrews; Lt Geo Patten, A C S
Lt C C Churchill; Lt W A Winder; Lt J W Patton

The following list of the passengers & crew, saved & lost, of the ill-fated barque **St John**, is furnished by Mr J B Munroe, of Boston, alien com'r.
Cabin Passengers lost: Mary Flanagan, Nancy Hannagan, & Mgt Hannagan, of Killinara, county of Clare; Bridget Quinn & Eliza O'Brien, of Inistivan, Clare. Steerage passengers lost: Ann Slatterly, Bridget Slatterly, Hugh Maddison, Mgt Keenan, of Inistivan; Bridget Connelly & 3 children, Patrick Sweney & wife & 9 children, of Kunnamara, county of Galway; Peter Greally & Jas Greally, of

Claronbridge, county of Galway; Patrick Corman, Miles Sweeney, Thos Burke-mother saved-Eliza Burke, Patrick Bruke, Misses McDermott-sisters-Mary Joyce & child, Catharine Fitzpatrick, Bridget Burke, Bridget Mulligan, Peggy Purky, Martha Purky, all of Galway; Michl Hannegan, Lalinch, county of Clare; Patrick Lahiff, John Lahiff, Thos Riley, Bridget Maddigan, of Kilfanora, county of Clare; Hugh Glynn, of Inistivan, county of Clare; John Belton, Mary Dolan, Thos Fahey, Bridget Fahey, Martha Fahey, Honora Donnelly, Honora Mullen, Catharine Heniff, & __ Heniff-sisters-Mary Cahill, Patrick Noonan, Mary Lanskey, Peggy Mullen, & sister's child, John Butler, county of Galway; Patrick McMahan, Bridget McMahan, Catharine McMahan, Mary Nalon, Mary Frowley, & child, of Kilmaly, county of Clare; John Dolan, Roan, county of Clare; Mary Freeman & child, Mr Eagan, wife & daughter, Martha Sexton, of Innis, county of Clare; Jeremiah Murphy, Jas Moran, Dysant, county of Clare; Jeremiah Murphy, Jas Moran, Dysant, county of Clare; Mgt Keenan, Miss Brooks, of Inistivan; Danl Byrnes, Mich Griffin, Catharine Burns, Peggy Mallon, Ellen Hassett, of Anch, county of Clare; Patrick McGrath, Jas McGrath, Winny Calvin, Mary Calvin, Mgt Kane, Mary McNamara, of Kilmally; Honora Lahiff or Rohan, John Lahiff or Rohan: Mary Curtin, Honora Mulkenan, Mary Mulkenan, Mgt Mulkenan, of county of Clare.
Crew lost: Antonio McDonough, Wm Angers, Wm Thompson, Edw Kennelly, Michl Conners, & 2 apprentice boys.
Passengers saved:
Austin Kean, 20
Catharine Flanigan, 20
Betsey Higgins, 21
Mary Kane, 21
Michl Fitzpatrick, 26
Michl Gibbon, 26
Barbara Kennelly, 20
Mary Slatterly, 20
Michl Redding, 24
Honora Counlin, 28-lost 3 children-sick at Lothrop's, Cohasset
Mary or Honora Burke, 27-lost 3 children-sick also.
Ofcrs & crew saved: Capt Oliver
Henry Cummeford, 1st Mate
Sailors
Henry O'Brien
Thos Walker
Michl Kennelly
Jas Flaherty
Wm Larkin
Andrew Forrest
Isaac Cummerford

Mrd: on Oct 11, by Rev Mr Hodges, Franklin L Buckingham to Miss Leona Adams, both of Wash City.

Mrd: on Oct 11, by Rev Wm Matthews, Geo Bartle to Miranda Ellis, daughter of Mr John Ellis, all of Wash City.

Mrd: on Oct 8, in Balt, by Rev Mr Clarke, Wm H Sloan, of Wash, to Miss Lucy O'Reilly, of Balt City.

Died; on Oct 14, Miss Mary Ann, only daughter of John Allen, of Wash City. After a long & painful illness, death came to her relief. Her funeral is this afternoon at half past 3 o'clock, from the residence of her brother.

Household & kitchen furniture at auction on Oct 17, at the late residence of Cornelius Cox, deceased, on I, between 9th & 10th sts. –Green & Tastet, aucts

Orphans Court of Wash Co, D C. Letters of administration on personal estate of Cornelius Cox, late of said county, deceased. –Caroline Cox, admx

Orphans Court of Wash Co, D C. Letters testamentary on personal estate of Moriah Byrne, late of Wash Co, deceased. –Jas F Haliday, C Buckingham, excs

TUE OCT 16, 1849
Annual meeting of the Md State Agricultural Society, held at Balt, last Fri, the following gentlemen were elected ofcrs for the ensuing year:
Pres: Chas B Calvert, PG Co
Vice Presidents:
John Glenn, Balt City
H G S Key, St Mary's Co
J G Chapman, Chas Co
Horac Capron, PG Co
Geo Weems, Calvert
J H Somerville, Anne Arundel
Alex Norris, Howard Dist
A Bowie Davis, Montg
David W Naill, Fred'k
Wm Dodge, Wash
Dr Saml P Smith, Alleghany
Geo Patterson, Carroll
Cor Sec: Geo W Dobbin, Balt
Rec Sec: Saml Sands, Balt
Curators:
W W W Bowie, of PG
J Carroll Walsh, of Harford
Jas G Cox, of Balt City

Wilson M Carey, Balt
Chas Carroll, Harford
Rev Jas McIntyre, Cecil
G S Holiday, Kent
Jas T Earle, Queen Anne
Col N Goldsborough, Talbot
T P Stewart, Caroline
Dr Jos E Muse, Dorchester
Wm H Jones, Somerset
John U Dennis, Worcester
G S Stevenson, D C

Treas: Jas McNeil, jr, Balt

Chas R Howard, of Balt Co
Martin Goldsborough, of Talbot
N B Worthington, of Anne Arundel

Election of the School Trustees & Police Magistrates, last night, Wash:
School Trustees:
Jas F Haliday
R Farnham
John D Barclay
V Harbaugh
T Donoho
Police Magistrates:
S Drury
John D Clark
S Grubb
J L Smith

P Bacon
J B Ellis
J M Roberts
Jas Adams
J E Morgan

T Donoho
B K Morsell
T C Donn
W Thompson

S Byington
P M Pearson

J W Beck
Jas Crandell
G McNeir

Mrd: on Oct 14, by Rev V Palen, Mr Chas C Edelin to Miss Mary Louisa Acton, both of Wash.

Mrd: on Oct 14, in Trinity Church, by Rev C M Butler, Mr Whitman C Bestor to Miss Selina Baldwin, both of Wash City.

Mrd: on Oct 11, in Wash City, by Rev Mr Samson, Mr Marion Fenwick to Miss Lavinia Killmon, both of Wash City.

Died: on Oct 14, at the residence of his mother, Mrs Julia Dement, in PG Co, Md, Geo Edw Dement, in his 21st year. His funeral is today at 12 o'clock.

Died: on Oct 3, at Parkersburg, Va, Mrs Virginia Harriet Murdoch, consort of John R Murdoch, & daughter of Jas H Neal, in her 39th year.

Died: on Sep 18, at his residence, *Willow Brook*, PG Co, Md, Thos Duckett, aged 43 years. He was exemplary in the discharge of the various relations & duties of life. He was an affectionate husband, fond parent, & kind master. He left 4 young children, who can never know the devoted affection of a parent to whom they could fly in the hour of danger & distress.

WED OCT 17, 1849
Convention for the formation of a Constitution for the State of Calif assembled in the Court House in Monterey on Sep 1, pursuant to the proclamation of Gen Riley. Nearly all the Delegates were present, & all the districts represented. The following is a list of the Delegates:
Puebla de San Jose: Kimball H Dimmick, Jos Aram, Jacob D Hoppe, Don Antonio M Pico, Elan Brown.
Monterey: H Wagar Halleck, Thos O Larkin, Lewis S Dent, Pacificus Ord, Chas T Botts.
San Francisco: Myron Norton, Edw Gilbert, Jos Hobson, Wm M Steuart, Wm M Gwin.
Sacramento: John H Suter, Jacob Snider, L W Hastings, J H Shannon.
Sonoma: Lyman W Boggs, Don Guadeloupe Vallejo, Robt Semple, Joel P Walker.
San Luis Obispo: Don A J Carruvius, Henry Tift.
Santa Barbara: Don Pablo Noriago
Ciudad de los Angelos: Don Manuel Domingas, A J Carrera, Abel Stearns, Dr Foster.
San Diego: Henry Hill, Miguel de Pedrorena.

Emancipation: Maj Wood, late of Darien, Ga, at his death, freed all his slaves, 150 in number, & left $5,000 to pay for their expenses to Liberia.

Yesterday, while Mrs Edw Coleman, of Harrison Co, was passing along Maine st in her carriage, a cart ran so close that the wheels of the 2 came in contact. This alarmed Mrs Coleman very much, & she sprang out of her carriage, on the side-walk in front of Mr Frazer's jewelry store. She called to her brother, who was in the carriage, fell & expired. She has been in delicate health for some time, supposed to be disease of the heart. –Lexington Adv

Noble Act: Mr Mortimer Barnes recently saved the life of the 18 year old daughter of Mr Geo Miller, when flames enveloped the wooden bldg, that she, her father, & her mother, were in. –Oswego Adv Extra

Died: on Oct 9, near the Cross Roads, Montg Co, Md, Mary Eliz Wilson, in her 21st year, daughter of Wm Wilson.

Wm Henry Bennett, son of Wm A Bennett, of Lynchburg, Va, left his father's shop on Sep 28, & has not been heard of since. No cause can be assigned for this painful circumstance. He is 19 years old, a tailor by trade. This announcement is to procure some information which may possibly relieve the family of their painful distress. -Virginian

Valuable property at auction: Oct 18: two 3 story brick houses, one on I st, the other on 24th st. –Jos Boulanger, G, near 17th st. -E C & G F Dyer, aucts

In Chancery: Mary King et al vs Chas King's heirs et al. The trustee in this cause has reported the following sales of Chas King's property, viz: dwlg house of said Chas King on 1st st, in Gtwn, with the ground attached, to Sarah King, for $605: part of lot 72, in old Gtwn, on Cherry alley, to Saml Cropley, for $1,225; 2 parts of lot 62, in old Gtwn, on Jefferson st, to Peter Von Essen, for $400. Court orders that the sales be ratified. –John A Smith

THU OCT 18, 1849

The Salem Register announced the death, on Oct 10, at Haverhill, Mass, of the Hon Leonard White, aged 82 years. He was the classmate & friend of John Quincy Adams, & before going to college, were fellow-students with Rev Mr Shaw, of Haverhill. They were of the class of 1787 at Hharvard.

New Post ofcs: established, discontinued, & changed the site & name of the following ofcs, during the week ending Oct 13, 1849:

Office	County, State	New Appointment:
Nottla	Cherokee, N C	A D Kilpatrick
Apple Grove	Morgan, Ala	Thos Ryan
Blue Spring	Morgan, Ala	S M J Benson
Brush Creek	Perry, Ala	Saml Becke
Jackson Camp	Tallapoosa, Ala	Geo Y Jarvis
Up Peach Tree	Wilcox, Ala	Jos J Mathews
Cypress	Bosier P, La	W Laskin
Milford	E Bat Rouge P, La	W L Burnett
Saline	Bienville P, La	Jas R Head
Cato Springs	Rankin, Miss	J A Nash
Battlefield	Lauderdale, Miss	Jas M Trussell
Calhoun	Lafayette, Ark	Robt G Harper
Clinton	De Witt, Texas	R H Chisolm
Hopewell's	Upshur, Texas	Jas W Jackson
Ten Mile Point	Prairie, Ark	Wm Deadman
Lost Creek	Breathitt, Ky	Jos E Haddix
Daysville	Todd, Ky	Geo H Day
Little Chute	Brown, Wis	M P Caulfield
Waterford	Racine, Wis	Saml C Russ
Clay	Wash, Iowa	Albert Allen

Copper Creek	Jackson, Iowa	Nathan Hixon
McGary's	Hancock, Ill	Geo Beals
Worton Hghts	Kent, Md	Wm Vannort
Falsington	Buck's, Pa	Jas Thompson
Oxford Valley	Buck's, Pa	John G Spencer
Collamer	Chester, Pa	Thos Baker
Genesee Ford	Potter, Pa	Isaac S Annis
Cole's Mills	Dela, Ohio	Hugh Cole
Unison	Dela, Ohio	Jas R Youell

Names & sites changed:
Moss Side, Alleghany, Pa, name & site changed to Coal Valley, & Orville A Lee appointed p m.
Kersville, Cumberland, Pa, name & site changed to Plainfield, & Thos Greason appointed p m.
Strode, Culpeper, Va, name changed to Farley, & Robt Wellford appointed p m.
Oak Hill, Overton, Tenn, name & site changed to Netherland, & Richd Potete appointed p m.

Missionaries for India: the ship **Arab** will sail from Boston on Thu next for Calcutta, having among her passengers the following Missionaries of the Baptist Board: Rev H M Campbell & wife, & Rev H E Knapp & wife, for Arracan; Miss H Eliz T Wright, Mrs Mary Prayton [wife of Rev D L Prayton, of Merqui] & daughter, & 2 young men, Karens, for Maulmain.

Wash Corp: 1-Ptn from J T Walker & others, for certain alterations in the license laws: referred to the Cmte on Police. 2-Act for the relief of John E Neale: referred to the Cmte of Claims. 3-Ptn of J H Woodward, praying remission of a fine: referred to the Cmte of Claims. 4-Bills referred to the Cme of Claims-relief of: Edw Hammersly; Thos Lewis; John H Mullen; Basil Simms; & Lawrence Callan. Also, act for refunding Jas C Cruser the amount of a fine. 5-Bills referred to the Cmte on Improvements: relief of Chas Stewart; of Walter Linkins; & of Thompson Nailor. Also, ptn from John Sched. 6-Ptn of John C Wade, praying remission of a fine: referred to the Cmte of Claims. 7-Ptn of Saml Grubb, in relation to a fine imposed on Robt Earle: referred to the Cmte of Claims.

In Chancery: Circuit Court of Wash Co, D C. Oct Term, 1849. John Thompson Mason, vs John A Wharton, Eliz his wife, & others, heirs at law of John Thompson Mason, deceased, & the excs of John Mason, deceased. John Marbury, the trustee, reports he has sold all that part of lot 80, in the orginal plan of Gtwn, to Alex'r Ray, for $2,600, & the purchaser has complied with the terms of sale. –John A Smith, clerk

Died: on Oct 17, after a short illness, Mr John Henry, in his 43rd year, a native of Germany, but for the last 18 years a resident of this place. His funeral is this evening, at 3 o'clock, from his late residence on G st, between 26th & 27th sts.

Died: on Oct 17, Jas O'Niel, for many years doorkeeper at the Pres' House, & late a messenger in the Post Ofc Dept. His funeral will take place this morning at 10 o'clock from the Infirmary, near the City Hall.

FRI OCT 19, 1849
Appointment by the Pres: Saml Frost, to be Appraiser of Merchandise for the Port of N Y, vice Geo W Pomroy, removed.

Robinson, who swindled several postmasters by representing himself as the nephew of Maj Hobbie, & was at last detected by the Evansville postmaster, has been convicted & sentenced to the Indiana penitentiary for 2 years.

Capt Forbes, of Boston, has been voted a silver medal by the members of Lloyd's for his gallant conduct in saving passengers from the wreck of the vessel **Chas Bartlett**.

Miss Ellen Jones' School for young Ladies will be re-opened on Oct 1, at the corner of H & 21st sts.

For rent: brick house on the corner of G & 6th sts, opposite the Episcopal Church [Mr Hodge's.] Inquire at the 3rd house next to the Baptist Church, on Va ave.

From Europe: News has been received from Sir John Franklin's exploring expedition, which is said to be surrounded by ice in Prince Regent's Inlet.

Report that Comorn has surrendered, & that the Hungarian Gen Gorgey has been shot by Count Zucika, whose brother was shot by order of Gorgey.

Mrd: on Oct 17, by Rev Elisha Ballantine, Thos J Johnston, of Miss, to Isabella, daughter of the late David Walker, of Wash City.

Mrd: on Oct 18, by Rev Jas Donelan, Jos P Mitchell to Mgt Ann Martin, all of Wash City.

Mrd: on Oct 18, by RevC M Butler, Mr John R Hendley, of Wash City, to Miss Mary Catherine Evans, of Alexandria.

Mrd: on Oct 17, at the Episcopal Church, Oak Grove, Va, by Rev Mr McGuire, Maj S L Lewis, of Wash, to Miss K E Bowcock, of Westmoreland Co, Va.

Mrd: on Oct 16, in Gtwn, D C, by Rev L F Morgan, Mr B Rush Dallam, of Harford Co, Md, to Miss Jane J Hepburn, of the former place.

SAT OCT 20, 1849
Household & kitchen furniture at auction on Oct 22, at the residence of Mr Henning, on North Capitol st, opposite the residence of Hon Judge Cranch.
-Green & Tastet, aucts

Military Posts of the 8th Dept:
Fort Polk: Co K, 4th Artl, Capt F E Hunt, commanding. Brasos Santiago.
Fort Brown: Cos E, H, & K, 1st Infty, [headquarters,] Brevet Lt Col T Morris, commanding. Brownville.
Ringgold Barracks: Co B, 4th Artl, & Co C, 1st Infty, Brevet Maj J H Lamotte, commanding. Brownville
Laredo: Cos G & I, 1st Infty, Lt E L Viele, commanding. Brownville.
Eagle Pass: Cos A, B, & F, 1st Infty, Brevet Maj Scott, commanding. Lavaca & San Antonio
Leona: Co C, 2nd Dragoons, Co F, 8th Infty, Brevet Lt Col Hardee, commanding. Lavaca & San Antonio.
Rio Seco: Co G, 2nd Dragoons, Co G, 8th Infty, Brevet Maj Longstreet, commanding. Lavaca & San Antonio.
San Antonio: Cos A & B, 8th Infty, [headquarters,] Maj Morrison, commanding. Lavaca & San Antonio
Fredericksburg: Co B, 2nd Dragoons, & Co K, 8th Infty, Lt Col Fauntleroy, 2nd Dragoons, commanding. Lavaca & New Braunfels.
Austin: Headquarters 2nd Dragoons, Col & Brevet Brig Gen Harney, commanding. Galveston.
Hamilton Creek: Co A, 2nd Dragoons, & Co C, 8th Infty, Capt A F Lee, 8th Infty, commanding. Galveston & Austin.
Leon River, near junction of Corquell creek, [new post to be established]-Cos D & I, 8th Infty, Brevet Lt Col Montgomery, commanding. Galveston & Austin.
Fort Graham: Co I, 2nd Dragoons, Co H, 8th Infty, Brevet Lt Col Montgomery, commanding. Galveston & AustinWest Fork of Trinity: Co F, 2nd Dragoons, & Co F, 8th Infty, Brevet Maj Arnold, commanding. Galveston & Austin.

Mrd: on Oct 18, by Rev S Pyne, D D, Robt Tansill, of the U S Marine Corps, to Anna Lucinda Bender, daughter of Maj Bender.

Mrd: on Oct 16, in St Mary's Church, by Rev Mathias Alig, Mr Philip Ennis to Mrs Catharine Rice, both of Wash City.

Died: on Oct 18, Jabez H, son of Wallace & Mary J Kirkwood, aged 6 years. His funeral is from the residence of his father, in PG Co, Md, on Oct 20, at 10 o'clock.

Wanted: a competent married man to take charge of the Farm of John F Clark.
—Green & Tastet, aucts

Situation wanted: a practical Florist & Vegetable Gardener, who thoroughly understands the business, wishes immediate employment. Apply to Henry Douglas, Florist & Seedsman, corner of 15th & G sts.

For sale: 2 story brick house on K st, I for sale. Three frame bldgs on Mass ave, for sale. Inquire of Mr J T Walker.

For rent: 2 rooms over the store of Simms & Sons, entrance from the avenue. Inquire of Simms & Sons.

Millinery: Mrs E Collison, 7th st, above H st. [Ad]

MON OCT 22, 1849
Wash Corp: every person who shall apply for a tavern or ordinary license shall produce to the mayor a certificate, signed by the Com'r, & 6 respectable freeholders of the ward in which such person resides; also 6 respectable freeholders residing in the neighborhood of the premises for which application for a license is made.
Applicants:
1st Ward: A Favier, square 119, on 19th st:
2nd Ward
E D & H A Willard, square 225, Pa ave
Michl R Coombs, square 349, Pa ave & 10th st
Conrad Finkman, square 292, Pa ave
Andrew Hancock, square 292, Pa ave
Jas Maher, square 256, E st north
Abraham Butler, square 254, F st north
Jas Shackleford, square 225, Pa ave
John Thomas, square 322, Pa ave
Henry Walker & John Rowlett, square 225, Pa ave
H Ridgway, square 226, Pa ave
3rd Ward:
Presley W Dorsey, square 428, 7th & I sts
M Talty, square 431, 7th st, west
John Foy, square 378, D st
M Talty, square 432, 7th st
Thos Baker, square 432, 8th & D sts
H Cook, square 407, D & 8th sts
J R Hendley, square 432, 7th & E sts
J H Eberbach, square 407, E & 8th sts
Wm G Howison, square 407, 8th & D sts
Geo Stutz, square 408, 9th st
C Klomann, square 431, 7th st
F Stutz, square 408, 9th st
4th Ward:
D H Branch & Co, Res 10, Pa ave
Jas Fitzgerald, Res 10, Pa ave
B O Sheckell, square 461, 7th st
John Williams, square 461, Pa ave & 6th st
Geo Tophan, Res 10, Pa ave
W W Campbell, square B, Pa ave
Wm Benter, square 491, Pa ave
P H King, square __, Res 10, Pa ave
John West, square 461, 7th st
C W Blackwell, square 491, Pa ave & 6th st
John H Clarvoe, square 461, 7th st
T P & M Brown, square 460, Pa ave
Ellen Sweeting, square 490, C st

5th Ward:
John Reiley, square Res 12, P ave
Jas Ragan, square 575, Pa ave
John Donovan, square Res, Pa ave
B Shad, B st
Patrick McGarvey, Pa ave
John Donovan, pa ave
Geo & Jno Dawson, square 688, A st
Jas Casparis, square 688, A st
6th Ward:
Notley L Adams, square 907, L st
John A Golden, square 928, 8th st
John Howard, square 355, 11th & G sts
Job Corson, square 355, Water & 11th sts
Peter Jones, 356 Water st

Freeholders: Ward/Neighborhood:

Jacob Acker	A F Kimmell	T P Brown
Nicholas Acker	J P Pepper	Geo Wilner
Wm J Wheatly	Jas Kelcher	C H Munck
J B Gardner	Franck Taylor	T Gunton
Jno C Fitzpatrick	And Small	Wm H Harrover
N C Towle	John M Farrar	Jos Harbaugh
Jos F Brown	Z D Gilman	Raphael Jones
Robt Brown	T P Brown	H Thorn
Jas Rhodes	John W Maury	Michl Talty
D E Kealey	P W Browning	F Mattingley
Jas Kealey	Jas Fitzgerald	Geo Handley
Michl Crane	Ch Lee Jones	Wm T Steiger
Matthew Trimble	Edw Simms	John F Boone
Jacob Smull	Wm H Upperman	Ebenezer Rodbird
Henry Hoffman	J M Johnson	W H Harrover
Jos Peck	Bonevender Shad	J D Hendley
A Coyle	Michl McDermott	J R Hendley
Levi Pumphrey	Michl McCarty	Thos Parker
Thos H Havenner	Thos Young	P Thyson
Jos H Bradley	Wm H Upperman	Wash Adams
W A Bradley	Wm Jackson	Jas H Shreeve
W Lenox	Thos Pursell	B F Morsell
Wm Greason	Marshall Brown	Jas P Phillips
Jas Fitzgerald	Horatio S Fitch	D S Waters
John Kelly	S Hyatt	C Buckingham
Jas McGraw	W B Kibby	Robt S Patterson
Michl McDermott	B F Middleton	Geo S Gideon
F Y Naylor	B L Jackson	S P Franklin
John T Killmon	F Cudlip	J C McGuire
Jas Dixon	Edw Simms	Jas K Plant
John N Coyle	J P Pepper	J R Queen
Richd Wallach	M Delany	J L Marceron

F S Walsh	Jas H Causten	Jas McColgan
T P Tench	Saml Stott	Christian Eckloff
R M Comly	Geo Krafft	Louis Lepreux
Thos Bayne	Thos Smith	Jno France
Jas Mitchell	Saml Redfern	C Uttermohle
J W Martin	A Hoover	J Aigler
Rich Wimsatt	F Schneider	Wm Morrow
L Thomas	S N Owen	John Brown
B W Riley	Geo Lamb	Nathl Plant
Geo Mattingly	S W Handy	Joel Downer
K H Lambell	Thos Miller	Augus Lepreux
Geo Hercus	Jas McCleary	Louis Lepreux
Wm Cooper	F Burch	Joel Downer
Henry Weeden	Thos Miller	Abraham Butler
Jas Maher	S P Franklin	B Willet
A J Joyce	E Lindsley	McClintock Young
Wm Fischer	Vincent Massi	E Simms
Saml Butt	Lewis H Schneider	Jas Larned
Edwin Green	Michal Sardo	Michl Nourse
Wm Mc L Cripps	Geo A W Randall	B W Reed
David Munroe	Michal Sardo	Allison Nailor

On Sun, a wherry containing Mr J Byrden & 2 young ladies who had acted as bridesmaids, [the parties having only been married that morning,] was proceeding up the river towards Putney, T Laidlaw, brother of the bride, having the management of the boat. Midway between Battersea & Wansworth, it came across the mooring chain of a barge which was at anchor. The women, in alarm, rose from their seats, & instantly the boat overturned, & the whole party was immersed in water. Unfortunately, the bride & Mary Ashdown, a bridesmaid, were drowned.
–Quebec Gaz, Oct 3

Mrd: on Thu last, at St Patrick's Church, by the Very Rev Wm Matthews, Arthur Hood, of Ga, to Miss Sarah C Roche, of Wash City.

Died: yesterday, Josiah Sprigg Chew, in his 25th year. His funeral is today at 3 o'clock, from his mother's residence on 8th st, between L & M sts.

Died: on Oct 4, Wm Sawkins, jr, in his 46th year, a native of England, & for many years a citizen of Balt.
+
Died: on Oct 9, at Cambridge, Ia, Judge John Test, for many years a Rep in Congress from that State. The former the eldest son, the latter a son-in-law of Wm Sawkins, of Wash City.

Warfield Academy, Howard District, Anne Arundel Co, Md. Rev R J Shepherd, A M, Mr Wm T Crapster: Assoc Principals. Winter session commences on the first Wed of Nov. Circulars may be obtained by addressing the Principals, Mathew's Store, Howard District, Md.

TUE OCT 23, 1849
Appointment by the Pres: John S Gallagher to be Third Auditor of the Treasury, vice Peter Hagner. [Oct 26th newspaper: Peter Hagner has been 56 years in public service- appointed when that ofc was created in 1817.]

Maj Thompson S Brown, late Engineer to the Erie Railroad, will soon leave this country for a 5 years' engagement with the Emperor of Russia, from whom he is to receive a salary of $12,000 per annum. He will be employed for the next 2 years in the completion of the great railroad from St Petersburgh to Moscow, a distance of 450 miles. Maj B is to fill the place made vacant by the death of our distinguished countryman, the late Maj Whistler. –Troy Budget

Mr Key, appointed by Govn'r Thomas to determine the point where the line between Pa & Md strikes the Delaware line, was in Elkton last week, & is about proceeding to the work. The Whig says the stone set at the point in question by Mason & Dixon is lost, & owing to the pecularities of the lines, it will be difficult to determine its place.

Mrd: on Oct 9, near Hannibal, Missouri, by Rev Mr Lorentz, Malcolm A Lindsley, formerly of Wash City, to Sophia P, daughter of Rev Wm Porter Cochran.

Died: on Oct 19, Wm Alfred, the 2nd son of Wm & Eliz A Hoover, aged 6 years & 6 months.

Died: Oct 22, Thos, son of Abraham & Eliz Clarke, aged 7 years & 7 months.

WED OCT 24, 1849
Household & kitchen furniture at auction on Oct 25, at the residence of the late R H L Villard, on Bridge st. –Edw S Wright, auct

Colt's Improved Repeating Pistols. Expecting to be absent in Europe for some months, all inquiries in relation to said arms may be addressed to J Knox Walker, Wash, who is empowered as my atty & genr'l agent to contract & receive orders for the delivery of said Pistols. –Saml Colt

A Lot of Ground for sale: bordering on the North Boundary st, but outside the city limits, adjoining the farm of Mr E Gilman: contains about 5½ acres. Apply to Z D & W H Gilman, Druggists.

Wash Corp: 1-Cmte of Claims: asked to be discharged from the further consideration of the ptn of John Bohlayer, jr. 2-Cmte of Claims: bill for the relief of Wm H Fletcher. 3-Cmte of Claims: bill for the relief of Wm Cammack, jr. 4-Ptns from Edw Hogan & John E Neale: severally referred to the Cmte of Claims.

Mrd: on Oct 12, in Wash City, by Rev Smith Pyne, D D, Wm Meade Robinson, of Louisville, Ky, to Miss Ann Mason, daughter of the late Prof Chas Bonnycastle.

Fishery for rent: at Md Point, on the Potomac. Apply to Henry Ferguson, Port Tobacco, Md, or to J B & C Ferguson, Light & Pratt sts, Balt, Md.

Port of Gtwn: Oct 19: arrived schnr **Mary Francis**, Mastin, Alexandria, salt to J A Grimes. Oct 22: arrived schnr **Samuel the First**, Pennington, Alexandria, salt to J A Grimes; schnr **Mobile**, Lewis, Havre de Grace, coal to W H Edes; schnr **Rio Grande**, Oxman, Phil, coal to F & A H dodge; schnr **Crescent**, Clarence, Salem, plaster to F Dodge; schnr **B L F**, Kirkwood, Port Deposite, lumber to J Libbey & M Duffy; packet steamer **Columbia**, Harper, Balt, to E Pickrell, & freight for the District; packet steamer **Washington**, Wood, Balt, to P Berry. –Advocate of yesterday.

The ladies & gentlemen of Wash, Gtwn, & Alexandria, are invited to our sale at the residence of Col Grice, on G st [the house formerly occupied by Hon Cave Johnson,] comprising the richest & best assortment of American cabinet Furniture.
-E C & G F Dyer, aucts

For rent: the house on H st, next west of the one occupied by Mr Campbell, between 17th & 18th sts. Inquire of Richd Smith.

THU OCT 25, 1849
Anniversary celebration at *Salt Lake*: from the Frontier [Iowa] Guardian of Sep 16. Jul 24th being the anniversary of the arrival of Presidents Young & Kimball, with the Pioneers, in the valley, the inhabitants awoke by the firing of cannon & martial music. The Pres of the State, 12, & bands, went to prepare the escort in the following order, at the house of Priest B Young, under the direction of Lorenzo Snow, J M Grant, & R D Richards. Horace S Eldridge, marshal, on horseback, in military uniform. 24 men carried a banner: The Zion of the Lord. 24 young ladies each carried the Bible & Book of Mormons, & a banner: Hail to our Chieftain. Newell K Whitney, Bishop; Thos Bullock, Clerk. John Smith, Patriarch. Brigham Young, Parley P Pratt, Chas C Rich, David Spencer, Willard Snow, Willard Richards, Heber C Kimball, John Taylor, Erastus Snow, D Fulmer, followed by 12 Bishops carrying flags of their wards.

Some months since the barn of Mr Henry Black, jr, of Wold Creek township, was burnt, an act of an incendiary. Another firing of his stacks of grain was discovered, & the guilty person was Mrs Black, his own aunt. She was arrested, & lodged in jail, but has since been bailed by her friends in the sum of $2,500. The causes are: Mr Jos Black, the husband of Mrs Black, died a few years since, & left his property to his nephew, Henry Black, jr, whom he had adopted [not having children of his own] with the agreement that he should support his widow during her lifetime. Mrs Black has felt much dissatisfaction with this arrangement, & has lived elsewhere at different periods, but for some time past has resided in a house on the farm which her nephew erected for her accommodation. She appears to have brooded over the subject.
-Mercer [Pa] Luminary

I have on hand a first-rate lot of Mules, at Smiths & Birch's livery stables, where I will be on the 24th thru the 26th. Persons wishing to purchase will please call & see for themselves. –John W Nichols

Furnished house for rent: containing 10 rooms. Inquire at A Holmead's grocery store, Market Space.

New Post ofcs: established for the week ending Oct 20, 1849:

Ofc	County, State	Postmasters:
N Hyde Park	Lomoille, Vt	Otis Wheeler
West Fitchburg	Worcester, Mass	Leonard C Sanborn
Monterey	Dutchess, N Y	Geo Pink
Smithtown	Suffolk, N Y	Simon B Wheeler
Shamong	Burlington, N Y	Nich S Thompson
Grafensburg	Adams, Pa	David Goodyear
Cross Kill Mill	Berks, Pa	Jacob Newcomb
Kossuh	Clarion, Pa	John Mimm
Zionsville	Lehigh, Pa	Chas W Wieand
Eagle	Warren, Pa	Noah Hand
Jeddo	Jefferson, Ohio	John Cooper
Crossanville	Perry, Ohio	Geo Hays
Gravelly Hill	Bladen, N C	Jas H Meredith
Free Will	Hind, Miss	E Coker
Bigby Ford	Monroe, Miss	Arthur M Mooney
Zavilia	Jasper, Texas	Thos B Huling
Silver Springs	Dallas, Ark	Albert G Phillips

Names Changed: Sedgwick Bay, Hancock Co, Maine, changed to Brooklin. Hankins' Creek, Sullivan Co, N Y, changed to Hawkins. Smithtown, Suffolk Co, N Y, changed to Smithtown Branch.

The remains of the late Gen Worth have been brought from Texas to New Orleans. Those of the late Col Duncan will be forthwith brought from Mobile, when the 2 lamented ofcrs, so often partners in victory, but at last united in death, will be conveyed to their final resting place in N Y, according to resolutions passed at a meeting of the City Council.

FRI OCT 26, 1849
Rumor has it that Walter Forward, of Pa, has been appointed Solicitor of the Treasury in the place of R H Gillet.

Orphans Court of Wash Co, D C. Letters testamentary on the personal estate of Jas Larned, late of said county, deceased. –E R Larned, excx

Boonsboro Odd Fellow: meeting of the Stockholders of the Weverton Mfgr Co, held on Oct 16: the following elected Directors of the Company:
Hon J G Chapman, Port Tobacco, Md [Re-elected Pres.]
Washington Berry, Wash, D C   Geo Jacobs, Waynesboro, Pa
P Frazer Smith, Westchester, Pa   Wm Lougheridge, Weverton, Md
Mason Kindell, Chestnut Hill, Pa
Gen Archibald Henderson, Wash, D C

Burring Machines: patent re-issued dated Jul 31, 1849. –Milton D Whipple, Lowell, Aug 27, 1849.

Death of an eminent composer. Chas E Horn died at Boston, where he has for 2 years been residing. He died on Mon at about aged 62 or 62. Few musical composers of our day will be found to have left a more enduring record than this distinguished artiste. –Evening Express

Mrd: on Oct 23, by Rev Wm H Pitcher, Mr Thos Oliver to Miss Mary J Hodgskin, all of Wash City.

Mrd: on Tue last, by Rev P B O'Flanagan, Mr John M Riley to Miss Jane Eliza Broders, of Gtwn, D C.

Died: on Oct 24, after a short illness, Ambrose White, a native of King Wm Co, Va, in his 74th year. He removed to this city in 1794, at which time he attached himself to the Methodist Episcopal Church, & continued an exemplary member of the same to the day of his death. His funeral is today, at 2 o'clock, from his late residence, on N J ave.

Died: on Oct 16, in Wash City, Mrs Emeline Bydelman, aged 39 years.

A young man, Cornelius Martin, was badly but not fatally stabbed last Tue on Pa ave, in an affray with some negroes, one of whom, Saml Adams, has been arrested & committed for trial by Capt Goddard.

On Wed, John Wade, a laborer, was seriously, but not dangersouly, injured, by the falling of some bricks upon his head while he was standing on the ground in front of the east portico. It was negligence on the part of the bricklayers.

The dwlg of Washington Berry, 2 miles north of the city, was robbed on Wed by burglars, who stole about $700 in money & sundry silver articles.
+
$250 reward: my house was robbed on Oct 24: among the articles stolen was a silver case marked Washington Berry; a silver tumbler marked Anna Maria Berry; one marked Eliza Thomas Berry; one marked Mary Louisa Berry; & one marked Thos Williams Berry. –Washington Berry

$2 reward for return of buffalo Cow, that left my residence on Oct 6.
–Robt R Hozard, 14th st, between B & C sts, near Long Bridge

SAT OCT 27, 1849
Balt Patriot: Gen Tobias E Stansbury died at his residence in Balt Co on Thu, at the advanced age of 93 years. He lived & died in the place where he was born. From the opening events of the Revolutionary war down to within a very recent period, he participated actively in Nat'l & State affairs.

A letter from *Notch House*, White Mountains, states that Mr Fred'k Strickland, son of Thos Strickland, Bart, of England, left the above house on Oct 19 with a party of others, to ascend the mountain. Because of the snow, the others returned, but Strickland pursued his journey. His lifeless body was found upon the mountains on Oct 21. He lost his way & perished.

New Nat'l Clothing Emporium, corner of 6th st & Pa ave. —Wm Marshall

$100 for runaway negro Wm Marshall, about 35 years of age. —John Hamilton, living near Port Tobacco, Chas Co, Md

For rent: house with or without furniture, at the corner of Washington & Dunbarton sts, Gtwn. Apply to T M Cassin, Gtwn.

Household & kitchen furniture at auction on Oct 30, at the residence of Mrs Hellen, on G, between 13th & 14th sts. —Green & Tastet, aucts

Mrd: on Oct 11, at the residence of Hon J R Underwood, Bowling Green, Ky, by Rev A C Dickerson, Watkins Addison, of D C, to Mary Jane, daughter of Col John Cox, of Gtwn, D C.

Died: on Oct 26, Mrs Bridget Ann King, in her 56th year. Her funeral is on Sun, at half past 3 p m, from her son's residence, on Pa ave.

Died: on Sat last, in Phil, Mrs Malvina Allen Campbell, wife of Jas Campbell, of that city, & daughter of the late Jas Wilson, of Alexandria, Va. This announcement will be unexpected to a numerous connexion in Va & D C.

MON OCT 29, 1849
Those who have made the improvements in the Nat'l Hotel, under the supervision of C B Calvert & Mr E D Willard, aided by Mrs Willard.
Messrs Finch & Son, painters
Mr Hayward, painter of signs & door numbers
*Messrs Dufief & Entwisle, carpenters
Mr Thos Lewis, bricklayer
Mr John W Thompson, plumber
Mr John M Porter, plasterer
Mr McKinstry, of the Wash Foundry, caster of the iron columns
Mr A Rutherford, marble-cutter
Mr Dreyer, fresco work
Mr S P Franklin & Mr D Moore, paper-hangers
Mr W H Harrover, tin work & roofing
Mr P Hevener, grate-setter
Mr F Lamb, gilder
Mrs Hutchins & Mrs Higgins, upholsterers
*Most of the alterations & improvements have been made under the immediate direction & suggestions of Messrs Dufief & Entwisle, who contracted for most of the work.

Augusta [Georgia] Chronicle says that Bennet Dozier, an inmate of the hospital in that city, while under delirum tremens, stabbed & killed Thos Hadaway, & severely wounded the keeper of the hospital, Chas T Rich, on Oct 18. Dozier was arrested.

Mrd: on Oct 23, by Rev Mr White, Mr Lemuel L Lusby to Miss Mary Ellen Bright, all of Wash City.

Mr Michl Wise, the Hair-restorer, from Rochingham Co, Va, will be in the vicinity of Wash City on Nov 1, when he will be prepared to administer to persons afflicted with baldness, provided a sufficient number, say 50, can be raised by that time.

Accidents from the N Y papers of Mon. 1-On Sat Andrell Seed, a workman in Grant & Darrick's store, South st, had his right leg broken by falling through a trap door. 2-Patrick Dixon, an emigrant, had his left arm borken by falling into the hold of a vessel. 3-Michl Howe, had his righ arm broken by a fall on the sidwalk in 27th st. 4-Augustus McBarth had his right arm broken by machinery in a saw mill in 5th st. 5-Fred'k Magin had his left hand crushed by a railway car, & his leg much injured.

City Ordinances-Wash: 1-Act for the relief of Thos Lewis: that the fine of $2.50 for an alleged violation in relation to carts, be remitted. 2-Act granting permission to Jeremiah Hepburn to weigh hay in the 5th Ward.

Desirable farm of 100 acres for sale: in Montg Co, Md, on the old road leading to Rockville, & adjoining the property of Mr Wm Hurdleston. Apply to W S Nicholls, Gtwn.

TUE OCT 30, 1849
Valuable farm for sale: I wish to sell my farm upon Jackson's river in Alleghany Co, Va: 2,720 acres: good 2 storied log dwlg & other out-bldgs. My friend, Mr Jas Crosby, residing upon the premises, will show the same. For terms apply to the undersigned, residing at Staunton. –John L Peyton

Maj David B Douglass, Prof of Math & Natural Philosophy at Geneva College, died in that village on Sat last. Obit in the Albany Evening Journal: Immediately after his graduation as Bachelor of Arts at Yale College, in 1813, he applied for the commision of Lt of Engineers, to which he was appointed on the recommendation of Gen Swift. In 1814 he joined the army on the Niagara frontier, under command of Gen Brown, & took part in the gallant action of Lundy's Lane. At the siege of *Fort Erie* he superintended, as Lt of Engineers, the repairs of the works under the very heavy guns of the enemy. On the night of the assault by the British troops he commanded a battery which was assailed by the 103rd British regt, which was most gallantly repulsed after repeated attempts to storm the works. For this exploit he received the brevet of Capt, & the commendation of his cmder, Gen Gaines, although not yet 21 years of age. Subsequently he was appointed to the presidency of Kenyon College, Gambia, Ohio.

Richd S McCulloch, Assayer of the U S Mint in Phil, was unanimously chosen Prof of Natural Philosopy, vice Elias Loomis, resigned, in the College of N J, at Princeton, on Wed.

Mrd: on Oct 25, by Rev Smith Pyne, Wm B B Cross to Anne Eliza, daughter of Thos Ritchie, all of Wash City.

Died: on Oct 24, of consumption, Mrs Minerva Brown, wife of Reuben Brown, aged 29 years, 7 months, & 8 days.

Died: on Oct 28, Mr John Voorhees, of the 6th Auditor's ofc, formerly of Trenton, N J, aged 64 years. His funeral is today at 3 o'clock, from his late residence, on E st.

Farm of 600 acres for sale near Staunton, Augusta Co, Va. The undersigned, wishing to give his undivided attention to the practice of law, offers for sale his farm: bldgs have been put up within the last 2 years. –Wm B Johnson

WED OCT 31, 1849
Geo W Thompson has been nominaed for Congress by the Democracy of the Wheeling District in the place of Alex Newman, deceased. Thos S Haymond is the Whig candidate.

Purser Wilson, of the U S Navy, died at Boston last Sat. He had been ill for some time of a bilious complaint.

Wash Corp: 1-Ptn of John F Callan, asking remission of a fine: referred to the Cmte of Claims. 2-Ptn of J Shedd: cmte discharged. 3-Ptn of Jas Williams, for remission of a fine: referred to the Cmte of Claims.

Circuit Court: summoned to serve as jurors during the present term:

Jas C Maguire	John Agg	John T Linman
F A Donn	Jas Towles	Wm R Riley
A W Miller	R S T Cissill	E F Brown
A Harvey	H C Williams	T C Farquhar
R B Clarke	Timothy Remick	Z W Denham
Robt Barry	B Willet	B S Baile
Wm H Minnix	Jonathan Prout	W Warder
P Simpson	Jonathan Y Young	John Wilson
R S Wharton	R Pettit	Chas K Good
F B Lord	E H Edelin	

$10 reward for return of a Pocket Book containing about $73, which was forcibly taken from his hands on Sat, in the Centre Market, by a white man, who ran off with his booty. –John Hutchison, C st, between 12th & 13th

Died: on Oct 29, at the residence of her mother, Mrs Worthington, after long & severe affliction, Mary Eliz, wife of N A Randall, of Wash City. Her funeral is at 2 o'clock this afternoon.

Died: on Oct 21, in Detroit, Maj Robt Forsyth, Paymaster U S Army, aged 51 years.

Died: on Oct 28, suddenly, of congestive scarlet fever, Howell, son of Wm P & Mary Agnes Williams, in his 3rd year.

THU NOV 1, 1849
Appointments by the Pres:
John C Clark to be Solicitor of the Treasury, vice Gillet, removed.
Thos L Smith to be First Auditor of the Treasury, vice Clark.

Promotions & appointments in the Navy, were made on Tue by the Pres:
Jas M McIntosh, to be a Capt in the Navy, vice Gwinn, deceased.
Wm F Lynch, to be Cmder, vice McIntosh, promoted.
Wm E Boudinot, to be a Lt, vice Lynch, promoted.
Van Rensselaer Morgan, to be a Lt, vice E C Anderson, resigned.
Richd T Allison, of Md, appointed Purser in the Navy, vice Nathl Wilson, deceased.
-Republic

Letters were received from Mr Bodisco, the esteemed Minister of Russia, [now on a visit of leave to his own country] dated at St Petersburg as late as the beginning of Oct, informing them that he would return to the U S early in the spring.

New Post ofcs: established for the week ending Oct 27, 1849:

Ofc	County, State	Postmaster
Tamworth Iron Works	Carroll, N H	Saml Merrill
Scotia	Schenectady, N Y	Geo Conde
Lafayetteville	Dutchess, N Y	Rugus White
Pentaquit	Suffolk, N Y	Seth R Clock
Hubbard's Corners	Madison, N Y	Wm T Manchester
Peytona	Boone, Va	Wm D Pate
Saldick	Preston, Va	E E Alford
Nathansville	Conecuh, Ala	Nicholas S Travis
Old Town	Coffee, Ala	Wm Holly
Trout Creek	St Clair, Ala	Henry W Box
Wellbourn	Coffee, Ala	A L Millican
Tripoli	Pishamingo, Miss	Wm J Nolin
Lapomba	Lafayette, Miss	Jack Stephens
Steen's Creek	Rankin, Miss	Nevil H Smith
Falling Spring	Clarke, Miss	N Gardner
Talasha	Newton, Miss	Wm H Jones
Conoochee	Emanuel, Geo	Benj E Brinson
Oakmulgee	Telfair, Geo	Duncan McRea
Olustee	Coumbia, Fla	Hansford R Alford
Bayou Pierre	Caddo P, La	Hilliard H Fatherrel
Lake Caraway	Carroll P, La	Jesse Kennedy
Beaver Ruin	Union, Ark	L H Driskill
Centre	Cass, Texas	Wm Mosley
Schockey's Prairie	Lamar, Texas	David H Davis
Mount Warren	Weakley, Tenn	Wm Jones
Point Mason	Benton, Tenn	W D Woodson
Beelsburg	Dickson, Tenn	John J Hinton
Bryant's Creek	Monroe, Ia	Chas G Carr
Bridgeton	Parke, Ia	John Briggs, jr

Rock Well	Bond, Ills	Peter Long
Rough & Ready	Hancock, Ills	Jacob S Peebler
Greenvale	Jo Daviess, Ills	Jonathan Jennings
Modrells Point	Cole, Ills	Wm J Kigly
North Fork	Ozark, Mo	Wm G Pumphrey
Summerville	Boone, Mo	David Jacob
Walnut Hill	Buchanan, Mo	R Jessee
Fairfield	Benton, Mo	Thos J Bishop
Fredericksburg	Osage, Mo	Ira E Tatum
Ewington	Clayton, Iowa	Ira E Briggs, jr
Fort Gaines	M T	J H McKinny
Marvin	Chautauque, N Y	Orlando Durkee

Names changed:
Fallsport, Wayne Co, Pa, changed to Hawley.
Maguire, Morgan Co, Ohio, changed to Claytons.
Rock & Cave, Hardin Co, Ill, changed to Cave in Rock.

Barnum's Hotel, St Louis, Oct 30. Two young Frenchmen calling themselves Count Gonzales de Montesquion & Count Raimond de Montesquion, arrived in this city from Chicago, & took apts at the Barnum Hotel. Last night, as Mr Barnum, the nephew of the proprietor, & J J Macomber, the steward of the house, were retiring to their chamber, one of the Frenchmen tapped on the gallery window. Mr Barnum pushed the curtain aside to look outside when the Frenchman fired a gun, a ball from which passed through Mr Barnum, & 2 buckshot lodged in the arm of Mr Macomber. The report of firearms alarmed the lodgers, & Mr Albert Jones, a coachmaker in 3rd st, who roomed adjoining, rushed to the door, where he was shot through the head & fell dead. Mr H M Henderson & Mr W H Hubble were wounded with buckshot. The assassin was pursued to his room & arrested. Both the gentlemen were arrested, & affected to be insane. Mr Barnum is still living, but not expected to recover. The trunks of the assassins were opened & letters found proving them to be Parisians of wealth & family. They both fired fatal shots. The funeral of Mr Albert Jones took place this evening. Oct 31-Barnum is still living. [Nov 21st newspaper: Mr Barnum has instituted as suit to recover the loss of the services & society of his son, he having been a minor at the time of his death. The damages are laid at $3,000, which is about the amount of the property found in the possession of the Montesquions, who have been fully committed to take their trial for murder.]

Died: last evening, after a painful illness of 12 years, Mrs Ariana W, consort of Wm G Deale, in her 54th year. Her funeral is on Fri at 2 o'clock, from the residence of her husband, on G, near 5th st.

Died: on Oct 29, at Albany, Dr Peter Wendell, Chancellor of the Univ of the State of N Y, aged 64 years.

Orphans Court of Wash Co, D C. In the case of Fred'k W Eckloff, adm of Thos H Army, alias Aymor, deceased, the Administrator & Court appoint Nov 20 next for settlement of the estate. –Ed N Roach, Reg/o wills

Circuit Court of Wash Co, D C-in Chancery, Oct Term, 1849. Edmund Hanley's excs, against Susan D Shepherd, widow & admx of Alex'r Shepherd, deceased, & Alex'r R Shepherd, Anna P Shepherd, Mary E Shepherd, Thos M Shepherd, Wm S Shepherd, & Arthur S Shepherd, heirs at law of said Alex'r Shepherd. Wm Redin, trustee in the above cause, reports the sale by him of the real estate of the late Alex'r Shepherd on Aug 6 last, when Columbus Alexander became the purchaser of part of lot 2 in square 286, with improvements thereon, for $810. –John A Smith, clerk

Port of Gtwn: Oct 30: arrived schnr **John Henry**, Hooper, from Salisbury, lumber to Jos Libbey; schnr **Caroline**, Chyandler, from Accomac, oats to J F Essex; schnr **Robert James**, Bell, from Accomac, oats to Waters & Wheatley; schnr **Expedition**, Guy, from Accomac, oats to Waters & Wheatley; schnr **Hornet**, Scott, from Phil, to E Pickrell & Co. Oct 31: brig **Delhi**, Hodgson, to John A Grimes.

FRI NOV 2, 1849
By virtue of 3 writs of fieri facias, at the suits of A Nailor, C Cammack, & Parker & Spalding, vs the goods & chattels of Thos Dumphrey, to me directed, I have seized & levied on one frame house, in square 383, Va ave & 10th st, & will be auctioned on Nov 28, in front of the premises. -O E P Hazard, Constable Wash Co

Wm Kirkparick vs Fred'k Grieb, adm of Henry Grieb-Judgment.
Tici & Hammond vs Fred'k Grieb, adm of Henry Grieb-Judgment.
Nov 6, at my ofc in the City Hall, Wash, I shall state the proportion of assets to which the judgments above named are entitled. The adm & his sureties are requested to attend. –W Redin, auditor

Appointment by the Pres: Amory Holbrook, of Mass, to be U S Atty for the district of Oregon, vice Jos J Coombs, who declines the ofc.

Winter Fashions: Mrs Annie Speir: Show rooms-D st, between 9th & 10th sts.

Mrd: on Oct 16, at Glasgow, Mo, by Rev F A Savage, John M Bronaugh, M D, formerly of Wash City, to Georgiana H, daughter of the late Judge John P Morris, of that town.

Died: on Oct 23, in Springfield, Mass, Hon John Howard, aged 58.

Fatal accident. John King, overseer to Mrs Berry, residing near Addison's Chapel, PG Co, Md, died on Wed last, at Upper Marlboro. On leaving the Agricultural Fair there, on horseback, the animal took fright on turning a corner of the street, when Mr King fell, broke his neck, & died on the spot.

Suitable reward for return of strayed & stolen buffalo Cow. –Ann W Whitwell, 4½ st.

Single & double-barrel guns for sale. Jno W Baden & Bro, Pa av & 6th.

SAT NOV 3, 1849
John McGinniss appointed Chief Clerk of the Treasury Dept, in place of McClintock Young, resigned. Geo Harrington appointed Clerk to the Assist Sec of the Treasury, vice McGinniss appointed Chief Clerk.

Wanted: 6 first-rate workmen on Ladies' fine work, to whom the highest wages & constant employment will be given. –John Mills, 6th st, Nat'l Hotel, Wash, to Ladies & Gentlemen's Fancy Boot & Shoe Maker.

Household & kitchen furniture at auction on Nov 6, at the residence & store of Mrs Stoops, Pa ave, near 18th st. –Green & Tastet, aucts

Philip Petona, a young man, died a few days ago near Easton, Pa, from the effects of a rat bite he received a few weeks ago. He died in great agony.

Mrd: on Thu last, by Rev Jas B Donelan, Mr John T Cochrane to Miss Ellen Manning.

Mrd: on Oct 17, in Lincoln Co, N C, by Rev Robt H Morrison, Peter K Rounsaville, of Lexington, to Miss Martha C Graham, daughter of the late John D Graham.

Mrd: on Oct 30, by Rev Mr Lewin, Dr H H Bean, of Chas Co, Md, to Mary A E, only daughter of Jas Miltimore, of Charlotte Hall, St Mary's Co, Md.

Died: on Oct 31, at the residence of his father, PG Co, Md, after a brief but severe illness, Wm C Brashear, Cmder in the late Navy of Texas, in his 37th year. Capt Brashear was formerly of the U S Navy, from which he resigned, to participate in the more active service of Texas during her struggle for independence. His death has fallen with a heavy blow upon a large circle of relatives & friends, who deeply mourn his loss.

Died: on Nov 2, in Wash City, after a short illness, Robt Jeremiah, 2nd son of Benedict & Martha Milburn, in his 5th year. His funeral is on Nov 4, at 2:30 p m, from the residence of Mr John M Willson, 4½ st, near the U S Arsenal.

Port of Gtwn: 1-Arrived Nov 1: brig **Corlann**, Flowers, Eastport, plaster to G Waters; schnr **Robert James**, Bell, Accomac, oats to Waters & Wheatley; schnr **Albatross**, Pritchett, Balt, tar to J N Fearson; schnr **Eagle**, Wilkins, Alexandria, wheat to C Wilson; schnr **Catherine**, Martha, Dashiel's, Phil, coal to John Dickson.

New Wood & Coal Yard: 14th & C sts. Orders left at J T Radcliff's grocery store, Odd Fellows' Hall, will be attended to. –Chas M Keys & Co

MON NOV 5, 1849
Fatal accident last Thu on the Columbia [Pa] Railroad, when the coupling of part of the train broke. Two men employed by the State, repairing the road near the spot, were struck. Linn was instantly killed, & Patton is not expected to live.

In the town of West Bradford, Pa, there is an old Churchyard in which stand 7 stones, side by side, covering the remains of the Hon Nathl Thurston & his 6 wives. They stand in order as follows:
Mrs Betsey Thurston, died Nov 25, 1790, aged 34.
Mrs Martha Thurston, died May 12, 1799, aged 32.
Mrs Huldah Thurston, died Sep 8, 1801, aged 21.
Mrs Clarissa Thurston, died Nov 14, 1803, aged 36.
Mrs Martha Thurston, died Jul 27, 1804, aged 25.
Mrs Mary Thurston, died Mar 3, 1808, aged 27.
Hon Nathl Thurston, died in Lansingburg, N Y, Oct 21, 1811, aged 56.
This case hardly beats a more modern one we knew of, a little nearer home. The deacon in one of our most prominent churches in this city, & his amiable better-half, form a queer instance in matrimony. The deacon is the 5th husband of the lady, while the lady is the deacon's 4th wife. Beat that, who can. --Connecticut paper.

Lawbreakers arrested in Arkansas: implicated in the recent outrages in the northwestern portion of Ark. Gen Wood called into requisition a considerable military force, & quiet in a great measure is restored. J N Everett, ___ Stathon, Robt Adams, Robt Cowin, Harry Love, Jesse Mooney, & Hanford Tutt were placed in the Marion Co jail to await their trial.

Died: yesterday, in her 65th year, Mrs Eliz Towers, formerly of Alexandria, but for many years past a resident of Wash City. Her funeral is tomorrow at 10 a m, from the residence of her son, on 6th st, between G & H sts.

Died: on Nov 1, at New Haven, Conn, Hon Elizur Goodrich, L L D, in his 89th year. He was one of the very few survivors among the men who figured in public life under the administration of Washington & the elder Adams. Since the death of the late Albert Gallatin, he is believed to have been perhaps the eldest survivor among the members of Congress during that period. He belonged to the Washington school of Federalists, & his removal from the ofc of Collector of Customs at New Haven, immediately on the accasion of Mr Jefferson to the presidency, gave occasion to the famous letter of Pres Jefferson, in which he avowed his principle of removal for political opinions. Mr Goodrich was for some time Prof of Law in Yale College, & for many years the efficient Mayor of New Haven. He has been retired for more than 20 years. He was an occasional visitant in our city, to his daughter, the late Mrs Henry L Ellsworth. He was wounded, & scarcely escaped being killed in the attack on New Haven, while he was a member of Yale College, during the Revolutionary war. He died without a struggle or groan.

New Haven [Conn] Palladium. Two more murders: two aged English people, Mr Chas Smith & his wife, who for some time have been the sole occupants of the solitary house upon the brow of East Rock, a short distance from the city limits, were found brutally butchered. Mr Smith was over 80 years old, & served for many years in the army of the Duke of Wellington, in the peninsular war, & other campaigns. The house had the marks of having been thoroughly searched for plunder.

For rent: 2 story brick dwlg house on 19th st, near L. Inquire of Mr Thos Smith, opposite the premises.

City Ordinances-Wash: 1-Act for the relief of Walter Linkins: to pay him the amount found due him according to the Surveyor's estimate for driving of bolers or large stone below the grade on K st. 2-Act for the relief of Wm Becket: that the fine imposed for an alleged violation in relation to bonds required from free negroes, be remitted: provided he pay the costs of prosecution; & that the sum of $5 is hereby appropriated to be paid to him.

Trustee's sale: by decree in Chancery, will offer at public sale at the court-house door, in Upper Marlboro, on Nov 12, all that tract or parcel of land on which Leonard H Chew resides, on the Nottingham road, containing about 3,330 acres, more or less. Good dwlg with necessary outbldgs. –Wm H Tuck, trustee

Sale of valuable real estate: by deed of trust, dated Jun 11, 1849, recorded in Liber J A S, #6, folios 314 thru 316, in the land records for Wash Co, D C. Sale on Nov 9, all the undivided interest of Geo W Frazier & Isabella C Frazier, his wife, in that part of lots 8 & 9, in square 787, in Wash City, at 3rd & East Capitol sts. –R T Morsell, trustee -Green & Tastet, auctioneers

H M Brackenridge, a member of the former Commission on Mexican Claims, will be in Wash in the course of Nov, & offers his services to claimants under the treaty. Address Andrew Eylie, Wash.

TUE NOV 6, 1849
The Jennings Family [See Sep 26, 1849 newspaper.] The immense estate has created quite an excitement in this country. In 1798 Wm Jennings died instestate, at age 97, in the county of Suffolk, a bachelor, leaving an estate then estimated at two millions of pounds sterling. For want of children, this immense property passed to more distantly connected relatives, the landed estates coming in the possession of the father of the present Earl Howe, & the personalty being divided between Mrs Lygon & Lady Andover. Attempts to disturb the distribution of the estate which had taken place at the time of Wm Jenning's death proved abortive. An account fo the death of Wm Jennings, & the mode in which his property was disposed of, may be found in the Annual Register for 1798, page 52, of the Chronicle. It follows from that account that the property never was in abeyance, but passed immediately into the possession of the heirs at law. This took place so long ago than any adverse claim not brough forward before 1818 would be barred by the statute of limitations, [3rd & 4th Wm IV, chapter 27,] which, after 20 years, not only takes away the forensic remedy, but actually extinguishes the right & title of the person out of possession. It would seem that attempts to set up a claim of it have long been hopeless. –Richmond Whig

Mscl: in 1786, Gen Washington imported 2 ploughs from England, because he found our own too inferior for good husbandry.

The L'Union Medicale of Sep 8, says, on Aug 23, Madame Labrune, a healthy married woman, residing a Langres, France, died from the effects of chloroform vapor. She wished to have a tooth extracted.

Appointments by the Pres: 1-John W Farrelly, to be Auditor of the Treasury for the Post Ofc Dept, vice P G Washington, removed. 2-Gabriel W Long, to be Indian Agent for the Chickasaws, vice A M M Upshaw, removed.

According to Mr Bancroft, the first Puritan settlers of New England are the parents of one-third of the population of the U S. In the first 15 years, the time when most of the immigration from England took place, there came over 21,000 persons. Their descendants in 1840 were estimated at 4,000,000. Each family has multiplied on the average to a thousand souls.

M Jean Baptiste Robillard, the oldest man in France, died Oct 1, at Fontenay, near Paris, at the age of 113 years, 4 months & 2 days. He was born in Jun, 1736, & retained the use of his faculties till the last moment.

Information wanted of Jas Hansbrough, about 24 years old, left Fauquier Co, Va, in Jan, 1845, & went to Harden Co, Ky, where he resided till Nov, 1845, where he left, intending to spend time in Lincoln Co, Mo, & then proceed to the Territory of Oregon. Since 1845 his relatives in Va have not heard from him & cannot ascertain his present locality. By the recent death of his father, Elijah Hansbrough, the exc of said deceased is anxious to hear of or from him. Any person who may have any information respecting Jas Hansbrough, will please address a letter to me on the subject, to Somerville, Fauquier Co, Va. –David Hansbrough, Exc of Elijah Hansbrough, deceased.

Admx sale of farming utensils, horses, cattle, hogs, corn, grain, & hay, at auction: on Nov 13, by order of the admx, at the farm owned by the late Dr Nicholas Worthington, 2 miles from the city, on the Wash & Rockville Turnpike, 7th st. –Catherine Pearson, admx -E C & G F Dyer, aucts

Philadelphia North American: advertisement by the administrators of Mr Claypoole, eminent printer, who died recently in this city, in his 93rd year, will dispose by public sale of the original manuscript of Washington's Farewell Address; a document which has been, & must continue to be, held in the highest estimation by the people of this county. We hope it will fall into the hands of the General Gov't, or some public institution by whom it will be suitably cherished. [Being acquainted with the handwriting of Pres Washington, I am satisfied that evey word in the text whether written in regular course or interlined, is his, & his alone. –W Rawle]

Rev Dr Hooper's Family School, in the country, Warren Co, near Littleton, N C. Next session will commence on the last Thu of Nov. –Rev W Hooper

Mrd: on Nov 4, in Wash, by Rev Mr Slattery, Mr John T May to Mrs Rosanna A Rust.

Mrd: on Nov 3, by Rev M Alig, Jas Barcley to Mary Fagan, of Wash City.

Died: on Nov 5, in her 14th year, Ellen Frances, eldest daughter of Richd White, of Wash City. Her funeral is today at half past 3 o'clock.

For sale or rent: 3 story brick house, formerly occupied by his excellency Mr Bagot, the British Minister, & more recently by the late Wm Hayman, situated on K st, near Gtwn. Inquire of Cmdor Stephen Cassin, in Gtwn, or of H C Spalding, in Wash.

WED NOV 7, 1849
Political movements in New Mexico. Santa Fe Republican of Sep 20: meeting held on Aug 21, of the citizens of Santa Fe Co on the organization of a proper Territorial Gov't. Capt W Z Angney presides, assisted by Rufus Beach & J W Folger as Vice Presidents, & Lewis D Sheets as Sec. Maj R H Weightman offered a preamble & resolutions, which were discussed by Messrs Messervy, Weightman, Houghton, Smith, Angney, West, Nangle, Ashurst, & Tuley. In another publication of the Republican, we observe that Lt Col Beall, who, in the absence of Col Washington, was then military commandant in New Mexico. Returns from all the counties, one precinct, Dona Ana, yet to be heard from, as follows:
Santa Fe: Manuel Alvarez, Capt W Z Angney, Dr E V Deroin
Taos: Antonio Jose Martin, Capt C St Vrain, Jose Martin, Antonio Leroux
Rio Arriba: Capt Chapman, Salbador Lucero, D J Nangle.
San Miguel del Bado: Manuel An Baca, Gregorio Virgil, Miguel Senayy Roemro
Bernalillo: Manuel Armijo, Ambroisio Armijo
Santa Anna: Tomas Baca, Miguel Montoya
Valencia: Judge Otero, JuanJose Sanches, Wm C Skinnger, Mariana Sylba

Rev John Black, D D, the oldest minister of the Reformed Presbyterian Church, & one of the earliest settlers of the city of Pittsburg, died at his residence in that city, last week, after a few days' illness, in his 82nd year.

Mrd: on Nov 5, by Rev Jas B Donelan, John A Ganbert to Miss Sarah Jane Peak, of Wash.

Mrd: on Nov 5, by Rev Mr Slattery, Mr Jas Sutton to Miss Frances M Lacey, both of Wash City.

Mrd: on Oct 16, in Perry Co, Ala, by Rev W M Smithe, Wm M Lapsley, of Cahawba, to Miss Emily A Barron, of Perry.

Died: on Nov 5, Margaret, the infant daughter of Fred'k & Mary E Whyte.

Sailing of Missionaries: Rev J L Mackey & wife, Rev J W Simpson & wife, & Rev J Best, Missionaries for Gaboon; Mr John S Brooks & wife, & Sarah Kinson, for the Mendi Mission; Mr Adolphus Pike, for Sierra Leon; Mr Jos Barry & wife & Mrs Webb, for Liberia, sailed from N Y on Sat in the brig **Lowder**, for Africa, under the auspices of the American Board of Com'rs for Foreign Missions.

Last Mon, the largest boat ever brought down the C & O Canal was the boat **Phineas Janney**, Gibson, from Harper's Ferry, with 911 barrels of flour, all delivered in perfect order in Gtwn. This boat was built in Wash City by Capt W Easby.

Tornado in Louisiana on Oct 15, swept over Terrebone. Mr Pierre Gerbeau's house was destroyed, & he was killed. His wife & children escaped, but were badly injured. Damaged: Mr Tanner's plantation; Messrs Thibodaux & Batey's sugar plantation; Maj Potts' plantation, & 2 frame houses, lately occupied by Mr Auguste Babin, on Bayou Bieu. –New Orleans Bee

Fatal mistake: Mrs Barker, wife of Zenus W Barker, for many years a resident of Sandusky, died suddenly on Oct 27, aged 51 years. She accidentally took strychnine in place of morphine. –Sandusky Clarion of the 29th.

Public sale of real estate: by decree passed by PG Co Court, as Court of Equity, in a cause wherein Myer Stone, Baptist Gray & Eliz his wife, are cmplnts, & David Stone, Priscilla Stone, & others, are dfndnts. Sale on Nov 16, the real estate of which David Stone, late of said county, died seized & possessed, called *Chance*, containing 166 acres more or less. The main road from the Long Old Fields to Alexandria runs through said estate. –N C Stephen, D C Digges, Trustees

Official: Zachary Taylor, Pres of the U S of A, recognizes Guillaume Alexandre Lebaron as Vice Consul of Sardina, for the port of Mobile, in the State of Alabama.

$3 reward for return of strayed or stolen middling sized red Cow. Deliver to my house on D st, between 9th & 10th sts. –John Foy

Household & kitchen furniture at auction, by the trustee, on Nov 9, at the residence of Jas Colburn, on 3rd st, near High st. –W Redin, trustee -E S Wright, auct

THU NOV 8, 1849
Biographical sketch of the life of the late Maj Alphonso Wetmore. He was born in Connecticut, & while a child, his father emigrated to Montg Co, N Y; at age 18 he entered the army, & participated with General's Scott, Ripley, Gaines, Towson, Brooke, Worth, Wool, Brady, & Kearny in the trying scenes of the Northern frontier. He returned from those campaigns with the loss of his right arm & an incurable wound in his right side. After the late war with Great Britain, Capt Wetmore was retained as Btln Paymaster in the 6th Regt of the U S Infty, & later appointed Paymaster, with the rank of Major of Cavalry. He remained in this position until 1832, when he resigned, & his connexion with the army closed. He collected & collated a Gazetter of the State of Missouri, the State of his adoption. With the aid of Col Chas Keemle, of St Louis, he was co-editor of the Missouri Sat News. After the failure of this newspaper, he was elected Justice of the Peace; then devoted his time to the practice of law; during the war with Mexico, he raied a regt, 1,000 strong. The regt was not accepted. –An ofcr of the old 23rd Regt Infty

Abraham Rackett was arrested in N Y on Sat on suspicion of stealing a certificate for $1,000 U S stock. It has been missing for about 10 years, & a few days ago a man from Boston says he received it from Rackett. –Boston Daily Adv

Gen Don Manuel Rincon, well known for his valor at the battle of Churubusco, lately died in the city of Mexico, highly respected as a soldier & a citizen.

Boy lost: was missed by his relatives, an Italian, about 13 years old, named Nicholas Bacigalupo. He speaks very little English. He was missed between Alexandria & Wash City, on the Va side of the river. His distressed relatives are at the German Hotel, 9th st, opposite the Republic ofc.

From Florida: correspondence of the Florida Republican: Pilatka, Oct 29, 1849. Gen Twiggs & his 2 daughters, & Majors Myers, Makall, & Brooks, of his staff, reached here yesterday. Capts Vogde's & Fowler's companies have been sent to *Fort Reid* & *Fort Gatlin*, & Capt Swartwout's to New Smyrna. Col Dimick's & Lt Chalfin's companies have returned to this place, & Capt Grafton's is now on its way here from Orange Springs. Col Steptoe's company is mounted, & will accompany the Gen back to Tampa. Sam Jones made his appearance at the last council: he is a tall figure, about 90 years old, hair perfectly white, & walks with a staff about 10 feet long. He is a fine looking & venerable man. Bowlegs assured the Gen that the 5th Indian of the party that made the attack upon Pease creek should be delivered to him. [Nov 10th newspaper: Bily Bowlegs is a fine looking fellow of 40, followed with great earnestness & dignity of manner.]

Mrd: on Nov 6, by Rev J R Eckard, Mr Alex'r R Seymour, of New Market, Va, to Miss Eliza McLean, daughter of Mr Jas Gaither, of Wash City.

Died: on Nov 7, Sophia Jane, aged 2 years, youngest daughter of John F & Jane E Tucker. Her funeral is today, at 2 o'clock, from the residence of her parents, near corner of 5th & E sts east.

Grand Millitary & Civic Ball of the Wash Light Infty on Nov 22. Managers:
No hats or caps will be admitted in the ball room.

Capt Jos B Tate	Jas Bousseau	Wm McM Payne
Lt John F Tucker	Geo Becker	Jos Stanley
Lt Wm H Clarke	Saml H Warner	W W S Kerr
Lt Jas V Davis	Jas Burdine	Edmund V Rice
Ensign J W Mead	Wm S Lewis	Geo Payne
Serg H Richey	Jos P Mitchell	Anselm Hatch, jr
Serg Jas Kelly	Benj F Beers	Jas King
Serg E Varden	Benj F Duvall	Ign F Mudd
Serg J O Warner	Wm Garner	Wm Goggin
Q M S W E Morcoe	Ed B Duvall	T T Sparrow
Andrw J Joyce	John S Finch	Thos Luxen
Jas Booth	Jos McQuen	P M Dubant
Jas Powers	John Pic	F Benter
Jas H Mead	P M Fisher	Wm Dalton

John Hutchinson	John M Judge	Wm Rupp
John Browers	Douglas West	Wm Bergman
C F M Powell	Arthur Stanford	Thos McGlocklan
Wm J Harris	John Corcoran	Jas Cammell
Wm Spalding	Francis Garcia	Jos Rasselte
Henry Fisher	Francis Holden	Chas Toomey
John L Day	Ephraim B Rodbird	F F Elgen
Lemuel Williams	Henry Khul	
Thos B Duvall	John Howell	

Tickets $1, to be had at Butts' Drug Store, N Hammond's, G W Cochran's, Jos Shillington's, D Keally's, & the door on the evening of the Ball.

FRI NOV 9, 1849
Firemen's & Citizen's Ball: the Anacostia Fire Co announce that their Annual Ball will be held on Nov 28, at their Hall, under the direction of the following managers:

Jonas B Ellis	Thos Goss	Jas Burdine
Wm Morgan	John Ober	Wm E Hutchinson
Jas H Meade	Jos Mitchell	

Household & kitchen furniture at auction on Nov 12, at the house recently occupied by Mr Greenleaf, on G st, & 14th sts. –Green & Tastet, aucts

Administrator's sale: estate of David C Claypoole, deceased. The Original Manuscript of Washington's Address. Will be sold, at public auction, at the Phil Exchange, on Feb 12, 1850. This paper, in the handwriting & bearing the signature of Washington, was presented by him to Mr Claypoole, the then editor & proprietor of the Daily Advertiser, which gazette Gen Washington had selected for its first publication. –Thos C Rockhill, Jas Peale, adms. Moses Thomas & Sons, aucts, 93 Walnut st, Phil.

Wash Corp: 1-Ptn from Saml Carusi: referred to the Cmte on Improvements. 2-Ptn from Saml Adams & others: referred to the Cmte on Improvements. 3-Cmte of Claims: bill for the relief of John F Callan. 4-Cmte of Claims: asked to be discharged from the further consideration of the ptn of Temple Sherman: discharged accordingly. 5-Bill for the relief of Wm Fensley: passed. 6-Cmte of Claims: discharged from the further consideration of the ptn of J E Neale: discharged accordingly. 7-Bill for the relief of J E W Thompson: referred to the Cmte on the Asylum: passed. 8-Ptn of John Crane & of Patrick Magee, praying remission of fines: referred to the Cmte of Claims.

The American mail-steamer **Washington**, from Southampton, brought to N Y, among the passengers: Hon Romulus M Saunders, of N C, late U S Minister Pleni to Spain; Hon Richd Rush, of Pa, late Envoy to France; Hon Wm H Stiles, of Ga, late Charge d'Affaires at Vienna; & Hon R P Flenniken, of Pa, late Charge d'Affaires at Copenhagen, each accompanied by his family.

Mrd: on Nov 4, in Christ Church, Pittsford, N Y, by Rev W L Childs, Minister of the Parish, Edw Snell to Mary Ann, eldest daughter of Ethelbert Wicking, all of Pittsford.

The Imperialist, Count Zichy, has expressed, in a letter to the Paris Presse, his indignation at the report that he had shot Gorgey in revenge for the death of his brother.

Died: on Nov 2, in Wash City, of consumption, aged 18 years & 6 months, Miss Sarah Eliz Franklin Martin, eldest daughter of the late Thos J Martin, of Portsmouth, Va, but formerly of Wash City. By this bereavement her widowed mother, grandmother, & other members of the family are much afflicted; but they sorrow not as those who have no hope.

SAT NOV 10, 1849
P Brightman, a young man, on a gunning excursion near Fall river, a few days ago, had his arm accidentally shatter. John England, who lived north of Carlinville, Ill, met his death on Oct 15, when seeing if his gun was loaded.

Sylvia Tory was lately burnt to death by her clothes taking fire in South Kingsburytown, R I. Her age was more than 112 years. She was imported from Africa when 8 years old, & leaves a daughter 87 years of age. Her eyesight was perfect up to the day of her death.

A son of Mr Hugh Nicar, near Lynchburg, Va, committed suicide on Thu week by hanging himself. He was about 11 years of age.

Information wanted of Jas Keogan, formerly of Castle Rue, Ire, who sailed from Liverpool for N Y in 1830. He was last heard from near Wash, D C. Any information of his whereabouts will be kindly received by his brother John, care of Edw Marklew, Hamilton st, between Schuylkill 3rd & 4th sts, Phil.

Agency for heirs at law & next of kin advertised for in the English newspaper. The undersigned has obtained from London an authentic list of the names of all deceased persons leaving property, for whose heirs at law or next of kin ads have appeared in the English newspapers during the last 50 years. The list contains 10,000 names. Applications for information by letter must be post paid. –Wm Chase Barney, at Wm Thompson's Adv Agency, Carroll Hall, Balt, Md.

The subscriber, late of the Pension Ofc, having for the last 7 years been employed on the various duties connected with the said ofc, tenders his services to the public in the prosecution of claims against the Gen Govt, embracing not only the Pension Ofc, but all other depts. –Thos Lumpkin, Willard's Nat'l Hotel

Clermont at Public Sale: the residence of the late Gen John Mason, in Fairfax Co, Va, will be offered by his excs on Dec 14 next. The estate comprises about 327 acres; 4 miles from Alexandria; mansion & its appurtenances are of the most ample & commodious description, overlooking the town of Alexandria. The place will be shown by Mr Butler, the overseer. For further information address the subscriber, the acting exc, at Winchester, Va. -Jas M Mason

Mrd: on Nov 8, in Gtwn, by Rev John W Everitt, Wm Lunsford, formerly of Warrenton, Va, to Miss Eliz Ann Payne, daughter of Mr Thos Payne, of Gtwn, D C.

Mrd: on Oct 8, by Rev Mr Lenahan, Mr John H Barr to Miss Frances Alcinda Brinsley, all of Wash City.

Mrd: on Oct 30, in Norfolk, at the residence of John Southgate, by Rev Geo Cummins, Wm C Yeaton, of Alexandria, Va, to Mary Frances, daughter of the late Col Edmund B Duvall, of PG Co, Md.

Died: last night, in Wash City, the Rev Jos Van Horsigh, for many years the beloved Pastor of St Peter's Church, on Capitol Hill, in his 53rd year. His funeral will take place tomorrow, at 3:30 p m, from his late residence, adjoining to the Church.

MON NOV 12, 1849
The remains of Gen Worth, Col Duncan, & Col Gates arrived at N Y in the steamer **Ohio** on Sat. They are to be interred by the city authorities of N Y, who have decided to have the funeral procession on Nov 15.

Mr John Lenthal, for a long time stationed at the Phil Navy Yard as Naval Constructor, has removed to Washington, because of his appointment as Chief constructor. Mr Richd Powell, engaged for many years as the assist of Mr Lenthal, is stated to have accompanied him to Washington.

The oldest college in the U S is Harvard Univ, at Cambridge, Mass, established in 1638; next is Wm & Mary, in Va. The institution was founded in Feb, 1692, under the name of the Univ of Wm & Mary. The 3rd was Yale College, at New Haven, established in 1700. –Union

Jacob Asker, Ex-Sheriff of N Y C, died on Tue in that city, in his 56th year.

An immense congregation attended the funeral of the beloved Pastor of St Peter's Church, Rev Jos Van Horsigh, which was solemnized yesterday in that ancient edifice. The funeral rites were performed by Fr Mathews & his associate, Rev Jas B Donelan. Dr Ryder, the Pres of Gtwn College united in the ceremony. The funeral discourse was delivered by Rev John E Blox. It is calculated that 2,000 persons went to the funeral who could not get admission into the church.

Fight at Columbia, Ark, on Oct 27, which has probably proved fatal to both parties engaged: Mr Archibald Goodlow & Romulus Payne, long friends & neighbors, & planters of high respectability. Some time ago Goodlow sold out all his property to a brother-in-law, throwing upon Payne a liability, as his endorser, for $10,000, which Payne had to pay. This begot a misunderstanding & hostility between them. The Court met at Columbia, on Sat last, when Goodlow attacked Payne with 2 revolvers. Payne rushed upon Goodlow with a pistol. Goodlow was quite dead. Payne was speechless & not expected to live. –New Orleans Delta

Fatal Powder Mill explosion on Tue week. Mr Danl Byerly, a native of Germany, employed in the mill of Messrs E & E Hammer, near Orwigsburg, Pa, was killed in the explosion. He was a young unmarried man.

There are at present 8 persons confined in the St Louis jail on the charge of murder: Jas Cassidy, for killing Saml Hefferman; Geo Lambert & his wife, for killing Michl Donavan; Geo W Lansdown, for killing Capt Howard; 2 Indians, for killing Mr Colburn, a Santa Fe trader, on the plains; Gonsalve & Raynard Montesquion, for the late murder at the City Hotel. –Reveille of Oct 31.

Mrd: on Nov 8, at Phil, by Rev Dr Ducachet, Wm Henry Beck to Mary Louisa Bayard, daughter of Hon Richd H Bayard.

Mrd: on Nov 7, at **Locust Wood**, the residence of J A Constant, on the Hudson, Jas C Douglass, U S Navy, to Ellen, daughter of Wm Sinclair, U S Navy.

Mrd: on Nov 7, at N Y, by Rev Francis Vinton, D D, August Belmont to Caroline Slidell, daughter of Cmdor M C Perry, U S Navy.

Mrd: on Oct 26, at Portsmouth, N H, at St John's Church, by Rev Dr Burroughs, Archibald H Lowery, of N Y, to Frances Austriss, daughter of Hon Levi Woodbury.

Mrd: on Nov 6, at Easton, Md, by Rev T L McLean, Rev Levi R Reese, of the Md Conference of the Methodist Protestant Church, to Miss Tamsey A Hughlett, of Talbot Co, Md.

Mrd: on Oct 31, at St Peter's Church, Phil, by Rev W Odenheimer, Jas Murray, of Annapolis, Md, to Catherine Stewart, daughter of the late Cmdor Murray, U S Navy.

Mrd: on Nov 8, by Rev Geo Adie, John Moore Orr, of Middleburg, Loudoun Co, Va, to Orra, eldest daughter of Dr Geo Lee, of Leesburg, Va. [Note: the bride is now Mrs Orra Orr.]

Died: on Nov 2, at Milwaukee, Wisc, after an illness of 10 days, in his 38th year, Dr John F Spalding, formerly of Chas Co, Md, leaving a disconsolate wife & an extended circle of friends to lament his early death.

Died: on Nov 9, of scarlet fever, Elizabeth, daughter of Geo C & Eliz Whiting, aged about 2 years.

Fire on Oct 18, consumed the house of John Townsend, jr, in Southport. Martin Townsend, about 14 years of age, & Jas H Hardy, nearly 8 years of age, were victims to the flames. –Chemung Democrat

TUE NOV 13, 1849
The first 3 American missionaries to Jerusalem were born among the Green Mountains of western Massachusetts, within 40 days of the same time, & within 30 miles of each other, viz: Rev Jonas King, D D, in Hawley; Rev Levi Parsons, in Goshen; & Rev Pliny Fisk, in Shelburne.

Confectionary re-opened, having secured the services of a first-rate workman. –Thos Havenner & Son, C st, between 4½ & 6th sts.

People's Convention for framing a Constitution for the State of Calif: held on Sep 1, at Monterey. Organization of the body was completed by the election of the following ofcrs: Robt Semple, Pres; Wm G Marcy, Sec; Caleb Lyons & J B Field, Assist Secs; W E P Hartnell & Henrique Henriques, Translators; J S Houston, Sgt-at-Arms; & Cornelius Sullivan, Door-keeper.
The following are the membeers admitted to seats in the Convention:
San Diego: Miguel de Pedrorena & Henry Hill
Los Angeles: S C Foster, J A Carillo, M Domingues, A Stearns, & Hugo Reid
Santa Barbara: P Laguerra & Jacinto Rodrigues
San Luis Obispo: Henry A Tefft & J M Cabarruvia
Monterey: H W Halleck, Thos O Larkin, C T Botts, P Ord, & L S Dent
San Jose: J Aram, K H Dimmick, J D Hoppe, A M Pico, & E Brown
San Francisco: E Gilbert, M Norton, W M Gwinn, J Hobson, W M Steuart, W D M Howard, Francis J Lippitt, A J Ellis, & R M Price
Sonoma: J Walker, R Semple, L W Boggs, & M G Vallejo
Sacramento: J R Snyder, W S Sherwood, L W Hastings, J S Fowler, W E Shannon, J A Sutter, John Bidwell, M M McCarver, John McDougal, E O Crosby
San Joaquin: J Mc H Hollingsworth, C L Peck, S Haley, B F Lippincott, T L Vermuile, M Fallon, B F Moore, Walter Chipman, J M Jones, & O M Wozencraft.

I hereby notify all persons that I will pay no debts contracted in my name by either of my children on & after this date; & I will enforce the law against any person or persons who may harbor or traffic with them without my knowledge.
-Michl Shiner, Navy Yard

Balt: our young & accomplished townsman, Teackle Wallis, has gone out in the steamer **Europa** as Com'r to Spain from out Gov't. He is a superior Spanish scholar, & well versed in that country.

From Calif: 1-Five mutineers on board the U S steamer **Ewing** were to be tried for an attempt to drown Passed Midshipman Gibson. 2-Hon A S Thurston, the U S Rep from Oregon, was among the passengers brought by the ship **Empire City**.

Port of Gtwn: Arrived, Nov 10, schnr **Pampero**, Murch, N Y to P Berry; schnr **Alverda**, Tolly, Petersburg, to J H King. Arrived, Nov 12: schnr **G Hoffman**, Ross, Phil, to P Berry; packet steamer **Columbia**, Harper, Balt, to E Pickrell & Co; propeller **Washington**, Wood, Balt, to P Berry.

Cigars, cigars: imported Havana Cigars. –Jas W Berry, 7th st

Mrd: on Nov 11, at Brown's Hotel, by Rev Mr Roszell, Mr Danl S Jasper, of Lynchburg, Va, to Miss Adelina E, daughter of N B Magruder, of Amherst, Va.

Mrd: on Nov 8, at ***Beall's Retreat***, Montg Co, Md, by Rev J W Everest, F J Bartlett, of Wash, to Martha S Beall, youngest daughter of Ninian Beall.

Mrd: on Nov 6, at Phil, by Rev Mr Garland, Mr P McDevitt to Miss Kate T McDevitt, all of Washington.

Died: on Nov 5, at Dayton, Ohio, of consumption, Mrs Rennelche W Schenck, wife of the Hon Robt C Schenck.

C Letmate, Watchmaker, Gold & Silversmith, 7th st, near the Patent Ofc. Repairs & makes new work in that line in the best manner.

$150 reward: the undersigned had his pocket picked this morning at the City Post Ofc [whilst awaiting the assortment of the mail] of a package containing $460, mostly in N Y funds. The above reward will be paid on delivery of the amount to Wm H Hemmick.

WED NOV 14, 1849
Pacific News: owing to the high wages paid to seamen in the merchant service at San Francisco, [being from $130 to $150 per month,] the greatest difficulty has been experienced, & the strictest surveillance required on the part of the naval ofcrs to prevent the men attached to the U S squadron from deserting. On Sep 13, as a boat's crew of 5 men, belonging to the U S schnr **Ewing**, attached to the service of the coast survey, effected their escape by suddenly seizing & throwing overboard Lt Gibson, the ofcr in command. The gallant ofcr dragged into the water with him 2 of his heartless assailants. Here a desperate struggle ensued; finding himself in danger of sinking from the weight of his clothes, he gave up the unequal contest. His cries for assistance were heard, & a passing boat picked him up. He was taken to the U S Hotel, pulseless & apparently lifeless, where, by the prompt & judicious treatment of Dr Bowie, of the Navy, respiration was established, & the circulation restored. At the latest date he was out of danger. The perpetrators were captured, & are to be tried by a court martial. They are: Beattie, Cummerford, Hall, & 2 brothers, Black. All are stated to be Englishmen, who shipped at Callao on the outward voyage of the **Ewing**.

We learn, unofficially, that Nixon White, of N C, has been appointed a Purser in the Navy, vice Wm B Hartwell, deceased.

Fatal casualty at the Navy Yard yesterday, at the battery, whilst experimenting with a large 32 pounder, which had been fired several times, the gun suddenly burst, instantly killing Mr Chas S McLane, a gunner in the U S Navy.

Wash Corp: 1-Bill for the relief of J E W Thompson: passed. 2-Bill for the relief of Thompson Nailor: postponed until Mon next. 3-Bill for the relief of David Miller: passed.

City Ordinances-Wash: 1-Act for the relief of Wm Fensley: that the fine imposed for an alleged violation relative to vending shoes, [he being a non-resident,] be remitted: that Hanson Brown, county constable, be required to surrender to said Fensley his watch, [now in his possession,] in good order, held by him as collateral security for said fine. 2-Act for the relief of Thos Greeves: the sum of $115.43 be paid to him, being the amount due to Greeves for work done in cleaning alleys & places.

Desirable farm, farming utensils, horses, cows & sheep at auction: on Nov 20, on the premises 100 acres of land in Montg Co, on the old road leading to Rockville, & adjoining the property of Messrs Wm Huddleston, Spates, & Baulcher. –Edw S Wright

Trustee's sale: by deed of trust from Franklin W Klickerman & Louisa his wife, [late Louisa Dixon, one of the heirs of Thos Dixon, deceased,] to Walter W Berry, dated Feb 24, 1844, recorded in Liber W B 106, folio 386, will be sold at auction, for the purposes of the said deed, on Dec 15 next, at the auction rooms of Edw S Wright, in Gtwn, all the undivided share & interest of the said Klickerman & wife of & in all the lots & hereditaments of the said late Thos Dixon, deceased, consisting of the following, in Gtwn, to wit: part of lot 184, in Beatty & Hawkins' addition, fronting 40 feet on High st; the south part of lots 146 & 147, in Bealle's addition to Gtwn, fronting 30 feet on Green st; also, lot 164, in Bealle's addition, fronting 60 feet on Olive st, & 99½ feet on Green st; & of & in lot 2, in square 820, in Wash City; with the dwlg-houses on some of the same. Terms: one-fourth of the purchase money in cash, & the residue at 6, 12, & 18 months, with interest from the day of sale. –W Redin, trustee -E S Wright, auctioneer

Desirable farm, farming utensils, horses, cows & sheep at auction: on Nov 20, on the premises 100 acres of land in Montg Co, on the old road leading to Rockville, & adjoining the property of Messrs Wm Huddleston, Spates, & Baulcher. –Edw S Wright

New Post ofcs for the week ending Nov 10, 1849:

Ofc	County, State	Postmaster:
East Craftsburg	Orleans, Vt	J W Simpson
West Otis	Berkshire, Mass	Ardon Judd
Banksville	Fairfield, Conn	John Banks
Monument Isl'd	Delaware, N Y	Chester Rood
Delaware Bridge	Sullivan, N Y	Paul A Tyler
Pinkney	Lewis, N Y	John J Goodenough
Mountain Hall	Berks, Pa	Hugh Lindsay
Davistown	Greene, Pa	Alpheus B Copland
Douglass	Montg, Pa	Aaron K Stauffer
Cecil	Washington, Pa	Robt Johnson
North Sewickly	Beaver, Pa	Jonthan Leet
Seisholtzville	Berks, Pa	H B Griffith
Caln	Chester, Pa	Isaac C Preston
Elk Dale	Chester, Pa	Saml Hughes
Radnor	Delaware, Pa	Thos R Petty
East Sandy	Venango, Pa	Wm Shorts
Portersville	Perry, Ohio	Philip Adams
Palermo	Carroll, Ohio	John Wert
Mill Creek	Williams, Ohio	Calvin Ackley
Pine View	Fauquier, Va	Geo H Stribling
Walnut Creek	Buncomb, N C	Luke L Branson
Howellsville	Robeson, N C	Edw B Patterson

Monticello	Pike, Ala	Jas A Brooks
Isney	Chostaw, Ala	Jos H S White
Ichepuckesassa	Hillsboro, Fla	Jacob Summerlin
Franksville	Claiborne P, La	D Franks
Alligator	St Mary's P, La	Stephen Delucky
Talahatah	Newton, Miss	Wm Lovett
Boggy Depot	Cherokee Na'r, Ark	Wm R Guy
Spring Hill	Navarre, Texas	G W Hill
Bethany	Pacola, Texas	Thos G Davenport
Young's Settlement	Bastrop, Texas	John Lytton
Coker Creek	Monroe, Tenn	Auctin Fry
Cookseyville	Crittenden, Ky	John Campbell
Brewersville	Jennings, Ia	J D P A M Chauncey
Roland	Gallatin, Ill	Felix G Harvey
Ball Point	Dallas, Mo	Lemuel Jones
Whitehall	Clark, Mo	Wm McKee
Grindstone	Daviess, Mo	John Osborn
Sextonville	Richland, Wis	Ebenezer M Sexton
Fall River	Columbia, Wis	Alfred A Brayton
Wells' Mills	Appanoose, Iowa	Ambrose Carpenter
Montacute	Polk, Iowa	John Houser
Lovelis	Monroe, Iowa	Theodous Davis
Nine Eagles	Decatur, Iowa	Allen Scott
Bear Creek	Poweshick, Iowa	Joshua C Talbott
Wassonville	Wash, Iowa	Jas Watters
Portland	O T	Thos Smith
Salem	O T	J B McLane
Vernon	C T	Gilbert A Grant
Collonea	C T	Jacob T Little
Sacramento City	C T	Henry E Robinson
Stockton	C T	Wm Hopkins
Benecia	C T	Chas W Haden
San Jose	C T	J D Hoppe
Sonoma	C T	L W Boggs

Names Changed: North Fitchville, Huron Co, Ohio, to Olena.
Lower Sandusky, Sandusky Co, Ohio, to Fremont.
Melton, Chicot Co, Ark, to Gaines' Landing.
Snow Creek, Maury Co, Tenn, to Santa Fe
Fall Branch, Wash Co, Tenn, to James' Cross Roads.
City West, Porter Co, Indiana, to Fillmore.
Naves' Store, Livingston Co, Mo, to Spring Hill.
Devereaux, Herkimer Co, N Y, to Stratford, Fulton Co.

Marshal's sale: by writ of venditiona exponas, on judgment of condemnation on a writ of attachment, issued from the Clerk's ofc of the Circuit Court of Wash Co, D C., to me directed, I shall expose to public sale for cash, on Nov 24, before the Court-house door, the following property: sundry empty Cigar boxes; lot of tobacco of various kinds, lot of common cigars, snuff boxes, bottles, cologne, scales, weights, tools, mattress & comfort. Seized & levied upon as the porperty of J W Beackley, & sold to satisfy Judicials 33 to Mar term, 1850, in favor of Chas R Danenhoover against said Beackley. –Richd Wallach, Marshal of D C

Died: yesterday, in his 61st year, Geo Sweeny, a native of Balt, but from early childhood a resident of Wash City. Prominently connected with its history, he was justly regarded by his fellow citizens of Washington as one of its most efficient & enlightened friends, & was repeatedly distinguished by tokens of their confidence. The community has lost a valuable member, his family a vigilant & kind protector, & his intimate associates a faithful & zealous friend. A Christian from conviction, he attested the sincerity of his faith by the cheerful performance of his duties to God & man. His funeral is this afternoon, at 3 o'clock, from his late residence on 7th st.

Mrd: on Nov 13, in Gtwn, D C, by Rev J W Everist, John R Heald, of Balt, to Eleanor Virginia, daughter of Jas F Essex, of the former place.

THU NOV 15, 1849
Levi Chamberlain, for 27 years secular superintendent of the Sandwich island mission, died at Honolulu on Jul 29, aged 57 years. He was a native of Dover, Vt.

Death of a venerable Marylander. Col Henry Maynadier, of Annapolis, died in that city on Sun last. He was 93 years of age, & participated in many of the stirring scenes of the Revolutionary war. He served with eminent distinction under Gen Washington, & at the battle of Brandywine, in the capacity of Surgeon in the Army, extracted a ball from the leg of Gen Lafayette. Col M was a fine specimen of a gentleman of the olden time, & was universally respected for his many virtues. –Balt Clip

A fire occurred in Portsmouth, Va, on Sun last, Jas Martin, a confectioner, was burnt to death in his bed.

Messrs Robbins & Treadwell, of N Y, are having built for Calif 450 or 500 houses of a story & a half in height & 15 by 25 feet; about 120 houses are now in process of construction for Capt Billings, who is also having 80 others built in Brooklyn-among them is a bowling alley & 2 hospitals. 120 houses have been constructed for Capt A Miner, to be shipped to Calif by the ship **Diadem**. Various firms have shipped portable section houses, to be carried over the Isthmus on pack-mules. An order for 30 or 40 more is being executed for Mr John Parrott, U S Minister at Mazatlan. Wm H Ranlett, of Augusta, Ga, is about to start for San Francisco with 50 dwlgs & stores, all complete & ready for setting up & use. –N Y Tribune

Two valuable tan-yards & skin-dressing establishments, & stock, at auction in Gtwn & Wash: by authority of several deeds of trust, made by Jas Colburn, Messrs Ward, Reynolds, & Waitt, & others, recorded in Liber W B 113, folios 181, #137, folio 388, & Liber J A S #7, folios 141 & 145: sale on Dec 17 next: valuable Tan-yard at Fayette & 2nd sts, in Gtwn, D C, favorably known as Baker's Tan-yard, & recently said Colburn's. Also, that valuable Skin dressing establishment, in Wash City, near the lower bridge on Rock Creek. –W Redin, trustee -Ed S Wright, auct

$5 reward for return of strayed or stolen bay Pony. –Philip Ennis, 6th st

Orphans Court of Wash Co, D C. Letters of administration on the personal estate of Ann Steuart, late of Wash Co, deceased. –Susan K Williams, Jereh Williams, adms

Died: on Oct 31, at Parkersburg, Va, Wm J Gardner, an esteemed & enterprising resident of that place.

Furnished 3 story brick house for rent, on I st. Apply to John W Simonton, Pa ave opposite Brown's Hotel.

By writ of fieri facias, I shall expose to public sale for cash on Nov 20, in Wash City, the following property, to wit: 1 carryall, 1 dark bay mare; & 1 bridle, seized & taken as the property of John Callan, & will be sold to satisfy a judgment in favor of Wm Lord. –A E L Keese

Household & kitchen furniture at auction on Nov 15, at the residence of Mrs Laub, on High st. –E S Wright, auctioneer

Valuable farm at auction: on Nov 26, that handsome tract of land belonging to the estate of Isaac C Smith, deceased, lying in Fairfax Co, Va, with 92½ acres of land. –Green & Tastet, aucts

Mobile Advertiser: Wreck of the barque **Elijah Swift**, Capt Nye, whilst on her way from N Y to New Orleans. Disaster occurred before daybreak on Oct 29, when, being anchored off the island-*Great Isaacs*, a violent storm sprung up causing her to drag her anchors & run upon some rocks, when she went to pieces in an hour. Among those lost were Parker Flower, 2nd ofcr, & Jas Lane, seaman, both of N Y, who lost their lives in endeavoring to save those of Mrs N A Bailey & Miss Henrietta P Ray, both cabin passengers. The rest of our number succeeded in reaching a place of safety. The next morning we found an infant, 6 weeks old, the son of Mrs Bailey; it had been washed upon the rocks the morning before, & had remained there 26 hours. It was alive, & apparently sustained but little injury. On the 3rd day we were rescued by the ship **Bangor**, Capt W J Philbrook, who answered our signals of distress, took us on board, & treated us with kindness. Those lost: Mrs N A Bailey, of New Orleans; Miss Candia, of N Y, about 11 years old; Miss Henrietta P Ray, of New Orleans, about 14 years old; Betsey, colored servant; also, a Frenchman, a German, an Irishman, & child, names unknown; & Parker Flower, Jas Lane, & Chas Robinson, of the crew. The 28 survivors arrived in Mobile on Nov 7, in a destitute condition, having lost everything except when they had on.

FRI NOV 16, 1849
Mr Jos T Kessler, Prof of Music, having returned to this city after an unavoidable absence, caused by ill health, now offers his services to the musical public. Any commands may be left for him at his residence, at Mrs Wise's Boarding-house, on 13th st, between the Avenue & E st.

Board of Com'rs on claims against Mexico met yesterday & examined new memorials:
Jas W Zacharie: case of schnr **Susan**
John Parrott: embargo of property
Asmus C Bredall: false imprisonment
Asmus C Bredall: case of schnr **Lodi**
C & H Childs: case of schnr **Cornelian**
Jonah Rogers, adm of Augustus Rogers: case of schnr **Nelson**
Atlantic Ins Co of N Y: case of brig **Splendid**
Jesse E Brown: case of schnr **Alert**
John J Palmer, receiver of American Ins Co of N Y: case of schnr **Isaac McKim**
Thos Morrison, surviving partner of Plumber & Morrison
Jos Mathieu Cucullu, adm of Simon Cucullu: case of schnr Isaac McKim
Memorials rejected: Memorial of John Parrott, in the case of the Mutador, as not complying with the rules. Memorial of Wm S Parrott, surviving partner of the firm of Parrott & Wilson, as not setting forth the facts whence arises the claim, except by referring to other cases. Memorial of Ann Y Kelly, admx of Henry Lee; 1st, not setting forth whether the person under whom the claim arose [he being domiciliated in a foreign country] was a subject of such country or had taken an oath of allegiance thereto; 2nd, it does not appear whether memorialist is a native or a naturalized citizen of the U S. Memorial of Sanford Kidder: expulsion from Tampico: as [the claimant being a resident in a foreign country] omitting to state whether or not he was a subject of that county, or had taken an oath of allegiance thereto.

Steamship **Falcon**, Oct 29, 1849. Meeting of the Passengers from N Y to Chagres, [transferred from the steamship **Ohio**, at Havana, on Oct 24, to the steamer **Falcon**, bound to Chagres,] John H Van Benthuysen, of N Y, appointed Pres, & Geo H Peck, of Vt, Sec. Resolved: that our thanks our due to Capt Harstein, Lt Commandant of the steamship **Falcon**, & to his ofcrs generally, for their attention & gentlemanly deportment throughout the passage; that we can safely commend the **Falcon** to the public as a vessel whose domestic arrangements are perfectly systematic, & whose fare generally must be satisfactory, & well calculated for the comfort of passengers.
Passengers:

John H Van Benthuysen, Pres
Geo H Peck, Sec
A H Hall, of Maine
David P Selling, of N H
John Osborne, of Mass
J E Caulker, of Conn
Saml Francis, of R I
J O Van Bergen, of N Y
Thos McCarter, of Pa

Danl Henry, of N J
Wm S Burch, of Wash, D C
R K Reid, of S C
Thos S Berrien, of Ga
Saml Truesdell, of Mo
Thos Regan, of Ind
J J Jackson, of Ill
John Ridley, of Panama

Resolved: We have heard with regret of the death of our respected colleague, Dr Nathl P Causin, who for more than a quarter of a century, has filled a distinguished place in our profession. –Robt King Stone, Sec: Medical Assoc of D C.

For rent: furnished house, about 3 squares east of the Pres' Mansion. Inquire to John J Joyce, F & 13th sts.

Writ of fieri facias, issued by Thos C Donn, J P for Wash Co: sale on Nov 20, opposite the Centre market: a new spring carryall, 1 dark mare, & 1 bridle, seized & taken as the property of John Callanan, & will be sold to satisfy a judgment in favor of B W Reed. -A E L Keese, Constable

Mrs Wellford is prepared to accommodate permanent or transient boarders with neat & comfortable single or double rooms: residence on 9th st, between D & E sts.

House to let: 2 story brick house on the corner of 6th & F sts. Apply to Dr C Boyle.

Jim Williams, negro, was arrested on Wed, charged with burglariously entering Mr John Major's house, [keeper of the Toll gate on 7th st,] & knocking down Mrs Major, in making his escape. Mr Major fired at him with a horse pistol, but missed him.

Bladensburg Female Academy will be opened on Dec 5, under the superintendence of Miss S A Bliss.

Sale by order of the Orphans Court of Wash Co, D C. Sale of wines, brandy, whiskey, Jamaican Rum & Champagnes, on Nov 23, in front of our Auction Rooms, in order to close the estate of the late R W Dyer, deceased. -Edw C & G F Dyer

SAT NOV 17, 1849
Mr Saml Usher, formerly postmaster of Kingfield, who was suspected & arrested, charged with robbing the mail, has at last been enabled to make manifest his innocence. It turns out that one of the richest & most influential men in Kingsfield, was active in his efforts to procure Usher's conviction, was the real robber. [Name not given.]

John B Dodd, arrested at Newark, N J, some weeks ago, for stealing Mr Crane's horse & carriage, & removed from Essex jail to Sussex Co, by habeas corpus, was sentenced to 6 years' imprisonment in the State Prison.

Splendid houses to let: subscriber is now prepared to rent both his houses, one on 11th st, the other on Pa ave, together with their furniture. Apply to Jos K Boyd.

Obit-died: on Nov 11, Rev Jos Van Horsigh. At an early age he commenced his ecclesiastical studies in his own loved country, Belgium. His idolizing parents & sister were there ministering to his necessities, & closing his dying eyes. Ordained in St Mary's Seminary, in Balt, Jul 24, 1823, he has been successively Pastor of St Patrick's Church, Balt, Norfolk, & Portsmouth, Va, where a beautiful edifice stands as a monument of his zeal in the cause of religion; & of St Peter's in Wash City, where his labors are well known.

Editor: the foreign journal has a Mr Arnold as the inventor of the Centrifugal Pump. The machine is the invention of Mr Gerret Erkson, now of Wash City, & at work on our canal. A patent is understood to have been applied for. -J

Mrd: on Nov 6, at Boston, by Rev Dr Peabody, Hon Robt C Winthrop to Mrs Laura Derby Welles.

Mrd: on Nov 15, by Rev Wm H Pitcher, Mr Saml C Espey to Miss Lydia Ann Thompson, daughter of Richd Thompson, all of Wash.

Mrd: on Nov 15, by Rev Wm H Pitcher, Mr Danl Tucker to Miss Mary Jones.

Mrd: on Nov 15, by Rev Wm Collier, Mr Wm H Goods to Miss Mary Ann Bradbury Stanley, eldest daughter of Thos Stanley, all of Wash City.

Mrd: on Nov 15, by Rev Mathias Alig, at St Mary's Church, Mr David Bucler to Frances Selly, both of Wash City.

Mrd: on Nov 15, by Rev Mr Roszel, Mr Wm R Simmons to Miss Eliza Jane Richardson, all of Wash City.

Mrd: on Nov 13, at Woodside, near Troy, N Y, by Rev Dr Halley, Brev Capt Irvins McDowell, Assist Adj Gen U S Army, to Helen, daughter of Henry Burden.

Died: on Tue last, Dr Nathl Pope Causin. His funeral is this morning, at 11 o'clock, from his late residence on 11th st.

Died: on Oct 27, in Leesburg, Loudoun Co, Va, Mrs Martha S Blincoe, aged 59 years & 10 days.

Died: on Nov 8, at the State Magazine, on Cooper river, Charleston Neck, [where he resided,] Col Wm Yeadon, closing a long life of uncommon activity & usefulness by a peaceful & happy death, at the advanced age of 72 years.

Mr Nelson Putney, the proprietor of a large private boarding house at White Plains, has been arrested, charged with a series of robberies. He came from Conn to White Plains in 1838, & it is supposed this thieving continued from then til the present time.
–N Y Mirror

MON NOV 19, 1849
N Y Legislature: State ofcrs elected:
Christoper Morgan, Whig, Sec of State
Washington Hunt, Whig, Comptroller
Freeborn G Jewett, Dem, Judge of Appeals
Levi S Chatfield, Dem, Atty Gen
Supreme Judges elected:
Wm Mitchell, Whig
John W Brown, Dem
Henry Hogeboom, Dem
Danl Cady, Whig

Alvah Hunt, Whig, Treasurer
Hezekiah C Seymour, Whig, Engineer
Fred'k Follett, Dem, Canal Com'r
Darius Clark, Dem, Inspector of State Prison

Fred'k W Hubbard, Dem
Wm H Shankland, Dem
Thos A Johnson, Whig
Jas A Hoyt, Whig

Worcester Shield: Elisha L Purnell, one of the most estimable citizens of *Snow Hill*, was killed on Mon by the bursting of the cylinder of a threshing machine which he was superintending.

Appointments by the Pres: Rosemond de Armas, to be Receiver of Public Moneys at New Orleans, La, vice Henry W Palfrey, removed. Woodson Wren, to be Register of the Land Ofc at Augusta, Miss, vice John S Howze, resigned.

The funeral to honor the gallant dead, Maj Gen Worth, Col Duncan, & Maj Gates, on Thu, in N Y, was the most brilliant civic & military display ever witnessed in that city. Upon its return from the Park about 12 o'clock, prayer was offered by Rev Dr De Witt, & an oration delivered by Mr John Van Buren. The remains of Gen Worth were interred in the Greenwood Cemetery; Col Duncan's were taken to Cornwall, his native town; & those of Maj Gates were interred on Govn'rs Island.

Phil papers announce the death of Col Henry Petriken, who was extensively & favorably kown throughout Pa. He was the first child born in Bellefonte, Centre Co, in 1798, a printer by profession & for years the editor of the Bellefonte Patriot, a member of the House & Senate, & deputy Sec of the Commonwealth.

The London papers announce the death of the Earl Albemarle, aged 78; Lord Talbot de Malahide, aged 83; & Chopin, the eminent pianist & composer in Paris.

A colored man, Chas Robertson, died recently in Carroll Co, Md, at the remarkable age of 103 years & 7 months.

A re-encounter in Louisville, Ky, on Sat week, between 2 young men, J H Owings & John Herr, resulted in the death of the latter. The charge was made by Herr that Owings had robbed him of some money. Each drew a pistol & fired. Owings is in jail.
-Public Journal

Terrible steamboat explosion took place on Nov 15, at New Orleans. The capacious steamer **Louisiana**, bound for St Louis, was about starting from her wharf, just as the wheels began to move, both her immense boilers exploded, shattering the boat almost to atoms. The steamer **Storm** & the steamer **Bostona** were lying alongside of her at the time, both of which were greatly damaged. The **Louisiana** was crowded with passengers, as well as the **Storm** & **Bostona**. It is supposed that 160 or more lives have been lost. Capt Kennon, of the **Louisiana**, has been arrested & held to bail in the sum of $8,000. The explosion is attributed to carelessness. [Nov 22nd newspaper: Victims of the steamer **Louisiana**, at New Orleans: Killed: Mr Knox, Andrew Bell, Levi Prescott, & Bensier Buckner, of Memphis; Mrs Moody, wife of the clerk of the steamer **Storm**; & R McMeckin. All these bodies have been found. Missing: J M King, of St Louis, & Elliott J Merring, of Cincinnati. Wounded: H W Buchanan, Marcus Milner, Saml S Smith, Thos M Merriwether, & Saml Conly, all from Ky; S Wilger, Indiana; Isaac Miller, Ohio; Mr Wolfe, Memphis; W Tucker, J Tucker, John E Tucker, Thos Hamser, & L O Reid, all from Mississippi; Capt Hopkins, of steamer **Storm**; Capt Dustin, Robt Price, & John Mason, of steamer **Bostona**.]

The little son, about 8 years old, of Rev T W Dorman, of Demopolis, Ala, was accidentally shot a few days since by a boy of about the same age, son of I A Traweek. –Linden [Ala] Argus

The subscriber gives notice that there are 8 vacancies in his Family Boarding School for Young Ladies, which he will be glad to occupy by daughters of Members of Congress or others. –R W Cushman, Indiana ave, Wash

Mrd: on Nov 15, in Winchester, Va, by Rev A H H Boyd, Mitchell H Miller, of Wash, D C, to Miss Sarah Clayton, only daughter of the late Jas C Williams.

Mrd: on Nov 15, at the residence of Capt J M Harvey, near Buchanan, Va, by Rev H H Paine, Col Thos P Mitchell, late of Ala, to Miss Virginia B, daughter of the late Col Harvey, of Fincastle, Va.

Died: Nov 18, in his 80th year, Richd Shekell, a native of Md, but for the last 36 years a resident of D C. His funeral is from the residence of his son, on D st, between 9th & 10th sts, today at 2 o'clock; whence he will be conveyed to Anne Arundel Co, Md.

Constable's sale: by order of distrain, from Jas Fitzgerald, against the goods & chattels of Thos Ragan: I have seized the following property, to satisfy rent due & in arrears to Jas Fitzgerald: 2 hogs, 1 bureau, 5 chairs, 1 washing tub, 1 waiter, & 1 spider: sale on Nov 22, in front of the Centre Market-house, & on the same day, at my house, near D Carroll's place, I shall sell the Hogs at auction, for cash, to satisfy said rent due & in arrears to said Jas Fitzgerald. –Wm Cox, Bailiff

Orphans Court of Wash Co, D C. Letters of administration on the personal estate of Nicholas Travers, jr, late of said county, deceased. –Elias Travers, adm

For rent: new handsome dwlg-houses, with basements, on E st, between 9th & 10th sts, now occupied by Mrs Voorhees, will be for rent Dec 1. Apply to Wm Orme.

TUE NOV 20, 1849
Sale of household & kitchen furniture at the residence of Mr Edw Mattingly, at Blagden's Wharf. –Green & Tastet, auctioneers

Eulogium on departed heroes: N Y C: delivered by Mr John Van Buren.
1-Collinson Reed Gates was the eldest son of Col Wm Gates, of the 3rd Artl, late Govn'r of Tampico. He was born at Niagara, N Y, in 1815, & graduated at West Point in 1836. He immediately joined the 1st Regt of Infty, under Gen Worth, in Fla. He was with the army in Mexico, & in most of the engagements which distinguished that war, commencing at Palo Alto. At the battle of Resaca de la Palma he was severely wounded, & was forced to return to this country to recruit. He was brevetted a Capt, & rejoining the army in Mexico he bore an honorable part in the engagements at Nat'l Bridge, Churubusco, Milino del Rey, Chapultepec, & at the gates of the city of Mexico. He was again wounded at Churubusco, & received a brevet of major. He returned with his regt to the U S, & subsequently accompanied them when ordered to Texas, where he died of cholera, at Fredericksburg, Feb 28 last, aged 34.

2-Jas Duncan was born in Cornwall, Orange Co, N Y, & was graduated at West Point in 1835; entered the army as a Lt in the 4th Regt of Artl, & served with honor under Gen Gaines in the Fla war. It was under Gens Taylor & Scott that this extraordinary young man ran the larger portion of his brief but brilliant career. The arm of the public service with which he was connected, & which indeed Ringgold, Bragg, Washington, Taylor, Ridgely, Magruder, & himself may be said to have created, was the light or flying artl. At Palo Alto, Resaca de la Palma, Churubusco, the gates of Mexico, & in the city itself, this formidable engine of destruction, brought to rare perfection within 10 years, by these men, carried carnage & dismay into the enemy's ranks, & gave victory to the American standard. The lamented Ringgold lived only to witness its first grand success at Palo Alto. Duncan used it with tremendous effect at Resada for the novel purpose of pursuing & routing a retreating army. He carried it to the capital of the Aztecs, & its effects were brilliant. Duncan rose by regular promotion to a captaincy; for his service at Palo Alto, he was brevetted a Major; at Resaca a Lt Col; & at Churubusco, & the city of Mexico a Colonel. On the death of Col Croghan he was appointed by the Pres Inspec Gen of the army, which gave him the rank of Colonel. He died at Mobile on Jul 2 last of the yellow fever, aged 38. [Nov 25th newspaper: correction by the Savannah Republican: Col Duncan did not belong to the 4th Artl. He commenced his career as Brevet 2nd Lt in the 2nd Artl; nor did he ever leave it until he was promoted to the ofc of Inspec Gen. –S R]

3-Gen Worth was a native of Hudson, in Columbia co, who, at the commencement of the war of 1812, was a clerk in a mercantile business. He was sec to Gen Lewis, & passed to that of Gen [then Col] Scott. For his gallantry at Chippewa, in 1814, he was brevetted a Capt, & 21 days afterwards, at Niagara, he gained a 2nd brevet as Major. After the war he was the instructor in tactics of the Cadets at West Point, & then transferred to the Watervliet Arsenal, when he became a Major of Ordnance. During the Seminole war, the 8th Regt of Infty was organized, & the command was given to Col Worth. He subdued the Seminole Indians with complete success, & at the close of the Fla war received the brevet of Brig Gen. He moved with Gen Taylor, as 2nd in command, from Corpus Christi to the Rio Grande, on the breaking out of the Mexican war, & a decision having been made ty that cmder which gave Gen Twiggs a priority in rank over Gen Worth, he returned to the U S & tendered his resignation to the Pres, which was not accepted. He received orders to join the army, & reached Mexico in season to bear a distinguished part in the battle of Monterey. When Gen Scott took command of the army in Mexico, he ordered Gen Worth to join him. He was the first American soldier to set foot on the shore at Vera Cruz, & would have been the first to enter the Halls of the Montezumes, if he had not been ordered to stop by the orders of his cmder, who bestowed this distinction upon Gen Quitman, another native son of N Y. When Worth joined Gen Lewis he was some 18 years of age. He was an affectionate father, & most attached husband, the idol of his family. It was thus that Mrs Worth, his son & 2 daughters, one of whom is the wife of Maj Sprague, followed him to San Antonio, in Texas, leaving another daughter, & the only remaining member of his family, in this city. He was seized with cholera on May 7 last, & died in several hours after his attack, aged 55, surrounded by his relatives & friends.

Furnished rooms for rent: on F st, between 17th & 18th sts, adjoining the printing ofc of Mr Alexander. Inquire on the premises, E Dove.

Circuit Court of Wash Co, D C: in Chancery. Bronaugh M Deringer, cmplnt, vs Wm Choppin & Archibald C Peachy, dfndnts. Deringer, by his bill alleges, that he sold & conveyed to the dfndnt, Wm Choppin, a tract of land in Wash Co, D C, containing 41 & 2/5th acres, more or less, & bounded as particularly set forth in the bill. In part payment for the land Choppin, executed to the cmplnt 4 notes, all bearing date on Sep 15, in 1847, all bearing interest from date, one payable Sep 15, 1848, for $500; another for $500 payable Sep 15, 1849; another for $1,000 payable Sep 15, 1850; another for $1,000 payable Sep 15, 1851; that to secure the punctual payment of the said sums, with interest at 6% per year, Choppin executed to Peachy a deed of trust on the land for the use & benefit of the cmplnt, & if Choppin failed to pay, the whole debt should by such default become immediately payable, the said deed of trust dated Sep 17, 1847, signed & sealed by Wm Choppin & his wife Matilda, Archibald C Peachy, & Bronaugh M Deringer, is exhibited as executed in pursuance of the original agreement & terms of sale. In case of default by said dfndnt, Choppin, the said trustee, Peachy, was authorized to sell the land to raise the money due to the cmplnt as in the deed of trust set forth fully. The bill alleges that Choppin hath possession of the land, & is in possession, but hath not paid to the cmplnt any part of said purchase money or interest, & is wholly in default. The trustee, Peachy, removed from D C to Calif before Sep 15, 1848, is now absent, & residing in Calif. The bill prays for a foreclosure of the dfndnt, Wm Choppin's, equity of redemption, & for a sale of the land. The 4th Mon in Mar next is assigned for the day of appearance & answer of said dfndnt, Archibald C Peachy. –Geo M Bibb, for cmplnt. Test, John A Smith, clerk

Mrd: on Nov 13, at Refuge, Chas Co, Md, by Rev Mr Ritromelli, Geo Brent to Catherine, eldest daughter of Hon Wm D Merrick.

Died: on Nov 18, Mrs Sarah Smith, aged 90 years, a native of Annapolis, Md, but for the last 27 years a resident of Wash City. Her funeral is at 3 o'clock, today, at the residence of her daughter, Miss Maccubbin, on Louisiana ave, near the City Hall.

Died: on Nov 14, in Wash City, Renwick Blair, & on Nov 17, Mary Virginia, eldest & youngest children of Isaiah & Ann Catherine Bartley.

Died: on Nov 15, Susana, infant daughter of Jas & Martha Riordan, aged 5 months & 15 days.

Fed Lodge #1 meeting at the Masonic Hall Nov 20, at 7 o'clock.
–G A Schwarzman, sec

$2 reward for return of a yellow Setter Dog, strayed or stolen on Oct 15.
–John M Kraft, corner of F & 12th sts.

For rent: 2 story brick dwlg at 8th & Mass & N Y aves. Apply to S C Barney, E st, between 6th & 7th sts.

Orphans Court of Wash Co, D C. Letters testamentary on the personal estate of Ann McKaraher, late of said county, deceased. –John Sessford, exc

WED NOV 21, 1849

Arrest in N Y on Fri last, of Saml Drury & his son, charged with the diabolical attempting in May last, to destroy the lives of Mr Thos Warner & his family by an infernal machine. [A small tin box filled with combustible matter.] On searching Drury's house at Astoria, jewelry, gold watches, diamonds, spoons, dies for counterfeiting & altered bills were found. Examination will take place in a few days. It will probably lead to a very extensive counterfeiting operation. –Eve Post

On Tue last Mr Halloway Fullerton, son of Judge Fullerton, of Minisink, came to his death by attempting to jump from one car to another while in motion, when he fell across the track, & a lumber car passed over his body, cutting him entirely in two. He was about 28 years of age. –Fishkill Standard

Orphans Court of Wash Co, D C. In the case of Sophia Prevost, admx of Henry M Prevost, deceased, the admx & Court have appointed Dec 8 next for settlement of the estate of said deceased, with the assets in hand. –Edw N Roach, Reg/o wills
-J H Hamilton, agent

Hon Geo W Hopkins, late Charge d'Affaires to Portugal, has returned to the U S, & was in Wash City yesterday on his way to his residence in Va.

Martin Harris, formerly of Palmyra, who was concerned with Joe Smith in originally proclaiming the Mormon faith, wrote the book of Mormon from Joe Smith's dictation. Harris raised funds for its publication by mortagaging his farm. He no longer goes with the Mormons, saying that they have got the devil just like other people. He abandoned them 15 years ago, when they assumed the appellation of "Latter-Day Saints," & bore his testimony against them by declaring that "Latter-Day Devils" would be a more appropriate designation. –Roch Amer

Zachary Taylor, Pres of the U S of A, recognizes Manual Armendari as Consul of the Mexican Republic for the Territory of New Mexico. Nov 20, 1849.

Balt, Nov 20. A young man named Haig, clerk in a fringe establishment of Balt City, committed suicide this morning by hanging himself. Unrequited love was the cause.

To let: 4 rooms or the whole house, near the ave. –J Galligan & Son, Pa ave.

Mrd: on Nov 20, by Rev S A Roszell, Mr Wm H Frazure to Miss Prudence E Suter, all of Wash City.

Died: on Nov 20, Thos Dove, a native of Md, but for the last 50 years a resident of Wash, aged 76 years. His funeral is from his late residence, on I st, between 9th & 10th, this afternoon, at 3 o'clock.

THU NOV 22, 1849

Hugh B Sweeny has been appointed to the vacant post of Notary of the Bank of Wash, in addition to that of Teller, which he has long filled. Mr Geo Venable has been appointed Discount Clerk to the same institution.

Rev T J Burroughs, who was some time ago suspended by the Phil Conference for killing Jas A Bishop on the Eastern Shore of Md, has formally withdrawn from the Church, & delivered up his ministerial credentials to the cmte which was appointed by the Conference to investigate his case.

Execution in Canada. Smith, a private soldier, was convicted of murder at the last Toronto assizes for shooting a fellow soldier, Eastwood. He was executed outside the city jail, in Toronto, last Wed. Smith alleged intoxication as the provocative to the deed.

Dr A D Chaloner, of Phil, has invented this new & useful instrument, consisting of a pair of slender steel forceps, 6 inches in length, & terminating in a cup-shaped cavity, whose edges are toothed. The instrument, when closed, is a probe, & then passed into a wound, the object found, the blades then opened, & the shot is caught & extracted. It should be in the hands of every member of the profession.

Mrd: on Nov 8, in Washington, Geo, by Rev R Lane, Dr Wm H Pope, of that place, to Mrs Eliza Chapman Davidson, of Fairfax Co, Va.

The U S war steamer **Princeton** has been demolished at the Charleston Navy Yard; she was built at Phil, under the supervision of Cmdor Stockton, by contract. On Sep 7, 1843, she was launched, & a short time after was purchased by the U S Gov't, & Cmdor Stockton was appointed to her command. In 1844 the Paixha_ Gun exploded on board of this vessel, killing several members of Mr Tyler' Cabinet, who were present to witness a trial of the huge instrument of death. The timber of the Princton was cut in N J & Dela, in 1842, only 1 year before she was launched, hence it must have been very green. The oak of which she was built was not of good quality. Mr Pook, the naval constructor, when questioned about the propriety of repairing her, estimated that it would cost at least $48,000, which would be about four-fiths the sum to build a new vessel, upon which she was condemned & ordered to be torn in pieces. The original cost of the **Princeton** was $60,000. Since her purchase she had been in constant service.

Mrs Henry Wall informs that she continues to give lessons on the Piano Forte at the residences of pupils. Mrs Wall has but recently arrived from Dublin, where she acquired the method of teaching pursued at the Royal Academy of London. Mrs Kesley's, Pa ave, south side, near 4½ st, Wash.

FRI NOV 23, 1849
Breach of promise of marriage was tried before Judge Lowrie in the Dist Court of Pittsburg on Fri last. The parties were Catherine Johnson against Jas W Reynolds, both occupying respectable positions in society. The dfndnt having been proved to be worth $3,000, the jury awarded $1,000 to the plntf.

The large & elegant mansion of Mrs Anna Jenkins, at Providence, R I, was entirely destroyed by fire on Tue, & the owner & a daughter perished on the premises. The fire originated in a furnace in the cellar, intended for warming the bldg. The younger Miss Jenkins was rescued by a ladder. Mrs Jenkins was a preacher of the Society of Friends.

Men distinguished for their patriotism have in all ages been distinguished for their longevity. No less than 13 of the 56 signers of the Declaration of American Independence lived to the patriarchal age of 81 & upwards, viz:

Chas Carroll, of Md, 95
Wm Ellery, of R I, 93
John Adams, of Mass, 91
Saml Adams, of Mass, 81
Robt Treat Paine, of Mass, 83
Benj Franklin, of Mass, 84
Wm Williams, of Conn, 81

Wm Floyd, of Long Island, 87
Thos McKean, of Pa, 83
Thos Jefferson, of Va, 83
Geo Wythe, of Va, 89
Matthew Thornton, of Ireland, 89
Francis Lewis, of South Wales, 90

Household & kitchen furniture at auction: on Nov 27, at the residence of Mr W G Deale, on G, near 5th st. –Green & Tastet, aucts

N Y papers record the death of Wm H Attree, who was, some years ago, considered as the best reporter in the country. His memory was tenacious to an extraordinary degree. -Phil North American [No date-current item.]

Wash Corp: 1-Ptn from Patrick McGawley: referred to the Cmte of Claims. 2-Cmte of Claims: asked to be discharged from the further consideration of the ptn of Mrs H B Macomb: agreed to. 3-Cmte of Claims: bill for the relief of Wm Clabaugh, agent of Wm Winn: passed. 4-Ptn of Owen McGee, praying remission of a fine: referred to the Cmte of Claims. 5-Cmte of Claims: asked to be discharged from the further consideration of the ptn of John Tenant: agreed to. 6-Cmte of Claims: asked to be discharged from the further consideration of the ptns of Jas Williams, & of Patrick McGee: agreed to. 7-Cmte of Claims: act for the relief of Jas H Shreeves & Harrison Taylor: which was read. 8-Cmte of Claims: asking to be discharged from the further consideration of the ptn of John C Wade: agreed to.

Medical Dept of the Army: Medical Board convened on Oct 15, in Phil, for examination of applicants for the appointment of Assist Surgeon in the Army, the following persons were examined & approved:

Isaac L Adkins, Dela
Robt O Abbott, Pa
Thos M Getty, Va
David L Magruder, Va

Wm J H White, D C
Rodney Glisan, Md
Elisha P Langworthy, N Y

Assist Surgeon Jas Simons was also examined by the same Board, & was found qualified for promotion.

N Y city papers: Jas W Webb, of that city, has received the appointment of Charge d'Affaires to Austria. From the Republic of yesterday: Jas W Power, of Pa, has been appointed Charge d'Affaires to Naples, vice T W Chinn, resigned.

Fayetteville, N C: last week Mr Alex'r C Simpson, who had died on Nov 8, [as was supposed from natural causes,] had been poisoned with arsenic. His wife is charged with the deed, & has escaped.

New Post ofcs: for week ending Nov 17, 1849:

Ofc	Postmaster	
County, State		
Big Tree Corners	Erie, N Y	Aaron Gould
New Brighton	Beaver, Pa	B B Chamberlin
Cushingville	Potter, Pa	Hose Cushing
Contreras	Butler, Ohio	John Hand
Green Bud	Sussex, Va	Chas B Champion
Price's Forks	Montg, Va	Josiah B Lancaster
Edray	Pocahontas, Va	Robt Moore
Farnham	Richmond, Va	Matthew Glenn, jr
Ringgold	Pittsylvania, Va	Iverson B Walters
Hornet's Nest	Mecklenberg, N C	C B Cross
Glade Mines	Hall, Geo	Jas M Chapman
Keaton's Shoals	Baker, Geo	Benj B Keaton
Pumpkiin Vine	Paulding, Geo	Evan Parson
Big Pord	Fayette, Ala	David Loftis
Edgefield	Pike, Ala	W M Reed
Lawrenceville	Henry, Ala	Jos Lawrence
Pleasant Ridge	Greene, Ala	Chas M Roberts
Scottsville	Claiborne P, La	Wm L Burton
Taylorsville	Smith, Miss	Geo C Anderson
Round Pond	Wayne, Miss	Wm W Lang
Buckatoney	Clark, Miss	Thos F Hicks
Hays' Creek	Carroll, Miss	John T Cain
Brasas Santiago	Cameron, Texas	Ambrose Crane
Live Oak	De Witt, Texas	John Scott
Anadarco	Rusk, Texas	Wm J Barry or Berry
Flora	Smith, Texas	Jas K Beane
Blue Hill	Williamson, Texas	Jos O Rice
Old Town	Phillips, Ark	Jas W Munsey
Cache	Saint Francis, Ark	Robt Adams
Walnut Ford	Newton, Ark	Job Christman
Seven Island	Roane, Tenn	Jos B Martin
Church Hill	Christian, Ken	W T Whitlock
Short Creek	Grayson, Ken	Henry Haynes
Brooklyn	Campbell, Ken	Saml Bassett
Mendon	Clayton, Iowa	J T H Scott
Menasha	Winnebago, Wis	Jas K Lush

Names changed: East Bloomfield, Crawford Co, Pa, changed to Spartanburg.
Norritonville, Montg Co, Pa, changed to Penn's Square.
East Euclid, Cuyahoga, Co, Ohio, changed to Euclid.
Euclid, Cuyahoga Co, Ohio, changed to Collamer.
Ridgeway, Charlotte Co, Va, changed to Rough Creek.
Graceville, Houston Co, Ga, changed to Henderson.
High Bridge, Cobb Co, Ga, changed to Boltonville.
Border, Harrison Co, Texas, changed to Jonesville.
Dallas, Grant Co, Indiana, changed to Jalapa.

New Strasburg, Cook Co, Ill, name changed to Thorn Grove.

Mrd: on Nov 21, by Rev Mr Lanahan, Veneranda E King to Sallie A, 2nd daughter of Thos Bayne, all of Wash City/

Circuit Court of Wash Co, D C-in Chancery. Ludine Baily, Eliz Wells, & Hannah Bargy, vs Jos Carbery & al. This suit is to procure a decree to permit the cmplnts to enter upon the land described in the bill, & elect & designate 2 acres thereof to be set apart as a mill-seat for the use of the cmplnts, as heirs at law of Jesse Baily, deceased. The bill states that the cmplnts are heirs at law of Jesse Bailey; & that Bailey, in his lifetime, to wit, in 1795, made a certain indenture, by which he conveyed to one Abner Cloud the premises therein mentioned & described, [with certain reservations,] known as *White Haven;* that the said Cloud has since died, leaving the dfndnts his heirs at law, & that they or some of them hold the said land; & that Susanna Cloud, one of said dfndnts, resides out of D C. Absent dfndnt to appear in this Court, in person or by solicitor, on or before Mar 25 next. –John A Smith, clerk -Carlisle & Ratcliffe, Solicitors for Cmplnts

SAT NOV 24, 1849
Appointment by the Pres: Chas R Railey, to be Collector of the Customs, Natchez, Miss, vice David C Hutchison, resigned.

The family of Mr Bodisco, [says the Gtwn Advocate,] had letters from him by the last arrival from Europe, in which he states that he will leave for this country in Jan next.

The Hon John C Lewis, late Speaker of the House of Reps of the State of Conn, died at New Haven on Tue night.

Silvester Roberts, paper maker, of North Amherst, Mass, accidentally fell into a caldron of boiling liquid which had been prepared for bleaching purposes, on Nov 12, & was mortally scalded. He died the next day. His age was 41, & he leaves a wife. An only child came to his death in a similar way not long since. –Worcester Spy

Vermont Judiciary: re-elected-Judges of the Supreme Court:
Stephen Joyce, Chief Justice   Danl Kellogg, 3rd Assist Judge
Isaac F Redfield, 1st Assist Judge   Hiland Hall, 4th Assist Judge
Milo L Bennet, 2nd Assist Judge   Luke P Poland, 5th Assist Judge

Elected last week by the Legislature of Georgia:
Geo W Harrison, Sec of State   S J Ray, State Printer
Wm B Tinsley, [Whig,] State   John Boston, Dir State Bank
Treasurer   ___ Sturgis, Solicitor Southern Circuit
Jas R Butts, Surveyor Gen
Ezekiel S Candler, Comptroller Gen

The jury in the case of Wm B Archer, recently tried at Richmond, Va, for forgery, was discharged on Tue, not being able to agree. 11 were for conviction & 1 for acquittal. The prisoner was remanded to jail.

On Monday a daughter of Danl Cameron, of Berlin, together with a daughter of Ira Cameron, of Middlesex, were drowned by falling accidentally through the railroad bridge near the mouth of Dog river, Vt. The girls were cousins, one aged 17, the other 10.

Mrs Eliz Barnett, a lady of Chester Co, Pa, recently died at Guthrieville, Pa, at the advanced age of 111 years. She retained her mental faculties to the last.

Fatal Accident. Mr Nathl Melchoir, a cutler by occupation, having a small shop in Conway's edge tool factory, on Pres st, Balt, was almost instantly killed on Wed by the bursting of a grindstone at which he was at work, a portion of it striking him in the head & facturing his skull.

Mrd: on Nov 22, by Rev Mr Collier, Mr Thos J Boswell to Miss Lucy Augusta Lemon, all of Wash City.

Mrd: on Nov 22, at Northeast, Cecil Co, Md, by Rev J W Arthur, Dr J E Marsh, of Kent Co, Md, to Miss Anne E Beatty, daughter of Wm Beatty, of Cecil Co.

Mrd: on Nov 15, in Winchester, Va, by Rev A H H Brown, Mitchel H Miller, of Wash, D C, to Miss Sarah Clayton, only daughter of the late Jas C Williams.

Mrd: on Nov 20, in Gtwn, D C, by Rev Peter B O'Flanigan, Fielder Suit, of PG Co, Md, to Mary E, eldest daughter of the late Thos O N May, of the former place.

Died: on Nov 23, Mrs Winifred McCarthy, in her 48th year. Her funeral is tomorrow, at 3 o'clock, from her late residence on F st.

Died: on Thu, of consumption, in her 16th year, Sarah Olivia Edmonston, 4th daughter of Franklin Edmonston, of Wash City.

For rent: 5 bedrooms, a parlor, & dining room, with a servant's room, in a good neighborhood. –Abraham Butler, F st, near 15th

By virtue of 2 writs of venditioni exponas: at the suits of E M Morrill, against the goods & chattels, lands & tenements, rights & credits of Jas Tucker: I have seized & taken in execution, lot 13 in square south of square 515, with a 2 story frame house; the same being a leasehold interest. Public sale on Dec 1. –H R Maryman, Constable

For rent: in Gtwn, a 2 story brick house, near Mrs Geo French's, with extensive back bldgs. Inquire of Dr Bohrer, Gay st, Gtwn.

Persons having claims against a balance due from the U S to the estate of Wm Ball, late a private in the Marine Corps, deceased, are to present them at the ofc of the 4th Auditor of the Treasury within 2 months from this date: Nov 23, 1849.

New Orleans Picayune of Nov 16. Explosion of the steamboat **Louisiana**, Capt Cannon, bound for St Louis, just backing out from the wharf at the foot of Gravier st, when the whole of her boilers burst, which resounded throughout the city. A part of the boiler cut a mule in two, killed a horse & the driver of a dray to which they were attached. Men were killed at a distance of 200 yards from the fragments of iron & blocks of wood, which carried death in all directions. Legs, arms, & trunks were scattered over the levee. Bodies were blown as high as 200 feet in the air, & fell in the river. Casualties, so far as we have been able to ascertain:
Killed: Robt Devlin, of Baton Ruge; Mr Gilmer, 2nd mate of **Louisiana**; Capt Edmonston, of St Louis; Andrew Bell, pilot of **Lousiana**; Mrs Robt Moody & child, [Mrs Moody was standing on the guard opposite the ladies' cabin, & was instantly killed;] Mr Roach, deck hand on the steamer **Storm**; Mr Knox, head steward on the **Storm**; a cabin boy on the **Storm**, name unknown; 2 men, names unknown, blown from the **Storm**; John Sullivan, news boy; the coachman of the St Charles Hotel; & several negroes & deck hands of the steamer **Bostona**. 30 bodies have been brought to the 2nd Municipality watchhouse, Baronne st.
Missing: Dr Thos M Williams, of Lafourche; Dr Bloudine, of Poite Coupee; Robt McMackin, clerk of the **Louisiana**; J J Gillespie, of Vicksburg; J Merring, of Cincinnati; Mr Wilson, grocer, of St Louis; Mr Edgar, oversee, of Wash Co, Miss; Sylvester Prescott & Eneas Crafft, of Memphis; Mr King, of the firm of J J Grey & Co, of St Louis; ___ Wolf, newsboy; Mr Elliott, clerk in the firm of Marsh & Ranlett, of this city. Merrick Morris, clerk in the firm of Small & McGill, of this city.
Wounded: Isaac Hait & Mr Rey, badly; S Davis, Mobile; Augustus Fretz; A Bird, planter; Capt Hopkins, of the **Storm**; John Mason, Mr Horrell, of this city; Mr Price, clerk, of the **Bostona**; Harvey W Bickham, Danl Eckerle, Henry Livingston, Isaac Garrison, Hugh McKee, Saml Fox, Wm Welch, Clinton Smith, John Evans, Wm Burke, John Laws, Wm Tucker, Henry Tucker, Jas Matthews, Juan Montreal, Wm Nee/Noe, Jas Welch, Jas Flynn, ___ McCarthy, H Rea, Thos Harrison, Missouri; Fred'k A Wood, Saml Corley, Ky; Crocket Harrison, Missouri. There are between 20 & 30 others whose names we are unable to learn.

MON NOV 26, 1849
The new Oregon appointees, Hon John P Gaines, Govn'r, Hon Wm Strong, Judge, & Geo E Hamilton, Sec, with their families, numbering in all 24, will sail from N Y on Dec 2, in the U S storeship **Supply**. They furnish their own stores for the voyage, the Gov't providing only for their passage.

From the Southern Literary Messenger. The *Natural Bridge* for Sale. By virtue of a decree of the Circuit Superior Court of Law & Chancery for Rockbridge Co, rendered on Sep 16, 1848, in the case of Jos Lackland vs Walter K Cole & others, I shall sell, at public auction, on Dec 3 next, the undivided $2/3^{rd}$s of that famous property known to the world as the *Natural Bridge* of Virginia. N B: I am requested by Col Jesse Wootten, of Henry Co, who is the proprietor of the other third, to say, that he is willing either to sell or lease his interest. He will be present at the sale. -S

Wash Ordinance: 1-Act for the relief of Geo Fosnaught: that $15.56 be paid to him for gravelling 11 st west to Pa ave, as certified by the Com'r of the 2nd Ward.

The New Orleans Delta of Nov 17 contains a list of persons killed, [whose bodies have been found,] some missing, & some wounded by the explosion of the boilers of the steamer **Louisiana**. Killed: Simeon Wolffe, Dr T M Williams, Maj Edmondson, Capt Rensaler Becker, Edw Hurlburt, Dr E J Marsh, E Cresswell, Peter Welsh, Evan Knox, Levi Prescott, Wm Brown, Richd Kelly, Andrew Bell, R Pell, Robt Devlin, John Sullivan, Alfred Watson, W C Read, Jos Chesman, Jacob N Craft, Dennis Abbott, John Handerlan, J H Myers, Edw Leyster, John Kelly, John Long, Wm Riley, Mr Simmons, Mr McMachin, W C Edgar, W H Graves. Missing: Mr Barrelle, John Deane, Marritt Morris, J Merring, J I Gillespie, Mr Wilson, Mr Edgar, Dr Beinville, John S Elliott, Jas Woods, Mr Champ, Jas Atkinson, Wm Green, Mr King, Lester Cottells.

Mr Kellogg is at present, in Balt, engaged by the request of the Balt bar, on a full length likeness of Chief Justice Taney. The back-ground of the picture will exhibit a view of the Supreme Court Chamber in the Capitol.

Jas Seering, a laborer in Hoe's factory in Sheriff st, N Y, while grinding a tool on one of the grindstones on Sat, had the fingers of his left hand caught between the stone & rest, & 3 of his fingers were ground off before the stone could be stopped.

Chas A Synder, a carpenter & worthy citizen, was shot dead at Phil last Fri, as he was passing along Girard ave, below 8th st, on his way home. It is believed to have been accidental. Three black men, with guns, seen at a distance, are presumed to have been firing at a mark.

On Fri, Mr Wm McCullum, son of Mr Jas McCullum, & that gentleman's partner in the White Lead & Shot Manufactory, at Saugerties, N Y, fell, by some unexplained accident, into the river, was carried off by the current & drowned. His body had not yet been discovered. He bore an excellent character.

The jury in the case of John Dunn, tried at Hoboken for the murder of his wife in July last, have found him guilty of murder in the 2nd degree. He was sentenced to 20 years hard labor in the State Prison of N Y.

Mrd: on Nov 20, by Rev Thos B Atkinson, D D, John D Gluck, of the U S Coast Survey, to H Mary, daughter of John H Duvall, of Balt.

Died: on Nov 11, in Wash City, Mr Jas Rollow, in his 21st year, formerly of Fredericksburg, Va.

Valuable business stand for sale: being the house & lot on Pa ave, next to the Odon bldg; lower story occupied by Mr Comly as a fancy store, & the 2nd story by Mr Throop, engraver. –Stanislaus Murray, or H H Dent

For rent: a double 2 story furnished house, now occupied by Capt Sawyer, U S Navy, Pa ave, near the West Market, 1st Ward. Inquire on the premises.

TUE NOV 27, 1849
In Chancery: Albert F Yerby & Adonis Yerby, cmplnts, against Caroline Lombardi, admx of Francis Lombardi, & Chas G Lombardi, & Laura Lombardi, his heirs at law, & Michl A Guista & Nicholas Callan, dfndnts. The parties above named, & the creditors of the late Francis Lombardi, are to attend at my ofc, in City Hall, Wash, on Dec 4, when I shall state an account of the personal estate of said Lombardi.
–W Redin, Auditor

We regret to learn that Hon Nathan F Dixon, member of Congress elect from R I, has resigned his seat in the House of Reps of R I.

Govn'r Ramsay, with the consent of the Council, has made the following appointments for the Territory of Minnesota: 1-Lorenzo Babcock, to be Atty Gen for the Territory. 2-Jonathan E McKusick, to be Auditor of Public Accounts. 3-Calvin A Tuttle, to be the Territorial Treasurer

A monument is about to be erected at New Haven, in the rear of the Centre Church, over the remains of Col John Dixwell, one of the judges who caused King Chas I to be condemned & executed. The remains were exhumed on Thu last & the skeleton was found in a tolerable state of preservation. The bones were put into a small box partly filled with earth, which was placed in the centre of the plot over which the monument is to stand. It is erected by Mr Dixwell, of Boston, a descendant of the Judge-the city of New Haven having given him permission to erect it where the body was interred, now the Public Green. Mr Dixwell died in 1668, at the age of 82.

Rt Hon Jas Grattan, eldest son of the late Henry Grattan, the great Irish orator & patriot, has sold out his Irish property, & intends settling in Va, in which State he has purchased 5,000 acres of land.

Mrd: on Nov 21, in the Catholic Church, at Winchester, Va, by Rev Mr Plunket, Nathan Loughborough to Miss Anna Henry Rose, youngest daughter of the late Robt H Rose.

Died: yesterday, aged 14 months, Thos H, 2nd son of John Randall & Louisa Smith Hagner, & grandson of Peter Hagner, of Wash City.

Circuit Court of Wash Co, D C-in Chancery. Geo Lowry, cmplnt, against Ann E Kervand, widow of Lazare Kervand, & Ann Louisa Kervand, Isabel Kervand, & J L Kervand, heirs at law, dfndnts. Wm Redin, Trustee, reports that he sold *Woodley*, before called *Pretty Prospect*, on heights above Gtwn, formerly the residence of P B Key, & now occupied by Mrs Kervand, & that the part sold consists of the dwlg house & out-bldgs, & 101 acres & 9 perches of land, attached to & surrounding the said dwlg-house & out-bldgs, as shown by the survey & plot of Lewis Carbery, County Surveyor, filed in the above cause: Lorenzo Thomas was the highest bidder & became purchaser at $50 per acre, $5,058.43; terms of sale complied with. –Jno A Smith, clerk

Valuable Loudoun lands for sale: decree of the Circuit Superior Court of Law & Chancery, for Loudoun Co, Va, pronounced on Oct 29, 1849, in the case of Saml Campbell & Co, vs Burr P Noland, adm with the will annexed of Geo Cuthbert Powell, deceased, & others, I will offer for sale, at public auction, on Dec 24, the following real property, belonging to the estate of the said deceased, viz: 1-**The** *Hill Farm*, in said county, adjoining the town of Middleburg, containing 460 acres; the mansion house is of brick, 2 stories high, & numerous out-bldgs. This farm is encumbered by the life estate of Mrs Catharine Powell in the mansion house & 40 acres of the adjoining land, with the privilege of fuel & fencing timber from the most convenient woodland of the estate, & will be sold subject to that incumbrance. I am authorized to sell the land entire. Also: 2 small houses & lots in Middleburg, now occupied by B P Noland & Geo W Shurman. Also, an undivided half of certain ground rents in Middleburg, subject to Mrs Catharine Powell's life estate in the same. These rents are worth annually about $200. –B P Noland, adm, with will annexed, of G C Powell, deceased.

$50 reward for runaway negro woman Jane Brent, about 22 years of age. She was of the number who ran off some time back & were captured aboard the boat **Pearl**. She left the place at which she was hired on Sat last. –J H Goddard, for the owner

By virtue of a writ of venditioni exponas, at the suit of Edw Rice, against the goods & chattels, lands & tenements, rights & credits of Mrs R King & Jas Bottomley: I have seized & taken lot 19 in square 566, with the improvements thereon; & will expose the same to public sale on Dec 27, in front of said lot & square. –H R Maryman, Cnstble

WED NOV 28, 1849
Public Records consumed. On Nov 8, the Court House of the parish of Claiborne [at Athens, La,] was consumed by fire, together with all the public records since 1828, embracing mortgages, marriages, sales, conveyances, judgments, & the private papers of Wm C Cope, the clerk of the District Court. Geo W Peets, atty at law, who kept his ofc there, was also a sufferer.

Wash Corp: 1-Cmte of Claims: asked to be discharged from the further consideration of the ptn of John M Kraft. 2-Ptn of Wm Rupp: referred to the Cmte of Claims. 3-Act for the relief of Jas Crutchett: referred to the Cmte of Claims. 4-Act for the relief of John Magar; relief of J F Wollard; & relief of J M Wright: severally referred to the Cmte on Police. 5-Payment of claim of Morris Holloran: referred to the Cmte on Improvements. 6-Ptn of John West for the remission of a fine; ptn of Jas Davis, for remission of a fine: both referred to the Cmte of Claims. 7-Bill for the relief of J E W Thompson: reported the same, & the amendment was agreed to. 8-Bill for the relief of Wm Cammack: passed. 9-Cmte of Claims: bill for the relief of Wm Clarbaugh, agent for Wm Winn: passed.

Circuit Court of Wash Co, D C-in Chancery. Henry Naylor, cmplnt, vs the widow & heirs-at-law of Edw W Clarke & others, dfndnts. E J Middleton, trustee in the above cause, reported to the Court that he had sold all that part of lot 11 in square 688, in Wash City, which he was authorized to sell, & Henry Naylor was the purchaser thereof, being the highest bidder therefore, at the sum of $810. –Jno A Smith, clerk

New Post ofcs for the week ending Nov 24, 1849:

Ofc	County, State	Postmaster:
North Elba	Essex, N Y	Dillon C Osgood
Mauton	Providence, R I	Wm S King
Robeson	Berks, Pa	John B Seidel
North West Mines	Houghton, Mich	D D Rockway
Peppers' Ferry	Montg, Va	Jesse Pepper
Clinch River	Russell, Va	Saml H Nash
Miami	Miami, Fa	Alexander Blake
Grant	Grant, _a	Jos W Baldwin
Rogersville	Henry, _a	Jabish Luallin
Kossuth	Boone, Ill	Asa H Manley
Piasa	Macoupin, Ill	Chas Falley
Troy Mills	Fulton, Ill	Wm Moore
Beaufort	Franklin, Mo	Wm M Simmons
Farmington	Jefferson, Wis	D M Aspinwall
Port Hope	Columbia, Wis	Jonathan Whitney
Willow River	St Croix, Wis	Philip Aldrich
Lynnville	Jasper, Iowa	Danl Stevens
Home	Van Buren, Iowa	Edw Hilles
Sugar Grove	Poweshiek, Iowa	N J Latimer

Names changed:
Bovina Centre, Dela Co, N Y, changed to Brushland.
South Chili, Monroe Co, N Y, changed to Clifton.
East Branch, Dela Co, N Y, changed to Havard.
Mount Seir, Mecklenburgh Co, N Y, changed to Mount Moriah.
Barnett's Creek, Ohio Co, Ky, changed to Buford.
Ebele, Putnam Co, Indiana, changed to Nicholsonville.
Linn, Adams Co, Indiana, changed to Linn Grove.
Petersburgh, Boone Co, Mo, changed to Burbunton.

Henry, son of Amos Dodge, of Albany, ran a pin into his arm above the elbow on Mon; on Tue he became ill, & on Wed he died.

The Presbyterian Church at Bethesda, Montg Co, Md, Rev R A Smith, Pastor, was entirely destroyed by fire on Nov 23. The fire caught accidentally upon the roof.

Hector Moore, a member of the St Louis bar, has been convicted at Memphis, Tenn, of the abduction of a negro, & sentenced to the penitentiary for 5 years.

Horace Jennison, of Newton, Mass, has obtained a verdict of $2,000 damages in a suit of slander against Wm White, of Watertown. The slander was an accusation of stealing tripe.

The steam saw mill of Col G B Locke, near Memphis, Tenn, was destroyed by fire on Nov 13, with the adjoining bldg. Loss about $15,000, insurance $4,000.

Two accomplished & experienced counterfeiters, Nelson Rector & Smith A Ellis, have been arrested in Huron Co, Ohio. They are now in Columbus jail.

Mrd: Nov 25, by Rev Mr Hodges, Chas N Garner to Lucretia A Cook, all of Wash City.

Died: on Nov 26, of paralysis, Miss Susan G Beall, in her 70th year. Her funeral is this morning, at 11 o'clock, at her late residence.

THU NOV 29, 1849
The Court-house at Quincy, Fla, was destroyed by fire on Nov 12, & all records not reclaimed by their owners, were destroyed.

A Naval Court-Martial was convened on Tue, on board the U S ship **Pennsylvania**, for the trial of 4 men attached to the U S sloop-of-war **Germantown**, who are charged with assaulting & beating an ofcr. The court is composed of the following ofcrs: Cmder John L Saunders, Pres; Cmders D G Farragut, T Aloysius Dornin, & R B Cunningham, & Lts John A Davis, Richd L Page, & Chas H Poor, members. Lt A Sinclair, Judge Advocate. –Norfolk Beacon

The Hon Thos H Blake died yesterday, at Cincinnati, after a short illness, which commenced on his return from a recent visit to Wash City. Col Blake was born in Md, but was reared in this District. 30 years ago he emigrated to Indiana, where he entered into the practice of the law & obtained considerable distinction.

Petersburg Intelligencer mentions the death of Mr Dandridge Spotswood, in his 64th year, who had been a resident there for about 45 years, having removed there from Orange Co. If we are not mistaken, he was a descendant of Govn'r Spotswood, who, according to Mr Chas Campbell's History of Va, made the first complete discovery of a passage over the Blue Ridge mountains, then a most difficult one, instituted the Tramontane Order, whose motto was Sic juvat transcendere montes, whose badge was a golden horseshoe. Mr Dandridge Spotswood's widow was a daughter of the famous Peter Franciso, whose life & adventures are so well known.

Col H L Scott, of Newton Co, has been appointed Assist Superintendent for the removal of the Choctaws, in the place of Rev T C Stewart, of Pontotoc. There are about 2,500 of this tribe still lingering in Mississippi, to the great injury of themselves & the annoyance & discomfort of their white neighbors. –Jackson [Miss] Southron

Died: yesterday, in Wash City, after a short illness, Mary Ann, aged 5 years, 2 months & 17 days, daughter of Dr Jos & Catharine Z Borrows. Her funeral is this afternoon at 3 o'clock, from the residence of her father on E, between 9th & 10th sts.

Furnished rooms for rent: on 12th st, between C & D sts. –M E Fowler

Boarding: Mrs Willis, corner of F & 13th sts.

Marshal's sale: writ of fieri facias: I shall expose to sale, for cash, on Dec 8, at the auction store of Edw C & G F Dyer, on Pa ave, the following goods & chattels: sundry materials-velvet, calico, netting, serge, & plaid cloth; woolen caps, 2 shawls, & 1 trunk, seized & taken as the property of John & Geo F Allen, & sold to satisfy Judicials 8, to Oct term, 1849, in favor of Robt Patterson & Wm C Patterson. –Robt Wallace, late Marshal of D C. -Edw C & G F Dyer

Constable's sale: by virtue of 3 writs of fieri facias; at the suit of Haslup & Weeden, against the goods & chattels of John Connor: sale on Dec 4, of one 4 wheeled carryall. -J F Wollard, Constable

For sale, or city property taken in part: **Hygeian Hall**, a snug Farm in Va, containing 85 acres; with a new barn, about 5 miles from Washington. Address Richd B Lloyd, Alexandria, Va. I have a bright mulatto boy, aged 16 years, pock-marked, light curly hair, called John Clavoe, strolling about the city. To any one taking him up I will give $10.

SAT DEC 1, 1849
Lt John Y Bicknell, of the U S Dragoons, died at Maryville, Tenn, on Nov 11. He participated in nearly all the battles in Mexico.

Commission of claims against Mexico: 1-Memorial of Clement Saracina, of Santa Fe Co, New Mexico, claiming as due to him, a citizen of the U S from the Republic of Mexico, of which he was then a citizen, $560.37. 2-Memorial of Francisco Saracina, of Santa Fe Co, New Mexico, claiming, on the same grounds as above, $2,447.87. 3-Memorial of Don Antonio Sandoval, of the same place, claiming, upon the same grounds, $27,546. The Board came to the opinion that the said claims are not embraced within the provisions of the treaty of Feb 2, 1848, between the U S & Mexico. Same were rejected.
4-Memorial of Terry & Angus, as amemded, claiming for destruction of property at the siege of Puebla. 5-Memorial of Geo A Gardiner, claiming for expulsion from his mines at San Luis Potosi. 6-Memorial of John C Jones, claiming for losses consequent upon the seizure & detention of schnr **Loriat**, was examined & received so far as it sets forth the claim of Jones in his own right, but rejected so far as the memorial joins a claim for personal injuries of another.

Rev J M P Atkinson, of Warrenton, Va, has received a call from the Bridge st Presbyterian Church of Gtwn, to become its Pastor, & it is probable he will accept.

Gen Thos Holland, of Mobile, was shot dead a day or two ago by J H McClintock, his clerk. The cause was jealousy. The murderer surrendered himself.

Mrd: on Nov 29, in Wash City, at the residence of John L Smith, by Rev Mr Gilliss, Her. H Heath, of Mich, & Anna Rosalba S Sheppard, of Wash.

Mrd: on Nov 26, in Phil, by Rev Dr Decachet, Elisha Riggs, jr, of Wash City, to Miss Mary Boswell, of Lexington, Ky.

Mrd: on Nov 21, in Richmond, by Rev M D Hoge, Mr Edw Martin to Miss Marie Vass, daughter of Jas C Vass, all of Richmond, Va.

The schnr **Diamond**, owned by Messrs W T Richmond & Co, commanded by Capt Stone, clears today for New Orleans & the West Indies, by way of the Illinois & Michigan canal & Mississippi river. The canal locks would admit her, & leave 4 inches to spare. This will be the first lake & ocean vessel ever passed over our canal, & settles the question as to our connexion with the ocean, even if old mother England should refuse the free navigation of the St Lawrence. –Chicago Journal

Trustee's sale of valuable property: on Dec 10, by deed of trust recorded in Liber W B 138, folios 157 thru 160, Land Records of Wash Co, D C: sale of all that part or parcel of lots 2 & 3 in square 322, designated as lots C, D, & E, of the subdivision made by John McClelland of said lots with the improvements. –J G Berret, trustee
-Edw C & G F Dyer

MON DEC 3, 1849
Boston, Dec 1. Last evening the mutilated remains of a body, supposed to be those of Dr Parkman, were found under the Medical College, where he was last seen alive. Prof Webster, of the College, was arrested upon suspicion of having committed the murder, & was lodged in jail. The whole affair is about to undergo a rigid investigation. [Dec 5th newspaper: the jaw & teeth which were found in Dr Webster's grate have been identified as those of Dr Parkman by his dentist who had operated upon them, & the family has claimed the remains & are preparing to inter them.] [Dec 10th newspaper: Dr Parkman's property is estimated about half a million. He was a large owner of real estate, making his collections himself. He bestowed much charity in an unostentatious way.]

Chas Mansfield, of Liverpool, & John Gallagher, of Phil, were drowned at Wilmington, N C, near Big Island, on Wed last, from on board the schnr **Boston**, of Yarmouth, Mass, bound to Gtwn & Alexandria, with a load of lumber. Mansfield was knocked overboard, by the fore-boom, in jibing, & Gallagher took a boat to rescue him. The boat capsized, & both sank before further assistance could be rendered.

Wash City Ordinances: 1-Act for the relief of Wm Clabaugh, agent for Wm Winn: to be paid $50, that being the value of a horse injured in passing over the bridge across Rock Creek, at K st north. 2-Act for the relief of Chas Stewart: sum of $23.27 be paid to Stewart for the elevation of the curb line on square 378.

Gen Duncan L Clinch, formerly of the U S Army, & subsequently a Rep in Congress from Georgia, died at Macon, on 28th ult, after an illness of 9 days. A braver soldier or a nobler hearted man it has never been our good fortune to know. [Dec 6th newspaper: to his amiable family his loss will be absolutely irreparable. His spotless fame is their best legacy.]

John Price, who murdered Geo W Campbell in May last, & whose trial was removed from Balt to Anne Arundel Co, has been found guilty of murder in the 2nd degree, & was sentenced by the Court to the penitentiary for 14½ years.

Niagara Falls, Nov 27. Yesterday a young woman of about 35 years, with her 2 sons, ages 4 & 6 years old, came by the train of cars, & took a room at the Eagle Hotel. She called for writing material & was not heard from until the next morning, when the boys rang the bell asking for their mother. Letters were on the table, one directed to Maj Miller, U S Army, one to Hom John Norvell, Detroit, Mich, & another to the proprietor of the Eagle Hotel; also the ringlets of one side of her head, her gold watch, 2 trunks of clothing, a silk purse with gold & silver coins, & a wedding ring. The children said they had come from Winchester, Va, & their father was in Florida. Her black crape shawl was found tied to the railing of the bridge to let her down upon the pier, to indicate to those who should look for her that her mind was made up for the fearful leap. Her father has been telegraphed, & the children have been kindly taken charge of by Hon Augustus S Porter. Copy of the letter addressed by Mrs Miller to Mr White, of the Eagle Hotel. My mind is made up. I have no wish to live any longer. I shall go where my body will never be recovered. No one shall gaze on my mangled remains. Please take care of my two little boys till they can be sent to Detroit, where their grandparents reside. They are the sons of Maj Miller, of the army, now in Florida, & grandsons of Hon John Norvell, Detroit, Mich. Please forward my letters & protect my children till some of their relatives come for them. Mrs J G Miller
Referring to the above, we find the following in the Buffalo Commercial Adv: It is reported that a lady here, answering to the description of Mrs Miller, left this city for the East in the express train this morning, & that there are circumstances leading to the belief that the apparent evidences of suicide are only *apparent*. Her friends will undoubtedly investigate the matter, & until they ascertain something which they desire to be communicated to the public, we shall do, as we would have others do if we were similarly situated, say nothing on the subject.
The Buffalo Republic confirms the intimation of the Commercial Adv: that the catastrophe is one of frailty, & not of self murder. It states that the lady who used the above signature returned to that city & departed thence in company with a gentleman who registered his name at one of the hotels as Henry Blakemer, of Phil.
[Dec 5th newspaper: We learn from the Rochester American of Sat, that Mrs Miller, who took care to have herself reported as having jumped over Niagara Falls on Mon week, has been arrested at Syracuse. She was running away with a young man named Blackmer, & had contrived the suicide to cover her retreat.]

Orphans Court of Wash Co, D C. Letters testamentary on the personal estate of Geo Sweeny, late of said county, deceased. –H B Sweeny, exc

Orphans Court of Wash Co, D C. Letters of administration on the personal estate of Wm Miller, late of Wash Co, deceased. –Mary Miller, admx

U S Patent Ofc, Dec 1, 1849. Ptn of Nathan Scholfield, of Norwich, Conn, praying for an extension of a patent granted to him for an improvement in Water-wheel & Steam Engine Regulator for 7 years from the expiration of said patent, which takes place on May 17, 1850. –Thos Ewbank, Com'r of Patents

$5 reward for the return of a lost Market Pocket, made of bedticking, containing a bead purse & money. Mgt Egelston, living on N Y ave, between 6th & 7th sts.

Mr Jas Montgomery, poet, completed his 78th year on Sunday week, & to commemorate the event, to raise a monument to his fame, his friends & neighbors, Mr & Mrs Saml Mitchell, & other residents at the Mount, invited Mr Montgomery, on Sat last, to plant a tree in the grounds belonging to that property. A purple beech was selected. Mr Montgomery acknowledged the compliment. –Sheffield [England] Independent

Capt E T Dustin, of Louisville, cmder of the steamer **Bostona**, died at New Orleans on Thu week from the wounds he received by the explosion of the steamer **Louisiana**.

On Nov 18, Mr Seaborn Jones, in his 40th year, came to his death, when his 12 year old son, stepped out of his house into the yard to shoot off his gun, & accidentally shot his father, killing him almost instantly. –Savannah Georgian

Mrd: on Nov 28, in N Y, at the city residence of Maj Gen Scott, Brevet Maj Henry L Scott, of the 4th Infty, & A D C, to Cornelia, daughter of Maj Gen Scott.

Mrd: on Nov 9, in N Y, by Rev T Jarvis Carter, J Watson Webb, Editor of the Courier & Enquirer, to Laura Virginia, daughter of Jacob Cram, of N Y.

Died: on Nov 1, on board the steamer **Franklin**, from Galena, Ill, to St Paul, Minn, in his 34th year, David Lambert, of N Y, for some years a resident of Wash City holding ofc under Gov't. He has left a wife & interesting boy in his 6th year to mourn his loss.

Ladies with letters in the Post Ofc, Wash, Dec 1, Wash, D C.

Andrews, Mrs Geo	Fraser, Mrs Re M	Johnson, Miss Eme
Arny, Mrs D S	Fields, Mrs R	Jones, Miss Nancy
Bestdering, Mrs A	Frazure, Mrs Sarah	Latruit, Mrs El'h
Brook, Miss Brena	Gardner, Ann	Lubey, Mrs Ellen
Brown, Miss Cath	Gardner, Miss El'h	Lane, Mrs Ellen
Burton, Mrs Clar	Goods, Mrs Mary	Lucas, Mrs Jemima
Branan, Mrs Eliz	Golden, Miss V	Lewis, Mrs Mary
Bassett, Mrs Eliza	Grant, Miss Louisa L	Miller, Mrs Ann
Barrett, Miss Em A	Hunt, Mrs Chas	Mulvey, Miss Betsy
Brooks, Miss A R	Hall, Miss Cornelia	Myer, Miss Con W
Bennett, Mrs Rose	Holsworth, Mrs	Madison, Mrs Jas
Bonnycastle, Miss N	Heath, Miss Eliza A	Murphy, Mrs H
Bowling, Miss M E	Hogg, Miss Jane	Mullikin, Mrs M
Burton, Miss Sarah	Hardia, Mrs Jos'e	McNerney, Miss E
Carter, Mrs Ann	Hill, Miss Marg	McCarty, Mrs Eliza
Conley, Mrs Jane	Hoban, Miss Mary	Nevin, Miss Eleanor
Callahan, Mary	Haymen, Mrs Nan	Nelson, Miss Marg't
Edwards, Ellen R	Higgins, Mrs Sarah	O'Brien, Mrs M-2
Eyre, Miss Sarah	Harris, Mrs S Jane	Page, Mrs B
Forbes, Mrs Ann M	Hurly, Miss Virginia	Proctor, Mrs July A
Francis, Mrs Ele'r	Harding, Mrs W W	Perry, Miss Jane M
Fitzhugh, Mrs Jane	Hannah, Miss Louisa	Posey, Miss Mar A
Forrest, Mrs Jane	Johnson, Mrs El'th	Riley, Miss El'h W

Rich, Mrs Eliz
Robinson, Mrs Elh
Reis, Louisa
Ready, Mrs Mouru
Read, Miss Rachael
Richardson, Mrs S A
Suter, Miss Ann U
Sherman, Miss Jane
Smith, Mrs Martha
Seely, Mrs Sarah A
Sanford, Miss Mary
Scott, Mrs M W

Smith, Mrs Ra A
Scott, Mrs Rebecca
Smith, Mrs Isaac C
Taylor, Mrs El's A
Taylor, Levi H
Taylor, Miss Lucin
Turner, Miss M
Throckmorton, Mrs Mary
Ward, Mrs Anna
Webster, Mrs
Washington, Mrs C

Wood, Mrs El'th
Walker, Mrs El'th
Wilson, Miss Har't
Wadsworth, Mrs H N
Whaley, Miss M A
Walsh, Mrs Lt J C
West, Mrs Mary A
Williams, Miss Ma
Walter, Priscilla
Willard, Mrs Sarah
Young, Miss Marg
-Wm H Bradley, P M

TUE DEC 4, 1849
Mr Wm Hampton, a much esteemed citizen of Jessamine Co, Ky, was drowned in the Ky river a few days since. He had plunged into the river to save a negro boy, but was seized by the drowning person & both drowned.

A few days since, the 2½ year old daughter of Jas Dawson, N Y C, tipped over hot tea at the table, & was so severely scalded that she died the same night.

Fatality among the sons of the late W Thompson, of New Haven, who visited Calif within the past year. 3 sons have perished within the past 4 months. Wm died on the route from Vera Cruz to the Pacific. Walter & Webster were both seized with a fever of the climate, from exposure when their small boat overturned in the San Francisco Bay. Walter died after a day's illness; his brother continued ill, & was most of the time deranged. While in this condition, he committed suicide on Sep 31. –St Louis Repub

Commission on Claims against Mexico: Dec 3, 1849. 1-The Board took up the case of Mrs Mgt Meade, widow of & sole excx of the late Richd W Meade: postponed it for the present. 2-Mr Geo Bowdoin, atty of Francis del Hoyo, in the matter of the claim of Francisco Aranas, now before this Board as one of the cases before the commission of 1839, left undecided by the umpire: further time needed for procuring certain proofs needful to his case, be given.

Criminal Court-Wash: gentlemen summoned to serve on the Grand Inquest:
Roger C Weightman, Foreman

Chas K Gardner
David English
Cahs H Wiltberger
Rezin Arnold
G C Grammer
C L Coltman
W B Scott
Lemuel J Middleton

Benj K Morsell
John Underwood
Geo M Kendall
Robt M Coombs
Henry Holt
John H King
W D Murdock
Thos Donoho

Bladen Forrest
John G Robinson
Saml Cropley
Robt Keyworth
Alex'r Ray
John T Sullivan
Theodore Wheeler

Died: on Oct 30, at Cape Girardeau, Mo, in her 22nd year, Miss Eliz Gantt, of Moulton, Ala, daughter of the late Dr Edw Gantt, who emigrated from PG Co, Md, many years ago.

Died: on Nov 18, on board the steamboat **Highland Mary**, on her trip from *Fort Snelling* to this city, after a short & severe illness, aged 33 years, Capt Leonidas Wetmore, of the 6th Regt of U S Infty. The deceased return home from Mexico in very bad health, from disease contracted in that country, & had not entirely recovered. He was stationed at *Fort Snelling*, on the Upper Mississippi, & was on his way to join his relatives in this city, on furlough to recruit his health, when he was attacked on the boat & died soon afterwards. The deceased was in several engagements with the Indians in the Florida war, & participated in the battles of Mexico; was at the storming of Vera Cruz, at Cerro Gordo, & in several hard-fought battles before the city of Mexico, at the battles of Churubusco, Molino del Rey, & San Antonio. He was escorted to the grave by several of his brother ofcrs, & his relatives & friends of this city. –St Louis paper

Mrs Ann H Clark's Fashionable Millinery: store, Bridge st, Gtwn. [Ad]

WED DEC 5, 1849
A CARD. Peter H Green, formerly a citizen of Mobile, recently a resident of Louisiana, presents himself to the members of the House of Reps as a candidate for the ofc of Sgt-at-Arms. Wash, Dec 5, 1849

Miss E Kimberly announces that she will read Shakespeare's play of Hamlet, on Dec 5, in Odd Fellows' Hall, 7th st. Tickets-$1.

Pleasant rooms, with best board, at Miss Gwynn's, *Smith's Row*, 1st st, Gtwn.

Rooms: 2 bedrooms & a parlor, furnished, for gentlemen only, on P ave, near 6th st. Inquire of Mrs Jas Davis.

Mrs Beveridge, boarding-house, Pa ave, between 4½ & 3rd sts: moderate terms.

Furnished apts for rent: on E st, between 9th & 10th sts. Mrs C Buckingham

Information received at the War Dept that Capt Marcy, of the 5th Infty, arrived at *Fort Washeia* on Nov 6 last, a little in advance of his command, which had escorted to Santa Fe a party of Arkansas emigrants en route for Calif. He reported that his men were all well, but that one of his ofcrs, Lt Montgomery P Harrison, [grandson of the late Pres of that name] had been killed by Indians near the Colorado river, in Texas, on Oct 7 last. He had ridden out from camp that day alone, to ascertain the proper road. No Indian signs had previously been seen, & no Indians were supposed to be near. He was found pierced in many places with arrows, & shot, as is supposed, with his own pistol. This young ofcr had many friends in Wash, & will mourn his untimely end.

Orphans Court of Wash Co, D C. Letters of administration on the personal estate of Wm Murphy, late of said county, deceased. –John Murphy, adm

Baton Rouge, La, late fire made a clean sweep of the properties of A Matta, R Beal & Son, J Huguet, J Mansker, T Pendergast, J & L Florence, J Turnis, J Garvin, A Theriot, John L Wolff, P Foley, Mrs Foster, R & F Sans, J McCalop, E F Phillipe, F Vincent, L Grandpre, & S Bear. The exertions of the soldiers, stationed at Baton Rouge, to arrest the progress of the flames, were most praiseworthy & untiring.

Wm Woodward has been convicted at Norfolk for forgery, & sentenced to the penitentiary for 2 years. There are still 79 distinct charges against the prisoner, of which the Grand Jury have found [including the one just disposed of] true bills.

Wash Corp: 1-Ptn from Jas F Haliday & others, in relation to a soap factory which is about to be established near 11th & C sts & Pa ave: referred to the Cmte on Police. 2-Acts for the relief of J F Wollard; of J M Wright, & of John Magar: passed. 3-Act for the relief of Robt Earle; & relief of Edw H Edelin: rejected.

Public sale: the subscriber offers his residence, 3 miles from Upper Marlboro, PG Co, Md, for sale: at public auction, on Dec 20: the whole of his personal property, consisting of between 30 & 40 negroes, almost all healthy & young. Also, a large lot of horses, cattle, tobacco, & all household & kitchen furniture. I intend removing out of the State. My house & lot in the town of Upper Marlboro is also for sale. This is the property formerly owned by Gov Pratt, & consists of a large brick dwlg house, covered with slate. –Thos W Clagett

Orphans Court of Wash Co, D C. Letters of administration on the personal estate of John Wilson, late of said county, deceased. –Wm Clark, adm

Circuit Court of Wash Co, D C: sitting in Equity. The U S vs Hosea H Smith & John Y Bryant. This case charges that the dfndnt Smith is indebted to the cmplnts in the sum of $1,000; that he is in insolvent circumstances; & that moneys not less than $100 nor more than $150, belonging to or claimed by him, are in the hands of the dfndnt Bryant. The bill prays a discovery of the amount of money belonging to or claimed by the dfndnt Smith, which came into the hands of the dfndnt Bryant, & of the facts under which it so came into his hands, & that such money which is now before decree may be in his hands, may be decreed to be applied to the discharge of the debt due by said Smith to the cmplnts; & that Bryant may be enjoined from paying out, & Smith from transferring, said moneys; & for further relief. Hosea H Smith resides out of D C. He is to appear before this Court, in person or by solicitor, on or before Apr 6 next.
–Jno A Smith, clerk

Same as above: The U S vs Hosea H Smith & Enoch Tucker. Moneys not less than $900 nor more than $1,000, belonging to or claimed by him are in the hands of the dfndnt Enoch Tucker. Hosea H Smith resides out of D C. He is to appear before this Court, in person or by solicitor, on or before Apr 6 next. –Jno A Smith, clerk

Mrd: on Nov 22, by Rev Mr Smith, Mr Henry J Hoyle to Miss Rebecca C Kurtz, both of Wash Co, D C.

Mrd: on Nov 29, in Gtwn, by Rev Mr Tillinghast, Mr Wm H Kurtz to Miss Susan R Cartwright, both of Wash Co, D C.

Mrd: on Dec 3, by Rev Mr Steele, Mr Geo K Jacobs, of Wash City, to Miss Louisa Nicholson, of Manchester, N H.

The late Mrs Govn'r Carroll, of Md: it was on the Sabbath, when the messenger of death summoned the subject of this notice. The wife & mother, has fallen sorrowfully, but not hopelessly. [No death date given-current item.]

For rent: new house, corner of H & 15th sts. Apply to De Chas S Frailey, of the Gen Land Ofc.

I will offer at public sale for cash on Dec 13, the personal property of Susan G Beall, at her residence, near the Anacostia Bridge, such as horses, cattle, sheep, corn, provender, & household & kitchen furniture, & many other articles. –Fielder Magruder

Note lost: payable Dec 27, given to Geo H Plant by Wm Walker, for $122. Payment has been stopped. Return to Alfred Richards, at the Brick Press, near the Eastern Branch.

Teacher wanted: at the upper Marlborough Academy: salary is $350 per annum. No one need apply except an experienced & professional teacher. –Jno B Brooke, Pres of the Board of Trustees of U M A.

$10 reward for return of lost pocket-book, containing about $35. Owner's name, R C Barton, & his license, with other papers, was in the book.

THU DEC 6, 1849
Chancery sale of valuable & eligibly situated house & lot. By decree of the Circuit Court of Wash Co, D C, sitting in Chancery: in the cause of Albert T & Adonis L Yerby vs Caroline Lombardi, widow of & admx, & Chas G & Laura C Lombardi, infants & heirs-at-law of Francis Lombardi, deceased, & others, I shall proceed to sell on Jan 3, on the premises, at public sale, all those 2 parts of lot 6 in square 348, in Wash City, on 11th st, near Pa ave, with new 2 story brick house & improvements thereon, of which said Francis Lombardi died seized & possessed, subject, to the lien created by a certain deed of trust from said Francis Lombardi & Caroline Lombardi, his wife, dated May 29, 1848, to Nicholas Callan, trustee, to secure the payment of $1,000 & interest, on which said sum of $1,000 there is an unexpired credit of 9 years from May 29, 1849, interest payable quarterly. If the terms of sale are not complied with in 3 days after the sale, the right to resell, at the cost & risk of the purchaser, is reserved. –Chas S Wallach, trustee -C W Boteler, auctioneer

Mrd: on Tue, by Rev John C Smith, Mr John H Thorn to Miss Mgt Espey, all of Wash City.

Mrd: on Dec 2, by Rev Mr Marks, Mr John Thos Hurley to Miss Cenia Taylor, of Wash City.

Mrd: on Dec 3, by Rev Jas Laurie, D D, Mr Jas Henning, of Gtwn, to Miss Ellen Graham, of Wash City.

Circuit Court of Wash Co, D C-in Chancery. John Withers, vs Jas Withers, Sarah Bayne, Edw F Tabb & Kitty Ann Tabb his wife, Allen C Hammond & Sarah Eliza his wife, Wm D Cunningham, Saml O Cunningham, Jas L Cunningham, John C Payne & Mary D his wife, John Long, Jas Anderson & Eliz his wife, Sarah Long, Abraham D Long, Mary Mellairn, Robt Merritt, Sarah Ann Mellairn, Eliz Winning, Benj Merritt, & Richd Wallach, exc of Jas Long, deceased, dfndnts. Jas Long, in his lifetime, being indebted to the cmplnt in a large sum of money, for the purchase money of lots A, B, & D, in the subdivision of lot 6 in square 460, in Wash City, on Jan 9, 1836, conveyed the said lots to the cmplnt, with a power of atty to the dfndnt, Jas Withers, to sell the same, on the failure of said Jas Long to pay the said purchase money at the time & times stipulated in the said deed & for the payment thereof. It further states that the said Jas Long, in his lifetime, entered into a written contract with the cmplnt to purchase a piece of ground adjoining the aforesaid lots, to pay part of the purchase money, & to secure the balance due by a deed of trust. That the said Long entered into possession under both purchases & paid large sums off money on account of each, but did not pay the whole of either, & died in 1848, leaving due on account of the purchase of lots A, B, & D about $15,260.87, which has been reduced by payments made since his death to the sum of $12,635.08, which, with interest from Apr 4, 1849, is still due & unpaid; & leaving due at his death, on account of his said second purchase, the sum of $4,180.71, with interest from Jan 1, 1848, which is still due & unpaid. That the said Jas Long left a will, which was proved in the Orphans Court of Wash Co, D C, & letters of administration were granted to the said Richd Wallach, who says he has no funds out of which to pay said debts; that the dfndnts, except the said Jas Withers & Richd Wallach, are the heirs at law of said Jas Long, & reside out of D C, & in the U S; that Jas Withers refuses to sell under the power given to him in the said deed from said Jas Long to said John Withers; & it prays the appointment of a trustee, & a sale of the property, & so much as may be found necessary to pay the said debts, & asks a publication against the absent dfndnts. This Nov 8, 1849, by the Court, is ordered that the said Jas Withers, Sarah Payne, Edw F Tabb, Kitty Ann Tabb, Allen C Hammond, Sarah Eliza Hammond, Wm D Cunningham, John C Payne, Mary D Payne, Jos E Payne, Sarah Ann Payne, John Payne & Mary D Payne his wife, John Long, Jas Anderson, Eliz Anderson, Sarah Long, Abaham D Long, Mary Mellairn, Robt Merritt, Sarah Ann Mellairn, Eliz Winning, & Benj Merritt be & appear in this Court, in person or by solicitor, before the 4th Mon of Mar next. —Jno A Smith, clerk

By virtue of an order of distress for house rent due to Stephen Clark by Lucy Swallwood, I will expose at public sale, for cash, on Dec 13, in front of the Centre Market, in Wash City, one mahogany sofa & a lot of carpeting.
—H R Maryman, Bailiff

Among the few absentees from the House of Reps is Mr Geo W Julian, of Indiana. Mr Julian had another attack of hemorrhage of the lungs on Tue, & he is quite ill. At 10 o'clock yesterday, he had another attack.

Accident on the Fitchburg railroad on Sat: 4 of the cars were thrown off, killing 4 laborers who were riding on them: David Barrus, Timothy Conner, Jas Ftiz Gibbins, & Mat McCan; the one injured was Patrick McGuire. —Boston Journal

House of Reps: third day & yet no Speaker of the House of Reps: 4 elections were held in addition to the 10 held on the preceding days. The last trial before adjournment yesterday was as follows:
Mr Winthrop: 99
Mr Cobb: 89
Mr Potter: 10
Mr Richardson: 8
Mr Root: 7
Mr Gentry: 5
Mr Cleveland: 3
Mr Allen: 1
Mr Kaufman: 1

St Louis, Dec 4. On Sat Mr Newton Weimer, brother of the late postmaster of this city, had an altercation in the street with Jas S Thomas, broker, of the house of Benoist & Co. Pistols were drawn, but through the interference of bystanders were not used. On Mon the parties met again: Weimer fired at Thomas, & Thomas returned the fire; 9 shots passed between them. Thomas was shot in the chest & Weimer, having exhausted his pistol, rushed on Thomas beating him on the head with a colt. Thomas shot Weimer through the body, of which wound he died in the evening. Mr Thomas may possibly recover. The affray originated thus: Mr Thomas had some time since, while Mr Weimer's brother was postmaster, failed to receive some large remittances of money sent by mails, & charged the p o with fraud. Mr Weimer, who was a clerk in the ofc resented.

Died: on Dec 4, in Wash City, Patrick Magee, a native of county Down, Ireland, but for many years a resident of Wash City. His funeral is this morning at 11 o'clock, from his late residence on 21st st.

For rent: 2 story house at 6th & G sts. Inquire of Mr Wilner, Paper Hanger, on 9th st.

Found, on Dec 1, one Sailboat, called **Friendship**. Owner can have same by calling on John Mansfield, *Greenleaf's Point*, & paying charges upon the same.

FRI DEC 7, 1849
Fatal accident on the Phil & Col Railroad on Wed last, resulting in the death of Mr Adam Yost, of Dillersville. While walking on the road, he discovered a train coming towards him, & stepped on the other track to avoid it, stepping in front of the other train.

Valuable improved property at auction: on Dec 12: the ***Columbian***, on the n w corner of 8th & E sts, owned & occupied by Mr J H Eberbach: house was built in 1842, expressly for the present owner. -Edw C & G F Dyer

Savannah Republican announced the retirement of Mr J Cameron, who had been conductor of one of the passenger trains in the Central [Ga] Railroad for 10 years & 3 months, & has traveled more than 50,000 miles. -Crescent

Criminal Court-Wash: Tue: Alice Haney was found guilty of grand larceny in stealing boots & wearing apparel. Being recommended to mercy by the jury, she was sentenced to 1 year's imprisonment at labor in the penitentiary. Wed: Wm Rawling, John Bell, & Lavinia Overton, free negroes, were all found guilty of receiving money known to have been stolen from Miss Labbe.

Jonathan Ogden, of Fulton, Oswego Co, was killed on Fri of last week, in a planning mill, when his large loose frock caught in an upright shaft as it revolved, whirling his body & severing his limbs by the knives of the planning machine.

Elkton Whig: a young man, Manlove, shot a man named Crow in Sassafras Neck, this week. Crow went into Manlove's father's barn & did not respond when called. Mr Manlove told him to shoot him, which he did. Next to Crow were 2 jugs of whiskey.

New Post ofcs for the week ending Dec 1, 1849:

Ofc	County, State	Postmaster
Belvidere	Lamoille, Vt	Randall Shattuck
North Evans	Erie, N Y	John Borland
Mindenville	Montg, N Y	Sylvester Yoran
Wegatchie	St Lawrence, N Y	A M Church
Kinderhook	Wash, Va	Wm Grant
Canaday Gap	Floyd, Va	Isaac Lemmans
Martin	Davidson, N C	John Rothrock
Bentonsville	Johnson, N C	Lawrence Peacok
Worth	De Kalb, Ala	Gideon Graham
Saint Paul	Clarke, Ala	Nathl Bradford
Makesville	Clarke, Miss	Jackson A Milhford
Saline Mills	Natchitoches P, La	Reuben Drake
Rock Creek	Yell, Ark	Alex'r A Scott
Pleasant Hill	Hopkins, Texas	Danl Hudson
Bridge	Kaufman, Texas	Ezra W Wiley
Cox's Store	Wash, Ten	Jas C Cox
Rockville	Monroe, Ten	Lewis Johnson
Jones' Mills	McNairy, Ten	Wm Jones
Altamont	Grundy, Ten	Robt Tate
Springersville	Fayette, _a	A E Pentecost
Richardson	Vermillion, Ill	Geo T Richardson
Elm Tree	Hancock, Ill	Wm Johnson
Somerville	De Kalb, Mo	Elisha Manning
Belle Point	Boon, Iowa	Jesse Hull

Names changed: Merrimack, Hillsboro Co, N H, changed to Reed's Ferry. Stockport, Wayne Co, Pa, changed to Stockport Station, Delaware Co, N Y. Cobham Depot, Albemarle Co, Va, changed to Cobham.
Walnut Branch, Fauquier Co, Va, changed to Saint Stephen.
Mount Pleasant, Wilkinson Co, Miss, changed to Holly Retreat.

Household & kitchen furniture at auction: on Dec 14, at **Bethel Cottage**, the residence of Mr J Crutchet, on North Capitol st, near the Capitol. -Green & Tastet, aucts

Mrd: on Dec 4, by Rev Mr Lanahan, John Calvin Shafer to Miss M A Virginia Powell, eldest daughter of G Powell, all of Wash City.

Mrd: on Dec 6, in Wash City, in the Church of the Ascension, by Rev L I Gilliss, Peter Lammond, of Ogdensburg, N Y, to Miss Mary C Robey, of Chas Co, Md.

Mrd: on Nov 14, at Bauden, Chowan Co, N C, Miss Nanniet, daughter of Chas E Johnson, to Dr R B Baker, of Woodville, Perquimans Co.

Died: on Dec 3, suddenly, after a few hours illness, at Sydenham, near Phil, [the residence of Hon Richd Rush,] Eugenia Frances, wife of J Murray Rush, of Phil, & daughter of the late John S Heister, of Reading, Berks Co, Pa.

Orphans Court of Wash Co, D C. Letters of administration on the personal estate of Rev Jos Van Horsigh, late of said county, deceased. –John F Ennis, adm

Anne Arundel lands for sale: on Dec 18, the *Crownsville Farm*, having a fine dwlg, with all other outbldgs; also a good store house. I will also sell another Farm, within 1 mile of the Crownsville farm. Call upon me in Wash, at Middleton & Beall's, Merchants, or at my brick-yard, North Capitol st. –Thos Crown

SAT DEC 8, 1849
Danl Moore, of Phil, has recoverd $3,000 damages from Geo W Watson. The plntf, in Jan last, was passing the carriage manufactory of the dfndnt, when his sign was blown down, by which the leg of the plntf was so badly shattered that amputation was rendered necessary. During his confinement Mr Watson contributed to the support of Moore's family, paid all his doctor's bills, & when he recovered offered him a permanent salary of $8 a week, which was refused, & the suit brought for damages. The verdict was a compromise between the parties.

On Dec 3, ofcr Philbrick arrested at the omnibus ofc, in Montg Place, Boston, a young man named Wm Howard, charged with writing to Mr S M Wells, of Jamaico Plain, one or more letters containing threats to burn his bldgs, in case a certain specified sum of money was not forwarded to the writer. He was held for trial at the municipal court.

H Bradley & Son's Cabinet, Chair, & Sofa Manufactory: corner of Pa ave & 13th, Wash.

For sale: house & lot on N Y ave. For terms apply to C W Pairo.

Late from Calif: The mutineers who attempted to murder Lt Gibson were condemned to death & executed on board the frig **Savannah**.

Jacob Hays, now in his 79th or 80th year, was on Monday sworn in for the 49th time as high constable, having been first appointed to that ofc by Mayor Livingston, in 1801. He was first appointed a marshal of N Y C in 1798.

Balt papers: Hon Benj C Howard had declined the appointment of U S Senator, tendered him by the Govn'r of Md, to fill the vacancy caused by the resignation of Hon Reverdy Johnson, & the Govn'r has made a new appointment by conferring the commission on David Stewart, of Balt, which will continue until a successor is elected by the Legislature, in the latter part of this month.

Jos Woodroe, aged about 50 years, who has resided near Port Deposite, Md, for a number of years, committed suicide on Wed last, by shooting himself with a musket. He has left a wife & a large family of children. No cause is assigned for the act.

Belmont for sale: as exc of the late Miss Mgt Mercer, I offer for sale, the estate called **Belmont**, in Loudoun Co, Va: consists of a large Mansion House, with about 600 acres attached thereon. **Belmont** is the site of a Female Seminary, which was under the management of the late Miss Mgt Mercer, which has been continued under Mrs Mercer. Address to the subscriber at **Belmont**, or to Chas L Powell, at Leesburg, Loudoun Co, Va. –Thos S Mercer, exc

Mr John Dunnman, on the San Jacinto river, Texas, had in 1837 thirty-three head of cattle. His stock of cattle now numbers over three thousand head. Out of the stock, he has supported a large family. –Texas Advocate

Died: yesterday, in Wash City, after a long & painful illness, Alfred Wallingsford, in his 43rd year. His funeral is tomorrow, from his late residence, on 4½ st, at 2 o'clock.

Died: on Nov 3, Ernest Lacy, infant son of J P & Clarissa Heiss.

MON DEC 10, 1849
Constitution for the State of Calif: San Jose designated as the permanent capital. Delegates signed: at Monterey, Calif, Oct 12, 1849. –B Riley, Bvt Brig Gen U S A, & Gov of Calif. H W Halleck, Bvt Capt & Sec of State.

Jos Aram	J D Hoppe	Antonio M Pico
Chas T Botts	Jos Hobson	Jacinto Rodriguez
Elam Brown	H W Halleck	Hugh Reid
Jose Anto Carrillo	L W Hastings	J A Sutter
Jose M Cavarrubias	J McH Hollingsworth	Jacob R Snyder
Elisha O Crosby	Jas McHall Jones	Winfield S Sherwood
Lewis Dent	Thos O Larkin	Wm C Shannon
Manuel Dominguez	Francis J Lippitt	Pedro Sansevain
K H Dimmick	Benj S Lippincott	Abel Stearns
A J Ellis	M M McCarver	W M Steuart
Stephen G Foster	John McDougal	R Semple
Pablo De La Guerra	Benj F Moore	Henry A Teffi
Edw Gilbert	Myron Norton	M G Vallejo
Wm M Gwin	P Ord	Thos L Vermu'e
Julian Hanks	Miguel De Pedrorena	Joel P Walker
Henry Hill	Rodman M Price	O M Wozencraft

Marshal's sale: writ of fieri facias, issued out of the Clerk's ofc at the Circuit Court of Wash Co, D C: sale on Jan 5, 1850, for cash: all the right, title, or claim of Eliza Davidson in & to the south half parts of lots 173 & 174, on Green st, in Beall's addition to Gtwn. Also 37 feet & 6 inches fronting on Wash st, being south half of lot 16, with improvements: seized & levied upon as the property of Mrs Eliza Davidson, & sold to satisfy judicials 10 to Mar term, 1848, in favor of the Pres & Dirs of the Bank of Wash. –Thos Woodward, Deputy to the late Alex'r Hunter, Marshal

War Dept: on Sep 26, Brevet Capt W H Warner, of the Topographical Engineers, was murdered by the Indians, on the Upper Sacramento, in Calif; & on Oct 16, Brevet Capt Herman Thorn, of the 2nd Infty, while in command of an escort with the Collector for the district of Monterey, was drowned whilst crossing the Colorado river, near the mouth of the Gila. Capt Warner wa shot down, 8 arrows having entered his body, by a party of 25 Indians.

Wash Ordinances: 1-Act for the relief of Jas M Wright, police ofcr of the 4th Ward, to be paid $80.89, the balance due to him on the settlement of his police accounts in full up to Jul 1, 1849. 2-Act for the relief of J F Wollard: to be paid $73, the amount for full settlement of his account, as police ofcr of the 3rd Ward, to Jun 30, 1849. 3-Act for the relief of John Magar, police ofcr of the 7th Ward: to be paid $65.73, the amount due to him on the settlement of his police account for the last 6 years, up to Sep 1, 1849. 4-Act for the relief of David Miller: fine imposed on him by Saml Grubb, for an alleged violation of an ordinance in relation to nuisances, be remitted, with all cost. The sum of $2 be paid to Miller. 5-Act for the payment of the claim of Morris Holloran: that $163.90 be paid to Holloran, the amount due him by the certificate of the Surveyor & Com'r of the Ward, for grading & gravelling F st north, between 2nd & 4th sts west.

Inquest was held on Sat last by Coroner Woodward, over the body of John Sipes, who, in a state of mania potu, junped out of the 3rd story of a bldg in the 1st Ward, so injuring himself, that he died in about 6 hours.

Circuit Court of Wash Co, D C-in Equity, Oct Term, 1849. Saml Redfern et al, vs Barbara A Parker et al. John E Ennis, the trustee in the above cause, reported he sold & disposed of part of lot 4 in square 141, in Wash City, on Nov 2 last, to A Nailor, for $660; he also reported that on Mar 31, 1849, he sold part of lot 3 in square 56, & the premises thereon, in Wash City, to Wm H Mosely, for $295. Terms of the sales have been complied with. –Jno A Smith, clerk

Dept of State: information received from John Black, U S Consul at the city of Mexico, of the death, at San Luis Potosi, on Aug 19 last, of Thos S Lewis, an American citizen, born in the State of Va.

Dr Mills, who was tried at Harrisburg, Pa, & convicted on the charge of seducing 3 sisters, was sentenced to 5 years' imprisonment in the Dauphin Co penitentiary, to $200 fine, & costs.

Pa Inquirer. Died: on Dec 5, at his residence in this city, Wm Short, in his 91st year. He has lived permanently in Phil for nearly half a century, was a native of Va. He was educated at Wm & Mary College, in the same class with the late Chief Justice Marshall. He was a member of the Exec Council of Va at an early age, & on the appointment of Mr Jefferson as Minister to France by the Congress of the Confederation in 1784, was joined with him as Sec of the Legation. Mr Short was appointed Charge d'Affaires to the French Republic, by Pres Washington, being the first U S Citizen nominated & appointed to a public ofc under the Federal Constitution. On his return to America, he retired altogether from public life, & selected Phil as his home, where he resided until his death.

Mrd: on Dec 4, by Rev Smyth Pine, Wm J Stone, jr, to Mary Frances, eldest daughter of Thos Green, all of Wash City.

TUE DEC 11, 1849
Naval Court Martial on board the U S ship **Pennsylvania**, at Gosport, on Nov 27, to try ____ Hillard, David Carter, Martin Gilmartin, & Fred'k Mowbray, of the crew of the U S sloop of war **Germantown**, for assaulting & beating an ofcr. The findings will not be discharged until the pleasure of the President is known. —Norfolk Herald

Col J B Weller has got into a difficulty with Maj Gray, of the Boundary Commission. A collision took place at San Diego, between them, in which Weller was shot in the leg; the hurt is slight. Mr Weller was not in any danger from it.

The Naval Gen Court Martial convened on board the U S sloop of war **Warren**, at anchor at San Francisco, on Nov 8, for the trial of the boat's crew, consisting of 5 seamen belonging to the U S surveying schnr **Ewing**, & after a thorough examination of the charges, found the accused, John Black, Jonathan Biddy, Wm Hale, Peter Black, & Henry Commerford, guilty of mutiny, & deserting with a boat belonging to the U S, from which they had previously thrown overboard passed midshipman Wm Gibson. The exteme penalty of the law was carried into execution on Nov 23, by hanging Peter Black at the fore yard arm of the U S frig **Savannah**, & John Black at the fore yard arm of the schnr **Ewing**, in presence of all the ships & vessels of the U S on the station. Com Jones had previously commuted the sentence of the other 3 prisoners to hard labor for the remainder of their term of service, 3 years.

On Dec 2, at New Orleans, the boiler of the locomotive exploded, instantly killing Jacob Hepps, the engineer, & so badly wounding John Chapman, fireman, that he too died.

Orphan's Court of PG Co, Md. Letters of administration, pendente lite, on the personal estate of Lloyd M Lowe, late of said county, deceased. —John H Lowe, adm; Sophia A Lowe, admx [Notice: I authorize & empower my brother, John H Lowe, the above named administrator, to settle the business connected with the administration of the said estate. -Sophia A Lowe, admx, Piscataway, Md]

Household & kitchen furniture at auction: on Dec 18 & 19, at the Columbian House, occupied by Mr John H Eberbach. -Edw C & G F Dyer

Household & kitchen furniture: by order of the Orphans Court of Wash Co, D C: at auction: on Dec 14, at the residence of the late John Boyle. -Edw C & G F Dyer

Mrd: on Dec 9, by Rev Mr Lanahan, Mr Saml E Douglass to Miss Eliz A Hauptman, daughter of Mr David Hauptman, all of Wash City.

Died: on Sat, in Wash City, after long & severe suffering, Ann Eliz, infant daughter of Anne Maria & Horatio R Maryman, aged 1 year & 4 months.

Furnished rooms to let, on Pa ave, between, 10th & 11th sts, over J F Kahl's Piano Store.

Rooms to rent at Mrs Stetson, south side of Pa ave, between 3rd & 4½ sts.

WED DEC 12, 1849
The newly appointed Charge d'Affaires to Venezuela, I Nevitt Steele, with his Lady, sailed from the Delaware yesterday, in the barque **Venezuela**, for Laguyra.

Criminal Court-Wash: Sat: 1-Caroline Russell, free colored girl, indicted for an assault on N B Van Zandt: found guilty & sentenced to 3 weeks in the county jail. 2-Thos Miles, free negro, indicted for receiving stolen property to the amount of $4.468, found guilty. Tues: Philip Parker, free negro, indicted for Sabbath breaking, found guilty.

Wash Corp: 1-Ptn of A Jackson, praying remission of a fine: referred to the Cmte of Claims. 2-Ptn of Wm P Howell, for the remission of a fine: referred to the Cmte of Claims. 3-Act for the relief of Hanson Brown: referred to the Cmte of Claims.

Mrd: on Jan 22 last, in Wash City, by Rev Mr Brown, I Nevitt Steele, of Balt, to Rosa L Davis, daughter of Hon John Nelson.

Commission on Claims against Mexico: 1-The Board will hear the cases of Baldwin, Chase, & the ship **Henry Thompson**, tomorrow. 2-The memorial of Thos Rowland, of New Mexico, claiming indemnity for losses incurred through the death, by an insurrection at Santa Fe in 1837, of certain civil ofcrs of the Mexican Gov't, who were then his debtors; & also for the destruction of certain of his goods at the same place in 1841, in consequence of a manifestation on his part to aid his unfortunate countrymen of the Texan expedition against Santa Fe, was presented & examined. The Board came to an opinion that the said memorial does not set forth a valid claim against Mexico, & it therefore rejected. 3-*The memorial as amended of Rhodo MacRae, of Fayetteville, N C, claiming, as mother of Alex H MacRae, a pension from the Mexican Gov't, was examined & received. [*Dec 14th newspaper: the memorial of Mrs Rhoda MacRae: the same is valid, & allowed the same accordingly, the amount to be awarded subject to the future action of the Board.]

Died: on Mon last, Levania Ann, aged 6 years & 12 days, 2nd daughter of Wm N & Ethelinda Johnson. Her funeral is this evening, at 3 o'clock, from their residence on Mass ave, between 9th & 10th sts.

THU DEC 13, 1849
Com'rs appointed by Chas Co Court to value & divide the real estate of Priscilla E Keech, late of Chas Co, deceased, notice to all whom it doth concern, we will meet at Dr Wm S Keechey's, on Feb 11, for making said partition. –Stouten W Dent, Josias H Hawkins, John Hamilton, Saml Core, Nicholas V Miles, Com'rs

Mrd: on Dec 11, by Rev G W Samson, Mr John F Havenner to Miss Ann Cooper, all of Wash City.

Mrd: on Dec 4, in Staunton, Va, by Rev T T Castleman, Norborne Berkeley, of Aldie, Loudoun Co, to Lavinia, daughter of Dr E Berkeley, of Staunton.

Died: on Dec 11, Mary Eliz, daughter of J W Brown, of the Treasury Dept, in her 17th year. Her funeral is today, at 2 o'clock, at her father's residence on 15th st, between L & M sts.

The partnership existing between Geo Barber & Robt Parkhill, blacksmiths & farriers, has been this day dissolved, the books having been transferred. Robt Parkhill alone is authorized to receipt. The undersigned hopes the patronage extended to the firm, will continue. –Robt Parkhill

FRI DEC 14, 1849
Wash City: Striking improvements at Gadsby's Hotel: the painting by Messrs T T & A Hurdel, is an excellent piece of work, deserving of commendation.

Criminal Court-Thu: convicts sentenced to the same prison:
Wm Rawlings, 1 year, commencing Dec 18.
John Bell, 1 year, commencing Dec 18.
Lavinia Overton, 18 months.
Frances West, 1 year
Frances West, 1 year, commencing at the expiration of the first sentence
Geo W Handy, 2 years
Eliza Simms, 2 years
Seymour Hooe, aged 78, 1 year
Catherine Allen, 18 months
Edw Hall, convicted of an assault & battery on the servant of the Mexican Minister, by fracturing his skull, to be imprisoned 9 months. He had been imprisoned since July.

On Sat last, in Camden, S C, Champion, eldest son of John M De Saussure, was killed by the accidental discharge of a gun in the hands of his younger brother, Douglas, both being on a hunting excursion.

Senate-Dec 13: 1-Mr Mason ask leave to withdraw from the files of the Senate, the papers of the heirs of Col David Morgan.

John Bromfield, of Boston, who is just dead, has left in his will a sum of $125,000 to different asylums, & to the town of Newburyport, for charitable purposes, $10,000. He left upward of $100,000 to relatives & friends. He was 70 years old in Apr last.

New Post ofcs for the week ending Dec 8, 1849:

Ofc	County, State	Postmaster
South Granby	Oswego, N Y	Jas Campbell
Fly Mountain	Ulster, N Y	Wm Van Wagoner
Port Mercer	Mercer, N J	John A L Crater
Jacksville	Butler, Pa	B C Jack
Snow Shoe	Centre, Pa	Saml Askey
Fairview Village	Montg, Pa	Sol Shultz
Sullivan	Tioga, Pa	Jas B Dewey
Fidelity	Miami, Ohio	Robt St Clair
Basnettsville	Marion, Va	B S Basnett
Shaver's Creek	Lee, Va	Geo B Melbourn
New Garden	Russell, Va	Thos W Davis
Oak Shade	Culpeper, Va	Presley Morehead
Station	Thomas, Ga	Jas S Godfrey
Goude's Precin'r	Clark, Ky	John Hughes
Bluffville	Carroll, Ill	N D French
St Peter's	Franklin, Ill	Francis Bower
Blue Creek	Franklin, Ill	M Mergenthal
Grindstone P'n	De Kalb, Mo	Geo W Smith
Jack's Forks	Texas, Mo	Reuben Harlow
Marietta	Jasper, Mo	Jos S Cone
Mount Vernon	Linn, Iowa	Elijah D Waln
South Ford	Wayne, Iowa	Benj Barker
Montezuma	Green, Wis	Oliver Cotton
Hortonville	Brown, Wis	Mason O Hubbard

Names changed:
Jay, Franklin Co, N Y, changed to Jay Bridge.
Ingle's Ferry, Pulaski Co, Va, changed to Lovely Mount.
Russellville, Marshall Co, Miss, changed to Harry Hill.
Harrisburg, Van Buren Co, Iowa, changed to Utica.

Commission of Claims against Mexico: 1-The memorial of John N Swazey, John Curtis, administrator of Abner Curtis, Wm Lewis, Jonathan Farnham, Abner Lane, [claimants in the matter of the seizure of the schnr **Eclipse**,] & of the proofs & documents connected therewith, & came to the opinion that the same is valid; allowed the same accordingly; & the amount to be awarded subject to the future action of the Board.

Trustee's sale of valuable Fred'k Co Land: by decree of Fred'k Co Court, in Equity: public sale on Dec 29, of a highly cultivated farm, *Araby*, containing 311 acres, more or less; formerly the Mansion Farm of Col John McPherson: lies 3 miles south of Fred'k. —Jas W Baugher, Lewis F Coppersmith, Grayson Eichelberger, Trustees, Fred'k, Md.

Fancy Dry Goods: Wm P Pouder, Pa ave, [upstairs] next door to Clagett & Co.

Newport Adv: Hon Wm Hunter died on Mon. His father was a Scotch physician, educated at Edinburgh, but settled in this town many years prior to the Revolution. It is said that he was one of the devoted band of Scotchmen who adhered to the last to the ill-fated house of Stuart, & that his emigration hither was the consequence of his participation in the rebellion of 1745. In 1755 he was surgeon to the troops raised by this State for the expedition against Crown Point, & it was in his tent that the brave Baron Dieskau breathed his last. About 1756 he delivered in this town the first course of anatomical lectures ever given in this country. His youngest child, the subject of the present notice, was born at Newport, in Nov, 1774, & received his father's name. He graduated at Brown Univ in 1791, & visited London & studied medicine under the guidance of his kinsman, the celebrated John Hunter. This profession was more his mother's choice than his. He studied law at the Inner Temple, in the same city, & became a pupil of Arthur Murphey, well known as the translator of Tacitus. He returned to Newport & was admitted to the bar at age 21; public career commenced in 1799, when he was chosen a Rep of Newport in the Gen Assembly; later he was chosen a Senator in Congress from this State; in 1834 he was appointed Charge to Brazil.

The Lexington Valley Star of Dec 6 says that two-thirds of the Natural Bridge were sold under a decree of Rockbridge Superior Court, on Mon, to Col Wooten, of Henry Co, [the owner of the other third,] for the sum of $6,600.

Died: on Dec 12, in Wash City, of consumption, Catharine Chism, in her 25th year. Her funeral is today, at 2 P M, at the residence of her brother, on I st, between 21st & 22nd sts.

Died: on Sat, at Norfolk, Va, Miles King, aged 63 years. Though secluded from society for the last 7 years by physical infirmity, the deceased was in his prime of manhood. He was an ofcr in Ott's efficient Norfolk Light Artl, while it was in service on this station during most of the period of the war of 1812; was elected to the Gen Assembly; in 1816 received the appointment of Navy Agent-for 11 years; again elected to the Gen Assembly; closed his public life in the ofc of Mayor,-for 13 years. Retired to the bosom of his family. -Norfolk Herald

SAT DEC 15, 1849
House of Reps: 1-Howell Cobb, of Ga, is chosen Speaker of the House of Reps of the 31st Congress. [After 45 votes there was still "no choice."]

U S Patent Ofc, Dec 14, 1849. Ptn of Isaac Adams, of Boston, Mass, praying for the extension of a patent granted to him for an improvement in power printing presses for 7 years from the expiration of said patent, which takes place on Mar 2, 1850.
–Thos Ewbank, Com'r of Patents

Senate: 1-Leave was granted to withdraw from the files the ptn & papers of Wm Woodbridge & Henry Chipman.

Mrd: on Dec 13, by Rev Wm Matthews, Josiah Read Bailey to Ann Eliz Laporte, all of Wash.

Mrd: on Dec 11, near Taneytown, Carrol Co, Md, by Rev Mr Grier, M W Galt, of Wash, to Mary Jane, daughter of Sterling Galt, of the former place.

Died: last evening, in Gtwn, Col John Cox, in his 75th year. In early life Col Cox moved to Gtwn, & was one of its most prominent & successful merchants. In the war of 1812 he was inspector of the military of the District & took an active part in the disastrous battle of Bladensburg. He was Mayor of Gtwn for more than 20 years in succession. He has left no enemy behind him, but a large circle of friends, & a large family of children & grandchildren to mourn his loss. His funeral is tomorrow at 3 o'clock, from the late residence of his son, Clement Cox, deceased, at the corner of Gay & Congress sts.

Household & kitchen furniture at auction: on Dec 20 & 21: 2 houses owned by Jos K Boyd, on D & 11th sts, commencing with the house on 11th st. –Edw C & G F Dyer

On Thu the warehouse in Water st, Gtwn, occupied by Messrs Burch & Morrow, tanners, was entirely destroyed by fire. It was thought that this fire was caused by an incendiary. Mr Morrow said that part of the bldg & stock were insured.

MON DEC 17, 1849
Rev Mr Perkins, Pastor of the Unitarian Church at Cincinnati, committed suicide last Fri, by jumping from the ferry boat into the river. He left his cloak, hat & memorandum book on the boat. He was doubtless laboring under temporary insanity. He leaves an interesting family, & was much esteemed by all who knew him.

Jas A Hicks, recently of Boston, & acting Spanish Consul, was lost overboard, off Bermuda, on his passage from N Y to St Thomas, whither he was going with his family for his health.

Fifty years ago, Dec 14, 1799, Washington died. –N Y Express

Criminal Court-Fri: 1-John Seitz, charge with 2 indictments with theft: guilty of stealing a barrel of flour; acquitted in the other case. Sentenced to 18 months in the penitentiary. 2-Mary Ann Mason, guilty of petit larceny: sentenced to 6 months in the county jail. 3-Loyd Lane, guilty of breaking into the house of John Skinner, but not with intent to steal, a motion in arrest of judgment having been made, it was granted by the court, & the dfndnt was discharged.

Died: on Dec 7, at Portsmouth, Va, after an illness of a few hours, Mrs Harriet Patton, wife of Dr Farley Patton, U S N, & youngest daughter of the late Anthony Buck, of Fredericksburg. She was a most affectionate wife & devoted mother. Her little ones are yet unconscious of the loss they have sustained.

More on the disappearance of Mrs Miller from Niagara Falls: in her letter to her father she says her little girl is in heaven: good-bye, my dear parents, brothers & sister. Don't forget to do all you can for Maj Miller. He has always been a kind husband. I G Miller [Mrs Miller is 26 years old: mother of 4 children, the oldest & youngest of whom died in early infancy. At Winchester, Va, her infant daughter was distressingly ill for several months. She married when she was 17½ years old; part of her education was received at the nunnery in Detroit; was a short time at the academic institution of Madame Greland, in Phil; & for some months at that of Miss English, of Gtwn, D C.] The prevalent opinion at the scene of the recent tragedy is more than probably correct. To that impression her relations must adhere till eradicated by indubitable evidence of a different & worse catastrophe.

Commission of Claims against Mexico: 1-Memorial of Nathan Barklay, administrator of Moses Nolan, of Desha Bunton, of Malcolm Sandeman & Co, of John W Bunto, of Harrison C Allensworth, of Jas M Gatewood, of Dexter Watson, of Silas M Knight, of Johnson H Alford, of Jas Love, administrator of Pallas Love, being taken up for examination, as also the proofs & documents connected therewith, the Board came to an opinion that the same are valid, & allowed the same accordingly: the amount to be awarded subject to the future action of the Board. 2-The memorials of Danl Davis, of Nathan Barklay, administrator of S Booker, of Nathan Barklay, administrator of B B Bolling, of Nathan Barklay, administrator of Alex'r C Dougall: examined, & for the present suspended.

Died: on Dec 15, at the residence of Mr Saml Cropley, Gtwn, Miss Mary Fulmer, aged 19 years.

Died: on Dec 3, in Wash City, Emily E, aged 7 months & 10 days, only daughter of W H & M E Falconer.

TUE DEC 18, 1849
New Minister from Great Britain: Rt Hon Sir Henry Lytton Bulwer, Privy Councelor, K C B, born in 1804; married in 1848 Hon Georgiana Charlotte Mary, youngest daughter of first Lord Cowley & niece of the Duke of Wellington; entered the diplomatic service in 1829; was attached to the courts of Berlin, Vienna, & the Hague till 1830; sent to Brussels on a 2nd mission of observation at the revolution in Belgium in 1830; elected member of Parliament for Wilton in 1830; for Coventry in 1831 & 32; for Marylebone from 1834 till 1837; was Sec of Legation & Charge d'Affaires at Brussels in 1835 & 36; Sec of Embassy of Constantinople in 1837; appointed Sec of Embassy at St Petersburgh at the close of 1838, but did not proceed thither, having been appointed Sec of Embassy at Paris in 1839. Appointed Minister Pleni at Madrid in 1843; negotiated the peace between Spain & Morocco in 1844; was dismissed by the Spanish Ministry in 1848. [From the British Peerage of 1849: extracted by the N Y American.]

Bridge over a small creek near the Covington depot, on the Georgia Railroad, was crushed on Thu with the weight of the immense new engine Oregon, & the entire train precipitated 50 feet, killing the conductor, Mr McCan, instantly. –Augusta Sentinel

Commission on Claims against Mexico: 1-Memorial of John Baldwin, claiming for the seizure & loss of a trunk of wearing apparel, a horse, & mule, being taken up: Board of the opinion the claim is not valid: not allowed. 2-Memorial of Henry Stevens, of Matamoros, claiming for expulsion from that town on Apr 12, 1846, was ordered to be received. 3-Memorial, as amended, of Ann Y Kelly, admx of Wm H Lee, claiming for losses by expulsion from Matamoros, under the Mexican decree of Sep 23, 1843.

Mrd: on Nov 22, at Vicksburg, Miss, by Rev Mr Patterson, Chas E Smedes to Martha Love, daughter of Dr R H Brodnax, all of Wash City.

Died: on Dec 17, Gillis R Taylor, in his 38th year. His funeral is this afternoon, at 3 o'clock, at his late residence, corner of Md ave & 6th st.

Died: on Dec 17, after a protracted illness, Martha A Arnold, wife of Wm H Arnold. Her funeral is tomorrow, at 4 o'clock, from her late residence on Capitol Hill.

Died: yesterday, Mary Rittenhouse, daughter of Jos E & Sarah W Nourse, aged 8 months. Her funeral will move at 1 p m today from the residence of Wm Nourse, 11th & N sts.

Died: on Dec 17, in Gtwn, Francis Dulany, aged 16 months, 3rd son of Caroline & Robt P Dodge. His funeral is at 3 o'clock this afternoon.

Household & kitchen furniture at auction: on Dec 22, by order of the Orphans Court of Wash Co, D C: at the residence of Mrs Stewart, 14th & G sts. -Edw C & G F Dyer

Lewisburg Chronicle: on Nov 15, the daughter of Mr Pennington, of Monroe Co, & the daughter of Mr Meadows, of Mercer, were drowned in New river. Mr Pennington, the father of one of them, tried to rescue them but failed before life was entinct. They were young ladies.

Teacher wanted in his family: gentleman capable of instructing a few small children in the elementary branches of English. Address J Waring, Chaptico, St Mary's Co, Md.

WED DEC 19, 1849
Accidents. 1-*Mr Andrews, a lawyer of New Haven put his head out of the window of the New Haven cars on Sat, as it was rounding the corner of Grand & Centre sts, in N Y C, & the down train happened to be passing at the time, when the baggage-car came in collision with his head, tearing off one ear & injuring him severely. He was taken to the hospital. 2-A conductor, Mr Palmer, while disconnecting the cars from the locomotive at Fishkill Landing, on Fri, fell off the platform, & the whole train passed over him, killing him instantly. [*Dec 20th newspaper: Mr Andrews died unexpectedly in the city hospital on Mon night.]

Wash Corp: 1-Ptn from Geo Stutz, for remission of a fine: referred to the Cmte of Claims. 2-Bill authorizing Chas Lenman to continue certain improvements on a frame house in square 140: passed.

Gentlemen's Wear: Wm Shuster & Co, corner of 7th & Pa ave. [Ad]

Fight between the Pawnee Indians & a Company of the U S Dragoons. Madison [Iowa] Statesman, of Dec 1. Mr P Sperry, of this place, who has been living at **Fort Laramie** the past summer, returned home on the steamer **Mary Blane** last Tue & informs that a battle took place of Oct 23 between Lt Ogle, of Co B, U S Dragoons, who were escorting the mail, & a party of Pawnee Indians. The Dragoons numbered only 20 strong, & the Indian force was 5 times that number. Lt Ogle demanded to know their intentions when they assembled around his men, & they began to show hostilities. He ordered his force, after firing upon them with their holster pistols, to charge with drawn sabres upon them, which they did, driving the Indians into a ravine, where it was impossible for the soldiers to act effectively on account of their horses. In the charge Lt Ogle had 6 men wounded, 2 mortally, he was struck in the mouth with an arrow cutting both lips & riddling his clothes completely, which did not prevent him from continuing at the head of his force. Lt Ogle succeeded in collecting his wounded, & was met by Maj Chilton, the commanding ofcr at **Fort Kearny**, with reinforcement.

New Post ofcs for the week ending Dec 15, 1849:

Ofc	County, State	Postmaster:
Greene	Kennebeck, Maine	Elijah Barreil
Eaton Centre	Carroll, N H	E Baker
Painesville	Chittenden, Vt	Henry Stanton
Moose's Meadow	Tolland, Ct	Alfred Anderson
Middletw'n Centre	Dela, N Y	Wm W Grant
South Franklin	Dela, N Y	Wm A Miller
Amboy Centre	Oswego, N Y	Jonathan Randall
Glass Creek	Barry, Mich	C J Brewer
Fort Ridge	Marshall, Va	Wm A Knox
Staunton	Granville, N C	John M Poole
Hopkin's Trun Out	Richland D, S C	Martin Cahill
Pawtuxet	Wakulla, Fla	John Bland
Crane's Forge	Assumption P, La	Thos J Crane
Dorchest	Claiborne, La	David H Courtney
Pleasant Valley	Yell, Ark	M Harkey
Brooks' Tan Yard	Macon, Ten	John R Brooks
Drennon's Ridge	Henry, Ky	B Barton
Leander	Graves, Ky	W Yancy Eaker
Lockport	Henry, Ky	Andrew Slinck
New Michigan	Livingston, Ill	Geo W Richards
Low Point	Woodford, Ill	Wm Dodds
Littletonville	Knox, Ill	Giles Cook
Big Neck	Adams, Ill	Jas Shannon
Cow Skin	Ozard, Mo	Wm Turner
Fas_ York	Macon, Mo	A McMullen
Hollister's Mills	Holt, Mo	Albert G Hollister
Martin's Mills	Buchanan, Mo	Wm W Brown
Cadiz	Green, Wis	Wesley Swank
Trenton's Corners	Dodge, Wis	Raymond S Castle

Shopiere Rock, Wis Louis P Harvey
Markesan Marquette, Wis S H H Wright
Soap Creek Davis, Iowa Wm Wells

Names changed:
Greene, Kennebeck Co, Maine, changed to Greene Depot.
Lippitt, Kent Co, R I, changed to Phenix.
Downsville, Dela Co, N Y, changed to Colchester.
Craig's Mills, St Lawrence Co, N Y, changed to Crary's Mills.
Tuscarora Valley, Juniata Co, Pa, changed to Pleasant View.
Petersburgh, Perry Co, Pa, changed to Duncannon.
Brereton, Somerset Co, Md, changed to Upper Trappe.
Coelebs, Pittsylvania Co, Va, changed to Bachelor's Hall.
Luthersville, Rowan Co, N C, changed to China Grove.
Crossville, Fayette Co, Ala, changed to Military Grove.
Wiley Bright, Kemper Co, Miss, changed to Centre Ridge.
Drane's Mills, Choctaw Co, Miss, changed to Steam Mills.
Mount Mourne, Panola Co, Texas, changed to Kinlock.
Walnut Creek, Stark Co, Ill, changed to West Jersey.

Commission on Claims against Mexico: 1-Memorial of Andrew Wylie, jr, administrator of Saml Baldwin, intestate, claiming for the seizure of a schnr, for imprisonment, & various losses & wrongs, was examined, & ordered to be received.

Court of Common Pleas in New Bedford this past week, Judge Hoar presiding. Three young men, Chas Thomas, Ursal Harrison, & Hiram Willey, charged with forcibly entering the house of Isaac Little, an aged citizen of Dartmouth, on Oct 6 last, & robbing & threatening the lives of the inmates, were found guilty, & sentenced to hard labor in the State prison for life.

Wm Emmert, Confectioner, Bridge st, Gtwn. P S: Weddings, balls, dinners, & other parties attended with despatch.

Household & kitchen furniture at auction: on Dec 19, at the residence of Mr C A Moenster, who is about to leave the city. –Green & Tastet, aucts

Furniture, crockery, & dry goods auction: on Dec 19, at the store of Thos B Brown, 7th & I sts. -Edw C & G F Dyer

THU DEC 20, 1849
Matthew L Bevan, a prominent merchant in Phil, died in that city on Fri last.

Dental Surgery: Wm P McConnell, ofc on Pa ave, nearly opposite Brown's Hotel, & next door to Hoover's Shoe Store. Ten years' residence in Wash City. Operations performed under the influence of Chloric-Ether can be accommodated.

For rent: large 3 story house, just erected, at H & 15th sts. Apply to Dr Chas S Frailey, Gen Land Ofc.

Montgomery Advertiser of Dec 15: burning of the Capitol of Alabama. All that remains of our once beautiful Capitol are crumbling walls. The fire was discovered yesterday, first issuing from the front portico, having originated on the roof. The clerks of the 2 houses saved all their papers, & the archives of the State, in the ofcs of the Govn'r, Sec of State, Treasurer, & Comptroller, were all saved. Most of the furniture was preserved from the flames.

East Braintree, Mass, Sunday last, Mr Jas T Loring hastened to the assistance of boys playing on the ice on a pond, but in his efforts to save others, he lost his life. He was a highly esteemed citizen. A lad named John Hill was also drowned.

Died: on Mon last, Mrs Ann Kerr, relict of the late Alex'r Kerr, of Wash City. Her funeral is at 1 o'clock, on Dec 21. To move from St John's Church.

Died: on Nov 21, a Broad Creek, PG Co, Md, in her 18th year, Maria Louisa Lyles, youngest daughter of the late Dr Thos C Lyles. She was a devoted daughter & affectionate sister. Upper Marlborough & Port Gibson, Miss, papers please copy.

FRI DEC 21, 1849
We are informed that Capt Seth Eastman, of the U S Army, has the reputation of being an artist of superior ability, & has arrived in Washington, where he expects he will remain for the winter. He has spent some 20 years on the frontiers, portraying upon canvass the manners & customs of the Indians.

Judge Morehouse, one of the Justices of the Supreme Court of N Y, died at Cooperstown on Dec 15.

A well dressed man was arrested yesterday at the railroad ofc, while attempting to rob Mr Francis H Edelen, of Chas Co, Md, of his pocket-book containing over $140.

Mrd: on Dec 18, by Rev Wm H Pitcher, Mr John A Moulden, of Wash, to Miss Ann Mary Hardt, of Rockville, Md.

SAT DEC 22, 1849
Rev Geo Johnson, a graduate of the Theological Seminary at Gambier, & but recently ordained a minister of the Protestant Episcopal Church, lost his life on Tue last, when accidentally shot by a gun he had in his room, that he was returning. It is supposed that in putting on his cloak it had become entangled in the lock of the gun, or he fell with the gun. -Columbus [Ohio] Journal

At N Y, on Tue, Jas Brant, a rigger, was killed instantly by a fall from the mainsail of the packet ship **Manhattan**. Also, Ann Boylan, killed by falling from a 3rd story, while washing windows. At night, Jas Phelan, going up Broadway, under the influence of liquor, fell into an area, & injured himself so that he died immediately.

Rev Moses Howe, seamen's preacher in New Bedford, Mass, formerly of Portsmouth, has been in the ministry 34 years.

Advices from Marion Co state that Jesse N Everett & Nelson Stratton, two of the principal actors in the recent outrages in Marion Co, have escaped from the jail at Smithville, & are now, with about 40 of their confederates, all armed, embodied within 6 miles of Yellsville. The whole country is in a high state of alarm. Capt Mitchell's company has been called out again, & were ready to move upon them & retake the prisoners, as soon as Gen Wood should arrive. –Little Rock Democrat, 7th

On Thu last Mr Josiah Heard & his sister-in-law, of North Berwick, attempted to cross Lake Winnepisseogee in a sleigh, & hired a man to show them the way. The ice gave way, & the whole party, together with the horse, went down & were drowned. Portsmouth [N H] Gaz, 17th

$50 will be given for the apprehension of 2 negro men, Benj Berry, about 23 or 24, & Perry Grose, about 20 or 21, who ranaway on Dec 9. –John H Skinner, near Nottingham, PG Co, Md

Mrd: on Dec 18, at Falling Spring, near Shepherdstown, Jefferson Co, Va, by Rev Mr Andrews, Geo W Hall, of Brookville, Montg Co, Md, to Mary Augusta, daughter of Jacob Moyan, of the former place.

The undersigned is desirous of ascertaining the residence of Anthony Gifford, or of Jas H Crossman, his son. He is now in Washington, in destitute circumstances, & any person who can give him information as to their location would confer a great favor. Any information left at this ofc will reach him. –Bradford F Crossman

MON DEC 24, 1849
Criminal Court-Wash-Sat: 1-Emmeline Shaw, indicted for stealing $60 in gold belonging to R R Goldin, was acquitted. 2-Swope Smith, charged with an assault & attempt to rob Mr Edelen, of Chas Co, Md, at the car ofc on Thu, was acquitted. 3-Eliz Butler, guilty of grand larceny: sentenced to 10 months in the penitentiary. 4-Wm Cropsey, a white boy, guilty of malicious mischief, in throwing stones at Wm P McConnell & at the his dwlg house: sentenced to 2 months in the county jail. 5-Geo W Wilson was found guilty of petit larceny in 2 cases.

Pottawatamie Indians arrived in Wash City, accompanied by Mr J C McCoy. They are from the Kansas river, 100 miles west of the State of Missouri, having visited Wash for the purpose of receiving their annuities for the current year. The 3 oldest members of the Party are bordering upon 80 years of age, & glory in the following names: Pat-e-go-shuck, or the Powerful Fish, Waub-seigh, or the Sturgeon with the White Skin, & Qua-qua-tah, or the Digging Bear. The 2 other individuals are educated Indians, & named Dr J W Barrow & J W Bourassa.

Orphans Court of Wash Co, D C. Letters of administration on the personal estate of Alfred Wallingsford, late of said county, deceased. –Eleanor Wallingsford, admx

Phil, Dec 21. Mr Baker, an aged lawyer of our city, died yesterday from injury received on Wed, by being struck with a tongue of a chaise, at 6th & Chestnut sts.

Mrd: on Dec 13, at N Y, by Rev Dr Skinner, Edmund Dwight to Harriet Allen, daughter of B F Butler, all of that city.

TUE DEC 25, 1849

Senate: 1-Ptn of Richd Chaney, relative to his claim or pre-emption to a part of the land now occupied by the town of *Fort Madison*: referred to the Cmte on Public Lands. 2-Memorial of Angelina B N Cook, widow of Col Wm J Cook, for compensation for services of her husband, in superintending & organizing Texas volunteers at Point Isabel, during the Mexican war: referred to the Cmte on Military Affairs. 3-Ptn & papers of Henry Simpson, adm of Stephen Simpson, deceased: withdrawn from the files. 4-Ptn & papers of Wm C Sterrett, withdrawn from the files: referred to the Cmte on Pensions. 5-Papers of a L Knickerbocker, withdrawn from the files: referred to the Cmte on Pensions. 6-Ptn & papers of Manuel X Harmony, withdrawn from the files: referred to the Cmte on Pensions. 7-Ptn & papers of Arel Spalding, withdrawn from the files: referred to the Cmte on Pensions. 8-Ptn & papers of N B Hill, adm of Gilbert Stalker, withdrawn from the files: referred to the Cmte of Claims. 9-Ptn & papers of Guion & McLaughlin, taken from the files: referred to the Cmte on the Post Ofc & Post Roads. 10-Ptn & papers of Capt McLellan's company of Florida volunteers be taken from the files of the Senate: referred to the Cmte on Military Affairs. 11-Ptn & papers of Saml W Chilson, be taken from the files: referred to the Cmte on the Post Ofc & Post Roads. 12-Ptn & papers Clements, Bryan & Co, be taken from the files: referred to the Cmte of Claims. 13-Memorial of N Nye Hall be taken from the files: referred to the Cmte on Pensions. 14-Ptn of papers of John Wormsley, & the ptn & papers of Sarah Crandell, be taken from the files of the Senate: referred to the Cmte on Pensions. 15-Ordered, that Catharine Oliphant have leave to withdraw her ptn & papers. 16-Mr Borland to introduce the following bills: pension to Mrs Nancy Featherstone. Relief of Cincinnatus Tousdale & John C Connelly. 17-Ptn of Thos N Carr, late Consul of the U S for the Empire of Moroco, asking compensation for diplomatic services near the Gov't: referred to the Cmte on Foreign Relations. 18-Ptn of Hugh W Dobbin, in behalf of himself & his 2 sons, Lodowick Dobbin & Wm W Dobbin, both deceased, praying compensation for services & sacrifices in the late war with Great Britain: referred to the Cmte on Military Affairs. 19-Ptn of Edmud Pavenstedt & Fred'k Schumacher, merchants of N Y C, asking to be released from liability on a custom-house bond: referred to the Cmte on Commerce. 20-Ptn of Ladislaus Wankoweiz & G Tochman, legal reps of the heirs of Thaddeus Kosciusko, deceased, asking the protection of the Gov't against certain alleged interference with their rights in the Court of the U S by the Emperor of Russia: referred to the Cmte on Foreign Relations. 21-Ptn of Thos M Taylor, a purser in the navy, praying to be released from liability for public money lost in consequence of the failure of a bank in which it was deposited: referred to the Cmte on Naval Affairs. 22-Claim of Hamilton P Bee, an ofcr in the army, asking reimbursement of money expended by him for the transportation of subsistence & quartermaster's store from Camargo, Mexico, to Loredo, Texas: referred to the Cmte on Military Affairs. 23-Ptn of Frances C Elliott, widow of Jesse D Elliott, deceased, late an ofcr in the navy, asking reimbursement of the expenses incurred by her late husband in receiving & entertaining the representatives of certain foreign Powers, while in command of the naval forces of the U S in the Mediterranean, between 1835 & 1839: referred to the Cmte on Naval Affairs.

Shocking accident at Burlington, Vt, on Mon: the trestles now in process of erection to connect the new bridge over the Onion with the grade at Winooski Falls, fell to the ground while 10 men were at work upon them. Mr Amos P Cutting, an overseer, from Lyme, N H, died; John Bland, an Irishman, was dreadfully lacerated about the hips, & after suffering a painful operation, died in the evening. Jas Kennedy, of Burlington, has his chest crushed, & died in a few hours. F D Cunitz, late of Phil, received some injury from the shock, but will probably recover. Henry Williams, of Colchester, suffered a compound fracture of the arm, & Wm Hoos, of Winooski, had his thigh broken in a shocking manner.

Army Order: War Dept: Gen Orders, 54: Adj Gen Ofc, Wash, Nov 30, 1849. Promotions & appointments in the U S Army, made by the Pres since publication of Gen Orders #38, of Jul 5, 1849.
I-Promotions:
Corps of Topographical Engineers.
2nd Lt Jos D Webster, to be 1st Lt, Jul 14, 1849, vice Hagner, deceased.
Brevet 2nd Lt Wm F Smith, to be 2nd Lt, Jul 14, 1849, vice Webster, promoted.
2nd Regt of Dragoons:
2nd Lt Alfred Pleasonton, to be 1st Lt, Sep 30, 1849, vice Lowry, resigned.
1st Regt of Artl
2nd Lt Saml F Chalfin, to be 1st Lt, Nov 6, 1849, vice Smith, deceased.
Brevet 2nd Lt Beekman DuBarry, to be 2nd Lt, Nov 6, 1849, vice Chalfin, promoted.
2nd Regt of Artl:
2nd Lt Chas Griffin, to be 1st Lt, Jun 30, 1849, vice Sears, resigned.
Brevet 2nd Lt Thos J Haines, of the 1st Artl, to be 2nd Lt, Jul 1, 1849, vice Griffin, promoted.
3rd Regt of Artl:
Brevet 2nd Lt Wm Silvey, to be 2nd Lt, Oct 31, 1849, vice McDonald, resigned.
1st Regt of Infty:
1st Lt Wm E Prince, to be Capt, Aug 31, 1849, vice Mumford, resigned.
2nd Lt Fred'k J Denman, to be 1st Lt, Aug 31, 1849, vice Prince, promoted.
Brevet 2nd Lt Danl Huston, jr, of the 8th Infty, to be 2nd Lt, Jun 30, 1849, vice Bradford, resigned.
Brevet 2nd Lt Wm H Lewis, of the 4th Infy, to be 2nd Lt, Aug 31, 1849, vice Denman, promoted.
2nd Regt of Infty:
2nd Lt Nelson H Davis, to be 1st Lt, Jun 8, 1894, vice Jarvis, deceased.
5th Regt of Infty:
Brevet 2nd Lt Thos Wright, of the 7th Infty, to be 2nd Lt, Oct 7, 1849, vice Harrison, deceased.
6th Regt of Infty:
2nd Lt Anderson D Nelson, to be 1st Lt, Nov 18, 1849, vice Wetmore, deceased.
Brevet 2nd Lt John L Tubbs, to be 2nd Lt, Nov 18, 1849, vice Nelson, promoted.
8th Regt of Infty:
1st Lt John Beardsley, to be Capt, Jun 28, 1849, vice Gates, deceased.
2nd Lt Thos G Pitcher, to be 1st Lt, Jun 26, 1849, vice Booker, deceased.
2nd Lt Geo E Pickett, to be 1st Lt, Jun 28, 1849, vice Beardsley, promoted.
2nd Lt Washington P Street, to be 1st Lt, Aug 4, 1849, vice Hanson, resigned.

Brevet 2nd Lt Wm T Mechling, of the 3rd Infty, to be 2nd Lt, Jun 26, 1849, vice Pitcher, promoted.
Brevet 2nd Lt Geo C Barber, of the 7th Infty, to be 2nd Lt, Jun 28, 1849, vice Pickett, promoted.
Brevet 2nd Lt Milton Cogswell, of the 4th Infty, to be 2nd Lt, Aug 4, 1849, vice Street, promoted.

II-Appointments.
Medical Dept:
Isaac L Adkins, of Delaware, to be Assist Surgeon, Nov 23, 1849.
Robt O Abbott, of Pa, to be Assist Surgeon, Nov 23, 1849.
Thos M Getty, of Va, to be Assist Surgeon, Nov 23, 1849.
Pay Dept:
Nathan W Brown, of N Y, to be Paymaster, Sep 5, 1849, vice Kirby, deceased.
Albert S Johnston, of Texas, to be Paymaster, Oct 31, 1849, vice Forsyth, deceased.

III-Casualties
Resignations:
Capt Wm H Swift, Coprs of Topographical Engineers, Jul 31, 1849.
Capt Wm Eustis, 1st Dragoons, Aug 4, 1849.
Capt Ferdinand S Mumford, 1st Infty, Aug 31, 1849.
1st Lt Albert Lowry, 2nd Dragoons, Sep 30, 1849.
1st Lt Grafton D Hanson, 8th Infty, Aug 4, 1849.
1st Lt Henry B Sears, 2nd Artl, Jun 30, 1849.
2nd Lt Saml B Maxey, 7th Infty, Sep 17, 1849.
Brevet 1st Lt Bedney F McDonald, 2nd Lt 3rd Artl, Oct 31, 1849.
Military Storekeeper Wm P Maulsby, Ordnance Dept, Jun 30, 1849.
Commissions vacated under the provisions of the 7th section of the act of Jun 18, 1846:
Capt John P J O'Brien, Assist Quartermaster, 4th Artl. [Staff commission only vacated.]
Deaths:
Col Jas Duncan, Inspector Gen, at Mobile, Ala, Jul 3, 1849.
Brevet Lt Col Saml McRee, Quartermaster, at St Louis, Mo, Jul 15, 1849.
Brevet Maj Collinson R Gates, Capt 8th Infty, at Fredericksburg, Texas, Jun 28, 1849.
Brevet Capt Leonidas Wetmore, 1st Lt, 6th Infty, on the Upper Mississippi river, Nov 18, 1849.
1st Lt Wm S Smith, 1st Artl, at Kingsbridge, N Y, Nov 6, 1849.
1st Lt Chas N Hagner, Corps of Topog Engineers, at Lavaca, Texas, Jul 14, 1849.
1st Lt Jacob J Booker, 8th Infty, at San Antonio, Texas, Jun 26, 1849.
1st Lt Chas E Jarvis, 2nd Infty, at Sonoma, Calif, Jun 8, 1849.
2nd Lt Montgomery P Harrison, 5th Infty, near the Colorado river, Texas, Oct 7, 1849. [Harrison-killed by the Indians.]
Paymaster Edmund Kirby, Brevet Col, at Avon Springs, N Y, Aug 20, 1849.
Paymaster Robt A Forsyth, at Detroit, Mich, Oct 21, 1849.
Transfers:
Capt Edw H Fitzgerald, Assist Quartermaster, to the 1st Dragoons, to take place on the Army Register next below Capt Carleton.
Capt Danl H Rucker, 1st Dragoons, to the Quartermaster's Dept, to take place on the Army Register next below Assist Quartermaster Reynolds.
Brevet 2nd Lt Edw D Stockton, of the 2nd Artl, to the 7th Infty.

Correction:
Brevet 2nd Lt Thos D Johns, of the 1st Infty, to be 2nd Lt of the 2nd Infty, Jun 8, 1849, vice Davis, promoted; instead of a 2nd Lt in the 1st Infty, Jun 30, 1849, as announced in the Gen Orders #38, of Jul 5, 1849.

Memorandum:
The name of Delancy F Jones, a 1st Lt in the 4th Infty, will hereafter be known & recognized in the Army as Delancy Floyd Jones, the surname of his family having been changed by the Legislature of N Y to Floyd Jones. -R Jones, Adj Gen

Jas P McKean has removed his Book-binding Establishment to Odd Fellows' Hall, & is prepared to execute all orders in his line of business with promptness & the best manner.

Mrd: on Dec 23, by Rev Mr Gilliss, Mr M H Waite, of Wash, to Miss Louisa H Hepburn, of Cleveland, Ohio.

Died: on Dec 24, at his residence near Wash City, Mr John Evans, in his 62nd year. His funeral will take place on Wed at 11 o'clock.

THU DEC 27, 1849
Commission on Claims against Mexico: Dec 24, 1849: 1-Memorial of Benj Godfrey, of Alton, Ill, claiming for certain illegal taxes & duties levied & exacted upon him at Matamoras during 1830 thru 1833, was examined & ordered to be received. 2-That of Bridget Burns, claiming for goods in a convoy captured or destroyed near Ramos, on or about Feb 17, 1847, being submitted & taken up for examination, the following order was directed to be entered: "Ordered, That, in the opinion of this Board, the case set forth in the memorial of Bridget Burns persents no valid claim against the republic of Mexico, & that it is therefore rejected." 3-Consideration of several memorials of Edgarend J Forestall, in his own right, & also as copartner & representative of the late firm of Gordon, Forestall & Co; of Jas Johnston, administrator of Jas P Wallace, & of Jos H Cucullu, adm of Simon Cucullu, claimants in the matter of the seizure of the schnr **Felix** at Tampico in 1825; as also to the consideration of the proofs & documents connected therewith, & came to an oinion-That the claim of the aforesaid Forestall is not valid, & not allowed. Like manner the claim of Jos H Cucullu, as not valid, & not allowed. The claim of Jas Johnston, administrator is valid, & allowed accordingly: the amount to be awarded subject to Board.

The Charleston Courier announces the death of Capt John Williamson, of the U S Ordnance Dept, which took place at his residence in Cannonborough, on Sunday last. He was a native of N J, & had nearly completed his 44th year of his age. He was educated at West Point, & graduated with much distinction. The Gov't works on the Chattahooche river, Fla, were built under his superintendence, & he more recently superintended the construction of the U S Arsenal near Charleston, where he resided at the time of his death. He was an accomplished ofcr, & highly appreciated for his worth.

The British man-of-war **Herald**, Capt Kellett, arrived at Mazatlan on Nov 13. She was in search of Sir John Franklin, but could not get any tidings of him.

The Western Military Institute, one of the best in the valley of the Mississippi, will be removed from Gtwn to the Blue Licks on Jan 1 next. Col T F Johnson, the principal or chief commandant, has been long & favorable known as an instructor of youth. The Messrs Holliday, to whom the **Blue Lick** property belongs, are gentlemen of intelligence & experience in the business of hotel keeping. –Frankfort Commonwealth

We learn from Mr Tyre Maupin, Editor & Proprietor of the Harrisonburg Republican, that his printing ofc, with every appertaining to it, was destroyed by fire on Mon last. Loss is about $25,000. Mr Maupin has a large family connexion. –Va Advocate

Death of the Prophet of the <u>Millerites</u>. Mr Wm Miller died at his home in Kompton, Wash Co, N Y, on Dec 20, aged 68 years. He was a native of Pittsfield, Mass, & during the last war with England served as a Capt of Volunteers on the Northern frontier. He began to speak in public assemblies on the subject of the Millennium in 1833, & in the 10 years which preceded the time which he had set for the confirmation of all prophecy, he labored assiduously in the Middle & Northern States: succeeded in building up a sect of some 30,000 or 40,000 disciples, which disappeared rapidly after the close of the day of probation in 1843, after which time Mr Miller himself did not often advocate or defend his views in public.

A letter from Las Vegas, dated Oct 27, gives some additional particulars respecting the murder of Mr Jas M White & his party. The murders were committed by a band of about 70 Apache Indians, near Point-of-Rocks, within 7 or 8 days travel of Santa Fe. The carriages of the victims were completely riddled with balls & the 5 men, Mr Jas M White, Wm Calloway, Mr Snowberger, Ben Thompson, a mulatto, & another gentlemen, lay near the carriages scalped, with evident signs of desperate fighting every where visible around the camp. A company of Mexicans came up soon after, but did not know of any harm, & were busy looking at the effect of the massacre, when they were surprised & attacked by the same body of Indians. They gained the hill but lost 4 men, & a mere boy was left for dead. Mr Hugh N Smith, the Delegate from New Mexico to Congress, on his way to this city, picked him up. Mrs White & her daughter were carried off captives by the Indians.

On Christmas day the dwlg of a colored man named Wells, residing at the Navy Yard caught fire, & 4 human beings fell victims to the flames: David Whittle, 35, who drove a hack for Wells [owner of the house,] Eliz Wells, 12, Philip Wells, 9 to 10, children of P Wells, & Eliz Shorter, aged 6 or 7, grandchild of P Wells. The chimney in the house had been swept the previous day, & the soot had been suffered to remain on the hearth. The fire communicated to a fire-board.

Mrd: on Dec 25, in Broadway Methodist Church, Balt, by Rev L F Morgan, of Wash, Jas W Deeble, of the latter place, & Nicea Fuller, of the former.

Mrd: on Dec 18, in Richmond, Va, by Rev Dr Empie, Robt E Scott, of Fauquier, to Miss Henningham, daughter of Jas Lyons, of Richmond.

Died: on Dec 24, Susan M G Hedgman. Her remains will, this morning, be removed from the residence of her brother, on 18th st, to the family burial place in Virginia.

Died: on Dec 23, at Phil, in his 21st year, Geo B Stone, student of medicine at the Univ of Pa, & youngest son of Wm H & Eliz J Stone, of Wash.

Died: on Dec 25, 2nd daughter of Thos & Frances Birch, aged 6 years & 10 months. Her funeral is today, at 3 o'clock, from her father's residence, on N Y ave, between 7th & 8th sts.

Persons having bills against the steamboat **Joseph Johnson** are to present them to Capt Corson or the undersigned before Jan 1 next. –Thos Parker, Chairman

FRI DEC 28, 1849
Senate: 1-Ptn of Wm Maxwell, heir of Josiah Maxwell, a Revolutionary ofcr, asking to be allowed commutation pay: referred to the Cmte on Revolutionary Claims. 2-Ptn of John Biddle, late register of the land ofc at Detroit, asking the reimbursement of money expended by him for extra clerk hire: referred to the Cmte on Public Lands. 3-Claim of Jonathan Kearsley, receiver of public moneys at Detroit, for the reimbursement of money expended by him for extra clerk hire: referred to the Cmte on Public Lands. 4-Ptn of Hiram Moore & John Hascall, asking a renewal of their patent for a harvesting machine: referred to the Cmte on Patents & the Patent Ofc. 5-Ordered, that the memorial & other papers in the case of John S Russworm, now on the files of the Senate: be referred to the Cmte on Revolutionary Claims. 6-Cmte on Printing, to whom was referred the memorial of the heirs of Kosciusko, reported in favor of printing the same: which was agreed to. 7-Ptn of F Maxwell, register, J A Langlois, receiver, Jacob Feaman, late register of the land ofc at Kaskaskia, Ill, asking to be allowed commissions on entries of military land warrants: referred to the Cmte on Public Lands. 8-Ptn of D Clapp & J H Murphy, register & receiver, & L R Noel & Wm E Russell, late register & receiver of the land ofc at Danville, Ill, asking to be allowed commissions on entries of military land warrants: referred to the Cmte on Public Lands. 9-Memorial of Mary A Watson, widow of Saml E Watson, late an ofcr in the marine corps, asking an increase of pension. This lady, observed Mr Clay, represents her husband, after having fought gallantly in the war with Mexico, died at Vera Curz; that application was made for a pension, & that a pension was granted to her at a rate below the rank of her deceased husband. She wishes Congress to increase the amount of the pension so as to make it correspond wih the rank he bore in the service of his country: referred to the Cmte on Pensions. 10-Ptn of Wm H Walker, for the heirs of Danl Walker, asking indemnity for French spoliations prior to 1800: ordered to lie on the table. 11-Ptn of Mr Geo F Warfield, asking compensation for losses sustained by depredations of public & private armed vessels of France, from the year 1793 to 1800: referred to the Cmte on Foreign Relations. 12-Ptn of David M Smith, of Niagara Co, N Y, asking a pension: referred to the Cmte on Pensions. 13-Ptn of Edw J Thomas, asking compensation for a horse abandoned by order of an ofcr of the U S in the Florida war: referred to the Cmte on Military Affairs. 14-Ptn of Jos T Walker, atty, in favor of sundry citizens of Florida, asking compensation for horses lost in the service of the U S: referred to the Cmte on Military Affairs. 15-Ptn of Kennedy & Darling, of Tampa, Fla, asking indemnity for injuries committed by the Seminole Indians in Florida: referred to the Cmte on Indian Affairs. 16-Ordered, that the papers in the case of Mrs Everett, widow of the late Alex'r Everett, now on the files of the Senate, be referred to the Cmte on Foreign Relations. 16-Ptn of the heirs of John Holden,

deceased, a revolutionary ofcr, asking compensation for his military services: referred to the Cmte on Revolutionary Claims. 17-Ptn of the heirs of Jacob Lathing, deceased, asking indemnity for French spoliations prior to 1800: laid on the table. 18-Ptn of Francis Rotche, co-heir of Wm Rotche & Sons, asking indemnity for French spoliations prior to 1800: laid on the table. 19-Ptn of A G Grover, a citizen of Springwater, N Y, asking such an amendment of the pension laws as will provide pensions for the heirs of Revolutionary ofcrs & soldiers who died prior to the passage of the act of 1818: referred to the Cmte on Pensions. 20-Memorial of Geo Adams, an ofcr in the U S marine corps, asking compensation for property lost during the Mexican war, & reimbursement of medical expenses incurred in consequence of a wound received in the engagement at the Natural Bridge: referred to the Cmte on Pensions. 21-Memorial of Geo Warfield & others, asking indemnity for French spoliations prior to 1800: laid on the table. 22-Memorial of Isaac Everett, exc of Harriet Barney, deceased, asking indemnity for French spoliations prior to 1800: laid on the table. 23-Cmte on Pensions: to inquire into granting a pension to Patsey Ellmore, for the services of her husband, Thos Ellmore, during the Revolutionary war in the Va line; & that the Sec of the Interior be directed to lay before the cmte the evidence in support of her application for a pension now in the Pension ofc. 24-Mr Clay has a ptn from a lady [Mrs Henry] whose husband he knew well. He served with great credit during the Revolutionary war, & in every war I believe that we have been engaged in. She prays for a pension. Referred to the Cmte on Pensions. 25-Ptn of Andrew Bankson, asking a grant of land for services rendered & property lost during the last war with Great Britain: referred to the Cmte on Public Lands. 26-Ptn of Lewis A Thomas & Thos Rogers, asking compensation for services in defending certain Sioux Indians, charged with murder, in the State of Missouri: referred to the Cmte on Indian Affairs. 27-Memorial of the heirs of Pascal Detchmendy, asking confirmation of their title to a tract of land in the State of Missouri: referred to the Cmte on Private Land Claims. 28-Ptn of Moses Paquett & Therese Brisbois, asking the confirmation of their title to an Indian reservation: referred to the Cmte on Public Lands. 29-Ptn from Abagail Shaler *S_ilwell, [Mr Clay remarked] is the sister of one of the wealthiest men I have known in public service, a man who was for a long time one of our consuls on the coast of Barbary & afterwards transferred to Cuba, where he died. The lady thinks that in the settlement of the estate of her deceased brother an allowance was refused which ought to have been made: referred to the Cmte on Foreign Relations. [*Could be Stilwell.]

Albany Evening Journal: In May last the troy cars ran off the track in Saratoga Co, killing the engineer & badly mutilating the fireman. John Tallmadge, a respectable farmer residing near the road was arrested & committed: witnesses were Jas Phayer & Jos Balfrey, alias Geo Parker. Balfrey said that Tallmadge arrived at Quebec on May 14 last, in the ship **Jessie**, from Limerick. Mr Scott-for the accused- found Mr Tallmadge arrived on May 25, the day after the railroad accident. He went to N Y to the ofc of the Emigrant Com'rs & found that Balfrey arrived there in Jul last. A man who had known both Phayer & Balfrey in Ireland, said they had bad characters. Phayer & Balfrey were arrested for perjury. The accused was released from prison, would go back to this family friends with a vindicated & unblemished reputation. Thus, after 6 months imprisonment, & at an expense of $2,000 in preparing his defence, Mr Tallmadge comes forth free alike from punishment & reproach.

The Newark Advertiser of Tue states that the schnr **Ellen Sedgwick**, Capt Beaston, was wrecked on the coast of N J during the severe storm of Sat last. All hands on board perished, with the exception of the mate, Mr Champney.

Norfolk papers: during the heavy blow on Sat last the windmill of Mr Wm C Moore, of Princess Anne Co, Va, near the Bay shore, was blown down, by which accident Mr Moore was instantly crushed to death. His son, & a young man named Pallet, were dreadfully injured.

The city of Lowell, by the verdict of the jury in the Supreme Judicial Court, is to pay Lyman Raymond, $9,975, as compensation for a broken knee pan, causing permanent lameness. He was injured by stumbling over a grate in the gutter, which stuck up some 2 inches above the curb-stone.

New Post ofcs for the week ending Dec 23, 1849:

Ofc	County, State	Postmaster:
Pottersville	Cheshire, N H	Aaron Smith
State Line	Berkshire, Mass	M D Schoonmaker
N Bridge Ctre	Worcester, Mass	Wm B Fuller
N Franklin	New London, Ct	Amos F Royce
N Monmouth	Kennebeck, Maine	John B Fogg
Transit Bridge	Alleghany, N Y	John Royce
State Bridge	Oneida, N Y	A Hess
Collamer	Onondaga, N Y	Henry E Peirce
Lee Centre	Oneida, N Y	O L Kenyon
Norton Hill	Greene, N Y	N Ramsdell
Blue Rock	Chester, Pa	Chas Tettew
River	Clarion, Pa	Jas Duncan
New Guilford	Franklin, Pa	Geo Tritle
Windridge	Greene, Pa	Robt Bristor
Dunmore	Luzerne, Pa	Geo P Howell
New Lebanon	Mercer, Pa	Jas H Leech
Baileysburgh	Perry, N Y	Jos Bailey
Woodbine	Carroll, Md	Basil Owings
Pricetown	Highland, Ohio	Jos Lambert
Penfield	Calhoun, Mich	Henry Parsons
Fowler's	Brooke, Va	A R Sharp
Blackshires	Marion, Va	Elias Blackshire
Buggabo	Wilkes, N C	O Sprinkle
Bethmont	Orange, N C	M C Stroud
Shooting Creek	Cherokee, N C	W R McConnell
Rickoe's Bluff	Gadsden, Fla	Wm McCelland
North River	Tuscaloosa, Ala	Chas F Jay
Strata	Montgomery, Ala	Elka Barnes
Jericho	Perry, Ala	Stephen S Poole
Pine Hills	Washita P, La	Jacob A Coons
Shoobota	Clark, Miss	Benj Blakeney
Stony Point	White, Ark	Jesse D Combs

Basham's Mills	Johnson, Ark	Jos A Stewart
Borland	Newton, Ark	Edw Hailes
Cash	St Francis, Ark	Geo W Wright
Monticello	Drew, Ark	J D Berry
Ash Spring	Harrison, Texas	John M Whitehorn
Biloxi	Newton, Texas	John C Lawhon
Kaufman	Kaufman, Texas	John W Field
4 Mile Prairie	Henderson, Texas	Mills Goodwin
Round Hill	Smith, Texas	A O Brian
Morales de Lavaca	Jackson, Texas	Jas Kerr
Walnut Valley	Marion, Ten	S B Bowles
Mount Nebo	Willaimson, Ten	John Richardson
Palo Alto	Lawrence, Ten	Jas W Perry
Stamper's Mills	Owen, Ky	Hugh Stamper
Haydon's	Owen, Ky	Jas Wilson
New Market	Marion, Ky	Henry H Carter
Eagletown	Hamilton, Ia	Jesse F Jackson
Deer Creek	Carroll, Ia	B H Smith
Catalpa Grove	Benton, Ia	Wm R Johnson
Carmargo	Jefferson, Ia	Amos Bussey
Stevens' Point	Portage, Wis	Wm Griffin
Bellefountain	Columbia, Wis	John S Bonny
Callamer	Sauk, Wis	Chester Mattson
Pleasant Plain	Jefferson, Iowa	Edw Hobson
St Jos Prairie	Dubuque, Iowa	John McCall
Cottage Grove	Wash, Min T	Jos W Tucker
Red Rock	Ramsey, Min T	John A Ford

<u>Names Changed:</u> Wilkinson, Windham Co, Conn, changed to Quinebaug.
East Solon, Cortlandt Co, N Y, changed to Taylor.
Campton, Bradford Co, Pa, changed to Merryall.
Carey's Academy, Hamilton Co, Ohio, changed to College Hill.
Earle, Lancaster Co, Pa, changed to Goodville.
Kern's Mills, Lehigh Co, Pa, changed to Eisenhart.
Hoysburgh, Alleghany Co, Md, changed to Winston.
Cool Spring, Wash Co, N C, changed to Scuppernong.
Larksville, Jones Co, Ga, changed to Griswoldville.
Hatter's Shop, Itawamba Co, Miss, changed to Mooreville.
Sangamon River, Cass co, Ill, changd to Robinson's Mills.
Camden, Schuyler Co, Ill, changed to Brooklyn.
Fair Plain, Whitesides Co, Ill, changed to Spring Hill.
Arena, Iowa Co, Wisc, changed to East Arena.
Polk Prairie, Columbia Co, Wisc, changed to Randolph.
Peneushr, Dallas Co, Iowa, changed to Adell.

Orphans Court of Wash Co, D C. Letters of administration de bonis non, with the will annexed, on the personal estate of John B Kerby, late of said county, deceased.
--John H Bayne, adm de bonis non, W A

From Calif: 1-Col R J P Allen, the special Mail Agent for Calif & Oregon, has returned from an official tour through the territory, & expected to return soon to the U S to report. 2-Col Collier, the new Collector, arrived at San Francisco & assumed the direction of the custom house. 3-Col A Johnson, Indian Agent for the Sacramento Joaquin valleys, had arrived at San Francisco. His official residence will be at Puebla de San Jose. 4-The following was under the heading of: the Calif newspapers contains the following notice of recent deaths, murders, & suicides. Four of the Rogers family who left N Y for Chagres in the steamer **Crescent City** in Dec last have since died. Mathew G Rogers, died of fever in Panama about Feb 1; the father, David Rogers, & David Rogers, jr, died a few weeks since on the Yuba river; & Leander breathed his last in this city on the 30th inst. 5-Died: on the 10th inst, after a lingering illness, of dysentery, Louis Tramble, printer, formerly of St Louis, Mo. Died: on Nov 11, after a long & painful illness, L D Ellis, of N Y, in his 26th year. Died, on the 2nd inst, Patrick Healy, formerly of New Haven, aged about 23 years. Died, on the 1st inst, on board barque **Clarissa**, Silas Wheeler, of N Y, of dysentery, subsequent to a relapse of typhus fever. Died: at San Francisco, on Oct 28, Wm Wallace Cook, of dysentery, formerly of Newark, N J, aged 23 years. Died: on Oct 27, in San Francisco, Mr John McCrackin, late of N Y, & formerly of Canada. Died: on the 5th inst, of consumption, Danl P Andrews, aged 22, late of Providence, R I. Fernando Flint, formerly of N Y, at one time a consul for Hanover & Brazil at Valparaiso, committed suicide on the 11th inst, at a house in this city, by blowing the upper portion of his head entirely off with a pistol. Henry Parks was found murdered in the Red Woods, on Nov 5, near the residence of Mr Chas Brown. An inquest was held on Sat last on the body of G W Tobey, who died suddenly on board the ship **Mentor**, in this port, on the previous day: verdict-excessive drunkenness. 5-Letter from Chas Hazleton, dated Sacramento, Nov 1, 1849. As myself & F S Leonard, of Worcester, Mass, were traveling on horseback from Nicholas rancho to the Yuba mines, on Oct 14, we were attacked by 11 Mexicans. I out ran them. When I looked back to see if my friend was following me, I saw them throw a lasso over his head & fastened him. I went back about an hour later, & found considerable blood on the ground, & have heard nothing of him since, & I expect he is murdered.

Christmas Day passed off in Wash City with few violations of the law. The firing of guns was more confined to enclosures & yards of private dwlgs. In Mr John A Donohoo's yard, on 7th & D sts, a gun burst in the hands of a German, F Ebeling, & so lacerated it that amputation will probably be necessary. He is attended by Dr Lieberman.

Commission of Claims against Mexico: 1-Memorial of Saml Toby, surviving partner of Thos Toby & Brother, of New Orleans, claiming for seizure & confiscation of the cargo of the Mexican schnr **Columbia**, in the mouth of Brasos, May, 1835, by the Mexican schnr **Montezuma**, was submitted, examined, & ordered to be received. 2-The cases of Benj Holbrook, in the matter of the ship **John**, & the one of John Bolden, but without coming to any final decisions thereon. Board adjourned.

Mrd: on Dec 27, by Rev L F Morgan, Saml A Peugh to Caroline S, youngest daughter of Anne Blanchard, all of Wash City.

Died: on Dec 26, Mr Wm Lloyd, in his 48th year. His funeral is at 11 o'clock, this morning, from his late residence on 13th st, near Md ave.
+
Members of the Columbian Encampment are to meet at the Hall this morning, to attend the funeral of Brother Wm Lloyd. –Fred Iddins, Scribe

Last Note: I do forewarn all persons from receiving a note of hand, payable to Susan G Beall, by Mr Selby B Scaggs. –Fielder Magruder, adm

SAT DEC 29, 1849
Wash Corp: 1-Ptn from Thos P Morgan for the erection of a wharf at the foot of G st: referred to Select Cmte. 2-Ptn from Caleb Sebastian for refunding of certain moneys: referred to the Cmte of Claims. 3-Ptn of Elias Barnes, praying the payment of a balance due him for certain work: referred to the Cmte on Improvements.

Jas G Gilchrist & Geo S Cox, Attys & Counsellors at Law & Solicitors in Chancery: ofc at Haynesville, Lowndes Co, Ala. [Ad]

Ravenscroft College, Columbia, Tenn, under the control of Bishop Otey & the Convention of the Protestant Episcopal Church: next session will begin on the first Mon in Feb. Prof Macleod is head of the household. Exec cmte: Rt Rev Jas H Otey, ex-officio Pres. Trustees: Andrew J Polk, Ashwood, Maury Co; Jas Walker, Columbia, Maury Co; & Rev E H Cresay, Ashwood Recto_ly, Maury Co.

Wash City Ordinance: 1-Act authorizing Chas Lenman to continue certain improvements on a frame house in square 140, on north L st, between 18th & 19th sts.

Count Arthur De Montesquiou, an elder brother of the 2 young Frenchmen of that name at present imprisoned in the St Louis jail for murder, arrived in that city on Dec 13, having started thither from France as soon as the news of the dreadful act of his brothers reached him.

MON DEC 31, 1849
Criminal Court-Wash: Fri last. 1-Lloyd Lane, guilty for attempting to break into the dwlg-house of John Shinnor. 2-Elijah Parker guilty for an assault upon & resisting a constable in the discharge of his duty. 3-Robt Burns guilty of assault only.
4-Lawrence Kennedy, guilty for lareny. Sat: 1-Free negro, W Adams, guilty of grand larceny.

The Richmond papers announce the death of Dr John Cullen, formerly Prof of Theory & Practice of Medicine in Hampden Sydney College. [No death date given-current item.]

Mr Griffin Theobolds, of Franklin, Ky, recently shot himself accidentally on a plantation on the Mississippi, & died from the wound.

Andrew Foster, one of the oldest & most esteemed merchants, died at his residence in N Y on Wed last, in the 78th year of his age.

Wash, Dec 27, 1849. The accounting ofcrs of the Treasury have reported Prosper M Wetmore, late Navy Agent of the U S at N Y, to the Solicitor of the Treasury, as a defaulter in the enormous sum of $558,000, & have recommended that prosecution shall be commenced against him forthwith. The surety in his official bond is only $30,000. Those who know Mr Wetmore, [says the Post,] will put no faith in this charge, until it is confirmed. Mr Wetmore assures the public, that whatever balance may be found to be due to the Gov't will be promptly paid.

Mrs Farnham, last winter, proposed to take charge of such females as desired to embark for a new home in Calif. She sailed from N Y, in the ship **Angelique**, with her 2 children & servant, & 2 or 3 female companions. She was left on the shores of Valparaiso, by the capt, in a destitute condition. Her servant had been induced by the capt to leave her & enter his service. For this & other controversies, a bad state of feeling seems to have grown up between them. On arriving at Valparaiso, Mrs Farnham went ashore to procure a new servant, but on returing to the ship, discovered the servant had no passport. She insisted upon returning to the city to procure on. She did so, & on her return, before her boat reached the ship, the capt set sail, abandoning her, without money or baggage, & carrying with him her 2 young children, the eldest not 7 years of age. The Boston Traveller says the people of Valparaiso promptly furnished her with the necessary means of prosecuting her journey to San Francisco. We can hardly conceive of any provocation sufficient to justify the apparent inhumanity of the capt's conduct.

Mrd: on Dec 20, at Williamsburg, by Rev S Malone, Alfred Briggs, of N Y, to Helen C Ironside, of Wash.

Mrd: on Dec 28, by Rev C M Butler, Mr Jas Hemsley to Miss Eliza Hall, both of Fairfax Co, Va.

Mrd: on Dec 28, by Rev C M Butler, Mr Thos J Hunter to Miss Mary E Odd, both of Chas Co, Md.

Mrd: on Dec 27, by Rev S A H Marks, Mr Jas Tucker to Miss Jane Maddox.

Mrd: on Dec 24, at the residence of Col Tuly, Clark Co, Va, by Rev Mr Hough, Dr Thos Hanse, of Calvert Co, Md, to Mary E, daughter of the late Capt H Garner, U S Army.

Mrd: on Dec 25, at the Church of Ascension, Balt, Md, by Rev Dr Atkinson, Jno W Spicknall, of Calvert Co, Md, to Lucie A, 2nd daughter of the late Capt H Garner, U S Army.

Female servant wanted, one who is honest, industrious, & capable of doing the general work of a family: good home & full wages, punctually paid, by application to Geo M Davis, at the Bank of the Metropolis, or Lewis Johnson, 11th & G sts.

Rev R R Gurley, our esteemed fellow citizen, has returned to his home in Wash City, in improved health, from a brief visit to the Colony of Liberia, in Alfrica.

Case of the heirs of Kosciusko: Circuit Court of Wash Co, D C-in Chancery. John G Ennis, adm de bonis non of Jos Zolkowski et al, vs Jonathan B H Smith, adm & trustee of the late Geo Bomford et al. On Sep 26, 1848, a bill was filed in this Court, having for its object to obtain discovery, account, & distribution of the personal estate of Gen Thaddeus Kosciusko, deceased. Said bill charges that Gen K made & executed 4 wills-one on May 5, 1798, by which he disposed of his property left in this country for certain charitable purposes; another, on Jun 28, 1806, by which he bequeathed to Kosciusko Armstrong $3,704, out of the same property; third, on Jun 4, 1846, by which he disposed of to sundry persons a portion of his property left in Europe, & then revoked all the wills & condicils made previously; fourth, on Oct 10, 1817, by which he disposed of the residue of his property left in Europe, leaving unrevoked the revoking clause of the will of Jun 4, 1816. Said bill further charges that, by reason of the revoking clause, the wills of 1798 & 1806 became a nullity, & cannot take effect, & prays that the estate of Kosciusko, left in this country, may be distributed among his next of kin. The said bill was demurred to by Jonathan B H Smith, adm & trustee of Geo Bomford, the deceased administrator of Kosciusko's estate, & also by the sureties to the probate bonds of said Bomford, from & against whom discovery & relief is sought. This Court, by a decision given on Dec 22, 1849, overruled their several demurrers, & suggested that it may perhaps be necessary that Kosciusko Armstrong should be made a party before final decree can be made in this case. An amended bill making said Kosciusko Armstrong a party to said original bill was therefore filed, praying that said Armstrong be ordered to answer the premises thereof relating to the will dated Jun 28, 1806, & charging that it is a nullity. The said amended bill further charges that subsequent to the filing of the original bill, to wit, on Feb 6, 1849, the probates of the wills of 1798 & 1806 have been revoked by the Orphans Court of Wash Co, D C. It appearing to the Court that said Kosciusko Armstrong does not reside within the jurisdiction of this court, it is, on motion of the solicitor of the cmplnts, [G Tochman,] this Dec 22, 1849, ordered that said dfndnt Kosciusko Armstrong be & appear before this court on or before the 1st Mon in May, 1850, to answer the original & amended bills of the cmplnts, & show cause why a decree should not pass as prayed by said bills; otherwise the same will be taken pro confesso. -W Cranch -Jno A Smith, clerk

A suit was brought by Lucius E Bulkely against C Bainbridge Smith & others this past week, to recover damages for alleged malicious prosectution in charging the plntf, [a counselor at law] with testifying in a case at the Common Pleas, brought by Mr Bradley, a hackney coachman, against dfndnts, that he [Mr B] had no interest in the result of the suit, whereas he had an interest, etc. A criminal cmplnt was made against Bulkely, who was acquitted of the charge & then brought the present suit. The jury yesterday rendered a verdict for plntf-$3,700 damages.
–N Y Mirror [etc as copied.]

Rev R R Gurley, our esteemed fellow citizen, has returned to his home in Wash City, in improved health, from a brief visit to the Colony of Liberia, in Alfrica.

Mr Jas B Huie, who went to Calif in command of one of the Louisville, Ky, companies, writes home that he is carrying on the auction & commission business in San Francisco, & is well pleased with his prospects.

In Chancery: Saml Redfern, cmplnt, vs Barbara A Parker & Jos Frazer, adms, & Geo W Parker, Thos J Parker, Jas M Parker, & Frances M Parker, & others, heirs of Thos T Parker, dfndnts. By an interlocutory order of the Circuit Court of D C, I am directed to state the account of the Trustee in the above cause, & the claims of the cmplnt & the other creditors of the late Thos T Parker, finally, & the proportion of assets due to each. I shall execute such order on Jan 7 next, at my ofc, in the City Hall, Wash, at 10 a m. Creditors who have not filed their claims are requested to do so. –W Redin, Auditor

In Chancery: Mary King, cmplnt, against Walter S Cox, adm de bonis non, & Geo King, Sally King, & Wm T Maddox & Anna Maria his wife, heirs at law of Chas King, dfndnts. By an interlocutory order of the Circuit Court of D C, I am directed to state the account of the Trustee in the above cause, & the claims of the cmplnt & the other creditors of the late Chas King, finally, & the proportion of assets due to each. I shall execute such order Jan 8 next, at my ofc, City Hall, Wash, at 10 a m. Creditors who have not filed their claims are requested to do so. –W Redin, Auditor

Washington Monument: 1-Resolved, that a cmte of 3 be appointed, whose duty it shall be to procure & forward to the Bldg Cmte of the Wash Nat'l Monument a block of Alabama marble: 4 feet long & 2 feet high, with a depth of about 12 inches, upon which they shall cause the following inscription to be made: Alabama Marble, Presented by the M W Grand Lodge of Ancient Free & Accepted Masons of the State of Alabama to the Washington National Monument Society. –Rufus Green, Grand Master; Amand Pfister, Grand Sec. Dec 6, A L 5849. 2-Resolved, that $200 be appropriated out of the funds of this Grand Lodge to aid in building the Wash Nat'l Monument, & that it be forwarded to Hon Elisha Whittlesey, Gen Agent, at Wash City. 3-Resolved, that a cmte be appointed, to address a circular to all of the sub-ordinate lodges under this jurisdiction, asking each of them to contribute a sum not less than $5 to the contemplated object, & that they forward the several amounts so given to Hon Elisha Whittlesey. Cmte on 1st Resolution: Brother W P Chilton, of Tuskegee; Brother J McCalet Wiley, of Clayton; Brother Amand P Pfister, of Montg, Cmte on 3rd Resolution: Brother Amand P Pfister, of Montg; Brother E M Hasting, of Montg; Brother Joel White, of Montg

Whereas the Columbia Topographical Society, conceiving it to be a duty they owe to the memory of the great Washington to contribute to the Nat'l Monument now erecting in Wash City, but being precluded by their laws from appropriating funds from their treasury for such purposes, have there. Resolved, that a cmte of one of the Society from each ofc be appointed to solicit donations from the members of the Society for the purchase of a suitable block of marble, to be placed in said monument in the name of the society. Cmte: M Caton, Jas English, J H Thorn, Geo Cochran.

The *President's House* will be open for the reception of visiters at 12 o'clock on New Years' day; also, that the receptions on Friday morning are dispensed with until further notice.

A

A W Johnson, 153
Abbe, 348
Abbot, 184, 320
Abbot of Mount Millery, 221
Abbott, 88, 169, 302, 320, 336, 378, 446, 451, 484
Abell, 167
Abernethy, 232
Abert, 87, 321
Abingdon, 203
Abney, 16
Aborn, 258
Abraham, 151
Abrahams, 396
Acadia, 217
Acaff, 384
Acker, 17, 25, 196, 408
Ackerman, 13
Ackles, 370
Ackley, 167, 433
Acklin, 289
Actios, 302
Acton, 184, 401
Adair, 310, 314
Adam, 49, 141
Adams, 1, 46, 47, 55, 79, 87, 91, 101, 104, 127, 144, 174, 176, 184, 192, 204, 211, 212, 258, 267, 270, 291, 294, 302, 305, 307, 325, 350, 354, 355, 357, 358, 374, 385, 388, 396, 400, 401, 403, 408, 413, 421, 427, 433, 446, 447, 474, 488, 492
Adamson, 349
Addington, 246, 248
Addison, 3, 9, 49, 53, 91, 99, 107, 109, 119, 277, 350, 354, 414
Adelphi Mills, 338
Adie, 430
Adkins, 446, 484
Adlum, 231, 262
Admiral, 153
Adoring Angels, 224
Agee, 28, 205
Agg, 375, 416
Agnew, 66, 365

Ahrens, 167
Ahumada, 280
Aigler, 47, 184, 409
Aiken, 176, 338
Aikin, 4
Ailer, 47, 184, 350
Ainsworth, 172
Aisquith, 136
Alberts, 76
Albertson, 238
Alderman, 107
Aldrich, 38, 54, 57, 64, 96, 454
Aldridge, 242
Aldunate, 286
Alert, 153
Alex Hamilton, 217
Alexander, 29, 88, 103, 121, 134, 138, 140, 184, 196, 234, 241, 274, 276, 279, 293, 381, 419, 442
Alford, 417, 476
Alger, 280
Algoma, 153
Ali, 342
Alice, 217
Alig, 225, 260, 378, 385, 406, 423, 439
Allen, 15, 27, 29, 33, 47, 49, 61, 62, 69, 77, 105, 114, 141, 165, 173, 178, 200, 211, 228, 231, 234, 239, 257, 290, 293, 302, 310, 314, 329, 339, 350, 355, 369, 376, 377, 385, 396, 399, 400, 403, 414, 434, 456, 465, 472, 482, 491
Allensworth, 476
Allison, 155, 291, 417
Allmand, 326
Allnutt, 279
Allston, 231
Alsop, 8
Alsworth, 282
Alva, 60
Alvarez, 424
Alvord, 266
Amazeen, 238
Ambler, 146
Amelia, 153
American, 153

American Eagle, 153, 217
American packet-ship, 280
Ames, 97
Ana, 424
Anderson, 1, 8, 10, 27, 47, 49, 56, 59, 71, 74, 75, 83, 88, 94, 133, 139, 159, 172, 184, 191, 203, 255, 256, 265, 302, 307, 321, 339, 355, 373, 397, 417, 447, 464, 478
Andover, 422
Andraud, 19
Andre, 164
Andres, 267
Andrews, 30, 40, 130, 146, 158, 231, 233, 249, 293, 352, 399, 459, 477, 481, 491
Andros, 369
Andross, 255
Angers, 400
Anglo Saxon, 154
Angney, 424
Angue, 95
Angus, 456
Annan, 278
Annis, 404
Ansman, 72
Anson, 10
Anthony, 219
Anthony Wayne, 155
Apperwolm, 204
Appleton, 139, 233, 358
Appointments by the Pres, 9, 10, 19, 22, 40, 108, 114, 117, 121, 131, 144, 147, 151, 161, 167, 170, 172, 176, 179, 180, 183, 191, 196, 200, 202, 203, 207, 211, 215, 219, 222, 223, 225, 228, 231, 233, 236, 237, 244, 246, 247, 252, 255, 259, 271, 274, 277, 289, 295, 299, 304, 310, 366, 371, 374, 399, 417, 423, 440
Araby, 473
Arago, 176
Aram, 393, 402, 431, 468
Aranas, 460
Archer, 123, 448
Archibald, 303
Arguelles, 383
Arguellis, 273

Arkansas Mail, 154
Armant, 286
Armendari, 444
Armijo, 424
Armistead, 35, 56, 96
Armstrong, 8, 38, 54, 73, 122, 129, 143, 192, 225, 242, 285, 296, 330, 494
Army, 418
Arndt, 196
Arner, 330
Arnold, 61, 72, 113, 123, 184, 270, 384, 406, 438, 460, 477
Arny, 459
Arredondo Grant, 18
Arth, 352
Arthur, 449
Asbury, 289
Ash, 259
Ashard, 89
Ashburton, 5, 214
Ashby, 310, 374
Ashdown, 8, 409
Ashford, 150, 213, 378
Ashland Row, 333
Ashley, 381, 385
Ashmead, 196
Ashton, 1, 170
Ashurst, 424
Asiatic Cholera, 260
Asker, 429
Askey, 473
Aspinwall, 23, 56, 151, 454
Astaburuage, 327
Astley, 43
Aston, 317
Astor, 114
Astor Opera House, 194
Atamasco, 22
Atcheson, 347
Atchison, 47, 103, 346
Atkins, 15, 215
Atkinson, 25, 37, 152, 376, 394, 451, 456, 493
Atlantis, 153
Attree, 446
Atwell, 378
Aubert, 286

Aubry, 209
Aud, 136
Audubon, 33, 145
Augell, 339
Austin, 1, 137, 167, 215, 238, 253, 278, 382
Austriss, 430
Avalanche, 154
Averill, 81, 211
Averll, 58, 63
Avery, 49, 172, 192, 208, 224
Ayer, 349
Aylward, 200
Aymor, 418

B

Babbitt, 127, 391
Babcock, 152, 452
Babin, 425
Baby, 286
Baca, 424
Bache, 51, 97, 205, 344
Bacigalupo, 426
Backenstos, 126, 153
Backus, 173, 183, 245, 374
Bacon, 47, 98, 158, 211, 213, 227, 276, 295, 320, 339, 353, 370, 401
Baden, 49, 176, 419
Badger, 96, 338, 381
Baeschlin, 350
Bagby, 333, 334
Baggett, 109
Bagley, 243
Bagot, 424
Bagwell, 295
Baile, 416
Bailey, 13, 113, 122, 167, 168, 180, 181, 191, 196, 203, 266, 302, 399, 436, 475, 489
Baily, 11, 230, 264, 323, 448
Bain, 341
Bainbridge, 124
Baird, 100, 200, 242, 265, 294, 329
Baker, 6, 14, 16, 17, 43, 52, 58, 66, 81, 127, 177, 284, 302, 339, 348, 358, 393, 404, 407, 435, 467, 478, 481
Bakewell, 12, 145

Balch, 328
Balclutha, 118
Balcomb, 183
Baldwin, 5, 16, 24, 25, 42, 71, 75, 122, 173, 184, 242, 295, 304, 335, 350, 402, 454, 471, 477, 479
Balfrey, 488
Ball, 88, 93, 193, 224, 227, 343, 358, 449
Ballantine, 77, 326, 338, 405
Ballard, 169, 229, 256, 265, 334
Ballman, 23
Baltimore, 352
Baltzell, 35, 348
Baltzer, 49, 268, 310
Bancroft, 356, 423
Banes, 1
Bangs, 222
Bankhead, 341
Banks, 47, 178, 189, 259, 389, 433
Bankson, 488
Bannatyne, 315
Baptista, 290
Barber, 49, 209, 255, 262, 270, 328, 352, 354, 358, 472, 484
Barbour, 89
Barclay, 401
Barcley, 423
Barco, 367
Barcroft, 184, 220
Bardin, 277
Bardis, 325
Barelli, 323
Bargy, 448
Barham, 340
Barker, 85, 137, 138, 140, 211, 276, 339, 364, 382, 391, 393, 425, 473
Barklay, 476
Barkley, 170
Barnard, 70, 119, 127, 151, 174
Barneclo, 3, 251
Barnes, 14, 19, 28, 45, 49, 82, 106, 202, 350, 352, 354, 358, 393, 402, 489, 492
Barnett, 272, 449
Barney, 38, 95, 111, 199, 428, 443, 488
Barnhill, 243

Barnitz, 67
Barns, 1
Barnum, 418
Barnum's Hotel, 418
Barny, 96
barque **Ada**, 387
barque **Adario**, 387
barque **C Devens**, 399
barque **Charles Bartlett**, 283
barque **Chester**, 388
barque **Chief**, 387
barque **Clarissa**, 491
barque **Danl Webster**, 387
barque **Elijah Swift**, 436
barque **Florida**, 218
barque **Floridian**, 131
barque **Hebe**, 60
barque **Hersiles**, 37
barque **Ionia**, 6
barque **Jane Blain**, 283
barque **Magnolia**, 387
barque **Maria**, 16
barque **Sarah**, 387
barque **St John**, 391, 397, 399
barque **Toulon**, 374
barque **Valhalla**, 387
barque **Venezuela**, 471
Barr, 48, 147, 350, 429
Barreil, 478
Barrelle, 451
Barrett, 5, 66, 211, 251, 352, 459
Barringer, 9, 45, 238, 242
Barron, 19, 184, 358, 424
Barrow, 46, 117, 152, 158, 210, 263, 481
Barrows, 275
Barrus, 464
Barry, 47, 147, 235, 317, 348, 390, 398, 416, 424, 447
Barstow, 369
Bartgis, 307, 314
Bartle, 400
Bartlett, 38, 49, 184, 283, 431
Bartley, 191, 443
Barton, 8, 27, 211, 219, 266, 290, 327, 380, 384, 463, 478
Bartow, 231, 246, 294
Basford, 295

Basnett, 473
Bassett, 42, 258, 447, 459
Bastianelli, 49, 169, 281
Bastion, 299
Batchelor, 134
Bateman, 249, 291, 350
Batemen, 121, 244, 302
Bates, 1, 16, 23, 39, 49, 55, 66, 75, 88, 103, 109, 138, 141, 144, 182, 184, 228, 243, 350, 354
Batesville, 154
Batey, 425
Battle, 94
Baudonin, 38, 54
Baudouin, 369
Baugher, 473
Baulcher, 433
Bawner, 341
Baxter, 1, 109
Bay State, 154
Bayard, 11, 17, 83, 180, 372, 430
Bayley, 209, 277, 336
Baylies, 189, 387
Bayliss, 349, 350
Bayly, 49, 100, 133, 184, 227, 235, 271, 331
Bayman, 120
Baynam, 222
Bayne, 47, 179, 202, 409, 448, 464, 490
Beach, 49, 98, 389, 396, 424
Beackley, 49, 190, 435
Beadle, 158
Beakley, 218
Beal, 367, 462
Beale, 91, 146, 184, 199, 253, 259, 269, 310, 323
Beall, 24, 43, 93, 127, 196, 218, 224, 227, 265, 267, 279, 307, 326, 347, 352, 353, 354, 424, 431, 455, 463, 467, 492
Beall's Park Enlarged, 295
Beall's Retreat, 431
Bealle, 322
Beals, 404
Bean, 2, 48, 250, 251, 350, 352, 353, 358, 420
Beane, 447

499

Bear, 462
Beard, 72, 302
Beardon, 97
Beardsley, 126, 350, 379, 483
Beardstown, 154
Bearley, 46
Beasely, 218
Beasley, 185, 188
Beaston, 489
Beattie, 432
Beatty, 25, 204, 449
Beaubarnais, 371
Beaulieu, 312
Beaumont, 294
Bebee, 33
Beche, 184
Becher, 214
Beck, 32, 68, 145, 150, 227, 235, 277, 401, 430
Becke, 403
Becker, 200, 333, 426, 451
Beckert, 281, 282
Becket, 32, 376, 422
Beckett, 188, 352
Beckham, 214
Beckley, 46
Beckman, 13
Beckwith, 388
Bede, 191
Bedell, 317
Bee, 24, 124, 126, 482
Beehler, 233
Beemer, 377
Beers, 164, 278, 282, 292, 426
Begg, 21
Begnam, 46
Beinville, 451
Beir, 84
Bekenhault, 268
Belden, 228
Belgar, 127
Belknap, 244
Bell, 40, 46, 52, 53, 66, 97, 198, 274, 289, 347, 350, 352, 354, 355, 388, 419, 420, 440, 450, 451, 466, 472
Bella Vista, 115
Belle Hatchee, 154
Belle Isle, 217

Belle View, 2
Bellinger, 291
Belmont, 430, 468
Belt, 192, 243, 278
Belton, 400
Beman, 8
Ben Rush, 154
Bender, 406
Benedict, 367
Benes, 96
Benet, 265
Benjamin, 81, 86, 233, 387
Bennet, 448
Bennett, 124, 128, 220, 267, 303, 403, 459
Benns, 199
Benoist, 465
Benson, 97, 122, 403
Bent, 163, 383
Benter, 52, 184, 407, 426
Benton, 92, 114, 131, 151, 168, 178, 370
Bequette, 196
Berault, 133
Berger, 49
Bergman, 49, 120, 427
Berkeley, 472
Berkeley Springs, 221
Berkley, 45, 287, 354, 366
Beron, 300
Berret, 457
Berrett, 257
Berrien, 437
Berry, 32, 48, 75, 109, 198, 212, 234, 243, 253, 291, 298, 302, 307, 322, 331, 339, 352, 355, 411, 412, 413, 419, 431, 433, 447, 481, 490
Berryman, 238, 276
Bertrand, 40, 399
Beschlin, 352
Bessee, 6
Best, 424
Bestdering, 459
Bestor, 46, 57, 184, 402
Bethel Cottage, 466
Bethune, 30
Bettincourt, 304
Bevan, 47, 479

Bevans, 88
Beveridge, 461
Bexle, 29
Bias, 21
Bibb, 173, 443
Bickham, 450
Bicknell, 456
Bicksler, 189
Biddle, 8, 146, 159, 290, 325, 487
Biddy, 470
Bidlack, 131, 145, 223, 233
Bidleman, 365
Bidwell, 431
Bier, 340
Bigelow, 320
Bigger, 118
Biggs, 114, 353
Bigman, 184
Bilings, 216
Billing, 358
Billings, 37, 138, 163, 435
Bingham, 16, 160
Bingman, 5
Binney, 11
Birch, 43, 80, 88, 99, 144, 190, 370, 411, 487
Bird, 176, 243, 344, 450
Birth, 190
Biscoe, 191, 204
Bishop, 61, 72, 120, 138, 139, 190, 213, 244, 312, 345, 382, 399, 418, 445
Bishop of Heliopolis, 29
Bishpam, 132
Bispham, 56
Bissell, 102, 121
Bissett, 390
Blache, 291
Black, 14, 35, 69, 112, 156, 191, 210, 223, 323, 347, 392, 411, 424, 432, 469, 470
Black Walnut Island, 210
Blackburn, 302
Blackburne, 248
Blackford, 16, 64
Blackiston, 348
Blackistone, 200
Blackmer, 458

Blacknall, 180
Blackston, 302
Blackwell, 52, 57, 62, 63, 107, 118, 302, 407
Blagden, 17, 87, 212, 236, 343, 350, 352, 354, 355, 389
Blague, 247
Blair, 124, 140, 184, 247
Blaisdell, 178
Blake, 29, 39, 54, 81, 103, 125, 184, 260, 273, 454, 455
Blakemer, 458
Blakeney, 489
Blaksler, 135
Blanchard, 28, 34, 108, 339, 491
Blanche, 1, 302
Bland, 478, 483
Blaney, 171
Blany, 132
Bleakley, 97
Bleecker, 160, 280, 341
Blincoe, 439
Bliss, 64, 276, 326, 358, 438
Blodget, 58, 63, 81
Bloomfield, 109
Bloudine, 450
Blount, 286, 304
Blox, 429
Bloxham, 308, 335
Blue Lick, 486
Blue Ridge, 154
Bluff, 200
Bluff Point, 245
Blunt, 113
Blythe, 11, 85, 225, 253
Boarman, 72, 184, 286, 291, 315
boat **Pearl**, 453
boat **Phineas Janney**, 425
boat **Phoenix**, 22
boat **William G Hackstaff**, 195
Bock, 46, 184
Bockley, 49
Boden, 145
Bodisco, 62, 116, 417, 448
Boerum, 302
Bogan, 184
Bogardus, 58, 325
Bogart, 201

501

Boggs, 13, 58, 63, 81, 96, 101, 203, 367, 394, 402, 431, 434
Bogus, 184
Bohlayer, 354, 393, 410
Bohrer, 52, 203, 355, 449
Bolden, 491
Boling, 278
Bolling, 476
Bolton, 72, 109, 133, 142, 272, 371
Bomford, 61, 100, 268, 494
Bonaparte, 2, 18, 116, 371
Bond, 211
Bonfils, 375
Bonifant, 348
Bonnell, 143
Bonner, 291
Bonneville, 264, 265
Bonny, 490
Bonnycastle, 242, 410, 459
Bonthorn, 358
Bonthron, 303
Bontz, 358
Bonzano, 40
Booker, 365, 367, 476, 483, 484
Boone, 212, 281, 315, 340, 348, 350, 353, 371, 408
Boone, J B, 350
Boorman, 29
Bootes, 234
Booth, 22, 264, 280, 426
Booystrom, 23
Boreas #3, 217
Borland, 34, 466, 482
Bornstein, 239
Borre, 352
Borremains, 190
Borreman, 358
Borremans, 291
Borrows, 162, 311, 386, 455
Bose, 396
Bosher, 85
Boshlin, 355
Bosman, 32
Boss, 122, 289
Boston, 58, 63, 448
Bostwick, 60
Boswell, 324, 342, 343, 449, 456
Bosworth, 4, 277

Boteler, 45, 46, 53, 88, 112, 135, 168, 273, 279, 298, 369, 379, 463
Bottomley, 453
Botts, 366, 394, 402, 431, 468
Boucher, 293
Bouck, 203
Boudinot, 417
Boughton, 229, 295
Boulanger, 227, 403
Boulton, 200
Boulware, 276
Bourassa, 481
Bourne, 334
Bousseau, 426
Boutch, 181
Bouvier, 109
Bowcock, 405
Bowdell's Choice, 132
Bowden, 211
Bowditch, 280
Bowdoin, 369, 460
Bowdon, 117, 210
Bowen, 19, 33, 46, 101, 184, 196, 207, 229, 246, 251, 354, 358
Bower, 47, 473
Bowers, 147, 333, 336
Bowie, 61, 132, 210, 224, 232, 284, 331, 348, 350, 397, 401, 432
Bowlegs, 426
Bowles, 490
Bowlin, 117
Bowling, 184, 302, 315, 322, 459
Bowman, 47, 153, 208, 248, 352
Bowyer, 75, 109, 111
Box, 417
Boy, 384
Boyce, 5, 117, 191, 376
Boyd, 48, 109, 196, 241, 285, 302, 313, 316, 358, 390, 438, 441, 475
Boyden, 242, 354
Boyington, 206
Boylan, 232, 480
Boylayer, 184
Boyle, 12, 102, 107, 118, 122, 133, 162, 184, 342, 438, 471
Boys, 109
Brackenridge, 422
Bradbury, 395

Braddock, 40, 285
Braden, 302
Bradford, 79, 237, 264, 266, 294, 308, 358, 466, 483
Bradle, 250
Bradley, 9, 87, 99, 212, 250, 252, 257, 289, 303, 306, 326, 358, 397, 408, 460, 467, 494
Bradley, 189
Bradshaw, 337
Bradwell, 309
Brady, 1, 47, 90, 128, 149, 182, 184, 204, 291, 302, 320, 354, 425
Bragaldi, 86
Bragg, 73, 114, 241, 442
Braisted, 201
Bramall, 16
Branan, 459
Branch, 52, 236, 291, 407
Brand, 241
Brandt, 13, 239
Brannan, 1, 365
Branson, 185, 433
Brant, 341, 480
Brashear, 420
Brashears, 47, 184
Brasher, 113
Bratt, 103
Bratton, 38
Brawner, 66, 164, 169, 392
Braxton, 46, 302
Breckenridge, 22, 170
Bredall, 437
Breese, 32, 192
Breeze, 225
Brenan, 17
Brennan, 201
Brenner, 49, 108
Brent, 12, 37, 58, 88, 106, 107, 151, 184, 205, 236, 285, 286, 291, 350, 355, 358, 383, 443, 453
Brenton, 147
Brentwood, 289, 300
Brereton, 45, 47, 49, 350
Bres, 287
Breshwood, 238
Brewer, 32, 478
Brian, 490

Bridges, 101, 376
Bridwell, 109
Briel, 49, 184
Brien, 398
brig **Analosta**, 321
brig **Andrew M Jones**, 387
brig **Antares**, 387
brig **Belle**, 133
brig **Carter Braxton**, 387
brig **Corlann**, 420
brig **Cybele**, 387
brig **Delhi**, 419
brig **Detroit**, 199
brig **Fidelia**, 36
brig **Floridian**, 135
brig **Forest**, 16
brig **Gil Blas**, 16
brig **Herald**, 387
brig **Leander**, 175
brig **Lola**, 222
brig **Lowder**, 424
brig **Meta**, 388
brig of war **Boxer**, 132
brig **Pandora**, 86
brig **Perfect**, 132
brig **Perry**, 171, 340
brig **Pope**, 22
brig **Restaurador**, 198
brig **Ruth**, 387
brig **Somers**, 84
brig **Splendid**, 437
brig **Susan**, 171
brig **Tarquina**, 387
brig **Volaute**, 222
brig **Wellingsley**, 387
brig **Wyandot**, 387
Briggs, 172, 224, 280, 417, 418, 493
Brigham, 21, 66, 96, 357
Bright, 49, 191, 225, 415
Brightman, 428
Brightwell, 358
Brindle, 290
Brindley, 60
Brinkley, 211
Brinsley, 429
Brinson, 417
Brintnall, 74
Brinton, 377

Brisbois, 488
Briscoe, 45, 49, 64, 184, 282, 291, 354, 358
Bristol, 330
Bristor, 489
Broadbent, 21, 53
Broadwater, 40
Brobson, 181
Brochar, 328
Brochus, 83
Brock, 25
Brodb't, 190
Brodback, 51
Brodbeck, 10, 349
Broders, 413
Brodhead, 171, 358
Brodnax, 477
Brogon, 242
Bromfield, 472
Bromley, 310
Bronaugh, 53, 419
Bronough, 109, 184, 302
Bronson, 314, 323
Brook, 398, 459
Brooke, 7, 49, 62, 127, 137, 161, 178, 217, 234, 243, 255, 314, 320, 358, 371, 386, 425, 463
Brookes, 276
Brooks, 9, 21, 88, 107, 109, 121, 126, 178, 184, 185, 207, 239, 249, 257, 281, 350, 352, 400, 424, 426, 434, 459, 478
Broscoe, 204
Brosnahan, 48
Broun, 31
Brower, 12, 49
Browers, 334, 427
Brown, 1, 8, 23, 27, 45, 47, 48, 49, 52, 55, 60, 76, 77, 79, 88, 90, 95, 100, 101, 104, 106, 111, 113, 114, 117, 119, 141, 145, 156, 157, 166, 169, 181, 184, 185, 188, 189, 190, 197, 201, 203, 211, 212, 215, 216, 219, 222, 229, 238, 242, 243, 251, 256, 257, 259, 261, 265, 268, 271, 272, 277, 297, 302, 304, 309, 311, 319, 327, 330, 332, 333, 343, 348, 350, 352, 353, 354, 355, 358, 365, 366, 379, 387, 388, 390, 394, 399, 402, 407, 408, 409, 410, 415, 416, 431, 432, 437, 439, 449, 451, 459, 468, 471, 472, 478, 479, 484, 491
Browne, 271
Brownell, 384
Browning, 8, 49, 65, 184, 320, 408
Brownson, 285
Bruce, 2, 144, 170, 269
Bruen, 214
Bruff, 26, 137, 345, 382
Brummill, 385
Brundege, 313
Brune, 396
Brunning, 47
Bruno, 27
Brunswick, 154
Brush, 18, 21, 72, 84, 94, 96
Bruswick, 109
Bruton, 192
Bryan, 1, 8, 34, 75, 85, 88, 96, 121, 198, 199, 227, 235, 248, 286, 301, 302, 309, 348, 482
Bryant, 26, 85, 98, 106, 109, 142, 195, 238, 327, 350, 376, 462
Bryarly, 136
Bryden, 142, 358
Bryne, 128
Buchanan, 56, 204, 327, 440
Buck, 38, 54, 83, 96, 275, 304, 336, 355, 383, 396, 475
Buckely, 355
Buckhart, 223
Buckingham, 100, 106, 107, 220, 243, 306, 392, 400, 408, 461
Buckland, 212
Buckley, 184, 190, 354
Buckmaster, 13
Buckner, 440
Bucknor, 58
Bucler, 439
Buete, 51, 184
Buffa, 133
Buffalo Tuck Combs, 169
Buffington, 84, 238
Buffum, 365
Buford, 122
Bulfinch, 358

504

Bulger, 1, 109
Bulkely, 494
Bull, 198
Bullard, 61
Bullitt, 86, 162, 233, 278
Bulloch, 299
Bullock, 226, 232, 388, 411
Bully, 51, 184
Bulow, 58
Bulwer, 476
Bunch, 380
Buneff, 350
Bunker, 215
Bunto, 476
Bunton, 476
Burbbayge, 283
Burch, 15, 109, 230, 290, 315, 328, 382, 409, 437, 475
Burchard, 271
Burche, 88, 138, 144, 181, 218, 257
Burckhartt, 395
Burden, 287, 439
Burdick, 106, 131, 191
Burdine, 426, 427
Burges, 219
Burgess, 30, 45, 57, 143, 184, 302, 305, 348, 350
Burgevin, 109, 281
Burghalter, 350
Burghatter, 45
Burghest, 200
Burgoyne, 162, 365
Burgundy, 54
Burgwin, 282
Burgwyn, 347
Burke, 196, 291, 397, 398, 400, 450
Burkleo, 323
Burleson, 27
Burlingham, 339
Burnap, 280
Burnet, 29, 169
Burnett, 86, 204, 229, 333, 354, 365, 379, 403
burning of the Capitol of Alabama, 480
Burns, 45, 47, 102, 131, 201, 242, 244, 263, 268, 358, 485, 492

Burr, 18, 45, 184, 242, 279, 304, 307, 326, 338, 340, 376
Burries, 97
Burrill, 46
Burriss, 6
Burroughs, 139, 213, 430, 445
Burrows, 302, 387
Burrum, 365
Burt, 384, 393
Burton, 276, 447, 459
Bury, 196
burying place, 333
Busey, 115, 179, 195, 378
Bush, 31, 109, 188, 278, 355
Bushnell, 88
Bussey, 490
Buthman, 48
Buthmann, 76
Butle, 184
Butler, 1, 3, 4, 26, 32, 41, 46, 52, 72, 74, 80, 97, 118, 121, 123, 159, 168, 176, 184, 185, 201, 204, 211, 219, 246, 253, 268, 293, 300, 302, 312, 315, 335, 337, 339, 340, 350, 352, 353, 354, 355, 357, 358, 374, 378, 400, 402, 405, 407, 409, 428, 449, 481, 482, 493
Butt, 36, 49, 184, 249, 251, 278, 409
Butterfield, 244
Butterworth, 79
Butts, 339, 427, 448
Bydelman, 413
Byerly, 429
Byington, 137, 235, 401
Byrd, 172
Byrden, 409
Byrens, 341
Byrne, 40, 109, 144, 184, 221, 272, 286, 324, 346, 357, 358, 401
Byrnes, 400

C

C Connor, 154
Cabarruvia, 431
Cabasa, 324
Cabell, 9, 210
Cabet, 76
Caden, 219, 281, 352

505

Cadet, 3
Cady, 439
Cahill, 400, 478
Caho, 3, 45, 49, 97, 145, 350, 353
Cahoe, 201
Cain, 109, 302, 346, 447
Caldwell, 21, 33, 39, 66, 96, 121, 189, 198, 241, 380, 382
Caledonia, 154
Calhoun, 6, 73, 144, 171, 234, 372
Calkins, 8
Call, 271
Callaghan, 27
Callahan, 33, 302, 459
Callan, 48, 49, 86, 100, 149, 169, 227, 235, 281, 282, 333, 341, 359, 404, 416, 427, 436, 452, 463
Callanan, 438
called **Friendship**, 465
Callimaki, 207
Callnan, 249
Calloway, 486
Calraw, 216
Calvert, 119, 188, 274, 305, 347, 401, 414
Calvin, 400
Cambria, 154
Cameron, 109, 137, 231, 311, 374, 449, 465
Cammack, 47, 268, 291, 341, 357, 410, 419, 453
Cammell, 427
Camp, 87
Campbell, 18, 29, 40, 47, 49, 52, 56, 66, 73, 77, 85, 88, 96, 102, 104, 107, 117, 177, 189, 208, 212, 255, 278, 294, 302, 305, 357, 358, 359, 370, 404, 407, 411, 414, 434, 453, 455, 457, 473
Camper, 254
Camron, 137
Canada, 276
Candia, 436
Candler, 448
Canfield, 96, 111, 204, 247
Cannon, 48, 149, 355, 374, 450
Cape Hatteras, 256
Capella, 97

Caperton, 236
Capron, 98, 138, 263, 330, 401
Car of Commerce, 154
Carar, 56
Carbery, 19, 87, 102, 150, 192, 220, 241, 247, 270, 287, 318, 324, 359, 448, 452
Carey, 46, 325, 401
Cargill, 23
Carhart, 115, 201
Carillo, 431
Carleton, 17, 484
Carley, 304, 312
Carlin, 48
Carlisle, 91, 329, 375, 381, 448
Carlysle, 39
Carman, 384, 395
Carmichael, 201, 287
Carnan, 200, 355
Carnes, 14, 33
Caroline Furnace, 193
Carothers, 276
Carpenter, 81, 215, 290, 304, 348, 353, 377, 434
Carr, 192, 223, 233, 417, 482
Carrera, 402
Carriel, 286
Carrillo, 468
Carrington, 96, 139
Carroll, 12, 109, 184, 196, 197, 200, 203, 213, 218, 236, 291, 317, 358, 359, 380, 381, 401, 441, 446, 463
Carroll Chapel, 299
Carroll Cottage, 314
Carroll's Woods, 397
Carruvius, 402
Carson, 5, 42, 96, 208, 212, 333, 399
Carter, 43, 49, 79, 87, 101, 107, 117, 131, 227, 249, 257, 294, 307, 326, 328, 341, 352, 392, 459, 470, 490
Carter Hill, 257
Cartwight, 160
Cartwright, 462
Carusi, 66, 92, 99, 427
Carver, 33, 158
Casady, 23
Casanave, 188, 350, 353
Casenove, 133

Casey, 109, 139
Cash, 188, 359
Caskin, 60
Casparis, 52, 188, 229, 408
Casper, 183
Cass, 10, 74, 86
Cassedy, 282
Cassel, 49
Cassell, 368
Cassidy, 221, 430
Cassin, 138, 382, 414, 424
Castee, 188
Casteel, 189
Castel, 48
Castle, 382, 478
Castleman, 472
Catalano, 352
Cate, 340
Cates, 254
Cathcart, 146, 148, 158, 227, 235, 257
Catholic Church, 314
Catlin, 23, 95, 152, 183, 244, 367
Caton, 2, 13, 34, 49, 75, 281, 282, 354, 495
Cattell, 382
Caulfield, 403
Caulk, 294
Caulker, 437
Causin, 247, 261, 348, 437, 439
Causten, 172, 409
Cavaignac, 2, 22, 262
Cavan, 31, 40, 96
Cavarrubias, 468
Cavenaugh, 143
Cavendy, 294
Cecil, 180
Cedar Hill, 386
Center, 96, 199
Chafee, 353
Chalfin, 426, 483
Chalmers, 333
Chalmette, 154
Chaloner, 445
Chamberlain, 119, 435
Chamberlin, 447
Chambers, 101, 220, 348
Chambliss, 101
Champ, 451

Champion, 447
Champlain, 154
Champlin, 96, 198
Champney, 489
Chance, 425
Chancellor, 339
Chandler, 89, 123, 125, 215, 242
Chaney, 72, 210, 276, 482
Chapin, 49, 225, 350
Chaplains, 130
Chaplin, 180
Chapman, 11, 37, 49, 78, 80, 109, 112, 126, 177, 192, 205, 245, 325, 359, 397, 401, 412, 424, 445, 447, 470
Charles, 205, 247
Charley, 189
Charlton, 274
Charter Oak, 154
Chase, 16, 121, 166, 244, 264, 267, 293, 339, 387, 471
ChasLarrabee, 95
Chatard, 232
Chatfield, 30, 64, 439
Chauncey, 56, 337, 352, 434
Cheeseman, 315
Cheever, 60, 97, 198, 279
Cheney, 11, 239
Cherrix, 399
Chery, 342
Cheshire, 1
Chesman, 451
Chester, 211
Chevalie, 319
Chevis, 302
Chew, 46, 271, 311, 338, 350, 409, 422
Chezum, 45, 122, 162, 168
Chief Jesus, 318
Child, 18
Childe Harold, 155
Childs, 39, 54, 57, 92, 145, 427, 437
Chilson, 482
Chilton, 478, 495
Chinn, 6, 96, 136, 233, 263, 382, 446
Chipman, 101, 325, 431, 474
Chiseltyne, 352
Chisholm, 226
Chisley, 268

Chism, 474
Chisolm, 403
Chittenden, 101
Choate, 280
cholera, 149, 260
Chopin, 440
Choppin, 286, 443
Choteau, 66
Chouteau, 96, 274
Chrismond, 91
Christian, 255
Christie, 42, 114
Christman, 447
Christopher, 153
Christy, 86, 109
Chubb, 139, 189, 191
Church, 466
Churchill, 1, 63, 399
Chyandler, 419
Cignani, 177
Cilley, 103
Cincinnati House, 309
Circassian, 154
Cissel, 291
Cissell, 47, 189, 350
Cissill, 416
Cisterian order of Trappists, 221
Civill, 259
Clabaugh, 446, 457
Claflin, 39, 54, 73
Clagett, 2, 49, 53, 63, 95, 172, 227, 247, 277, 348, 358, 364, 462, 473
Clamorgan, 95
Clapham, 381
Clapp, 101, 271, 487
Clapper, 15
Claray, 366
Clarbaugh, 453
Clare, 204, 291
Clarence, 411
Clark, 1, 27, 32, 39, 40, 47, 49, 54, 56, 64, 96, 123, 129, 131, 148, 162, 170, 179, 188, 189, 199, 200, 243, 256, 262, 266, 274, 290, 299, 304, 313, 319, 322, 327, 332, 338, 343, 346, 352, 353, 355, 374, 383, 401, 406, 417, 439, 461, 462, 464

Clarke, 4, 5, 46, 48, 49, 66, 93, 99, 107, 108, 119, 121, 124, 132, 153, 168, 189, 211, 219, 224, 236, 243, 279, 284, 285, 287, 304, 338, 339, 342, 343, 352, 359, 378, 390, 400, 410, 416, 426, 453
Clarksville, 153
Clarvoe, 52, 165, 407
Clary, 302
Clavadetacher, 49
Clavoe, 456
Claxton, 13, 88
Clay, 29, 34, 71, 93, 132, 240, 371, 381, 487, 488
Claypoole, 115, 423, 427
Clayton, 54, 94, 98, 148, 225, 236, 273, 441, 449
Cleandrinking Farm, 365
Cleary, 281, 282
Clemantine, 346
Clemens, 142
Clement, 352
Clements, 62, 88, 116, 188, 230, 291, 298, 352, 358, 359, 369, 396, 399, 482
Cleopatra, 177
Clermont, 119, 168, 428
Clermorne, 378
Cleveland, 293, 339, 465
Clic, 38, 54
Click, 64
Cliff, 357
Clifford, 22, 376
Clinch, 33, 457
Clintick, 290
Clinton, 219, 381
Clitch, 49, 174
Clock, 417
Clokey, 5, 12, 45
Cloon, 290
Closkey, 188
Cloud, 448
Clough, 201
Clure, 282
Cluskey, 208, 223, 226, 310
Clusky, 235
Coad, 167
Coakley, 1

Coates, 5, 109
Coats, 362
Cobb, 109, 209, 465, 474
Cobbs, 58, 63, 81, 95
Coberly, 78
Coburn, 359
Cochran, 8, 49, 53, 72, 258, 276, 349, 410, 427, 495
Cochrane, 420
Cockbill, 26
Cocke, 29, 145
Cockey, 348
Cockrell, 27, 49, 53, 243, 350, 353, 354, 355
Coddington, 2, 149, 358
Coe, 215
Coes, 320
Coffee, 124, 267
Coffey, 115, 384
Coggshall, 118
Cogswell, 38, 55, 59, 93, 96, 199, 243, 266, 484
Coit, 210
Coke, 352
Coker, 412
Colburn, 4, 23, 34, 85, 354, 425, 430, 435
Cole, 5, 38, 54, 59, 73, 83, 93, 94, 118, 148, 149, 196, 200, 239, 242, 269, 291, 348, 404, 450
Colegan, 243
Coleman, 27, 118, 200, 240, 259, 338, 397, 402
Coles, 355
Colhoun, 348
Colison, 36
Collamer, 98
Collard, 12, 343
Collier, 117, 118, 122, 208, 234, 244, 276, 284, 324, 342, 349, 439, 449, 491
Collins, 53, 79, 82, 118, 184, 189, 211, 249, 284, 299, 337, 355, 359
Collison, 109, 407
Colman, 45
Colony of Connecticut, 170
Colony of Rhode Island, 180
Colquhoun, 12

Colquitt, 102
Colston, 226
Colt, 70, 131, 188, 207, 410
Coltman, 325, 460
Columbus, 49, 178
Colvin, 188
Comb, 328
Combs, 44, 49, 52, 158, 189, 348, 367, 489
Comly, 28, 49, 409, 451
Commerford, 470
Common, 30
Comorn, 405
Comstock, 144
Conagan, 355
Conant, 379
Conaway, 1, 348
Concordia, 154
Conde, 417
Condy, 19
Cone, 473
Confidence, 154
Congress burial ground, 26
Congress Cemetery, 273
Congressional burial ground, 316
Congressional Burial-ground, 117
Congressional Burying Ground, 170
Conklin, 144, 331
Conkling, 38
Conlan, 51, 189, 350
Conley, 42, 95, 198, 459
Conly, 440
Connecticut, 154
Connell, 345, 366
Connelly, 33, 39, 44, 359, 399, 482
Conner, 352, 355, 464
Conners, 400
Connolly, 101, 189, 359
Connor, 45, 48, 51, 53, 355, 456
Conolly, 36
Conover, 1, 215, 294, 301
Conrad, 314
Conradt, 303
Conroy, 49, 140, 190
Constant, 430
Contee, 132, 294
Convers, 208
Converse, 395

Conway, 236
Coodey, 61, 111
Coody, 93, 159
Cook, 12, 49, 52, 93, 111, 118, 170, 189, 198, 242, 259, 264, 276, 302, 315, 322, 348, 353, 379, 381, 395, 407, 455, 478, 482, 491
Cooke, 48, 81, 124, 144, 164, 232
Cookendorffer, 359
Cookman, 289
Cooley, 14, 349
Coolidge, 179, 209
Coombe, 282
Coombs, 69, 198, 310, 407, 419, 460
Coon, 80, 377
Coons, 359, 489
Cooper, 23, 41, 81, 84, 113, 117, 127, 169, 181, 228, 302, 340, 346, 354, 409, 412, 472
Coot, 136
Coote, 202, 358
Cope, 8, 453
Copland, 433
Copp, 51, 52
Coppersmith, 473
Cora, 154
Corcoran, 13, 74, 82, 99, 159, 205, 242, 352, 359, 375, 389, 427
Core, 472
Corkery, 207
Corkran, 72
Corley, 450
Corman, 400
Cornelia, 398
Cornell, 250
Corning, 197, 206
Cornish, 319, 352
Cornwall, 357, 371
Corrigan, 190
Corse, 1, 57
Corser, 93
Corson, 52, 58, 189, 280, 352, 399, 408, 487
Cortlan, 250
Corwin, 29
Costigan, 48, 359, 378
Costin, 46
Costing, 30

Cottage Farm, 276
Cottells, 451
Cotton, 107, 473
Cotton Factory, 237
Couch, 73
Coule, 107
Coulson, 348
Coumbs, 137
Counlin, 400
Courtney, 396, 478
Couts, 394
Couvillier, 96
Couvillion, 63
Couvillon, 70
Covell, 366
Cover, 141, 272
Covillon, 58
Cowan, 225, 384
Cowell, 144
Cowherd, 196
Cowin, 421
Cowles, 113
Cowley, 330, 476
Cowman, 132
Cowperthwaite, 314
Cowton, 174, 347
Cox, 19, 25, 62, 107, 109, 137, 192, 204, 211, 237, 241, 251, 281, 282, 297, 309, 330, 344, 352, 383, 401, 414, 441, 466, 475, 492, 495
Coxe, 192, 294
Coxen, 53, 179, 359
Coy, 256
Coyle, 24, 28, 44, 47, 49, 88, 188, 223, 235, 243, 257, 305, 307, 408
Coyler, 29
Cozens, 298
Crabb, 34
Cracton, 247
Crafft, 450
Craft, 451
Crafts, 116
Cragen, 321
Craig, 102, 122, 243, 271, 338
Craighill, 101
Craigin, 370
Crain, 102
Cram, 459

Cramer, 302, 304
Crampsey, 189
Crampton, 283
Cranch, 54, 308, 494
Crandall, 80
Crandell, 26, 54, 165, 192, 195, 213, 287, 298, 344, 352, 401, 482
Crandle, 47
Crandlel, 302
Crane, 6, 51, 133, 136, 222, 408, 427, 438, 447, 478
Crapen, 93
Crapster, 409
Crater, 473
Craumer, 147
Craven, 294, 327, 329, 359
Cravens, 102
Crawford, 33, 37, 52, 87, 94, 98, 100, 108, 129, 339, 358
Creighton, 232
Cresay, 492
Cressey, 308
Cresson, 29
Cresswell, 451
Creutzfeldt, 51
Creutzfelt, 191
Crier, 109
Crim, 255
Cripps, 17, 188, 282, 409
Crittenden, 123, 128, 129, 136
Crocker, 53
Crockett, 160, 348
Crockson, 13
Crogan, 353
Croggon, 219
Croghan, 22, 128, 442
Crome, 180, 197, 393
Cromwell, 12, 20, 52, 115
Cronin, 147, 230
Crooks, 109
Cropley, 403, 460, 476
Cropsey, 481
Crosby, 374, 415, 431, 468
Cross, 61, 114, 188, 251, 347, 350, 359, 415, 447
Crossan, 180
Crossman, 17, 38, 481
Crosson, 151, 281

Crow, 466
Crowell, 182
Crowinshield, 336
Crowley, 88, 166, 350, 390
Crown, 342, 353, 467
Crowninshield, 333
Crownsville, 342
Crownsville Farm, 467
Croxall, 272
Croyean, 366
Crozer, 312
Crozier, 176, 203, 310
Cruit, 189, 373
Crump, 189, 243
Crumpton, 385
Cruser, 368, 404
Crusor, 169, 222
Crutchet, 466
Crutchett, 169, 189, 453
Cruttenden, 350, 358
Cucullu, 437, 485
Cudlip, 324, 408
Cull, 47
Cullen, 397, 492
Culloma Mills, 318
Culverwell, 137, 219
Cumly, 47
Cummeford, 400
Cummerford, 400, 432
Cumming, 56, 266
Cummings, 61, 213
Cummins, 27, 339, 350, 356, 429
Cummiskey, 257, 285
Cunitz, 483
Cunningham, 71, 128, 149, 197, 267, 348, 455, 464
Cunobelin, 3
Curd, 170
Curl, 327
Curley, 364
Currier, 238
Curry, 315, 355
Curson, 251, 346
Curtani, 398
Curtin, 25, 51, 400
Curtis, 72, 180, 200, 339, 365, 473
Cushing, 13, 332, 447
Cushman, 180, 206, 269, 341, 441

Custer, 34
Custis, 163
Cutter, 374
cutter **Petrel**, 135
cutter **Walcott**, 22
Cutting, 109, 483
Cutts, 291
Cuvillier, 330, 359
Cuyp, 177
Czar Nicholas, 371

D

d'Lagnel, 122
D'Urban, 217
Dabney, 195
Dacy, 260
Dade, 152, 368
Daguerre, 134
Dailey, 275
Dale, 48, 216, 359
Daley, 352, 359
Dall, 56
Dallam, 121, 396, 405
Dallan, 12
Dallas, 9, 205
Dalrymple, 316
Dalton, 2, 46, 302, 426
Daly, 48, 318
Dalzel, 200
Dameron, 58, 63, 73, 96
Damerson, 85
Damron, 38, 54
Dana, 58, 63, 92, 245
Dandy, 101
Danenhoover, 435
Danford, 179
Daniel, 41
Dankworth, 185
Dant, 14, 282, 364
Danube, 217
Darby, 23, 34, 96, 152, 326
Darden, 6, 96
Dare, 263
Darling, 328, 487
Darly, 25
Darne, 300
Darnell, 336
Darracott, 348

Darrick, 415
Dart, 175, 366
Dashiel, 420
Dashiell, 106, 128, 173, 267, 330
Dau, 377
Daut, 359
Davenport, 6, 96, 101, 245, 434
David, 25, 185
Davidge, 323, 324
Davidson, 9, 71, 103, 123, 234, 312, 326, 359, 377, 445, 469
Davies, 110, 219, 238, 391
Davis, 1, 16, 24, 25, 44, 46, 47, 49, 51, 53, 59, 61, 63, 64, 70, 72, 73, 77, 80, 82, 90, 92, 96, 101, 107, 109, 110, 118, 148, 169, 176, 179, 185, 189, 190, 193, 194, 211, 212, 213, 233, 236, 246, 250, 251, 258, 262, 268, 275, 280, 294, 304, 316, 320, 343, 348, 350, 353, 355, 357, 359, 365, 366, 374, 375, 376, 382, 383, 387, 394, 395, 397, 398, 401, 417, 426, 434, 450, 453, 455, 461, 471, 473, 476, 483, 485, 493
Davison, 147, 223, 318
Davy, 49, 396
Dawes, 276, 326
Dawson, 5, 27, 43, 52, 106, 121, 153, 408, 460
Day, 9, 30, 183, 202, 340, 350, 353, 355, 359, 374, 403, 427
Day, 185
de Armas, 440
de Baillou, 225
de Bodisco, 251
De Buys, 97
De Forest, 248
De Forrest, 246
de Garno, 72
De Groff, 242
De Hefner, 364
De Kalb-steamer, 154
De Kay, 59
de Krudener, 384
de la Forest, 177
De La Guerra, 468
De Lano, 265
De Lareintrie, 330

De Maen, 139
De Main, 226
De Maine, 69
de Malahide, 440
De Milhau, 69
de Montesquion, 418
De Montesquiou, 492
De Neale, 100
De Necker, 396
de Pedrorena, 394, 402, 431
De Pedrorena, 468
De Russey, 33, 264
De Russy, 264, 267
De Saules, 352
De Saussure, 472
De Selding, 117, 121, 203, 262
de Silva, 20
de Stoeckly, 251
De Vico, 133
De Vos, 105
De Witt, 440
Dead, 267
Deaderick, 203
Deadman, 403
Deale, 251, 418, 446
Dean, 57, 112
Deane, 451
Deaney, 12, 124, 319
Deany, 123
Dearborn, 76, 385
Deas, 113, 153, 173, 235, 264, 323
Deavon, 302
Debaugn, 109
Deblois, 244
DeBree, 326
Decachet, 456
Decatur, 8, 44, 61, 74, 160
Deckman, 51
Dee, 42
Deeble, 268, 276, 310, 486
Deent, 185
Deevers, 45, 259, 350
Deffner, 242
Defiance, 154
Deitz, 359
DeKalb, 85
DeKoven, 19
DeKrafft, 103, 282

DeKraft, 282
del Hoyo, 460
Del Sarto, 105
Delacroix, 286
Delance, 49
Delaney, 88, 169, 334
Delano, 109, 276
Delany, 1, 49, 107, 175, 189, 252, 408
Delavan, 237
Dell, 40
Dellet, 6
Deltro, 46
Delucky, 434
DeMaine, 235
Demar, 1
Demaree, 136
Dement, 185, 191, 225, 344, 402
Demilt, 392
Denahy, 205
Denby, 324
Deneale, 45, 46
Denear, 109
Denham, 72, 355, 416
Denike, 242
Denison, 335, 372, 384
Denman, 237, 483
Dennis, 84, 401
Dennison, 184
Denniston, 215
Denny, 267
Dent, 30, 101, 126, 231, 315, 327, 344, 350, 366, 394, 402, 431, 451, 468, 472
Derham, 110
Deringer, 443
Dermott, 185
Deroin, 424
Desaules, 76
DeSaules, 185
Desha, 24, 77
Deslonde, 285, 286
Desmond, 293
Detchmendy, 488
Devans, 327
Devaughn, 185, 190, 246
Devens, 202
Deveny, 49
Deveraux, 204

Devereux, 291
Devers, 350
Devlin, 75, 450, 451
Devoe, 201
Devouge, 366
Devries, 348
Dew, 49
Dewdney, 185, 246, 251, 254, 333
Dewey, 108, 131, 323, 473
Dexter, 67
Deyorle, 9
Dezeny, 201
Dibbin, 15
Dick, 145, 302, 350, 359
Dickens, 249
Dickerson, 414
Dickey, 339
Dickins, 298, 300
Dickinson, 2, 117
Dickson, 10, 69, 192, 322, 420
Die Vernon, 155
Diel, 1
Dielman, 92, 285
Dies, 21
Dieskau, 474
Dieson, 209
Dietz, 137, 150
Digges, 168, 295, 322, 338, 348, 359, 425
Digging Bear, 481
Diggs, 46, 352, 355, 359
Dillon, 48, 179, 396
Dillow, 185
Dilworth, 304
Dimick, 126, 381, 426
Dimmick, 107, 365, 393, 402, 431, 468
Dimock, 68
Dinkgrave, 271
Dinkins, 349
Dinsman, 82
Diny, 110
Disher, 302
Dismond, 48
Distin, 184
Ditson, 327
Divine, 325
Dix, 14, 18, 70, 75, 83, 128, 133

Dixey, 295
Dixon, 301, 326, 348, 384, 408, 415, 433, 452
Dixwell, 452
Dobbin, 34, 189, 401, 482
Dobbyn, 281, 282
Dobyus, 121
Dockerty, 381
Dockhard, 134
Dodd, 6, 309, 350, 438
Dodds, 271, 478
Dodge, 11, 26, 38, 43, 123, 124, 234, 243, 322, 329, 345, 401, 411, 454, 477
Dods, 49
Dodson, 88, 90, 95, 227, 352, 355
Dogins, 109
Dolan, 170, 398, 400
Doland, 34, 398
Dolci, 105
Domingas, 402
Domingues, 431
Dominguez, 468
Donadieu, 262
Donaghe, 108
Donaldson, 11, 52, 106, 231, 371, 392
Donavan, 430
Donelan, 73, 84, 133, 151, 163, 178, 204, 214, 219, 220, 221, 230, 239, 314, 342, 364, 405, 420, 424, 429
Donellan, 143
Donevan, 281, 282
Doniphan, 49, 83
Donn, 42, 49, 51, 137, 227, 234, 250, 316, 359, 399, 401, 416, 438
Donnelly, 398, 400
Donnohan, 223
Donoho, 106, 144, 185, 215, 320, 401, 460
Donohoo, 48, 88, 227, 292, 491
Donovan, 48, 52, 181, 262, 271, 354, 408
Dooley, 53, 185, 281, 282
Doran, 78, 269
Dorman, 441
Dorn, 144
Dornin, 225, 455

Dorsey, 18, 52, 138, 143, 161, 200, 289, 307, 340, 382, 398, 407
Dortch, 70
Dosier, 185
Doty, 371
Doudin, 302
Dougall, 476
Dougherty, 110, 144, 166, 182
Doughty, 102
Douglas, 48, 89, 97, 198, 310, 406
Douglass, 39, 46, 69, 88, 185, 211, 227, 228, 235, 251, 352, 353, 387, 415, 430, 471
Douty, 290, 348
Dove, 57, 70, 88, 91, 185, 227, 235, 243, 350, 353, 359, 376, 388, 442, 444
Dovilliers, 183
Dow, 78, 227, 235, 243, 257, 261, 297, 336
Dowell, 45, 348
Dowley, 304, 359
Dowling, 5, 13, 150, 350, 355, 359
Downer, 180, 185, 205, 409
Downes, 160, 192, 327, 336
Downey, 45, 315, 339
Downing, 25, 45, 62, 350
Downs, 39, 54, 64, 118, 185
Dowson' Row, 131
Dowson's Row, 116, 230
Doyle, 318, 354
Dozier, 414
Drake, 196, 213, 330, 352, 466
Draper, 10, 233, 281
Drayton, 180, 206
Drennen, 219
Drew, 61, 269
Dreyer, 414
Driesbach, 62
Driskill, 417
Druett, 359
Drumond, 56
Drury, 49, 53, 190, 192, 235, 260, 284, 364, 366, 367, 401, 444
Du Barry, 265
Du Bernard, 315
Du Bose, 102
Duane, 99, 205

Dubant, 278, 426
Dubarry, 381
DuBarry, 483
Dubois, 75, 113, 120
Dubosq, 37
Ducachet, 430
Ducatel, 168
Ducket, 1
Duckett, 132, 373, 402
Duckworth, 49
Dudley, 170, 217, 278
Duell, 252
Duer, 81, 295
Dufendorf, 395
Duff, 45, 65, 355, 359
Duffer, 4, 56
Duffey, 27, 150
Dufief, 258, 414
Dugas, 323
Duke, 288
Dukes, 91
Dulany, 19, 46, 106, 189, 352, 477
Duling, 387
Dumnor, 184
Dumphrey, 31, 419
Dumphy, 188
Duncan, 29, 40, 42, 60, 110, 122, 128, 208, 210, 212, 234, 247, 261, 266, 286, 289, 330, 337, 412, 429, 440, 442, 484, 489
Duncanson, 227, 235
Duncas, 63
Dunham, 395
Dunlap, 1, 115, 350, 354
Dunlop, 161, 306, 359
Dunmead, 322
Dunn, 49, 175, 183, 334, 359, 451
Dunnavant, 238
Dunning, 179
Dunnington, 185, 191, 328
Dunnman, 468
Dunwell, 185
Dupont, 2
Durant, 153, 207
Durkee, 418
Dusenbury, 86
Dushani, 274
Dustin, 71, 459

Duther, 242
Duvall, 45, 48, 49, 50, 70, 72, 77, 79, 85, 109, 185, 212, 213, 292, 348, 382, 426, 427, 429, 451
Dwight, 101, 109, 145, 482
Dye, 38, 55
Dyer, 27, 35, 37, 64, 86, 88, 103, 107, 109, 127, 134, 185, 208, 245, 250, 302, 315, 316, 332, 343, 350, 353, 357, 359, 364, 438, 456
Dyson, 53, 185, 189, 302, 330, 350
Dyvernois, 190

E

Eaches, 100, 274
Eagan, 47, 400
Eaker, 478
Eames, 22, 81, 222
Earl, 185, 220, 281
Earl Albemarle, 440
Earle, 46, 310, 360, 401, 404, 462
Early, 29
Earpe, 181
Easby, 1, 100, 150, 172, 179, 305, 355, 425
Eastern Burial Ground, 32
Eastman, 377, 480
Easton, 211, 390
Eastwood, 445
Eaton, 73, 99, 124, 201, 304, 352, 359, 381
Eaves, 384
Ebeling, 353, 491
Eberbach, 52, 384, 407, 465, 470
Eberbech, 373
Eberhart, 84
Eccleston, 314
Eckard, 77, 426
Eckbert, 69
Eckel, 40, 53
Eckerle, 450
Eckhardt, 190
Eckhart, 360
Eckle, 393
Eckloff, 239, 303, 352, 360, 409, 418
Eddins, 339
Eddy, 8, 44, 277

Edelen, 243, 310, 322, 355, 376, 480, 481
Edelin, 2, 47, 185, 190, 277, 291, 322, 352, 401, 416, 462
Edes, 42, 144, 243, 350, 411
Edgar, 30, 128, 228, 450, 451
Edgerton, 386
Edgewood, 236
Edgeworth, 234
Edmonds, 180
Edmondson, 121, 451
Edmonston, 28, 47, 50, 65, 69, 112, 137, 449, 450
Edney, 233
Edward Bates, 154, 155, 217
Edwards, 17, 84, 94, 103, 161, 185, 195, 199, 212, 228, 253, 254, 360, 459
Eels, 25
Egan, 50, 98
Egelston, 458
Ehrmancroutt, 354
Ehrmantrout, 51
Eichelberger, 473
Eichhorn, 185, 189
Elder, 346
Eldon, 214
Eldridge, 340, 411
Elgar, 287
Elgen, 427
Elgy, 381
Eliason, 43
Eliot, 69, 360
Elisha, 353
Eliza Sewart, 217
Elkinton, 159
Ellery, 73, 446
Ellett, 101
Ellicott, 35, 239, 360
Ellicott's Mills, 108
Elliot, 11, 85, 174, 185, 190, 234, 307, 352, 360, 397
Elliott, 32, 43, 66, 76, 80, 129, 134, 234, 246, 304, 450, 451, 482
Ellis, 13, 18, 49, 58, 66, 72, 84, 88, 107, 170, 227, 235, 241, 275, 320, 365, 387, 393, 400, 401, 427, 431, 455, 468, 491

Ellmaker, 196
Ellmore, 488
Ellsworth, 421
Elterman, 98
Elwell, 260
Elwes, 7
Elwood, 360
Ely, 90, 210, 215, 239
Elzey, 122, 359
Emack, 316
Embassy, 217
Emerson, 67, 93, 199, 223, 354, 355
Emert, 185
Emery, 212, 353, 354, 368, 369
Emmert, 479
Emmet, 116
Emmett, 13
Emmonds, 279
Emmons, 16, 21, 35
Emory, 44, 140
Emperior of Russia, 482
Emperor of Austria, 146
Emperor of Russia, 194, 333, 410
Empie, 486
Enfield Chase, 140
England, 88, 257, 428
Engle, 200
Engles, 384
Englis, 203
English, 13, 23, 101, 215, 266, 282, 287, 324, 359, 360, 365, 460, 476, 495
English 74, **Vesuvius**, 133
Ennis, 17, 47, 138, 150, 185, 204, 221, 243, 257, 281, 282, 291, 302, 350, 360, 406, 436, 467, 469, 494
Entwisle, 24, 414
Epilepsy, 164
Eppes, 5
Erichsen, 330
Erie, 42
Erkson, 438
Erskine, 327
Erving, 360
Eslin, 249, 281, 354
Esling, 136
Eson, 56
Espey, 88, 439, 463

Essex, 419, 435
Essington, 132
Estep, 161
Etter, 192
Etting, 180
Eudora, 217
Eustis, 280, 484
Evans, 27, 28, 72, 77, 96, 117, 143, 185, 218, 225, 249, 278, 316, 326, 331, 343, 344, 348, 384, 390, 392, 395, 405, 450, 485
Everest, 431
Everett, 7, 14, 280, 282, 372, 421, 481, 487, 488
Everhart, 141
Everist, 118, 435
Everitt, 428
Eversfield, 42
Ewbank, 196, 245, 287, 458, 474
Ewell, 78
Ewing, 19, 94, 98, 121, 200, 228, 282, 320, 367
executed in England, 197
Eylie, 422
Eyre, 302, 459

F

Facsi, 242
Fagan, 110, 163, 201, 423
Faherty, 281, 282
Fahey, 398, 400
Fairbanks, 342
Fairchild, 388
Fairfax, 37, 335, 355
Fairfield, 1, 10
Fairman, 281
Falcon, 36
Falconer, 476
Fales, 360
Fallansbee, 391
Falley, 454
Fallon, 431
Farelly, 153
Faris, 66
Farley, 309
Farmer, 395
Farnandis, 348

Farnham, 50, 69, 80, 171, 211, 213, 320, 401, 473, 493
Faron, 131
Farquhar, 416
Farragut, 455
Farrah, 52
Farrar, 23, 50, 89, 137, 185, 408
Farrell, 105
Farrelly, 423
Farren, 87
Farrington, 39
Farrow, 39, 55
Fatherrel, 417
Fauble, 135
Fauntleroy, 406
Favier, 52, 306, 354, 355, 378, 407
Faxall, 43
Fay, 312
Feaman, 374, 487
Fear, 348
Fearson, 48, 150, 185, 189, 420
Featherston, 110
Featherstone, 482
Fedesco, 184
Feeney, 185
Feeny, 165, 365
Felch, 58
Fendall, 87, 149, 252, 254, 273, 277, 387
Fenderich, 138
Fensley, 268, 427, 432
Fenwick, 80, 281, 282, 360, 402
Feraille, 4
Fergerson, 352
Ferguson, 158, 216, 230, 251, 259, 368, 384, 410
Ferrall, 48, 161, 227
Ferrando, 142
Ferris, 281, 282, 398
ferry-boat **Bedford**, 320
ferry-boat **Hoboken**, 76
Fessenden, 252
Fetterman, 291
Few, 214
Field, 19, 23, 265, 431, 490
Fields, 459
Filhiol, 271
Fill, 148

Fillebrown, 134
Fillmore, 74, 88, 99, 332, 334
Filson, 237
Finch, 97, 198, 214, 414, 426
Finckel, 211
Fink, 12, 185
Finkel, 333
Finkman, 52, 185, 407
Finley, 38, 86
Finly, 302
Finnegan, 220, 250
Finotti, 337
Finsley, 281
Fire in Charleston, S C, 194
first white child, 263
Fischer, 9, 50, 145, 360, 409
Fish, 345
Fishe, 110
Fisher, 1, 3, 34, 46, 51, 66, 215, 231, 236, 243, 291, 302, 352, 353, 355, 426, 427
Fisk, 113, 360, 395, 430
Fister, 185, 354
Fitch, 62, 89, 196, 202, 297, 387, 408
Fithian, 232
Fitler, 389
Fitnam, 48, 50, 69, 89, 147, 185, 281, 305, 364
Fitter, 290
Fitton, 185
Fitz, 126, 202, 204, 228, 289, 371
Fitzgerald, 5, 33, 48, 52, 76, 90, 153, 185, 217, 222, 223, 281, 282, 354, 407, 408, 441, 484
Fitzhugh, 12, 49, 90, 99, 182, 218, 298, 300, 335, 459
Fitzpatrick, 107, 225, 281, 325, 360, 397, 398, 400, 408
Flag Hill, 394
Flagg, 206, 249
Flaherty, 400
Flanagan, 96, 397, 398, 399, 413
Flanigan, 83, 400, 449
Flannegan, 9
Fleishchmann, 233
Fleming, 46, 133, 185, 297
Flemmins, 148
Flenner, 2, 47, 53, 57, 310

Flenniken, 427
Flesher, 367
Fletcher, 1, 60, 82, 84, 88, 94, 179, 280, 285, 350, 353, 368, 410
Fleury, 281, 282
Flinn, 12, 26
Flint, 209, 491
Flood, 28
Florence, 462
Flournoy, 39
Flower, 63, 70, 96, 436
Flowers, 420
Floyd, 152, 229, 236, 446
Flusser, 103
Flynn, 213, 450
Fogg, 489
Foley, 62, 79, 150, 462
Folger, 424
Follansbee, 69, 185, 270
Follen, 280
Foller, 48
Follett, 439
Folly, 242
Foltz, 9
Fontaine, 231, 324
Fontane, 96, 198
Foote, 27, 46, 77, 150, 223, 233, 261, 291, 295
Forbes, 1, 118, 242, 323, 360, 367, 405, 459
Force, 87, 172, 185, 357, 364
Ford, 1, 38, 54, 67, 145, 149, 185, 203, 204, 282, 290, 291, 302, 332, 355, 399, 490
Forde, 205
Forest, 1, 23, 360, 376
Forest Home, 321
Forestall, 485
Forman, 255, 325
Forney, 103
Forrest, 9, 168, 185, 192, 200, 225, 263, 358, 366, 400, 459, 460
Forstall, 286
Forster, 140, 394
Forsyth, 75, 128, 142, 267, 416, 484
Fort Brooke, 130
Fort Brown, 406
Fort Clinton, 162

Fort Collville, 195
Fort Columbus, 265, 374
Fort Colville, 25
Fort Crawford, 27
Fort Erie, 230, 415
Fort Gaines, 130, 418
Fort Gatlin, 426
Fort Gibson, 43, 93, 129, 130
Fort Graham, 406
Fort Independence, 171
Fort Johnson, 267, 368
Fort Johnston, 265
Fort Kearny, 112, 130, 241, 390, 478
Fort Knox, 112
Fort Laramie, 130, 234, 312, 382, 390, 478
Fort Leavenworth, 130, 234, 241, 265, 371, 390
Fort Mackinac, 130, 265
Fort Madison, 482
Fort Marcy, 130
Fort McHenry, 265
Fort Monroe, 130, 265
Fort Montgomery, 112, 162
Fort Morgan, 130
Fort Moultrie, 130
Fort Pemmaquid, 255
Fort Pickens, 130
Fort Polk, 406
Fort Porter, 112
Fort Reid, 426
Fort Sacramento, 107
Fort Scott, 130
Fort Smith, 235
Fort Snelling, 130, 234, 461
Fort Townson, 130
Fort Washeia, 461
Fort Washita, 130
Fort Wayne, 64, 112, 147, 152
Fort Winthrop, 112
Forte, 291
Forward, 18, 412
Fosdick, 376, 385
Foshee, 354
Fosnaught, 368, 373, 450
Foss, 310
Fossett, 360

Foster, 1, 29, 68, 230, 238, 255, 386, 402, 431, 462, 468, 492
Foulkes, 360
Four Farms, 270
Fowble, 137
Fowle, 342
Fowler, 50, 52, 121, 139, 191, 223, 296, 304, 346, 360, 371, 372, 373, 426, 431, 455
Fox, 24, 39, 352, 355, 371, 450
Foy, 52, 65, 137, 213, 407, 425
Foyles, 300
Fraeler, 36, 185
Fraelig, 249
Frailey, 202, 463
Fraler, 67
Frame, 5, 58, 62
France, 81, 114, 191, 409
Francis, 163, 287, 437, 459
Francisco, 384
Franciso, 455
Frank, 48, 177, 189, 302, 352
Franklin, 19, 50, 88, 105, 107, 138, 151, 153, 176, 205, 227, 235, 281, 294, 399, 405, 408, 409, 414, 485
Franklin Row, 180, 261, 279
Franks, 434
Fraser, 127, 253, 341, 360, 459
Frasier, 50
Frazer, 35, 84, 166, 266, 402, 495
Frazier, 39, 76, 164, 227, 353, 385, 422
Frazure, 444, 459
Frealer, 48
Frech, 97
Frederick, 62
Freedy, 360
Freeland, 288, 352
Freeman, 3, 58, 62, 92, 127, 168, 193, 203, 244, 398, 400
Freer, 107, 360
Freiere, 286
Freire, 286
Frelinghuysen, 30
Freme, 213
Fremont, 35, 86, 114, 128, 139, 142, 146, 151, 158, 175, 209, 218, 291

French, 13, 42, 69, 77, 124, 125, 205, 235, 248, 253, 260, 273, 313, 318, 323, 384, 385, 390, 449, 473
Fretz, 450
Friend, 335
Friendship, 247
Frier, 321
frig **Congress**, 38, 42
frig **Guerriere**, 160
frig **Independence**, 132
frig **Lawrence**, 84
frig **Mississippi**, 174, 180
frig **Philadelphia**, 8, 16
frig **Philadephia**, 74
frig **Potomac**, 160
frig **Raritan**, 103, 241, 372
frig **Savannah**, 81, 467, 470
frig **St Lawrence**, 26
Frink, 384
Frisby, 185
Frisse, 185
Frochlick, 219
Froehlich, 220, 229
Froehlig, 250
Frolic, 217
Frost, 72, 113, 129, 137, 143, 405
Frothingham, 13
Frowley, 400
Fry, 350, 434
Frye, 69, 88, 107, 195
Fugate, 96
Fuggitt, 53
Fugitt, 48, 350, 353, 354
Fulgham, 385
Fuller, 1, 19, 33, 96, 97, 169, 198, 222, 229, 243, 302, 330, 360, 486, 489
Fullerton, 384, 444
Fulmer, 32, 66, 250, 286, 304, 411, 476
Fulton, 8, 39, 171, 278
Funk, 50
Furlong, 360

G

Gaar, 38, 78
Gabby, 136
Gabler, 302

Gachle, 167
Gadsby, 99, 135, 219, 283
Gadsby's Hotel, 472
Gaehle, 92
Gage, 166
Gaines, 34, 61, 73, 128, 230, 237, 266, 267, 313, 386, 415, 425, 442, 450
Gaines Plantation, 226
Gainor, 281, 282
Gaither, 50, 251, 324, 426
Gale, 271, 278, 364
Gales, 29, 150, 273
Galignani, 133
Galigo, 172
Gallagher, 172, 410, 457
Gallaher, 238
Gallatin, 214, 317, 421
Galligan, 47, 168, 444
Gallispie, 355
Gallop, 208
Gallot, 235
Gally, 318
Galt, 50, 71, 261, 352, 475
Gamage, 96
Gamble, 172
Game, 10
Gammage, 58, 78, 198
Ganbert, 424
Gannon, 46, 178, 185, 224, 228, 243, 353, 376
Gansevoort, 269
Ganson, 239
Gantt, 61, 110, 147, 259, 461
Garchell, 224
Garcia, 13, 160, 166, 427
Gardier, 348
Gardiner, 90, 257, 315, 456
Gardner, 19, 26, 119, 143, 185, 195, 225, 289, 341, 360, 389, 408, 417, 436, 459, 460
Garfield, 219
Garison, 38
Garland, 11, 29, 229, 264, 265, 431
Garner, 110, 185, 190, 349, 368, 426, 455, 493
Garnet, 80
Garnett, 62, 86, 355, 360
Garr, 54, 242

Garratt, 137
Garret, 63
Garrett, 159, 189, 211, 239, 396
Garrettson, 190
Garrison, 6, 54, 66, 96, 199, 301, 330, 450
Garrot, 97
Garver, 348
Garvin, 203, 462
Gary, 242
Gasne, 15
Gasquet, 286
Gass, 360
Gassaway, 62, 88, 234
Gaston, 286
Gates, 12, 42, 140, 180, 298, 319, 429, 440, 441, 483, 484
Gatewood, 259, 476
Gaulden, 276
Gautier, 50, 185, 337
Gawney, 58, 63, 89
Gay, 131, 140
Gayle, 108
Geary, 365
Gedney, 201, 371
Geffers, 46, 48
Gehman, 339
Geisinger, 371
Gelston, 360
Gen Green's Row, 137
Gengenback, 353
Gentry, 465
Genzenbach, 136
George, 352, 367, 396
Gerard, 14
Gerbeau, 425
Germon, 110
Gerry, 120
Gess, 184
Getting, 115
Gettings, 145
Getty, 385, 446, 484
Gherardi, 327
Ghiselin, 84
Ghislin, 340
Gibbins, 464
Gibbon, 400
Gibbons, 205, 397

521

Gibbs, 1, 55, 88, 93, 134, 310, 347
Gibson, 2, 9, 127, 153, 167, 185, 191, 236, 310, 344, 350, 425, 431, 432, 467, 470
Giddings, 10
Gideon, 89, 162, 227, 235, 257, 393, 408
Gifford, 481
Giger, 260
Gignoux, 177
Gilbert, 53, 283, 332, 365, 393, 402, 431, 468
Gilchrist, 492
Gildemeister, 42, 231
Gildermeister, 350
Gilead, 167
Giles, 13
Gill, 216, 264, 360
Gillatt, 348
Gillen, 321
Gillespie, 99, 113, 201, 207, 354, 450, 451
Gillet, 64, 384, 412, 417
Gillett, 66, 84
Gilliam, 327, 336
Gillies, 360
Gillis, 57, 75, 326
Gilliss, 25, 96, 202, 220, 315, 392, 456, 467, 485
Gillmore, 265
Gillot, 177
Gillroy, 325
Gilman, 50, 136, 324, 408, 410
Gilmartin, 470
Gilmer, 450
Gilstrap, 376
Giltner, 395
Gingenback, 350
Ginter, 236
Gipson, 289
Girard, 63
Girard Estates, 63
Girdletree Hill, 399
Gittings, 250, 316, 346
Given, 105
Giveney, 352
Giveny, 350
Givney, 355

Gladmon, 185
Glassup, 301
Glaze, 348
Gleason, 385
Glenn, 196, 342, 401, 447
Glick, 53, 185, 353, 354
Glisan, 446
Glossbrenner, 199
Glover, 105, 298
Gluck, 451
Glynn, 75, 96, 198, 205, 400
Goddard, 48, 121, 140, 185, 251, 281, 304, 413, 453
Goddin, 101
Godey, 158, 160, 175
Godfrey, 25, 395, 399, 473, 485
Godfroy, 5
Godon, 218
Godwin, 324
Goebel, 100
Goetz, 132, 134
Goggin, 190, 372, 426
Goins, 352
Gold, 6
Golden, 20, 408, 459
golden horseshoe, 455
Goldin, 52, 481
Golding, 11, 46, 52, 189
Goldsborough, 26, 121, 185, 360, 371, 395, 397, 401
Goldsmith, 185, 289, 350
Goldstein, 258
Gollady, 121
Gondolier, 155
Gooch, 285
Good, 416
Goode, 217, 222, 276
Goodenough, 433
Goodlow, 429
Goodmanson, 299
Goodrich, 117, 185, 360, 421
Goodrick, 192
Goods, 439, 459
Goodsell, 228
Goodson, 72
Goodwin, 4, 161, 193, 490
Goodyear, 412
Gor, 229

Gordon, 1, 4, 69, 72, 88, 161, 167, 185, 189, 193, 219, 227, 235, 239, 242, 247, 257, 269, 302, 340, 360, 390, 485
Gorey, 5
Gorgey, 405
Gorham, 47, 239, 283
Gorman, 82, 105, 139
Gorter, 313
Gorton, 339
Goslin, 110
Gosnell, 210
Goss, 340, 427
Goszler, 43, 291
Gothard, 46
Gott, 95
Gough, 284
Gould, 84, 108, 282, 379, 447
Gouverneur, 4, 264, 266
Gove, 38, 55, 80
Govn'rs Island, 440
Gow, 169
Gowin, 367
Graeff, 76, 103
Graffenreid, 102
Grafton, 381
Graham, 1, 9, 10, 70, 114, 124, 149, 185, 242, 251, 286, 420, 463, 466
Grammar, 57
Grammer, 26, 45, 195, 313, 389, 460
Grandpre, 462
Granger, 126, 239
Grant, 93, 96, 119, 126, 150, 185, 297, 411, 415, 434, 459, 466, 478
Grason, 373
Grattan, 452
Graves, 39, 55, 80, 451
Gray, 19, 50, 108, 110, 140, 151, 185, 210, 211, 229, 295, 340, 348, 360, 395, 396, 425, 470
Gray Eagle, 155
Gray's tract, 167
Grayson, 51, 64, 75, 126, 365
Greally, 399
Greason, 185, 341, 404, 408
Great Father, 33
Great Mills, 198
great paintings, 269

Greaves, 185
Greely, 160
Green, 2, 10, 16, 17, 24, 42, 48, 50, 72, 78, 80, 88, 97, 104, 106, 137, 151, 182, 184, 185, 191, 199, 204, 205, 215, 219, 257, 266, 274, 291, 296, 307, 314, 335, 347, 350, 352, 354, 360, 365, 366, 375, 397, 409, 451, 461, 470, 495
Green Mountain Boys, 33
Greene, 15, 101, 108, 295
Greenfield, 48, 261
Greenholtze, 214
Greenhow, 178, 395
Greenleaf, 29, 143, 281, 282, 284, 360, 427
Greenleaf Point, 313
Greenleaf's Point, 465
Greenwell, 232
Greenwood, 61, 155, 214, 258
Greenwood Cemetery, 440
Greer, 1, 78, 94, 100, 287, 302, 347, 373
Greeves, 251, 268, 297, 323, 432
Gregg, 108, 377, 392
Gregory, 17, 103, 246, 295, 307, 348, 360
Gregson, 103
Greland, 476
Grey, 1, 94, 244, 317, 450
Grice, 55, 141, 379, 411
Grieb, 174, 419
Grier, 67, 96, 127, 199, 294, 475
Griffeth, 137
Griffin, 47, 72, 169, 198, 200, 400, 483, 490
Griffith, 8, 10, 20, 149, 185, 191, 218, 276, 300, 397, 433
Griffiths, 152, 242, 367
Grigg, 41
Grigsby, 302, 340
Grimes, 46, 110, 117, 170, 185, 302, 352, 393, 411, 419
Grimsly, 193
Grinder, 7, 350
Grinnell, 89, 334, 343
Griscom, 8, 159, 315
Griswold, 211, 301, 396

Groenvelt, 360
Groghan, 40
Groning, 310
Grooms, 24
Grose, 481
Gross, 47, 189, 231, 258, 299, 312
Groupe, 354
Grousset, 159
Grover, 238, 352, 488
Grubb, 19, 150, 281, 314, 385, 401, 404, 469
Grupe, 48, 140, 185
Gude, 299
Gueneman, 353
Guerrant, 72
Guerrero, 365
Guest, 42, 115
Guido, 177
Guild, 11, 128
Guion, 482
Guista, 452
Gungs, 75
Gunn, 302
Gunnell, 88, 131, 141, 175, 243, 350, 360, 375
Gunnison, 180
Gunston Hall, 119
Gunter, 95
Gunton, 190, 247, 342, 345, 360, 408
Gurley, 77, 198, 299, 493, 494
Guthrie, 211
Guttierez, 286
Guy, 388, 419, 434
Guyer, 185, 354
Guyon, 21
Guyot, 280
Gwaltney, 84
Gwatkin, 36
Gwin, 35, 365, 402, 468
Gwinn, 255, 392, 417, 431
Gwynn, 286, 461
Gwynne, 177

H

Habersham, 341
Hackney, 360
Hadaway, 414
Haddix, 403

Haddock's Hills, 386
Haden, 434
Hagar, 354
Hager, 354
Haggatt, 201
Haggerty, 46, 48
Hagley, 162
Hagne, 186
Hagner, 120, 300, 410, 452, 483, 484
Haig, 444
Haigh, 246, 271
Haight, 365
Hailes, 490
Hailstock, 110
Haines, 55, 69, 189, 265, 350, 352, 483
Hainline, 255
Haislep, 353
Haislip, 350
Hait, 450
Hale, 26, 29, 32, 183, 290, 470
Haler, 158, 175
Halerman, 110
Hales, 87
Haley, 365, 431
Haliday, 107, 274, 320, 401, 462
Hall, 9, 16, 19, 20, 26, 29, 31, 35, 47, 48, 50, 55, 67, 89, 91, 92, 93, 99, 100, 106, 110, 114, 117, 120, 139, 140, 141, 145, 149, 150, 152, 160, 172, 174, 175, 190, 191, 193, 194, 195, 197, 206, 213, 216, 224, 227, 235, 236, 240, 242, 255, 257, 264, 267, 281, 286, 302, 306, 315, 327, 334, 353, 354, 385, 397, 432, 433, 437, 448, 459, 472, 481, 482, 493
Halleck, 221, 366, 394, 402, 431, 468
Haller, 126, 153
Halley, 439
Halliday, 226, 235, 253, 380
Hallowell, 372
Halpin, 28
Halstead, 242
Halsted, 215
Hambleton, 348
Hamer, 97
Hamersley, 186, 190, 315, 354

Hamilton, 2, 69, 77, 85, 115, 152, 180, 196, 215, 223, 252, 255, 275, 286, 352, 361, 444, 450, 472
Hammer, 327, 429
Hammersley, 297
Hammersly, 310, 365, 404
Hammett, 180
Hammitt, 276
Hammond, 105, 118, 124, 125, 142, 223, 256, 265, 369, 419, 427, 464
Hamner, 367
Hampton, 83, 341, 352, 460
Hamser, 440
Hanbury, 1
Hance, 288
Hancock, 52, 101, 153, 186, 407
Hand, 132, 206, 232, 301, 412, 447
Handerlan, 451
Handley, 50, 101, 408
Hands, 216, 226, 235, 315, 378
Handy, 5, 12, 20, 48, 133, 144, 186, 218, 225, 251, 307, 344, 385, 409, 472
Haney, 466
Hanfler, 302
Hanks, 393, 468
Hanley, 272, 419
Hanlon, 253
Hanly, 185
Hanna, 349
Hannagan, 399
Hannah, 459
Hannegan, 100, 400
Hanning, 1
Hansbrough, 423
Hanse, 231, 493
Hansel, 110
Hansell, 360
Hanson, 33, 63, 85, 110, 115, 185, 212, 243, 285, 307, 331, 350, 397, 483, 484
Haralson, 371
Harauh, 186
Harbaugh, 50, 140, 213, 320, 401, 408
Hardaway, 93
Hardcastle, 44, 140
Hardee, 197, 406
Hardenbrook, 224

Hardesty, 2
Hardia, 459
Hardin, 1, 90
Harding, 13, 52, 54, 96, 198, 279, 374, 459
Hardt, 480
Hardy, 30, 114, 133, 140, 430
Hare, 314
Harford, 110
Hargraves, 249
Harkey, 478
Harkness, 119, 186, 194, 207, 251, 305, 310, 350
Harlan, 391
Harley, 14, 21
Harling, 351
Harlow, 367, 473
Harmon, 100
Harmony, 8, 21, 58, 83, 94, 482
Harney, 406
Harohman, 351
Harper, 48, 50, 60, 61, 227, 330, 338, 403, 411, 431
Harrington, 46, 220, 246, 249, 257, 367, 420
Harris, 18, 35, 39, 42, 102, 106, 145, 175, 185, 189, 242, 291, 317, 352, 365, 376, 427, 444, 459
Harrison, 7, 10, 18, 19, 42, 46, 67, 79, 93, 110, 135, 145, 159, 170, 172, 185, 200, 201, 208, 222, 270, 307, 325, 331, 344, 365, 396, 448, 450, 461, 479, 483, 484
Harrover, 50, 74, 95, 297, 329, 375, 408, 414
Harry, 219, 246
Harry Hill, 155
Harshan, 344
Harshman, 45, 344
Harshorn, 1, **188**
Harstein, 437
Hart, 144, 185, 205, 344, 345
Hartley, 72
Hartnell, 431
Harton, 330
Hartshorn, 348, 386
Hartslein, 209
Hartwell, 432

Harvey, 47, 48, 53, 82, 136, 164, 281, 282, 286, 305, 350, 353, 354, 375, 416, 434, 441, 479
Harwell, 330
Harwood, 205
Hascall, 131, 487
Haskell, 149, 167, 366
Haslup, 338, 456
Hassell, 64
Hassett, 400
Hassler, 48, 190
Hasson, 256, 265
Hasting, 495
Hastings, 402, 431, 468
Hatch, 13, 47, 53, 126, 203, 350, 354, 426
Hatfield, 105
Hatten, 152
Hatton, 259
Haughery, 72
Hauptman, 110, 471
Haven, 13, 236, 293, 308, 365
Havener, 307, 354, 355
Havenner, 69, 408, 430, 472
Havens, 304
Havilland, 367
Haw, 236, 243
Hawbecker, 28
Hawes, 125, 179
Hawke, 249
Hawkins, 185, 189, 207, 348, 355, 377, 381, 472
Hawkinsk, 365
Hawks, 59
Hawley, 160
Hawthorne, 228
Hay, 361
Hayard, 50
Hayden, 80, 284, 312
Hayes, 208, 233, 312, 395
Hayfield, 77
Hayman, 361, 424
Haymen, 459
Haymond, 416
Hayne, 48, 178
Haynes, 396, 447
Haynie, 245
Hays, 147, 292, 385, 412, 467

Hayward, 414
Haywood, 391
Hazard, 17, 29, 232, 251, 330, 375, 389, 419
Hazel, 259, 355
Hazell, 279, 281
Hazle, 361
Hazleton, 491
Head, 403
Heald, 93, 301, 435
Healey, 58
Health Report, 148
Healy, 64, 97, 285, 491
Heany, 281
Heard, 284, 481
Heath, 456, 459
Hebb, 260
Hebert, 287
Hedge, 108
Hedgman, 486
Hedrick, 85
Hefferman, 430
Heintzelman, 153
Heiskell, 100, 379
Heisler, 191
Heiss, 84, 468
Heister, 355, 467
Heiter, 357
Heitmiller, 185
Helfenstein, 215
Hellen, 199, 414
Helme, 397
Hemans, 348
Hemmick, 432
Hempstead, 191, 192
Hemsley, 493
Hendershott, 9
Henderson, 87, 97, 113, 180, 207, 246, 257, 273, 294, 381, 412, 418
Hendley, 52, 141, 405, 407, 408
Hendren, 238
Hendrew, 255
Hendrick Hudson, 155
Hendrickson, 153, 234
Henif, 398
Heniff, 400
Henley, 46, 165, 203, 261, 361
Henn, 207

Henning, 48, 88, 186, 405, 463
Henningham, 486
Henrie, 30, 96, 318
Henrie, 198
Henriques, 431
Henry, 144, 169, 172, 189, 229, 246, 248, 292, 326, 336, 341, 348, 355, 357, 378, 396, 404, 437, 477, 488
Hensel, 339
Henshaw, 69, 79, 88, 125, 182, 257, 289
Henson, 110
Hepburn, 50, 90, 152, 285, 316, 326, 333, 376, 405, 415, 485
Hepps, 470
Herald, 155
Herbert, 271
Hercules, 163
Hercus, 47, 48, 409
Herman, 328
Hermann, 321
Herndon, 211, 341
Herold, 185
Herr, 84, 440
Herran, 217
Herrick, 1, 13, 349, 387
Herriman, 194
Herring, 39, 54, 81
Herrity, 399
Herron, 171
Hersey, 92
Hertmiller, 28
Hertmuller, 350
Hess, 169, 186, 489
Hessett, 273
Hestley, 110
Heston, 145
Hetricks, 110
Heuderbert, 252
Hevener, 414
Hewett, 219
Hewison, 354
Hewit, 128
Hewitt, 18, 101, 244
Hewson, 295
Heydon, 50
Heywood, 215
Hibernian, 155

Hibert, 83
Hickey, 106, 110, 247
Hickman, 136, 185, 186, 188, 303
Hicks, 176, 185, 196, 322, 334, 351, 374, 447, 475
Higby, 275
Higdon, 360
Higgins, 50, 102, 259, 269, 286, 289, 294, 313, 325, 367, 387, 397, 400, 414, 459
Highland Hall, 347
Highland Mary, 155
Hight, 102
Hilbus, 220
Hill, 30, 31, 47, 57, 65, 67, 76, 89, 104, 107, 110, 129, 141, 186, 192, 202, 219, 227, 233, 235, 243, 264, 266, 282, 291, 331, 339, 350, 352, 353, 361, 368, 381, 383, 388, 394, 402, 431, 434, 459, 468, 480, 482
Hill Farm, 453
Hillard, 470
Hillary, 84
Hilleary, 43, 138
Hilles, 8, 454
Hills, 50, 138
Hilts, 268
Hilyard, 48
Himmelwright, 397
Hinchman, 159
Hinckley, 180
Hind, 349
Hindes, 242
Hinds, 38, 55
Hines, 48, 190
Hinson, 339
Hinton, 289, 296, 417
Hiram, 250
his 6 wives, 421
Hiss, 186
History of Md, 32
Hitton, 241
Hitz, 42, 48, 50, 120, 185, 251
Hix, 60
Hixon, 404
Hoar, 479
Hoban, 282, 302, 361, 459
Hobbie, 93, 185, 405

Hobbim_, 105
Hobolochitto, 155
Hobson, 338, 365, 393, 402, 431, 468, 490
Hocker, 87
Hockett, 96, 199
Hodge, 41, 48, 89, 385, 405
Hodges, 57, 196, 209, 258, 292, 307, 342, 343, 400, 455
Hodgkin, 29
Hodgkins, 143
Hodgskin, 413
Hodgson, 8, 419
Hodson, 231
Hofflein, 349, 384
Hofflin, 355
Hoffman, 51, 110, 186, 246, 348, 396, 408
Hogan, 246, 355, 410
Hoge, 457
Hogeboom, 39, 55, 439
Hogeboon, 90
Hogg, 395, 459
Holabid, 266
Holbrook, 57, 419, 491
Holden, 5, 13, 58, 63, 70, 96, 352, 427, 487
Holding, 233
Holiday, 401
Holin, 1
Holland, 1, 21, 116, 171, 268, 291, 350, 352, 392, 456
Hollen, 110
Holliday, 486
Hollidge, 186
Hollige, 251
Hollingsworth, 301, 431, 468
Hollins, 361
Hollister, 72, 377, 478
Hollohon, 361
Holloran, 453, 469
Holly, 417
Holme's Island, 26
Holmead, 48, 50, 227, 287, 411
Holmes, 9, 10, 117, 196, 210, 221, 264, 281, 289, 334, 381
Holpain, 367
Holsworth, 459

Holt, 58, 460
Holtzman, 29, 85, 361
Holyrod, 186
Homans, 11
Homas, 186
Homer, 155
Hone, 160
Honing, 50
Hood, 1, 101, 339, 399, 409
Hooe, 50, 88, 102, 257, 472
Hook, 17
Hooker, 125, 126
Hooper, 140, 276, 419, 423
Hoos, 483
Hoover, 47, 53, 206, 226, 235, 257, 261, 355, 361, 382, 409, 410, 479
Hope, 53, 174
Hopkins, 69, 91, 112, 243, 273, 366, 392, 434, 440, 444, 450
Hopkinson, 244
Hoppe, 394, 402, 431, 434, 468
Hopper, 242
Horn, 148, 413
Hornbeck, 104
Horne, 80
Horner, 38, 46, 193
Horning, 186, 297, 341, 354
Horrell, 450
Horsey, 54
Horsigh, 239
Horsthamp, 186
Horstkamp, 48
Horton, 38, 54
Hoskins, 373
Hotchkiss, 11, 17, 93, 96, 236
Houcke, 281
Hough, 189, 191, 302, 493
Houghton, 165, 169, 424
Houneus, 5
House, 301
Houser, 434
Houston, 285, 313, 327, 370, 431
Hovenburgh, 330
How, 184
Howard, 1, 28, 50, 123, 185, 202, 203, 211, 221, 238, 250, 257, 277, 354, 355, 361, 365, 393, 397, 401, 408, 419, 430, 431, 467, 468

Howe, 39, 54, 72, 126, 185, 251, 387, 415, 422, 480
Howell, 5, 48, 153, 189, 256, 427, 471, 489
Howes, 365, 387
Howison, 407
Howlan, 53
Howland, 59, 108, 262
Howle, 185
Howlett, 281, 282
Howze, 440
Hoye, 200
Hoyes, 105
Hoyle, 462
Hoyt, 377, 439
Hozard, 413
Hubball, 118
Hubbard, 117, 158, 196, 210, 230, 236, 253, 268, 271, 361, 389, 439, 473
Hubbell, 44
Hubble, 418
Huddleston, 433
Hudson, 105, 108, 231, 266, 466
Huger, 9, 32, 103, 126
Hugerty, 350
Huggins, 50
Hughes, 23, 48, 72, 103, 127, 151, 158, 175, 191, 231, 242, 317, 328, 341, 344, 350, 351, 433, 473
Hughlett, 430
Huguenin, 50, 120
Huguenot, 32
Huguet, 462
Huie, 142, 494
Huling, 412
Hull, 96, 170, 198, 347, 466
Humbird, 376
Hume, 1
Humes, 48
Humphreys, 84, 181, 290, 353
Hunt, 8, 28, 88, 127, 196, 239, 263, 270, 361, 377, 380, 406, 439, 459
Hunter, 30, 34, 68, 80, 101, 103, 113, 145, 170, 171, 178, 203, 204, 207, 253, 254, 264, 266, 267, 284, 302, 326, 327, 341, 367, 469, 474, 493
Huntington, 60, 76, 97, 117, 198

Huntsman, 347
Hurdel, 472
Hurdleston, 415
Hurlburt, 135, 451
Hurley, 282, 361, 463
Hurly, 459
Hurst, 222, 236
Huske, 228
Huson, 67, 72
Hussey, 283
Husted, 271
Huston, 483
Hutchins, 20, 118, 215, 348, 414
Hutchinson, 37, 58, 276, 304, 427
Hutchison, 147, 416, 448
Hutter, 27, 101, 128, 267
Huttleson, 329
Hutton, 361
Huxley, 365
Hyatt, 50, 227, 238, 287, 361, 379, 408
Hyde, 43, 74, 182, 184, 190, 223, 302, 327, 350, 389
Hyder, 258
Hyer, 134
Hygeian Hall, 456
Hyman, 151
Hynson, 192
Hyslop, 9, 317

I

Iardella, 48, 137
Ickis, 366
Iddins, 351, 492
Inauguration Hall, 100
Inch, 361
Independent Tract, 270
Indermaurer, 361
Indian Collection, 23
Ingle, 26, 50, 79, 110, 143, 161, 186, 195, 212, 243, 251, 255, 326, 361, 394
Inglehart, 238
Ingraham, 352
Inscow, 91
Iredell, 159
Ireland, 200
Iron City, 155

Ironside, 493
Irvin, 117
Irvine, 105, 129, 147
Irwin, 201
Isaac McKim, 437
Isaac's Additon, 295
Isaac's Park, 295
Isaacs, 186, 354
Isham, 285
Isherwood, 165, 224
Isley, 242, 268
Israel, 115, 179, 228, 242
Ives, 139, 182

J

J J Hardin, 155
Jack, 47, 139, 335, 473
Jackson, 17, 30, 48, 95, 108, 110, 113, 118, 123, 126, 143, 163, 184, 186, 190, 215, 219, 227, 231, 257, 284, 289, 323, 326, 327, 338, 353, 377, 380, 403, 408, 437, 471, 490
Jackson City, 26
Jacob, 151, 418
Jacobs, 38, 114, 242, 249, 412, 463
Jaffray, 246
Jamar, 348
James, 47, 50, 67, 110, 189, 340
Jameson, 150, 315
Jamieson, 46, 186
Jamison, 24, 340
Janeway, 29
Janney, 223
Janny, 94
Janvrin, 387
Jarboe, 45, 50, 230, 361
Jardin, 378
Jardine, 186
Jarvis, 242, 385, 403, 483
Jasper, 46, 431
Jay, 489
Jebb, 342
Jefferies, 192
Jeffers, 22, 361
Jefferson, 59, 146, 421, 446, 470
Jeffrey, 93
Jenison, 389

Jenkins, 23, 40, 102, 286, 335, 387, 396, 445
Jenks, 4, 176
Jenness, 219
Jennifer, 186
Jennings, 47, 352, 355, 377, 418, 422
Jennison, 454
Jessee, 418
Jessop, 142
Jesuits, 328
Jesup, 186, 273, 282
Jeter, 276
Jett, 192
Jewel, 367
Jewell, 137
Jewett, 121, 191, 260, 291, 361, 439
Jilliard, 50
Jimenez, 27
Johns, 1, 248, 253, 264, 265, 281, 336, 485
Johnson, 12, 13, 15, 17, 22, 23, 26, 27, 29, 35, 38, 44, 45, 48, 50, 55, 57, 58, 59, 60, 61, 62, 70, 76, 77, 90, 96, 98, 107, 108, 110, 112, 120, 139, 141, 147, 149, 159, 170, 172, 186, 189, 191, 195, 212, 224, 227, 231, 235, 241, 248, 249, 251, 260, 266, 273, 286, 298, 301, 302, 303, 310, 313, 323, 326, 327, 339, 341, 351, 352, 355, 361, 368, 374, 377, 379, 390, 391, 408, 411, 416, 433, 439, 445, 459, 466, 467, 468, 471, 480, 486, 490, 491, 493
Johnston, 7, 9, 24, 36, 86, 89, 124, 126, 152, 153, 180, 264, 267, 278, 368, 394, 405, 484, 485
Johnstone, 302
Joice, 398
Jolly, 57, 351, 353
Jonas, 167
Jones, 1, 4, 7, 8, 9, 11, 13, 15, 21, 22, 26, 29, 36, 40, 46, 48, 50, 52, 58, 72, 84, 87, 90, 96, 101, 102, 103, 107, 110, 115, 116, 117, 127, 129, 130, 131, 139, 143, 145, 146, 149, 161, 162, 166, 174, 175, 186, 189, 191, 193, 197, 201, 224, 227, 235, 236, 238, 240, 242, 252, 256, 264,

267, 273, 276, 281, 291, 302, 314, 317, 340, 349, 351, 352, 353, 354, 355, 361, 366, 367, 370, 375, 376, 378, 388, 399, 401, 405, 408, 417, 418, 426, 431, 434, 439, 456, 459, 466, 468, 470, 485, 490
Jordan, 175
Jordon, 108
Josephs, 33
Josiah Lawrence, 155, 156
Joslin, 377, 395
Jost, 51, 52, 186
Jounett, 170
Joyce, 3, 45, 48, 278, 352, 409, 426, 437, 448
Judah, 126
Judd, 433
Judge, 39, 54, 427
Judson, 46, 121, 383
Judy, 113
Julia, 217
Julian, 464
Junkins, 274
Junnicutt, 257

K

Kahl, 119, 471
Kain, 112
Kalahan, 31
Kalb, 358
Kale, 189
Kalkman, 98
Kalorama, 258, 387
Kama, 274
Kanan, 398
Kane, 48, 84, 106, 200, 340, 361, 372, 397, 398, 400
Kansler, 302
Kap, 157
Kapp, 238
Karar, 241
Karens, 404
Karna, 274
Kase, 290
Kathrens, 269
Kaufman, 45, 186, 351, 465
Kavanaugh, 361
Kay, 238

Keaho, 181
Kealey, 186, 408
Keally, 278, 427
Kean, 400
Kearn, 397
Kearney, 192, 225
Kearnin, 201
Kearns, 218
Kearny, 37, 81, 102, 425
Kearsley, 487
Keaton, 447
Kecheval, 371
Kechler, 330
Kedglie, 45, 356
Keech, 110, 472
Keechey, 472
Keef, 296
Keefe, 186
Keefer, 330
Keeling, 136
Keemle, 425
Keenan, 254, 399, 400
Keeney, 13, 67
Keese, 390, 393, 436, 438
Kehl, 47
Kehoe, 148
Kehrer, 51, 207
Keiffer, 204
Keim, 196, 290, 303
Kelcher, 46, 408
Keleher, 269
Kelig, 352
Kell, 246, 325
Keller, 26, 132, 203, 275
Kellett, 485
Kelley, 219
Kellogg, 1, 108, 265, 310, 319, 448, 451
Kellum, 238, 247
Kelly, 24, 42, 136, 150, 201, 281, 339, 343, 355, 408, 426, 437, 451, 477
Kemble, 32, 41, 158, 293
Kemp, 203
Kendall, 93, 186, 460
Kendrick, 19, 46, 234, 330, 361
Kenely, 397
Kengla, 43
Kenly, 331, 348

Kennady, 357
Kennaugh, 10
Kennedy, 60, 88, 106, 110, 222, 225, 257, 346, 347, 417, 483, 487, 492
Kennelly, 398, 400
Kennerly, 380
Kennon, 440
Kenny, 315
Kent, 108, 200, 202, 233, 273, 348, 355
Kenyon, 489
Keobel, 353
Keogan, 428
Keough, 261
Kepler, 110
Keppler, 186
Ker, 29, 234
Kerbaugh, 72
Kerby, 7, 44, 281, 490
Kerfoot, 90, 261, 275
Kern, 175, 218
Kerne, 158, 209
Kerr, 71, 170, 278, 331, 348, 361, 426, 480, 490
Kerrnan, 384
Kersey, 51, 141, 222
Kervand, 66, 389, 452
Kerwin, 8
Kesley, 445
Kessler, 287, 436
Ketchum, 234
Kettlewell, 209
Key, 9, 188, 284, 326, 354, 361, 389, 401, 410, 452
Keyes, 245
Keys, 420
Keyworth, 50, 102, 186, 355, 361, 460
Khul, 427
Kibball, 47
Kibbey, 309, 346, 353
Kibble, 190
Kibby, 50, 353, 408
Kickham, 351
Kidd, 93
Kidder, 437
Kidney, 140
Kidwell, 241, 361
Kiernan, 201, 361

Kigly, 418
Kilano, 60
Kilburn, 153
Kilby, 180
Kilgour, 348
Kilian, 50
Killian, 186
Killmon, 48, 402, 408
Kilmon, 227
Kilpatrick, 403
Kimball, 100, 380, 385, 411
Kimber, 8
Kimberly, 36, 461
Kimmell, 188, 408
Kincart, 40, 66
Kindell, 412
King, 3, 6, 9, 11, 32, 33, 43, 46, 47, 48, 52, 63, 72, 86, 91, 108, 110, 111, 117, 138, 139, 142, 146, 158, 162, 164, 168, 169, 175, 186, 191, 203, 205, 211, 229, 237, 239, 254, 281, 282, 284, 286, 291, 311, 328, 335, 351, 352, 353, 361, 367, 370, 391, 403, 407, 414, 419, 426, 430, 431, 440, 448, 450, 451, 453, 454, 460, 474, 495
King Chas I, 452
King of Sardinia, 270, 288
King of Sweden, 371
Kingman, 186, 361
Kingsbury, 58, 62, 63, 70, 75, 138, 264, 265
Kinneraly, 142
Kinney, 2, 38, 54, 58, 63, 73, 81, 155, 156, 228, 230, 376
Kinniffe, 325
Kinsey, 69, 88
Kinsley, 46
Kinsman, 304
Kinson, 424
Kinzie, 152
Kirby, 186, 267, 327, 343, 484
Kirk, 115
Kirkham, 93, 126
Kirkparick, 348, 419
Kirkpatrick, 174
Kirkwood, 338, 365, 406, 411
Kit Carson, 217

Kitchen, 357
Kite, 159
Kitsen, 57
Klack, 110
Kleiber, 53, 235, 250
Kleindienst, 52, 354
Kleiss, 372
Klickerman, 433
Kline, 132
Kloffer, 186
Klomann, 52, 407
Klopfer, 88
Kloppher, 361
Klots, 385
Knabe, 92, 167
Knaggs, 4, 25
Knapp, 72, 404
Knickerbocker, 39, 482
Knight, 8, 45, 121, 132, 178, 203, 243, 288, 293, 327, 351, 352, 356, 381, 476
Knott, 1, 50, 65, 112, 186, 351, 352, 354
Knowles, 313, 342, 361, 391
Knox, 144, 203, 440, 451, 478
Kohler, 365
Kontz, 43
Kosciusko, 4, 482, 487, 494
Krafft, 50, 186, 349, 354, 361, 393, 409
Kraft, 384, 443, 453
Kramer, 302
Krause, 163
Kremer, 395
Kuhl, 51, 186
Kuhns, 43
Kurtz, 160, 361, 368, 462

L

La Clede, 274
La Motta, 299
la Rosa, 286
Labadie, 301
Labarbe, 286
Labbe, 380, 466
Labeaume, 295
Labrune, 423
Lacey, 259, 424

Lack, 33
Lackland, 450
Laclede, 155
Lacon, 16, 39, 55
Lacy, 28, 57, 468
Ladd, 208, 224, 232, 250
Lady Madison, 155
Lafayette, 5, 32, 164, 435
Lafferty, 148
Laguerrra, 431
Lahey, 398
Lahiff, 398, 400
Laidlaw, 409
Laidler, 361
Laidley, 127
Lakin, 236
Lalleman, 328
Lally, 258
Lamartine, 2
Lamb, 120, 180, 197, 202, 210, 335, 409, 414
Lambel, 362
Lambell, 186, 257, 351, 354, 409
Lambert, 145, 430, 459, 489
Lambright, 53
Lamden, 56
Lamkin, 1
Lammond, 190, 467
Lamotte, 406
Lamson, 330
Lanahan, 77, 115, 239, 381, 448, 467, 471
Lancaster, 286, 291, 447
Lance, 286
Landers, 365
Landon, 54, 92, 315
Landrick, 45, 64, 186, 352
Landry, 196
Lane, 50, 122, 129, 190, 252, 330, 331, 347, 353, 387, 436, 445, 459, 473, 475, 492
Lang, 447
Langford, 56
Langhorne, 84
Langley, 45, 93, 163, 351
Langlois, 487
Langton, 112
Langtry, 103

Langworthy, 446
Lanham, 245
Lanier, 384
Lankford, 348
Lanman, 74, 210, 234
Lanphier, 316
Lansdale, 110
Lansdown, 430
Lansing, 258, 292
Lanskey, 400
Laplace, 310
Laporte, 281, 282, 475
Lapsley, 424
Larken, 366
Larkin, 28, 121, 263, 394, 400, 402, 431, 468
Larmour, 292
Larned, 26, 123, 186, 195, 299, 303, 381, 409, 412
Larner, 89, 173
Larrabee, 72, 81, 240
Larzaere, 357
Larzelere, 295
Laskey, 69, 88, 281, 282, 386
Laskin, 403
Lasky, 190
Latham, 24, 47, 101, 161, 188, 310, 334
Lathing, 488
Lathrop, 261
Latimer, 141, 297, 454
Latmite, 351
Latrobe, 169, 229
Latruit, 459
Latruitte, 91
Laub, 48, 186, 291, 436
Laughrey, 331
Laurel, 155, 263
Laurie, 29, 77, 186, 193, 197, 198, 211, 298, 307, 331, 463
Lautner, 69
Lauxman, 186
Lauxman, Martin, 351
Lavalette, 38, 192
Lavallette, 42, 225
Lavender, 186, 190
Law, 55, 87, 174, 186, 362
Lawhon, 490

Lawler, 21
Lawrason, 296
Lawrence, 50, 78, 94, 100, 203, 219, 226, 253, 273, 275, 280, 284, 288, 317, 362, 447
Lawrenson, 150
Laws, 450
Lawson, 128, 186, 280, 315, 330
Lawton, 277
Lay, 282
Laydon, 263
le Beaume, 399
le Blank, 92
Le Cage, 80
Le Couteulx, 285, 286
le Roy, 262
Lea, 110, 332
Leachy, 72
Lear, 264, 265
Learned, 208
Leary, 39, 48, 121, 249
Leave, 94
Leavenworth, 101
Lebaron, 425
Lechman, 310
Leckie, 282
Leddy, 48, 190, 352
Lederer, 186
Ledgwick, 190
Ledoni, 13
Ledwith, 56
Lee, 1, 38, 43, 46, 47, 53, 54, 68, 70, 84, 88, 103, 107, 110, 125, 128, 148, 150, 153, 194, 246, 275, 302, 326, 348, 351, 352, 356, 362, 387, 396, 404, 406, 408, 430, 437, 477
Leech, 246, 489
Leef, 35
Leeper, 192
Leet, 118, 433
LeFevre, 242
Lefferts, 201
Leffler, 190, 219
Legare, 269
Legg, 252
Leggett, 21
Lehaul, 43
Lehman, 51, 106, 186

Leib, 332
Leigh, 62, 198, 273
Leiller, 310
Leitch, 110, 249
Leixear, 190
Lekmann, 297
Leland, 35, 196
Lemmans, 466
Lemmon, 84, 396
Lemmons, 260
Lemon, 449
Lenahan, 104, 429
Lenkins, 323
Lenman, 353, 354, 356, 477, 492
Lennox, 357
Lenox, 29, 45, 87, 89, 107, 141, 162, 170, 218, 228, 235, 243, 338, 362, 379, 408
Lent, 13
Lenthal, 429
Lenton, 348
Leokron, 322
Leonard, 128, 267, 280, 365, 491
Lepretre, 285, 286, 291
Lepreux, 48, 186, 268, 409
Leroux, 424
LeRoy, 13
Lerrion, 120
Lesene, 35
Lesley, 15
Leslie, 136, 267, 294
Letherman, 256, 265
Letmate, 432
Lettle, 377
Levallette, 42
Leverett, 38, 54, 79, 95, 122
Levering, 333, 396
Levy, 31
Lewin, 420
Lewis, 1, 8, 28, 46, 50, 53, 61, 81, 103, 115, 132, 136, 137, 138, 170, 179, 186, 190, 196, 207, 215, 224, 251, 266, 292, 297, 304, 305, 310, 315, 316, 326, 330, 335, 336, 351, 353, 356, 362, 386, 395, 404, 405, 411, 414, 415, 426, 442, 446, 448, 459, 469, 473, 483
Lewisville, 161

Leyster, 451
Libbey, 67, 411, 419
Liberia Packet, 299
Lieberman, 491
Ligen, 97
Lightfoot, 155
Ligon, 225
Lilley, 106
Lilly, 98
Limerick, 220
Linard, 31
Lincoln, 183, 191, 201, 302, 347
Lindday, 122
Lindley, 86
Lindsay, 129, 148, 301, 361, 433
Lindsey, 45, 103, 345
Lindsley, 25, 29, 50, 186, 190, 281, 365, 409, 410
Lingford, 303
Linkins, 179, 351, 352, 354, 404, 422
Linman, 416
Linn, 420
Linnard, 153
Linsley, 259
Linson, 385
Lintell, 248
Linthicum, 362
Linton, 88, 243, 257, 282
Liomin, 186
Lippard, 47
Lippincott, 159, 431, 468
Lippitt, 365, 393, 431, 468
Liscomb, 145
Litchfield, 101, 110
Litle, 186
Little, 3, 17, 38, 124, 147, 186, 228, 231, 251, 351, 434, 479
Little Missouri, 155
Livingston, 13, 101, 201, 233, 365, 450, 467
Llangollen, 229
Llewellyn, 275
Lloyd, 65, 110, 135, 137, 212, 227, 235, 298, 305, 336, 353, 405, 456, 492
Locke, 110, 381, 454
Locker, 158
Lockey, 251

Lockwood, 39
Locust Wood, 430
Lodge, 110
Loeby, 110
Loeser, 99
Loffland, 36
Loftis, 447
Logan, 254, 362
Lokey, 351
Lomas, 254
Lomax, 336
Lombardi, 452, 463
London, 39, 352
Long, 113, 114, 123, 129, 246, 362, 418, 423, 451, 464
Longacre, 213
Longaere, 361
Longfellow, 308
Longstreet, 173, 406
Looby, 46
Loomis, 323, 415
Lord, 48, 107, 186, 196, 251, 288, 352, 376, 416, 436
Lorentz, 410
Lorillard, 5
Loring, 4, 67, 111, 242, 277, 293, 339, 480
Lorraine, 105
Lothrop, 280
Lott, 283
Lottier, 276, 379
Loughborough, 291, 452
Lougheridge, 412
Louis, 110
Lounds, 347
Love, 127, 268, 311, 421, 476
Lovegrove, 170
Lovejoy, 36, 110
Lovel, 9
Loveless, 351
Lovell, 89, 271, 283
Loverage, 220
Lovett, 258, 434
Low, 366
Lowe, 190, 207, 336, 370, 470
Lowery, 430
Lowndes, 87, 107, 388
Lownds, 43

Lowrey, 13, 88
Lowrie, 29, 445
Lowry, 38, 55, 65, 96, 124, 143, 203, 224, 243, 266, 276, 281, 362, 389, 452, 483, 484
Loyall, 113
Loyd, 72, 313
Luallin, 454
Lubey, 459
Luby, 81
Lucas, 1, 190, 302, 315, 351, 392, 459
Lucchesi, 169, 324
Luce, 341, 367
Lucero, 424
Lucius, 376
Luckett, 43, 80
Ludlow, 86
Ludlum, 242
Lugenbeel, 126
Lukins, 1
Lummons, 46
Lumpkin, 29, 428
Luncy, 50
Lundy, 15, 336
Lunsford, 428
Lunt, 1, 202
Lunts, 283
Lurman, 396
Lusby, 50, 186, 352, 415
Lush, 447
Luskey, 165
Luther, 233
Luti, 105
Lutz, 361
Luxen, 179, 426
Lygon, 422
Lykins, 340
Lyle, 59
Lyles, 480
Lyman, 292, 376
Lynam, 72
Lynch, 58, 62, 89, 243, 273, 351, 356, 359, 417
Lynde, 110
Lynn, 386
Lyon, 112, 121, 274, 292, 346, 356
Lyons, 351, 431, 486
Lytle, 55, 71, 93, 381

Lytton, 434

M

MacAboy, 310
Macarius, 221, 256
Macaulay, 162, 253, 328
Mace, 348
Macgill, 147
MacGill, 121
Macgowen, 2
Macguire, 105
Macintosh, 83
Mackay, 127, 262, 390
Mackenheimer, 212
Mackey, 299, 424
Macklern, 5
Maclay, 123, 299
Macleod, 492
Maclin, 128, 267
Macmurdo, 6
MacMurdo, 310
MacNee, 312
Macomb, 95, 97, 137, 232, 376, 446
Macomber, 418
MacPherson, 179
Macrae, 368
MacRae, 471
Macrea, 97
Macready, 194
MacRee, 290
Maddigan, 400
Maddison, 399
Maddox, 192, 204, 259, 289, 354, 362, 493, 495
Madeori, 55
Madison, 32, 146, 272, 273, 275, 351, 459
Madlam, 34
Maelin, 267
Maeulete, 280
Maffit, 172
Magar, 81, 251, 313, 338, 352, 368, 453, 462, 469
Mage, 46
Magee, 53, 239, 317, 354, 356, 368, 427, 465
Maget, 336
Magill, 266
Magilton, 264
Magin, 415
Magle, 353
Maglenen, 71
Magner, 231
Magness, 314
Magnus, 190
Magraw, 196, 206
Magruder, 26, 47, **88**, 132, 138, 147, 161, 174, 186, 193, 227, 243, 291, 302, 322, 334, 336, 338, 344, 351, 353, 385, 431, 442, 446, 463, 492
Maguire, 105, 150, 157, 179, 187, 189, 259, 282, 351, 356, 416
Mahan, 219
Mahappy, 231
Mahar, 352, 356
Maher, 52, 281, 282, 317, 323, 341, 368, 407, 409
Mahon, 53
Mahoney, 200, 325
Mail, 155
mail-steamer **Washington**, 427
Maine, 339
Major, 345, 438
Major Barbour, 155
Makall, 426
Makay, 353
Malan, 303
Mallicotte, 176
Mallock, 384
Mallon, 400
Mallory, 55, 310
Malon, 190
Malone, 186, 493
Maloney, 127, 271
Mamluke, 217
Man, 158
Manchester, 417
Mandan, 217
Manders, 110
Mangum, 57
Mankin, 186, 327, 352
Mankins, 189
Manley, 277, 454
Manlove, 466
Manly, 34, 63, 192

Mann, 47, 169, 228, 229, 236, 280, 344
Manning, 131, 293, 341, 420, 466
Mannion, 205
man-of-war **Herald**, 485
Mansfield, 201, 247, 457, 465
Mansker, 462
Mantaluke, 155
Mantz, 243
Manuel, 158
Many, 41, 230
Mapes, 242
Maratti, 177
Marble, 210
Marbury, 141, 237, 247, 404
Marceron, 89, 324, 408
Marchand, 4
Marcoe, 205
Marcy, 19, 431, 461
Marden, 137
Marengo, 155
Maria, 27
Maria Thomas, 154
Markey, 45
Markham, 340
Markle, 290
Marklew, 428
Markoe, 46, 205
Marks, 143, 186, 289, 463, 493
Markwood, 214
Marlborough, 362
Marll, 95
Maron, 282
Marriott, 19, 200, 354
Marron, 282
Marsh, 29, 31, 70, 117, 210, 223, 233, 366, 449, 450
Marshal, 323
Marshal Ney, 217
Marshall, 19, 20, 26, 32, 64, 84, 94, 98, 106, 110, 115, 136, 146, 189, 220, 223, 266, 274, 303, 307, 314, 321, 348, 353, 367, 414, 470
Martell, 33, 322
Martha, 217, 420
Martha Washington, 157
Martin, 1, 10, 28, 34, 38, 50, 53, 62, 79, 81, 88, 158, 166, 189, 198, 213, 231, 234, 243, 289, 297, 316, 331, 344, 345, 348, 352, 356, 362, 365, 376, 386, 405, 409, 413, 424, 428, 435, 447, 457
Martini, 258
Marvel, 388
Marvin, 117, 210
Mary, 155
Mary Monica, 314
Maryman, 3, 149, 164, 268, 449, 453, 464, 471
Masell, 356
Masi, 36, 50, 172, 186
Maslbury, 301
Mason, 19, 38, 43, 46, 100, 106, 110, 119, 128, 141, 159, 168, 186, 191, 229, 232, 242, 248, 262, 276, 286, 287, 303, 313, 326, 335, 338, 352, 354, 355, 362, 404, 410, 428, 440, 450, 472, 475
Massee, 395
Massey, 362
Massi, 409
Massie, 30
Masters, 233
Mastin, 411
Mater, 325
Mathew, 409
Mathews, 204, 209, 286, 290, 301, 325, 387, 403, 429
Mathiot, 304
Matlock, 70, 270
Matson, 197
Matta, 462
Matthew, 238
Matthews, 77, 94, 183, 209, 230, 260, 291, 397, 400, 409, 450, 475
Mattingley, 282, 408
Mattingly, 47, 257, 294, 362, 388, 409, 441
Mattson, 490
Maulsby, 484
Mauns, 186
Maupin, 486
Mauro, 306
Maury, 5, 9, 51, 71, 87, 88, 107, 112, 172, 188, 227, 235, 257, 286, 392, 408

Maveracke, 192
Maverick, 192
Maxcy, 277
Maxey, 484
Maxwell, 29, 50, 203, 227, 304, 374, 487
Maxy, 25
May, 26, 88, 95, 122, 227, 242, 246, 257, 268, 278, 282, 288, 299, 336, 340, 423, 449
Mayes, 200
Mayfield, 72
Maynadier, 435
Maynard, 6
Mayo, 192, 225, 336
Mays, 95
Mayson, 238
Mazureau, 224
McAboy, 259
McAdams, 244
McAfee, 94
McAffee, 83
McAllister, 196, 267
McAndrew, 198
McArann, 73, 327
McArthur, 62, 148, 266
McAtee, 291
McAvoy, 62
McBarth, 415
McBeth, 312
McBlair, 88, 135, 272, 393
McBoal, 323
McBridge, 25
McCabe, 285
McCaleb, 169
McCall, 153, 252, 490
McCalla, 261
McCallum, 310
McCalop, 462
McCampbell, 136
McCan, 464, 476
McCandless, 45
McCandlish, 233
McCann, 103
McCarter, 437
McCarthy, 50, 281, 282, 392, 449, 450
McCarty, 36, 101, 219, 362, 408, 459
McCarver, 431, 468

McCauley, 35, 192, 250, 366
McCauly, 53
McCelland, 489
McCeney, 243, 375
McCerren, 362
McCleary, 409
McClellan, 126, 153, 203, 384
McClelland, 16, 31, 327, 457
McClellen, 181
McClery, 50, 186, 278, 352
McClintock, 215, 456
McClung, 233
McClure, 265
McClurg, 222
McColgan, 281, 282, 409
McCollum, 225
McCombs, 349
McConnell, 352, 370, 479, 481, 489
McCorkle, 132, 362
McCormick, 19, 53, 86, 164, 191, 200, 226, 235, 281, 289, 332, 356
McCorry, 310
McCoy, 187, 238, 330, 481
McCracken, 208
McCrackin, 491
McCreary, 30, 345
McCulloch, 196, 203, 415
McCulloh, 3, 223, 253
McCullon, 132
McCullough, 170
McCullum, 451
McCully, 170, 226
McCutchen, 353
McDaniel, 103, 141
McDermot, 118
McDermott, 46, 186, 300, 398, 400, 408
McDevitt, 53, 350, 354, 431
McDonald, 47, 93, 152, 153, 195, 199, 200, 201, 352, 359, 483, 484
McDonogh, 29
McDonough, 319, 400
McDougal, 431, 468
McDowell, 9, 10, 84, 168, 439
McDuell, 70
McDuffie, 150
McElfresh, 115, 163, 313
McEllegett, 376

McElrath, 54
McEnery, 225
McEwen, 58, 63, 83, 95
McFarlan, 25, 326, 388
McFarland, 101, 302
McFarlane, 25
McFaul, 10
McFerray, 248
McFerrin, 248
McGarry, 326
McGarum, 51
McGarvey, 46, 52, 354, 408
McGarvy, 259
McGaun, 186
McGavock, 12
McGawley, 446
McGee, 115, 213, 222, 317, 446
McGill, 123, 264, 290, 450
McGinn, 383
McGinniss, 420
McGlocklan, 427
McGlue, 251, 351, 377
McGrann, 398
McGrath, 87, 400
McGraw, 408
McGregor, 69, 190, 262
McGuire, 201, 213, 277, 405, 408, 464
McHatton, 366
McHenry, 106, 110, 207, 257, 397
McIlhaney, 134
McIlvain, 29
McIntire, 9, 51, 101, 186, 225, 280
McIntosh, 54, 58, 62, 67, 89, 94, 102, 266, 417
McIntyre, 102, 191, 397, 401
McKaig, 331, 348
McKane, 2
McKaraher, 134, 443
McKay, 200, 201
Mckean, 190
McKean, 46, 183, 346, 390, 446, 485
McKee, 35, 64, 81, 434, 450
McKeever, 265
McKelden, 356
McKenney, 243
McKenny, 2
McKie, 158

McKim, 187, 392, 396, 437
McKinley, 201, 348
McKinny, 418
McKinstry, 414
McKissack, 129
McKnew, 261
McKnight, 7, 15, 207, 305, 395
McKusick, 452
McLain, 76, 77, 326
McLane, 9, 29, 66, 79, 96, 172, 234, 300, 316, 432, 434
McLaughlin, 35, 77, 110, 219, 274, 325, 482
McLean, 158, 264, 274, 426, 430
McLellan's, 482
McLeod, 2, 138, 308, 312, 323
McMachin, 451
McMackin, 450
McMahon, 32
McMannen, 57
McMeckin, 440
McMullen, 478
McMurray, 69
McNair, 12
McNally, 60
McNamar, 46
McNamara, 400
McNamee, 69, 98, 257, 352
McNeeney, 351
McNeil, 401
McNeill, 228
McNeir, 130, 243, 401
McNerhany, 45
McNerney, 459
McNew, 110
McNier, 191
McNorton, 186
McNutt, 203
McParlin, 128
McPhail, 264, 266
McPherson, 53, 101, 140, 145, 187, 317, 354, 473
McPorril, 301
McQuay, 187, 189
McQuen, 426
McQuiston, 225
McRa, 246
McRae, 68, 199, 215

540

McRea, 199, 417
McRee, 127, 484
McShane, 397
McSherry, 32, 66, 73
McVean, 9, 331
McVey, 148, 268
McVickar, 317
McWhorter, 211
McWilliams, 250, 362
Meacham, 55
Mead, 110, 209, 252, 278, 426
Meade, 9, 30, 74, 196, 427, 460
Meadows, 477
Meashaw, 314
Mechlen, 134
Mechlin, 88, 186, 248
Mechling, 484
Meckins, 381
Medici, 177
Medill, 222
Meeker, 23, 75, 117
Meekes, 398
Mehagan, 9
Meigley, 186
Meigs, 362
Meinengen, 303
Mejia, 27
Melbourn, 473
Melcher, 281
Melchoir, 449
Mellairn, 464
Mellen, 332
Mellon, 96
Melrose, 347
Melvin, 295
Menan, 5
Mendall, 139
Mendota, 155
Menze, 45
Mercer, 29, 46, 283, 290, 307, 326, 468
Merchant, 122, 123, 127, 319
Meredith, 94, 98, 144, 273, 376, 385, 412
Merford, 327
Mergenthal, 473
Meridian Hill, 211
Merrett, 301

Merrick, 348, 443
Merrill, 126, 301, 365, 370, 417
Merriman, 231
Merring, 440, 450, 451
Merritt, 204, 464
Merriwether, 191, 440
Merry, 18, 314
Merton, 242
Messervy, 424
Messrs Ray's Mill, 237
Metcalf, 213
Metero, 156
Methodist Burial Ground, 312
Mettier, 40
Meyers, 56
Michael Angelo, 177
Mich-an-no-pee, 43
Michler, 248
Michoud, 235
Mickham, 110
Mickle, 364
Mickum, 50
Middleton, 24, 29, 36, 57, 79, 88, 196, 227, 235, 243, 279, 286, 287, 294, 315, 326, 332, 352, 353, 356, 408, 453, 460, 467
Milbourn, 65
Milburn, 44, 140, 150, 187, 209, 362, 420
Miles, 103, 362, 471, 472
Miley, 228
Milford, 39, 55, 75
Milhford, 466
Milkburne, 301
Millar, 242
Miller, 3, 8, 17, 26, 33, 38, 40, 50, 54, 64, 72, 73, 77, 78, 81, 88, 89, 110, 112, 120, 136, 141, 148, 153, 156, 184, 186, 187, 189, 190, 192, 195, 211, 212, 215, 227, 235, 239, 242, 246, 249, 260, 264, 268, 275, 278, 282, 296, 351, 353, 354, 356, 366, 373, 375, 396, 398, 402, 409, 416, 432, 440, 441, 449, 458, 459, 469, 476, 478, 486
Millerites, 486
Millican, 417
Milligan, 1, 90, 269, 300

Milliken, 16
Millikin, 64, 75, 93
Millis, 201
Mills, 12, 45, 47, 60, 65, 110, 136, 152, 183, 190, 215, 288, 310, 351, 352, 354, 360, 385, 420, 469
Millwood, 342
Milner, 440
Milnor, 242
Miltimore, 420
Milwaukie, 155
Mimm, 412
Miner, 362, 435
Mines, 114, 255
Minnix, 179, 338, 416
Minor, 67, 214, 294, 295, 340
Minot, 219
Minturn, 343
Mirkem, 243
Mish, 294
Missouri, 155
Missouri Mail, 155
Misterer, 351
Mitchel, 257
Mitchell, 38, 47, 49, 55, 56, 65, 93, 144, 176, 182, 228, 252, 271, 291, 315, 320, 326, 405, 409, 426, 427, 439, 441, 459, 481
Mitchem, 256
Mithoff, 396
Mizner, 222
Mockbee, 45
Moenser, 282
Moenster, 215, 479
Moffat, 380
Moffatt, 152, 395
Moffett, 334
Moffitt, 251
Mogul, 156
Mohin, 187
Mohler, 299, 341, 349, 351
Mohun, 91, 107, 281, 282, 351
Monae, 234
Monahun, 163
Moncini, 257
Moncrieff, 201
Mondawmin, 328
Mongtomery, 97

Monona, 155
Monroe, 4, 56, 93, 110, 146, 199, 334, 356
Montague, 291
Montauk, 217
Montcalm, 324
Monterey, 155
Montesquion, 430
Montez, 301
Montgomerie, 221
Montgomery, 62, 69, 80, 93, 199, 214, 339, 406, 459
Montholon, 291
Montoya, 424
Montreal, 450
Moody, 440, 450
Mooney, 191, 412, 421
Moore, 39, 50, 52, 53, 56, 66, 81, 96, 121, 147, 161, 171, 189, 190, 191, 198, 210, 217, 221, 231, 260, 262, 264, 266, 286, 293, 314, 323, 326, 336, 351, 352, 363, 385, 394, 414, 431, 447, 454, 467, 468, 487, 489
Moorehead, 54
Moorhead, 257, 335
Moors, 31
Morales, 177
Moran, 17, 46, 50, 353, 362, 400
Morcoe, 219, 278, 426
Mordecai, 127
More, 80
Morehead, 88, 95, 199, 313, 473
Morehouse, 220, 480
Morel, 41, 299
Morell, 50, 112
Morely, 138
Moreno, 56, 234
Moreton, 134
Morfit, 100, 183
Morgan, 8, 13, 26, 34, 61, 72, 77, 88, 95, 110, 115, 142, 145, 174, 175, 180, 181, 186, 193, 195, 196, 210, 211, 215, 225, 262, 273, 294, 316, 320, 324, 348, 352, 356, 357, 364, 390, 391, 401, 405, 427, 439, 472, 486, 491, 492
Moriarty, 247
Morin, 158

Morison, 150, 248
Morley, 190
Morly, 207
Mormon, 444
Mormons, 250, 411
Morphy, 310
Morrell, 59
Morrice, 282
Morrill, 449
Morris, 4, 42, 105, 110, 123, 125, 126, 186, 192, 194, 207, 225, 234, 239, 242, 268, 273, 275, 280, 281, 282, 294, 303, 307, 326, 372, 406, 419, 450, 451
Morrison, 12, 50, 72, 96, 97, 123, 149, 184, 326, 337, 406, 420, 437
Morrow, 25, 173, 236, 370, 409, 475
Morse, 93, 110, 190, 256, 286, 387
Morsell, 9, 57, 118, 150, 161, 165, 179, 190, 192, 227, 279, 287, 401, 408, 422, 460
Morsman, 242
Mortimer, 50, 179, 201
Morton, 93, 110, 132, 201, 225, 241, 268, 270
Morton, 291
Moseley, 19
Mosely, 219, 371, 469
Moses, 262
Mosher, 59
Mosley, 417
Moss, 117, 289
Mott, 40, 143, 295, 365
Moulden, 480
Moulthrop, 387
Mount, 14, 177, 186, 303
Mount Pleasant, 321, 387
Mount Vernon, 163
Mountz, 48
Mouton, 286
Mowbray, 470
Mower, 152
Mowry, 81
Moxley, 138
Moy, 321
Moyan, 481
Mucklow, 328

Mudd, 8, 47, 89, 110, 147, 251, 254, 257, 320, 368, 426
Mulkenan, 400
Mulkennan, 398
Mullady, 72
Mullen, 46, 149, 197, 222, 398, 400, 404
Mulligan, 381, 400
Mullikin, 68, 132, 189, 246, 336, 354, 372, 459
Mullin, 186, 188
Mullins, 46, 102
Mulloy, 12, 26, 45, 251
Mulvey, 459
Mumford, 483, 484
Muncaster, 147, 354
Munch, 46, 50
Munck, 187, 408
Munro, 87, 329
Munroe, 213, 268, 397, 399, 409
Munsey, 447
Murch, 431
Murdick, 362
Murdoch, 402
Murdock, 247, 333, 460
Mure, 186
Murillo, 177
Murphey, 474
Murphy, 15, 25, 32, 39, 54, 81, 110, 137, 187, 206, 208, 225, 252, 282, 289, 356, 371, 383, 400, 459, 461, 487
Murray, 37, 53, 60, 81, 82, 110, 159, 186, 189, 201, 223, 227, 238, 243, 281, 282, 294, 315, 335, 344, 430, 451
Murtagh, 353
Muse, 103, 327, 401
Mussey, 376
Musson, 162
Mustin, 186
Myer, 150, 243, 459
Myerle, 24, 34
Myers, 38, 40, 55, 58, 63, 66, 80, 81, 85, 123, 196, 242, 268, 426, 451
Myrick, 196
Mytton, 379

N

Naif, 72
Naile, 395
Naill, 307, 401
Nailor, 48, 50, 88, 182, 188, 216, 303, 330, 341, 362, 393, 404, 409, 419, 432, 469
Nairn, 50
Naish, 376
Nalley, 51, 187
Nalon, 400
Nangle, 424
Napier, 93
Napoleon, 2, 6, 18, 22, 76, 207, 371
Nash, 2, 41, 66, 225, 271, 276, 403, 454
Nathan Hale, 156
Natural Bridge, 450
Naudain, 33
Nauman, 124, 125, 153
Naylor, 19, 32, 46, 52, 106, 107, 143, 180, 192, 251, 257, 332, 380, 408, 453
Neal, 402
Neale, 213, 222, 291, 317, 351, 356, 362, 383, 393, 404, 410, 427
Neally, 207
Nee, 450
Needham, 215
Neil, 354
Neilson, 250
Nelson, 45, 110, 151, 233, 236, 279, 459, 471, 483
Nepp, 351
Nesmith, 48
Netcher, 177
Neville, 324
Nevin, 459
Nevins, 227
Nevitt, 66, 96
Nevitte, 70
New Post ofcs, 330, 348, 367, 376, 395, 403, 412, 417, 433, 447, 454, 466, 473, 478, 489
New Post Ofcs, 339, 384
New Uncle Sam, 217
Newbold, 136
Newcomb, 412

Newell, 304, 315
Newhard, 104
Newlin, 339
Newman, 99, 110, 336, 345, 416
Newmyer, 353
Newton, 2, 21, 64, 75, 84, 95, 143, 166, 187, 213, 227, 234, 281, 282, 336, 365
Nicar, 428
Nice, 276
Nicholas, 22, 321, 491
Nicholls, 187, 295, 415
Nichols, 153, 190, 215, 297, 304, 309, 411
Nicholson, 9, 71, 214, 294, 376, 463
Nicking, 2
Nicoll, 33
Nicols, 392
Niebergall, 303
Niepce, 134
Niles, 63, 69
Nimmo, 238, 265
Noble, 39, 54, 71, 96, 191, 199, 212, 351
Nock, 14
Noddles's Island, 192
Noe, 450
Noel, 152, 371, 487
Noell, 50, 53
Noer, 351, 355
Noerr, 180, 187
Nokes, 187
Nolan, 476
Noland, 193, 291, 453
Nolin, 417
Noonan, 400
Nooney, 140
Norbeck, 50, 356
Norfleet, 114
Noriago, 402
Norris, 55, 72, 96, 118, 216, 242, 323, 401
North, 301, 341
North Alabama, 156
North America, 156
North View, 255
Northerman, 163, 216
Northern, 377

Norton, 14, 25, 61, 362, 365, 393, 402, 431, 468
Norvell, 264, 458
Norwood, 241
Notch House, 413
Nott, 224
Nourse, 4, 68, 95, 104, 158, 183, 187, 211, 298, 326, 362, 409, 477
Noyes, 5, 47, 282
Nugent, 162, 187, 355
Nutt, 68, 101, 203, 204
Nutting, 384
Nye, 66, 108, 152, 436

O

O'Bannot, 248
O'Brien, 153, 242, 264, 281, 367, 398, 399, 400, 459, 484
O'Callahan, 242
O'Conner, 249
O'Connor, 44, 281, 282
O'Dell, 50, 53
O'Donnel, 392
O'Donnell, 50, 88, 114, 281
O'Donnoghue, 282
O'donoghue, 187
O'Donoghue, 47, 48, 291, 351, 355
O'Donohue, 291
O'Driscoll, 231
O'Flanegan, 2
O'Grady, 247
O'Hare, 48, 393
O'Keefe, 275
O'Leary, 356
O'Neal, 72, 281
O'Neale, 82, 162, 187, 197, 247, 362
O'Neil, 214
O'Neill, 317
O'Niel, 405
O'Niell, 136
O'Reilly, 2, 56, 93, 400
Oak Hill, 300
Oak Hill Cemetery, 62, 122
Oakland, 284
Oakley, 26
Oaks, 153
Ober, 13, 48, 209, 269, 353, 427
Odborn, 242

Odd, 493
Odd Fellow, 156
Odenheimer, 430
Oella No 2, 156
Oellers, 87
Oelrichs, 246
Ofensteink, 352
Offutt, 8, 291, 297
Ogden, 128, 191, 222, 242, 275, 332, 466
Ogilvie, 240
Ogle, 140, 478
Ohl, 39, 54, 71, 96, 199
Olcott, 92
Old Brandon, 172
Old Clipper, 157
Old Uncle Sam, 217
Older, 348
oldest college, 429
Oldham, 170
Oley, 308
Oliphant, 482
Oliver, 2, 136, 156, 179, 209, 400, 413
Olroyd, 228
Omsted, 339
Ord, 366, 394, 402, 431, 468
Orem, 91, 189
Organ, 301
Orme, 48, 50, 235, 251, 282, 353, 441
Orphan Asylum, 204
Orr, 187, 320, 362, 430
Osborn, 87, 434
Osborne, 256, 291, 356, 437
Osburn, 163, 323
Osgood, 13, 454
Otero, 424
Otey, 29, 492
Otis, 101
Ott, 42, 306, 474
Otten, 201
Otterback, 187, 351, 355
Ottison, 287
Oueto, 318
Ould, 91, 261
Ouseley, 282
Ousley, 281, 346
Outton, 170
Overton, 466, 472

545

Oviatt, 395
Owen, 138, 190, 193, 340, 356, 382, 409
Owens, 42, 119, 174, 187, 294
Owings, 440, 489
Oxen Hill, 212
Oxman, 411
Oyster, 32, 189, 191, 305, 362

P

Paca, 397
Pacheco, 10, 17, 27, 61
packet **Liberia**, 76
packet ship **Henry Clay**, 343
packet ship **Oxford**, 325
Packete, 113
Paddock, 215
Padres, 376
Padsworth Farm, 132
Page, 19, 46, 58, 72, 103, 187, 196, 215, 236, 316, 322, 325, 366, 455, 459
Pageet, 178
Pageot, 37, 74
Paggett, 99
Paige, 264, 371
Paine, 117, 191, 264, 441, 446
Painter, 46
Pairo, 117, 191, 216, 305, 467
Palen, 229, 366, 401
Palestine, 156
Palfrey, 440
Pallet, 489
Palmer, 14, 21, 106, 132, 204, 341, 377, 437, 477
Pane, 303
Paquett, 488
Paralto, 281
Paredes, 242
Parish, 44, 110, 137
Parke, 50, 265, 352
Parker, 20, 38, 50, 51, 52, 92, 103, 110, 141, 169, 187, 190, 200, 221, 225, 227, 275, 295, 303, 304, 309, 311, 323, 333, 334, 341, 353, 354, 355, 362, 365, 408, 419, 469, 471, 487, 488, 492, 495
Parkhill, 472

Parkin, 275
Parkman, 457
Parks, 38, 42, 233, 263, 330, 340, 390, 395, 491
Parmelee, 170
Parmenter, 108
Parran, 136
Parris, 187, 215
Parrish, 225, 382
Parrot, 240
Parrott, 42, 286, 287, 363, 435, 437
Parson, 447
Parsons, 52, 83, 141, 202, 243, 268, 280, 387, 430, 489
Parton, 352
Pascoult, 2
Past Events, 263
Pasteur, 113
Pate, 417
Pat-e-go-shuck, 481
Patrick, 127, 250
Patten, 367, 399
Patterson, 22, 50, 72, 100, 110, 113, 135, 141, 161, 192, 196, 237, 243, 257, 290, 307, 341, 365, 392, 401, 408, 433, 456, 477
Patton, 67, 339, 362, 399, 420, 475
Paul Jones, 155, 156
Paulding, 26, 84
Paule, 110
Paulin Le Grand, 96
Pavenstedt, 482
Paxton, 189
Payne, 4, 17, 18, 21, 23, 32, 58, 62, 71, 82, 95, 111, 148, 189, 213, 233, 246, 291, 297, 303, 310, 351, 352, 355, 362, 376, 426, 428, 429, 464
Peabody, 280, 291, 438
Peachey, 370
Peachy, 365, 443
Peaco, 77, 190
Peacok, 466
Peak, 424
Peake, 187, 198, 260, 362, 363
Peale, 427
Pearce, 102, 397
Pearson, 33, 162, 227, 235, 289, 296, 343, 353, 355, 362, 397, 401, 423

546

Pease, 310
Pechin, 305
Peck, 152, 187, 201, 288, 351, 352, 355, 391, 408, 431, 437
Peddicord, 189
Peebler, 418
Peed, 42
Peel, 187
Peerce, 204, 227, 276, 353
Peet, 237
Peets, 453
Peetsch, 356
Pegg, 353
Pegram, 269
Peirce, 489
Peitch, 268
Pekin, 156
Pelham, 191
Pelican, 156
Pell, 451
Pelouze, 101
Pemberton, 153
Pendergast, 462
Pendergrast, 294
Pendleton, 210, 380, 383
Penn, 295
Penniman, 95
Pennington, 131, 141, 411, 477
Penny, 158, 303, 339
Penrose, 13, 123, 129
Pentecost, 466
Peoples, 365
Pepper, 408, 454
Percival, 27, 97
Perine, 70
Perkins, 3, 50, 58, 63, 81, 86, 117, 187, 265, 329, 353, 365, 379, 394, 475
Perrie, 282
Perrin, 151, 378
Perrine, 83, 315
Perry, 5, 50, 58, 97, 142, 179, 192, 227, 236, 244, 257, 306, 335, 348, 387, 396, 430, 459, 490
Peter, 104, 278
Peters, 45, 52, 160, 180, 238, 303, 341, 356
Peterson, 7, 187, 234, 351

Petherbridge, 242
Petit, 377
Petona, 420
Petriken, 440
Pettes, 108
Pettibone, 173, 187, 310, 354, 368
Pettingall, 236
Pettit, 187, 196, 416
Petty, 97, 433
Peugh, 491
Peyton, 86, 233, 313, 324, 331, 389, 415
Pfister, 495
Phayer, 488
Phelan, 480
Phelphs, 11
Phelps, 29, 71, 85, 91, 96, 161, 178, 199, 239, 259, 294, 317, 352, 356
Philbrick, 467
Philbrook, 436
Philips, 110, 254, 340, 371
Phillipe, 462
Phillips, 52, 69, 88, 119, 160, 174, 180, 190, 261, 273, 277, 295, 314, 353, 367, 408, 412
Phillips' Mill, 347
Phinney, 211, 293
Piano Grove, 132
Pickara, 209
Pickell, 106
Picket, 107
Pickett, 233, 483, 484
Pickin, 2
Pickrell, 30, 82, 159, 362, 411, 419, 431
Pico, 394, 402, 431, 468
Pierce, 29, 30, 37, 52, 119, 192, 249, 331
Pierson, 271
Pifer, 103
Piggott, 181, 339
Pike, 270, 424
Pikering, 113
Pilcher, 38, 55, 70
Piles, 54
Pilling, 52
Pilot, 156
Pim, 227

Pindell, 170
Pine, 470
Piney Point, 321
Piney Woods, 156
Pink, 412
Pinkney, 175, 230
Pise, 286
Pitcher, 7, 115, 163, 198, 230, 326, 413, 439, 480, 483, 484
Pitman, 118
Pitt, 382
Pix, 78
Pizarro, 80
Pizzini, 286
Plant, 187, 191, 251, 268, 292, 351, 356, 408, 409, 463
Planter, 156
Plater, 228, 338
Platt, 42, 183, 265, 340
Pleasanton, 187
Pleasants, 85, 193, 281
Pleasonton, 273, 291, 483
Plough Boy:, 156
Plowden, 214
Plume, 365
Plumer, 307, 331
Plummer, 56, 96, 101
Plunket, 452
Pocahontas, 263
Poe, 291, 391
Poelzel, 23
Poindexter, 17, 90, 92
Poisel, 97
Poiser, 201
Poland, 448
Polk, 74, 98, 102, 110, 132, 149, 171, 200, 207, 231, 237, 238, 240, 261, 308, 332, 382, 492
Pollard, 58, 63, 92
Pollard's Row, 234
Polley, 42
Pollock, 269, 363
Pomeroy, 99, 237, 239, 247
Pomroy, 405
Pond, 200, 201, 323
Pone, 176
Pons, 362
Pooder, 53
Pook, 445
Pool, 242
Poole, 95, 145, 233, 478, 489
Poor, 67, 93, 366, 455
Poore, 234, 386
Pope, 37, 138, 161, 243, 244, 260, 331, 445
Pope Pius IX, 160
Popham, 151
Poplar Ridge, 132
Porter, 10, 11, 78, 88, 125, 126, 144, 153, 200, 224, 232, 239, 242, 269, 295, 396, 414, 458
Posey, 179, 459
Post, 365
Posten, 251
Potete, 404
Potosi, 469
Potter, 99, 110, 236, 465
Potts, 425
Pouder, 473
Poulson, 115
Poultney, 130, 152, 225
Pound, 385
Pounds, 270
Poussin, 100
Powell, 46, 149, 187, 192, 197, 202, 219, 229, 253, 269, 345, 368, 376, 427, 429, 453, 467, 468
Power, 446
Powerful Fish, 481
Powers, 203, 224, 303, 349, 426
Prairie Bird, 156
Prairie State, 217
Prall, 18
Prather, 187, 213, 351, 355, 356, 362
Pratt, 34, 36, 156, 250, 315, 343, 363, 387, 396, 411, 462
Pray, 113
Prayton, 404
Prentiss, 58, 63, 81, 144, 176, 187, 192, 303
Presbyterian Church, 454
Prescott, 163, 440, 450, 451
President's House, 495
Preston, 94, 98, 245, 354, 362, 433
Pretty Prospect, 389, 452
Prettyman, 57, 104

Preuss, 35, 139, 142
Prevost, 257, 444
Price, 2, 81, 148, 206, 256, 276, 362, 365, 393, 431, 440, 450, 457, 468
Pridgen, 367
Prince, 127, 327, 483
Prince of Hayti, 153
Pritchard, 247, 286
Pritchett, 420
Proctor, 2, 459
propeller **Hartford**, 175
propeller **Washington**, 431
Prospect Hill, 72, 145
Proulin, 158
Proulx, 175
Prout, 7, 362, 416
Prouty, 238
Provest, 51
Prunty, 339
Public Records consumed, 453
Pulizzi, 187, 351
Pullen, 170
Pumphrey, 187, 190, 227, 247, 297, 303, 309, 362, 368, 408, 418
Pumphry, 52
Punis, 247
Purcell, 46, 187, 224
Purdy, 45, 114, 305, 309, 351, 354, 355, 356
Purky, 400
Purle, 303
Purnell, 397, 440
Pursell, 50, 408
Putnam, 152, 228
Putney, 439
Pye, 388
Pyne, 18, 97, 164, 258, 273, 406, 410, 415
Pynell, 46

Q

Quaker Hill, 394
Quantril, 174
Qua-qua-tah, 481
Queen, 88, 107, 137, 175, 209, 227, 235, 291, 303, 315, 386, 408
Queen Elizabeth, 252
Quesenberry, 205

Quigley, 51, 246, 353
Quigly, 282
Quin, 393
Quinche, 276
Quincy, 180
Quincy, Fla, 455
Quinen, 398
Quinn, 95, 339, 378, 398, 399
Quitman, 97, 332, 368, 442

R

Rabbitt, 110
Rabourg, 363
Rackett, 426
Racoon Ford, 270
Radcliff, 24, 65, 183, 190, 226, 227, 235, 250, 364, 420
Radcliffe, 88
Radetzky, 176
Ragan, 47, 225, 351, 354, 408, 441
Ragen, 378
Ragsdale, 4
Raiford, 147
Railey, 29, 45, 448
Raimy, 190
Rain, 259
Rainey, 192
Raleigh, 198, 263
Raleigh Register, 390
Raley, 351
Ralls, 384
Ralph, 79
Ralston, 29
Rambler, 156
Ramsay, 95, 230, 286, 452
Ramsdell, 489
Ramsey, 100, 141, 187, 203, 204, 291, 352
Rand, 211, 321
Randall, 47, 48, 93, 102, 103, 161, 180, 187, 277, 286, 409, 416, 478
Randals, 2
Randolph, 18, 26, 195
Randon, 8
Raney, 46, 356
Rankin, 304
Ranlett, 435, 450
Rantoul, 202

549

Raphael, 177
Rappitti, 187
Rasch, 106
Raspail, 2
Rasselte, 427
Ratcliff, 309, 312, 365
Ratcliffe, 85, 249, 336, 448
Rathburn, 285
Rathburn's Hotel, 369
Raub, 184, 187
Ravoux, 234
Rawle, 423
Rawling, 466
Rawlings, 50, 120, 187, 351, 355, 472
Rawlins, 184, 323
Rawls, 114
Ray, 13, 71, 164, 192, 404, 436, 448, 460
Rayburn, 225
Raymond, 38, 54, 81, 242, 489
razee **Independence**, 215
Rea, 450
Read, 71, 176, 192, 324, 327, 333, 345, 451, 460
Reader, 110
Ready, 51, 271, 351, 460
Ream, 30
Rearden, 91
Record of weather, 195
Rector, 20, 244, 455
Red Man of Calif, 31
Red Wing, 217
Reddall, 199
Redding, 247, 397, 400
Redfern, 63, 108, 119, 187, 221, 249, 336, 351, 409, 469, 495
Redfield, 448
Rediks, 303
Redin, 55, 87, 149, 150, 159, 174, 194, 250, 272, 292, 297, 351, 389, 419, 425, 433, 435, 452, 495
Reed, 2, 33, 39, 48, 95, 110, 135, 138, 152, 181, 187, 241, 377, 380, 395, 399, 409, 438, 447
Reeder, 11
Reese, 77, 95, 103, 106, 139, 321, 349, 430
Reeve, 31

Reeves, 14, 285, 296
Regan, 437
Regnald, 84
Regnes, 122
Reichenbach, 106
Reid, 50, 201, 285, 431, 437, 440, 468
Reiley, 408
Reilly, 356
Reily, 363
Reindollar, 84
Reiner, 303
Reintz, 352
Reinz, 351
Reis, 460
Reiss, 187
Reitz, 210, 226
Remick, 167, 416
Rencher, 64, 76
Rendenstein, 242
Rene, 105
Reneau, 44
Rensselaer, 86
Resin, 351
Retter, 187
Rey, 450
Reynes, 5
Reynolds, 29, 72, 128, 153, 203, 247, 263, 266, 267, 325, 435, 445, 484
Rhea, 39, 117
Rhett, 264
Rhoads, 161
Rhodes, 35, 187, 351, 355, 371, 408
Rhorch, 303
Rice, 11, 13, 48, 64, 103, 179, 303, 351, 363, 374, 406, 426, 447, 453
Rich, 110, 269, 388, 411, 414, 460
Richard, 162
Richards, 2, 110, 143, 194, 220, 351, 381, 394, 411, 463, 478
Richardson, 144, 158, 184, 187, 189, 203, 211, 225, 248, 251, 276, 289, 310, 317, 351, 394, 439, 460, 465, 466, 490
Richey, 426
Richie, 159
Richmond, 382, 457
Rickard, 286
Ricketts, 206

Riddall, 30
Riddell, 103
Riddle, 79, 87, 96, 161, 340
Riddley, 242
Rider, 108, 392
Ridgeley, 21
Ridgely, 103, 125, 442
Ridgley, 50
Ridgway, 214, 239, 354, 407
Ridley, 437
Rieman, 396
Riffle, 5
Rigby, 28
Rigdon, 48, 363
Rigg, 74
Riggles, 190
Riggs, 46, 193, 300, 352, 363, 375, 456
Riley, 50, 51, 85, 106, 138, 187, 201, 278, 282, 306, 318, 351, 354, 356, 373, 400, 402, 409, 413, 416, 451, 459, 468
Rincon, 426
Rind, 56, 114
Ringgold, 156, 267, 442
Ringo, 259
Rio Grande, 156
Riordan, 187, 303, 443
Ripks, 168
Ripley, 126, 127, 162, 425
Risey, 331
Risley, 117
Ritchie, 9, 80, 164, 261, 273, 415
Ritman, 72
Ritromelli, 443
Rittenhouse, 477
Ritter, 51, 356
Rives, 29, 118, 141, 210, 349
Rix, 356
Rixey, 337
Rixeyville, 337
Roach, 17, 53, 63, 119, 187, 204, 216, 269, 291, 341, 351, 355, 394, 418, 444, 450
Robards, 102
Robbins, 435
Robert Fulton, 154, 156
Robert Weightman, 156

Roberts, 24, 38, 48, 54, 58, 62, 81, 127, 187, 196, 234, 271, 272, 299, 303, 320, 330, 356, 364, 401, 447, 448
Robertson, 20, 80, 111, 115, 161, 187, 191, 194, 251, 265, 390, 391, 440
Robeson, 11
Robey, 363, 467
Robidoux, 175
Robillard, 423
Robinet, 276
Robins, 278
Robinson, 50, 79, 86, 95, 99, 102, 103, 110, 112, 116, 119, 121, 131, 139, 151, 187, 199, 209, 215, 226, 227, 232, 251, 259, 286, 290, 317, 332, 350, 351, 356, 390, 392, 405, 410, 434, 436, 460
Robron, 348
Roby, 48
Rochart, 48
Roche, 88, 97, 409
Rock Creek, 375
Rockhill, 427
Rockway, 454
Rockwell, 114, 326
Rodbird, 408, 427
Rodes, 170
Rodgers, 2, 9, 42, 61, 76, 84, 106, 172, 208, 221, 222, 230
Rodier, 303
Rodrigues, 431
Rodriguez, 96, 468
Roemele, 48
Roemro, 424
Rogers, 2, 55, 61, 62, 87, 110, 168, 174, 175, 211, 231, 271, 274, 289, 339, 366, 367, 396, 437, 488, 491
Rohrbaugh, 216
Rohrer, 158
Roland, 33, 123, 153, 193, 341
Rolfe, 263, 335
Roll, 293
Rollan, 356
Rollin, 2, 104
Rollins, 2, 51, 103, 149
Rollow, 451
Romaine, 201

Roman, 268
Rondbush, 339
Rood, 433
Rooker, 337
Root, 246, 348, 465
Rope, 268
Ropes, 387
Rosa, 177
Rose, 2, 45, 60, 72, 110, 117, 187, 363, 452
Rose Hill, 255
Rose Hills, 386
Rosedale, 205
Rosenstock, 46, 47, 187, 222, 241, 317, 368
Rosevelt, 211
Ross, 42, 46, 66, 79, 85, 101, 111, 141, 151, 176, 177, 181, 187, 203, 206, 236, 248, 266, 303, 431
Rossell, 69
Rosser, 211
Rossi, 3
Rossiter, 384
Rossitter, 91
Roszel, 221, 439
Roszell, 115, 431, 444
Rotche, 488
Rotchford, 394
Roth, 281, 282
Rother, 306
Rothrock, 466
Roths, 355
Rothschild, 221
Rothwell, 5, 212, 226, 235, 245, 342, 358, 363
Rounsaville, 420
Roura, 331, 337
Rousby, 205
Rovira, 76
Rowan, 105, 133, 371
Roward, 363
Rowe, 239
Rowland, 191, 321, 325, 389
Rowles, 255
Rowlett, 340, 407
Roy, 266
Royall, 356
Royce, 308, 489

Royston, 367
Rozell, 206
Rubens, 105
Rubens, 177
Rucker, 484
Ruckle, 201
Rudd, 327
Ruff, 47, 125, 338, 352
Ruggles, 126
Ruland, 19
Rundal, 397
Runnells, 356
Runnels, 366
Rupert, 51
Rupp, 5, 12, 26, 51, 66, 82, 169, 187, 222, 268, 281, 292, 427, 453
Ruppell, 51
Ruppert, 282
Rush, 171, 427, 467
Rusk, 200, 207
Russ, 403
Russell, 5, 50, 96, 123, 126, 143, 168, 172, 180, 200, 201, 203, 215, 231, 271, 284, 303, 310, 374, 379, 381, 390, 471, 487
Russey, 264
Russworm, 299, 487
Russy, 264
Rust, 292, 423
Rutherford, 219, 270, 414
Rutledge, 180
Ryan, 368, 386, 403
Ryder, 274, 429
Ryland, 338
Rynders, 253
Rynex, 77, 212
Ryon, 48, 227, 269, 334, 352, 353, 391

S

Sabastian, 52
Sackett, 271
Sagathy, 72
Salinas, 233
Salona Farm, 161
Salt Lake, 411
Saltmarsh, 97
Sammons, 285

Sampayo, 94
Sampson, 28, 211, 261, 351
Samson, 10, 77, 91, 218, 225, 232, 270, 402, 472
Samuels, 51, 193
Sanborn, 412
Sanches, 424
Sanchez, 176, 365, 393
Sandel, 241
Sandeman, 476
Sanders, 26, 303
Sanderson, 234
Sandford, 226
Sandoval, 456
Sands, 53, 104, 200, 307, 372, 401
Sandy Hill, 399
Sanford, 180, 200, 327, 460
Sanger, 97
Sangfitt, 303
Sangston, 348
Sans, 462
Sansevain, 393, 468
Saracina, 456
Sarah, 217
Sardinian Minister, 149
Sardo, 409
Sargent, 71, 112, 162, 203, 233, 274
Sasser, 2, 88
Saunders, 19, 58, 63, 70, 144, 150, 179, 187, 195, 213, 242, 247, 257, 264, 310, 364, 385, 427, 455
Saur, 187, 190, 213
Savage, 51, 96, 198, 277, 281, 286, 362, 419
Savoy, 2
Sawkins, 409
Sawyer, 101, 143, 188, 367, 451
Saxon, 239
Saxton, 62, 266
Sayre, 173
Sayres, 206
Scaggs, 492
Scallan, 363
Scanlan, 111
Scantland, 7, 96, 301
Schanks, 243
Schaub, 136
Sched, 404

Schemerhorn, 13
Schenck, 99, 191, 208, 221, 236, 329, 432
Schermerhorn, 69
Schlegel, 258
Schley, 56, 309, 371, 397
Schmit, 232
Schneider, 409
schnr **Abby Hammond**, 166
schnr **Albatross**, 420
schnr **Alert**, 437
schnr **Alverda**, 431
schnr **Amelia**, 60
schnr **B L F**, 411
schnr **Bandicott**, 171
schnr **Boston**, 457
schnr **Calista**, 374
schnr **Caroline**, 419
schnr **Catherine**, 420
schnr **Chesapeake**, 388
schnr **Coll Castle**, 275
schnr **Columbia**, 491
schnr **Constellation**, 167
schnr **Cornelian**, 437
schnr **Crescent**, 411
schnr **Diamond**, 457
schnr **Eagle**, 387, 420
schnr **Eclipse**, 473
schnr **Elizabeth**, 387
schnr **Ellen Sedgwick**, 489
schnr **Empire**, 372
schnr **Ewing**, 432, 470
schnr **Expedition**, 419
schnr **Felix**, 485
schnr **Flirt**, 87
schnr **G Hoffman**, 431
schnr **Hornet**, 419
schnr **Isaac McKim**, 437
schnr **John Allyne**, 334
schnr **John Henry**, 419
schnr **John Lillie**, 181
schnr **Laconic**, 81
schnr **Lodi**, 437
schnr **Loriat**, 456
schnr **Mary Francis**, 411
schnr **Mobile**, 411
schnr **Montezuma**, 491
schnr **Morris**, 172

schnr **Nelson**, 437
schnr **Pampero**, 431
schnr **Rio Grande**, 411
schnr **Robert James**, 419, 420
schnr **Spartacus**, 388
schnr **Susan**, 437
schnr **Taney**, 327
schnr **Ticonie**, 16
schnr **William Henry**, 108
schnr **Zenobia**, 240
Schofield, 102
Scholfield, 220, 363, 458
Schoolcraft, 333
Schoonmaker, 489
Schott, 5, 27
Schriner, 166
Schucking, 386
Schuermann, 372
Schumacher, 396, 482
Schureman, 9
Schwaitze, 353
Schwarts, 32
Schwartz, 50
Schwartze, 188
Schwarzman, 159, 443
Schweitzer, 187
Scofield, 395
Scolley, 39
Scott, 14, 29, 45, 48, 49, 53, 87, 97,
  117, 120, 126, 131, 138, 140, 160,
  170, 187, 203, 206, 236, 246, 252,
  292, 298, 311, 353, 363, 386, 406,
  419, 425, 442, 447, 455, 459, 460,
  466, 486
Scoville, 330
Screven, 123, 126
Scrivener, 235, 381
Scrivenner, 363
Scrivner, 253, 284
Scull, 99
Sea Bird, 156
Sea Gull, 157
Seabring, 339
Seabury, 67, 335
Seaman, 327
Seamans, 108
Sears, 50, 210, 227, 483, 484
Seaton, 9, 106, 117, 227

Sebastian, 9, 492
Secor, 275
Sederer, 355
Sedgwick, 122, 191
Sedwick, 126
Seed, 415
Seely, 460
Seering, 451
Seevers, 136
Segar, 122
Seidel, 454
Seidell, 348
Seip, 384
Seitz, 26, 183, 188, 356, 393, 475
Seixas, 201
Selby, 351, 399
Selden, 92, 101, 111, 257, 289, 356
Seldner, 353
Sellhausen, 51
Sellick, 201
Selling, 437
Selly, 439
Semmes, 48, 49, 81, 107, 120, 175,
  223, 227, 283, 286, 291
Semoice, 21
Semple, 394, 402, 431, 468
Sencheimer, 47
Seney, 214
Sengstack, 342, 351, 352, 353
Sergeant, 205
Serrin, 143, 251, 352
Sessford, 1, 34, 90, 251, 252, 352, 443
Seston, 16
Setzer, 323
Seufferle, 187
Sevier, 15, 22, 24
Sewall, 74, 85, 111, 187, 233, 243,
  282, 363, 391
Seward, 333, 384
Sewart, 15
Sewell, 242
Sexton, 21, 66, 96, 400, 434
Seybold, 74
Seybolt, 49
Seymour, 41, 125, 204, 297, 315, 352,
  426, 439
Shaaff, 253
Shackelford, 52, 159

Shackleford, 407
Shacklett, 351
Shad, 341, 408
Shadd, 52, 188, 190, 354, 356
Shaeffer, 50
Shaer, 234
Shafer, 215, 467
Shaffer, 21, 96, 199
Shakespeare, 105, 461
Shaler, 488
Shankland, 252, 439
Shanks, 47, 51, 184, 318
Shannehar, 225
Shannon, 46, 402, 431, 468, 478
Shaops, 62
Sharp, 489
Shattuck, 466
Shaub, 355
Shaw, 51, 93, 149, 158, 187, 190, 215, 269, 348, 403, 481
Sheahan, 213
Sheatham, 121
Sheckell, 188, 407
Sheckells, 190
Sheckels, 52, 191
Shedd, 162, 222, 248, 317, 355, 416
Sheehey, 3
Sheet, 160
Sheets, 46, 424
Sheffield, 246
Sheid, 47
Shekell, 281, 282, 286, 441
Shekells, 243
Shelby, 22, 121
Sheldon, 84, 94, 97
Shelladay, 191
Shepard, 36, 93, 247, 326, 392
Shephard, 40, 252
Shepherd, 9, 58, 111, 126, 248, 272, 409, 419
Shepley, 244
Sheppard, 29, 65, 123, 129, 216, 319, 456
Shepstone, 274
Sherburn, 101
Sheriff, 348
Sherk, 269

Sherman, 9, 15, 161, 242, 258, 271, 289, 294, 377, 427, 460
Sherurne, 44
Sherwood, 145, 189, 431, 468
Shields, 197, 352
Shillington, 51, 71, 278, 427
Shimer, 290
Shiner, 431
Shinner, 314
Shinnor, 492
ship **Adelphi**, 283
ship **Admiral**, 104
ship **Akbar**, 387
ship **Ambassador**, 387
ship **Angelique**, 171, 211, 493
ship **Annie Tift**, 6
ship **Arab**, 404
ship **Architect**, 33, 94
ship **Bangor**, 436
ship **Belle Isle**, 217
ship **Belle of the West**, 293
ship **Byron**, 387
ship **Cambria**, 82
ship **Carthage**, 387
ship **Channing**, 329
ship **Christoval Colon**, 13
ship **Constitution**, 392
ship **Crescent City**, 99, 114
ship **Dale**, 327
ship **Diadem**, 435
ship **Edward Bates**, 217
ship **Edward Everett**, 16
ship **Empire City**, 431
ship **Enterprise**, 151, 176
ship **Erebus**, 176
ship **Eudora**, 217
ship **Europa**, 92
ship **Flavio**, 387
ship **Franklin**, 99, 116
ship **Friendship**, 387
ship **General Montgomerie**, 221
ship **Germantown**, 336
ship **Grey Eagle**, 37
ship **Henry Kneeland**, 167
ship **Henry Thompson**, 471
ship **Herald**, 86
ship **Humboldt**, 242
ship **Independence**, 226, 294

ship **Investigator**, 176
ship **Isaac Newton**, 389
ship **Ivanhoe**, 309
ship **J M Ryerson**, 90
ship **James Mitchell**, 38, 55, 80
ship **Jessie**, 488
ship **John**, 491
ship **John Jay**, 387
ship **Juniata**, 315
ship **Kingston**, 275
ship **Magnolia**, 37
ship **Manhattan**, 480
ship **Maria**, 220
ship **Mary & Adeline**, 9
ship **Mentor**, 491
ship **Ohio**, 23, 371
ship **Oriental**, 387
ship **Pennsylvania**, 176, 455, 470
ship **Plymouth**, 371
ship **Russell**, 388
ship **S Baldwin**, 388
ship **Sheridan**, 319
ship **South America**, 298, 387
ship **Splendid**, 387
ship **St Denis**, 308
ship **St Lawrence**, 388
ship **Susan Drew**, 387
ship **Talma**, 387
ship **Terror**, 176
ship **Wm Sprague**, 387
ship **Xylon**, 60
Shipley, 140
Shipman, 201
Shippen, 301
ships **Ontario & Ashburton**, 329
Shiras, 147, 336
Shocco Springs, 274
Shoemaker, 96, 159, 199, 243, 370
Shooke, 339
Short, 29, 470
Shorter, 111, 187, 188, 486
Shorts, 433
Shover, 193
Showers, 114
Shreeve, 118, 408
Shreeves, 446
Shreve, 189, 372
Shriver, 111, 298, 397

Shroeder, 363
Shryock, 363, 374
Shubrick, 132, 150, 160, 215, 294
Shufeldt, 172
Shultz, 473
Shultze, 366
Shumway, 200, 201
Shunk, 102, 348
Shurman, 453
Shuster, 51, 132, 133, 206, 232, 309, 478
Shutheo, 336
Shutt, 98, 106
Shutz, 353
Shy, 170
Sibellich, 230
Sibilich, 183
Sibley, 21, 111, 351, 355, 365, 395
Sibly, 356
Sidebotham, 363
Sidell, 242
Sigler, 147
Sill, 101, 161
Silliman, 179
Silsbee, 104
Silvers, 303
Silvey, 265, 483
Sim, 61
Simington, 106
Simmes, 331
Simmonds, 79
Simmons, 35, 37, 96, 288, 341, 351, 365, 439, 451, 454
Simms, 48, 49, 51, 88, 115, 187, 188, 213, 227, 251, 254, 259, 283, 289, 303, 351, 352, 355, 368, 385, 404, 406, 408, 409, 472
Simonds, 87
Simons, 215, 446
Simonson, 129, 234
Simonton, 8, 71, 75, 153, 436
Simpers, 348
Simpson, 12, 14, 20, 51, 67, 87, 111, 126, 140, 171, 180, 212, 250, 331, 352, 363, 381, 416, 424, 433, 446, 482
Simpsonville, 140
Sims, 131

556

Sinclair, 19, 84, 165, 242, 340, 430, 455
Singleton, 247
Sinsheimer, 353
Sioussa, 187
Sipes, 469
Sipher, 268
Sirian, 269
Sister Martina, 323
Sisters of Charity, 296, 323
Sisters of Mercy, 314
Sitgreaves, 153
Siuss, 348
Sizer, 41
Skerrett, 232
Skidmore, 111, 189, 353
Skiles, 56
Skilling, 287
Skillman, 278
Skinker, 193
Skinner, 15, 97, 199, 209, 254, 348, 395, 475, 481, 482
Skinnger, 424
Skirving, 34, 51
Slack, 67
Slacum, 58, 64, 75
Slade, 50, 209, 313, 348, 355, 385
Slater, 173
Slatery, 398
Slatford, 232
Slatterly, 398, 399, 400
Slattery, 423, 424
Slaughter, 123, 215, 283
Sleight, 188
Slemons, 385
Slicer, 34, 77, 98, 115, 261
Slidell, 106, 389, 430
Slight, 137, 373
Slinck, 478
Sliver, 72
Sloan, 373, 400
Sloanaker, 113
Sloat, 19
Slocumb, 178
Sloo, 225, 255
sloop of war **Germantown**, 296, 470
sloop of war **Jamestown**, 133
sloop of war **John Adams**, 269

sloop of war **Vandalia**, 334, 341
sloop of war **Warren**, 470
sloop **Philomel**, 240
sloop-of-war **Dale**, 222
sloop-of-war **Germantown**, 87, 455
Slosson, 196
Slye, 137, 336, 338
Small, 297, 309, 408, 450
Smallwood, 46, 147, 152, 191, 254, 273, 351, 352
Smedes, 477
Smethurst, 192
Smith, 2, 6, 8, 12, 13, 20, 22, 25, 38, 39, 42, 43, 44, 46, 48, 54, 66, 71, 72, 76, 77, 82, 85, 87, 92, 96, 97, 98, 99, 100, 101, 104, 105, 106, 111, 114, 116, 117, 124, 125, 127, 132, 133, 135, 136, 142, 148, 150, 153, 163, 167, 169, 173, 176, 179, 180, 183, 188, 191, 192, 198, 200, 201, 204, 208, 210, 211, 212, 215, 216, 217, 218, 232, 236, 242, 246, 248, 250, 255, 258, 259, 261, 263, 265, 266, 267, 274, 281, 282, 285, 286, 295, 301, 303, 306, 307, 310, 313, 315, 316, 317, 321, 322, 326, 327, 328, 333, 336, 337, 338, 340, 343, 345, 346, 348, 351, 352, 355, 356, 363, 365, 366, 367, 372, 373, 377, 378, 380, 382, 386, 391, 392, 396, 397, 401, 403, 404, 409, 411, 412, 417, 419, 421, 422, 424, 434, 436, 440, 443, 444, 445, 448, 450, 452, 453, 454, 456, 460, 462, 463, 464, 469, 473, 481, 483, 484, 486, 487, 489, 490, 494
Smith's Row, 461
Smithe, 424
Smiths, 411
Smithson, 46
Smithsonian Institute, 179
smokes his cigar, 146
Smoot, 43, 85, 91, 176, 187, 192, 197, 290, 291, 351, 383, 390
Smtih, 180
Smull, 408
Smyth, 79
Smythe, 82

Snavely, 38, 54, 70
Sneed, 391
Snell, 427
Snelling, 123, 126
Snethen, 219
Snider, 268, 402
Snively, 385
Snodgrass, 21, 79
Snow, 411
Snow Hill, 213, 440
Snowberger, 486
Snowden, 179
Snyder, 175, 268, 384, 431, 468
Snyders, 105
Solomon, 101
Somerville, 356, 401
Sommers, 381
Sonoma, 394
Soper, 230, 248
Sorrel, 158, 256, 265
Sorrell, 381
Sothoron, 48, 96, 99, 199
Soule, 29, 68, 387
South America, 217
Southgate, 429
Southward, 165
Southwick, 42
Southworth, 8
Spafford, 201
Spalding, 37, 72, 291, 295, 374, 419, 424, 427, 430, 482
Spangler, 232
Sparks, 280, 370
Sparrow, 426
Spates, 433
Spaulding, 337
Speake, 17, 311
Speaks, 352
Speed, 328
Spegle, 3
Speiden, 9, 42, 75, 202
Speir, 419
Spencer, 56, 57, 64, 93, 95, 152, 277, 322, 348, 370, 404, 411
Sperry, 478
Spicer, 356
Spicknall, 493
Spieden, 294

Spignall, 187, 189
Spillman, 340
Spilman, 374
Spinotti, 350
Spofford, 13
Spohr, 372
Spooner, 35
Spotswood, 455
Spotts, 232
Spottswood, 263
Sprague, 29, 128, 173, 442
Spratt, 101
Sprenkel, 369
Sprice, 132
Sprigg, 363
Spriggs, 187
Spring Valley, 212
Springland, 231
Springman, 187, 189
Spurling, 45, 349, 351, 388
Squier, 142
Sr Mary Bernard, 204
St Clair, 45, 473
St Felix, 13
St Inigoes, 220
St Jean, 111
St John, 310, 364
St John's, 284
St John's [N B], 111
St Joseph's Forest, 284
St Louis Oak, 157
St Peters, 217
St Vrain, 424
Stacy, 271
Stadden, 77
Staffon, 47
Stafford, 38, 55, 58, 63, 81
Staites, 326
Stake, 348
Stakes, 2
Stalings, 187
Stalker, 31, 482
Stalkes, 31
Stallings, 38, 202
Stamp, 200
Stamper, 490
Stanard, 273
Stanfield, 372

Stanford, 427
Staniford, 123
Stanley, 187, 335, 426, 439
Stansbury, 172, 209, 413
Stanton, 13, 124, 313, 478
Stanyon, 312
Staples, 233
Stapp, 246
Stark, 65, 205, 276, 374
Starkweather, 256, 384
Starr, 228, 377
Staten Island, 194
Stathon, 421
Stauffer, 433
Ste Martin, 271
Stealy, 39
steamboat **America**, 321
Steamboat casualties, 153
steamboat **Champion**, 157
steamboat **Chas Hammond**, 206
steamboat **De Soto**, 380
steamboat **Emily**, 231
steamboat **Empire**, 200
steamboat **Highland Mary**, 461
steamboat **James Adams**, 31
steamboat **Joseph Johnson**, 280, 487
steamboat **Louisiana**, 450
steamboat **Ohio Mail**, 41
steamer **Algoma**, 297
steamer **Alleghany**, 304
steamer **Bostona**, 440, 450, 459
steamer **Buckeye**, 380
steamer **Buffalo**, 182
steamer **California**, 228, 242
steamer **Canada**, 290
steamer **Charles Carroll**, 105
steamer **Columbia**, 278, 282, 411, 431
steamer **Crescent City**, 22, 201, 242, 491
steamer **Elite**, 345
steamer **Embassy**, 242, 268
steamer **Empire**, 208, 212, 224, 232
steamer **Europa**, 356, 431
steamer **Ewing**, 431
steamer **Falcon**, 37, 209, 437
steamer **Franklin**, 459
steamer **G W Coffee**, 381
steamer **General Pike**, 176

steamer **Globe**, 252
steamer **Hardee**, 345
steamer **Isaac Newton**, 345
steamer **Louisiana**, 440, 451, 459
steamer **Mary**, 206
steamer **Mary Blane**, 478
steamer **Mary Kingsland**, 381
steamer **Memphis**, 241
steamer **Michigan**, 204, 332
steamer **Mount Vernon**, 366
steamer **New Orleans**, 173
steamer **Niagara**, 86
steamer **Ohio**, 389, 429
steamer **Orus**, 242
steamer **Panama**, 23, 242
steamer **Princeton**, 445
steamer **Queen City**, 378
steamer **Richland**, 25
steamer **Rip Van Winkle**, 208
steamer **Severn**, 376
steamer **St Joseph**, 206
steamer **Storm**, 440, 450
steamer **Tecumsch**, 388
steamer **Visiter**, 357
steamer **Walker**, 221
steamer **Washington**, 411
steamer **White Cloud**, 217
steamer **Yazoo**, 235
steamers, 217
steamers **Autocrat, De Witt Clinton**, 217
steamers **Mary, Phenix, San Francisco, & Dubuque**, 297
steamers **United States, Acadia, & Britannia**, 92
steamship **Caledonia**, 221, 338
steamship **Crescent City**, 151
steamship **Europa**, 283
steamship **Falcon**, 165, 437
steamship **Galveston**, 133
steamship **Gladiator**, 381
steamship **Ohio**, 437
Stearns, 402, 431, 468
Stebbins, 10
Steele, 125, 126, 170, 239, 248, 278, 463, 471
Steenbergen, 314
Steer, 51, 272, 393

Steger, 191
Steiger, 408
Stem, 21
Stenant, 268
Stenson, 42
Stephen, 425
Stephens, 42, 56, 103, 113, 417
Stephenson, 59
Stepper, 187, 356
Stepperfeldt, 158
Steptoe, 399, 426
Sterrett, 92, 482
Stetson, 60, 280, 471
Stettinius, 150, 305
Steuart, 127, 130, 267, 365, 393, 402, 431, 436, 468
Stevens, 25, 47, 51, 101, 107, 190, 215, 232, 289, 381, 387, 454, 477
Stevenson, 2, 34, 69, 111, 196, 242, 253, 351, 353, 355, 365, 401
Steward, 203, 303
Stewart, 2, 12, 46, 48, 51, 59, 72, 88, 107, 131, 163, 181, 187, 192, 201, 208, 220, 231, 250, 320, 323, 330, 341, 351, 363, 375, 401, 404, 430, 455, 457, 468, 477, 490
Stickney, 219
Stiles, 167, 299, 318, 427
Stille, 160, 166
Stillman, 308
Stilwell, 488
Stirman, 192
Stith, 152, 193, 287
Stock, 187
Stockett, 72
Stockman, 59
Stockton, 84, 169, 229, 266, 323, 347, 445, 484
Stodard, 238
Stoddard, 117
Stoddert, 6, 78, 294
Stoep, 395
Stokely, 38, 55
Stone, 9, 45, 111, 127, 140, 150, 164, 195, 201, 216, 232, 242, 248, 278, 321, 347, 425, 437, 457, 470, 487
Stoneall, 238
Stonestreet, 279, 313

Stoops, 16, 48, 138, 190, 220, 282, 291, 420
storeship **Erie**, 272
store-ship **Lexington**, 232
storeship **Supply**, 84, 340, 450
Storm, 190, 310
Storms, 327, 349
Stott, 51, 351, 387, 409
Stowe MSS, 214
Strange, 13
Stratton, 481
Straub, 355
Street, 38, 483, 484
Streeter, 106
Stribling, 433
Strickland, 207, 413
Stringfellow, 276
Stringham, 192, 225
Strohecker, 171
Strong, 259, 269, 377, 450
Strother, 221
Stryhos, 303
Stuart, 81, 102, 125, 126, 188, 193, 203, 387, 474
Stubbs, 187
Stuck, 51
Stucker, 340
Studley, 381
Stuebgen, 100
Stull, 19, 296
Stump, 242
Stump Hill, 394
Sturdevant, 290
Sturgeon with the White Skin, 481
Sturgis, 323, 448
Stutz, 52, 139, 341, 354, 407, 477
Succhesi, 217
Suddards, 269
Sue, 63, 69
Suechesi, 180
Suezineau, 385
Suggett, 2
Suit, 160, 220, 449
Sulivane, 373
Sullivan, 10, 134, 187, 257, 289, 342, 376, 396, 431, 450, 451, 460
Sully, 153
Sulser, 113

Sultana, 155, 157
Summerlin, 434
Summers, 92, 232, 244
Summons, 285, 296
surrender of Rome, 280
Suter, 228, 243, 303, 319, 329, 402, 444, 460
Sutherland, 72, 76
Sutter, 431, 468
Sutton, 38, 46, 55, 65, 107, 164, 170, 191, 296, 424
Suwanee, 157
Suydam, 380
Swagart, 356
Swallwood, 464
Swan, 152, 157, 392
Swaney, 398
Swank, 478
Swann, 52, 111, 159, 210, 232, 284, 379, 392
Swartwout, 64, 426
Swartz, 363
Swatara, 157
Swazey, 473
Swearing, 190
Swearingen, 249
Sweeney, 267, 386, 400
Sweeny, 51, 69, 88, 107, 135, 209, 227, 235, 257, 282, 335, 360, 435, 444, 458
Sweeting, 52, 352, 407
Sweetser, 105
Sweetzer, 10
Sweiger, 355
Sweitzer, 147, 152
Sweney, 399
Swett, 269
Swift, 205, 363, 415, 484
Switzer:, 101
Swope, 38
Swords, 127
Sykes, 124
Sylba, 424
Syles, 279
Symes, 267
Symmes, 264, 308
Synder, 451

T

Tabb, 464
Tabler, 111
Tagart, 348
Tagert, 300
Taglioni, 217
Tait, 142, 251, 254
Talbert, 352, 353, 356
Talbot, 84, 96, 199, 253, 297, 310, 351, 387
Talbott, 182, 434
Talcott, 116, 126, 127
Taliaferro, 79, 89, 117, 162
Tallmadge, 89, 264, 488
Talma, 157
Talmadge, 191, 329
Talpin, 158
Talty, 52, 407, 408
Taney, 98, 451
Tanner, 152, 188, 425
Tansey, 385
Tansill, 42, 119, 406
Tappan, 244
Tarlton, 188, 258, 287, 347, 396
Tarrall, 388
Tarver, 111
Tascoe, 352
Tasset, 182
Tastet, 188, 257, 375
Tate, 51, 85, 98, 106, 227, 278, 426, 466
Tattnall, 42
Tatum, 269, 418
Tavenner, 16, 47
Tavern Stand, 394
Tay, 356
Tayloe, 113, 171, 318, 363
Taylor, 3, 9, 20, 25, 28, 33, 37, 38, 39, 42, 43, 49, 51, 54, 61, 62, 64, 65, 69, 71, 73, 74, 77, 78, 80, 86, 87, 89, 91, 92, 96, 98, 99, 115, 117, 122, 127, 128, 129, 140, 145, 149, 153, 162, 168, 169, 182, 188, 190, 201, 215, 222, 234, 239, 242, 246, 258, 263, 269, 276, 290, 291, 295, 296, 303, 313, 318, 323, 327, 334, 335, 341, 345, 350, 351, 352, 363,

368, 373, 389, 397, 408, 411, 425,
442, 444, 446, 460, 463, 477, 482
Tazewell, 61
Teague, 299
Teakle, 384
Teeney, 51
Teffi, 468
Tefft, 431
Telegraph, 157
Temple, 77, 212, 369
Templeman, 51
Temples, 348
Ten Broeck, 205, 248
Ten Eyck, 22
Tenant, 106, 189, 446
Tench, 49, 88, 114, 164, 188, 351, 409
Teneirs, 105
Tenent, 191
Tenney, 188
Tepe, 331
Terrett, 106, 294
Terrill, 101
Territy, 351
Terry, 456
Terwilliger, 349
Test, 409
Tete, 286
Tettew, 489
Tevis, 265
Tew, 330
Thacker, 95
Tharp, 19
Thatcher, 95
Thaw, 138
Thaxter, 211, 310
Thayer, 291
The Birchland Tract, 270
The Landing of Columbus, 23
The Meadows, 270
The Winder Tract, 270
Theobald, 327
Theobolds, 492
Theriot, 462
Thibodaux, 35, 425
Thom, 9
Thoma, 188
Thomas, 1, 12, 13, 17, 26, 45, 51, 52,
  60, 72, 87, 95, 127, 137, 145, 164,
188, 199, 242, 277, 281, 282, 303,
304, 319, 320, 326, 344, 348, 349,
351, 352, 355, 356, 365, 385, 397,
399, 407, 409, 410, 427, 452, 465,
479, 487, 488
Thomason, 96
Thompson, 2, 8, 14, 15, 37, 38, 46, 52,
55, 57, 63, 64, 67, 69, 89, 108, 111,
145, 147, 150, 162, 165, 188, 190,
200, 201, 213, 255, 262, 289, 295,
305, 315, 316, 342, 352, 363, 370,
400, 401, 404, 412, 414, 416, 427,
428, 432, 439, 453, 460, 486
Thomson, 25, 111, 200, 228
Thorburn, 42
Thorn, 122, 123, 125, 126, 351, 408,
463, 469, 495
Thornely, 235
Thornley, 49
Thornton, 2, 38, 51, 55, 111, 128, 446
Thorp, 271, 371
Thos, 471
Threlkeld, 365
Thrift, 159
Throckmorton, 460
Throop, 356, 451
Thrower, 271
Thruston, 146, 192, 216, 381
Thumb, 189
Thurber, 33
Thurston, 421, 431
Thyson, 47, 184, 350, 355, 388, 408
Tibbets, 348
Tibbits, 280
Tiber, 1
Tiber Mill, 183
Tici, 419
Tidball, 122, 220, 266, 314
Tiffany, 2, 396
Tift, 402
Tilgham, 291
Tilghman, 23, 42, 188, 242, 348, 397
Tilley, 91, 102, 112, 286
Tillinghast, 30, 462
Tillman, 286
Tillson, 101
Tilyard, 78
Timand, 353

Timberlake, 94
Time and Tide, 157
Timms, 41
Timour, 217
Tims, 213, 363
Tinckler, 351
Tindall, 113
Ting, 369
Tinkler, 177
Tinklers, 273
Tinsley, 10, 448
Tintoretto, 177
Tippett, 189
Tipton, 372, 377
Titian, 105
Tobey, 491
Toby, 491
Tochman, 482, 494
Tod, 42
Todd, 47, 90, 106, 178, 188, 201, 220, 271, 275, 288, 388
Todlschnider, 355
Todtschinder, 51, 188
Tointon, 342
Tolly, 431
Tolson, 243
Tomlinson, 184, 351
Tompins, 345
Tompkins, 5, 12, 45, 58, 63, 73, 75, 85, 95, 105, 127, 128, 189, 250, 286, 332
Tonants, 72
Tone, 116, 133, 141
Tooler, 304
Toomer, 281
Toomey, 384, 427
Topham, 52, 188
Tophan, 407
Topping, 56
Torbett, 13
Torre, 286
Torrente, 286
Tory, 428
Totten, 9, 76, 103, 167, 172, 273
Tousdale, 482
Tower, 125, 126
Towers, 71, 88, 144, 235, 257, 421
Towle, 39, 54, 73, 261, 408

Towles, 334, 416
Town, 381
Towner, 233
Townley, 303, 351
Townsend, 267, 365, 430
Towson, 87, 97, 127, 425
Trabue, 313
Tracy, 238
Trader, 348
Tramble, 491
Tramontane Order, 455
Trapnel, 57
Trappist Monks, 256
Trask, 323
Traveller's Rest, 22
Travers, 13, 49, 141, 165, 188, 349, 351, 354, 374, 396, 441
Travis, 111, 417
Traweek, 441
Treadway, 242
Treadwell, 435
Treatler, 90
Tree, 153
Treichel, 167
Trenton, 157
Treppnell, 138
Trevitt, 61, 248
Trezavani, 2
Trias, 269
Triay, 259
Tribon, 38, 54
Tribore, 64
Tributary, 157
Tricou, 286
Trigg, 236
Trimble, 49, 408
Tritle, 489
Trivier, 30
Trock, 363
Trook, 282
Trotter, 170, 340
Trousdale, 33, 39
True, 2, 280
Truesdell, 298, 437
Truman, 138
Trumbo, 348
Trumbull, 136, 164, 183
Trundle, 159

563

Trunell, 291
Trussell, 403
Tschiffely, 188
Tubbs, 234, 483
Tuck, 58, 72, 238, 290, 295, 422
Tucker, 19, 25, 50, 51, 56, 80, 107, 119, 151, 188, 226, 242, 262, 274, 285, 294, 303, 310, 324, 354, 363, 381, 396, 426, 439, 440, 449, 450, 462, 490, 493
Tuley, 37, 424
Tulip Hill, 277
Tullock, 170
Tuly, 493
Tunstell, 95
Tupper, 208
Turk, 365
Turnbull, 126, 135
Turner, 46, 47, 52, 58, 115, 169, 170, 180, 192, 217, 237, 240, 353, 363, 382, 460, 478
Turnis, 462
Turpin, 2, 197, 340
Turton, 188
Tuthill, 201
Tutt, 121, 421
Tuttle, 385, 452
Twichell, 228
Twiggs, 8, 44, 74, 97, 426, 442
Twine, 353
Twiss, 214
Twomey, 317
Twomy, 222, 368, 373
Tygart, 348
Tyler, 10, 93, 101, 111, 151, 169, 199, 229, 245, 258, 264, 278, 349, 355, 433, 445
Tyson, 51, 53, 322

U

Udegraff, 357
Ulshoeffer, 317
Uncle Ben, 157
Uncle Harkless, 163
Uncle Sam, 157
Underbill, 201
Underhill, 383

Underwood, 29, 61, 238, 259, 281, 414, 460
Ungerer, 2
Uniach, 351
<u>Unitarian Church</u>, 331
Upperman, 49, 227, 391, 408
Upshaw, 240, 423
Upton, 395
Usher, 233, 438
Uttermohle, 409
Uttermuhle, 351
Uttermule, 390

V

Vail, 89, 93
Valentine, 47, 242
Vallambrosano, 177
Vallejo, 394, 402, 431, 468
Van Alen, 13, 86, 233
Van Allen, 382
Van Antwerp, 207
Van Benthuysen, 437
Van Bergen, 437
Van Bokkelen, 125
Van Buren, 4, 122, 128, 244, 267, 270, 280, 296, 440, 441
Van Coble, 363
Van Dyke, 177
Van Everdingen, 105
Van Goyen, 177
Van Havre, 305
Van Horn, 248
Van Horne, 82, 153
Van Horsigh, 91, 371, 429, 438, 467
Van Horsign, 280, 324
Van Kleeck, 171
Van Kleek, 24
Van Lear, 32
Van Name, 384
Van Ness, 84, 94, 98, 123, 129, 180, 267, 318
Van Os, 177
Van Patten, 119, 282, 318, 363
Van Rensaelaer, 30
Van Rensselaer, 417
Van Resick, 213
Van Reswick, 320, 338, 354, 355
Van Riswick, 2

Van Tyne, 134
Van Vleit, 241
Van Vorhes, 310
Van Wagoner, 473
Van Wormer, 241
Van Wyck, 326
Van Zandt, 147, 150, 188, 326, 393, 471
VanBuskirk, 111
Vance, 89, 252
Vancoble, 277
Vandelcher, 282
Vanderhorst, 326
Vanderlyn, 23
Vandervert, 16
Vandrecourt, 46
Vanhorsigh, 36, 198, 246, 342, 378
Vanhorsign, 334
Vanmeter, 170
Vannort, 404
Vanveghton, 231
Vanvliet, 234
Vanzant, 51
Varden, 426
Vashaw, 312
Vass, 457
Vaucluse, 37, 117
Vaucluse Vein, 117
Vaughan, 215, 263, 369
Vellerino, 242
Venable, 51, 188, 243, 444
Verdaile, 120
Vergnol, 182
Vermillion, 138, 281
Vermu'e, 468
Vermuile, 431
vessel **Chas Bartlett**, 405
vessel **Investigator**, 151
vessel **North Star**, 151
vessel **Plymouth**, 195
Vial, 18, 68
Vickers, 335
Vidal, 39
Viele, 406
Viers, 145
Vigo, 60, 77, 93
Villard, 98, 363, 410
Vincent, 80, 101, 462

Vinson, 202, 279
Vinton, 99, 430
Vioget, 365
Virgil, 424
Visser, 51, 121, 188, 347, 355, 396
Vivans, 387
Vodgers, 381
Vogde, 426
Von Essen, 47, 403
Von Schmidt, 14
Vonnessen, 228
Vonnessin, 243
Voorhees, 63, 81, 165, 416, 441
Vorhees, 108
Voss, 51, 197
Vroom, 29, 370

W

W H Day, 157
Wachten, 242
Waddell, 246, 294
Wade, 83, 126, 245, 395, 404, 413, 446
Wadman, 303
Wadsworth, 260, 460
Wager, 111
Wagerman, 85
Waggaman, 389
Waggoner, 355
Wagler, 363
Wagner, 353
Wainwright, 97, 269, 319
Waite, 139, 141, 169, 175, 215, 387, 485
Waitt, 435
Wakeling, 355
Walbach, 128
Walbridge, 264
Waldron, 96, 198
Walke, 394
Walker, 9, 11, 16, 21, 25, 29, 52, 57, 61, 72, 85, 97, 101, 103, 107, 111, 122, 125, 139, 142, 144, 150, 179, 188, 206, 207, 212, 230, 231, 236, 243, 245, 247, 266, 267, 303, 339, 351, 355, 364, 368, 375, 385, 394, 400, 402, 404, 405, 406, 407, 410, 431, 460, 463, 468, 487, 492

Wall, 47, 49, 89, 138, 184, 227, 445
Wallace, 77, 90, 91, 96, 148, 153, 170, 189, 196, 198, 207, 212, 216, 222, 249, 252, 273, 348, 368, 456, 485
Wallach, 18, 88, 89, 92, 104, 107, 252, 273, 408, 435, 463, 464
Wallar, 111
Waller, 225, 273, 356
Walling'd, 51
Wallingsford, 468, 481
Wallis, 91, 188, 431
Waln, 473
Walsh, 51, 205, 401, 409, 460
Walter, 284, 396, 460
Walters, 145, 303, 447
Wanderlish, 188
Wankoweiz, 4, 482
Wannall, 51
Wannell, 251
Ward, 38, 39, 51, 54, 68, 72, 73, 81, 93, 164, 196, 205, 212, 225, 226, 240, 303, 322, 328, 332, 351, 354, 355, 364, 435, 460
Wardell, 138
Warden, 170, 351, 388
Warder, 159, 278, 351, 354, 356, 416
Ware, 42, 111, 170
Waresch, 72
Warfield, 396, 487, 488
Warhurst, 388
Waring, 18, 178, 232, 477
Wark, 242
Warley, 215
Warner, 68, 165, 182, 188, 227, 351, 426, 444
Warner Hall, 346
Warnock, 93
Warren, 171, 299, 388
Warriner, 51
Warrington, 9, 273, 367, 371
Wash City, 317
Wash Nat'l Monument, 37
Washburn, 323
Washington, 18, 27, 32, 39, 55, 85, 91, 97, 136, 138, 146, 150, 158, 163, 164, 188, 198, 199, 203, 215, 216, 266, 279, 282, 288, 290, 338, 355,
356, 421, 422, 423, 424, 427, 435, 442, 460, 470, 475, 495
Washington Monument, 495
Watchman, 348
Water, 354
Waterfield, 51
Waterloo, 220
Waters, 145, 196, 228, 241, 251, 282, 301, 351, 354, 356, 408, 419, 420
Watkins, 62, 69, 289
Watmough, 180
Watrous, 335
Wats, 72
Watson, 18, 44, 85, 87, 93, 103, 121, 144, 220, 238, 317, 353, 451, 467, 476, 487
Watters, 434
Watterston, 16, 87, 320
Wattle, 372
Watts, 40, 242, 268, 384
Waub-seigh, 481
Waugh, 30
Waver, 51
Way, 306
Wayne, 33
Weaser, 351
Weaver, 43, 216, 277
Webb, 38, 47, 49, 56, 57, 70, 111, 112, 145, 159, 170, 183, 207, 226, 252, 257, 278, 354, 355, 391, 446, 459
Webber, 44
Weber, 35, 188
Webster, 2, 29, 115, 312, 328, 330, 351, 356, 457, 460, 483
Weed, 75
Weede, 330, 382
Weeden, 26, 409, 456
Weedon, 76
Weeks, 171, 303
Weems, 119, 348, 401
Weichmann, 393
Weightman, 29, 36, 63, 67, 106, 243, 424, 460
Weimer, 465
Weir, 76, 177, 367
Weiss, 352
Welch, 342, 388, 450

566

Wellborn, 367
Weller, 24, 140, 168, 201, 242, 470
Welles, 3, 438
Wellford, 303, 404, 438
Wellington, 167
Wells, 28, 57, 102, 188, 213, 216, 272, 316, 342, 371, 448, 467, 479, 486
Welner, 53
Welsh, 47, 49, 122, 196, 286, 451
Wendell, 72, 356, 418
Werden, 222
Werner, 188, 303
Wert, 433
Weser, 45
West, 2, 43, 52, 72, 80, 165, 242, 268, 313, 353, 407, 424, 427, 453, 460, 472
Westbrook, 225
Westcott, 8, 51, 264
Westerfield, 317
Westerhood, 397
Weston, 33
Westwood, 157
Wetherbee, 90
Wetmore, 425, 461, 483, 484, 493
Weyer, 299
Weyer's Cave, 299
Weyrick, 191
whale ship **Uncas**, 195
Whalen, 353, 363
Whaley, 188, 460
Wharton, 380, 397, 404, 416
Wheat, 150, 308
Wheat, 308
Wheatley, 47, 49, 106, 107, 364, 419, 420
Wheatly, 151, 408
Whedbee, 143, 267
Wheeler, 19, 51, 103, 243, 250, 278, 304, 339, 354, 362, 377, 386, 391, 412, 460, 491
Whelan, 294
Whicher, 38, 54, 152
Whipple, 140, 412
Whistler, 194, 248, 333, 410
Whitaker, 89
Whitall, 123
Whitcomb, 303, 357

White, 28, 33, 35, 37, 38, 44, 51, 54, 66, 96, 102, 107, 130, 141, 150, 159, 192, 196, 200, 203, 204, 228, 243, 248, 257, 263, 270, 274, 277, 291, 293, 299, 308, 317, 348, 353, 358, 395, 403, 413, 415, 417, 424, 432, 434, 446, 454, 486, 495
White Cloud, 217
White Haven, 448
White Rose, 157
Whiteford, 348
Whitehead, 25, 238
Whitehorn, 490
Whitehouse, 317
Whitford, 247
Whiting, 140, 141, 226, 257, 300, 430
Whitlock, 447
Whitlocke, 188
Whitman, 31
Whitmarsh, 17, 341
Whitmen, 37
Whitmore, 131, 135, 140
Whitney, 5, 27, 111, 214, 219, 250, 260, 340, 411, 454
Whittaker, 233
Whitten, 93
Whittett, 38, 54, 64
Whittingham, 105
Whittle, 486
Whittlesey, 29, 51, 87, 90, 145, 179, 195, 223, 495
Whitwell, 188, 307, 346, 364, 419
Whyte, 424
Wiber, 281
Wicking, 427
Wickliffe, 86, 104, 317
Wicks, 171
Wieand, 412
Wiesler, 303
Wight, 183, 326
Wilbur, 203, 239, 277
Wilcox, 108, 120, 139, 188, 222, 241, 353
Wilder, 23, 151, 269
Wildes, 211
Wiler, 304
Wilerson, 2

Wiley, 169, 229, 243, 257, 466, 479, 495
Wilger, 440
Wilkerson, 188, 251
Wilkes, 82, 89, 489
Wilkins, 51, 248, 250, 324
Wilkinson, 14, 83, 92, 103, 173, 238, 279, 313, 323, 353
Willard, 52, 128, 247, 273, 281, 282, 355, 356, 407, 414, 460
Willcox, 246
Willer, 242
Willet, 148, 188, 409, 416
Willets, 295
Willey, 479
Williams, 2, 6, 12, 17, 23, 26, 29, 30, 38, 40, 41, 43, 47, 51, 52, 55, 62, 63, 65, 68, 73, 89, 93, 96, 108, 111, 118, 119, 124, 126, 128, 137, 139, 144, 161, 167, 188, 189, 190, 195, 199, 203, 204, 208, 209, 215, 218, 222, 226, 242, 246, 260, 266, 268, 271, 275, 286, 296, 303, 311, 314, 318, 330, 336, 338, 344, 351, 354, 363, 365, 366, 372, 376, 379, 397, 407, 413, 416, 427, 436, 438, 441, 446, 449, 450, 451, 460, 483
Williamson, 2, 12, 38, 54, 73, 88, 99, 269, 300, 303, 313, 351, 485
Willickman, 188
Willis, 136, 138, 200, 201, 218, 226, 277, 455
Willow Brook, 373, 402
Wills, 286, 357
Willsey, 222
Willson, 49, 57, 420
Wilmer, 324
Wilner, 408, 465
Wilson, 2, 11, 23, 25, 32, 34, 38, 47, 49, 54, 57, 71, 72, 73, 79, 96, 98, 102, 106, 108, 111, 113, 116, 118, 139, 141, 144, 145, 149, 164, 165, 167, 174, 181, 188, 189, 190, 191, 195, 201, 207, 227, 232, 234, 235, 243, 251, 279, 285, 292, 295, 330, 335, 348, 351, 353, 354, 356, 361, 364, 381, 396, 399, 403, 414, 416, 417, 420, 450, 451, 460, 462, 481, 490
Wiltberger, 150, 168, 181, 226, 235, 375, 460
Wimer, 18
Wimsatt, 49, 251, 409
Winans, 29
Winchester, 86, 188, 368
Winder, 12, 89, 134, 180, 322, 399
Windsor, 138
Winfield, 305
Wing, 334
Wingate, 73
Wingerd, 72
Winks, 372
Winless, 316
Winn, 170, 194, 233, 446, 453, 457
Winning, 464
Winship, 123, 394
Winslow, 115, 294
Winston, 365
Winter, 51, 88, 107, 227, 235, 257
Winthrop, 11, 99, 112, 210, 369, 438, 465
Wirgman, 115
Wirt, 227, 235
Wirt, 188
Wise, 45, 88, 111, 139, 142, 161, 200, 213, 215, 246, 260, 341, 345, 353, 356, 415, 436
Wiseman, 22, 71, 72
Wishback, 345
Wislizenus, 95
Wisner, 269
Wisong, 344
Wistar, 144, 205, 371
Wister, 159
Witherell, 252
Withers, 2, 215, 266, 363, 464
Witter, 192
Wittner, 51
Wizlizenus, 199
Wolcott, 242
Wolf, 60, 450
Wolfe, 307, 440
Wolff, 462
Wolffe, 451
Wolfley, 23

Wollard, 140, 188, 189, 251, 341, 353, 453, 456, 462, 469
Wonderlick, 355
Wood, 2, 5, 15, 111, 153, 180, 248, 256, 265, 280, 290, 328, 339, 345, 351, 364, 375, 392, 402, 411, 421, 431, 450, 460, 481
Woodbridge, 125, 126, 325, 474
Woodbury, 234, 271, 430
Woodeard, 356
Woodhull, 69, 201, 236, 304
Woodlands, 247
Woodlawn, 258
Woodley, 66, 84, 389, 452
Woodroe, 468
Woods, 30, 83, 126, 211, 292, 342, 351, 396, 451
Woodson, 417
Woodward, 51, 253, 254, 262, 284, 303, 312, 316, 318, 364, 365, 404, 462, 469
Woodyard, 2
Wool, 425
Woolard, 107, 291
Woolley, 311, 316
Wooten, 474
Wootten, 450
Wootton, 132
Worcester, 7, 355
Worle, 72
Wormley, 4, 47, 356
Wormsley, 482
Worrell, 288
Worsley, 111
Worth, 82, 97, 104, 173, 178, 210, 265, 266, 289, 319, 387, 412, 425, 429, 440, 441
Worthin'n, 51
Worthington, 25, 151, 159, 174, 183, 289, 300, 323, 339, 343, 374, 397, 398, 401, 416, 423
Worwick, 67
Wovermans, 105
Wozencraft, 431, 468
Wren, 341, 384, 440
Wright, 43, 47, 49, 50, 66, 68, 72, 82, 86, 101, 111, 157, 204, 218, 237, 242, 251, 266, 268, 271, 297, 349, 353, 356, 363, 365, 368, 389, 404, 433, 453, 462, 469, 479, 483, 490
Wroe, 49
Wyandotte, 157
Wyatt, 5, 67
Wylie, 94, 479
Wyman, 53
Wynkoop, 290, 312
Wyse, 57
Wythe, 446

Y

Yallabusha, 157
Yancey, 207
Yard, 327
Yates, 47, 238
Yazoo, 157
Yeadon, 439
Yeardley, 263
Yeates, 223
Yeatman, 52, 189
Yeaton, 429
Yell, 260
Yerby, 67, 88, 452, 463
Yonge, 5, 38, 54, 96, 199
Yool, 4
Yoran, 466
York, 247
Yost, 465
Youell, 404
Young, 2, 21, 23, 26, 36, 44, 47, 49, 52, 62, 71, 80, 88, 89, 95, 96, 103, 111, 132, 137, 141, 159, 163, 166, 180, 188, 189, 193, 195, 203, 244, 253, 270, 276, 282, 283, 291, 297, 303, 316, 324, 326, 338, 355, 364, 378, 380, 382, 399, 408, 409, 411, 416, 460
Young Plymouth, 195
Younge, 271

Z

Zacharie, 437
Zachary Taylor, 157
Zamora, 222
Zantzinger, 30, 199, 386
Zeilin, 42
Zell, 221

Zevely, 212
Zichy, 428
Zimmerman, 72, 81, 92, 196, 340, 394

Zolkowski, 494
Zucika, 405
Zurbaran, 177

Other Heritage Books by the author:

National Intelligencer *Newspaper Abstracts Special Edition: The Civil War Years Volume 1: January 1, 1861-June 30, 1863*

National Intelligencer *Newspaper Abstracts Special Edition: The Civil War Years Volume 2: July 1, 1863-December 31, 1865*

National Intelligencer *Newspaper Abstracts 1850*

National Intelligencer *Newspaper Abstracts 1849*

National Intelligencer *Newspaper Abstracts 1848*

National Intelligencer *Newspaper Abstracts 1847*

National Intelligencer *Newspaper Abstracts 1846*

National Intelligencer *Newspaper Abstracts 1845*

National Intelligencer *Newspaper Abstracts 1844*

National Intelligencer *Newspaper Abstracts 1843*

National Intelligencer *Newspaper Abstracts 1842*

National Intelligencer *Newspaper Abstracts 1841*

National Intelligencer *Newspaper Abstracts 1840*

National Intelligencer *Newspaper Abstracts, 1838-1839*

National Intelligencer *Newspaper Abstracts, 1836-1837*

National Intelligencer *Newspaper Abstracts, 1834-1835*

National Intelligencer *Newspaper Abstracts, 1832-1833*

National Intelligencer *Newspaper Abstracts, 1830-1831*

National Intelligencer *Newspaper Abstracts, 1827-1829*

National Intelligencer *Newspaper Abstracts, 1824-1826*

National Intelligencer *Newspaper Abstracts, 1821-1823*

National Intelligencer *Newspaper Abstracts, 1818-1820*

National Intelligencer *Newspaper Abstracts, 1814-1817*

National Intelligencer *Newspaper Abstracts, 1811-1813*

National Intelligencer *Newspaper Abstracts, 1806-1810*

National Intelligencer *Newspaper Abstracts, 1800-1805*

www.ingramcontent.com/pod-product-compliance
Lightning Source LLC
Chambersburg PA
CBHW071712300426
44115CB00010B/1395